MACAULAY

MACAULAY

The Shaping of the Historian

by JOHN CLIVE

 Alfred A. Knopf   New York   1973

THIS IS A BORZOI BOOK
PUBLISHED BY ALFRED A. KNOPF, INC.

Copyright © 1973 by John Clive

All rights reserved under International and Pan-American Copyright Conventions.
Published in the United States by Alfred A. Knopf, Inc., New York, and
simultaneously in Canada by Random House of Canada Limited, Toronto. Distributed
by Random House, Inc., New York.

Library of Congress Cataloging in Publication Data

Clive, John.   Macaulay: the shaping of the historian.

Includes bibliographical references.
1. Macaulay, Thomas Babington Macaulay, Baron, 1800–1859. I. Title. DA3.M3C5
907'.2'024 [B]   72–8727 ISBN 0–394–47278–0

Manufactured in the United States of America

Published March 23, 1973
Second Printing, April 1973

For B.B., L.B.,
F.L.F., E.R.F.

CONTENTS

ILLUSTRATIONS

SOME ABBREVIATIONS
AND SHORT TITLES USED IN THE NOTES

Errington MSS	MS and typescript collection of Thomas Babington Macaulay letters, in the possession of Mrs. Reine Errington.
Huntington MSS	Macaulay Family MSS, Henry E. Huntington Library, San Marino, California.
I.O.L.	India Office Library.
Margaret Macaulay, *Recollections*	*Recollections of a Sister of T. B. Macaulay* (privately printed, London, 1864).
Morgan MSS	Macaulay MSS, Pierpont Morgan Library, New York.
T.B.M.	Thomas Babington Macaulay.
Trinity Correspondence	Correspondence of Thomas Babington Macaulay, Trinity College, Cambridge.
Trinity Journal	Thomas Babington Macaulay's "Journal," Trinity College, Cambridge.
Trinity MSS	Macaulay MSS, Trinity College, Cambridge.
Works	*The Works of Lord Macaulay* (Albany edition, 12 vols., London, 1898).

ACKNOWLEDGMENTS

IN THE COURSE OF WRITING THIS BOOK, I HAVE INCURRED MANY OBLIGA-
tions. For permission to cite manuscript material and for other
courtesies extended to me, I should like to thank the Master and
Fellows of Trinity College, Cambridge, the librarians of the Henry E.
Huntington Library, Pierpont Morgan Library, India Office Library,
Harvard College Library, John Rylands Library, University of Not-
tingham, University of Newcastle upon Tyne, Duke University, Uni-
versity College, London, as well as Mrs. Reine Errington, Mrs.
Humphry Trevelyan, Mrs. Mary Moorman, Mrs. Pauline Dower,
Mr. Gordon Ray, and the Duke of Portland.

The John Simon Guggenheim Memorial Foundation and the
American Council of Learned Societies awarded me grants that enabled me to work on this book; and the Center for Advanced Study
in the Behavioral Sciences at Palo Alto, California, made it possible
for me to spend a year in those pleasant surroundings. I am very
grateful to these three corporate benefactors.

A number of individuals read all or parts of the manuscript and
offered helpful advice. Others drew my attention to particular
problems. Among them were Bernard Bailyn, Kenneth Ballhatchet,
Kitson Clark, Richard Friedman, Peter Glazebrook, Donald Graham,
Charles Gray, Leopold Haimson, Joseph Hamburger, H. J. Hanham,
Jenifer Hart, Howard Mumford Jones, Anthony Lester, Standish
Meacham, A. N. L. Munby, Robert Robson, Carl Schorske, Zeph

Stewart, William Thomas, the late G. M. Trevelyan, and Robert Lee Wolff. I owe thanks to all of them. But my chief obligation is to Thomas Pinney, who generously shared with me his immense knowledge of Macaulay and saved me from many errors. The responsibility for those remaining is mine alone.

I have been fortunate in my publishers and editors. David Farrer read the entire manuscript and made many valuable suggestions. William Koshland has been consistently helpful and encouraging. Mrs. Jane N. Garrett has been a fine editor. I should also like to thank Mrs. Ann Adelman for her exemplary copy editing. Mrs. Kay Bruner rendered invaluable help with the index.

PROLOGUE

THE SUBJECT OF THIS BOOK IS NOT THE EMINENT VICTORIAN, THE Macaulay of the collected *Essays* and *Speeches,* the *Lays of Ancient Rome,* the *History of England*—works that made him a household word in the English-speaking world, and gained him his country's first "literary" peerage. It is, rather, the outsider, the "parvenu" (as he once called himself)—awkward, ugly, impecunious—who by sheer talent and energy won the respect of the Whigs, and a seat in the cabinet before the age of forty. This volume concludes before the Queen was crowned, and before any of his major works had made their appearance. Its aim is to trace some of the forces—familial, intellectual, political, and personal—which helped to shape the man and the historian.

MACAULAY

I

ZACHARY AND SELINA

ZACHARY MACAULAY, THE HISTORIAN'S FATHER, HAS HIS OWN PLACE IN history. For many years he was in the van of the great struggle for the abolition of the slave trade; and his stern presence broods over any account of the "Clapham Sect," that highly effective pressure group of "Saints" who lived within earshot of one another on the outskirts of London during the early years of the nineteenth century and devoted their energies, their substance, and their not inconsiderable wisdom in the ways of this world to humanitarian and philanthropic reforms. The story of how Zachary Macaulay became one of its members, a sequence of sin and corruption, coincidence and conversion, exemplifies that sort of spiritual odyssey, a favorite with the Evangelicals, to which in retrospect the label "foreordained" could most easily be attached.

Zachary was born in Inverary in 1768, the son and grandson of Scottish Presbyterian ministers who were in their turn descended from embattled Highland chiefs. It was a doubly fierce heritage. His father could not afford to provide him with a university education. By the time he was fourteen years old, he had taught himself Greek and French and had started to work in the countinghouse of a Glasgow merchant. There, according to an autobiographical memoir which he wrote at the age of twenty-nine, he became acquainted with a group of university students whose facility in dialectical argument cost him his faith. At the same time, his business acquaintances introduced him to hard drinking. He had no taste for this, but joined in with them because they told him that it provided ground for glorying rather than sin. His driving ambition, characteristic of him throughout his life, was such that he was not content to remain ordinary, even in deviation from virtue. He eradicated from his mind every trace of religious belief. Moreover, using weapons from the formidable armory of his new oracle David Hume, he made it his pastime to shake the faith of those of his companions who were still firm. Not only did he himself drink heavily; he tried regularly to drink all his companions under the table as well. And, he recalled, in the conventionally florid language of the Evangelical confessional mode:

When I was not draining the midnight bowl, I was employed in wasting the midnight oil by poring over such abominable, but fascinating works as are to be found under the head of novels in the catalogue of every circulating library.[1]

After two years of this mode of life, he left Glasgow for the West Indies. He wanted to go abroad because sober reflection, to which he was led by an unspecified "circumstance" that occurred at the end of 1784, had convinced him that this was the only way of extricating himself from the "labyrinth" in which he had become involved. A distant relative who had once been Governor of Jamaica persuaded Zachary's father to let the youth try his fortune there. A few months later, not yet seventeen, he found himself in the position of under-manager, or bookkeeper, on a sugar plantation worked by slave labor. His initial squeamishness over the sufferings these laborers had to undergo soon gave way to callous indifference. In a letter to a friend, written in 1785, he pictured himself "in a field of canes, amidst perhaps a hundred of the sable race, cursing and bawling, while the noise of the whip resounding on their shoulders, and the cries of the poor wretches, would make you imagine that some unlucky accident had carried you to the doleful shades."[2] Even in this degraded condition he kept up his taste for reading and derived some comfort from Horace and Voltaire; but more solid comfort, as he later remembered, came from his own vanity and firmness of nerve.

Four years went by. Then he received a letter from an uncle in London, offering him an advantageous position upon his return.

1. Margaret Knutsford, *Life and Letters of Zachary Macaulay* (London, 1900) , 5.
2. Ibid., 8.

And so, against the wishes of his father who, like many other clergymen of the time, felt no particular moral revulsion toward slavery
and the slave trade, he arrived back in England in 1789, in his
twenty-first year. This is where the short autobiographical memoir
ends. As far as his spiritual state was concerned, the tide was about to
turn. But one must not imagine that in depicting his preconversion
state, Zachary painted an entirely black canvas. This is not merely
the familiar tale of absolute depravity before the miraculous moment
of illumination. When writing their memoirs, Evangelicals tended to
accentuate the negative, to depict themselves as totally sunk in sin
before the descent of grace. But it is clear, even from Zachary's own
testimony, that his tough physical constitution (impaired from birth
by lack of vision in one eye), weathered in early youth a serious
accident to his right arm which resulted in years of pain and repeated
surgery, as well as, later on, dangerous bouts of ill-health in Jamaica;
it is also clear that his tough moral constitution repeatedly asserted
itself during the years when it was being most severely tested. The
pleasures to which he had given himself in Glasgow never interfered
with his attention to business. In fact, his employers presented him
with a large gratuity when he departed for Jamaica. On the voyage
out, he resolved to abstain from excessive drinking, and he stuck to his
resolution. On the voyage home, he made a similar resolution with
regard to gambling, one he was able to keep "with few deviations."
And he recalled that while in the West Indies he had retained
throughout a kind of high-mindedness which kept him from complaining even when most wretched, and which, at considerable risk,
made him take the part of young men who, like himself, were being
tyrannized by the overseers on the plantation. All this he remembered himself. From another source we learn that he tried, and
failed, to reform the "mischievous habits" of the slaves.[3] Possibly this
failure had as much as anything else to do with setting him eventually against slavery and the slave trade.

It is important to stress the persistence of these positive moral
traits in his character in order to clarify the nature of the conversion
he underwent upon his return to England. The Evangelicals were
men and women mostly of middle-class origin who had been touched
by the same fire of faith and conversion that John Wesley had used
to set alight the dying embers of Gospel religion in the indifferentist

3. Thomas Babington to Zachary Macaulay, April 9, 1793, Macaulay Family MSS,
Henry E. Huntington Library, San Marino, California (referred to henceforth as Huntington MSS).

spiritual atmosphere of the eighteenth century. Wesley's converts had been largely among the humble and downtrodden, many of them in those increasingly heavily populated areas of the new industrial Britain for which the still medieval parish system of the Church of England had made no provision at all. Wesley himself, it is true, remained a clergyman of the Church throughout the course of his long and incredibly active life. But Methodism could not be contained within the Establishment. In seeking out the very dregs of society, in proclaiming the absolute equality of rich and poor before God, the Methodists offended against that strictly hierarchical social system of eighteenth-century England of which the Church, closely tied to the aristocracy, was part and parcel. Thus, by the end of the century, the Methodists had broken away from the established Church. But their message found a responsive chord in some clerics and laymen who were determined to work for a spiritual revival and a reformation of society from within the Church. Evangelical religion demanded above all a change of heart, a rebirth in Christ vouchsafed by divine grace to those strong in the faith. But this kind of conversion did not at all signify the end of sin and the attainment of a permanent equilibrium. In many ways it portended the beginning rather than the end of struggle. For neither trust in God's Providence nor confidence in one's ultimate salvation meant that the forces of this world had suddenly been vanquished. The convert's new-found faith gave him the means to identify his enemies, as well as the weapons with which to stand them off. But he could not afford to rest. He had to be his own general, foot soldier, and, above all, his own war historian. For he knew that he would be held to account for losses and blunders.

We do not know much about Zachary Macaulay's actual conversion, though the subsequent record of his spiritual life fills innumerable pages of his diaries and journals. There is design in this. One of his complaints against the Methodists was to be that some of their number would fix in retrospect upon some single, crucial event which had led to their change of heart. This was wrong. It was the Gospel, above all, not any part of mere human experience, that deserved to be enshrined as the agent of conversion. Grateful remembrance, however, was duly rendered by Zachary on many occasions to the person who had helped to open his own heart to the Gospel, and to the place where his new life in Christ had had its beginning. The person was Thomas Babington, and the place his country seat, Rothley Temple in Leicestershire. It is here that chance and coincidence enter into the story.

In 1787 Thomas Babington, a young Leicestershire country gentleman with strong Evangelical views, had taken a trip to the Scottish Highlands in the company of his friend Aulay Macaulay, Zachary's brother. They stopped for a few days at the family manse. And there Babington met and fell in love with one of the daughters of the house, Jean. They were married shortly thereafter, and settled at Rothley Temple. When Zachary returned from the West Indies, he found that his father had died. So he went to stay for some time with his sister Jean, to whom he had always been close, and his brother-in-law. The years on the plantation had left him hardened and boorish in manner, completely unaccustomed to the warmth and affection of the family circle gathered together at Rothley Temple. Domesticity of this kind made for a welcome change. But an even more welcome change turned out to be that, as he put it some years later, he found his better self, all principles of rectitude, all desires superior to "those of the beast, which perish," at his brother-in-law's house.[4]

At some point during his stay, he underwent the change of heart that made him into an Evangelical. He never forgot what he owed to Babington, who soon realized what an ardent disciple he had helped to recruit for the cause. He could even bring himself to write personal letters to Zachary on a Sunday, which when any other correspondents were involved must count as a profanation of the Sabbath. For, "when you come into my mind, my thoughts generally take a turn which makes them as proper for this as for any other day."[5] Evangelicalism was indeed a cause as well as a way of life. The Evangelical's obligation was to glorify God. This meant taking action in the world; not only in obedience to the God of Scripture, but also in response to the Holy Spirit, present in each convert's soul.[6]

The long and ultimately successful battle for the abolition of the slave trade, to which the Evangelicals were to devote themselves for so many years above all else, was at this time in its opening stages. It was a foregone conclusion that Zachary, given his experiences in Jamaica and his newly found faith, would join it. It was certainly at Rothley Temple that he became convinced of the iniquity of the trade.[7]

An opportunity soon arose. The prospects of which his uncle had

4. Zachary Macaulay to Selina Mills, February 12, 1797, Huntington MSS.
5. Thomas Babington to Zachary Macaulay, July 30, 1794, Huntington MSS.
6. See Trygve R. Tholfsen, "The Intellectual Origins of Mid-Victorian Stability," *Political Science Quarterly*, LXXXVI (1971), 80–3.
7. Thomas Babington to Zachary Macaulay, April 9, 1793, Knutsford, *Zachary Macaulay*, 24.

written him had, in any event, failed to materialize; and he found it difficult to settle down in England. At this juncture, one of the leading Clapham "Saints," the wealthy banker Henry Thornton, asked his friend Babington to name a reliable person who would be prepared to report back to him on the current state of affairs in the Negro settlement of Sierra Leone in West Africa. Babington had by then become so impressed with his brother-in-law's character and views that he recommended him. Zachary sailed at the end of 1790, to a troubled scene. Three years earlier, under the sponsorship of the philanthropist Granville Sharp and some leading Evangelicals, a group of about four hundred settlers, mainly slaves liberated by Lord Mansfield's historic judgment putting an end to slavery on English soil, had sailed to the West Coast of Africa. There a tract of land had been purchased for them, and there they were to found a free and democratically governed black community in the very heartland of the slave trade. It was not a success. Surrounding native tribes attacked and burned the settlement. Many of the settlers found it hard to gain a livelihood and drifted away. But Sharp and his friends, among them Thornton, Babington, and Wilberforce, did not give up so easily. While they were working for the abolition of the slave trade by act of Parliament in England, they wanted to be able to point to a place where blacks could live in peace and freedom in their native land. Furthermore, many among them were businessmen just as much as philanthropists. The Sierra Leone Company, which they proceeded to form and which was incorporated in 1791, was a commercial enterprise that promised a return to the shareholders who had invested in it even though trade was to subserve "the Honourable Office of introducing to a Vast Country long detained in Barbarism the Blessings of Industry and Civilization."[8]

The company was allowed by Parliament to make its own laws for those concerned in its affairs; so that what had originally started out as a self-governing province was now a colony under the control of absentee directors. This control they exercised through a governor and a council. Zachary, who had returned to England in the spring of 1792 after proving himself as an observer in Sierra Leone, was sent out again as one of the council members a few months later. He became governor in 1794. By that time, a fresh group of settlers had arrived from Nova Scotia, consisting of former slaves who had been on the Loyalist side during the war of the American Revolution and

8. Christopher Fyfe, *A History of Sierra Leone* (London, 1962), 31.

who had subsequently escaped to Canada. Like the other settlers, they found conditions in Sierra Leone far less idyllic than they had been led to believe. The next few years called forth all of Zachary's toughness of spirit and character. What his directors at home regarded not merely as a philanthropic but also as a moneymaking proposition, the settlers on the spot were more apt to look on above all as a place of refuge and freedom. Zachary never had any doubt about where his own duty lay. And he worked literally night and day to carry it out. It must be said that in so doing he gives much more the impression of a stern and ruthless colonial administrator than of a humanitarian savior of souls and protector of the oppressed. This should not mislead one about the strength of his principles where the iniquities of the slave trade were concerned. But the historian of Sierra Leone is right in pointing out that he lacked emotional sympathy with his subjects.[9] In his case, as with some of the other prominent Evangelicals, one is sometimes led to wonder whether abnegation, austerity, and devotion were not primarily self-administered tests of character and only secondarily the products of love for one's fellow men.

Macaulay's journals during this period tell the story of disaffected and sometimes openly rebellious settlers, many of them sunk in sloth, riddled with venereal disease, beset with domestic quarrels, and responding no better than the slaves in Jamaica to his efforts to reform them. Ironically enough, in view of his Jamaican experience, Zachary on at least one occasion ordered some of them to be punished by flogging. It seems clear to us today that the settlers had some legitimate complaints. For example, before coming out, the "Nova Scotians" had been promised that they would never have to pay rent for their land. But the company found it necessary to charge quit-rents. As far as Zachary was concerned, however, the quit-rent issue was merely a pretext used by the settlers to cover their deep-seated moral deficiencies.[10]

Then, in the autumn of 1794, came the bombardment and sacking of the settlement by French revolutionary forces—apparently less impressed by the Declaration of Human Rights than by the prospect of loot. Zachary had been worried about the virus of revolutionary agitation spreading from France to England.[11] Now the revolution had unexpectedly come, not to Britain, but to Africa. He never

9. Ibid., 73.
10. Zachary Macaulay to Selina Mills, December 5, 1797, Huntington MSS.
11. Zachary Macaulay to Thomas Babington, July 30, 1794, Huntington MSS.

forgot the manner of its arrival. But while he had no use at all for what he called "the present ruinous system that has deluged Europe with blood,"[12] it would be quite wrong to characterize him as a Burkean conservative, in sympathy with the aristocracy. He was critical of the sort of people who indignantly rejected every rational expedient for conciliating the affections of the lower orders around them, unwilling to make any concessions in their direction lest their dignity should appear to be truckling to plebeian baseness.[13] Unlike Burke, he encomiastically linked the American and French revolutions, seeing in both alike lessons to the ages of what might be done by men's love of liberty when those men were willing to pay in lives as well as property for it.[14]

In 1795, Zachary's health broke down from anxiety and overwork. The directors of the Sierra Leone Company called him back to London. It is characteristic of the man that in spite of the state of his health he chose a slave ship as his means of transport part of the way, in order to observe at first hand how the blacks were being treated during the infamous "middle passage" from Africa to the West Indies. Actions of this kind help to bring home to us the incredible self-discipline of the man whose repelling appearance, Thornton had felt it necessary to assure the previous governor, belied deeper feelings.[15]

Those feelings were aroused during his visit to England when he met his future wife, Selina Mills, at the house of Hannah More and her sister. It is hard to imagine a more appropriate *mise-en-scène* for an Evangelical engagement. For Hannah More, though like some of the others a nonresident, was very much a part of the Clapham Sect. Born in 1745, the daughter of a West Country schoolmaster, she had at first devoted her precocious and considerable talents in part to teaching in a boarding school for young ladies which she and her sisters opened in Bristol, and in part to the cultivation of literature and conversation. Soon her reputation grew beyond the bounds of Bristol. For a time she was the toast of London literary society. Dr. Johnson reveled in her company; Garrick called her "Nine" because she embodied in her person the accomplishments of all the Muses. She had always been religiously inclined. But shortly after the deaths, in quick succession, of Garrick, Johnson, and her father, she underwent a conversion which made her abjure the pleasures of London.

12. Zachary Macaulay to Selina Mills, February 4, 1797, Huntington MSS.
13. Zachary Macaulay to Selina Mills, March 25, 1797, Huntington MSS.
14. Zachary Macaulay to Selina Mills, February 22, 1797; Knutsford, *Zachary Macaulay*, 164.
15. Fyfe, *Sierra Leone*, 49.

Henceforth, she was "Saint Hannah," as Horace Walpole called her, the leading propagandist of the Evangelicals, the confidante of all the chief Claphamites, the embattled schoolmistress of the Mendip poor.[16] With the proceeds from her writings she purchased a house in Bath and a cottage at Cowslip Green, near Bristol. After spending three days with her and her sisters at Bath shortly after his return to England, Zachary wrote that he had enjoyed in their conversation something of a foretaste of Heaven: "How much does such an interview loosen and weaken our earthly ties, and set our souls as it were on fire for immortality."[17]

In the event, his visit to the More sisters considerably strengthened his earthly ties. For in the course of it he met and fell in love with his future wife, Selina Mills, the mother of Thomas Babington Macaulay. Selina was the daughter of Thomas Mills, a Bristol bookseller, stationer, and binder, and a devout Quaker. Many years later one of his granddaughters remembered him "talking incessantly of Jacob Behmen [Boehme]."[18] The very few of his letters that have been preserved evince an unremittingly earnest and devout religious temperament, with none of that sense of humor for which Lord Macaulay is said to have been grateful to his mother's side of the family. As it happens, the future historian is the subject of all these letters. In one of them, written to his daughter a few months after his grandson's birth, he expressed the hope that the boy would follow her as she walked in the footsteps of Christ, "so that when he, in whom is now hid our spiritual life, shall appear; may you and yours be of the number of his Jewels, and shine as stars in the Kingdom of his glory."[19] Selina had written to her father that the baby (Tom) looked like him. His reply was that even if their outward features did not correspond exactly, "we shall have in the internal Root of our minds a strong likeness, a resemblance that we have proceeded from the same corrupt stock, and shall need a translation, or separation from the Tree of our wicked nature, in order to our being ingrafted into the true one, before ever we shall bear fruit pleasing and acceptable to our heavenly Father."[20] In another letter about his grandson, written twelve years later, he expressed the hope that divine

16. See Ford K. Brown, *Fathers of the Victorians: The Age of Wilberforce* (Cambridge, 1961), on this last aspect of her activities.

17. Zachary Macaulay to John Campbell, January 12, 1795, Huntington MSS.

18. Hannah, Lady Trevelyan's account for her son George Otto of reminiscences of her brother, Thomas Babington Macaulay, 3. Macaulay MSS at Trinity College, Cambridge (henceforth referred to as Trinity MSS).

19. Thomas Mills to Selina Mills Macaulay, May 21, 1801, Huntington MSS.

20. Idem.

grace would attach his mind "to that blessed object in whom are hid all the treasures of our heavenly wisdom and divine knowledge; and may the holy Jesus fix his abode within him, so will he be beloved of God, and esteemed by all good men."[21] One reason for the historian's turning so violently against the Quakers and all they stood for later in life no doubt lay in his aversion to this particularly unctuous mode of expression.

Selina did not become a Quaker. She received her own education at the school conducted by the More sisters at Blagdon, some ten miles from Bristol. And she must have come to share their Evangelical views. For they grew to like her so much that they took her into their own household, and made her a joint proprietor of their school in Park Street, Bristol. In fact, they became so fond of her that when it became evident to their sharp eyes that Zachary and Selina were attracted to each other, they even resorted to unworthy and rather discreditable stratagems to keep her from leaving them. Zachary had been too shy to declare himself. Later on, he wrote to Selina that the reasons for his reserve lay both in his not wishing to take advantage of her "impressibility," which was the trait in her character that first struck him, and in his fear that Hannah More's "eagle eyes" might suspect too much were he less studiously reserved.[22] The story goes that on the occasion of Zachary's farewell visit to the sisters, before his return to Sierra Leone, Hannah More told him, supposedly in the interests of her sister Patty, who was particularly attached to Selina, that, in fact, Selina was indifferent to him. But at this point Selina was heard sobbing in an adjacent room. Her heart was revealed, and the young couple became secretly engaged before Zachary sailed back to Africa from Portsmouth early in 1796. Prior to his departure, he sent his future wife a book of sermons on the evidences of Christianity, as well as the Methodist hymnbook.

Zachary's original intention, fiercely and successfully opposed by the More sisters, was to have Selina follow him to Sierra Leone as a missionary. But by the autumn of 1796 he had given up this project. At that time he wrote to Babington that the constant disturbances among the settlers as well as the state of his health had induced him to change his mind about permanent residence in Africa.[23] But he

21. Thomas Mills to Selina Mills Macaulay, December 20, 1813, Huntington MSS.

22. Zachary Macaulay to Selina Mills, February 9 and 10, 1797, Huntington MSS.

23. Zachary Macaulay to Thomas Babington, September 28, 1796, Huntington MSS. A few months later, he wrote to Selina that it might still be his duty to return to Sierra Leone; in which event he hoped that he could be sure of not hearing "dehortatory counsel" from her. Zachary Macaulay to Selina Mills, January 31, 1797, Huntington MSS.

did not return to England until 1799. And during the interim he kept in touch with Selina through a special "Journal"—really a series of letters sent off when ships sailed homewards—which, unlike Selina's letters to Zachary in this period, has survived. It is an extraordinary correspondence, which sheds a great deal of light on the psychology of Evangelicalism as well as on the character of the two people conducting it. For these are letters full of probings into the human heart, carried out with exceptional frankness and intensity. Even compliments were hedged about with moral import. Thus, when Zachary wrote to Selina that he had always admired the way she dressed, he was quick to add that this was *not* because he attached much weight to external appearances, but because he regarded it as the outward sign of a well-ordered mind.[24]

For Zachary, as for all devout Evangelicals, every bout of self-indulgence had to be turned into an occasion for self-denial. Yet he admitted that he himself was sometimes weak enough to let his attention wander from the dry details of accounts, figures, and reports in order to gaze at Selina's portrait.[25] On the second anniversary of their engagement, having duly accused himself of "littleness" in attaching too much significance to anniversaries, he told her that the Catholics might worship their Saints, the French revolutionaries liberty, but that *he* would say his vows to *her:* "You shall be my tutelar Saint. Your smile shall cheer me, your counsel shall guide me, your example shall animate me, your love shall lighten my labours, and your intercessions shall bring down on me the blessing of Heaven."[26] Ultimately, however, neither compliments nor expressions of affection but, rather, repeated and merciless analyses of character, motives, and transgressions provide the keynotes for these remarkable love letters.

The Evangelical discipline was founded on the immovable rock of absolute trust in the power and Providence of God. On the question, for instance, of whether he and Selina would meet in another world, Zachary wrote to her: "My own mind is abundantly satisfied of the certainty of this knowledge."[27] But, for the rest, conversion brought not peace, but a sword—a sword wielded just as much against the snares and temptations that beset one's own soul as against the evil and deceit of the world outside. The enemy was within as well as without. Only the truth could make one free. "Truth at all costs"

24. "1798," Knutsford, *Zachary Macaulay,* 195–6.
25. Zachary Macaulay to Selina Mills, February 9, 1797, Huntington MSS.
26. Zachary Macaulay to Selina Mills, February 1798, Huntington MSS.
27. Zachary Macaulay to Selina Mills, January 31, 1797, Huntington MSS.

was part of the Evangelical creed—including the cost of pain and self-laceration. Thus Selina had sudden fears that "recommendation" (by others) rather than love was the chief source of her attachment to Zachary. She had evidently written him to that effect, for he deemed it necessary to reply at length, pointing out that recommendation did not, after all, preclude judgment. "Did Miss H[annah]'s telling you for instance that I was an old man," he asked, "blind your eyes? Had it not in fact the contrary effect?"[28] Then he went on to argue that, in fact, the level of intensity of one's critical sense stood in direct proportion to the level of intensity of one's imaginative expectation, and so allayed her fears.

Selina was just as eager to make certain that his judgment of her had not been clouded as she had been to make certain that *her* judgment of *him* had not been swayed by extraneous factors. She had evidently indicated to him that she believed he was putting too much value on her understanding. Zachary bluntly reassured her that this was not so; that "tho' lovers in general may be too apt to exaggerate," he had fixed his expectations below rather than above the line of truth—strange and unique reassurance in the correspondence of lovers! Besides, he added, it was not her brilliant talents, her refinement of taste, nor her ability that attracted him, but her heart above all. With a psychological subtlety worthy of a Laclos, he continued:

It was rather a hard task you imposed on me, to doubt the soundness of your understanding in the moment you were giving me the most convincing proof of it, by detecting your own errors in judgement and pointing them out with a nicety of discrimination.[29]

Evangelicalism has often been dubbed the religion of the heart. Zachary was mortified when a Scottish Presbyterian minister (John Clarke) preached a sermon in Sierra Leone on the text "God is Love" that was full of proofs from reason and classical allusions, instead of being what it ought to be, "a heart-affecting discourse."[30] Yet the constant seeking after truth in motive and character could engage one's dialectical faculties as deeply as any problem in logic. The immediate effect was destructive. But what was destroyed was hypocrisy, vanity, pretense. And one could build upon what remained, using contrition, work, and prayer as materials. In a rela-

28. Zachary Macaulay to Selina Mills, February 10, 1797, Huntington MSS. In fact, she was one year older than he was—which shows the lengths to which the Miss Mores were willing to go to keep her with them.

29. Zachary Macaulay to Selina Mills, March 25, 1797, Huntington MSS.

30. Zachary Macaulay to Selina Mills, April 21, 1798, Huntington MSS.

tionship between two persons this meant a frank and not necessarily unwelcome recognition that the attraction between them derived as much from complementary faults as from complementary virtues. Certainly this was far better than to lay claim to virtues that did not exist. Zachary noted, for instance, that he and Selina had grappled with the same kind of spiritual enemy. "Perhaps," he wrote, "we shall not be the less helpsmeet [sic] for each other for having an experiential knowledge of those peculiar trials to which each is exposed." He was, in fact, thankful that she had in some small degree experienced the same evils that weighed him down. For this made him hopeful of her sympathy and indulgence, her counsel and assistance.[31]

What, then, were the evils that weighed him down? On his twenty-ninth birthday he listed them in the journal he was keeping for Selina: Want of warm enough love of God, patience too easily exhausted by trifles, readiness to think bad thoughts of others, even (and this came surprisingly from a man who worked from dawn to midnight) indolence and procrastination. "I do not know," he wrote with his usual honesty, "that I am ever absolutely idle, but I often nod over my work."[32] His main "Baal," the worst sin of all, was his pride, his love of praise, his excessive "strength of manner." His brother-in-law Babington, addressing Zachary in the role of "censor" (a role Zachary himself had assigned to him) shortly before his marriage, singled out impatience, self-confidence, and love of praise as his principal faults, and an excess of natural ardor of mind and firmness of character as his principal defects.[33]

We shall see Zachary reprimanding his son Tom again and again for the very qualities he had exposed in himself with such merciless frankness:

A disputatious turn of mind—an impatience of opposition or contradiction—the adoption of rash and immature counsels. An over-fondness in uttering opinions hastily, and perhaps intemperately conceived, while yet crude and undigested. A strong manner and imposing tone in uttering these. An eagerness to talk on subjects of which I know little with a view to the praise of intelligence. An unreasonable assumption of powers and authority which do not belong to me, at least exclusively.[34]

31. Zachary Macaulay to Selina Mills, March 25, 1797, Huntington MSS.
32. Zachary Macaulay to Selina Mills, May 2, 1797, Huntington MSS.
33. Thomas Babington to Zachary Macaulay, August 6, 1799, Knutsford, *Zachary Macaulay*, 232.
34. Zachary Macaulay to Selina Mills, March 25, 1797, Huntington MSS.

It is worth pointing out that Zachary wrote this at a time when, in his capacity of acting governor, he was enforcing some very stern measures on behalf of his directors in London. The company was trying to cut the losses it had incurred as a result of the French sacking and other disasters. Settlers from Nova Scotia threatened to riot over the issue of quit-rents. Macaulay in his turn announced that order would be enforced, if necessary with the use of the gallows. He wrote to Selina that the real issue was not at all the matter of quit-rents (he called that a mere pretext), but the fact that the settlers lacked moral fiber. The root cause of the disturbances, he felt, lay in the "retrogradation" of moral improvement among them, in their licentiousness, and their impatience of every wholesome restraint.[35] Here is one vital ingredient in the Evangelical attitude to social problems, one that was responsible for their blindness to much suffering. If the root causes of discontent and distress could be assumed to be always essentially moral, then it followed that little or nothing needed to be done to improve physical conditions.

Men like Zachary Macaulay would work themselves to exhaustion in the cause of slave trade abolition, while at the same time remaining seemingly oblivious to the social injustices they themselves perpetuated in the name of duty. Zachary never doubted the rectitude of his régime as governor. What surprised and disappointed him was the recalcitrance of the human material. In Jamaica, we recall, he had been unable to reform the "mischievous habits" of the slaves; and that had been one of the causes which had led to his conversion at Rothley Temple. Now, in Sierra Leone, strengthened by his new-found faith, he was still unable to eradicate the equally mischievous habits retained by freedmen. This, indeed, was one reason for his request (in 1798) to be sent home. Did he ever question the fundamental assumption behind his continued disappointment? There is no evidence that he did. There is evidence that each failure drove him toward more and more rigorous self-examination. Perhaps it was something within himself, some trait of worldliness, some inner weakness, that prevented him from influencing other people. Sir Toby's question: "Dost thou think because thou art virtuous, there shall be no more cakes and ale?" applies here.

One wonders how many of his self-confessed faults—"no doubt this is a black list which requires no small allowance of candour to peruse with undiminished regard"[36]—Selina found herself sharing with

35. Zachary Macaulay to Selina Mills, December 1, 1797, Huntington MSS.
36. Zachary Macaulay to Selina Mills, March 25, 1797, Huntington MSS.

him. The sole blemish that relentless and practiced faultfinder Thomas Babington could discover in her was too much haste in forming and expressing her opinions, which in any event were apt to be too decisive.[37] But to Zachary she revealed another failing, and it is one that illuminates the heritage bequeathed to their son, who, for his part, was to value it more than anything else: daydreaming, wandering thoughts, an unbridled imagination. Sometime in the course of 1797 Selina wrote to Zachary, asking him to lay down some rules for her which could serve as a cure for her wandering thoughts. This hit a tender spot. For he, too, so he informed her, was subject to the very same disease and had as yet found no infallible remedy for it. To be sure, he was able to fix his unimpeded attention on the Scriptures by reading them in Greek, with the help of a dictionary. He was able to fix it on sermons—"I was for a long time particularly prone to this wandering during sermons"—by taking notes of striking observations or oddities of expression on the part of the preacher and by constructing an outline of the sermon. But paying strict attention during public prayers he found more difficult:

I have knelt down with, as I thought, a strong resolution of keeping my mind fixed, and on rising have found to my mortification and sorrow that I had arranged the whole plan of an important trading expedition, drawn up an able reply to some objections that had been made to our proceedings, fought a battle with two privateers, and sunk one of them, or enjoyed the delights of a meeting with you in Park Street while I ought to have been employed in mourning over sin, pleading for pardon, or pouring out prayers and intercessions for all men.

The imagination was lawless, he told her. Desultory thoughts tended to arise, and the difficulty became greater during times of alarm than it was in times of calm. Interesting incidents and things that appealed to our restless passions were formidable assailants. "By stating the difficulty I have no intention of lessening the obligation."[38]

Here speaks the man who in his youth was peculiarly susceptible to novel reading and to all that was romantic and extravagant; who spent much of his time making up speeches for ladies delivered from the hands of robbers and assassins or adjusting the particulars of some intriguing affair of honor; and whose imagination drove him on the occasion of a journey into the interior of Sierra Leone to

37. Thomas Babington to Zachary Macaulay, July 20, 1797, Knutsford, *Zachary Macaulay*, 148.
38. Zachary Macaulay to Selina Mills, February 19, 1797, Huntington MSS.

visualize himself on his deathbed, making speeches to Selina and talking to Babington, in such a way that the native boy accompanying him was moved to ask solicitously whether he was tired.[39]

He well knew the cause of these wandering thoughts. It was the sinful love of this world, the ramification of corruption which "like the Indian fig, 'embowering endless,'" tainted all our powers and spread its deadly, noxious shade over our affections.[40] The human imagination was one of its weapons. Take the Methodists, for instance. They held that the genuineness of works performed after conversion depended on sensible impressions made upon the imagination at the time of conversion. Then many of them were misled into feeding themselves with the corrupt manna of past experience, "while neglecting the milk of the Word."[41] Imagination was not an enemy to be easily conquered. "Do not complain of disappointment," Zachary wrote, in reply to a letter of Selina's seeking his advice on the subject of how to go about that conquest, "if you find my remarks puerile and inadequate. I was myself expecting from you some aid on this point."[42]

It is worth noticing this dimension of Zachary Macaulay's personality, this powerful and uncontrollable imagination hidden behind the forbiddingly dour mask he presented to the outside world, the staid manner, stern look, and grave deportment for which he became known.[43] A friend of Zachary's, a certain Winterbottom, felt impelled to tell him that when engaged in business he looked so grave as almost to frighten him.[44] It was his peculiarity, Sir James Stephen wrote much later, "to conceal, as far as possible, his interior life, under the veil of his outward appearance," that is, an earnest and monotonous expression. How successful he was in this concealment is best shown by the fact that Stephen himself was capable of calling Zachary's mind "not naturally imaginative."[45]

Zachary was fully aware of his gloomy exterior—on the occasion of one of his annual birthday stocktakings, he reprimanded himself for being too reserved, for habits such as that of sitting at the break-

39. Knutsford, *Zachary Macaulay*, 5; Zachary Macaulay to Selina Mills, February 2, 1797, Huntington MSS.

40. Zachary Macaulay to Selina Mills, February 12, 1797, Huntington MSS.

41. Zachary Macaulay to Selina Mills, April 25, 1797, Huntington MSS.

42. Zachary Macaulay to Selina Mills, February 19, 1797, Huntington MSS.

43. See John Campbell Colquhoun, *William Wilberforce, His Friends and His Times* (2nd ed., London, 1867), 235.

44. Winterbottom to Zachary Macaulay, July 1796, Knutsford, *Zachary Macaulay*, 142.

45. Sir James Stephen, *Essays in Ecclesiastical Biography* (4th ed., London, 1860), 545, 547.

fast table intent on business and not talking to others.[46] Selina was evidently worried, before her marriage, about this side of her future husband's personality. It was she who had asked Winterbottom, when he called on her in England, whether Zachary was not inclined to be too gloomy at times. His tactful answer was that in spite of appearances this was not the case; though he added (in a burst of understatement) that her fiancé could not be said to be inclined to the high flow of spirits. "She seemed pleased," he reported to Zachary.[47]

Zachary went out of his way to tell Selina that he had never known low spirits, even at the lowest points in his circumstances. Some hidden spring was always touched, the elasticity of which, till then concealed, seemed to throw off the weight.[48] But after Zachary's return to England in 1799, Babington still felt it necessary to advise his brother-in-law to make special efforts to adjust his temperament to that of "a pious, affectionate, and amiable wife." Hours of relaxation, he wrote, were among the most useful as well as the most pleasant seasons of matrimonial life, provided that they did not occur too frequently, and that the source of enjoyment was pure and hallowed. Zachary must not merely drag his "fellow-traveler" over deserts and through swamps, or bury her in the depths of a forest. Rather, he should lead her through cheerful cornfields and pastures, and occasionally "go out of [his] way a little to show her a flowery meadow or a winding stream."[49]

Three weeks after this letter was sent, on August 26, 1799, Zachary and Selina were married in the parish church of St. Augustine in Bristol. We are told that after the wedding the More sisters, desolate, retired to a private room in order to sob their fill. But if they still bemoaned the fate they apprehended for Selina, as well as their loss, they might have spared themselves their tears. It turned out to be a very happy marriage. Selina had no taste for society of any sort. Her only intimate friend throughout her life was her sister-in-law, Jean Babington. What she liked best was to remain at home with an interesting book. Zachary, on the other hand, led an active life of business and public affairs. Soon after his return, he was appointed secretary to the Sierra Leone Company at a salary of

46. Zachary Macaulay to Selina Mills, May 2, 1797, Huntington MSS.
47. Winterbottom to Zachary Macaulay, June 1796, Knutsford, *Zachary Macaulay*, 142.
48. Zachary Macaulay to Selina Mills, January 30, 1797, Huntington MSS.
49. Thomas Babington to Zachary Macaulay, August 6, 1799, Knutsford, *Zachary Macaulay*, 234.

£400 a year. He was active in the Religious Tract Society, the Church Missionary Society, and the Society for the Suppression of Vice—to name but a few. Like most of the leading Evangelicals, he loved to be gregarious in good causes. He is said to have regretted the fact that his wife was by temperament too retiring. But he always relied on her affection and her good sense. His letters to her, written during his frequent absences from home, never lost the utter candor and devotion of the love letters from Sierra Leone.

Since very few of her letters have been preserved, she remains from the time of her marriage a rather dim figure. The existing letters reflect her constant worry about his overworking. "It is a poor compensation to me," she wrote him in 1823, "to be told by every-body that you do the work of four men."[50] They also reflect the voice of a woman of sense as well as sensibility. One catches occasional echoes of this voice. In 1807, when the Macaulays were about to move into a new house, she expressed her annoyance with the servants who had not done the washing according to her instructions: "I wish you could tell them that I expect they have the three counterpanes, and sheets, and everything in the house perfectly clean, as I ordered. I am sorry," she added, "they made us so many rooms. What shall we do with them? We must shut up three or be ruined."[51] But her growing family was to take care of the space problem.

We get another glimpse of her common sense in action a few years later, when she reported to Zachary one of Hannah More's frequent and lugubrious intimations of almost immediate death. "I think she will outlive her two sisters," was her wry comment.[52] It reminds one of Zachary's treatment of a Sierra Leone settler who, pretending that rats had eaten up his papers of entitlement, claimed more rations than were due him. On Zachary's refusing to give him anything at all, "he found means next day to recover the paper from the rats."[53] Tom Macaulay's parents could not be accused of harboring many illusions about the ways of this world.

50. Selina Mills Macaulay to Zachary Macaulay, July 26, 1823, Huntington MSS.
51. Selina Mills Macaulay to Zachary Macaulay, July 11, 1807, Huntington MSS.
52. Selina Mills Macaulay to Zachary Macaulay, August 24, 1816, Huntington MSS.
53. Knutsford, *Zachary Macaulay*, 55.

II

CHILDHOOD

ON AN EARLY SUMMER'S DAY IN 1811, THOMAS DE QUINCEY'S MOTHER was engaged in writing a letter to her son when "a curious little Boy . . . arrived with a Note in his hand from Hannah More, begging us to receive him for a couple of days." The boy's cleverness and voracious appetite for reading—the first evening at her house he devoured half the *Mysteries of Udolpho*—led her to call him a "Baby genius." She found him amusing beyond expression. He reminded her, she wrote her son, of no less a person than Coleridge. But, she went on, "he says such extraordinary things that he will be ruined by praise."[1] Her prediction proved to be false. But her reaction to the young Tom Macaulay was by no means unique. He was without a doubt one of the most gifted children of his or any other generation.

Thomas Babington Macaulay was born at Rothley Temple on October 25, 1800. The first time Selina saw her son she repeated the lines of Isaac Watts's cradle hymn:

> *Mayst thou live to know and fear Him,*
> *Trust and love Him all thy days*
> Then *go dwell for ever near Him,*
> *See His face, and sing His praise.*[2]

1. Mrs. De Quincey to Thomas, June 8, 1811, Alexander H. Japp, ed., *De Quincey Memorials* (2 vols., London, 1891) , II, 92–5.
2. Selina Mills Macaulay to Thomas Babington Macaulay (referred to henceforth as T.B.M.) , May 28, 1813, Sir George Otto Trevelyan, *The Life and Letters of Lord Macaulay* (enlarged and complete ed., London, 1908) , 33.

Her choice must have pleased her brother-in-law, Thomas Babington, since a few years later he remarked in his *Practical View of Christian Education in Its Earliest Stages* that a truly Christian education ought to begin with Watts's hymns for children sung in the nursery.[3] For Zachary, as for all Evangelicals, children—and there were to be eight more after Tom—were nothing less than sacred trusts; and none more sacred than the eldest son, who, literally from the cradle onwards, displayed such extraordinary talents. Within a few months of his birth his mother noted the effectiveness of his strategy of singing as hard as he could in order to test whether she was *really* angry when she tried to quiet him.[4] Half a dozen years later, already famous in Clapham as "Clever Tom," omnivorous reader from the age of three, epic poet, and master of repartee, he was hard at work on a compendium of universal history. "We ought to be grateful," Zachary wrote to Selina at this time, "that it has pleased God to give us such a soil to work upon. May we be enabled to cultivate it in such a manner that it may bear fruit to God's glory."[5]

The family had moved to Clapham from Birchin Lane in the City of London in 1802. In the course of the previous year, Zachary had set up in business as a shipowner and merchant, trading with Africa and the East Indies. For some years the business prospered exceedingly. Zachary's energies and industry were such that he was able to continue and intensify his efforts on behalf first of the abolition of the slave trade and, when that had been accomplished (in 1807), of the abolition of slavery itself. He also found time for many years to edit the *Christian Observer*, the monthly periodical of the Evangelical Party.

Clapham, then still a rustic retreat from the busy life of the town, was the headquarters of the "sect" which derived its name from the place. Here, in pious and well-ordered amity and—let it be added—solid material comfort, resided the principal "Saints" and their families: Wilberforces, Grants, Thorntons, as well as Macaulays. Here parliamentary strategy for the great abolitionist battles was argued and decided; and the military progress of Napoleon (whose appearance on the stage of history one and all believed to have been foretold in the Old Testament) anxiously charted. Here were to be

3. Thomas Babington, *A Practical View of Christian Education in Its Earliest Stages* (Boston, 1818), 81.

4. Knutsford, *Zachary Macaulay,* 250.

5. Zachary Macaulay to Selina Mills Macaulay, July 10, 1807, ibid., 279.

found emissaries from the oppressed and abused throughout the world, come to seek critical counsel, financial aid, and crusading zeal, and finding inexhaustible reservoirs of all three. It is hardly suprising in the circumstances that the little boys at Mr. Greaves's day school in Clapham took a great interest in the parliamentary elections of 1806 (which saw Henry Thornton returned as MP) and in the final, successful battle for slave trade abolition that followed immediately.

Activity in the world, so that the souls of others might be saved, represented, however, only one part, and that the less important, of the message inscribed upon the Evangelical banner. The securing and preserving of one's own spiritual health remained the first order of business, and one by no means neglected in the household of Zachary Macaulay, where Sundays meant two sermons in church as well as an additional one read by the head of the family at home. It must not be supposed (though it often is) that the children of the "Saints" were expected by their parents to lead lives entirely grim and gray. The theater was out of bounds for them. But there were games of blindman's buff at Wilberforce's house. There were costume parties, at which on more than one occasion Tom made his appearance as Napoleon Bonaparte. There was even, to use Zachary's own phrase, an occasional "dissipated afternoon," in the course of which Tom, to his great delight, was taken to see a conjurer.[6] Thomas Babington's tract would not forbid parents to unbend with their children. "Most certainly," he wrote, "they may, and ought, frequently to relax with them, and even to take pains to make them happy by joining in their little amusements. But," he was quick to add, "they may combine this course of proceeding extremely well with a constant recollection of the immortal nature and high value of their children, for whom Christ died, and with a suitable behaviour towards them."[7]

This was certainly the approach chosen by Zachary and Selina; and, for a time at least, it appears to have had its intended effect upon their son. On his visits to Barley Wood, the country home of the More sisters, he did not merely engage in his favorite pastime of baking plum and apple pies or read for the first time, with mingled

6. Thomas Babington Macaulay's "Journal," preserved at Trinity College, Cambridge (henceforth referred to as Trinity Journal), May 28, 1853; E. M. Forster, *Marianne Thornton: A Domestic Biography 1797–1887* (New York, 1956), 54; Lord Teignmouth, *Reminiscences of Many Years* (2 vols., Edinburgh, 1878), I, 4; Zachary Macaulay to Selina Macaulay, Knutsford, *Zachary Macaulay*, 277.

7. Babington, *Practical View*, 45.

horror and delight, Coleridge's *Ancient Mariner;* standing on a chair, he also preached to the amazed field hands.[8] We hear of him at the age of eight, a slim, blue-eyed, fair-haired figure, vigorously opposing in a school debate the removal of the seat of the ancient Roman government from Rome to Vei; and addressing an appeal to the people of Travancore to embrace the Christian religion.[9] Hymns as well as epic poems like "The Battle of Cheviot" flowed from his pen:

> *Thy wrath is like a burning fire,*
> *Thy goodness all the good admire.*
> *Thy word restores the dawning day,*
> *At Thy command bright lightnings play.*[10]

But for Zachary it was not enough that his son's exuberant imagination should feed on the pietistic atmosphere of Clapham. Superior talents, when properly channeled, could work for the greater glory of God. At the same time, they could all too easily be productive of occasions for pride and self-indulgence. His own experience had taught him that only the severest self-discipline could make those occasions resistible. It was this lesson that he wished to pass on to his precocious son from the beginning. Tom's first wholly preserved letter to his father, written at the age of seven, struck a note that was to resound through their correspondence for almost twenty years. It began: "My dear Papa: I am sorry that my writing did not please you"—and ended with the hope that he would be able to improve it.[11]

Zachary was at great pains to supply a critical counterweight to the adulation proffered by adults to the boy's extraordinary abilities. In doing so, he hoped to be able to curb certain disturbing tendencies his son showed from an early age, all of which could be traced to his exceptional gifts. Thus, Hannah More wrote to him when Tom was ten that his son, being brilliant himself, was inclined to underrate people who were not in some degree considerable, or

8. Knutsford, *Zachary Macaulay,* 278; Trevelyan, *Life and Letters,* 25; Stanley Hutton, *Bristol and Its Famous Associations* (Bristol, 1907) , 94.

9. *Recollections of a Sister [Margaret] of T. B. Macaulay* (privately printed, London, 1864) , 90 (referred to henceforth as Margaret Macaulay, *Recollections*) ; Trevelyan, *Life and Letters,* 22.

10. Lionel Horton-Smith, ed., *Hymn by Lord Macaulay: An Effort of His Early Childhood* (2nd ed., Cambridge, 1902) , 8.

11. T.B.M. to his father, July 8, 1807, Knutsford, *Zachary Macaulay,* 279.

distinguished in some way or other. She had tried to explain to him that people without such distinction could nevertheless be valuable and worthy.[12] His playmates, we are told, would come crying to Tom's mother with the complaint: "Tom will play at Homer! I can't play at Homer!"—while he was already distributing roles, assigning to himself that of Achilles.[13]

Along with conceit went a tendency to what his father, at least, considered to be idleness. Presumably, since things came so easily to him, he did not find it necessary to spend much time studying. When no exercises had been sent home as promised from a holiday at Clifton, Zachary felt bound to comment that "we find, at least in the case of some persons (whether Tom Macaulay be in the number is best known to himself) that relaxation instead of acting as a stimulus to labour seems only to produce total inaction as to anything useful."[14] Furthermore, Tom's handwriting and general neatness still left so much to be desired that improvement in both respects was made a condition for any further excursions to Barley Wood. Hannah More herself felt that the boy needed more competitors—"he is like the prince who refused to play with anything but kings."[15] Zachary, on the other hand, put primary emphasis on the need for that constant discipline he himself was too busy to provide. What school would best supply discipline as well as competition?

Some time after the historian's death, one of his younger sisters, by then herself an old lady, regretted that her brother had not been sent to one of the great English public schools. "Those who knew and loved him best," she wrote, "will acknowledge that in many respects his character would have been improved and his influence greater had he been so trained."[16] Tom's parents, she added, thought that a public school education would have proved inimical to his religious development. In fact, Zachary had seriously considered moving his family from Clapham to Westminster, so that Tom would be able to attend the famous public school there as a day boy, yet be under domestic supervision the rest of the time. Hannah More approved of this idea, convinced that the hard study and severe discipline to be found at Westminster would tie down the boy's roving mind and pin his desultory pursuits to a point. At the same time, she warned that

12. Hannah More to Zachary Macaulay, May 1820, Knutsford, *Zachary Macaulay*, 288.
13. Margaret Macaulay, *Recollections*, 5–6.
14. Zachary Macaulay to T.B.M., June 6, 1811, Huntington MSS.
15. Hannah More to Zachary Macaulay, August 7, 1812, R. Brimley Johnson, ed., *The Letters of Hannah More* (London, 1925), 147.
16. Fanny Macaulay, "Domestic Portrait of T.B.M.," Huntington MSS.

"throwing boys headlong into these great public schools always puts me in mind of the practice of the Scythian mothers, who threw their new-born infants into the river; the greatest part perished; but the few who possessed great natural strength, and who were worth saving, came out with additional vigour from the experiment."[17]

Perhaps the force of this warning outweighed the thought of the possible advantages. Perhaps Selina, more tender-hearted than Zachary, objected to the scheme. In any event, the boy was sent away to a private boarding school at Little Shelford, in Cambridgeshire, which was presided over by the Rev. Matthew Preston, a onetime fellow of Trinity College, Cambridge, and a clergyman closely connected with leading Evangelical circles. Wilberforce had sent his oldest son there, too. Leaving home was a heavy blow for Tom, who confided to his mother within a week of going: "I do not remember being ever more gloomy in my life than when I first left Clapham."[18] His first letters home were blotted with tears.[19] Suddenly he found himself "a child among young men . . . crying for my papa and mamma and sisters, among hardened thoroughbred schoolboys."[20] Public schools possessed no monopoly on roughness and bullying. His mother obeyed his request not to subject him to jokes "which I would willingly dispense with" by addressing her letters to him as "Mr." rather than "Master" Macaulay.[21]

The combination of evident homesickness and pre-eminent intellectual talents generally tends to act as an irresistible challenge to bullies. Tom had to absorb more than his share of beatings, though he speaks of himself as much too wise and perhaps a little too proud to let his assailants perceive that their aggressions were having an effect on him.[22] His slovenly habits were a further challenge. Preston reportedly gave Tom's schoolfellows full permission to comb, brush, and towel him forcibly whenever necessary.[23] It is hardly

17. Hannah More to Zachary Macaulay, August 7, 1812, Johnson, ed., *More Letters*, 147–8.

18. T.B.M. to his mother, February 3, 1812, Correspondence of Thomas Babington Macaulay, Trinity College, Cambridge (henceforth referred to as Trinity Correspondence).

19. Fanny Macaulay, "Domestic Portrait of T.B.M.," Huntington MSS.

20. T.B.M. to his mother, March 4, 1819, Trinity Correspondence.

21. T.B.M. to his mother, September 15, 1813, Knutsford, *Zachary Macaulay*, 308.

22. In a letter to his mother, January 31, 1815, Trinity Correspondence, T.B.M. singled out an older boy named Wilson who used to beat or taunt him ten times a day. Perhaps he took his revenge for being bullied by becoming, as he put it, a champion wasp-killer at school. Trinity Journal, August 19, 1854.

23. Frederick Arnold, *The Public Life of Lord Macaulay* (London, 1862), 18.

surprising that he came to decide that the homesickness of the Swiss mountaineer was to his own "maladie du Clapham" as chickenpox to smallpox.[24]

He did not find any real comfort in Zachary's reminder that Christ had left *His* father for thirty years and had encountered many troubles, yet faced them cheerfully.[25] What saved him from lapsing into melancholy, he told his mother, was his school work and his outside reading.[26] He writes a long paper on the subject of the French Revolution and makes it a rule to eat neither supper nor lunch, and only a very sparing breakfast, until he has completed it.[27] "Against my conscience," he takes the negative side in a school debate on whether the Crusades were beneficial; one of his principal arguments being that they were impelled by superstition, and served to confirm the minds of the people in it.[28] Above all, he reads on his own, sitting alone in his study, protected from intrusion by a bolt "as strong as an elephant and as thick as ever mortal man beheld." Preston lends him some books, on condition that he finish one completely before asking for the next. Hannah More sends him an occasional two guineas, to be used to build up his library. He requests that the money be spent to buy him historical works—Hume, Smollett, Adolphus—but preferably French literature: Corneille and above all (if his father will give his consent on moral grounds) Molière.[29]

He might with some justice have entertained high hopes of obtaining the desired parental approval of his first reading choice. For had he not become acquainted with Molière and Richardson during an Easter visit in 1813 to that most prominent of Evangelical divines, Dean Milner, the president of Queens' College, Cambridge? Many years later he remembered Milner's talk about these authors, full of gaiety and interest.[30] It may have been this demonstration that even leading Evangelicals could be broadminded which emboldened him to recommend Dryden's verse paraphrase of some of Boccaccio's tales to his mother.[31] That volume, to be sure, contained none of the

24. T.B.M. to his mother, January 31, 1815, Trinity Correspondence.
25. Zachary Macaulay to T.B.M., August 15, 1813, Knutsford, *Zachary Macaulay*, 307.
26. T.B.M. to his mother, September 9, 1813, Trinity Correspondence.
27. Selina Mills Macaulay to Zachary Macaulay, May 27, 1814, Huntington MSS.
28. T.B.M. to his mother, May 17, 1813, Huntington MSS; T.B.M. to his father, March 23, 1813, MS in the possession of Mr. Gordon Ray.
29. T.B.M. to his father, May 7, 1814, August 25, 1814, Trinity Correspondence.
30. Mary Milner, *The Life of Isaac Milner* (London and Cambridge, 1842) , 560–1.
31. T.B.M. to his mother, August 23, 1815, Trevelyan, *Life and Letters*, 42.

"Comical Tales"! Nonetheless, he was on safer ground when he opted for Cowper's rather than Pope's Homer. "Pope," commented the thirteen-year-old scholar, "was not well acquainted with Greek."[32] Hume's *History of England* he found wanting in religious principle, and he felt impelled to reprimand Smollett for his ridiculous mixture of levity and anti-fanaticism at every mention of religion.[33]

Meanwhile, aided by his prodigious memory, a heritage from his father,[34] he made excellent progress in his studies. Preston, who moved his school from Little Shelford to Aspenden Hall in Hertfordshire in 1814, had occasion to praise Tom to Hannah More for his disposition and his learning.[35] Miss More herself never ceased to be astonished at the amount of reading Tom was able to pour in, and the amount of writing he was able to pour out. She enjoyed nothing more than his visits to Barley Wood. "Sometimes," she reported, "we converse in ballad-rhymes, sometimes in Johnsonian sesquipedalians; at tea, we condescend to riddles and charades."[36] Even Zachary, always chary with praise, was greatly impressed with his son's diligence; though he reminded him that this ought to stem from a sense of duty rather than from a desire for distinction.[37] He took pride in Tom's verses to the memory of William Pitt—"a little nonsense here and there, and some historical inaccuracy—but the lines flow well, and the leading idea is certainly not amiss"[38]—and in his "Vision" (1814), wherein the genius of Africa reproached Britain for neglecting the interests of the slaves in that year's Treaty of Paris. Zachary's brother, General Colin Macaulay, showed his nephew's poem to the great Duke of Wellington himself, who declared himself pleased with it.[39] Zachary and Selina visited Aspenden Hall in October of 1815 to hear Tom, now head boy of the school, declaim in the role of "Coningsby impeaching Harley, Earl of Oxford, for blasting Marlborough's laurels by the Peace of Utrecht."[40] Obviously delighted,

32. T.B.M. to his mother, September 4, 1813, Huntington MSS.

33. T.B.M. to his mother, October 26, 1814, Trinity Correspondence.

34. Zachary Macaulay recalled having committed to memory all of James Thomson's "Spring," the greater part of "Winter," and most of the striking pages of "Summer" and "Autumn," "without design." Knutsford, *Zachary Macaulay*, 171. Whenever information on any subject was required by the "Saints," Wilberforce used to say: "Let us look it out in Macaulay." Trevelyan, *Life and Letters*, 47.

35. Hannah More to Zachary Macaulay, November 15, 1814, Arthur Roberts, ed., *Letters of Hannah More to Zachary Macaulay* (London, 1860), 58.

36. Hannah More to Zachary Macaulay, ibid., July 21 [1815], 83–5.

37. Zachary Macaulay to T.B.M., April 5, 1813, Knutsford, *Zachary Macaulay*, 298.

38. Zachary Macaulay to Hannah More, December 26, 1814, Huntington MSS.

39. Knutsford, *Zachary Macaulay*, 318.

40. Zachary Macaulay to Hannah More, October 18, 1815, ibid., 326.

Zachary described the occasion to his friend and chief counselor, Hannah More.

Yet relations between father and son were not always easy. There was a flippant as well as an indolent strain in the lines Tom had addressed to his teacher:

And if at Eastertide thou mak'st us work,
Thou mightst as well have been a Jew or Turk.

Hadn't the boy had enough holidays? And, in any event, was a holiday really such a good thing? Then, it seemed, Tom did not like decimals. His father, on the other hand, happened to be very fond of this species of calculation, which had helped him considerably in his business transactions. He would wish to recommend respect and even a passion for decimals to his son—"if I had any hope of success in my recommendation."[41]

Any young schoolboy could be expected to have a liking for holidays and an aversion to figures. But as he entered adolescence, Tom's likes and dislikes, and the reasons he gave for them, departed in a remarkable fashion from the conventional pattern. Why, he asked his mother in a letter written in French, spend so much time in the study of ancient literature? It might show man's progress from barbarism to elegance; but works of equal merit were surely to be found in the modern languages, including English. And as for progress—"Peut-être on peut se promettre le retour d'un âge d'or quand les jeunes demoiselles entreront dans nos universités et deviendront Senior Wranglers."[42] Why, he asked his father in a long letter a few months later—which he took care to call "speculative," since he was actually engaged in reading two Greek tragedies a week at the time of writing—why must we moderns have classical models when the ancients did without them? Euripides was his particular *bête noire:* "Scenes which would have been hissed off an English stage with the unanimous execrations of pit, boxes, and of galleries, no sooner appear in a Greek clothing than all the terms of applause which language affords are lavished on their meanest puerilities." Like Patroclus in the armor of Achilles, like the ass in the lion's skin, they triumphed not by their merit but their clothing. The Renaissance might well have been dazzled by the luster of the classics: "A farthing candle will almost blind with its light one whose eyes have been long

41. Zachary Macaulay to T.B.M., March 15, 1814, Trinity Correspondence.
42. T.B.M. to his mother, June 1, 1816, Trinity Correspondence.

accustomed to the darkness of a cellar. But shall its lustre be therefore considered as equal to the brightness of the sun?"[43]

One may well wonder what went through Zachary's head as he read his son's letter. The style must have struck him: eloquent, forceful, ablaze with metaphor and simile. As for the substance, it was plain that Tom's annoyance with the classics was temporary—the result, he reported, of the spleen he had felt as his head ached over an unintelligible, defective, and mutilated chorus of Aeschylus or a punning prologue of Euripides, stuffed with geology and commonplace proverbs. In fact, barely three weeks later, the young scholar announced that Demosthenes had once again put him in a good humor with the classics.[44] But more striking than his complaints about the Greeks was the particular sort of common sense he showed as a critic, based on the assumption that men were too easily taken in by mere antiquity; that it was the "Greek clothing" and not the actual worth of certain works of literature that had given them a reputation they did not deserve. It was in the service of truth, the confounding of sham and pretense, that Zachary daily wielded his practiced scalpel against the tumors of sin outside and within him. Tom's strong love of truth was one of the qualities in his character that most pleased Zachary.[45] Now, as he saw evidence of his son's ability to "strike through the mask," might he not have wondered when and whether it would be turned to higher uses?

After the boy had been at Preston's school for little more than a year, Selina's father, the old Quaker, had expressed the hope to his daughter that divine grace might soon descend upon his grandson.[46] Zachary clearly shared this hope. For it was his own conversion experience at Rothley Temple that had given his life meaning and focus. Worldly success and intellectual achievements were as nothing, unless with the aid of grace they could be turned to God's service. He was convinced, we are told on good authority, that if his own qualities of concentration, energy, industry, and patience could only be joined with his son's rather disorderly genius, a being might be formed who could regenerate the world.[47] How he must have wished for the divine lightning to strike Tom's heart, as it had his own! Perhaps because he was afraid that the very act of putting his wish in

43. T.B.M. to his father, October 24, 1817, Trinity Correspondence.
44. T.B.M. to his father, November 11, 1817, Trinity Correspondence.
45. Zachary Macaulay to Hannah More, January 30, 1816, Huntington MSS.
46. Thomas Mills to Selina Macaulay, December 20, 1813, Huntington MSS.
47. Hannah, Lady Trevelyan, "Reminiscences," 18, Trinity MSS.

writing might inhibit its fulfillment, he never (as far as we know) did so directly to him, though he certainly did all he could to lay a groundwork of piety and discipline. But he or, more likely, Preston must have talked to the boy about the need for that faith which alone could bring about the descent of grace. For, many years later, the historian was to note in his journal: "Nobody who has lived with our high Evangelicals can doubt that they consider faith as a thing which a man is to be urged to get, and chidden for not having."[48]

It is possible, indeed, that being "chidden" too severely had just the opposite effect from the one intended. Looking back, Tom's favorite sister Hannah castigated Preston's religious training as "woefully mistaken," and referred to his "exaggerated Evangelicalism" and his "queer, suspicious temper."[49] The historian himself once recalled that Preston had kept the Sabbath by being in a bad temper.[50] Perhaps Preston drove too hard, forgetting that his star pupil was adept not merely in the classics and debating but also in seeing through cant. What is certain is that he told Zachary in October 1815 that while Tom was "the most correct" boy he had ever known, he desired to see in him "more unequivocal indications of decided piety."[51]

The boy was not outwardly irreligious. Only the previous year, Preston had singled out to Hannah More Tom's reverence for religion.[52] And Zachary declared himself satisfied with his son's moral improvement and his disrelish for all that was low and sensual. But, to use the phraseology of his father-in-law, the Holy Jesus had not fixed his abode within him. Thus, Zachary noted with pleasure how anxious Tom was to obtain his parents' and his master's approbation—but added: "May he become equally intent to please his God."[53] Almost two years later, when his son's schooldays were about to come to an end, the father's comment was: "So far all is well. May God give him his grace."[54]

It may well be that neither Preston nor his school was to blame for

48. Trinity Journal, November 27, 1859.

49. Hannah, Lady Trevelyan, "Reminiscences," 25–6, Trinity MSS.

50. Dorothy Alston, "Some Personal Recollections of Lord Macaulay," London Mercury, XVIII (1928), 59.

51. Zachary Macaulay to Hannah More, October 18, 1815, Huntington MSS.

52. Hannah More to Zachary Macaulay, January 15, 1814, Roberts, ed., More Letters, 58.

53. Zachary Macaulay to Hannah More, January 30, 1816, Huntington MSS.

54. Zachary Macaulay to Hannah More, December 24, 1817, Huntington MSS.

Tom's unconverted state; that, rather, it was related to a temperamental difference between father and son which it would be simplistic to regard as merely the reaction of a sensitive youth of genius
to a strict paternal regimen. It is perfectly true that (as Tom's sister
Hannah was to point out in a memoir written after her brother's
death) the boy's faults were particularly those with which Zachary
had no patience. The father was precise, neat, accurate, calm, and
self-controlled. The son was careless and, above all, impetuous. But
what lends the difference between father and son particular poi-
gnancy and also helps to account for Zachary's increasing concern is
the fact that some of the character traits recognized and deplored in
the son by the father were identical with those against which Zachary
had had to force himself to wrestle with such vigilance, even after his
conversion. Pride, disdain for society, an excessively vivid imagination—were these not the self-same qualities which the Governor of
Sierra Leone had time and again confided to his journal with such
merciless candor and without ever being able to extirpate them to his
satisfaction? Now they seemed to have been visited upon his first-
born.

Tom was loud-mouthed and conceited, impatient of the company
of those inferior to him in ability (which was to say almost all
company), and far more intent on writing poems and reading novels
than on the salvation of his soul. Furthermore, he lacked good
manners, was careless in deportment and personal appearance, and—
what accentuated these qualities—grew fat and ungainly after a fever
at the age of sixteen.[55] Hannah recalled remarking once to her
father that Tom was like Forester, the eponymous hero of Maria
Edgeworth's novel: intelligent, frank and generous, but at the same
time ill-mannered, scornful of the common forms of civilization, and
carrying his love of independence to such an extreme that, in the
words of Miss Edgeworth, "he was inclined to prefer the life of
Robinson Crusoe in his desert island to that of any individual in
cultivated society." Zachary's vehement reply was: "But I do not
want him to be like Forester!"[56] Nor did Zachary want him to be
like that part of himself which, even with the aid of divine grace, he
had been able to put behind him only at the cost of a struggle that

55. Margaret Macaulay, *Recollections*, 32. Already in 1813 (April 26), T.B.M. wrote
to his father: "I am glad that Mamma is satisfied with my defence on the topic of exercise; and I assure her that though the current opinion here is that I shall grow tall there
is not much suspicion of my being thin." MS in the possession of Mr. Gordon Ray.
56. Hannah, Lady Trevelyan, "Reminiscences," 24, Trinity MSS.

had left its marks on his personality as well as on his grim and forbidding appearance.

That is, no doubt, why he kept hammering away at Tom's weaknesses: "Loud-speaking, affected pronunciation in reading, late lying in bed, neglect of cleanliness"—thus ran a summary reminder in a letter to the fifteen-year-old boy.[57] "Wisely, but rather cruelly . . . as a damper to his genius," Hannah More commented,[58] he set Tom the task of compiling the index to the thirteenth volume of the *Christian Observer*. Not without a touch of irony, the boy proudly announced its appearance to Miss More, together with that of Scott's *Lord of the Isles*, Southey's *Roderick*, and Wordsworth's *Excursion*.[59]

Tom was to have his revenge for the index. One of his next appearances in the *Christian Observer* was as the anonymous author of a letter in defense of fiction. "Severe indeed is the cynic," Candidus [Tom] remarked, who would "preclude the English ladies from any lighter studies than Butler's *Analogy* and Hooker's *Ecclesiastical Polity*"; especially when even the novels of Smollett and Fielding taught lessons of virtue through characters like Joseph Andrews and Parson Adams.[60] It was a remarkable letter—remarkable for the closely formulated ethical approach which got it past the eagle eye of his father, the editor, whose own library of fiction was then confined to a few titles of the order of the Rev. James Beresford's *Talents Improved or The Philanthropist;* remarkable as well for the fact that Tom himself had not even read Fielding's novels when he wrote the letter, and had had to rely for his information about them on his schoolfellow Malden.[61]

There is evident in all this a prankish strain of gaiety and panache of the sort which had earlier made him respond to his father's pleas to be less loud by a resolve to speak in a moderate key, except (he added) when speaking at the same time as three others, or when praising the *Christian Observer* or the Rev. Matthew Preston and his sisters.[62] This strain was bound ultimately to bring all of Zachary's disciplinary efforts to nought. "I like to see him as boyish as he is studious," Hannah More wrote about him when he was fifteen, "and

57. Zachary Macaulay to T.B.M., February 22, 1815, Trinity Correspondence.
58. Hannah More to Zachary Macaulay, February 2, 1815, Roberts, ed., *More Letters,* 73–4.
59. T.B.M. to Hannah More, January 16, 1815, ibid., 69–70.
60. "Observations on Novel Reading," *Christian Observer,* XV (1816), 784–7.
61. Margaret Macaulay, *Recollections,* 92.
62. T.B.M. to his mother, April 11, 1814, Trevelyan, *Life and Letters,* 36.

that he is as much amused with making a pat of butter as a poem."[63] His intellect and his reputation, she added, were getting better every day; but the child in him was still preserved.

Her observation was just. Tom's literary tastes and opinions were taking form, some to remain unchanged through a lifetime. He had already decided that Wordsworth was a bore, that he himself preferred London with its smoky atmosphere and its muddy river to the pure air of Hertfordshire.[64] Nature, he declared, "is the last goddess to whom my devoirs shall be paid." The subjects that interested and enchanted him were not the changing seasons, but rather "men and women, the camp, the court, the city, and the senate."[65] And, above all, the splendid achievements of great men past and present—of Pitt, of Wellington, yes, even of Napoleon. "Was there ever such a man as Bonaparte?" he asked his mother at the time of the escape from Elba. "All my detestation of his crimes, all my horror at his conduct, is completely swallowed up in astonishment, awe, and admiration at the more than human boldness of the present attempt."[66]

Precocious and cocksure judgments on life and letters, an ardent imagination, a pronounced temperamental difference from his father's austere view of life—did all these traits portend a desire to strike out for himself, to face the world on his own? Nothing could be further from the truth. He continued to respect his father and to do his best to please him. But Zachary's temperament was such that it rarely, if ever, permitted him to acknowledge such pleasure, when rendered. That did not make the relationship between father and son any easier. It was his mother whom Tom loved, with passionate devotion. In a letter written to her from Cambridge in 1821 that cries out to be called Proustian he recalled that "there is nothing which I remember with such pleasure as the time when you nursed me at Aspenden." He had been thinking back to that time in the course of a bout, just surmounted, of illness and hypochondria.

How sick, and sleepless, and weak I was, lying in bed, when I was told that you were come! How well I remember with what an ecstasy of joy I saw that face approaching me, in the middle of people that did not care if I died that night except for the trouble of burying me. The sound of your voice, the touch of your hand, are present to me now, and will be, I trust in God, to my last hour.

63. Hannah More to Zachary Macaulay, July 21, 1815, Roberts, ed., *More Letters*, 84.
64. T.B.M. to Hudson, August 22, 1815, Trinity Correspondence.
65. T.B.M. to Hudson, November 5, 1815, Trinity Correspondence.
66. T.B.M. to his mother, March 23, 1815, Trinity Correspondence.

He was almost ready to bless his illness and low spirits for bringing these images before him.[67]

Tom's letters to his mother during the period of his boyhood are his most sparkling and revealing, often quite unlike those to his father, which tended to be serious, guarded, and necessarily defensive in tone. And, as the family grew in number, his strong need for giving and receiving affection found new objects and sources. "As for the three little darlings," one letter from school concludes, "tell Fanny that I did not leave her the mumps intentionally, and Hannah that I think that Senna Tea is nasty but that it must be taken; and give Margaret a kiss."[68] "When I come home," he concluded another letter a few weeks later, "I shall, if my purse is sufficient, bring a couple of rabbits for Selina and Jane, and something for John and Henry and Fanny and Hannah, and little pretty Margaret."[69]

He lived for the holidays. In the summer of 1814, the family (except for Zachary) spent a few days at Brighton. Tom brought the scene of his little sister's and brother's sea-bathing vividly to life for the benefit of his absent father. Fanny, it seemed, was

actually petrified and overwhelmed by horror and amazement at finding herself precipitated from the tremendous height of the stairs of the bathing machine (or, as Misery Beresford[70] calls it, of the sea-hearse) into the raging deep. The bathing women, I am informed, animated and encouraged them to take the dreadful leap, by blandishments of a very remarkable kind. When Henry made his appearance upon the stairs they saluted him thus: "Come my darling, come my pretty prince, come my king, come, defence of his country."[71]

But spending the holidays at home in Clapham matched and exceeded the pleasures of the seaside; especially when his sisters and brothers were old enough to constitute an admiring audience. Here, in the evenings, when as a special treat reading aloud from novels was permitted, he entertained them with passages from *Sir Charles Grandison;* and here, loved and adored, the prince who would only play with kings could doff his crown and be at ease.

67. T.B.M. to his mother, March 25, 1821, Trevelyan, *Life and Letters,* 73.

68. T.B.M. to his father, February 26, 1813, MS in the possession of Mr. Gordon Ray.

69. T.B.M. to his father, May 8, 1813, MS in the possession of Mr. Gordon Ray.

70. The nickname was based on Beresford's authorship of *The Miseries of Human Life.*

71. T.B.M. to his father, July 11, 1814, MS in the possession of Mr. Gordon Ray.

III

CAMBRIDGE

MUCH HAS BEEN WRITTEN ABOUT MACAULAY'S ABIDING AFFECTION FOR Trinity College, where Zachary observed his son and his Clapham friend and fellow freshman Henry Thornton dining in Hall for the first time in October 1818, "plying their knives and forks with great vigour and without seeming to feel themselves strangers."[1] It was an affection derived from the feeling of social liberation, the talk, the companionship, and perhaps, above all, the sense of being part of a great tradition that his years there gave him.

Trinity, after all, had been the place

> . . . *where Bacon caught*
> *The first faint gleam of manly thought,*
> *That broke on that benighted age*
> *To guide the wanderings of the sage:*
> *Where Newton traced the secret cause*
> *Of moving worlds and nature's laws:*
> *Where Dryden touch'd his potent lyre*
> *With inspiration's earliest fire.*[2]

More recently, Byron had kept his bear there. It would have been surprising had not Macaulay's ardent imagination caught fire in such

1. Zachary Macaulay to Selina Mills Macaulay, October 18, 1818, Huntington MSS.
2. [Anon.], *Ode to Trinity* (1812).

a place, and no less surprising had he not taken full advantage of the opportunities for independent reading, forming friendships, and expanding his intellectual horizon which Cambridge provided. True, he vowed to Zachary that he meant to regard the university mainly as an armory of those weapons he needed in order that both of them, father and son, might one day triumph together over the enemies of humanity. To Hannah More he wrote that he did not wish to loiter among the magazines while the battle was raging.[3]

He firmly assured his uncle Babington, who was worried about the dangers of excess in collegiate life, that "the necessity of accepting wine-invitations, or of attending dinner-parties is, I am fully convinced, a factitious necessity."[4] From these and some of his other letters from Cambridge one might indeed gain the impression that his time was occupied solely with academic tasks of the highest seriousness,—particularly his ill-fated attempts to master algebra and trigonometry—interrupted only for the purpose of attending prayers: "If I rise at four the chapel breaks into my morning studies," ran his complaint to Zachary. "If I sit down after dinner, it interrupts me immediately again."[5] To one contemporary he was pointed out as the great man of his year, with the added comment that "it is hardly possible to suppose that a person with so heavy and unintellectual a countenance can possess any talent." From the same source we catch a glimpse of him: a short, ungainly figure, reciting the opening chorus of the *Persae* in his Greek class.[6]

He could certainly be pleased with his academic achievements. In the College Examination of Freshmen (May 1819), he ranked fourth in the first class. He won the coveted Craven Scholarship in 1821, of which, he recalled many years later, he "was as proud . . . as a peacock of his tail."[7] He gained the chancellor's gold medal for his poem "Pompeii" and recited it before him and a distinguished audience in July 1819, having ordered a black silk waistcoat especially for the occasion.[8] Yet he himself later confided to his sister

3. T.B.M. to his father, October 23, 1818, Knutsford, *Zachary Macaulay*, 343; T.B.M. to Hannah More, November 4, 1818, Trinity Correspondence.

4. T.B.M. to Thomas Babington, December 5, 1818, Trinity Correspondence.

5. T.B.M. to his father, November 16, 1818, Houghton Library MSS, Harvard University.

6. Richard Perry, *Contributions to an Amateur Magazine in Prose and Verse with a Preface, and Additional Notes containing some Account of the late Lord Macaulay, the Author's Fellow-Collegian and Early Friend* (London, 1861), 300.

7. Trinity Journal, December 2, 1857.

8. T.B.M. to his father, February 24, 1820, Trinity Correspondence.

Margaret that he never worked hard at Cambridge and that he was more idle than many of the men, "empty bottles," in the *argot* of the place, who were "plucked."[9] Granted his phenomenal memory and quickness of mind, the use of the term "idle" about himself must always be taken with a grain of salt. Still, there was something to what he recalled.

We do not, of course, hear of him indulging in the usual pastimes of fashionable Cambridge students of his generation: going to Newmarket races "à la tandem"; "barracking to Bury, Huntingdon, or Colchester to kick up a row at the ball"; billiards; boating; playing cricket on Parker's Piece, or "racketing away in the Tennis Court"; and "kissing rustic maidens."[10] As far as he was concerned, dissipation and idling at Cambridge meant conversation, not kissing; novel reading, not Newmarket. Reading Shelley's "Euganean Hills" (he disliked it) or Marmontel's *Memoirs,* which gave him his first acquaintance with the society of the Ancien Régime in France and which remained for some time his favorite book; or whiling away evenings in discussing the respective merits of Cromwell and Charles with his friends—all that was much to be preferred to mathematics. " 'Discipline' of the mind!" he exclaimed in a letter to his mother. "Say rather starvation, confinement, torture, annihilation! But it must be. I feel myself becoming a personification of Algebra, a living trigonometrical canon, a working table of Logarithms." And signed himself "your most miserable and mathematical son."[11]

At first he lived in Jesus Lane, in lodgings outside the college. Later he had rooms in Trinity, within earshot of the plashing of the fountain in Great Court. Within a few months of his arrival, he reported to Zachary that he had become "rather a favourite."[12] Nicknames are a sure sign of such a position. Macaulay, whose habits of neatness had not improved with age, was known as "the man with the neckcloth"; or, to distinguish him from a cousin who bore the sobriquet "bear," as "Beast Macaulay."[13] We catch sight of him talking at breakfast while a college servant was cleaning his boots; drinking a concoction of chopped hay instead of tea when both his purse and his tea cannister were temporarily at a low ebb; moving

9. Hannah, Lady Trevelyan, "Reminiscences," 32, Trinity MSS.
10. [J. M. F. Wright], *Alma Mater: By a Trinity Man* (2 vols., London, 1827) , I, 185–6.
11. T.B.M. to his mother, "1818," Trevelyan, *Life and Letters,* 64. On Shelley and Marmontel, see Trinity Journal, September 5, 1856, and December 28, 1854.
12. T.B.M. to his father, January 25 [1820], Trinity Correspondence.
13. Margaret Macaulay, *Recollections,* 33; [Wright], *Alma Mater,* I, 218.

into new rooms in Trinity and hoping that the mattress would be dry, "and that I shall not be eaten up by the rats who are not unfrequently tenants of these venerable haunts"—in short, savoring some of the joys and trials of undergraduate life.[14]

Among those joys writing poetry ranked very high; and it was poetry of the most diverse kinds, written in many different modes: a Hebrew eclogue on the young women of Israel going to bewail each year the sacrifice of Jephthah's daughter; a Jacobin song for 1792; some anonymous verses entitled "Tears of Sensibility," intended as a parody, but like enough to have been taken seriously by his mother as well as by the editor of the *Morning Post,* where they appeared; an apostrophe "To Woman":

> *The Poet is thy priest. To thee he rears*
> *A temple and an image in his heart*
> *And feeds thine altar's consecrated fires*
> *With the sweet frankincense of fond desires.*[15]

Whether those particular lines were addressed to a specific person or were more in the nature of a conventional poetic exercise it is not possible to say, though the latter seems more likely.

At one point during his Cambridge years Macaulay had fancied himself half in love with his cousin, Mary Babington. We hear of him trying to impress her one summer by his brilliant talk, while rowing her around the lake at Rothley Temple. "But," he later remembered, "her conversation soon healed the wound made by her eyes."[16] For her part, she had thought him remarkable but too conceited, and had not been fond of him. But that was in retrospect.[17] Apart from this brief episode, we know of no other. His real passion, and Zachary, in a letter to Hannah More, used the very word to describe it, continued to be his love of domesticity.[18] The keen sense of deprivation he suffered whenever he was away from home remained undiminished.

14. Three glimpses, in order: Arnold, *Public Life,* 22; T.B.M. to his father, November 24, 1819, Trinity Correspondence; and T.B.M. to his father, February 12, 1821, Huntington MSS.

15. "Tears of Sensibility" (1821), Trevelyan, *Life and Letters,* 77; "To Woman" (July 1822), MS in the possession of the author.

16. Lake scene based on information from typescript "Aunt Eliza's Story" (1875), a memoir by Eliza Rose Conybeare of life at Rothley Temple. I owe this reference to Thomas Pinney.

17. Margaret Macaulay, *Recollections,* 54. Mary Babington married James (later Sir James) Parker in 1829.

18. Zachary Macaulay to Hannah More, August 31, 1819, Huntington MSS.

In 1826 he was to publish in the *Edinburgh Review*[19] an article little known today, on "The London University," an eloquent testimonial to the establishment of the new University College in London. It contained some trenchant reflections upon the deleterious effects of the collegiate system and, more especially, upon the distaste for domestic life that was apt to develop in students living under it. "The system is monastic," he wrote, "and it tends to produce the monastic selfishness, inattention to the convenience of others, and impatience of petty privations." To the argument that a young student at London University living at home would be made idle by the society of his mother and sisters, Macaulay replied that, on the contrary, his ambition would at the same time be animated and consecrated by daily intercourse with those dearest to him and most inclined to rejoice in his success. "For our part," he observed,

when a young man is to be urged to persevering industry, and fortified against the seductions of pleasure, we would rather send him to the fireside of his own family than to the abodes of philosophers who died centuries ago,—and to those kind familiar faces which are always anxious in his anxiety, and joyful in his success, than to the portrait of any writer that ever wore cap and gown.

The diarist Henry Crabb Robinson, knowing of the young Macaulay's attachment to Cambridge and Trinity, expressed amazement that he of all people should have been capable of seeing so clearly the negative effects of the college system.[20] He would have been less amazed, had he been able to look over Macaulay's shoulder eight years earlier and seen him write to Hannah More: "I am no great admirer of this monastic life. I love the cheerful blaze of a domestic hearth, and reciprocation of mixed conversation and mixed company, too well to relish the state to which I am here necessarily doomed";[21] or had he been able to hear him argue for the advantages of married fellows against Henry Thornton, referring no doubt to "that pitiable being, an old Fellow of a College, without domestic ties or liberal views or capacities of literary enjoyment, or sense of benevolent pleasures."[22] Home, since 1818 no longer in Clapham

19. *Edinburgh Review*, XLIII (1826), 315–41; reprinted in John Clive and Thomas Pinney, eds., *Thomas Babington Macaulay: Selected Writings* (Chicago, 1972), 3–33.

20. Edith J. Morley, ed., *Henry Crabb Robinson on Books and Their Writers* (3 vols., London, 1938), I, 341.

21. T.B.M. to Hannah More, November 11, 1818, Trinity Correspondence.

22. For argument with Thornton, see Dorothy Pym, *Battersea Rise* (London, 1934), 82; quotation from T.B.M. to Hannah More, November 11, 1818, Trinity Correspondence.

but Cadogan Place in central London, remained the primary focus of Tom's existence. To one or the other of his sisters, who adored him, he wrote almost daily. "The very interest their affection leads them to take in his pursuits and in mine also," Zachary told his wife, "is elevating to young minds expanding into life and action."[23]

The father did not always sound such a laudatory note when he viewed his son's activities and character. To the occasions for strain that existed between them another was added during these years: politics. It will not do, however, to exaggerate their differences in this sphere. One is often told that Macaulay came up to Cambridge a convinced Clapham-bred Tory, and underwent a dramatic conversion to Whiggism there, having first passed through a Radical phase. But it is well to remember that not all Evangelicals were die-hard Tories, mainly concerned with stemming the French revolutionary tide. Such certainly existed, the More sisters among them. Late in life Macaulay recalled Patty More's high Toryism and how she considered everybody who did not agree with her a traitor, robber, or murderer. Significantly, he added the comment that Wilberforce, Thornton, his uncle Babington, and his father were too liberal in politics for her.[24] We have already seen that, in spite of his experience in Sierra Leone, Zachary had been able to discern the more constructive aspects of the French Revolution. He was no blind admirer of the established order, especially when this term had reference to the privileged rule of aristocracy. In 1814 he urged Tom to remember that Napoleon's occupation of the continental states had done a great deal of good; sweeping away tyranny, abuses, and superstition. Even English Radicals like Burdett and Cochrane, however bad their spirit, however false and mischievous their principles, had made no small contribution. Thus, Burdett had played a major role in the abolition of flogging in the British army. And the democratic fearlessness of the Radicals kept in check to some extent the outrageous profligacy of the high aristocracy. He himself was finding it hard to choose between the lying and seditious harangues of the democrats and the debauches of Belvoir Castle.[25]

This letter of Zachary's epitomizes the political attitude of a great many leading Evangelicals: respect for those of whatever party persuasion who were fighting abuses which they, too, wanted to see

23. Zachary Macaulay to Selina Mills Macaulay, November 25, 1820, Knutsford, *Zachary Macaulay*, 365.
24. Trinity Journal, February 21, 1859.
25. Zachary Macaulay to T.B.M., February 28, 1814, Trinity Correspondence. Belvoir Castle was the seat of the Duke of Rutland.

removed; disdain for aristocratic immorality; and hatred for democracy. The Evangelicals were Tories largely because it was the younger Pitt who had at one and the same time stood forth staunchly against the "armed doctrine" of the French Revolution and (somewhat less consistently) against the slave trade. They were against democratic radicalism, not only because they accepted a stratified society, providentially ordained, but also because radicalism meant to them, above all else, atheism.

Not surprisingly, the young Macaulay had caught the patriotic note during the Napoleonic wars. He was optimistic about the eventual outcome and dismissed the gloomy prognoses of his master Preston as those of "a very despairing politician."[26] His imagination responded impartially to heroic deeds and great occasions on either side. It was set ablaze equally by the memory of Pitt and by the daring of Bonaparte's escape from Elba. Anti-radicalism, as well as patriotism and admiration for great men, had characterized his schoolboy attitude toward politics. When not yet fifteen, he had managed to gain Hannah More's approbation for producing a satire on Radical reform entitled "Clodpole and the Quack Doctor."[27] Some months later he referred to "Orator" Hunt, one of the leading Radicals, as "this staple hunter of Reform who rushes on to his object through hedges and ditches, not caring how much dirt he may splash through, or how many honest passengers he may trample down in his way. . . . At Aspenden, such is our loyal zeal that I would not advise him to venture within the precincts of the park."[28] His sister Hannah later recalled that her brother came up to Cambridge sharing the very liberal Toryism of Zachary and his set.[29] The word "liberal" should be emphasized. In one of his first letters from Cambridge, Macaulay reported to his father that, except for one splendid sermon, all he had heard in church was "wretched indeed, half-political, half-polemical trash, against parliamentary reform and predestination and Bible Society."[30]

Of course, parliamentary reform could mean many things. It all depended upon who was demanding it: moderate Whigs were convinced the time had come to put an end to the aristocratic predominance buttressed by corruption which had characterized the

26. T.B.M. to his mother, September 15, 1813, Knutsford, *Zachary Macaulay*, 309.
27. Hannah More to Zachary Macaulay, July 21 [1815], Roberts, ed. *More Letters*, 85.
28. T.B.M. to his mother, December 9, 1816, Trinity Correspondence.
29. Hannah, Lady Trevelyan, "Reminiscences," 28–9, Trinity Correspondence.
30. T.B.M. to his father, November 4, 1813, Trinity Correspondence.

eighteenth-century parliamentary system and felt that this system was out of date in an age marked by the economic predominance of the middle classes (most of whom could not vote) in the new manufacturing towns (most of which were not represented in Parliament). Democratic Radicals, on the other hand, were fed up with the harsh Tory régime of repression and proscription which had followed Waterloo, and preached universal suffrage at mass meetings to hungry thousands deprived of work and livelihood by the postwar depression. It was a meeting of this sort that supplied the occasion for a real clash over politics between Zachary and his son.

In August 1819, Manchester yeomanry charged into a crowd gathered to hear "Orator" Hunt hold forth on the subject of parliamentary reform in St. Peter's Fields. Eleven people were killed and several hundred others wounded. Three weeks before this "Peterloo Massacre" (as it came to be called), Zachary had attributed the "ignited state" of Manchester in great part to the "inimical supineness" of the government in failing to be more vigilant in suppressing seditious publications.[31] Now his son expressed sympathy for the very people who must have drawn inspiration from those publications. It was certainly not an isolated act of sympathy on Tom's part. The reaction against the bloodshed of Peterloo transcended class lines. Even some of the Whig aristocracy took the side of the victims. But the Tories defended the action; and Zachary loyally supported them. Selina wrote to Tom that both she and his father were very uneasy about his views and wondered whether he had been initiated into any democratic societies at Cambridge.

We do not have her letter, but we have her son's eloquent reply. The Tory loyalism of his Aspenden Hall days had evaporated in the face of his moral outrage. He informed her proudly that his opinions, good or bad, had been learned not from Radical politicians, but from Cicero, Tacitus, and Milton. They were opinions which had produced men who had ornamented the world and redeemed human nature from the degradation of ages of superstition and slavery. (Tom had early mastered the knack of strategically reminding his father of his favorite cause.) "I may be wrong as to the facts of what occurred at Manchester," he went on. "But, if they be what I have seen them stated, I can never repent speaking of them with indignation. When I cease to feel the injuries of others warmly, to detest wanton cruelty, and to feel my soul rise against oppression, I shall

31. Zachary Macaulay to Hannah More, August 31, 1819, Knutsford, *Zachary Macaulay*, 349.

think myself unworthy to be your son." He was willing to admit that his ideas might be crude. But, he pointed out, it was inevitable that any person of reflection, however young, engaged in studying the history and politics of other nations must form certain notions on such subjects and apply them to his own country. The letter ended respectfully and submissively. Even if he were to be rewarded by the position of a Hampden or a Cromwell as a result of standing forth in the democratic cause, he would rather have his lips sealed on the subject than give his father and mother a single hour of uneasiness.[32]

The Peterloo correspondence represents the single, explicit political altercation between Tom and his father. In spite of Tom's indignation over the Massacre, he continued to share his father's sentiments about popular democratic movements. Neither Cicero nor Tacitus nor Milton would ever teach him otherwise. In 1821 he wrote to Zachary:

The conduct of the rabble of the jury, and of [the Radical] Sheriff Waithman, sometimes turns me for a few hours into a Tory. I now and then fear that I shall be a perfect jure-divino man, if these things go on. . . . Of all the *ocracies,* blackguardocracy is surely the worst, and if the liberties of the country are to be taken away, I hope that we shall at least have the privilege of being choked like the Duke of Clarence in Malmsey wine, not drowned in a filthy kennel.[33]

The elder Macaulay undoubtedly agreed. Political differences between father and son were not really sufficiently serious to precipitate a serious breach. As Zachary began to find more sentiment for the abolition of slavery among the Whigs than among the Tories, he himself moved in the same direction as his son.

Nor did undoubted differences of religious temperament lead to such a breach.

> *Oh, be your hearts and tongues the same*
> *While singing the Almighty's name*

had been the plea of the eight-year-old Tom in his role of hymnologist. Was he able to follow his own injunction? In 1819 he was considering the Church as well as the law as a profession; in part (so Zachary reported to Hannah More) because his love of domesticity was so great that the chance of an earlier settlement had a special

32. T.B.M. to his father, September 1819, Trinity Correspondence.
33. T.B.M. to his father, September 8, 1821, Trinity Correspondence.

appeal for him.[34] How serious the young Macaulay really was about this at the time we have no way of knowing. There may have been some wishful thinking in Zachary's report of his son's feelings on this question. It came in a letter replying to Hannah More's plaintive: "I am afraid he [Tom] must be a lawyer. What a pity! But really his talents seem irresistibly to lead that way."[35] Zachary was certainly pleased when he heard from Henry Thornton that Tom had formed a party at Trinity "for reviving the obsolete practice of making the responses at Chapel," and had persevered in this in spite of surprise, stares, whispers, and sneers on the part of his fellow students. But having praised the new party's respect for ritual, Zachary added, significantly: "God grant that their hearts may feel its influence."[36]

The hope he doubtless continued to entertain that the great change would come to his son as it had once come to him gradually flagged. One straw in the wind was Tom's refusal, in the course of a reading party in Wales in 1821, to participate in a Bible Society there.[37] Another, that, apart from attendance at Trinity Chapel (which was compulsory), he tended to avoid going to church services whenever possible.[38] But whatever his own hopes and disappointments, this was a subject on which the father would not press his son. Thus his comment on a possible career in the Church for Tom was: "If his life should be prolonged, he certainly does not seem likely to be a neutral character, however his lot in life may be cast—and my anxieties therefore are more . . . with respect to his principles and motives of action than the particular sphere in which he is to act."[39]

What did lead to a real crisis of confidence between the two was neither politics nor religion, but rather Zachary's continuing feeling that his son seemed to resist, now as before, the lessons of discipline so carefully inculcated upon him since babyhood. There were the

34. Zachary Macaulay to Hannah More, August 31, 1819, Huntington MSS.

35. Hannah More to Zachary Macaulay, August 24, 1819, Roberts, ed., *More Letters*, 131.

36. Zachary Macaulay to Selina Mills Macaulay, November 6, 1820, Huntington MSS. This was not the first time that T.B.M. had taken up that cause. In a letter of 1814, Hannah More had praised his "heroic exertion about the responses of the Church," pointing out that it was this emphasis on a social mode of worship that distinguished Evangelicals from Dissenters. Hannah More to Zachary Macaulay, "1814," Roberts, ed., *More Letters*, 64.

37. Trevelyan, *Life and Letters*, 74.

38. Henry Thornton recalled that T.B.M. would meet him on Sunday after morning service to go for a walk, "saying that, though he had not attended the service, he had given the example of piety by coming to the church door." Dorothy Alston, "Recollections," *London Mercury*, 60.

39. Zachary Macaulay to Hannah More, August 31, 1819, Huntington MSS.

perennial complaints about Tom's novel reading. Zachary evidently failed to be impressed by his son's argument that books of amusement were to men what toys and sugarplums were to children; and that the poet who amused his reader for a spare hour might claim "to be considered as an inferior labourer in the same field of benevolence with the liberators of Africa, the explorers of our prisons, and the nurses of our hospitals."[40] One wonders how these analogies sat with the recipient of this letter, who wanted to feel temporal things as "nothing but dung, nay less, compared with heavenly."[41]

A report reaching Zachary that his son had become known in Cambridge as "The Novel Reader" produced a paternal reprimand, warning of waste of time. This, in turn, elicited a cutting letter from the indignant culprit, who maintained that the confusion of knowledge of modern literature with the reading of fiction, which lay behind the nickname, occurred among men

who are mere mathematical blockheads; who plod on their eight hours a day to the honours of the Senate House; who leave the groves which witnessed the musings of Milton, of Bacon, and of Gray, without one liberal idea or elegant image, and carry with them into the world minds contracted by unmingled attention to one part of science, and memories stored with only technicalities.

As far as wasting time was concerned—and here the tone became truly acidulous—"I cannot afford to sacrifice a day every week in defence and explanation as to my habits of reading. I value, most deeply value, that solicitude which arises from your affection for me: but let it not debar me from justice and candour."[42] Zachary was not the sort of person to be unduly moved by ringing declamations; especially when the evidence from Cambridge continued to indicate room for doubt about the correct apportionment of his son's time. When Tom did not do as well in mathematics as had been expected, his father expressed the conviction that this was due to his son's preference for what he sarcastically called "more tasteful pursuits."[43]

Among these pursuits, Macaulay's role in the Cambridge Union Society certainly came to hold high rank. Then, as now, the Oxford and Cambridge Unions served as nurseries for future statesmen and parliamentary orators. All the bright young men of Macaulay's day—

40. T.B.M. to his father, February 5, 1819, Trinity Correspondence.
41. Zachary Macaulay to Selina Mills Macaulay, September 20, 1821, Knutsford, *Zachary Macaulay*, 370.
42. T.B.M. to his father, January 5, 1820, Trevelyan, *Life and Letters*, 70-1.
43. Zachary Macaulay to Hannah More, July 12, 1820, Huntington MSS.

Charles Austin, the Villiers brothers, Praed, Moultrie—proved their mettle in debate at the Union; and young John Stuart Mill, among others, came to Cambridge to watch and to be instructed in what Bulwer-Lytton celebrated as

> *That club-room, famous then,*
> *Where striplings settled questions spoilt by men,*
> *When grand Macaulay sat triumphant down,*
> *Heard Praed reply, and long'd to halve the crown.*[44]

Macaulay came to wield considerable power in the Union; and he later sometimes reproached himself with having wielded it tyrannically. John Moultrie, a Cambridge contemporary, recorded this vivid account of him in verse:

> *A presence with gigantic power instinct,*
> *Though outwardly, in truth, but little graced*
> *With aught of manly beauty—short, obese,*
> *Rough-featured, coarse-complexioned, with lank hair,*
> *And small grey eyes,—in face (so many said)*
> *Not much unlike myself,—his voice abrupt,*
> *Unmusical;—yet, when he spake, the ear*
> *Was charmed into attention, and the eye*
> *Forgot the visible and outward frame*
> *Of the rich mind within; with such swift flow*
> *Of full, spontaneous utterance the tongue*
> *Interpreted the deep impassion'd thought,*
> *And poured upon our sense exhaustless store*
> *Of multifarious learning.*[45]

In the course of an extended parody of a Union debate, another contemporary, Winthrop Mackworth Praed, himself a glittering star in the Cambridge firmament of his time, described Macaulay's intervention in debate in these terms:

> *But the favourite comes, with his trumpets and drums,*
> *And his arms and his metaphors crossed;*
> *And the audience—O dear!—vociferate "Hear!"*
> *Till they're half of them deaf as a post.*

44. [Edward Bulwer-Lytton], "St. Stephen's," *Blackwood's Edinburgh Magazine*, LXXXVII (1860), 294.

45. John Moultrie, "The Dream of Life," *Poems* (2 vols., London, 1876), I, 421–2.

The parodied speech itself dealt with a defense of the British constitution against the spread of Jacobinism, and was, of course, heavily larded with elaborate imagery, from the hyena that was heard howling until its raving, which had once excited dismay, provoked nothing but disgust, to the English nation, "which, while so many cities have been a prey to hostile fires, has never seen her streets lighted up but with the blaze of victorious illumination." The whole performance was characterized by Praed as:

> *Oratoric*
> *Metaphoric*
> *Similes of wondrous length;*
> *Illustration,*
> *Conflagration.*
> *Ancient Romans,*
> *House of Commons,*
> *Clever Uriel*
> *And Ithuriel,*
> *Good Old King,*
> *Everything.*[46]

It might be added that one reason why similes in such abundance are to be found in Macaulay's early writings and speeches was that, according to his own later testimony, he had great difficulty at first in thinking of any at all. He then deliberately set out to cultivate that particular talent, and inevitably ran into the opposite extreme.[47]

What did he talk *about?* So tense had been the political atmosphere in Cambridge after Waterloo that in 1817 the university authorities felt it necessary to prohibit Union meetings altogether. In 1821 the Union was allowed to resume its debates, on condition that no topics of current political interest—which meant topics concerning events later than 1800—were to be touched upon. There was, of course, an obvious way out of that prohibition. It was possible to treat historical topics in contemporary terms. Current political sentiment could easily find expression in debates about the French Revolution, or the merits of Pitt and Fox, or the chief parties and personalities of the Great Rebellion. The records of the Union

46. Winthrop Mackworth Praed, "The Union Club," *Essays* (London, 1887), 212–13. For specimens of T.B.M.'s oratory at the Union, see [Robert Aris Willmott], *Conversations at Cambridge* (London, 1836), 133–144. Arnold, *Public Life,* 28, considered these specimens "tolerably fair."

47. Margaret Macaulay, *Recollections,* 33.

during the years when Macaulay participated in its debates—he was, for a time, secretary—include such topics as "Is the political conduct of John Hampden deserving approbation?" "Was the conduct of England towards Ireland (up to the year 1800) deserving approbation?" "Is the political conduct of Mr. Fox (up to 1800) deserving of our approbation?" Nonpolitical topics were also debated on occasion, for example, "Is the study of works of fiction pernicious?" (Macaulay, not unexpectedly, spoke for the negative.) "Is Wordsworth or Lord Byron the greater poet?" No debate was possible upon the last topic, "because of the turbulent state of the society."[48]

It is hard to categorize Macaulay's political line unequivocally on the basis of what the Union records tell us. He defended the political character of George III against Praed; but he also joined the latter in defending the political conduct of Charles James Fox. He spoke in favor of the superiority of the English constitution to the American; but he also propounded the desirability of a reform of the House of Commons. It is worth remembering that Macaulay himself later recalled of his own years at Cambridge that whenever anyone enunciated a proposition, all possible answers to it would rush into his head at once; and that on those occasions he would have no politics except the opposite of those professed by his interlocutor at the time.[49] A rumor circulated during this period according to which members of the Union, assigning future parliamentary roles to one another, gave the "progressive" side to Macaulay and the "retardative" side to Praed.[50] That may or may not have been the case. But of Macaulay's oratorical powers there could be no doubt. Between 1822 and 1824, the side he maintained as a principal speaker for or against the proposition triumphed in fourteen out of those seventeen debates of which the results were recorded.[51]

To his fellow members of the Union, then, Macaulay soon came to appear as a heroic figure, the almost invincible champion orator. But as far as his parents were concerned, he long remained the gifted youth who would not work hard enough at things he did not like and whose personal habits left much to be desired. In contrast—hardly

48. *Laws and Transactions of the Union Society, Revised and Corrected to January 1830* (Cambridge, 1830), 55. Also 20–22, 26.

49. Trevelyan, *Life and Letters*, 88.

50. Morley, ed., *Henry Crabb Robinson*, I, 393. After he had become a Member of Parliament, Praed objected to the story that he was being "pitted" against Macaulay, which shows the currency that rumor must have had. Derek Hudson, "Macaulay," *Notes and Queries*, CCV (1960), 202. Praed, in fact, became a Tory. See pp. 189–93.

51. *Laws and Transactions of Union*, 20–36.

accidental—to Zachary's gloomy fastidiousness were his inability to dress correctly, his clumsiness, and his forgetfulness in practical matters. Starting out on a holiday trip, for instance, he first forgot his watch and then lost the key to his bag so that a blacksmith had to be fetched.[52] "Poor Tom," was Selina's reaction to this story. "I almost pity him for his double misfortunes. I hope however he has learnt wisdom by them."[53] "Almost pity" . . . Selina knew her husband. If this was a plea in extenuation of a fault, it had to be couched judiciously.

She was soon impelled once again to try to mollify the father's stern attitude toward his son. This time the occasion was more serious, and marked a genuine crisis in the relationship between Zachary and Tom. The only road to an honors degree from Cambridge University at this time led by way of the mathematical tripos examination. It is true that some of the colleges, notably Trinity, awarded their fellowships to men of outstanding talent, regardless of mathematical ability. But this was the rare exception rather than the rule. An honors degree was the normal prerequisite. Macaulay's tutor, Monk, later the author of a famous *Life* of the great Greek scholar Bentley, produced a pamphlet deploring a state of affairs in which very gifted men often saw colleagues with much less scholarship and industry than their own receiving greater rewards than they themselves did, only because they had no mathematical bent. "This," Monk wrote in proposing the addition of classical and theological tripos examinations, "is neither an imaginary nor an overstated case."[54]

There can be little doubt that Macaulay, who specifically applauded this pamphlet,[55] was one of those Monk had in mind as he wrote. For that very year he had been "gulfed" in mathematics, that is, had failed to obtain a position on the tripos list while nevertheless being permitted to proceed to an ordinary degree. He had had a special reason for hoping for better things from this examination. Demonstrated proficiency in mathematics was required of those competing for the chancellor's Classical Medal; and on this, having won the Poetry Medal in 1819 and again in 1821, Tom had his eye. So the end of December 1821, which found the Macaulay family in

52. Zachary Macaulay to Selina Mills Macaulay, July 5, 1821, Huntington MSS.

53. Selina Mills Macaulay to Zachary Macaulay, July 6, 1821, Huntington MSS.

54. "Philograntus" [J. H. Monk], *A Letter to the Right Reverend John, Lord Bishop of Bristol, Respecting an Additional Examination of Students in the University of Cambridge and the Different Plans Proposed for that Purpose* (London, 1822), 11.

55. T.B.M. to his father, February 28, 1822, Houghton Library MSS, Harvard University.

Brighton for the Christmas holidays, found a despondent Tom, by his own choice, grinding away at mathematics in Cambridge.[56] The sacrifice this represented can best be appreciated if one remembers that the intensity of his hatred of mathematics was matched only by the intensity of his love of a domestic Christmas.

It had all been to no avail. This was Tom's first academic failure, and his family was stunned by it. To have been "gulfed" was bad enough. His sister Hannah always remembered how her mother took her into her room to tell her about what had happened: "For even then it was known how my whole heart was wrapped up in him, and it was thought necessary to break the news."[57] But it was the manner of the defeat that Zachary considered far more disgraceful than the defeat itself. In a letter to Hannah More, he reported to her that Tom had entered the Senate House to take the examination; but that, finding after two days of struggle that he would be outdistanced by his competitors, he had withdrawn from the conflict. Those who knew Cambridge had told the father that his son had done the right thing, since low honors could be considered worse than none. "But," Zachary wrote, "we are disappointed, and he is sadly depressed on seeing how much we are so." He concluded the letter by observing that a great deal of good could come of the whole business in the end; especially in view of Tom's remorse and low spirits arising from the thought that he might have done better had he given up some of his "miscellaneous reading."[58]

Selina, too, was concerned with the moral benefits of the disaster. She hoped that it would serve to moderate those evil propensities which her son's former successes had given birth to; that he would adopt a less lofty tone, and learn to sympathize with the less gifted. But she was even more concerned with the effect Zachary's severe reprimands would have on their son at this particular moment of defeat and depression. "I am sure you will feel as strongly as myself," she wrote to her husband, "that all moral to be discovered from this unfortunate event must be delayed for a little time, in order to be of use." Once due time had passed, she would not spare him. For she, too, had found his behavior showing want of "manliness of mind." After all, he had outstripped his competitors so many times. Now he should just have done his best, and then stood by the event—instead of withdrawing.[59]

56. Zachary Macaulay to Hannah More, December 27, 1821, Huntington MSS.
57. Trevelyan, *Life and Letters*, 61.
58. Zachary Macaulay to Hannah More, January 23, 1822, Huntington MSS.
59. Selina Mills Macaulay to Zachary Macaulay, January 19, 1822, Huntington MSS.

We do not have any direct evidence of Tom's state of mind at this point. He must have been particularly chagrined by the reaction of his parents, his father's especially. During the previous months a crisis of confidence between father and son had, in any event, been brewing. In August, replying to Zachary's reprimands for some remarks Tom had made about the King's behavior, Tom had written that he did not mind so much about whether these remarks had been right or wrong as about the relationship of trust between himself and his father. If he could not freely write what was on his mind to those he loved, he would have to start composing state papers instead of letters. "Perfect love casteth out fear." And, for his part, he loved those best who showed enough confidence in his regard and candor to trust him with their foibles.[60] A few days later, evidently in reply to his father's assurance that he had meant well, Tom in turn assured him that "I never looked upon any of your remarks but as proving the most sincere affection and concern for my welfare. I quite acquiesce in the justice of your observations."[61] But some strain shows through the very conventionality of tone in which this dutiful acquiescence is rendered.

The writer, after all, was now over twenty-one. He was aware of his own genius, and admired by those who had come into contact with it. Why should he still be treated like a little boy? What he yearned for was affection and understanding; what he got was cold water thrown on his ebullience. Yet under the ebullience lay great, almost excessive, sensibility. Selina knew this better than Zachary. That is why she used all her considerable resources of tact in attempting to moderate her husband's severity. A few weeks after the examination failure, and perhaps under its impact, Tom's thoughts turned once again to the Church as a profession.[62] In view of the fact that he had really plumped for law three years earlier and had been entered at Lincoln's Inn in January 1822, this seems to indicate a general state of confusion and uncertainty about himself and his future during that spring and summer.

Confirmation of this is to be found in Selina's reply to a letter of Zachary's complaining once again about their son's inattention and want of punctuality. The explanation was, she wrote, that he had not been well for some time. He had grown thinner "and very absent and uncomfortable about himself." Perhaps Zachary was disposed to

60. T.B.M. to his father, August 31, 1821, Trinity Correspondence.
61. T.B.M. to his father, September 12, 1821, Huntington MSS.
62. Zachary Macaulay to Selina Mills Macaulay, April 2, 1822, Huntington MSS.

see his son's faults too strongly. His evil star seemed to prevail at present; everything seemed to be going wrong. What was required on these occasions, she gently reminded her husband, was great forbearance and discretion. She prayed that Zachary would receive wisdom from on high to manage Tom "at this critical period of his life." The strategy she recommended was to re-establish a relationship of complete confidence between father and son—a suggestion which indicates that by this time that relationship was wanting. To know the worst of another person's faults was to derive some comfort. "I am obliged to encourage myself with this conviction," she continued in this very moving letter, "when I discover in one and another things which discourage me and often cause me to shed many a tear in secret. In *him* there are many of the materials which form a great character, with some things I generally deplore."[63]

In reply, Zachary must have attempted to reassure her about his own kindness and forbearance toward Tom. For, a few days later, Selina informed her husband that it was only because she was convinced of his goodwill that she had hinted what she had in her previous letter: "He has often said to me: 'My dear mother, I hope that you and my father will always speak to me decidedly and openly when alone of my faults. I think I may venture to say, I shall always be gratified, and try to alter. But never talk *at me:* it is not generous and wounds me worse than I can tell you.' " And to that his mother added one heartfelt sentence: "I shall be glad when he has done with College."[64]

It would be false, then, to regard Tom's years at Trinity entirely through the golden haze that suffuses the pages of his nephew's biography. They brought defeat as well as triumph; strain as well as joy. The friendships and the talk of Trinity could not make up for the absence from home. The conflict of temperament between father and son was bound to make itself felt. And it left its scars. Some of Macaulay's comments later in life give evidence of this. In 1831, during the Reform Bill struggle, he noticed the great humanitarian and abolitionist Buxton smoking in the writing room of the House of Commons. "My father," he remarked to his sister Hannah, "will not believe it. He holds smoking, eating underdone meat, liking high fame, lying late in a morning, and all things which give pleasure to others and none to himself to be absolute sins. Is not that

63. Selina Mills Macaulay to Zachary Macaulay, June 9, 1822, Huntington MSS.
64. Selina Mills Macaulay to Zachary Macaulay, June 22, 1822, Huntington MSS.

an undutiful reflection?''[65] Twenty years later he confided to his
journal that he respected his niece "Baba" (Margaret Trevelyan)
more than any other human being, "more, I am sure, than I ever
respected my father.''[66]

Looking back years later, Macaulay could not help but feel that he
had never had "quite the encouragement and appreciation from
[Zachary] which he received from others"; and that the course his
father had pursued toward him during his youth was "not judicious.''[67] That the strain between father and son never became a
break was primarily due to the son's continued willingness to yield,
at no little cost to his own inclinations, when confronted by the
paternal wrath. A striking example of such an accommodation on his
part occurred not too long after the crisis of confidence of 1822
when, in response to his father's objections, Tom agreed to suspend
his contributions to *Knight's Quarterly Magazine*.

Knight's Quarterly was really the successor to a periodical called
The Etonian published by Charles Knight at Windsor, of which the
first number appeared in October 1820. It accepted contributions
from old Etonians at the universities, including several close friends
of Macaulay's at Cambridge, notably Winthrop Mackworth Praed,
poet and wit. Some time later, Knight decided that the quality of the
contributions merited a wider appeal; and so, by now settled in
London, he began to plan the new journal, the first number of
which appeared in the summer of 1823. Praed, a brilliant scholar
both at Eton and Cambridge, had presided (in the guise of "Pere-
grine Courtenay") over the elaborately masked society which, so its
columns revealed, constituted the editorial committee of *The Etonian*. Now, retaining the same pseudonym, he took charge of the new
periodical.

This is how he introduced it to his readers. It was, he wrote, the
production of a group of young men:

Some of us have no occupation, some of us have no money, some of us are
desperately in love, some of us are desperately in debt, many of us are
very clever, and wish to convince the public of the fact. . . . We will go
forth to the world once a quarter, in high spirits and handsome type, and
a modest dress of drab, with verse and prose, criticism and witticism, fond
love and loud laughter; everything that is light, and warm, and fantastic,

65. T.B.M. to Hannah Macaulay, July 30, 1831, Huntington MSS.
66. Trinity Journal, June 12, 1851.
67. Hannah, Lady Trevelyan, "Reminiscences," 16–17, Trinity MSS.

and beautiful, shall be the offering we will bear, while we will leave the nation to the care of the parliament, and the church to the Bishop of Peterborough. . . . Our food shall be of the spicy curry, and the glistening champagne;—our inspiration shall be the thanks of pleasant voices, and the smiles of sparkling eyes.[68]

It was of this high-spirited company that Macaulay became a member, probably through the agency of one of his younger Trinity friends, either Praed himself or John Moultrie, another veteran of *The Etonian,* and the poet to whom we owe some vivid descriptions of the Cambridge of his time. "Tristram Merton" was Macaulay's pseudonym (the initials remained the same as his own), and under that name he wrote some extraordinary contributions for *Knight's.* Extraordinary first of all because their scope and variety indicated the wide range of knowledge and learning of their author: essays on Dante and Petrarch, love poems, a review of Mitford's *History of Greece,* a disquisition on the evils of West Indian slavery, an "epic of the future" entitled "The Wellingtoniad," dramatic reconstructions of historical scenes from ancient Greece and Rome, allegories about the French Revolution and Napoleon, an imaginary conversation between Milton and Cowley on the subject of the Civil War—all these flowed easily from his pen within the space of a few months.

But what emerges from the pages of *Knight's* even more strongly than "Tristram Merton's" talent is his personality. While what he wrote to his father assumed more and more the character of "duty letters"—without sparkle, without gaiety, without *joie de vivre*—all these qualities abounded in his contributions to *Knight's;* as well as a vision of the world far different from that universe of sin and suffering, austerity and painful introspection with which he had grown up. Here we find a pagan world of wine, women, and song, bearing little, if any, resemblance to those expressions of duty, industry, and domestic piety that still characterized his letters to his father. It is hard to decide how much should be made of this discrepancy. No young man ever lives the life he describes to his parents. And it is clear that the Macaulay known to his friends at Trinity had for some time been quite different from the earnest young student concerned about the danger of wine parties and the particular modes of conducting chapel services. To what extent his imagination created an obverse of the Evangelical dispensation to serve as a counterfoil to a universe he could not yet afford to discard except in his thoughts; to

---

68. *Knight's Quarterly,* I (1823), 1.

what extent, on the other hand, the world he depicted in *Knight's* was indeed a reflection of a side of his personal life of which his biographers know nothing is a question that will in all probability always remain unanswered. Macaulay, like many men who begin life as child prodigies, was a consummate actor. The sole protection that such people have against the continuous impingement of dullness, mediocrity, and inferior talents is the ability to adopt various personae adequate to dealing with what must always appear to them an outside world found wanting. It is difficult to glimpse the "real" identity behind the camouflage, especially when the person involved is clever enough to hide the traces of that real identity from all but himself and a few intimates. What is certain is that these contributions to *Knight's Quarterly* reveal fresh, and in some ways unexpected, dimensions of Macaulay's personality—undoubtedly set down with all the more relish just because he could incorporate them in fictitious forms.

There are, to start with, the love poems, one to "Rosamond" and one to a "Fair Maid of France"; conventional enough in tone and expression, perhaps, but still a long way from the atmosphere of Clapham. To Rosamond the poet sang:

> *How fondly could I play for hours*
> *with thy long curling tresses,*
> *And press thy hand and clasp thy neck*
> *with fanciful caresses,*
> *And mingle low impassioned speech*
> *with kisses and with sighs,*
> *And pore into the dark-blue depths*
> *of those voluptuous eyes.*

And this was his entreaty to that "Fair Maid of France" whose "foreign accents dear" had captivated him:

> *By thy parting, by thy smiles,*
> *And by all the varied wiles,*
> *Which so sweetly won me,*
> *Laughter, blushes, sighs, caresses,*
> *By thy lips and by thy tresses,*
> *Sometimes think upon me.*[69]

69. Ibid., 219–20.

The "Fragments of a Roman Tale," a vignette of Rome at the time of the Catilinarian conspiracy, depicted Caesar as the chivalrous hero who saves the beautiful Zoe from being ravished by Clodius. "Give up such a lovely woman to that drunken boy!" Caesar exclaims. "My character would be gone for ever." But the dashing and lighthearted Caesar—"I live only for glory and pleasure," he tells Zoe—has another and more tender side. When she fears for his safety, and tells him that she finds it hard to bear his distress, he is unable, in Macaulay's words, to compose the brow which had confronted the frown of Sylla [sic] and the lips which had rivaled the eloquence of Cicero. "He hid his face on her bosom, and burst into tears. With sobs long and loud, and convulsive as those of a terrified child, he poured forth on her bosom the tribute of impetuous and uncontrollable emotion."[70] In short, Caesar is in love. It is hardly a coincidence that Macaulay here chose as his hero a man in whose personality outward nonchalance, self-possession, and light banter served to hide a fundamentally emotional nature in search of true love and affection—someone like "Tristram Merton" himself.

Not that this aspect of Macaulay's character entered into the portrait that the editors of *Knight's* painted for their readers. They described him as:

A short manly figure, marvellously upright, with a broad neck-cloth, and one hand in his waistcoat pocket. Of regular beauty he had little to boast; but in faces where there is an expression of great power, or of great humour, or both, you do not regret its absence.

There followed what must have been one of the first of later innumerable parodies of Macaulay's style and subject matter—here his admiration for ancient Athens, his romantic worship of beautiful women from the pages of history, the sense of immediacy he managed to communicate in his attitude toward the past:

They were glorious days for old Athens [he said] when all she held of witty and of wise, of brave and of beautiful, was collected in the drawing-room of Aspasia. In those the brightest and noblest times of Greece, there was no feeling so strong as the devotion of youth, no talisman of such virtue as the smile of beauty. Aspasia was the arbitress of peace and war, the Queen of arts and arms, the Pallas of the spear and of the pen: We have looked back to those golden hours with transport and with longing.

---

70. *The Works of Lord Macaulay* (Albany edition, 12 vols., London, 1898), XI, 214–17 (referred to henceforth as *Works*).

Here our classical dreams shall in some sort wear a dress of reality; he who has not the piety of a Socrates, may at least fall down before as lovely a divinity; he who has not the power of a Pericles may at least kneel before as beautiful an Aspasia.[71]

There ensues some banter among the "courtiers," who are said to constitute the editorial board of the periodical. Macaulay is told that he is taking up too much time, and asked to speak more to the purpose. In reply to this reprimand, he at once compares himself (still in the course of this affectionate parody) to the poor Prince in the Arabian Tales who must be frozen into stone before he is able to finish his task. "For the love you bear us," one of the courtiers then remarks, "a truce to your similes: they shall be felony without benefit of clergy, and silence for an hour shall be the penalty." The threat of silence and the ban on his similes enrages "Tristram," who explodes with: "A penalty for similes! Impossible! Paul of Russia prohibited round hats, and Chifu of China denounced white teeth; but this is atrocious." And so he continues, irrepressible, with learned references to Zoroaster and Mahomet.[72]

Already, then, we find traits that were to become hallmarks of his mature style: a love of elaborate similes, a plethora of learned illustrations culled from the history and literature of all mankind, and, above all, an outpouring of speech hard, if not impossible, to arrest:

> *To him there was no pain like silence—*
> *No constraint so dull as unanimity.*[73]

Macaulay's connection with *Knight's* was short-lived. In a touching effort to propitiate his father, he had made sure that the first number would contain a long article by himself on the subject of West Indian slavery; needless to say, an attack on the institution. But the effort did not succeed. What he considered to be the prevailing frivolous tone of the journal was too much for Zachary, more especially "Tristram Merton's" two love poems. He expressed himself accordingly. And so, on June 20, 1823, the dutiful son wrote as follows to Charles Knight, the publisher:

You are probably aware that there are among my family connections several persons of rigidly religious sentiments. My father, in particular,

71. *Knight's Quarterly*, I (1823), 7.   72. Ibid., 7–8.
73. Moultrie, "Dream of Life," *Poems*, I, 422.

is, I believe, generally known to entertain in their utmost extent what are denominated evangelical opinions. Several articles in our first number, one or two of my own in particular, appeared to give him great uneasiness. I need not say that I do not in the slightest degree partake of his scruples. Nor have I at all dissembled the complete discrepancy which exists between his opinions and mine. At the same time, gratitude, duty, and prudence, alike compel me to respect prejudices which I do not in the slightest degree share.

So, for the present, he went on, he must desist from taking any part in the magazine. It was a sacrifice that gave him considerable pain, since *Knight's* had formed a connecting tie between some very dear friends, from whom he would now be separated probably for a very long time, and himself. He hoped to renew his connection—in fact, some poems of his did appear in the third number. Knight was to tell only four intimate friends—including Moultrie and Praed—of the enforced decision.[74]

It is not hard to imagine Macaulay's feelings as he wrote this letter. At Cambridge he had left Evangelicalism behind him. He had made his own friends, he had triumphed in debate, he had been able to give full expression to his poetic temperament, to the "Tristram" part of his nature. Yet now he was still being judged by the standards of a world to which, in some ways at least, he no longer belonged; and forced to confess to those closest to him among his contemporaries that he must needs surrender to a paternal edict with which he profoundly disagreed. It could not have been an easy letter to write.

Reason had bowed once again to the father's powerful will. But it is possible to discern a new note in a letter to Zachary in which Tom defended himself against the accusation that he had introduced, in the shape of *Knight's Quarterly,* an "immoral book" into the Macaulay household. "I have only to say," he wrote, "that I await your arrival with great anxiety, unmingled, however, with shame, remorse, or fear."[75] It was clearly becoming more difficult for Tom to offer his father the kind of unquestioning obedience he had given him while a schoolboy. Yet a breach between the two was unthinkable. The Evangelical family ethos was far too strong for that. Rebellious and aggressive feelings must certainly have been evoked by the father's treatment of his son. But they were repressed and internal-

74. T.B.M. to Charles Knight, June 20, 1823, Charles Knight, *Passages of a Working Life during Half a Century, with a Prelude of Early Reminiscences* (3 vols., London, 1864–5), I, 304–5.

75. T.B.M. to his father, July 9, 1823, Houghton Library MSS, Harvard University.

ized. A *modus vivendi* was reached. Zachary's pride in Tom's achievements gradually began to outweigh the censoriousness that had marked his attitude toward him for so long. From the time Tom left Cambridge in 1823, his career as a lawyer now definitely determined upon, Zachary never again attempted to check his son's mode of life or the expression of his opinions.

Tom, for his part, while not in any way surrendering his hard-won independence, always showed a touching solicitude for his father's welfare as well as a moderate amount of zeal for the cause perpetually closest to Zachary's heart, the abolition of slavery. He also took upon himself without complaint the ever-increasing burden of contributing to the support of the Macaulay family. Zachary's business, from which he increasingly withdrew in order to devote himself to the anti-slavery campaign, no longer prospered as before. Already in 1822 Tom had taken on two pupils paying a hundred guineas between them for being tutored by him during the coming academic year, so as to relieve his father of some of the expenses for his support.[76] In 1824, having failed to do so the year before, he won a Trinity fellowship, tenable for seven years not necessarily spent in residence. Quite apart from its prestige, this provided him with what almost amounted to financial independence at a time when he no longer wished to be a burden to his father. He was now preparing for the Bar, which in those days meant mainly being privately tutored or reading on one's own in such fields as property law, special pleading, and equity. He took an occasional trip to Cambridge to speak at the Union. But, for the most part, he lived at home, now Great Ormond Street, Bloomsbury, where, in 1823, the family had moved from Cadogan Place to less expensive quarters. It was to this address that there suddenly descended in the autumn of 1825 a rain of dinner invitations to the newly discovered literary lion, the author of the essay on Milton in the August number of the *Edinburgh Review*.

76. T.B.M. to his father, July 26, 1822, Trevelyan, *Life and Letters*, 78.

IV

WHIG

How did Macaulay become a Whig? While at Cambridge, he himself is reported to have remarked to a contemporary (Hampden Gurney) : "I have been a Tory; I am a Radical; *but I never will be a Whig.*"[1] Thus the question assumes a double dimension. What or who was it that brought Macaulay under the influence of Radical ideas? And how did he, then, end up in the Whig camp after all? We have already had occasion to point out that Zachary's Toryism was not of the intransigent variety; but that nevertheless at the time of the Peterloo Massacre (1819) a real conflict had opened up between father and son, one in which Tom had taken the anti-repressive side, and had imputed his own libertarian sentiments to Cicero, Tacitus, and Milton. But that had hardly been a "radical" act. Support for the victims of Peterloo had been widespread, and bore little if any relation to radicalism at the time, a movement consisting of several different strands which had in common only an attitude of protest against both Whigs and Tories and against the assumption that birth or preferment should by themselves confer political power.[2]

The Radical movement included on the one hand men like Cobbett and Burdett, who advocated parliamentary and suffrage reform as a means of returning to the rule of a pre-commercial,

1. Trevelyan, *Life and Letters,* 56.
2. See William Thomas, "Whigs and Radicals in Westminster: the Election of 1819," *Guildhall Miscellany,* III (1970) , 174–216.

"natural" aristocracy; and on the other hand the intellectual disciples of Jeremy Bentham, who questioned all established customs, institutions, and procedures by applying to them the sole criterion of their present utility. It was one of the latter, Charles Austin, who was credited by Macaulay's sister Hannah with changing her brother's views at Cambridge in a more liberal direction. It was Austin, she wrote, who "inoculated him with his great admiration for American institutions, absence of state religious endowments, and a disposition to question everything hitherto considered settled. This," she added, "was a great grief to his mother and eldest sister."[3]

Austin must have been a formidable figure. The best description of him and his powerful influence is to be found in John Stuart Mill's *Autobiography*. Mill there recalled that Austin was the first person of intellect whom he met on the ground of equality. He remembered him conveying to all the impression of unbounded strength, "together with talents which, combined with such apparent force of will and character, seemed made to dominate the world." It was his belief, Mill wrote, that "much of the popular notion of the tenets and sentiments of what are called Benthamites or Utilitarians, had its foundation in paradoxes thrown out by Charles Austin."[4] Austin's influence at Cambridge, Mill remarked, was no less than a historical event. "For to it may in no small degree be traced the tendency towards Liberalism in general, and towards the Benthamic and political-economic form of Liberalism, which showed itself among a portion of the more active minded young men of the higher classes, from this time to 1830."[5] Mill was certainly right in remarking on Austin's particular influence in the Cambridge Union. We have a vivid description of Austin's bent of mind in Moultrie's *Dream of Life,* one that nicely complements Mill's:

> to his eye,
> *Whatever was ideal, seem'd untrue:*
> *The hopes which he profess'd of earthly good*
> *Were limited to that which he could see,*
> *Hear, taste, or feel—ease—pleasure—all the joys*
> *Which wait on wealth—the exercise and use*

3. Hannah, Lady Trevelyan, "Reminiscences," 29, Trinity MSS.

4. Jack Stillinger, ed., *The Early Draft of John Stuart Mill's Autobiography* (Urbana, Ill., 1961), 83. To get some sense of Austin's learning and polemical power, see his "The *Quarterly Review:* Greek Courts of Justice," *Westminster Review*, VII (1827), 227–68.

5. Ibid., 82.

Of intellect:—in all things he appear'd
A strict utilitarian. Yet the man
Was nobler than his creed, and though he mock'd
At things, which, to us poets, seem'd almost
The breath of human life—romantic love—
Chivalrous honour—patriotic zeal—
And loyal self-devotion—there were times
When even these very themes would kindle up
The better soul within, and he became,
Unconsciously, the enthusiast he despised.[6]

It is, of course, always very difficult to determine exactly the extent of one person's influence upon another. Certainly, Austin's strong personality appears to have been one of the few by which even Macaulay, always formidable himself, was awed. We know that at the Union Macaulay was ever ready to speak on the opposite side of any question; and he may have derived his own skeptical attitude toward received truths and accepted shibboleths from contact with his friend. How much else he really derived from him is open to question. Benthamite or Utilitarian doctrine consisted of a mixture of things: classical economics and secularism, a psychological and ethical system based on the maximization of pleasure and the minimization of pain, and a generally dim view of the status quo arising from the skepticism with which the master and his disciples confronted *idées reçues* and established institutions. Utilitarianism had potentially strong democratic tendencies built into it, since the desire for the greatest happiness of the greatest number, which had first set Bentham upon his path, eventually led him through practical experience—given the general indifference to his projects and ideas on the part of the governing classes—to the conclusion that the interests of the governors and those they governed would become truly identical only when the people as a whole governed themselves by means of universal suffrage.

But not all Benthamites went that far. Charles Austin, apparently, was one who did not. "He told me," so one of his contemporaries recalled, "that, in his most Radical days, he had never desired universal suffrage; he thought that, if mankind ever became perfect enough for universal suffrage, they would be perfect enough to do without the suffrage." Austin, according to the same source, was

6. Moultrie, "Dream of Life," *Poems*, I, 427.

more of an anti-ecclesiastical than a democratic liberal.[7] Thus one must take care not to exaggerate the extent of Austin's own radicalism. It is likely that those elements of Benthamism which he transmitted to Macaulay lay in the realm of a generally questioning attitude toward all things established. Many years later, Macaulay was to recall: "How Bentham ever imposed on me at all I cannot now understand: and yet he imposed on me less than on any person, I think, who entered life at the same time with me in the same circumstances."[8] As for admiration of American institutions, which, according to Hannah, her brother absorbed from Austin, we find this entry in Macaulay's journals for 1838: "When I left College it was the fashion of young liberals—*I cannot say that it was ever exactly mine*—to consider the American institutions as the very model of good government." (Italics mine.) [9]

In later life Macaulay may have played down the extent to which he had once fallen under Benthamite and "American" influence. But it is worth pointing out that even the essay which shows him most closely approaching Benthamite ideas in the sphere of politics demonstrates at the same time the limits of his radicalism. This is his review of Mitford's Tory-oriented *History of Greece,* which appeared in *Knight's Quarterly* in 1824. Here he strongly opposed Mitford's dictum that popular government must always turn out to be a curse. "The fact is," Macaulay wrote, "that a good government, like a good coat, is that which fits the body for which it is designed." The best government was that which both desired and knew how to make the people happy. This was possible only in a pure democracy. So that a government might be solicitous only for the interests of the governed, it was necessary for the interests of the governors and the governed to be identical. The interests of subjects and rulers would not coincide until the subjects themselves became the rulers.

Still, Macaulay, like Austin, did not advocate democracy pure and simple. What was crucial was not so much rule by the people, but, rather, rule by an *educated* people. The sad fact was (and here Macaulay brought forward good Benthamite doctrine) that though people were always desirous to promote their own interests, it was doubtful whether in any community they had ever been sufficiently educated to understand them. In England, for instance, the rights of the many had generally been asserted on their behalf (and against their will) by the few. There, too, though it was clear that free trade was one of the greatest blessings a government could confer upon a

7. Lionel and Beatrix Tollemache, *Safe Studies* (London, 1884) , 222–3.
8. Trinity Journal, October 21, 1849.   9. Trinity Journal, December 27, 1838.

people, it might well be doubted whether a liberal commercial policy would find any support from a Parliament elected by universal suffrage. The happiest state of society was one in which the supreme power resided with the whole body of well-informed people. Until such time as great statesmen might succeed in extending the power of the people in relation to the extent of their knowledge, it was not right to praise or to condemn institutions *abstractly*. From the despotism of St. Petersburg to the democracy of Washington there existed scarcely any form of government which might not, hypothetically at least, be the best possible.[10]

The essay on Mitford's *History* shows that Macaulay firmly believed in free trade, and felt that ideally the interests of governors and governed should coincide. Moreover, he did not shrink in horror from the vision of popular government—in another part of the world. But the keynote of his argument is hardly democratic. Rather, it stresses the force of particular circumstances in shaping particular forms of government, and puts great emphasis on the need for education as a prerequisite for participation in government. All this no doubt owed something to Austin and, perhaps via Austin, something to Bentham.

What of the Whigs in the 1820's? One must not imagine that there were then in existence confronting one another two parties—Whig and Tory—with diametrically opposed aims, platforms, historical memories, and means of support: On the one hand, the dominant Tories—hidebound, aristocratic reactionaries, opposed to all progressive men and measures, upholders of privilege in all things; on the other, the Whigs, a courageous minority—libertarian, reformist, middle-class, carrying on the exalted principles of the seventeenth century in the nineteenth; still battling against despotism and tyranny, as represented by their rivals. This picture would be nothing but a caricature of the real situation. It is true that the Tory government, having led the nation to victory in the war against Napoleon, had retained a monopoly of power since then; and that the Whigs, hampered in part by their pacific attitude during that war, in part by internal dissension and lack of leadership, were the opposition group trying to get into power. It is also true that in Scotland, where Jeffrey, the editor of the *Edinburgh Review,* resided and wrote, the two parties stood in a more clearly antithetical position to each other than they did elsewhere. Scottish politics had long been under the thumb of the English government of the day; and the

10. T.B.M., "Mitford's History of Greece" (1824), *Works,* XI, 371–3.

reaction against sympathy evoked by the French Revolution had struck particularly hard there.

But the political situation in England was more complex. In many ways it is perfectly legitimate, and not merely paradoxical, to regard the Tories of the early 1820's as far more "progressive" than their Whig opponents. On their front bench in the House of Commons sat Canning, carrying out a foreign policy supporting liberalism abroad, a policy that in Latin America had just called a new world into existence to redress the balance of the old; Peel, beginning his great series of reforms in the field of administration; and Huskisson, intent upon introducing classical economic measures designed to lead to the reduction of duties, less protection for agriculture, and increased free trade. From the time of the younger Pitt onward, the Tories had been proponents as well as executors of Adam Smith's economics, and this had gained them, in large measure, the support of the commercial classes. To be sure, the government consisted mainly of peers. But some of these came closer to the ideal of the professional politician than to that of aristocracy; not landowners, but self-made men who had reached their eminence by sheer ability.[11]

Certainly, too, the Tories had a reactionary, stand-pat wing, consisting of men like Eldon, the Lord Chancellor, who was so opposed to change of any kind that he refused to stop wearing his wig in bed, even though it gave him headaches; or ultras like Lords Bexley and Westmorland. It was this wing which sometimes drove the more liberally inclined Tories to despair, and which led Palmerston, then one of them, to remark in 1826 that the real Opposition was "the stupid old Tory party." A measure of Tory support traditionally came from the country squires and the smaller landowners. But it is worth noting that it was precisely some of these men who during the twenties blamed the system of rotten boroughs for the fact that Parliament could be induced to pass measures threatening the protectionist agricultural interest; and who therefore began to demand parliamentary reform, hoping that a broader system of voting and representation would prove advantageous to their interests. This, of course, was a demand that went counter to the majority of Tory opinion; and, *a fortiori,* its motivation went counter to the motivation for parliamentary reform on the part of those wholly or partially imbued with radical opinions.

The Whigs, on the other hand, were much more the party of the

11. See W. R. Brock, *Lord Liverpool and Liberal Toryism, 1820–1827* (Cambridge, 1941).

aristocracy, of really large landowners, of "connections," of the famous "cousinhood." They had forfeited certain chances for national popularity by the lukewarm attitude some of them showed during the Napoleonic wars. They had difficulty in recruiting able and widely respected leaders, in part because they were split into many disparate factions and groups that found it hard to pull together, ranging as they did from democratically inclined Radicals on the left to complacent aristocrats on the right. On the subject of parliamentary reform, the cause that was to unite them in 1832, they blew hot and cold during the 1820's. The sole issue on which most of them could be said to have taken a consistent stand since the start of the century was that of "emancipating" the Irish Catholics, that is, allowing them to sit in both Houses of Parliament. It was on this question, as well as on that of parliamentary reform, that the Tories were most vulnerable as the party of reaction; though even here the government contained some members (e.g., Canning and Castlereagh) who took a liberal view of the matter. In fact, Lord Liverpool, upon becoming Prime Minister in 1812, had declared the Catholic emancipation issue to be a "neutral" one, as far as the government was concerned.

It was only natural that there should have been attempts from the Whig side to fuse with the more liberally inclined members of the opposite party. Canning was the center of such fusion hopes, not only because of his well-known liberal views on foreign policy, but even more because he was thought to favor Catholic emancipation. Henry Brougham, the most brilliant and imaginative figure in the Whig ranks during the 1820's, attempted to engineer such a fusion in the course of the early 1820's. In 1806 Brougham had entered Parliament, as Macaulay was to do twenty years later, as a protégé of Lord Lansdowne, who (as Lord Henry Petty) had pursued his studies at Edinburgh University along with the leading *Edinburgh* reviewers, and had absorbed there the elements of a Whiggism more progressive than the predominant variety. Brougham had been fully aware of the necessity of a Whig-popular alliance for the survival of the party and had wanted to make himself the catalyst for such an alliance. This he had not thus far been able to accomplish.

Two powerful personalities helped to propel Macaulay toward the Whigs. One was his father. The other was Brougham. Brougham and Macaulay were to become bitter enemies in later life; which is probably the main reason why Sir George Otto Trevelyan in the biography of his uncle tended to minimize Brougham's influence on him. But Brougham should be given his due in this regard. As a personality he was vain, difficult, and obstreperous. Bagehot later remarked that he had the devil in him. But the Whigs had need of him. He was a brilliant parliamentary speaker—Macaulay was to call him the best he heard during his lifetime. He was seemingly omniscient. Above all, he was engaged in trying to bring Whiggism up to date, attempting to get it in touch again with the people at large—without, however, turning it in any sense into a "democratic" movement.

He himself had originally come to the Whigs as much by accidental circumstances as by intention based upon political principles. He had never been quite fully accepted by the aristocratic leaders of the Whig Party, but his intelligence and power were such that they could hardly be ignored. He had taken up a variety of causes, including free trade, the fate of the wretched Queen Caroline in 1820, and then Catholic emancipation, in order to further his aims. At one point, he had hoped to effect a junction of the Whigs with the more liberal elements of the Tory Party in this period. Yet neither Grey, the Whigs' titular leader, nor Canning on the Tory side was in fact prepared to enter into such an alliance at this time. In this matter Brougham was also hampered by his own left wing, Radicals like Burdett, Lambton, and Hume. The moderate Whigs—including Lansdowne and, in a manner of speaking, now Brougham himself— were, for instance, willing to accept the disenfranchisement of the Irish forty-shilling freeholders (county voters) as a price for Tory acceptance of Catholic emancipation. But the Radicals would not go along with this concession.[12]

Brougham called himself a Radical in 1825, but then went on to explain to his correspondent that "of course when we use the word *Radical* it is only for shortness and not as meaning Hunt and Cobbett."[13] It was only natural that at this point he was anxious to dissociate himself from any sort of linkage with democrats. He was certainly not of their persuasion. But he could, with justice, call himself a radicalizer of the Whig Party who was aware that if that party was to have any chance of regaining power, it could only do so by giving up its splendidly aristocratic isolation and putting out feelers to the people at large.

In 1823 Brougham, a staunch ally of the "Saints" in their campaign against slavery, addressed a letter to Zachary Macaulay on the subject of his son's future in politics. He had heard of Tom's great abilities from Howick, Lord Grey's son, one of Macaulay's fellow

12. See Arthur Aspinall, *Lord Brougham and the Whig Party* (Manchester, 1939) .

13. Brougham to Shepherd, October 14, 1825, Brougham MSS, University College, London.

students at Cambridge; and now "would fain impress upon you (and through you, upon him) a truth or two which experience has made me aware of, and which I would have given a great deal to have been acquainted with earlier in life from the experience of others." Brougham had heard that Tom possessed great talent for public speaking. In order to develop that talent he (himself one of the universally acknowledged orators of the age) advised Tom first of all to acquire the habit of speaking easily and fluently, which could be accomplished in a variety of ways—by easy writing, the custom of talking much in company, and by speaking in debating societies, "with little attention to rule, and more love of saying something at any price, than of saying anything well." That was the first stage. The second consisted of converting this style of easy speaking into "chaste eloquence."

There was only one way of doing this—and that was to study the proper models: Burke, Fox, and Windham among the moderns. But, above all, "if he would be a great orator, he must go at once to the fountainhead, and be familiar with every one of the great orations of Demosthenes." Cicero's orations (which Brougham assumed Tom had by heart in any event) were beautiful, but not of much use. What was far more important was that Tom should enter into the spirit of Demosthenes' speeches, "follow each turn of the argument, and make the absolutely perfect and most chaste and severe composition familiar to his mind." From Demosthenes one could learn how much might be done by the skillful use of a few words and the rigorous rejection of all superfluities. "In this view," Brougham continued, "I hold a familiar knowledge of Dante to be next to Demosthenes." In answer to the objection that imitation of those models would not do for the present time, he went on to assure Zachary that he himself had never made so much play as when almost translating from the Greek. He had, for instance, composed the peroration for his famous House of Lords speech in defense of Queen Caroline after reading and repeating Demosthenes for three or four weeks. Lastly, it was essential that all one's finest rhetorical passages be written out and prepared word for word in advance. "Now," the letter concluded, "would he be a great orator or no? In other words, would he have almost absolute power of doing good to mankind in a free country, or no? So he wills this, he must follow these rules."[14]

14. Henry C. J. Clements, *Lord Macaulay, His Life and Writings* (London, 1860), 24–7. See T. Fowell Buxton to Hannah Buxton, March 14, 1823, A.J.C. Hare, ed., *The Gurneys of Earlham* (2 vols., London, 1895), II, 12. Buxton had read Brougham's letter to Zachary Macaulay that very day, and immediately decided to apply his counsel to his own sons.

A member of another prominent Evangelical family, James Stephen, remembered hearing at the time of the letter Brougham wrote to Zachary about his son. In sponsoring the young Macaulay, Stephen felt bound to add, however, Brougham had been like the man who brought up a young lion which finally bit his head off.[15] The young lion himself wrote to his father that he was gratified by Brougham's kindness, and that it would be good to follow his counsel and begin his legal studies at once.[16] As we saw, he did so, returning only to take the fellowship examinations.

One can only speculate how much of his own actual rhetorical practice he based on the advice contained in Brougham's letter. He was no doubt familiar in any event with the models mentioned in Brougham's letter; and it may be pure coincidence that later that year he published an article on the "Principal Italian Writers" in *Knight's Quarterly,* in the course of which he observed that he had heard "the most eloquent statesman of the age" remark that next to Demosthenes Dante was the writer who ought to be most attentively studied by anyone who desired to obtain national eminence.[17] Nor need his own method of always preparing his speeches carefully in advance have had any necessary connection with Brougham's advice. But to have received a letter of this kind—"it made a great noise," Stephen recalled—from a leading Whig statesman of the time, who was a friend of his father's to boot, could not have been without effect on his own view of his political prospects.

But the connection with Brougham went beyond this letter. For it was the alliance of Brougham and Zachary Macaulay in the cause of abolition that played an important role in bringing Tom into public prominence, both as a speaker and as a writer. In 1823, the Quaker philanthropist Thomas Fowell Buxton had, at the urging of Wilberforce, become the new parliamentary leader of the abolitionists. In May of that year he moved a resolution recommending abolition with as much expedition as might be found consistent with the regard for the well-being of all parties concerned. Canning's retort to this resolution was to procrastinate. He proposed that the Privy Council be charged with undertaking the amelioration of the condi-

15. Philip Whitwell Wilson, ed., *The Greville Diary, Including Passages hitherto withheld from Publication* (2 vols., New York, 1927), II, 153. It seems that James Stephen had taken Brougham to Clapham years before to dine with Zachary Macaulay, and had told him that he would find a prodigy of a boy there, of whom he must take notice.

16. T.B.M. to his father, March 15, 1823, Trinity Correspondence.

17. *Works*, XI, 276.

tion of the slaves. An Order in Council promulgated a new code for Trinidad, one of the Crown colonies. The hope was expressed that other colonial legislatures, even in colonies that were not under the Crown, would follow suit. But this did not happen. Instead, riot and insurrection broke out in those territories near Trinidad which had taken no action on behalf of the slaves. One of these riots occurred in Demerara (British Guiana) where John Smith, an independent clergyman representing the London Missionary Society, conducted a chapel for Negroes. Smith was found guilty of helping to stir up insurrection, and died in prison of a previous illness while awaiting execution of his sentence.[18] Here, then, was a martyr.

The Evangelicals, meanwhile, disgusted by Canning's less than energetic interest in the cause closest to their hearts, began to think that they could derive more satisfaction from an alliance with the Whigs, and moved away from their traditional Tory allies. At the suggestion of Zachary Macaulay, Brougham took a leading part in the campaign that followed. He brought the case of missionary Smith before the House of Commons, and demanded that the Minutes be laid before Parliament. In a speech in the House on June 1, 1824, he reviewed the case in detail and supplied proof of Smith's innocence. Later that month, on June 25, there took place in London at Freemason's Hall, then the largest public assembly rooms in England, a meeting of the Society for the Mitigation and Abolition of Slavery, founded by Zachary in 1823. In the audience and on the platform were many prominent persons, including a representative of the royal family; the Whig historian and philosopher Sir James Mackintosh; the venerable Wilberforce; Brougham; and, of course, Zachary Macaulay. It was a proud moment in his life. For one of the principal speakers was his son Tom, who here made his first appearance as a public orator outside the precincts of the university. It was, by all accounts, a remarkable début.

Of the British slaveowners in the New World the speaker remarked that they outdid all the military despots and all the frantic Jacobins of the Old. Their tender mercies, he said, were more cruel than the vengeance of Dundee; their little fingers thicker than the loins of Alva. Robespierre chastised with whips; but they chastised with scorpions. As for the argument that, in fact, masters did not abuse the power with which they were invested *vis-à-vis* the slaves, this could only be called an argument which, if true, would demon-

18. For details, see Raymond Cowherd, *Protestant Dissenters in English Politics, 1815–1834* (Philadelphia, 1942), 54–7.

strate that there was no truth in experience, no consistency in human nature; that history was a fable, and political science a juggle, the wisdom of our ancestors madness, and the British constitution a mere name. "Let us break up the benches of the House of Commons for firewood, and cut Magna Charta into battledores!"[19] Brougham, in the *Edinburgh Review*, called Macaulay's performance "so signal for rare and matured excellence, that the most practised orators may well admire how it should have come from one who then, for the first time, addressed a public assembly."[20] The *Morning Chronicle* called him "a youth of whom high expectations have been formed which he will not disappoint."[21] Letters of congratulation poured in on Zachary. After Tom's speech, which was applauded and cheered for several minutes, he had tears in his eyes. For him this was the fulfillment of a dream: his son speaking on behalf of the sacred cause, and moving such a distinguished assembly with his oratory. Characteristically, though, on the walk home after the meeting, he said to him: "By the way, Tom, you should be aware that when you speak in the presence of royalty, you should not fold your arms."[22]

The Tories, in the shape of the *Quarterly Review*, not unexpectedly offered more fundamental criticisms. Sarcastically, the *Quarterly* reviewers referred to the speaker's having taken rather more pains than were necessary to prove that slavery was not a blessing. From beginning to end, they wrote, Macaulay's speech consisted of studied invective against the past and present conduct of all persons connected with the West Indian colonies. Brougham, too, became a target of attack because of the alleged intemperance of one of his speeches the previous April: "Two speeches more calculated to insult and exasperate every individual interested in our West India colonies cannot well be conceived."[23] It is not without significance that Brougham had been in the audience while Macaulay spoke; that the *Quarterly*, stung to the quick by the younger man's address, linked it with Brougham's in obloquy; and that Brougham himself, in the *Edinburgh Review*, the *Quarterly*'s predecessor and chief rival, went out of its way to praise the speech in such lyrical terms. It was probably in response to a request from Brougham to Zachary that in January 1825, Tom first made his appearance in the great Whig periodical, the *Edinburgh Review*, with an anti-slavery arti-

19. *Quarterly Review*, XXXII (1825), 510–11.
20. *Edinburgh Review*, XLI (1824), 226.
21. *Morning Chronicle*, June 26, 1824.
22. Knutsford, *Zachary Macaulay*, 424.
23. *Quarterly Review*, XXXII (1825), 510–14.

cle on "The West Indies."[24] Here, then, is the genesis of Macaulay the *Edinburgh* reviewer—recommended by Brougham, the outstanding Whig in the House of Commons, by virtue of his untiring productivity as a writer the most powerful member of that group of *Edinburgh* pioneers who had the most influence over Jeffrey, the editor; the same Brougham now allied with the Evangelicals in the cause of the emancipation of the slaves. It was by no means an accident that Macaulay's first *Edinburgh* article dealt with West Indian slavery.

A freewheeling approach to reviewing, in which the volume reviewed became not much more than an occasion for a piece the author would have written in any event, was the peculiar hallmark of the *Edinburgh,* founded in 1802 in the "Athens of the North" by some brilliant young men, for the most part Whig lawyers with time on their hands and no regular occupation. By the 1820's this periodical had become one of the chief and most feared arbiters of taste for the educated British reading public, as well as one of the principal supports of the Whig Party.

It was in the *Edinburgh* that Jeffrey had castigated Wordsworth's *Excursion* with a devastating "This will never do"; that Sydney Smith had poked clerical fun, as only he could, at Methodists and intolerant anti-Catholics; that Brougham had propounded scientific education and law reform. Unafraid of established reputations, merciless in pursuit of dullness and pomposity as well as Toryism, the *Edinburgh*'s authoritative voice—bolstered by a policy of anonymity giving it *ex cathedra* force—was listened to with respect all over educated Europe. Neither brilliance nor learning nor wit was lacking in it; after all, it included contributors of the caliber of Mackintosh, Malthus, and "the Smith of Smiths." Now Macaulay joined their ranks.

The "West Indies" essay, which in many respects echoed Macaulay's contribution to *Knight's* on the same subject a year and a half earlier, is of interest chiefly on two accounts. First, because it stresses the importance of historical *situation* as a determining factor of modes of moral behavior, and as an explanation of crimes which should not necessarily be held to discredit the sensibilities of those who committed them. "If Henry VIII had been a private man," Macaulay wrote, "he might have torn his wife's ruff, and kicked her lap-dog. He was a King, and he cut off her head."[25] (Note, by the way, how "ruff" and "lap-dog" quite easily and naturally conjure up

24. See Jane Millgate, "Father and Son: Macaulay's *Edinburgh* Debut," *Review of English Studies,* XXI (1970), 159–67.
25. *Edinburgh Review,* XLI (1825), 476.

a sixteenth-century tableau.) That a drover goads oxen, or a fish-monger crimps cod, or the Spanish Inquisition burns Jews, or an Irish gentleman torments Catholics is not necessarily due to lack of feeling on the part of those who commit these acts. Each of these persons would shrink from any sort of cruel employment, except that to which his *situation* has accustomed him. It is of some in-terest to find this relativistic notion of the importance of situation, or historical context, as a factor in historical explanation in a writer so often lightly charged with applying indiscriminately the standards of his own time to the past.

The second significant theme running through this abolitionist article is that of anti-colonialism, closely modeled upon the ideas of James Mill about this subject, which we know Macaulay had been studying. The notion of the West Indies as a source of vast wealth and revenue to the mother country Macaulay brands as an absurdity. He inveighs against the colonial Empire as such, settlements which have cost England much blood and money, but have not really accomplished anything of use to her.[26]

The Tory *Blackwood's* dismissed the review as "the ravings of a boy, who evidently has not yet mastered the first rules of Watts' Logic," and its author as "a clever lad, though pert and absurd in the most ludicrous degree, when he attempts to discuss subjects of this sort of character and importance."[27] But then, just a few months previously, the author of this very passage, William Maginn, had himself tried to persuade the founder of the journal, William Black-wood, to approach Macaulay as a prospective contributor, since, on the basis of his articles for *Knight's*, he appeared to him to be "the very cleverest young man at all dabbling in periodicals."[28] If Black-wood pursued the quest, he was unsuccessful; for Macaulay was no longer to be captured by the Tories. The connection with the *Edinburgh,* begun under the auspices of Brougham and Zachary, was to last for twenty years.

The "West Indies" piece led Jeffrey to request another article, more literary in substance; and in August 1825 there appeared in the *Edinburgh Review* an article, forty-two pages in length, ostensibly devoted to a critical discussion of Milton's *Treatise on Christian Doctrine, Compiled from the Holy Scriptures Alone,* a long-lost work of the poet which had recently come to light and had now been

---

26. Ibid., 483.
27. [William Maginn], *Blackwood's Edinburgh Magazine,* XVII (1825) , 468, 470.
28. Alan L. Strout, "William Maginn as Gossip," *Notes and Queries,* CC (1955) , 265.

translated from the original Latin by Charles R. Sumner, Bishop of Winchester from 1826 and a brother of the Archbishop of Canterbury. Like all articles in the *Edinburgh,* this one was anonymous. But its tone and substance were so original, its impact on the educated British public so great, that its authorship could not long be kept secret. It was this article which established Macaulay's fame and opened the way for his career both as essayist and as Whig politician. It was probably when he received this article in manuscript that the formidable editor of the *Edinburgh Review* wrote to its author: "The more I think, the less I can conceive where you picked up that style." It was the only compliment he ever received about which Macaulay was known to boast in later life. But it was by no means the only one he received at the time. Trevelyan wrote that the effect of "Milton" on the reputation of its author was instantaneous. "Like Lord Byron, he awoke one morning and found himself famous."[29]

What was there in the Milton article that helped to make it such a sensation? Style, indeed, was one of the chief factors contributing to its electric effect, an effect which the subject alone would certainly not have been able to exert. It is true that in the authentic *Edinburgh* tradition the matter of the essay itself ranged far beyond Milton's *Treatise on Christian Doctrine.* That was merely the peg on which Macaulay hung his observations about Milton's prose, poetry, and politics, as well as an elaborate comparison of Milton and Dante; not to speak of an analysis of the political struggles of seventeenth-century England, the roles played in them by the principal parties and personages involved, and their relevance to the contemporary English scene.

The Bible, the Greek tragedians and historians, the Italian poets of the Renaissance, English men of letters from Shakespeare to Cowley and Dryden, to Johnson and Burke and Swift—all were mobilized to illustrate and support the author's judgments. This was more than mere piling on of book learning; it was part of the setting for the phrases which sparkled and scintillated through the essay: "As the magic lantern acts best in a dark room, poetry effects its purpose most completely in a dark age." Dr. Johnson was "as ill qualified to judge between two Latin styles as a habitual drunkard to set up for a wine-taster." . . . "The men who demolished the images in Cathedrals have not always been able to demolish those which

29. Trevelyan, *Life and Letters,* 85–6.

were enshrined in their minds." Milton's fondness for Euripides was reminiscent of "the beautiful Queen of Fairy-land kissing the long ears of Bottom." . . . "In proportion as men know more, and think more, they look less at individuals and more at classes. They therefore make better theories and worse poems." Milton's poetry could be compared to Alpine scenery: "The roses and myrtles bloom unchilled on the verge of the avalanche."

Many politicians of our time are in the habit of laying it down as a self-evident proposition, that no people ought to be free till they are fit to use their freedom. The maxim is worthy of the fool in the old story, who resolved not to go into the water till he had learnt to swim. If men are to wait for liberty till they become wise and good in slavery, they may indeed wait for ever.[30]

Similes, epigrams, pungent invective, and striking illustrations studded the essay as raisins a cake. If anything, it was, so Gladstone aptly quoted Milton, "dark with excessive bright"; and, in the words of another powerful critic looking back on it, "overloaded with gaudy and ungraceful ornament."[31] The latter critic was none other than Macaulay himself, passing mature judgment upon his youthful masterpiece. For masterpiece it was, certainly in the old sense of a piece of work by which the craftsman gained recognition as a master from his guild.

It was not an entirely new masterpiece, for it contained many choice phrases and illustrations previously used by Macaulay in his speeches and writings. Praed's comment had substance: "In the new number of the *Edinburgh Review* there is a very brilliant paper on Milton by Macaulay. It is too full of his conceits, however, and rather disappointed me, because I remember almost every metaphor and simile applied by him in conversation or in public speaking to some different subject, although they are all strung together with wonderful ingenuity."[32]

Thus the stylistic groundwork for the Milton essay had been well laid. But this was no less true of its guiding ideas. Here, too, Macaulay, in developing his main theses, drew on themes long familiar

30. T.B.M., "Milton" (1825), *Works*, VII, 6–7, 9, 10, 16, 23, 30, 43.

31. W. E. Gladstone, *Gleanings from Past Years, 1843–1878* (7 vols., London, 1879), II, 273; T.B.M., author's preface, *Critical and Historical Essays of Lord Macaulay* (3 vols., Boston, 1900), I, xii.

32. Derek Hudson, *A Poet in Parliament: The Life of Winthrop Mackworth Praed, 1802–1839* (London, 1939), 126. See P. L. Carver, "The Sources of Macaulay's *Essay on Milton*," *Review of English Studies*, VI (1930), 49–62, for T.B.M.'s borrowings from his own previous writings and, wittingly or unwittingly, from Hazlitt.

to him. Take, for instance, the first key idea of the essay; one that runs through many of Macaulay's subsequent writings, and one crucial for an understanding of his thought. It postulates various stages, ranging from "rudeness" to "refinement," in the progress of civilization, and belongs in origin to the "Scottish" school of philosophical historians, such as Robertson, Ferguson, and Millar, whose ideas were transmitted to the first *Edinburgh* reviewers by way of the lectures of Dugald Stewart at the University of Edinburgh. Macaulay had read and memorized Millar and Robertson at school. From them he had learned that the history of mankind evolved in a series of stages. Each stage affected all aspects of society—political, economic, and cultural. Thus, the initial "rude" stage did not merely witness primitive forms of economic organization; it also produced particular forms of the poetic instinct, marked at this stage by the natural expression of passions and emotions. Civilization advanced and brought in its train not merely the division of labor and the growth of new classes and institutions, but also the sort of poetry, drama, and criticism appropriate to each later stage. Sismondi, also one of Macaulay's favorite authors since his schooldays, propounded something similar. In young nations, he wrote in his *Historical View of the Literature of the South of Europe,* literature was all feeling, inspiration, eloquence, and natural imagination. Then analysis succeeded creativity, and the intellect rose over native talent.[33]

The same thesis was widely maintained in England in the course of the eighteenth century. From mid-century on, a good deal of critical writing was built around an attempt to reground all thinking about poetry in the light of what seemed to be the superior originality and greater immediacy and universality of subject and appeal of the poetry of earlier periods.[34] Just five years before Macaulay's "Milton," Thomas Love Peacock in his essay on "The Four Ages of Poetry" had pointed out that those who lived in rude and uncivilized periods expressed themselves naturally in a poetic manner. As reason gradually gained the ascendant over imagination and feeling, poetry dropped into the background.[35]

Writing in this tradition of thought, Macaulay began his essay on

33. J. C. L. de Sismondi, *Historical View of the Literature of the South of Europe* (4 vols., London, 1823) , I, 1–8. The French edition had appeared in 1813, and Macaulay read it with enthusiasm three years later. See T.B.M. to his parents [March, 1816], Trinity Correspondence.

34. See W. Jackson Bate, *The Burden of the Past and the English Poet* (Cambridge, Mass., 1970) .

35. H. F. Brett-Smith and C. E. Jones, eds., *Works of Thomas Love Peacock* (10 vols., London, 1924–34) , VIII, 5–11.

Milton by examining, and eventually dismissing as false, the supposition that poets in the seventeenth century could more easily compose epics than their predecessors in earlier ages. Not at all, was Macaulay's reply to this view. It was, in fact, in the early, the "rude" stages of mankind's development that the imagination held easy and indisputable sway. In an analogy he was often to repeat, Macaulay compared those who lived during that first stage of society to children, easily terrified by monsters and the dark, quick to endow phenomena of nature with mysterious and supernatural significance. Then it was "natural" for the singer and the poet to give their imagination full rein, to speak to the heart rather than to the mind and the brain. By the time Milton wrote, however, this had become immeasurably more difficult. For the rise of civilization had brought with it not merely the twin boons of wealth and liberty, but also increase of knowledge, particularly scientific knowledge. Gradually, the critical supplanted the imaginative faculties, and it became far harder for the poet's imagination to exert itself.

For Macaulay, the thesis of advancing stages of civilization did not carry with it the postulate of illimitable progress. It was his assumption that when refinement had reached the ultimate point, decay would set in; and the process of advancement from rudeness would then begin all over again, perhaps in some other part of the globe. This cyclical idea was to appear in its most striking form in his essay on Ranke's *History of the Popes* (1840), in which he visualized the traveler from New Zealand standing on a broken arch of London Bridge to sketch the ruins of St. Paul's Cathedral. But it had exercised fascination over Macaulay very much earlier than that. At the age of sixteen he quoted to his father (from memory) a passage from Sismondi in which the latter anticipated a Europe without her current advantages and without the power she now exercised over the most remote regions of the habitable globe: "Her cities may sleep in the dust. Her temples may fall as the Capitol and the Pantheon have fallen already." Some other people might arise in the Orinoco mountains, or in the forests of New Holland (so Macaulay cited Sismondi), who would one day reflect back upon western Europe and would contemplate the names of Newton and Tasso as instances of the fruitless struggle maintained by genius against the destiny that decreed everything human must perish.[36]

Not only was progress not unlimited. It could not even be maintained that each succeeding stage of civilization brought with it only

36. T.B.M. to his father, May 14, 1816, Trinity Correspondence.

advantage. There was loss as well as gain. I think it would be wrong to assume, as some do,[37] that in his Milton essay Macaulay altogether welcomes the more enlightened and rational period of the seventeenth century as against the "ruder" beginnings of human history. Whatever may have been gained in refinement, sensibility, and knowledge was offset by a concomitant loss of imagination, emotional power, and directness. That Milton's epic poetry was achieved in a civilized age made its author all the greater for having been able to retain some of these "primitive" elements in an age uncongenial to them. In recognizing this, Macaulay recognized at the same time the importance of these qualities, signs though they were of earlier and more barbarous times. He was torn between regret at the loss of these natural expressions of emotion, imagination, and originality appropriate to a primitive age, and his sense of pride in the progressive development of enlightenment, liberty, wealth, and the critical faculty. One able, recent critic has found the key to Macaulay's personality in this ambivalent posture and has depicted him as someone who in spite of his repeated celebrations of progress and civilization really wanted to live in the distant past.[38] Putting it this way seems to me to be taking too literally what for Macaulay essentially remained an intellectual rather than a personal dilemma.

Macaulay is often described as an "Augustan," an heir of the eighteenth-century classical literary tradition, violently opposed to the more lyrical, more emotional mode of the Romantic poets. This is too simplistic a view. Macaulay, it is true, came to be known as an inveterate enemy of Wordsworth, and even to take a certain pride in his celebrity on this account. But the main reason for his hostility to that poet was his attempt to erect a metaphysical system on the basis of natural objects and ordinary men and women. It was not by any means the Lake poets' stress on the heart rather than the head, on feelings rather than ratiocination, that alienated Macaulay.

He certainly preferred the humanism of Dante and Shakespeare to what he called the literary fashion for nature of his own time. Self-consciously urban and common-sensical, he lacked any true feeling for Wordsworth's philosophy. What is it that we go to see in *Hamlet*,

37. For example, Walter E. Houghton, *The Victorian Frame of Mind, 1830–1870* (New Haven, Conn., 1957), 123. But see also the interesting article by Ronald Weber, "Seer and Singer: Macaulay on the Historian as Poet," *Papers on Language and Literature*, III (1967), 210–19, which suggests that T.B.M. inserted the figure of the ideal historian, i.e., himself, into the poetic void of modern, enlightened society.

38. George Levine, "Macaulay: Progress and Retreat," *The Boundaries of Fiction: Carlyle, Macaulay, Newman* (Princeton, N.J., 1968), 79–163.

he asked in his *Knight's* essay on the principal Italian writers. A reed shaken by the wind? A small celandine? A bed of daffodils? Or a mighty and wayward mind laid low? "It may perhaps be doubted," he went on, "whether the lakes and the hills are better fitted for the education of a poet than the dusky streets of a huge capital."[39] But he was far from oblivious to the genius of the Lake school of poetry; pointing out, for instance, that the finest works of the imagination were always produced in times of political convulsion—Shakespeare during the Reformation, Wordsworth during the French Revolution.[40] In another of his essays for *Knight's Quarterly*, he went out of his way to remark that the admiration of the multitude did not make Tom Moore a greater poet than Coleridge.[41] And, in his essay on the elder Pitt, he applied to Chatham Wordsworth's lines:

> He still retained,
> 'Mid such abasement, what he had received
> From nature, an intense and glowing mind.[42]

Macaulay was not so much an Augustan as someone who, along with a great many sensitive contemporaries, confronted the problem of finding himself in a transitional period between generations. Not so much, perhaps, an eighteenth-century "survival" in a romantic age—a definition which postulates that people can be fitted into appropriate time slots—as himself expressive of the dilemma faced by those in the early nineteenth century who could neither bring themselves to embrace the new nor to preserve the old without serious reservations, but felt drawn to both in varying degrees.

The idea that it was in the "rude" state of society that great original works were most frequently produced had its corollary in the fact that the world owed a large proportion of the original works produced in more polished ages to men of low station and little education. This Macaulay had already stressed in his essay on the principal Italian writers in *Knight's*. "Had Bunyan and Defoe been educated gentlemen," he wrote there, "they would probably have published translations and imitations of French romances 'by a person of quality.' I am not sure that we should have had Lear if Shakespeare had been able to read Sophocles."[43]

In part, then, the essay on Milton was a celebration of the great-

39. *Works*, XI, 271–2.   40. Ibid., 261.
41. "On the Athenian Orators" (1824), *Works*, XI, 345.
42. "William Pitt, Earl of Chatham" (1834), *Works*, VIII, 364.
43. *Works*, XI, 256.

ness of a poet who had been able to exert the power of his imagination on a heroic subject in a rationalistic age. But only in part. For any essay on Milton written in the early nineteenth century was almost bound to be as much a political manifesto as a piece of literary criticism; and this one was no exception. The *locus classicus* of critical comment on Milton was Dr. Johnson's essay in *Lives of the Poets*. There Johnson had dubbed Milton's political notions those of "an acrimonious and surly republican," and had described him as one who having justified the murder of his King (Charles I) then sold his services and his flatteries to a tyrant (Cromwell).[44]

Macaulay's relationship to Johnson throughout his life proved to be complex—a mixture of admiration, affection, and misunderstanding. In his essay on "The Athenian Orators" in *Knight's* he had gone so far as to talk of "that arrogant absurdity which, in spite of his great abilities and virtues, renders him [Johnson], perhaps, the most ridiculous character in literary history."[45] There can be little doubt that his own essay on Milton was intended as a repudiation of what he considered to have been Johnson's libels. Macaulay's approach was not that of the Romantic poets, who tended to celebrate Milton as a thorough revolutionary claiming inspiration both from the Heavenly Muse and the Holy Spirit, and who, "after the failure of his millennial expectations from the English Revolution, had kept his singing voice and salvaged his hope for mankind in an epic poem."[46] It was, rather, to see Milton from within the context of the politics of the 1820's, and to pay homage to him as one of the chief representatives of a well-defined political tradition.

In one of his youthful poems, Macaulay had called on Freedom to

> *Still on our children pour the holy ray*
> *Which sooth'd the gloom of Sidney's parting day.*
> *O'er Ham[p]den's life its beams of glory pour'd*
> *And hallow'd Milton's life and Marlbro's sword.*
> *Let dazzled nations bend before the blaze,*
> *And distant tyrants tremble while they gaze.*[47]

44. Samuel Johnson, *The Lives of the Most Eminent English Poets with Critical Observations on Their Works* (2 vols., Charlestown, S.C., 1810) , I, 102, 77.

45. *Works,* XI, 340–1.

46. M. H. Abrams, "English Romanticism: The Spirit of the Age," Northrop Frye, ed., *Romanticism Reconsidered: Selected Papers from the English Institute* (New York, 1963) , 45.

47. Quoted by T.B.M. as poem written for his master, Preston, at Aspenden. T.B.M. to his father, November 28, 1817, Trinity Correspondence.

The three names whose glory these lines celebrate—Hampden, Milton, Sidney—belong to the hagiography of radical Whiggism. Their bearers were heroes and martyrs for "The Good Old Cause," the Commonwealth side in the Great Rebellion of the seventeenth century. The poem, written by Macaulay at the age of seventeen, shows that his encomiastic view of what these men stood for—the main burden of his Milton essay—goes back to his schooldays; and that even then, there was some relation between this view and his attitude to contemporary English politics. We recall that Milton, along with Tacitus and Cicero, was one of those who helped to inspire his dismay at the Peterloo Massacre.

Certainly, the events of the seventeenth century continued to have a particular fascination for Macaulay throughout his youth and early manhood. In 1821, while on his way to Wales for a holiday, he wrote to his mother: "I had rather see my Jenny again, or argue with Selina [both sisters] for half an hour about the Long Parliament, than contemplate all the wonders that art has done for Stowe, or nature for Piercefield."[48] We know that Macaulay's sister Selina was, like his mother, particularly upset about the turn his political views took at Cambridge;[49] so that it is not hard to imagine what side of the argument *she* was on. In the course of the next year Macaulay won the prize given annually at Trinity College for the best essay on "The Character and Memory of William the Third," which he turned into a paean of praise for its subject: "To have been a sovereign, yet the champion of liberty, a revolutionary leader, yet the supporter of social order, is the peculiar glory of William."[50]

His own favorite essay among those he contributed to *Knight's Quarterly* took the form of an imaginary conversation held in 1665 between two poets—Cowley and Milton—one a confirmed Royalist, the other a staunch Republican. It took place while they were sailing on the Thames one fine summer evening. The subject was the Civil War, now a generation in the past; more specifically, the justice or injustice of the execution of Charles I, and the character of the Long Parliament responsible for that deed. Cowley cries out against the lawlessness of the execution, the deluge of blood it brought in its trail. Milton replies that the deluge was, in fact, a blessed flood, like that annual overflowing of the Nile which leaves fertility in its wake.

---

48. T.B.M. to his mother, July 10, 1821, Trinity Correspondence.
49. Hannah, Lady Trevelyan, "Reminiscences," 29, Trinity MSS.
50. A. N. L. Munby, "Germ of a History: Twenty-three Pages of a Macaulay Cambridge Prize Essay," *Times Literary Supplement*, May 1, 1969, 469.

Charles, he maintains, was more of a villainous huckster than a great King. In response to Cowley's protestation that he had, after all, been a proper gentleman and a great prince who died bravely, Milton hammers home the point that he failed to keep his promise to Parliament to observe the Petition of Right. The important fact was his tyranny, not his virtuous private character. He lived like a tyrant; and, just because he died like a martyr, his public crimes should not be forgotten. Milton, in this imaginary conversation as well as in his actual political writings, went so far as to justify the legality, though not the fact of the King's execution while admitting that, in the end, it may have hindered rather than helped the liberties of England.[51] That these ideas, here put into the mouth of Milton, were also Macaulay's is clear from the fact that they reappear, this time as his own, in the Milton essay.

This is what Macaulay has to say there about Charles I's personal virtues:

We charge him with having broken his coronation oath—and we are told that he kept his marriage vow! We accuse him of having given up his people to the merciless inflictions of the most hot-headed and hard-hearted of prelates—and the defence is, that he took his little son on his knee and kissed him! We censure him for having violated the articles of the Petition of Right, after having, for good and valuable consideration, promised to observe them—and we are informed that he was accustomed to hear prayers at six o'clock in the morning![52]

And, while he does not approve of the King's execution, he strongly endorses Milton's defense of that act, once it had been committed:

The very feeling which would have restrained us from committing the act would have led us, after it had been committed, to defend it against the ravings of servility and superstition. For the sake of public liberty, we wish that the thing had not been done, while the people disapproved of it. But, for the sake of public liberty, we should also have wished the people to approve of it when it was done.[53]

The extent to which the English Revolution fired his imagination is apparent from two vigorous ballads he wrote in 1824, one Royalist, the other Puritan. One, entitled "The Cavalier's March to London," contained these lines:

51. "A Conversation between Mr. Abraham Cowley and Mr. John Milton, touching the Great Civil War" (1824), *Works*, XI, 310–22.
52. *Works*, VII, 38–9.   53. Ibid., 45.

> *Quarter?—Foul fall your whining noise,*
> *Ye recreant spawn of fraud!*
> *No quarter! Think on Strafford, boys.*
> *No quarter! Think on Laud.*
> *What ho! The craven slaves retire.*
> *On! Trample them to mud,*
> *No quarter!—Charge. No quarter!—Fire.*
> *No quarter!—Blood!—Blood!—Blood!*[54]

The ballad written on behalf of the other side was entitled "Battle of Naseby," and celebrated that decisive defeat of the Royalist forces:

> *Down, down, for ever down*
> * with the mitre and the crown,*
> *With the Belial of the Court,*
> * and the Mammon of the Pope;*
> *There is woe in Oxford Halls;*
> * there is wail in Durham's stalls.*
> *The Jesuit smites his bosom:*
> * the Bishop rends his cope.*[55]

Were one to show these excerpts from the two poems to anyone who had no preconceptions about Macaulay and to ask such a person which of them expressed its author's "real" political sentiments, the answer would surely have to be that it was impossible to tell. If anything, the Royalist poem with its savage lilt and its climactic cry for blood might appear to be the more genuinely felt. To us, who know from the Milton essay and from Macaulay's other writings where his sympathies lay, there is a lesson worth learning here. The lesson lies in the capacity for impartiality of Macaulay's imagination. It is often the case that in his poetry he celebrates both sides in some great battle or political contest, drawn to his theme as much by the grandeur and excitement of the historical struggle as by current political sympathies.

To read aloud verses like his "Cavalier's March to London" or his "Jacobin Song for the Year 1792":

> *Let trembling despots fly the land*
> *To shun impending danger*
> *We'll stretch forth a fraternal hand*
> *To hail each glorious stranger . . .*[56]

54. *Works*, XII, 458.   55. Ibid., 456.
56. No date, initialed "T.B.M.," Huntington MSS.

makes nonsense of the charge so often brought against him that extreme partisanship prevented him from sympathizing with certain historical movements. On the contrary. The problem here is of quite a different sort; namely, to fathom why his most moving and deeply felt occasional poems so often turn out to be those in which he concerned himself with what, ideologically speaking, must have been for him the enemy. Is this due to the fact that there was in him, deep down, a sympathy for lost causes (Jacobites, Jacobins, Royalists during the Civil War), which could only find expression when he turned from prose to verse? Did he then take special pains to be just to the side which did *not* fundamentally engage his support? Or was there perhaps in his character some streak of contrariness, of basic rebelliousness, which must assert itself in this form since, for familial and prudential reasons, it could do so in no other?

Whatever the answer to these questions, it is well to remember that Macaulay's preoccupation with the seventeenth century was based not merely on his own past interests or his romantic attraction to the period. In taking up the cudgels on behalf of Milton in his essay for the *Edinburgh Review,* he was quite consciously making himself a link in a long-raging historiographical controversy, one involving not merely questions of historical interpretation, but basic political orientations and value judgments as well. At issue in this long-standing conflict were the utility and the justice of the great English Revolution of the seventeenth century. Had Charles I claimed extraordinary rights and powers? Was the Long Parliament justified in bringing about his execution? What were the character and effect of Cromwell's role? Two principal lines of thought may be distinguished. One owed its dominance to the fact that its spokesman was the great philosopher David Hume, whose *History of England,* written in the 1750's, still held the field in Macaulay's time. According to Hume, the early Stuarts did not really overstep their rights in any way, since under the "despotic" Tudors the privileges of Parliament had not been clearly defined. Thus, he reserved his condemnation not for them, but for the cant, hypocrisy, and bigotry that were to be found on the side of the Puritan Party.[57]

Hume regarded the execution of Charles as one more proof of the madness of the people, the furies of fanaticism, and the danger of

57. For all this, see Thomas Preston Peardon, *The Transition in English Historical Writing, 1760–1830* (New York, 1933) and Duncan Forbes, ed., *The History of Great Britain: The Reigns of James I and Charles I* (Harmondsworth, 1970). On the extent of Hume's "Toryism," and its Scottish context, see Forbes's introduction and Hugh Trevor-Roper, "David Hume as a Historian," *Listener,* LXVI (1961), 1103–19).

mercenary armies. Cromwell's conduct he called one continual violation of justice: He was "devoted to religion, tho' he perpetually
employed it as the instrument of his ambition; his crimes were
derived from the prospect of sovereign power, a temptation, which is,
in general, irresistible to human nature." For Hume the Independents represented the very height of extravagance and fanaticism,
holding as they did "enthusiastic" doctrines of predestination; keeping pace in their political with their religious views in aspiring to a
total abolition of the monarchy and aristocracy; and projecting
entire equality of rank and order in the Republic-to-be.[58] Hume's
powerful and elegant style helped to make his *History* widely read
and enormously influential.

The other side, for a long time, had found no historian of comparable ability to state its viewpoint. As Professor Trevor-Roper puts
it, "against Hume's sophisticated and elegant 'tory' history, successive Whig pens had squeaked in vain." One of Macaulay's own distant
relatives, Catharine Macaulay, had written a *History of England
from the Accession of James I to the Revolution* as a libertarian
manifesto. In it she praised the opponents of Charles I as "the
greatest men England ever produced," and called the Long Parliament the world's greatest monument of human virtue.[59] The Scottish philosophical historian James Millar, in his *Historical View of
the English Government,* had made the point (*contra* Hume) that
Charles's claims to absolute monarchy were inconsistent with the
original constitution and the fundamental laws of the kingdom.
Millar condemned Charles's execution not on moral grounds (he
merited the highest punishment), but for utilitarian reasons. Was it
really wise, given the circumstances of the time, to execute the
King?[60] Macaulay was familiar with both these works. He admired
Millar, but he called Catherine Macaulay's book more distinguished by zeal than by either candor or skill. Yet, as he pointed out
in his "Milton," Hume had managed to hold the field in great part
through sheer literary brilliance.

The fact that the chief historiographical tradition ran in favor of
the Royalist side should not make us forget, however, that its opponents left behind an important political legacy. That was the tradi-

58. Forbes, ed., *Hume,* 687, 580, 571–2.

59. Hugh Trevor-Roper, ed., Lord Macaulay, *Critical and Historical Essays* (London, 1965), 12; Peardon, *Transition,* 80.

60. John Millar, *An Historical View of the English Government* (4 vols., 4th ed.,
London, 1818), III, 220, 329.

tion of the Commonwealthman, recently elucidated by Professors Caroline Robbins and John Pocock. This tradition of radical Whiggism was based on the works of political pamphleteers such as Harrington, Sidney, Milton, and Locke. It was carried on in various ways throughout the course of the eighteenth century—by means of Dissenting sermons, pamphlets, some historical writings such as Catharine Macaulay's and Millar's. It played an important role in the American Revolution. And it is very much alive in Macaulay's Milton essay. For Milton was a key figure in that tradition. He had, after all, justified not only the Great Rebellion, but also the execution of Charles I. And this was pretty strong medicine, not just for Tories like Dr. Johnson, but for many Whigs as well. During the eighteenth century, as Professor Robbins points out, the Whigs as heirs of the Hanoverian settlement and the Revolution of 1688 saw themselves above all as guardians of stability. Most of them did not, for obvious reasons, wish to dwell unduly on any connection between the innovators and levelers of the period 1640–60 and the sober and restrained makers of the Glorious Revolution.[61] Only the most radical would dare take that line.

Thus, Milton on the killing of Kings became a touchstone of the authentic Commonwealth tradition. And by the early 1820's some fresh voices were raised, which took fundamental issue with Hume's view of seventeenth-century English history. So George Brodie, in his *History of the British Empire* (1822), maintained that the Stuarts supplanted with their tyrannical rule what had in effect been a limited monarchy; that Charles, not Parliament, was to be blamed for the fact that the ensuing struggle turned into bloodshed; and that the Commonwealth period was one of great achievement. In the *Edinburgh Review*, Jeffrey differed from Brodie as to the necessity for the King's death, and the merits of the Long Parliament and the Commonwealth, but emphasized that he differed still more from Hume in these matters.[62]

John Stuart Mill, discussing the same book in the Radical *Westminster Review*, not surprisingly took a far more vigorous anti-Humean line, in agreement with Brodie. Charles I, Mill pointed out, had voluntarily plunged his country into the horrors of civil war for

61. Caroline Robbins, *The Eighteenth-Century Commonwealthman* (Cambridge, Mass., 1959), 3. See also J. G. A. Pocock, "Machiavelli, Harrington, and English Political Ideologies in the Eighteenth Century," *Politics, Language, and Time: Essays on Political Thought and History* (New York, 1971), 104–47.

62. *Edinburgh Review*, XL (1824), 92–146.

the gratification of his own appetite for power. Next in immorality to a monarch capable of this must be declared the historian (Hume) who could bring himself to praise such an action. The object of Mill's article was to show that Charles deserved punishment; though whether, under a good government, he should have been put to death was a question not of justice but of policy.[63] This view was close to that of Charles Austin who, we are told, quite simply thought the execution of Charles had been a political necessity.[64]

It may appear strange that such strong feelings could still be elicited almost two hundred years later about men and events long past; though, if we want an analogy, we need only think of the continuing power of the controversies regarding the French or Russian revolutions over the minds of future generations. Views on either side of such questions were strongly held; especially when the questions became paradigmatic of the future course of domestic politics. Thus Jeffrey, writing to Brougham, who had suggested a potential reviewer for Hallam's *Constitutional History,* replied that he had heard that book much abused not only for its dullness, but for a strong leaning "against the men of the republic—the founders of our liberty—and on the whole the purest and most venerable characters" in English history.[65] It was in such terms—not meant for public consumption, since they appeared in a private letter—that the editor of the leading Whig periodical referred to the men of the Commonwealth.

When Macaulay in his Milton essay endorsed Milton's defense of Charles I's execution and compared his successor to Belial, while praising Oliver Cromwell as another George Washington, these judgments were therefore invested with a significance not merely historiographical. And the same was true of one of the most eloquent passages in that essay, in which Macaulay paid a glowing tribute to the Puritans, admitting their "absurdities," yet strongly denying the accusation often brought against them that they were mere vulgar fanatics:

We regret that a body to whose courage and talents mankind has owed inestimable obligations had not the lofty elegance which distinguished some of the adherents of Charles I, or the easy good-breeding for which the court of Charles II was celebrated. But, if we must make our choice,

63. *Westminster Review,* II (1824) , 390, 397.
64. Tollemache, *Safe Studies,* 216.
65. Jeffrey to Brougham, November 18, 1827, Brougham MSS, University College, London, No. 22, 138. In the end, it was Macaulay who reviewed Hallam.

we shall, like Bassanio in the play, turn from the specious caskets which contain only the Death's head and the Fool's head, and fix on the plain leaden chest which conceals the treasure. . . . People who saw nothing of the godly but their uncouth visages, and heard nothing from them but their groans and their whining hymns, might laugh at them. But those had little reason to laugh who encountered them in the hall of debate or in the field of battle. These fanatics brought to civil and military affairs a coolness of judgement and an immutability of purpose which some writers have thought inconsistent with their religious zeal, but which were in fact the necessary effects of it. . . . We do not hesitate to pronounce them a brave, a wise, an honest, and an useful body.[66]

It is not unlikely that the young essayist, following in the footsteps of the man whom at that time he called the greatest statesman of the age, may have found at least positive inspiration for this passage from Brougham. Addressing the House of Commons on June 1, 1824, on the subject of missionary Smith, Brougham had spoken of the Independents as a body much to be respected for their numbers, "but far more to be held in lasting veneration for the unshaken fortitude with which in all times, they have maintained their attachment to civil and religious liberty, and, holding fast by their own principles, have carried to its uttermost pitch the great doctrine of absolute toleration." Their ancestors, Brougham went on, were men to whom England would always acknowledge a boundless debt of gratitude, as long as freedom was prized among Englishmen. "For they, I fearlessly proclaim it, *they*, with whatever ridicule some may visit their excesses, or with whatever blame others, *they*, with the zeal of martyrs, the purity of the early Christians, the skill and the courage of the most renowned warriors, gloriously suffered, and fought, and conquered for England the free constitution which she now enjoys!"[67] Note particularly the phrase, "I fearlessly proclaim it." To be encomiastic about the seventeenth-century Puritans during the 1820's was more than merely passing a certain historical judgment. It was one way of taking sides against the Establishment, of declaring one's allegiance to the "good old cause," to the popular, the anti-aristocratic, side.

It becomes all the more illuminating, therefore, to observe Brougham's reaction to his disciple's Milton essay, which contained not only such glowing terms of praise for the seventeenth-century Puritans, but also such forthright condemnation of their opponents. This is what Brougham wrote to a correspondent about the article;

66. *Works*, VII, 51–4.
67. June 1, 1824, Henry Lord Brougham, *Speeches* (4 vols., Edinburgh, 1838), II, 53.

having first called it an extraordinary, a very wonderful performance, for such a young man:

Really I derived so much pleasure from seeing the true faith so inimitably preached by so young a disciple, that I thought you would partake of the same pleasure—namely of thinking that the good cause will not want supporters when *we* are gone. I thought it enough to have made the House of Commons hear patiently of "the just and necessary punishment inflicted on C[harles] I," and "the *execution* of the blessed martyr," etc.—but I never ventured further than saying "it was wiser to conquer the tyrant than to trust him"—nor so far as to call Charles II Belial and compare Cromwell [before his fall] to Washington.[68]

This was praise indeed. And it shows us not only that Macaulay had firmly aligned himself with the Whigs, but that he had taken a more radical line than Brougham himself at this time and had placed himself solidly into the Commonwealthman tradition.

The specific political issue of the 1820's which had doubtless helped to fire Macaulay's wrath against the Tories was that of Catholic emancipation, that is, the admission to Parliament of Irish Catholics. Brougham had just been rebuffed by Canning in the matter of a projected fusion between the Whigs and the liberal Tories, because Canning, who was personally pro-Catholic, did not believe that public opinion was at this point ready to support Catholic emancipation. Probably he was right about that. Much to Brougham's annoyance Canning refused, in 1825, either to try to commit the government to the Catholic cause or to vote in the negative on a parliamentary bill that outlawed the so-called Catholic Associations which had been formed in Ireland in support of emancipation.

In historical terms there were certain elements of paradox in Whig advocacy of the Catholic cause and Tory opposition to it during the 1820's. For it could be said that the Glorious Revolution of 1668–9, the foundation of Whig predominance in the eighteenth century, was forged in the very crucible of anti-Catholicism. The settlement of 1689 had specifically set out to preserve the Protestant succession. True, the Tories had played their part in bringing about the "abdication" of James II and his replacement by William and Mary. But in the course of the early eighteenth century it was the Tory Party which became tainted with Jacobitism, that is to say, with a Stuart threat to the Revolution settlement that was only finally removed with the defeat of the uprising of 1745.

68. Brougham to William Shepherd, September 21, 1825, Brougham MSS, University College, London.

Now it was the Tories, and on this question they had much of public opinion behind them, who were concerned about the Catholic danger. The rationale of those opposed to emancipation was that if the Irish were to be empowered to send Roman Catholic Members of Parliament to Westminster, there would then be Catholics able to exert jurisdiction over the Church of England—an impossible situation from the point of view of any strong Church-and-King supporters. And it was the Whigs who not only found their liberal attitude on the Catholic question winning them nothing but opprobrium in the country, but who saw with chagrin that, of all people, their old "reactionary" enemies had suddenly set themselves up as residuary legatees of the Glorious Revolution. In May 1825, at the very time when Macaulay must have been contemplating, if not preparing, his Milton essay, Lord Eldon gave an account to his friend Lady Bankes of a celebration of the defeat of a Catholic Relief Bill in the House of Lords: "A most sumptuous and splendid set-out at the Duke of York's. . . . Twenty-four rejoicing Protestants round the table. . . . We drank the forty-eight [the size of the majority in the Lords], the year 1688, and the glorious and immortal memory of William III."[69] A public dinner was held, also, at which the Duke of York, the most vehement anti-Catholic in the royal family, proposed a toast to "the glorious and immortal memory of William," to wild acclaim.[70] All of this was, of course, reported in the press.

It was these events which help to account for Macaulay's remark in the Milton essay that the principles of the (Glorious) Revolution had never been so grossly misrepresented as in the present year (1825).[71] William III, after all, was, as we know, already then one of Macaulay's heroes, one of the chief preservers of that British freedom which the young essayist had celebrated since his schooldays. To have the ultra-Tories now capture in illegitimate fashion both the hero and the hero's cause, in other words, the Revolution of 1688, was more than Macaulay could stomach. And so he went on to comment in mocking fashion that in Tory eyes William III was being celebrated only because he had campaigned against the Irish Catholics. Furthermore, he took pains to establish the thesis that James II was expelled not because he was a Catholic, but because he

69. Lord Eldon to Lady Bankes, May 23, 1825, Horace Twiss, ed., *The Public and Private Life of Lord Chancellor Eldon, with Selections from his Correspondence* (3 vols., London, 1844), II, 554.

70. James G. Croswell, ed., *Macaulay's Essays on Milton and Addison* (New York, 1902), xviii.

71. *Works*, VII, 33. On the Catholic question and its relation to party at the time, see G. M. Trevelyan, *The Two-Party System in English Political History* (Oxford, 1926).

was a tyrant. If Macaulay could prove, as he attempted to in his essay, that those who supported the Glorious Revolution must in all logic also support that other, earlier revolt against royal tyranny, the Great Rebellion, then he would place the Tories into one of two equally embarrassing positions: Either to deny that their principles had anything at all to do with 1688, and thus to lose a valuable part of their appeal to Parliament and to public opinion outside; or to stick to 1688, and be forced thereby to support the regicides of the 1640's, clearly an impossible line for them to take. Needless to say, it is doubtful whether the Milton essay actually posed this cruel dilemma for any Tory readers. It was a clever debating point, neatly scored by an experienced Union debater. It was also a point that Macaulay had obvious pleasure in making. One can imagine his reaction on hearing that Lord Eldon had become one of the worshippers at the shrine of 1688—that was going too far, and he was not going to permit such a misappropriation to pass unchallenged.

How, then, sum up Macaulay's political position in 1825, at the time of the Milton essay? Perhaps it is possible to go beyond some of the conventional explanations of his early political beliefs. Some hold that he was, in some miraculous fashion, "born a Whig"; others, that he started out in life as a Tory and was then converted to Whiggism at Cambridge through the efforts of Austin and other friends at the Union; others still, that he "ratted" from Toryism to Whiggery for personal advantage, since the latter party offered better prospects of a career to a young man in the 1820's.[72] Had he in fact done so, it would in the context of the time not have been as reprehensible as the word, used in the twentieth century, makes it sound. The two most talented young statesmen of the age, Canning and Brougham, could be accused of similar transgressions. This view of Macaulay would have to be based both on his initial Toryism, and upon the fact that the Tories, having been in power for so many years, had become a weak and tired party; that it was clear in the midtwenties that sooner or later, probably sooner, the Whigs would come back in; and that with them would come the vigor and energy which alone could attract young men beginning a political career. But that was far from being the case. Indeed, we have seen that if one is to judge the energy and vigor of parties according to the degree of progressiveness displayed, it would be hard, in some important respects, not to choose the Tories over the Whigs in the 1820's, certainly in terms of foreign and economic policy. And at that time it

72. This last view in George Saintsbury, *Collected Essays and Papers, 1875–1920* (2 vols., London, 1923), II, 231.

was not at all certain that the Whigs, split on every issue except that of Catholic emancipation, were marching united toward inevitable triumph.

But the point is that Macaulay did not really join their ranks from opportunistic motives, though happy enough to accept a seat in Parliament when Lord Lansdowne eventually made him the offer. One of the cardinal considerations was certainly his father. We have seen that there existed tensions in the relationship between Macaulay and his father. We have seen that the result of these tensions may well have been repressed feelings of antagonism under the outward continuance of manifestations of filial obedience and piety. But, given the family situation, it seems out of the question that the dutiful son would enter political paths diverging explicitly from those his father trod. Perhaps it is worth recalling that in the letter to Zachary in which the young Macaulay expressed his sympathy with the victims of the Peterloo Massacre, he went out of his way to add:

Were my opinions as decisive as they are fluctuating, and were the elevation of a Cromwell or the renown of a Hampden the certain reward of my standing forth in the democratic cause, I would rather have my lips sealed on the subject than give my mother or you one hour of uneasiness.[73]

Now, as we know, the elder Macaulay had drifted away from the Tories on the issue of slave emancipation. This cause was now being taken up by the Whigs; and specifically by Brougham, who had in any event taken considerable interest in the young Macaulay's political career. Brougham could be safely emulated, since not only was he, along with Canning, the most brilliant statesman of the age, but, beyond that, was now associated with Zachary in the cause closest to his heart.

This is not to say that Macaulay's politics could be identified with his father's. Zachary would hardly have sanctioned the radical Commonwealthman tradition of "the good old cause" which his son so eloquently propounded in his essay on Milton. This, it must be stressed, was far removed from the beliefs even of the more conservative wing of the Whig Party. But one must remember that the Whig tradition had, so to speak, two legs to stand on; or, as Lord Acton put it, a double pedigree.[74] One was the line leading from the Roundheads and Milton to Sidney and to Charles James Fox. The other, the

73. T.B.M. to his father, September 1819, Trevelyan, *Life and Letters*, 69.
74. Acton, *Home and Foreign Review*, quoted in David Mathew, *Acton: The Formative Years* (London, 1946), 152.

tradition of the old English lawyers, leading from Selden to Somers to Burke. Acton's comment on these two traditions was that there was more ground for civil war between these two branches of the family than ever there had been between Cromwell and King Charles.

For Acton, the Roundhead tradition was one that maintained the right of every people to choose and therefore to change its own rulers; one in which legitimacy of resistance was tested not by the laws of the land, but by the consent of the people. On the other hand, the tradition sustained by the Whig lawyers made both people *and* King subject to the law, each bound to avenge any breach of the constitution by the other.[75] Acton wanted to separate out as "true" this latter, conservative Whig tradition, one that combined acknowledgment of the divine will over the will of man with absolute exclusion of any arbitrary principle. It was not just Toryism that had been characterized by arbitrary elements. Locke, too, in Acton's view, by deriving civil society from contract, had introduced into political theory as arbitrary a principle as any that put the King above the law; and should therefore not hold a proper place in the real Whig canon.[76]

Acton went on to maintain that Macaulay had been saved from the wrong path by his admiration for Burke. Indeed, men like Macaulay and Sir James Mackintosh—an immense intellectual influence on the Whigs of the early nineteenth century, someone who had traveled the road from his anti-Burkean *Vindiciae* to what amounted to worship of Burke's general outlook—enabled the Whigs to have the best of both worlds. But Macaulay does not really lend himself to the kind of neat categorizing to which Acton (and others since) have subjected him. It was indeed largely the case that in him, as in others, the radical Whig tradition became overlaid by more conservative, Burkean attitudes. Largely, but not entirely. To some degree, radical and conservative elements continued to coexist in his view of politics. This was not merely a matter of Whiggish eclecticism. It was also the result of a position in society never wholly secure, and of a temperament naturally attuned to paradox, iconoclasm, and the unexpected.

In his essay on Milton, however, Macaulay had certainly ranged himself firmly within the radical line of the Whig tradition. How firmly we have seen by way of Brougham's admiration for the

75. Ibid., 152–3.   76. Ibid., 154.

manner in which he had aligned himself with "the good cause." It seems likely, then, that what Macaulay had meant by telling Gurney that he had been both a Tory and a Radical but would never be a Whig, was that looking at the Whigs of his time he could not recognize in them the continuation of the tradition of Milton and Cromwell. Given the state of the Whig Party in the 1820's, he can hardly be blamed for this. What it is important to remember, however, is that with all the overlapping and conflation of Whig and Tory ideas, with all the (justified) talk of Tories being in many ways more liberal than Whigs during this period, with all the social similarities (both parties essentially branches of the titled and moneyed aristocracy) which the *Westminster Review* delighted in pointing out, there were still certain dividing lines that fundamentally separated the two parties. One was certainly that upon which Macaulay took his stand in his essay on Milton: the heritage of Cromwell and the Roundheads. It is precisely because the current politics of the 1820's were so amorphous, so given to overlapping and confusion, that seventeenth-century disputes and parties played such an important role, for Macaulay and others. We sometimes have a tendency to think of history in its relation to politics as a series of checkpoints, in relation to which contemporary problems and issues can be examined and compared. Moreover, Marx has familiarized us with the dictum that a conscious reliving of historical memories and analogies can make farce out of what once was tragedy. However, in a period like the 1820's in England, history could become an enkindling agent, supplying touchstones and confrontations lacking in the contemporary situation. This is what happened here. The other dividing line was that of parliamentary reform. True, as we have seen, some extreme Tories took up this question from particular motives of their own. True, as well, that the Whigs were not united on it. Nevertheless, it was clear that if public opinion was ever to exert sufficient pressure to render parliamentary reform an essential measure sponsored by any party that wished to remain in power, it would be the Whigs rather than the Tories who alone could and would take their stand in its favor. And, inevitably, men like Macaulay would then be ranged on the Whig side.

V

EDINBURGH REVIEWER

IN FEBRUARY 1826 MACAULAY WAS CALLED TO THE BAR. HE JOINED the northern circuit at Lancaster in the course of the following month. It was his father's fond hope that, since his son did not seem destined for the Church, he would gain distinction in the legal profession. He should perhaps have known better. For Tom's oratorical successes at the Union had given him a taste for politics; and though, with the rest of his fellow barristers, he spent his share of time on circuit, he appears to have had great difficulty in obtaining briefs. Hannah More, while lamenting that Tom was not rich enough to be in Parliament—"he would eclipse them all"—thought that "with such a gift of the gab . . . he cannot fail to excel at the Bar."[1] But in spite of Brougham's advice, Macaulay could not bring himself to regard the routine of legal activity as anything but tedious. His thoughts and ambitions were elsewhere. He much preferred sitting in the Strangers' Gallery of the House of Commons, listening to the debates, to cadging briefs. It was clearly his supreme ambition to become a member of that body, not an easy thing to accomplish for a youth without aristocratic family connections or independent means.

He got a taste of active politics in the summer of 1826, when he went to Leicester in order to help William Evans, a cotton manufacturer with abolitionist and pro-Catholic sentiments, contest a seat in the parliamentary election of that year. In the journal kept by

1. Hannah More to Marianne Thornton, December 1825, Huntington MSS.

Macaulay's sister Selina we can still sense the excitement of his second political baptism by fire. (The first had occurred during his student days in Cambridge when, at an election meeting there, he was hit full in the face with a dead cat.) Evans, anticipating a hard contest and the possible necessity of obtaining legal advice about electoral procedures and returns, informed the elder Macaulay in May that he might require his son's professional services. Selina, always the loyal and adoring sister, noted in her journal that she hoped it *would* be a hard contest so that it would give her brother a chance to show his mettle.[2]

Her hopes were fully realized. At the end of the month, Macaulay was called to Leicester, and was soon put to work writing election handbills. Leicester was a good example of the unreformed franchise in action. It was one of those boroughs in which all freemen had the vote. The (Tory) corporation, anticipating the election of 1826, enrolled eight hundred honorary freemen between 1822 and 1824. For the actual polling, which lasted two weeks, both sides seem to have brought in electors from as far away as France. All this doubtless intensified the violence and tumult usual on these occasions. The Exchange was nearly sacked; yeomanry and militia had to be called in to disperse the mob; and 128 rioters ended up in jail.[3] At one point, Macaulay was determined to rush out to confront the mob— did he have Brougham's letter of advice in mind?—and was only prevented from doing so by being told that it would be exceedingly unprofessional to proceed in this manner.[4] Both Whigs contesting seats, Evans and Denman, emerged at the bottom of the poll; and legal protests for the Whig side proved of no avail. But Macaulay's uncle, Thomas Babington, who, though habitually a Tory, had proposed Evans's candidacy (Zachary, too, had spoken on his behalf in London, which shows the extent to which the Whigs' capture of the anti-slavery issue under Brougham's aegis was turning Tory Evangelicals away from their traditional party affiliation) told Selina that Tom had done very well. When the lawyers on the other side had spoken in a rude and disrespectful manner, her brother had forestalled unpleasantness by behaving with both spirit and good humor.[5]

---

2. Selina Macaulay, Journal, May 12, 1826, Huntington MSS.

3. R. W. Greaves, "Roman Catholic Relief and the Leicester Election of 1826," *Transactions of the Royal Historical Society*, 4th series XXII (1940), 199–223; W. Biggs to Sir George Otto Trevelyan, April 14, 1885, Macaulay Manuscripts in the Pierpont Morgan Library, New York (henceforth referred to as Morgan MSS).

4. Selina Macaulay, Journal, June 14, 1826, Huntington MSS.

5. Ibid., June 15, 1826.

After it was all over, Evans expressed his thanks to Macaulay for the many pleasant hours and the valuable professional services he owed him; while the latter, in turn, appreciated Evans's frankness in pointing out to him his deficiencies as a public speaker—an unexpectedly humble note.[6]

Some months later, in another venture on behalf of the cause of Catholic emancipation, Macaulay and some of his university friends now resident in London chartered a stagecoach, filled it with Cambridge M.A.'s, and arrived in Cambridge just in time to be able to reverse a university Senate petition against the Catholic claims.[7] Macaulay may have had this expedition in mind when he lampooned the opponents of the Catholic claims in a rollicking election ballad entitled "The Country Clergyman's Trip to Cambridge," which related the journey of a coachload of High Tory clerics on their way to cast "Protestant" votes in the election (1827) for the Cambridge University parliamentary seat. The coach, "a casket of learning and brotherly love," included such staunch divines as

> Dr. Nimrod, whose orthodox toes
> Are seldom withdrawn from the stirrup;
> Dr. Humdrum, whose eloquence flows,
> Like droppings of sweet poppy syrup;
> Dr. Rosygill puffing and fanning,
> And wiping away perspiration;
> Dr. Humbug, who proved Mr. Canning
> The beast in St. John's Revelation.[8]

Macaulay was becoming famous. That acute observer, Henry Crabb Robinson, encountered him at a dinner party in the autumn of 1826, and confided to his journal that here was one of the most promising of the rising generation he had seen for a long time. He had, so Robinson remarked, a good face—"not the delicate and expressive features of a man of sensibility and genius, but the strong lines and well-knit limbs of a man sturdy both of body and mind." His opinions were liberal, and yet he was by no means a "vulgar radical."[9] Macaulay no longer had the forum of the Cambridge Union, where he could express, mold, and defend his opinions. But

6. William Evans to Zachary Macaulay, June 28, 1826, Selina Macaulay, Journal, June 20, 1826, Huntington MSS.

7. Trevelyan, Life and Letters, 106.

8. T.B.M., Works, XII, 487.   9. Morley, ed., Henry Crabb Robinson, I, 341.

he had a new forum, a debating society in London founded by John Stuart Mill, which included not only some of his old Cambridge friends (such as Charles Austin, Praed, and the Villiers brothers), but also other young men of promise and influence, of varying shades of opinion. Fortnightly debates were held during the winter months at Freemasons' Tavern in Chancery Lane. Subjects such as the influence of the aristocracy (good or bad?) were debated. While the Radicals and the Whigs were well represented, there seemed to be some difficulty in finding spokesmen for the Tory point of view.[10] Macaulay's effectiveness in these debates was enhanced by his having studied political economy for a year in London with his cousin George Babington, a future doctor.

What else was Macaulay doing during these years, the period of the late 1820's? Until 1829 he lived at home in Great Ormond Street, a constant source of pleasure and entertainment to his family—and more especially to his sisters. We have glimpses of him arguing with his maternal aunt Virtue at breakfast about whether it was proper to persecute people for their religious views (his sister Selina, who chronicled this quarrel in her journal, noted that there was no love lost between aunt and nephew, and that arguments between them were apt to become rude and violent) ;[11] dining out in society at Lady Davy's, where he met the Countess of Cork, who invited him to a "rout" where Canning was expected and who angered him by her story that she broke off her acquaintance with Hannah More when the latter "turned good"; and inspecting in the company of his sister Selina the brand-new building in Gower Street of University College, London—completed so quickly that it reminded the girl of Aladdin's enchanted palace. (It was a particular source of pride to her that her brother Charles's was the first student voice to be heard in the new university.[12])

Macaulay's relationship with Brougham remained on the whole cordial and close during these years; though by the summer of 1828— a foretaste of things to come—he had concluded what most of Brougham's contemporaries felt, that when one came to know him, he turned out to be superficial and uncertain.[13] But several times they went on circuit together in the North, and it was Brougham who in 1827 recommended Macaulay to Lord Lyndhurst, the Tory

10. Michael St. John Packe, *The Life of John Stuart Mill* (London, 1954), 69–72; *Autobiography of John Stuart Mill* (New York, 1924), 88–90.

11. Selina Macaulay, Journal, October 7, 1826, Huntington MSS.

12. Ibid., November 5 and 7, 1828.

13. T.B.M. to his father, July 31, 1828, Trinity Correspondence.

Lord Chancellor, to fill a vacant Commissionership of Bankruptcy—describing him on that occasion as "the greatest genius now coming into the profession," and someone who had written the very best things he had read of late years.[14] It was a tribute both to Brougham's power and to Lyndhurst's broadmindedness that Macaulay got the office in January of 1828. Its emoluments came to about £250 a year, which, with his Trinity fellowship (£210 a year) and the money he received for his *Edinburgh Review* articles (around £200 a year), gave him a moderate income.[15]

This was more than a boon for Macaulay's love of independence—it was an economic necessity. For Zachary, who at one point, according to his own estimate, had been worth £100,000, had handed over control of his firm in 1823 to his nephew Thomas Babington, who, along with the elder Macaulay's cousin Kenneth, proceeded to ruin the company by excessive spending. By 1827 Zachary's fortune was consumed.[16] Early in 1828, Selina Macaulay told her daughters that she and they might have to leave London and settle somewhere in the provinces where they would be able to live more cheaply.[17] This did not, in fact, happen. Yet family circumstances clearly became straitened. Tom did his best to cheer up his father, assuring him in the late winter of 1829, for instance, that "come what may, the conveniences of life, independence, our personal respectability, and the exercise of the intellect and the affections, we are almost certain of retaining: and everything else is a mere superfluity." Above all, he advised him to keep up his health and spirits.[18] Zachary, however, was unable to follow this counsel. By the autumn of the same year he was beginning to suffer from increasing debility of mind and body; and though a gradual recovery set in, it was never quite complete.[19]

The political situation during these years—1825 to 1830—was characterized by the general dominance of a liberal trend. Peel had written to Croker in 1820:

14. Knutsford, *Zachary Macaulay*, 442. There were seventy commissioners, known to some as the Chancellor's Septuagint. Lyndhurst did not know T.B.M., and made the appointment solely on Brougham's recommendation. Lyndhurst to Milman, November 29, 1861, Trinity MSS.

15. For two of his three articles against the Utilitarians (1829) he received 80 guineas. See Paul M. Zall, "Selina Macaulay's Diary," *Bulletin of the New York Public Library*, LXVI (1962), 440–3.

16. Fyfe, *Sierra Leone*, 166–7.

17. Selina Macaulay, Journal, February 1, 1828, Huntington MSS.

18. T.B.M. to his father (from Lancaster), March 14, 1829, Trevelyan, *Life and Letters*, 109.

19. Selina Macaulay, Journal, October 3, 1829, Huntington MSS.

Do not you think that the tone of England—of that great compound of folly, weakness, prejudice, wrong feeling, right feeling, obstinacy, and newspaper paragraphs, which is called public opinion—is more liberal—to use an odious but intelligible phrase—than the policy of the Government? Do not you think that there is a feeling, becoming daily more general and more confirmed—that is, independent of the pressure of taxation, or any immediate cause—in favour of some undefined change in the mode of governing the country?[20]

He was a good prophet.

The real opposition to progressive measures of any kind continued to sit on the government front benches, in the shape of the die-hard Tories. Otherwise, all factions and groups were concerned, in one way or the other, with "improvement." The outstanding statesman during these years was George Canning, who had shown his liberal tendencies in his foreign policy, and who was personally convinced of the need for emancipating the Irish Catholics though, for tactical reasons, perpetually reluctant to pledge the government to this step. After a stroke suffered by Lord Liverpool put an end to the latter's long-lived government in February 1827, Canning succeeded him. And several Whigs, Lord Lansdowne in the lead, joined him in a coalition cabinet. It had long been Brougham's aim to bring about such a coalition. One of its salutary effects, to his mind, was a probable split in the Tory Party. In the event, the ultra-Tories did resign from the Canning cabinet. Into the period of the Canning ministry falls the anecdote of Macaulay's seeing Brougham (who had been made a King's Counsel in May 1827) in his new silk gown, and wearing an unpowdered wig known as a "Canning," probably (so Tom, who dearly loved a pun, suggested to his sister) because its namesake was a new Whig.[21] Indeed, for many Whigs it was difficult not to recognize Canning as one of their own at this point. No one knows what would have happened to the state of parties in England at this time if the coalition ministry had lasted. But Canning died suddenly, in August 1827. Tory ministries succeeded, first that of the ineffectual "Goody" Goderich, then that of the far from ineffectual Duke of Wellington. And for a while there seemed to be truth in Brougham's prophecy, made in October, that distinctions such as Loyalist and Jacobin, Whig and Tory, Court and Country, would

20. Peel to Croker, March 23, 1820, Louis J. Jennings, ed., *The Correspondence and Diaries of the Late Right Honourable John Wilson Croker* (2 vols., New York, 1884), I, 155-6.

21. Selina Macaulay, Journal, June 8, 1827, Huntington MSS.

soon be replaced by the two great divisions of "Liberal" and "Illiberal," which would "divide, but we may be sure most unequally, the suffrages of the Nation."[22] For the Iron Duke proved himself sufficiently malleable to preside first over the repeal of the Test and Corporation Acts (1828) and then, during the year following, over Catholic emancipation. The latter measure, especially, appeared to presage a new political era. John Stuart Mill wrote to Gustave d'Eichthal that it "has given a shake to men's minds which has loosened all old prejudices, and will render them far more accessible to new ideas and to rational innovations on all other parts of our institutions."[23]

It is true that the reversal of long and earnestly held Tory attitudes on these subjects represented by such steps set the stage for a certain amount of discomfiture during the Reform Bill debates a few years later. (Macaulay was to remind Peel during one of those debates that he was present in the House in 1827 when Peel said he would *oppose* the repeal of the Test and Corporation Acts, as well as parliamentary reform.) But for the moment the Duke's "About, turn!" order had the result of disarming the Whigs for whom, after all, Catholic emancipation had for many years been just about the sole issue upon which they could all agree. Indeed, at this point it was the ultra-Tories who were muttering about the need for parliamentary reform, so that the people of England should not be deprived of expressing their real views. These, it was (probably correctly) assumed, were anti-Catholic. But because they were represented in Parliament not by their chosen spokesmen, but by mere mouthpieces from rotten and pocket boroughs, doing their patrons' (and the government's) bidding, "un-English" measures such as emancipation could be foisted upon them.

One cannot, in truth, speak in this period of a "grass-roots" liberalism held down by a reactionary upper class. In fact, the ordinary Englishman was as likely to be anti-Catholic as the worst ultra. It was the liberal section of the aristocracy, along with the liberally inclined middle class, which helped to bring the pressure that forced Wellington to execute his volte-face. To say that "popular" and "liberal" were hardly synonymous during these years is not to imply the complete absence of democratic radicalism. This was the period when Benthamite ideas were discussed and disseminated by

22. [Henry Brougham], "State of Parties," *Edinburgh Review*, XLVI (1827), 431.
23. Mill to d'Eichthal, March 11, 1829, Francis E. Mineka, ed., *The Earlier Letters of John Stuart Mill, 1812–1848* (2 vols., Toronto, 1963), I, 28.

the Utilitarians, who had founded their own periodical, the *West-minster Review,* in 1824 to serve as a counterweight not only to the Tory *Quarterly* but to the Whig *Edinburgh* as well. In the very first number of the *Westminster,* James Mill, in a brilliant piece of polemical writing (for which the research was done by his son John Stuart), accused the *Edinburgh* reviewers of being at bottom just as much supporters of the existing order, represented by the aristocracy, as were their ostensible rivals, the critics of the *Quarterly.* The evidence for this, devastatingly presented by the Mills, was constant seesawing on the part of the *Edinburgh* on all important political issues. A seemingly radical view in one number would be contradicted by a conservative view of the same question in the very next number, and so on.

To lump together, as the Mills did, the chief organs of the Tories and the Whigs as written respectively by aristocratic retainers and time-servers—though certainly a brilliant pre-Marxist exercise in the class analysis of society—was in fact to do a major injustice to the long battle against reaction and privilege waged by the *Edinburgh* from the moment of its founding, on issues ranging from Catholic emancipation to the abolition of spring-guns and flogging in the army, from law court reform to a qualified defense of the French Revolution, put forward at a time when it was still widely held, certainly by the *Quarterly,* to have been the work of the archfiend. It would have been more accurate to have pointed out that there was indeed an alliance of sorts between the *Quarterly* and the *Edinburgh.* But its objective was not so much to preserve the English aristocracy as to save English society as a whole from revolution and democracy. In that sense a class analysis of, say, the Reform Act of 1832 begins to have meaning. The Canning coalition of 1827 seemed to confirm the Radical view that there was little or no difference between the major parties and their respective chief supporters. But for someone like Brougham (an *Edinburgh* veteran, and by no means the least anti-aristocratic), support of that coalition was first of all a means to power; and power meant an opportunity to try to change the Whig Party from an aristocratic coterie to a more broadly based middle-class party.

In this endeavor Macaulay was to play a significant part. Outwardly the story of his career during the five years after the appearance of the Milton essay may be summed up in terms of his progress from briefless lawyer to Commissioner of Bankruptcy and Member of Parliament, ready to assume his role in the most important debates of that generation. But the real story lies elsewhere, in the essays that followed that on Milton. For it was those essays that gained him both Brougham's patronage and his own parliamentary seat. They were, let it be recalled, occasional pieces, written quickly and not intended by their author to live for more than a brief period. This should be kept in mind by all who read them. They should not be judged as pieces composed for posterity; and Macaulay was certainly the last person who wanted to have them so judged. He long resisted republication of his essays in book form. It was only in 1842, after American publishers had put out several editions of the essays uncorrected and just as they had appeared in the *Edinburgh Review,* that he consented to an English edition, which appeared the following year and became one of the greatest best-sellers of the century.

Recently, however, the essays have had an undeservedly bad press. Again and again, they have been called superficially brilliant but essentially shallow. Some of the guiding ideas of the early essays have come under the interdict of those suspicious of the "Whig interpretation of history," who find in them notions of progress, optimism, and materialism repugnant to a less sanguine age.[24] There will be no attempt here to exonerate them from those charges, nor, on the other hand, to present yet another bill of particulars chronicling their youthful extravagances and their errors. They *are* uneven productions, marred by all sorts of faults. There seems little point, nowadays, in reading them in the manner of the teacher reading his students' examinations, awarding good and bad marks. The essential question, is, rather: Are they still worth reading today? If not, there is no sense in chalking up errors and issuing belated reprimands. If, on the other hand, the answer to this question be affirmative, then the next step is to inquire what profit the present-day reader can derive from their perusal, apart from the sheer pleasure of being a spectator at a literary fireworks display. That pleasure should not be taken lightly. For, whatever Macaulay's faults in this regard—exaggeration, repetition, forced paradoxes and antitheses, excessive amounts of highly colored writing—he remains always unmistakably himself, ever capable (even in the most unpromising territory) of surprising, delighting, and instructing his readers by the felicity of a phrase or the shrewdness of an observation.

The essays under discussion in this chapter, with the possible exception of the "Machiavelli," are not Macaulay's famous show-

24. See, e.g., Pieter Geyl, "Macaulay in His Essays," *Debates with Historians* (New York, 1958), 30–47.

pieces—the "Clive," the "Hastings," the "Chatham." They deal with miscellaneous subjects, ranging from a strictly political and opportunistic plea for support of the coalition ministry of 1827 to an essay on the social and industrial capacities of Negroes, from a cudgeling of the minor poet Robert Montgomery to an extended discussion, in the essay on Hallam's *History,* of modern English constitutional history. One must be prepared, certainly, to recognize their shortcomings. On the other hand, one must also admire the vigor of thought and the intellectual penetration which enabled Macaulay in his twenties to achieve in these fugitive pieces insight and illumination still of interest to us today.

Two leading ideas are to be found in these early essays. The first is that in order to grasp the realities of political power and of men's behavior in society, one must not accept the doctrines, badges, symbols, and phrases of publicists and politicians at their face value, but must see them within the context of the general moral atmosphere of their particular time. The second is that this all-important "spirit," or moral atmosphere, is to a great extent produced by "circumstances." These circumstances are closely linked to the social and political institutions of given periods in history; and those periods in turn are seen as parts of particular stages in the development of Western society.

Where did Macaulay derive these guiding ideas? The answer must include at least two sources: the Scottish historical school, including Hume, with its sociological emphasis, its assumption that the progress of societies from rudeness to refinement was shaped as much by circumstances as by individuals; and those aspects of Benthamite influence to which he responded positively—distrust of phrasemaking and clichés, refusal to be taken in by what people said and wrote without asking why they did so. The disposition of Macaulay's mind and personality provided a fertile soil for these particular influences to fall on. From his earliest youth, indeed, from his childhood, Macaulay had been engaged in a perpetual battle against shams, against being taken in by mere names and appearances. It is only necessary to recall the attitude expressed in letters to his father about the slavish adoration of the classics as against the study of modern, particularly English literature. That attitude was not unrelated to his Evangelical upbringing. "After the straitest sect of our religion," he once remarked, "I was bred a Pharisee." But, as we have seen, that breeding did not "take"—at least, not in the manner intended.

The Evangelical creed, once the fine frenzy of the initial impulse had passed, was peculiarly liable to a decline from heartfelt piety and genuine devotion to self-righteousness and hypocrisy. The declension was more characteristic of the second than of the first generation of Evangelicals. But the danger was there from the beginning. The temptation to testify too readily to one's own conversion—who, after all, could gainsay the testimony of personal experience?—the temptation to make one's own pious observances the occasion for censoriousness about others less assiduous, these must have been ever present, even within the Clapham Sect. And young Tom Macaulay, growing up in the midst of Evangelicals, sent to school with their sons, taught by Evangelical clergymen, must have early found opportunities to exercise his considerable intelligence in the exposure of cant. His histrionic talents helped here. For, easily capable of acting any part himself, he was all the better able to spot imposture and affectation in others. All this proved helpful, both in debate and in the writing of history, which, after all, is to a great extent a process of penetrating disguises and uncovering what is hidden. There was danger here, too, of course. For in rejecting the accepted and the traditional, the great temptation was to reverse them, to adopt habitually a posture of contrariness. This may be one reason why Macaulay's essays are marked by an excessive use of paradox. Yet, on the positive side, his almost instinctive ability to get to the root of the matter, to probe for the essential under the superficial, the bone beneath the skin, served him well as a historian.

Let us consider some examples. There is, first of all, the article on Machiavelli, written perhaps in tribute to a favorite of Macaulay's idol Bacon, certainly in tribute (eloquently expressed at the end of the essay) to the Italian states then fighting for freedom from Austrian domination. What, Macaulay asked, was the explanation for the various contradictions that were to be found in the thought of Machiavelli? Was the moral opprobrium that had long descended upon him and his works justified? To obtain an answer to these questions, Macaulay turned in the first place to the particular political circumstances of medieval Italy, where the predominance of strong municipal institutions and the relative insignificance of the feudal nobility helped to support liberty, and with it commerce, empire, science, and taste. Having contrasted the opulent and enlightened states of Italy in the Late Middle Ages with the less advanced, "ruder" countries of the North, Macaulay returned to the theme of the rule of the towns which had contributed not only to the early greatness but also to the early decline of the Italian states. The key here was the army. For while hunters and shepherds, and later on even peasants, had the time to devote themselves to military service for at least a part of each year, this was not possible for men engaged in commerce or manufactures, who had little time for war. In Renaissance Italy, the solution to this problem lay in the institution of mercenaries. But built into this solution was an ultimately fatal devaluation of valor, courage, and self-sacrifice—all moral qualities tied to a *citizen* army—and a corresponding emphasis on cunning, craft, and cleverness.

In similar fashion Macaulay explained, in his essay on Hallam's *Constitutional History,* why the statesmen of the reign of Charles II lacked steadiness of principle, and even "that vulgar fidelity to party which, in our time, it is esteemed infamous to violate."[25] The reason was that these men developed quick and active talents, rather than firm and masculine virtues, because they had been trained during a period of civil war and revolution. They were, in Macaulay's words, "men of combinations," and thus for them (as for Talleyrand in a later revolutionary period) apostasy was not so heinous a crime as it was considered by men whose experience lay in stable circumstances.[26]

Thus, in this essay on Machiavelli, Macaulay employed the contrast—derived in all probability from his reading in the Scottish school—between the values and achievements of "rude" and of "polished" societies, a contrast we have already encountered in the essay on Milton, where it was used as a yardstick for matters literary and aesthetic. Milton, it may be recalled, deserved special praise for having transcended the spirit of his particular time—not favorable to the epic—by writing an epic masterpiece. In his essay on Dryden (1827) Macaulay, employing the same approach, explained why Dryden was more of a critical than an imaginative poet. The rise of civilization, the gradual extinction of primitive and barbaric elements, meant more scope for the critical intellect, less for the poetic imagination.

In the essay on Machiavelli, however, the contrast between "rude" and "polished" served to illuminate two distinct sets of moral qual-

25. T.B.M., "Hallam's Constitutional History" (1828), *Works,* VII, 297. This is doubtless a reference to the Canning coalition. See [T.B.M.], "The Present Administration," *Edinburgh Review,* XLVI (1827), 245–67.

26. The distinction between "lions" and "foxes" has been employed in this century by Vilfredo Pareto as part of his sociological system. Pareto used the term "combinations" to characterize the "foxes." Arthur Livingston, ed., Vilfredo Pareto, *The Mind and Society* (4 vols., New York, 1935), IV, 1515–16.

ities admired in different parts of fifteenth-century Europe. In northern Europe, still more valorous and "ruder" than the South, the qualities generally despised were timidity, fraud, and hypocrisy. In Italy, on the other hand, these same qualities, when used inventively, tended to evoke not so much contempt as admiration. It must be remembered, by the way, that Macaulay wrote his essay over a generation before the appearance of Jakob Burckhardt's classic analysis of the Italian Renaissance spirit. While it would be plainly absurd to credit the *aperçus* in the article on Machiavelli with a major anticipation of Burckhardt, it should be said that in at least one important respect he went beyond the Swiss historian. While Burckhardt succeeded unforgettably in limning the moral qualities of the Italians during the Renaissance, painting a kaleidoscopic picture, Macaulay tried to go more deeply into what may have caused the prevalence of those often contradictory traits which Burckhardt was to be satisfied in depicting.

Macaulay's originality here went beyond his general thesis. He was always ready to supply concrete examples, taken either from history, from fiction, or from contemporary analogies. His sister Margaret thought that the remarkable clearness of her brother's style derived in some measure from his habit of conversing with very young people (i.e., his brothers and sisters) to whom he had a great deal to explain and impart.[27] Citing examples, to make the unfamiliar familiar, was part of this process. The particular example used in the Machiavelli essay to illustrate the different value systems of North and South has been called with respectful humor, by no less an authority than the sociologist Paul Lazarsfeld, the first projective test in history, that is, the first example of a method of testing public opinion whereby reactions to certain carefully chosen questions or situations elicit sentiments indicative of the general moral and emotional attitudes of different groups confronted with these questions and situations.

What Macaulay did, in order to clarify his point that falsehood and dissimulation were not always (as in nineteenth-century England) regarded with disapprobation, was to imagine the respective reactions to the story of Shakespeare's *Othello* on the part of "Northern" and Italian readers. For northern readers or audiences, Iago would have been the villain, detested for his wicked plots against the Moor. On the other hand, for an Italian audience there would have been something to admire in Iago's wit, clearness of judgment, and skill in dissimulation. Lazarsfeld writes:

27. Trevelyan, *Life and Letters*, 131.

It is clear what Macaulay is striving for. He wishes someone had conducted attitude studies in Florence and in London of the fifteenth century. Let us suppose that a polling agency existed at the time, and was hired by Macaulay to test his hypothesis. In a somewhat facetious way, we can imagine how they might have proceeded. The Othello story could have been written up in one or two paragraphs, without giving either Othello or Iago any advantage. Pretests could have been conducted to make sure that the wording was quite unbiased. (Perhaps they might have concealed the fact that Othello was a Negro because that might bias some respondents.) The crucial question would have been: How many Florentines and Londoners, respectively, approve of Iago, how many of Othello, and how many say "don't know"? Nothing less, but hardly much more, would have been needed to provide empirical evidence for Macaulay's brilliant conjecture.[28]

"Brilliant conjecture" is a good phrase for this and other, similar flashes of historical speculation in these early essays. For Macaulay might, of course, be quite wrong. Some fifteenth-century Englishmen would surely have been able to "set the murd'rous Machiavel to school." But even when he is wrong, he is both interesting and stimulating in the questions he raises and the fresh way in which he examines old historical issues.

Macaulay assumed that ideas and sentiments were shaped by the society in which they had their being. Machiavelli exalted liberty at the same time that he advised dissimulation. This was no mystifying paradox. It ought to be seen as a more forcible expression on the part of a great thinker of the generally received moral maxims of his time. One must not judge the past in terms of one's own contemporary moral standards. "He alone reads history aright, who, observing how powerfully circumstances influence the feelings and opinions of men, how often vices pass into virtues and paradoxes into axioms, learns to distinguish what is accidental and transitory in human nature from what is essential and immutable."[29] It should be added that Macaulay did not go all the way in this surprisingly modern moral relativism. Having concluded that *The Prince* belonged to the age rather than the man; having found that Machiavelli's advice to place means above ends could be explained in terms of his situation, Zachary's son still found it necessary to make the comment that the book's "immorality" was a great blemish. In similar fashion, having in the essay on Hallam's *History* put Charles II's and Alger-

28. Paul Lazarsfeld, "The Historian and the Pollster," Mirra Komarovsky, ed., *Common Frontiers of the Social Sciences* (Glencoe, Ill., 1957) , 244.
29. T.B.M., "Machiavelli" (1827) , *Works*, VII, 84–5.

non Sidney's dealings with the French into the context of the party
strife of the period (which tended to diminish patriotism), he felt
bound to remark that the pecuniary transactions in question must
still be regarded as "offensive."[30]

Two little-known reviews of Macaulay's, not published in his
collected *Essays* but undoubtedly his, offer further evidence for the
sharpness of sociological insight to be found in his writings of this
period. One concerns the "Social and Industrial Capacities of Negroes."[31]

A certain Major Thomas Moody, a commissioner appointed by the
Colonial Office to report on the condition of some liberated African
slaves who had been settled at Tortola, had stated in his report that
there existed an instinctive and insuperable aversion between the
white and black races, which would and could never be removed. As
a "proof" of this, Moody had cited the fact that even in those American states where slavery had been abolished, Negroes were still
regarded with disgust and contempt. In dealing with this argument,
Macaulay first adduced the Baconian rule that "when . . . phenomena can be explained by circumstances which, on grounds distinct from those phenomena, we know to exist, we must not resort to
hypothetical solutions."[32] Then he proceeded to demolish Moody,
perhaps not too difficult a task. But the process of demolition is still
well worth watching. Let Moody prove, Macaulay wrote, that there
was a "natural" aversion between black and white in a society in
which personal bondage never existed! The relevant arguments
should not be based on "instinct," but on society and economics. The
sort of question to be asked, in other words, was why, in England, a
lady would not marry a tinker. The *real* cause for the reluctance on
the part of whites to marry Negroes was to be sought not in physical,
but in political and moral circumstances. Change these, Macaulay
wrote, and the rest would take care of themselves.

As for the major's argument that slavery was needed to make men
work in torrid zones, this, too, became sterile when brought up
against the economic facts of life. Because the free African preferred
six shillings to sixpence, "we are told that he has a natural and
invincible aversion to agriculture. Because he prefers wealth to

30. T.B.M., "Hallam" (1828), ibid., 309.
31. *Edinburgh Review*, XLV (1827), 383–423. This essay, with an introductory note
by John Clive and Anthony Lester, has recently been reprinted in *Race*, XIII (1971–2),
133–64.
32. T.B.M., "Negroes," *Edinburgh Review* (1827), 388–9.

poverty, we are to conclude that he prefers repose to wealth."[33] It was all a question of economics, not of "physical causes." Plantation work exerted no stimulus on a sluggish mind. *That* was why skilled labor fetched such a high price in the West Indies—and why it was preferred by the Negroes. As for the Negroes' alleged reluctance to work more than the minimum hours necessary to earn their sustenance, this too, had economic and not physiological causes. After all, English laborers were known to keep "Saint Monday" as well as Sunday, if the rest of the week's wages sufficed for their upkeep. Coercion was not the answer to this problem, else the spinners of Manchester and the grinders of Sheffield ought to be coerced, too. (It did not occur to Macaulay that perhaps they were!) Macaulay concluded the essay by assuring the major that "a little knowledge of history is now and then very useful to a person who undertakes to speculate on politics."[34] By using his historical knowledge, by treating the problem of Negro "inferiority" not in the terms set by prejudice and ignorance, but in terms of man's moral, political, and economic behavior in various places and during various periods in the past, Macaulay asserted what twentieth-century anthropologists have confirmed, that there was nothing inherently inferior in the Negro race.[35]

Another early essay of Macaulay's appears equally modern and to the point today, this one published in 1826, on "The London University." It was written in praise of University College, London, then founded but not yet built; and what it had to say about the deleterious effects of collegiate life in Oxford and Cambridge in engendering a distaste for domestic life in the students has already been adverted to in the chapter dealing with Macaulay's undergraduate years at Cambridge.[36] University College was the first secular institution of higher learning in England, and as such was considered an evil thing by Tories, by the Church, and by the greater part of the aristocracy. Here again, Macaulay applied the abrasive power of his common sense to the arguments of his opponents. Several themes on which he liked to discourse may be found running through the article. There was, first of all, the issue of a possible threat to society represented by the extension of education to the lower classes. Macaulay was quite clear as to where he stood on this subject. Against the enemies

33. Ibid., 399.   34. Ibid., 404–5, 419.

35. See the use made of this essay by Marie Jahoda, *Race Relations and Mental Health* (Paris, 1960), 16–17.

36. See above, p. 40.

of education, who maintained that it rendered the poor arrogant and discontented, and that the ignorance of the people was the best security for their virtue and repose, he argued forcibly that arrogance was not an absolute moral quality, but, rather, the result of the particular situation in which one man found himself in relation to another. If the entire society were rising in intelligence together, no such feelings would exist.[37]

The important thing was that those who were going forward should feel that they were doing so as part of a general movement that embraced all classes. Since it was plainly impossible to unteach the poor, it was essential to teach those who could, by comparison, be called the rich, that is, the middle class. For that was a class which, "while it is too numerous to be corrupted by government is too intelligent to be duped by demagogues, and . . . though naturally hostile to oppression and profusion, is not likely to carry its zeal for reform to lengths inconsistent with the security of property and the maintenance of social order."[38] Thus Macaulay here plays a clever variation on the theme of education as a counter-revolutionary force. His message is not so much Educate the poor, as You can't stop the education of the poor, whatever you do. So you'd better see to it that those above them in the social scale are well educated. Not for the last time, Macaulay finds a way of linking the general progress of society with social stability.

Certainly, Macaulay was himself ready to do his own share of teaching the poor. In 1828 he negotiated with the Society for the Diffusion of Useful Knowledge, dedicated—under the principal leadership of Brougham—to "the imparting of useful information to all classes of the community," about writing a history of the Stuarts for the Society. He proposed to begin with an introductory view of the state in which society and opinions had been left at the death of Elizabeth. Into the body of the history, wherever he was able to do so with perfect security as to truth, he intended to introduce characteristic anecdotes and speeches, rendering, for instance, King James's broad Scots verbatim.[39] Even though this particular book— one might well see in it the germ of the *History of England*—was not written, Macaulay retained as one of his chief aims in his historical writing that of making himself clearly understood to the ordinary reader without formal education.

37. Sociologists today talk of "relative deprivation." T.B.M. may be said to have been talking here of "relative accumulation."

38. T.B.M., "The London University," Clive and Pinney, eds., *Macaulay*, 6–7.

39. Thomas Flower Ellis to Brougham, September 14, 1828, Brougham MSS, University College, London.

What of the argument, put forward by the enemies of University College (and in this group there were Dissenters as well as Anglicans), that it would be a university without religion? Macaulay's reply to them was that since the new university (unlike the Oxford and Cambridge colleges) was to be nonresident, religion could well be taken care of in the home. Among the readers not satisfied with that reply was John Henry Newman, who may or may not have known that Macaulay was the author of the essay on London University. In the fifth of his *Discourses on the Scope and Nature of University Education,* Newman adverted to the essay as a prime example of that school of thought which desired a divorce between religious and secular knowledge. "Writing as he does," he remarked about the author of the essay, "with liveliness and wit, as well as a profession of serious argument, this Reviewer can scarcely be quoted with due regard to the gravity which befits a discussion such as the present." In fact, he felt compelled to ask his audience at the Catholic University of Ireland to pardon him, "if, in my desire to do justice to him and his cause in his own words, I suffer him to interrupt the equable flow of our discussion with unseasonable mirth."[40]

He then proceeded to express his fundamental disagreement with two of Macaulay's illustrations. In reply to the shocked reaction of those who were appalled by the prospect of a university without religion, Macaulay had cited the example of a student of surgery who also took courses in political economy and in modern languages. As far as religious observances were concerned, this same student did what he or his family thought most advisable. What was wrong with that? Newman had an answer. Whatever might be said of political economy, neither setting fractures nor learning languages could properly be considered a branch of philosophy. "It is not more wonderful that such trials of skill or of memory can safely dispense with Theology for their perfection, than that it is unnecessary for the practice of gunnery or the art of calligraphy."[41]

Macaulay's other illustration had conjured up a vision of daughters who were educated at home, by different teachers: "The music master, a good Protestant, comes at twelve; the dancing master, a French philosopher, at two; the Italian master, a believer in the blood of St. Januarius, at three." The parents are in charge of their daughters' religious instruction. Why was such a situation so differ-

40. John Henry Newman, "Discourses on the Scope and Nature of University Education," Geoffrey Tillotson, ed., *Newman, Prose and Poetry* (Cambridge, Mass., 1965), 440.
41. Ibid., 440–1.

ent from that of a student at the new university? Newman replied to this question with one of his own: "Looking simply at his argument, I ask, is it not puerile to imply that music, or dancing, or lessons in Italian, have any thing to do with philosophy?" Then he went on:

It is plain, that such writers [as the author of the essay] do not rise to the very idea of a University. They consider it a sort of bazaar, or pantechnicon, in which wares of all kinds are heaped together for sale in stalls independent of each other; and that, to save the purchasers the trouble of running about from shop to shop; or an hotel or lodging house, where all professions and classes are at liberty to congregate, varying, however, according to the season, each of them strange to each, and about its own work or pleasure; whereas, if we would rightly deem of it, a University is the home, it is the mansion-house, of the goodly family of the Sciences, sisters all, and sisterly in their mutual dispositions.[42]

Making due allowance for the heightening of their respective positions produced by these two masters of English rhetoric, it is still worth underlining the genuine conflict between two very different philosophies of education that exists here. For Newman, secular learning and theology, both part of a coherent system of universal knowledge to be taught at universities, were inseparable. Else disorder and ruin would ensue. For Macaulay, education was an essentially nonreligious activity; and, as far as he was concerned, the university needed to teach no universal system, but only what its students freely chose to learn. The issue, thus dramatically joined between Newman and Macaulay, is still very much with us.

If, indeed, there were to be religious instruction at University College, Macaulay had argued, would not disputes invariably ensue? Concrete images as well as a sort of Swiftean humor abound in Macaulay's depiction of existing differences within the Church of England: "Whether it is proper to take in a Sunday newspaper, to shoot a partridge, to course a hare, to subscribe to a Bible Society, to dance, to play at whist, to read Tom Jones, to see Othello—all these are questions on which the strongest difference of opinion exists between persons of high eminence in the hierarchy."[43]

One of Macaulay's favorite devices, the use of mimicry and parody, made its appearance in his reply to those critics who fulminated against the shocking temptations of London for students residing there. For their benefit Macaulay conjured up most movingly the

42. Ibid., 441.
43. T.B.M., "The London University," Clive and Pinney, eds., *Macaulay*, 10.

idyllic atmosphere of Oxford and Cambridge, where all the men were philosophers and all the women vestals:

There, simple and bloodless repasts support the body without distressing the mind. There, while the sluggish world is still sleeping, the ingenuous youth hasten to pour forth their fervent orisons in the chapel; and in the evening, elsewhere the season of riot and license, indulge themselves with a solitary walk beneath the venerable avenues, musing on the vanity of sensual pursuits, and the eternity and sublimity of virtue.[44]

In a serious vein once again, Macaulay went on to point out that London in fact supplied two elements lacking in Oxford and Cambridge, both morally beneficial: the society of older men, and of younger women. The latter, especially, would serve to preserve students "from that brainless and heartless Yahooism, that disdain of the character of women, and that brutal indifference to their misery, which is the worst offence, and the severest punishment of the finished libertine."[45]

What of the pietistic associations, intellectual and historical, to be found in the Oxford and Cambridge colleges, associations which, we know, counted a great deal with the fellow of Trinity who was the author of this article? Here he made short shrift of them. Pictures and statues of Newton and Erasmus, it appeared, did not seem to prevent drunkenness and bad grammar. Having defended the new university, Macaulay registered his complaints against the old foundations—their wealth and privileges, their overemphasis on the classics and mathematics as against modern languages and learning. "We have known the dates of all the petty skirmishes of the Peloponnesian War carefully transcribed and committed to memory by a man who thought that Hyde and Clarendon were two different persons."

The colleges at Oxford and Cambridge, Macaulay wrote, induced industry only in those who expected to receive prizes and fellowships. The rest were idle. And why was this the case? Here again, Macaulay looked at and then discarded the conventional explanation lying closest to hand, that this idleness was due to the indolence and the levity of youth. That was not the point at all. It was, rather, that these young men lacked a *motive* for learning. They attended the ancient universities, not in order to learn but in order to acquire privileges that would stand them in good stead later on.[46] This was the substance under the shadow, the concrete reality underneath the rationalizations and the clichés.

44. Ibid., 11.   45. Ibid., 13.   46. Ibid., 29.

This probing beneath the obvious and the merely verbal is one of the hallmarks of Macaulay's early essays. We get a strong sense in them of the deceptive nature of language when used in different historical contexts, or when employed merely as ritual. Thus, Macaulay began his essay on Hallam's *Constitutional History* by saying that every political school had its doctrines for the initiated, and its visible symbols, forms, and fables for the vulgar. Pitt clubs, for instance, continued to adore restrictions on worship and on trade in spite of Pitt's own (contrary) views about these subjects. "On the other hand, the cause for which Hampden bled on the field and Sidney on the scaffold is enthusiastically toasted by many an honest radical who would be puzzled to explain the difference between Ship Money and the Habeas Corpus Act."[47]

Macaulay returned to this theme again in one of his essays against the Utilitarians (1829), where he examined the changing meaning of words in different historical situations. In the Convention Parliament, for instance, "Original Contract" meant the co-ordinate authority of the three estates. By "tomorrow" the meaning of the phrase might well change to denote annual parliaments and universal suffrage. Similarly, the term "Glorious Constitution" had meant everything in turn: Habeas Corpus, the suspension of Habeas Corpus, the Test Act, the repeal of the Test Act; just as the term "greatest happiness" had meant many different things to many different people.[48]

Words and phrases, then, must be understood in their particular context. Macaulay had championed this view in his essay on History (1828), in which he blamed Plutarch and the school of historians associated with him for attempting to apply concepts of patriotism and liberty, which in Greece had sprung from local and occasional causes, to the citizens of a big empire. There was nothing essentially and eternally good about Greek patriotism, a feeling which in other circumstances could turn states into gangs of robbers, lend peculiar atrocity to war, and generate that worst of all political evils, the tyranny of nations over nations. Plutarch and his school "conceived of liberty as monks conceive of love, as cockneys conceive of the happiness and innocence of rural life, as novel-reading sempstresses conceive of Almack's and Grosvenor Square, accomplished marquesses and handsome Colonels of the Guards."[49]

47. T.B.M., "Hallam," *Works*, VII, 225.
48. T.B.M., "Westminster Reviewer's Defence of Mill" (1829), *Works*, VII, 405–6.
49. T.B.M., "History" (1828), *Works*, VII, 187.

The abuse of language perpetrated by these historians had had ill effects not in England (where there existed indigenous traditions of liberty and patriotism) but on the French revolutionaries. Without this school of historians, Macaulay maintained, "the government of a great and polished nation would not have rendered itself ridiculous by attempting to revive the usages of a world which had . . . never existed except in the description of a fantastic school of writers." Many atrocities committed during the course of the Revolution sprang from such misapplication of words.[50]

Macaulay, then, tried to separate the realities of institutional life and historical change from the verbal carapaces abusers of language often built around them. "We hear of essentially Protestant governments and essentially Christian governments," he wrote in his marvelously terse and powerful essay on the "Civil Disabilities of the Jews" (1831); "words which mean just as much as essentially Protestant cookery, or essentially Christian horsemanship." Why a man should be less fit to exercise the powers of government "because he wears a beard, because he does not eat ham, because he goes to the synagogue on Saturday, instead of going to the church on Sundays, we cannot conceive." It was certainly better to have one's shoes mended by a heretical cobbler than by a person who had subscribed to the Thirty-Nine Articles, but had never handled an awl. It was patently absurd to permit Jews to own parliamentary boroughs but not to sit in Parliament. As long as money meant power, and as long as Jews were not forbidden to make money, they possessed power in any event. "An elector of Penryn will take ten pounds from Shylock rather than nine pounds nineteen shillings and eleven pence three farthings from Antonio."

Once again, Macaulay pointed to circumstances and situations to account for qualities that anti-Semites seemed to think were innate. It was ridiculous to accuse English Jews of lack of patriotic feeling as long as they did not possess the privileges of native Englishmen. They felt exactly the way their situation impelled them to feel. "The statesman who treats them as aliens, and then abuses them for not entertaining all the feelings of natives, is as unreasonable as the tyrant who punished their fathers for not making bricks without straw."

50. Ibid., 191. The same point was made by T.B.M. in his essay on Machiavelli, in which he noted the difference between the Greek citizen's duty to sacrifice all to the state (then really constituted by the totality of citizens), and the epigonic Romans, who continued to use the cant phrases about a country to which they owed nothing. *Works*, VII, 106.

Thus, it was at the level of social and institutional change that Macaulay searched for historical explanations of contemporary phenomena. This was true not merely of his historical essays, and of those dealing with current problems such as slavery and higher education, but also of such pieces of literary criticism as his essay on Robert Montgomery's *Poems,* a work of demolition of an inferior poetaster who had been puffed into a prominence from which Macaulay set out to topple him. This particular review was, for the most part, a vigorous diatribe against Montgomery's ineptness, the derivative nature of his verse, his banality. But all that was placed within the larger historical context of the transition from patronage to puffing which had occurred because since the eighteenth century the public had gradually taken the place of the patron.[51]

It is tempting to claim too much for Macaulay as a systematic social thinker, to build occasional brilliant flashes of speculation and insight into a sociological system. This temptation must be resisted. Yet there is a common denominator in his methodological approach in these various essays in the term "circumstances." It was "circumstances" that created and explained the ambivalent values of Machiavelli's time. It was "circumstances" that supplied the answer to the question as to why whites shrank from marrying Negroes. It was to the "circumstances" of every generation that higher education was supposed to adapt itself. It was the "circumstances" of their respective times that made the comparison between Cromwell on the one hand, and Washington and Bolivar, on the other, perfectly reasonable. As Macaulay pointed out in his essay on Dryden, it was a fallacy to have too much faith in what could be accomplished by great individuals in history. People were disposed to hate by misery, and to love by happiness; outstanding men were shaped by their age. That applied as well to the great discoveries, such as the theory of fluxions or the principles of political economy. The theory of rent, for example, was expounded by different individuals without knowledge of each other, during the same period of time.[52]

Now, "circumstances" is one of those umbrella words under which may be subsumed a great variety of meanings. Marxists talk of the crucial role of economic circumstances; Benthamites in the tradition of eighteenth-century associationist psychology talked of the way in

---

51. T.B.M., "Mr. Robert Montgomery's Poems" (1830) , *Works,* VII, 506–7. For his comments on the Jews, see T.B.M., "Civil Disabilities of the Jews" (1831) , *Works,* VIII, 3–9.

52. T.B.M., "John Dryden" (1828) , *Works,* VII, 116–17.

which it would be possible and desirable to change character and personality through a change of circumstances; later on in the nineteenth century, "circumstances" must have become so common an explanation—and often vindication—of misery, vice, and anti-social behavior that W. S. Gilbert was able to parody it in *Ruddigore:*

> *But be so kind to bear in mind,*
> *We are the victims of circumstances.*

What did Macaulay mean by the word? Did he have any consistent meaning in mind at all? For an answer to this question, it is worth looking at the essay on History in which he set down his desiderata for the perfect historian. It is here that Macaulay expounded a notion of social history which he himself was able, later on, to demonstrate triumphantly in the third chapter of his *History of England.* Less emphasis on courts and cabinets, more on how all classes of people lived and worked, and spent their leisure—that was the essence of his prescription. It owed a great deal to his reading of Scott's novels; it may have owed something to his favorite, Bacon, who had called for a history of mechanical inventions and scientific experiments, as part of a history of learning;[53] and it owed most of all to Macaulay's own poetical and imaginative temperament, nurtured (as we have seen) on fiction, and from his earliest youth preoccupied with the dramatization of history.

What is less well known about this essay than its programmatic statement is the *manner* in which Macaulay justified the shift of emphasis in historical subject matter that he was proposing. The major part of the essay is devoted to a capsule history of European historiography, in which its stages are tied to particular states of society existing in various periods. Thus the faults of Herodotus, those of a "simple and imaginative mind," are said to be due to the fact that it was "natural" for him to write in the manner he did, since in his time most of what could be learned about the past had to come from tradition and popular ballads, and not from books. The Peloponnesian War changed the Greek character. As civilization "advanced," the Athenians became less visionary and less simple-hearted. In an environment of logic and sophistry, in which thousands of

53. In *The Advancement of Learning.* See J. R. Hale, ed., *The Evolution of British Historiography from Bacon to Namier* (Cleveland, Ohio, 1964) , 17; for Scott's influence, see H. R. Trevor-Roper, *The Romantic Movement and the Study of History* (London, 1969) .

intellects speculated about life and government, history could not retain its old character. It became less gossipy and less picturesque, more accurate and more scientific. A new type of personality flourished in an atmosphere in which ties of party had superseded those of country, in which revolution and counter-revolution became events of daily occurrence. Macaulay, then, postulated that each historical era tended to develop its own characteristics, and that these were reflected in its literary—in this case its historiographical—production. Thucydides, living in a time "prolific in desperate and crafty political adventurers," could not possibly, therefore, have written in the manner of Herodotus.[54]

In finally approaching the question why modern historians were so much better philosophers than their ancient counterparts, Macaulay linked this phenomenon to a broader historical inquiry. Why had there occurred such extraordinary advances in modern times of the moral sciences in general, in subjects like the principles of government, political economy, and legislation? The invention of printing, and the resulting ease in the diffusion of ideas, were part of the answer. The other part, one that impelled Macaulay to enter upon a lengthy digression on European history, was that the European nations had generally become less exclusive. The Greeks had admired only themselves; the Romans had admired themselves and the Greeks. There followed Caesaro-despotism, effacing all national peculiarities and eventually ushering in a "Chinese" state of "tottering, drivelling, paralytic longevity."[55] Then came two revolutions: Christianity, which changed men accustomed to being turned over like sheep from tyrant to tyrant into devoted partisans and obstinate rebels; and the barbarian invasions, which—like the Great Fire of London—chastened and cleansed as they destroyed. "It cost Europe a thousand years of barbarism to escape the fate of China."[56]

Then came the beginning of a "second civilization" that was to witness numerous states united by ties of international law and common obligation in active and fruitful competition, one with the other. In the nineteenth century, as Macaulay was to point out elsewhere[57] (much in the spirit of Edward Gibbon's "Observations" on the causes for the fall of the Roman Empire), there was no longer

54. T.B.M., "History," *Works*, VII, 170–83. It is always difficult to remember, of course, that Herodotus and Thucydides were, at least for a part of their lives, contemporaries.
55. Ibid., 204.
56. Ibid., 206.
57. T.B.M., "Mill on Government" (1829), *Works*, VII, 362.

any fear for civilization from the hostilities of savage nations; though there remained the possibility of a malady of destruction being engendered within the bosom of civilization itself. Macaulay envisioned the occurrence of such an internal barbarism, which, significantly enough in view of his obsession with this theme in almost all his essays during this period, he linked with democracy. This new barbarism might lead to a situation where two or three hundred years hence, a few lean and half-naked fishermen would share the ruins of London with owls and foxes, wash their nets amid the remnants of the London docks, and build their huts out of the capitals of one of the city's stately cathedrals.

Thus optimism about the state of European civilization, present and future, remained tempered by some dark forebodings. Yet in the essay on History Macaulay laid stress on the positive advantages for modern historians of having had at hand far more empirical evidence of varying modes of behavior than their predecessors. This had enabled them to become effective generalizers, outdoing previous historians in the art of deducing general principles from facts. On the other hand, the trouble with modern historians (Macaulay cited Gibbon, Hume, and Mitford as evidence) was that they tended to fall into the opposite error of distorting facts to suit general principles. This, Macaulay commented, was not necessarily deleterious; since opposite interpretations of what happened in history—say, radical and conservative versions in the field of Greek history, where Grote was just about to come out in reply to the Tory Mitford—could then compete before the tribunal of the public, which was left to judge.

What had suffered in this process of different ideologies competing for favor before the public was the art of narration, of "interesting the affections and presenting pictures to the imagination." And it was here that Macaulay announced his own program for writing a novel kind of history, for becoming, in effect, a poet or bard suitable for the age.[58] The knowledge of past events was valuable only insofar as it led readers to form just calculations with respect to the future. And the sort of history which did not do this, though it might be full of battles, treaties, and commotions, was useless. Clearly, Macaulay felt that the circumstances of his own times, and, even more important, the circumstances of the future, called for a new

58. See Weber, "Singer and Seer," *Papers on Language and Literature*, 210–19; and David Fong, "Macaulay: The Essayist as Historian," *Dalhousie Review*, LI (1971), 38–48.

kind of history, one differing in its emphases from the traditional stress put on politics and wars. For the most important revolutions in the history of mankind were noiseless, and consisted not of violent physical conflict, but of changes in manners and morals, the transition of communities from power to wealth, from knowledge to ignorance, and from ferocity to humanity. Bishop Watson had compared geologists to gnats mounted on an elephant, laying down theories as to the whole internal structure of the animal from the phenomenon of its hide. That image was unjust to geologists, but very applicable to "those historians who write as if the body politic were homogeneous, who look only on the surface of affairs, and never think of the mighty and curious organisation which lies deep below."[59]

Macaulay issued a plea for more attention to be paid by a new school of historians to the life and culture of society as a whole. Sometimes the most valuable materials for the historian might seem on the surface to be insignificant discards and fragments. Yet it was these which often constituted the real substance of history:

At Lincoln Cathedral there is a beautiful painted window, which was made by an apprentice out of the pieces of glass which had been rejected by his master. It is so far superior to every other in the church, that, according to the tradition, the vanquished artist killed himself from mortification.[60]

The novels of Sir Walter Scott exemplified this parable, since he had used in a manner which might well excite historians' envy those fragments of truth that they had thrown scornfully behind them.

The important revolutions in history, Macaulay concluded, were almost always the consequence of moral changes that both preceded and were of far more significance than mere "public measures." Thus, his account of the history of historical writing was closely tied to his account of the major trends in European history as such, and to his view of his own time. Historians in the past wrote as they did because certain circumstances in their society, primarily moral, impelled them in that direction. The force that now should by rights be moving them to delve into society in depth rather than merely in the surface terms of politics and wars was, by definition, *the* most powerful force acting upon their own period.

What, then, was that force? Without a doubt, the democratic

59. T.B.M., "History," *Works*, VII, 214.   60. Ibid., 217.

tendencies of the time. As wealth and civilization increased, in the continuous advance from a rude to a refined state of society, they percolated downwards. Just as the poor were now becoming literate and educated, just as the middle ranks were advancing all along the line—so, too, their activities and style of life in the past were becoming altogether appropriate, indeed, essential subjects for the historian's pen. This does not mean that Macaulay himself desired political democracy. Far from it. It could be argued that it was because he did not that he realized how essential it was to make room to some extent—certainly in the past, if not in the present—for those who had been so long outside the historian's purview. Social history could play the role of social anodyne. Placing really important historical changes into the context of a general moral atmosphere rather than into one of politics and public affairs tended to diminish, or blur over, the significance of contemporary confrontations of rich and poor, progress and reaction, in the political sphere. The winds of change that were blowing could be said to be separate from party strife, unpolitical, and, therefore, all the more to be heeded. By enlisting the spirit of the time on one's side, one might be able to make it work in a preservative rather than in a revolutionary direction. Here, historiography and politics blended into one, just as in the essay on London University education and politics had been similarly joined together.

Reading this and other early essays of Macaulay should make one think twice before accepting the time-honored convention that the streams of historical writing ran so very differently in England and on the continent of Europe. It is doubtless true that in Macaulay there cannot be found in their pristine form those key ideas of German *Historismus* that appear first in Herder and Goethe, and later in the work of Carlyle, who is usually said to be a unique figure in British historiography in his explicit departure from eighteenth-century norms. Yet, in his stress on the "spirit" of particular epochs in history, in his (admittedly limited) relativism, and his desiderata for the writing of a different kind of history, Macaulay did in fact place himself within the camp of the new, romantic history. The spirit of *his* time was doing its work.

The "spirit of the age" was particularly important in Macaulay's approach to both history and the contemporary scene, since it was closely tied in his mind to a general schema of the growth of civilization. The ramifications of this schema extended inwards into domestic English history as well as upwards into contemporary English politics. Its basic tenet was that on the whole (here he followed Hume) the progress of civilization had been favorable to liberty, and had brought in its train increase of wealth as well as diffusion of knowledge. Macaulay most fully developed his own belief in progress in his attack on Robert Southey's *Colloquies*, where he championed the industrial age against the poet's nostalgia for older and happier times in the generation before the Reformation. Once a people attained civilization and prosperity, he wrote, there could be no retrogression, except by means of violent and terrible calamities, such as the barbarian invasions, or the desolation of Italy in the early sixteenth century. History was full of the signs of this "natural progress of society." The industry of individuals created wealth faster than governments could squander it. Thus, Britain had been getting richer and richer; her laboring classes were better housed and fed than they had been three hundred years before; they received better medical care; they lived longer. The advantages of civilization had outweighed the pressures of population.[61]

The gradual growth of wealth and knowledge as well as their increased diffusion in modern Western history were taken as axiomatic. As agents in historical change they really had far more significance than political and constitutional arrangements which, in the end, merely reflected them. The trouble with the Royalist Party in the seventeenth century, for instance, was that its members did not perceive the signs of the times, in other words, did not see that growing wealth and growing knowledge had made it impossible for monarchies of the Middle Ages to exist upon their old footing.[62] The privileges of the House of Commons, for which the people had fought in the seventeenth century, which they had then held to be synonymous with their liberty had by now (the nineteenth century) become nearly as odious as the rigors of martial law. Why? Because the seventeenth-century conflict took place between Crown and Parliament. But from the middle of the eighteenth century onwards a realignment in this conflict had occurred, leaving the people on one side, and Crown and Parliament combined on the other. After those privileges that had once entirely belonged to the House of Commons had fallen under the control of the Crown, the greatest safeguard of public liberty had come to reside in the publication of parliamentary debates. "The gallery in which the reporters sit has become a fourth estate of the realm."[63] In one striking phrase

61. T.B.M., "Southey's Colloquies on Society" (1830), *Works*, VII, 489–501.
62. T.B.M., "Hallam," *Works*, VII, 270.   63. Ibid., 319.

(which he was the first to use), Macaulay penetrated beneath the formal structure of politics to put his finger on the new great force of public opinion, which was coming to absolute power in his own time and which was itself clearly linked both to increased wealth more widely distributed in the society and to a more general diffusion of knowledge.

A great revolution in public feeling had taken place recently, because Parliament which, during Stuart times, had confined its role to one of checking and complaining, had now drawn unto itself all of the vices and all of the unpopularity of executive government. This led Macaulay to the theme of parliamentary reform, which he discussed here not merely as a desirable political measure, but also within a definite historical framework. The question had been of no importance before 1688, since Parliament was then dependent upon the support of the people. But after 1688, a happy and useful, but by no means a "glorious" revolution (there had indeed been something degrading in the necessity for foreign aid),[64] Parliament had on the whole become aristocratic both in temper and interest. "It is very far from being an illiberal and stupid oligarchy; but it is equally far from being an express image of the general feeling." It was therefore unpopular. And Macaulay correctly forecast (at a time, by the way, when by no means all Whigs agreed on this point) that reform would be the question of the period. "The public attention may be for a time diverted to the Catholic claims or the Mercantile code; but it is probable that at no very distant period, perhaps in the lifetime of the present generation, all other questions will merge in that which is, in a certain degree, connected with them all."[65]

In prescribing a remedy, Macaulay eschewed any technical discussion of franchise extension and redistribution of seats, and cut through to the heart of the matter: class representation. The only way in which an otherwise inevitable struggle could be prevented, in which the tragedies of the seventeenth century could be forestalled, was by reforming in time in order to preserve, was for some statesman to reconcile the two great branches of the "natural" aristocracy, capitalists and landlords. It was essential so to widen the base of the government as to interest in its defense the middling class—"that brave, honest, and sound-hearted class, which is as anxious for the maintenance of order and the security of property, as it is hostile to corruption and oppression."[66]

Thus, in Macaulay's view, parliamentary reform was a historical

64. Ibid., 310–11.   65. Ibid., 323–4.   66. Ibid., 324.

necessity rather than a mere political nostrum. For the increase of wealth and the diffusion of knowledge had given the middle classes a position in English society which must find reflection in the House of Commons, if a revolutionary situation, in the shape of an alliance between middle and lower orders, was to be averted. Macaulay explicitly stated his view of what was to be done at the very end of his three essays against the Utilitarians, written in 1829: "Our fervent wish, and we will add our sanguine hope, is that we may see such a reform in the House of Commons as may render its votes the express image of the opinion of the middle orders of Britain."[67]

He wrote those three essays in order to establish a definite line of demarcation between the Utilitarian school and the Whigs. It will be recalled that the Utilitarians had declared war against the *Edinburgh* in 1824. Now these articles struck back at the *Westminster*. By the late 1820's the Utilitarians had come to represent to both Brougham and Macaulay the danger of unbridled democracy, of which they appeared to be agents. There was nothing inevitable about this linkage between Benthamism and democratic ideas. Bentham himself was converted to these ideas by James Mill in 1808, at a time when he was in a state of intense depression over the way in which the English governing classes had steadfastly ignored his reform proposals. But Bentham's conversion did not, of course, signify that all those who *did* see merit in these proposals would therefore follow him on the road he had taken. Like Marx, like Coleridge, Bentham was the kind of seminal thinker who attracted fanatical disciples, but whose ideas reached far beyond those disciples to a much wider public, which often accepted them only in part or saw something sound in them without going all the way with James Mill's view of their political consequences. Macaulay's difference at this point was with James Mill.

The first of his three articles against the Utilitarians was entitled "Mill's *Essay on Government.*" That essay, written in 1820 for the *Encyclopaedia Britannica,* had been intended by Mill to serve both as an example of Utilitarian logic and, as such, as the most efficacious sort of propaganda for the cause of Benthamite political reform. It was an attack on the Whig doctrine favoring representation of "interests" rather than numbers. Mill's assumption was that universal (male) suffrage was the most desirable arrangement. But in answer to the question as to how far the suffrage might safely be restricted, Mill argued that if the "middle rank," the wisest and most virtuous

67. T.B.M., "Utilitarian Theory of Government" (1829) , *Works,* VII, 449.

part of the community, had the vote, then lower-class opinion, formed by that middle rank, would be in accord rather than at enmity with it. In that sense the essay could be read as a paean to the middle class; and that probably accounts for Mill's telling a correspondent at the time he was writing the essay that "you need be under no alarm about my article *Government*. I shall say nothing capable of alarming even a Whig, and he is more terrified at the principles of good government than the worst of Tories."[68] But, as W. R. Carr has recently pointed out, this "middle rank" argument of Mill's was designed to support the position that the franchise could safely be widened to include all classes in the community. Certainly someone like Macaulay, well acquainted with Austin, John Stuart Mill, and other young Philosophical Radicals through many a debate and discussion in which he had been engaged with them, probably on the subject of this very essay, was fully aware of the democratic drift of Mill's thought.[69]

Macaulay's own political views in the late twenties were still very much in line with the views of Brougham, whose radicalism the latter took great pains to distinguish from the democratic variety. In 1827 Macaulay had written an article in the *Edinburgh,* defending the Canning coalition. There, he had issued a warning about what would happen if the extreme Tories, who had seceded, ever returned to office. There would ensue a period of real repression. And the result? "A revolution, a bloody and unsparing revolution—a revolution which will make the ears of those who hear of it tingle in the remotest countries, and in the remotest time."[70]

Everyone knew that the English "middling orders" were attached to their country's institutions. But that attachment was not blindly partial. They saw the faults as well as the merits of the system, and they showed a growing desire for having those faults removed. If, while their wish for improvement was becoming stronger and

68. James Mill to Napier, September 10, 1819, Alexander Bain, *James Mill: A Biography* (London, 1882), 188.

69. Wendell Robert Carr, "James Mill's Politics Reconsidered: Parliamentary Reform and the Triumph of Truth," *Historical Journal,* XIV (1971), 553–79. See also William Thomas, "James Mill's Politics: 'The Essay on Government' and the Movement for Reform," *Historical Journal,* XII (1969), 249–84, and Joseph Hamburger, "James Mill on Universal Suffrage and the Middle Class," *The Journal of Politics,* XXIV (1962), 167–90. Mill wrote to McCulloch on August 18, 1825, that his essays were "the textbooks of the young men of the Union at Cambridge." Bain, *Mill,* 292. This particular essay was reprinted in 1824 and again in 1828 in pamphlet form; and this last reprint was the formal occasion for T.B.M.'s review.

70. [T.B.M], "Present Administration," *Edinburgh Review,* XLVI (1827), 260.

stronger, the government were to become worse and worse, the consequences would be obvious. For, within their ranks, there was arising

a Republican sect, as audacious, as paradoxical, as little inclined to respect antiquity, as enthusiastically attached to its ends, as unscrupulous in the choice of its means, as the French Jacobins themselves,—but far superior to the French Jacobins in acuteness and information—in caution, in patience, and in resolution.

These were the Philosophical Radicals—totally devoted to metaphysical and political science; averse to the fine arts, elegant literature, and the sentiments of chivalry; arrogant, intolerant, and impatient of all superiority. Because of those qualities, these men, "in spite of their real claims to respect," would remain unpopular as long as the people were satisfied with their rulers. But under an ignorant and tyrannical ministry, obstinately opposed to even moderate and judicious innovations, their ideas would become influential, and "the public, disgusted with the blind adherence of its rulers to ancient abuses, would be reconciled to the most startling novelties." A strong democratic party would be formed within the educated class. And there would then come about what was most to be feared—an alliance between the multitude and a large portion of the middling orders. This in turn would bring with it the risk of a major revolution that would turn Manchester into Lyons and Stowe into Chantilly.[71]

Macaulay himself, as we know, had been influenced to some extent by the Utilitarians. Indeed, he was to use Mill's own reassuring argument in the *Essay on Government* that parliamentary reform would not necessarily mean the abolition of either the monarchy or the House of Lords, in one of his own speeches in favor of the Reform Bill.[72] He shared the feeling of the Philosophical Radicals that Parliament had become too aristocratic a body.[73] He also shared their suspicion of the frivolous upper classes—those estimable persons (as he put it in his essay on University College) "who think that the whole dignity of man consists in living within certain districts, wearing coats made by certain tailors, and eschewing certain meats and drinks."[74] Elsewhere, he referred to "a kind of logic which the privileged orders alone are qualified to use, and which, with their

71. Ibid., 260–1; 267.　　　72. That of March 2, 1831, T.B.M., *Works*, XI, 419–20.
73. T.B.M., "Hallam," *Works*, VII, 323.
74. T.B.M., "The London University," Clive and Pinney, eds., *Macaulay*, 8.

other constitutional distinctions, we earnestly pray that they may long keep to themselves."[75]

He also approved of the Philosophical Radicals' admiration for the middle ranks, "that brave, honest, and sound-hearted class."[76] And he certainly shared their principal economic ideas, derived from the classical economists. In his essay on Southey's *Colloquies,* he used these in order to annihilate, to his own satisfaction, Southey's paternalistic economic notions. The state, he wrote, might be permitted to erect buildings for public purposes. But there it must stop. "We firmly believe that £500,000 subscribed by individuals for railroads or canals would produce more advantage to the public than five millions voted by Parliament for the same purpose."[77] Calderón's play *La Gran Cenobia,* which Macaulay read in India in 1835, contains the following lines:

> *Let them be wretched and suffer, since*
> *Heaven made them poor, heaven knows why.*
> *Am I able to correct it?*

Next to these lines Macaulay wrote in the margin: "A good answer to Southey and Sadler."[78]

What he could *not* share were the ultimate political aims of the Utilitarians. For him they conjured up the specter of revolution. But it was not merely differences in political ideas which separated him from them. Even more important, there were fundamental differences in temperament. Macaulay's ardent, romantic nature, his sense of the dramatic, his great imaginative capacities—all were alien to the ascetic, "Euclidean" view of life of the Utilitarians. In his essay on Canning's ministry he had defined the gulf between him and them in memorable phrases: "All that is merely ornamental—all that gives the roundness, the smoothness, and the bloom, has been excluded. Nothing is left but nerve, and muscle, and bone."[79] Philosophical pride, he went on to say, had done for them what spiritual pride had done for the Puritans, had made them averse to fine arts, elegant literature, and chivalry. It was this aspect of their character and doctrine that Macaulay excoriated in his first article on Mill and the

75. [T.B.M.], "Present Administration," *Edinburgh Review,* 252.
76. See above, p. 125.
77. T.B.M., "Southey's Colloquies," *Works,* VII, 474.
78. Calderón, *Comédias* (4 vols., Leipzig, 1827–30), I, 94. Houghton Library, Harvard University.
79. [T.B.M.], "Present Administration," *Edinburgh Review,* XLVI (1827), 261.

Millites—pointing to their contempt of ignorance, their antipathy to sentiment and eloquence, their affectation of "quakerly plainness." It may be surmised that he spoke from the heart when he remarked bitterly that the strongest arguments, "when clothed in brilliant language, seem to them so much wordy nonsense."[80] Surely, both at the Cambridge Union and at the London Debating Society, he must more than once have undergone the experience of being told that his own elaborate eloquence, his own sparkling and inventive wit, his own striking phrases and historical analogies, had nothing to do with the case. Here, then, was a chance for revenge.

The formal argument of Macaulay's charge against the Utilitarians, however, concerned their rationalism, their *a priori* methods, their vain attempts to deduce a science of politics from certain assumptions about the propensities of human nature. Against this methodology, Macaulay exalted what he called Baconian induction as the sole means of arriving at truth in political science. But his own article, as Popper has pointed out,[81] is less an exemplar of the inductive method than a largely successful attempt to confute Mill's assumptions about human nature and politics by means of references to history and experience. He upbraided Mill for believing that the preservation of property was the first and only object of government, pointing out that government must exist for the protection of persons as well as property, that the greatest possible happiness of society was not necessarily attained (as Mill claimed) by ensuring to every man the greatest possible quantity of the produce of his labor.[82] As an example, possibly remembering his studies of Machiavelli and his times, Macaulay cited the practice of vindictive assassination, where the assault had absolutely nothing to do with the assailant's attempt to get hold of someone else's property.

In this example there may be found a clue to Macaulay's general

80. T.B.M., "Mill on Government," *Works*, VII, 329; see also his remark in "Southey's Colloquies," ibid., 467: "We despise those mock philosophers, who think that they serve the cause of science by deprecating literature and the fine arts."

81. On T.B.M.'s own method, see Sir Karl Popper, *The Open Society and Its Enemies* (2 vols., Princeton, N.J., 1950), I, 544–5, as a corrective to Mill's *Autobiography*. See also J. C. Rees, "A Note on Macaulay and the Utilitarians," *Political Studies*, IV (1956), 315–17, in which T.B.M. is credited with the discovery of the "naturalistic fallacy" before Sidgwick and Moore.

82. There is a nice ironical touch here if one remembers (following A. J. Ayer) that the Utilitarian theory, with its emphasis on the general as opposed to sectional interests, and its attachment to the principle that each individual counted for one and only one, marked the first step from the older theories of government which represented its primary function as the defense of property or the maintenance of privilege. See A. J. Ayer, "Freedom and Happiness," *New Statesman*, September 18, 1964, 390.

attitude toward the Utilitarians, quite apart from the political differences which separated him from them. He could not abide what he thought was their failure to allot a proper place to the irrational elements in human behavior, their failure to do justice to the complexity of human nature as revealed both in history and in experience. Thus: "Innumerable martyrs have exulted in torments which made the spectators shudder; and, to use a more homely illustration, there are few wives who do not long to be mothers."[83]

Admitting that in pursuing this line of argument he might be exposing himself to the reproach of sentimentality, "a word which, in the sacred language of the Benthamites, is synonymous with idiocy,"[84] Macaulay pointed out, as against Mill's emphasis on aristocratic and monarchical rapacity, that King and Aristocracy were not merely in pursuit of physical pleasure, but that such motives as love of ostentation and fame, the desire to gain the good opinion of others, and the dread of posthumous censure were at least equally powerful. He backed up this argument with a series of examples drawn from different spheres of contemporary history and experience. Why, for example, was the position of an English wife different from that of her Italian or Turkish counterpart? If love of domination over others were indeed everywhere the principal trait in human nature, then this difference in situation would not exist. However, it was simply not true that people merely wished to dominate; they also wished to be loved and esteemed. Then he neatly turned this part of the argument in a political direction by stating that if the criterion were need, it was far more likely that the poor would plunder the rich than vice versa. The greater the inequality of conditions, the stronger the motives for spoliation.

In a democracy—and this, according to Macaulay, would come about if Mill's own doctrines were brought to their logical conclusion—the rich would be pillaged. This was not true of the United States, since in that country there existed plenty of the cheap accessories of life, and wages were high. But it was a different story in countries where the great majority of the people had to live from hand to mouth, where a great deal of wealth was amassed by the few.

83. T.B.M., "Mill's Essay on Government," *Works*, VII, 367. In her "The Victorian Ethos: Before and After Victoria," *Victorian Minds* (New York, 1968), 288–9, Gertrude Himmelfarb calls T.B.M.'s own stance "evangelized utilitarianism," since he emphasized the fact that some people's pleasure was to do what was not necessarily pleasurable, i.e., to behave as they ought to behave. Christianity, unlike the Utilitarians, admitted the existence of that "ought."

84. Ibid., 338.

Once again, Macaulay conjured up the specter of revolution. When abuses were linked to property, as in the France of 1789, revolution was sometimes justified. But this was clearly not the case in England, where it was the higher and middling orders who served as "the natural representatives of the human race." To be sure, *their* interest might be opposed to that of their poorer contemporaries; but, what was more important, it was identical with that of future generations. It was they who, if Mill had his way, and democracy ensued, might well disappear and be replaced by those lean and half-naked fishermen, washing their nets amid the remains of the London docks.

It was in line with these reflections that Macaulay, at the end of his third and last article against the Utilitarians, stated his own political views, advocating such a reform of the House of Commons as would render its votes the express image of the middle orders of Britain. Some sort of pecuniary qualification he held to be necessary. But every decent farmer and shopkeeper was to have the franchise.[85] This, ironically enough, was exactly what Mill had recommended in his pamphlet. And one might wonder what all the fuss was about, were it not for the fact that Macaulay, though insisting that he was arguing with the method and not the substance of Millite thought, was in fact treating the Philosophical Radicals as democrats. He did so, in part because he himself thought he knew the real direction in which their doctrines were tending, in part because he wished to make it abundantly clear that Whiggery of the *Edinburgh* stamp wanted to separate itself completely from this tendency.

In his condemnation of James Mill's deductive method, Macaulay found a sympathetic reaction in none other than Mill's son, John Stuart, who came to admit that Macaulay's arguments had persuaded him that his father had been both too narrow and too singleminded in his approach.[86] Politics apart, this was indeed the principal burden of the three essays against the Utilitarians. It was not true, Macaulay wrote in the second essay,[87] that all men would always act

85. T.B.M., "Utilitarian Theory of Government," *Works*, VII, 449.

86. Mill, *Autobiography* (New York, 1924), 110–13. "That in his own mind James Mill was not as simple-minded or dogmatic as his essay suggests is very likely. . . . Yet the fact remains that he wrote what looks very much like a scientific treatise on politics, rather than a proposal for parliamentary reform." Shirley Robin Letwin, *The Pursuit of Certainty* (Cambridge, 1965), 200.

87. T.B.M. wrongly assumed that Bentham himself had replied to his first essay and that now, in his second essay, he was in his turn replying to Bentham. But the actual author of the defense had been a Philosophical Radical named Poulett Thompson. John Stuart Mill wrote of him: "He has an understanding like a pin, going very far into a thing, but never covering a larger area of it than the portion of a pin's point." J. S. Mill to Carlyle, October 22, 1832, *Early Letters*, I, 127.

alike; for example, plunder their neighbors if they could. Men were placed in very different situations. Some had all they needed; others did not. Their respective behavior could not be postulated from any general assumption about human nature; but, rather, grew out of their particular circumstances.

What if we apply this approach to Macaulay himself? Is it possible to relate the leading ideas in his early essays to his own particular situation and circumstances during the late 1820's? He himself would certainly not have wanted to see the many sharp insights which punctuate these articles expounded by later commentators as any sort of system. For he repeatedly stressed the ephemeral nature of his periodical pieces. Thus, in taking issue with Macvey Napier (Jeffrey's successor as editor of the *Edinburgh Review*) over some excisions the latter had made of some of the most "pointed and ornamental" sentences in the "Southey" review, Macaulay argued:

Now for high and grave works—a History, for example, or a system of political and moral philosophy—Doctor Johnson's rule, that every sentence which the writer thinks fine ought to be struck out, is excellent. But periodical works like ours, which, unless they strike at the first reading, are not likely to strike at all, whose whole life is a month or two, may, I think, be allowed to be sometimes even viciously florid. Probably in estimating the real value of any tinsel which I may put upon my articles, you and I should not materially differ. But it is not by his own taste, but by the taste of the fish, that the angler is determined in his choice of bait.[88]

Those critics who, over the years, have censured Macaulay for his extreme formulations, the excessive glitter of his style, and his strident tone, should have remembered that he himself thought of all this as "tinsel."

Part of the situational context, therefore, lies in the exigencies of periodical writing—then or at any time. For another part, we must, of course, look to politics. The *Edinburgh Review* was a political, as well as a literary, journal, an organ of the Whig Party; and since "Milton," Macaulay's political ambitions and, to a great extent, his financial security, were tied to it and steadily growing. His chief "sponsor" in these years was Henry Brougham; and it seems reasonable to assume that the latter, during these years the most prominent statesman on the Whig side, as well as the most powerful of all the contributors to the *Edinburgh Review*, continued to exert consider-

88. T.B.M. to Macvey Napier, January 25, 1830, M. Napier, ed., *Selection from the Correspondence of the late Macvey Napier, Esq.* (London, 1879), 77.

able influence on Macaulay's politics. To take just one example: In 1827 it was Brougham who, among the Whigs, was the most determined to enter the Canning coalition, and who, at the same time, referred to the Radicals as intolerable atheists and bloody-minded republicans—"a set of drivellers who call themselves a kind of *doctrinaires,* and hold opinions subversive of all liberty."[89] Macaulay pressed home both these points of view in his *Edinburgh* article on "The Present Administration" during the same year.

But Macaulay's politics during the twenties must be seen in a broader context than that of the *Edinburgh* and Brougham. He was increasingly preoccupied with the fear of domestic revolution, and his writings show a continuous consciousness of this, whether in reminding his readers in one place that they were in the position of Englishmen at the time of James I, or in another, of Frenchmen at the time of Turgot.[90] This fear of revolution also emerged in less obvious ways. It was certainly present in his repeated assurances to the poor and the working classes[91] that they were now better off than ever before. Not that the objects of these assurances would be likely readers of the *Edinburgh.* But Macaulay surely intended to produce an antidote to what the Radical leaders were telling the same classes, that they had never been so badly off and that they ought therefore to be doing something about it.

The same sentiment lay behind his advocacy of more education for the poor; for it was Macaulay's belief that it was education alone which could turn irresponsible and potentially revolutionary mobs into citizens who would not abuse the privilege of the franchise. It was this sentiment which figured largely in his interpretation of modern European history. For the result of putting contemporary social and political tensions into a wider historical context was to blunt their edges and to weaken their contours. As civilization ineluctably advanced, as wealth increased, as science, literacy, industry, and technology increasingly flourished, it became a matter of course that more and more elements of the population would demand their rights; and would, by virtue of their education, be able to exercise them. Opportunities had been missed by the governing classes—in England in the seventeenth, in France in the eighteenth century. Disturbances and threats from rising classes were, in fact,

89. Aspinall, *Brougham,* 145.

90. T.B.M., "Hallam," *Works,* VII, 325; "Present Administration," *Edinburgh Review,* XLVI (1827), 264.

91. See especially T.B.M., "Southey's Colloquies," *Works,* VII, 491–7.

nothing novel. And they could be taken in stride, if the correct measures were taken, the proper concessions made in time, and previous mistakes, illustrated in history, avoided.

It was not only recent European history that taught these lessons. The story of civilization itself, with its steady advance from barbarism not only toward increased wealth, but toward a greater sharing in this wealth on the part of wider and wider elements of the population, put into perspective the social pressures of the Industrial Revolution. These could become very dangerous, if the governing classes set their face too vehemently against them. For they were part of the unfolding process of history itself, and therefore could be modified, but not eliminated. We tend to think of the German tradition, leading from Hegel to Marx, as the model of nineteenth-century inevitabilist theories of history. But in some ways the writers of the Scottish historical school, and people like Macaulay who took sustenance from it, were just as much inevitabilists; though, needless to say, for the latter it was not the eventual triumph of the proletariat, but, if anything, its eventual "bourgeoisification," which served as the desired end. In this sense, looking at recent history, Macaulay has proved to be not such a bad prophet.

These are some of the "situational" factors which should be kept in mind in reading Macaulay's early essays. Transcending them was, of course, the spirit of the age—a phrase much used at that particular period, by Hazlitt (in 1825), for example, and a few years later by John Stuart Mill, as titles of important essays. Macaulay himself, as we have seen, considered the moral and intellectual atmosphere of particular epochs in history to have been of the utmost significance. What of the spirit of *his* age? Two elements, especially, should be stressed here, the Romantic and the improving. Because of his antipathy, from his earliest youth, to the mystical and metaphysical aspects of the writings of the Lake poets, it is all too easy to categorize Macaulay as an anti-Romantic, his feet firmly set in the eighteenth century. However, we have already found that in his proposals for a new kind of history Macaulay went beyond the neo-classical mode. And, as M. H. Abrams has pointed out,[92] he was quite capable of employing eighteenth-century critical principles "ungratefully," to elevate Scott, Wordsworth, and Coleridge over their poetic predecessors, because they imitated nature better.

Certainly, Macaulay's temperament was constitutionally averse to

92. M. H. Abrams, *The Mirror and the Lamp: Romantic Theory and the Critical Tradition* (New York, 1958), 28.

mawkish sentimentality, to the democratic connotations of the Lake poets' linguistic innovations, to the whole idea of a transcendental nature embodying profound truths. He responded to Byron rather than to Wordsworth, even to the point of writing some lines in imitation of the former at the age of nineteen.[93] Now it can be argued that Byron was more "Regency" than "Romantic," that there remained a great gulf fixed between the Byronic and the Wordsworthian attitude to nature and the human condition. Here our concern is not so much to link Macaulay to individual poets, as to characterize his attitude in the large. What we find—and this reflects the mood of the period—is an exaltation of heart over head, of feeling over cold reason.

Given his family heritage, it would have been surprising indeed to find him personally incapable of deep emotion. But one must also pay some attention to the attitudes that emerge in his early essays. We have seen him castigating the Utilitarians for their "Euclidean" dryness. We have seen him praising Milton for writing his great poems in an atmosphere uncongenial to the epic imagination. In his essay on Dryden, which belongs to this same period, Macaulay defended that poet's "critical" cast of mind as inevitably belonging to the atmosphere of the age. But he nonetheless recognized the lack: Dryden's imagination "resembled the wings of an ostrich. It enabled him to run, though not to soar."[94] In the realm of political thought, Macaulay demanded a due regard for the great variety of human motives and passions against the mathematical cast of mind of the Utilitarians. In the realm of literature, he called for imagination and feeling against the merely critical and cerebral. In the realm of historiography, he looked for inspiration to Scott's novels, to new ways of engaging the affections and the imagination of readers. Thus, the romantic atmosphere of the age found specific reflection in Macaulay's leading ideas.

An equally important component of the spirit of the age was the general emphasis on "improvement." The 1820's in England witnessed a widespread concern with "improving" society, and this concern was by no means the monopoly of a single political party or group. The years after Waterloo saw serious fluctuations of the economy, much distress, and a great deal of resulting social tension.

---

93. *Weep not for me. Thou canst not know*   *How calmly face the sting of woe,*
    How souls like mine confront their fate.   *The sneer of scorn, the frown of hate.*
                                        Trinity MSS.
94. T.B.M., "Dryden," *Works*, VII, 158.

The ultra-Tories in both Houses of Parliament may have wanted to shut themselves off from all this, or to eliminate it by regression. But almost everyone else proposed solutions and reforms of varying kinds. Some, like Cobbett and Southey, wanted to try to return to a golden age in the past, to a society predominantly agricultural and patriarchal. Benthamites, in contrast, looked for remedies to new codes of law, to be promulgated by a truly democratic Parliament, as well as to the diffusion of knowledge to mechanics and workingmen. The Evangelicals, meanwhile, continued to work for the moral regeneration of society. In the urge for improvement, party lines often crossed and amalgamated. Liberal Tories, men like Huskisson, Peel, and Canning, were just as progressive in introducing and backing modern principles of political economy and administration as the main body of the Whigs who carried on the battle for Catholic emancipation. James Mill was a friend of Zachary Macaulay's; Brougham took over the leadership of the abolitionist campaign from Wilberforce. Whigs, Utilitarians, and Evangelicals collaborated in the founding of University College, London.

Macaulay himself, as we remember, from the time of his first coming to Cambridge, was fired with the ideal of working for the good of humanity, of changing the world. He lost the religious impulse which originally lay behind this desire. But the wish itself he retained, as is apparent in his writings and in his politics during these years. It is interesting to note, for instance, that in his *Knight's Quarterly* review (1824) of Mitford's *History of Greece,* where he first enunciated his proposals for a new kind of social history, he based this necessity on yet another, and that was to take account of the improvements made in the past to better the condition of mankind:

Paltry skirmishes and plots are reported with absurd and useless minuteness; but improvements the most essential to the comfort of human life extend themselves over the world, and introduce themselves into every cottage, before any annalist can condescend, from the dignity of writing about generals and ambassadors, to take the least notice of them.[95]

The new history he called for must include all that was not too trivial to promote or diminish the happiness of man. Thus the desire for improvement bore a direct relationship to Macaulay's view of the writing of history.

95. T.B.M., "Mitford's History of Greece" (1824), *Works,* XI, 390.

138 — MACAULAY

The particular demands of the periodical medium, politics, the general atmosphere of the period—all these must be taken into account as formative forces that went into the making of Macaulay's essays. Finally, personal factors entered in. There is no doubt that he wrote his articles on the "Disabilities of Negroes" and on University College, London, in part to please his father, who was deeply involved in both causes. Almost thirty years after he wrote the former, for instance, we find an entry in his journal which recalls how much pleasure that essay had given to Zachary.[96] And if his father inspired some of the essays, others owed their existence to his own thin-skinned tendency to take offense easily, the extreme sensitivity of a young man of no great social standing who was fighting his way upwards in a world in which privilege still went with birth. In Cambridge, his friends had thought him notable both for generosity and vindictiveness.[97] His sister Margaret, who kept a journal about her brother in 1831, recorded therein that Tom long remembered and deeply felt anything in the form of a slight: "His articles against Mr. Mill he wrote because he had heard that Mr. Mill had said in hearing something of it, 'What! Macaulay—I will smash him to atoms.' " Once he had taken his revenge, however, her brother forgave easily. He told her: "I have quite forgiven Mill for what he said, I have quite forgiven C. for having called me a barrister."[98]

"C." was the Tory diarist and politician John Wilson Croker, whose edition of Boswell's *Johnson* Macaulay had savaged in the *Edinburgh Review*. In the Reform Bill debates of October 1831, Croker had sarcastically remarked that "the honourable and learned member for Calne [Macaulay], though only a practising barrister in title, seemed to be in reality the most efficient member of the Government."[99] Macaulay had been contemptuously called a "barrister" before—in fact, a "bit barrister" as well as "an impertinent puppy," by John Wilson, "Christopher North," in the Tory *Blackwood's*.[100] Southey was one of Wilson's heroes. Thus he took strong exception to Macaulay's disrespectful treatment of the *Colloquies*, and prophesied that the reviewer, evidently a "clever lad," would remain such, and nothing more, for the rest of his days. Macaulay was be-

96. Trinity Journal, October 4, 1856.
97. T.B.H. himself told this to his sister Margaret, November 27, 1831. Margaret Macaulay, *Recollections*, 59.
98. November 27, 1837, ibid., 59–60.
99. T.B.M. to Ellis, October 17, 1831, Trevelyan, *Life and Letters*, 180.
100. April 1830. R. S. Mackenzie, ed., John Wilson, *Noctes Ambrosianae* (5 vols., New York, 1866), III, 449.

coming notorious as someone who hit hard and who evidently hurt his victims. He had already incurred the wrath of Thomas De Quincey in the *Edinburgh Saturday Post*, for his article supporting the Canning coalition. De Quincey linked Macaulay's views to "the ferocious *sansculotterie* of the Whig *parvenus*," and characterized his style as being stamped with youth, levity, inexperience, and audacity. "Every sentence seems saturated with its separate charge of quicksilver; and paragraph after paragraph roll off in volleys of minute explosions, flashes, raps, and bounces, like the small artillery of a schoolboy, or a feu-de-joye of squibs, and crackers."[101]

If the young Macaulay's essays elicited hostile criticism from the Tory side, that was only to be expected, and could be reckoned as a compliment to their effectiveness. But the essays brought him not merely the reputation of a bumptious youth on the warpath, but the supreme reward he had been looking for during these years—a seat in the House of Commons. In February of 1830, Lord Lansdowne, one of the moderate Whig leaders, who had been greatly impressed by Macaulay's three articles against the Utilitarians, offered him the vacant seat of Calne, a "pocket" borough under his control. There was striking irony in this situation, quite apart from the unavoidable anomaly of a parliamentary reformer's accepting such patronage. For it was Lord Lansdowne's father, the Earl of Shelburne, who in the 1780's had first taken Jeremy Bentham under his wing, and had given him his entry into Whig society. Now, Shelburne's son rewarded the man who had fiercely attacked Benthamite ideas with a seat in Parliament. Of course, Bentham's views had changed radically in 1808, when his friendship with James Mill had completed his conversion to democracy. And Lord Lansdowne himself could almost be considered an honorary *Edinburgh* reviewer, having (as Lord Henry Petty) received his education in that city, along with the founding members of the *Review*.

We have a description from the hand of Tom's sister Selina of what transpired during Lord Lansdowne's interview with Macaulay, in the course of which the offer of a seat was made. There was no man in England, Tom told him, to whom he would as soon owe obligation. But he *must* have complete freedom, both from personal conviction and for his father's sake, on the anti-slavery question. Lansdowne acceded to this condition at once, saying that he was far from expecting universal or servile accord from Tom; that, in fact,

101. *Edinburgh Saturday Post*, August 4, 1827; Stuart M. Tave, ed., *New Essays by De Quincey* (Princeton, N.J., 1966), 43–5.

what had greatly weighed with him in making the offer, was his high private and moral character. No expenses were involved for Tom. All he had to do was to spend a few days at Bowood, Lord Lansdowne's country seat, and engage in a little token electioneering.[102]

From Bowood, on February 10, 1830, Macaulay wrote his father that he found the house splendid and elegant—"I never saw any great place so thoroughly desirable for a residence"—that he got along very well with Lansdowne's son, Lord Kerry, and that great quantities of beer and potatoes were consumed by all present, including Lady Lansdowne. As far as the canvassing was concerned, he reported, he had even succeeded in winning over the single refractory burgess, out of about twenty voters, who during the last election had had the temerity to oppose the Lansdowne interest.[103]

About a week later, he was back in London, unanimously elected; and took his seat in the House on February 18. There was one discordant note: Brougham. Selina reported in her journal that Brougham was exceedingly angry about her brother's unexpected good fortune. Hitherto, Tom had always shown the greatest regard for him; indeed, Tom was indebted to him for his office of Commissioner of Bankruptcy. But now Brougham was jealous. In fact, Tom felt that Brougham had been jealous of him for some time, owing to his success in the *Edinburgh Review,* and had in an underhanded way prevented him from being offered the editorship after Jeffrey's retirement. (For this she had Jeffrey's authority.) The two of them, Brougham and Macaulay, apparently stood side by side in the Chamber at the oath-taking ceremony. But Brougham took no notice of Tom, and turned his back to him without speaking. His "excuse" for this behavior was that the seat should have gone to Denman, a much older and more experienced Whig, who had been Brougham's chief associate in the defense of Queen Caroline. But Selina's comment in her journal was that jealousy must be at the bottom of it.[104]

102. Selina Macaulay, Journal, February 11, 1830, Huntington MSS.

103. T.B.M. to his father, February 10, 1830, Trevelyan, *Life and Letters,* 110–11.

104. Selina Macaulay, Journal, February 20, 1830. She was wrong. On February 10, T.B.M. had written to his father that if Brougham, in publicly blaming Lansdowne for having given the vacant seat to T.B.M., meant that it should have gone to Denman, then "I can forgive, and even respect him, for the feeling which he entertains." Trevelyan, *Life and Letters,* 111. That was, in fact, what Brougham *had* meant. See Brougham to Creevey, 1830: "Ld. Lansdowne brings in young Macaulay, which may be all very well as far as he is concerned, but it gives all of us who are Denman's friends serious annoyance and regret." Herbert Maxwell, ed., *The Creevey Papers: A Selection from the Correspondence and Diaries of the late Thomas Creevey, M.P.* (New York, 1904), 550.

This was but a cloud on the horizon. For the moment, Macaulay was delighted with his situation, and eager for the active life of politics. As far as he himself was concerned, he wrote to Zachary, he would not hesitate to give up the law if it came to a "momentous" choice between law and politics. But the (financial) interest of his family had to be considered; and so he would have to see just how successful a public man he would prove.[105] This said, he duly took his seat in the House of Commons.

105. T.B.M. to his father, February 10, 1830, Trevelyan, *Life and Letters,* 111.

VI

THE REFORM BILL

RECENT SCHOLARSHIP ON THE REFORM ACT OF 1832 HAS ALMOST made it appear a basically conservative measure, which, far from granting power to the middle classes, in fact served to preserve the predominance of the landed interest and of the aristocracy in English politics and society. Those who reason thus base their case on two sets of arguments, one taken from the arrangements proposed and established by the bill, the other from its actual consequences. From the first set, it appears that more parliamentary seats were in fact given to the counties than to the new industrial towns; and that in the redrawing of boundaries which followed passage of the bill, voters in urban and rural constituencies were rigorously separated, so that the latter would more than ever before constitute spheres of the landed interest. From the second set of arguments, based on what we know of the subsequent course of nineteenth-century English history, it emerges clearly that the Reform Act did not lead to middle-class predominance in either politics or society. The composition of cabinets continued to remain aristocratic. The number of merchants and financiers in the House of Commons did not substantially increase. The £10 householders seemed to love a lord as much as their more affluent fellow voters. Networks of local influence still outweighed middle-class self-consciousness as electoral factors.

Can it be properly argued from all this that the Reform Act was not as much of a watershed as historians have assumed hitherto?

That, because it left things pretty much as they had been, it ought not to be regarded as a major turning point in modern English history? There are some obvious points to be made on the other side. Thus, while the proponents of reform vehemently reiterated its "finality," it was clear to many, including those who warned of "a leap in the dark," that, once embarked upon the path of reform, it would not be easy to stop at an arbitrary point, such as the £10 householder. Radical leaders had mobilized working-class pressure on behalf of the bill, and this had helped its eventual passage. Yet most of the working class was still without the vote. Once the *principle* of constitutional reform had been recognized, it was only a question of time before a demand for wider reforms would arise.

The historian must, in any event, separate the actual consequences of the Reform Act from the state of opinion at the time the bill was debated in Parliament. Can these debates be dismissed as mere rhetoric? Hardly. While most of public opinion throughout England was persuaded of the virtues of the bill, this was not equally true of MP's, as the closeness of the vote (302:301) on the occasion of the second reading of the bill on March 22, 1831, amply demonstrated. The House of Lords was set against the bill and could only be brought to pass it in the end by means of the threat of a royal creation of peers. It would be a mistake to maintain that all support for the bill was middle-class, all opposition aristocratic. One need only remember the aristocratic composition of Lord Grey's Reform cabinet, and recall that some of the most vigorous opponents of the bill, such as Peel, took pride in having themselves sprung from the middle classes. One can, however, ask this question: If the Reform Bill was so clearly intended to serve the interests of the aristocracy, why did not all the members of that class give it their enthusiastic support?

One sometimes gets the impression from recent historians that the whole business was some sort of plot, a stratagem that "took in" those clamoring to become part of the political system, because it redounded in the end to the benefit of the governing classes. If so, it must have been an extremely well hidden plot, for it was certainly not apparent to many of those who were to benefit from it. Even some of those who did believe that if the bill were to be a final constitutional adjustment, it would continue to give an immense preponderance to the landed interest, still recognized its revolutionary implications. For, as one of them, the future Lord Campbell, wrote at the time, "people would not be satisfied till universal suffrage and the ballot were tried."[1] Would it not make sense to say that, as in any major social or political crisis, revolutionary or not, different interest groups are to be found on the side advocating change, taking cover under an ideological canopy broad enough to cover both those who are proposing changes in order to justify and help to preserve a particular social system, and those who wish to transform it?

Macaulay certainly believed that the result of the Reform Act would primarily be to increase the power of the middle classes and the industrial towns, as against the power of the aristocracy and the landed interest; just as Lord Grey believed that the passage of the bill was necessary primarily in order to save the throne and the aristocracy. That both proved to be right underlines the fact that English liberalism in the nineteenth century witnessed conjunction rather than conflict between middle class and aristocracy.

We have seen that Macaulay had expressed his beliefs about the need for parliamentary reform in the *Edinburgh Review,* before the Whig leaders came to advocate reform as their policy. It was his good fortune to have been brought into Parliament in time to participate in a debate in which he could give voice to views he had for some time been advocating in his writings.

THE BARE OUTLINES OF WHAT PARLIAMENTARY REFORM INVOLVED ARE soon told. In one of his speeches on the subject, Macaulay summed them up as follows:

It destroys nomination; it admits the great body of the middle orders to a share in the government; and it contains provisions which will, as I conceive, greatly diminish the expense of elections.[2]

Two chief defects in the existing system had long been apparent; and, from the middle of the eighteenth century onwards, had come under severe criticism. But whereas in the eighteenth century it had been the undue power of the Crown that had been the chief target for reformers, in the nineteenth century it was the excessive power of

1. John Lord Campbell to George Campbell, March 4, 1831, Mary Hardcastle, ed., *Life of John Lord Campbell, Lord High Chancellor of Great Britain* (2 vols., Jersey City, N.J., 1881), II, 36.

2. December 16, 1831, *Works*, XI, 482.

the landed interest that served as the chief point of attack. About the first defect, all that need be said here is that at a time when the Industrial Revolution was in full blast, and the English manufacturing system had become one of the world's wonders, cities such as Manchester, Birmingham, and Leeds sent no representatives to Parliament; while, on the other hand, decayed boroughs sometimes consisting of no more than a few old houses and a handful of inhabitants, sometimes of neither, had the right to send Members. The second defect lay in the borough franchise, which, in contrast to that in the counties—where all forty-shilling freeholders had the vote—was diverse to the point of absurdity, resting as it did as often as not on anachronistic medieval usages. It ranged from universal male suffrage in a few places to a situation in many others where only the co-opted corporation or "freemen" of the borough, resident and nonresident, or only those paying certain customary taxes, possessed the vote. It often went with a house or a certain plot of ground, whether occupied or not.

This inevitably led to votes being openly bought and sold; and, in turn, to the so-called nomination boroughs, usually controlled by powerful landowners who could nominate whomever they chose—primarily members of their family, often younger sons; secondarily bright young men of promise—to sit for them. It was in this way that Lord Lansdowne had been able to nominate Macaulay for his "pocket" borough of Calne in Wiltshire.[3] The system had worked on the whole satisfactorily during the eighteenth century. It could be argued that, in functional terms, it had helped to supply needed majorities for the government of the day; even though in this way it became part of the machinery of patronage, mutual obligation, and corruption that helped make the political wheels go round. Apart from this functional argument, it could be maintained that while there existed nothing like numerical representation—which in any case smacked of democracy and which none but extreme Radicals called for—at least the major interests of a country still predominantly agricultural were represented "virtually."

Toward the end of the eighteenth century, reforms of various kinds were indeed proposed, not merely by Radicals, but by statesmen as moderate as Burke and Pitt. But the French Revolution, followed by the "Terror" and the Napoleonic wars, effectively put a

3. It was his intention that T.B.M. should have the seat until his son, Lord Kerry, had come of age. Lansdowne to William Smith, March [1830], Duke University Library MSS. I owe this reference to Thomas Pinney.

stop to serious reforming attempts. Waterloo, as we have seen, was followed by Peterloo. While the working classes were told by Radical orators such as Hunt that redress for their economic grievances must come from a House of Commons more popularly elected and thus more sympathetic to their plight, while Bentham and his disciples looked to an extension of the suffrage as the principal means by which their program for the removal of abuses could be put into practice, neither of the great political parties was willing to adopt parliamentary reform as its cause. Both could, if they wished, look back to a parliamentary reform tradition—the Whigs to the young Grey and his Friends of the People at the time of the French Revolution, the Tories to the younger Pitt's motions on the subject in the House of Commons. But the liberalization of the Tories during the 1820's, carried out by men such as Peel, Huskisson, and Canning, extended in the main to financial, foreign, and administrative policies. The Whigs, on the other hand, were divided about the issue. Catholic emancipation was the only platform on which they could all agree to stand.

It was not a popular platform, since "no-popery" sentiment was still very strong among all classes in England. And, in the event, it collapsed under them when the Tories, confronted with the threat of revolution in Ireland, made their *volte-face* under Wellington's command, and—to be sure, with the aid of the Whigs—emancipated the Catholics in 1829. It was then that the cause of parliamentary reform gained some unexpected recruits. For it was the ultra-Tories who had long been the strongest defenders of the Protestant constitution in Church and State, that is, of an exclusive and privileged status for the established Church. And it was they who now felt betrayed by the Duke of Wellington. Had it not been for the rotten boroughs under his control, they argued, he would not have been able to subvert what were to them sacred principles, by enabling first of all Dissenters and, a year later, Roman Catholics to take their places in the House of Commons, capable there of casting their votes on matters affecting the established Church. Everyone admitted that public sentiment had largely been against emancipation. It was the system of rotten boroughs that had made it possible for the great betrayal to occur. Thus the ultras deserted Wellington in 1829, just as the Canningites had deserted him during the previous year. And in their anger some of these ultra-Tories were ready to aid and abet those Whigs—and at this point that did not include by any means all the leading ones—who were prepared to make the question of parlia mentary reform their own from a very different motive: return to political power.

The Whigs were beginning to feel that the only hope for getting back into power, having for so long been deprived of it, was to resume once again their traditional alliance with the people, re-cemented during the Queen Caroline affair of 1820; and, therefore, to take up the question of parliamentary reform because in the popular mind it was becoming the most urgent question of the hour. It was in fact, as we have seen, one of those issues which different sections of the population embraced, expecting different things from it. The Whigs saw it as the master key to political power. The work-ing classes, suffering great distress during the hard winter of 1830, were being told by men like William Cobbett that nothing would be done about their miseries until the composition of Parliament was changed. Only then could a stop be put to repressive legislation and to economic policies that took no account of their sufferings. The middle classes, of course, saw it as a long-overdue recognition of their rights.

In Birmingham, a Political Union—destined to be the most power-ful of many such—was formed late in 1829, under the chairmanship of the banker Thomas Attwood. It was a "Political Union of the Lower and Middle Classes of the People," whose object it became "to collect and organize the moral power of the country for the restora-tion of the people's rights, to conciliate the passions, the prejudices, and the interests of all, and to bring all to unite in one common bond of union together."[4] These unions were to serve the dual purpose of bringing to bear and yet containing within safe bounds popular pressures for reform; and, as such, they played an important role both in achieving eventual passage of the act and avoiding major violence in the course of the agitation for it.

At this point, early in 1830, someone like Lord Grey was not fully convinced of the necessity for parliamentary reform, feeling that public opinion was not yet ripe for it. Then, in June, came the death of George IV, who had been closely attached to the Duke of Welling-ton as well as unalterably opposed to Grey, and whose general politi-cal tendencies were openly anti-reformist. His successor, William IV, the "Sailor King," did not share his predecessor's prejudices about these political personalities; and, though in fact by no means sympa-thetic to popular aspirations, was supposed by the general public to

4. "Proceedings" of the Birmingham Political Union, quoted by Asa Briggs, *The Age of Improvement* (London, 1959), 247–8.

favor reform. The Whigs began to hope that at the forthcoming elections—which had to follow upon the death of a monarch—they might do well enough to gain power. Those elections were still in progress when news arrived in England of the French July Revolution, which, in three bloodless days, had driven Charles X from his throne, with the French middle and working classes acting in concord to depose him.

The effect of this news on the elections themselves was not as great as historians had up to recently supposed, since the borough contests had already been concluded when it arrived. But there is no doubt that the spectacle of a successful and bloodless revolution against despotism and privilege across the Channel played its part in encouraging those who were, in any event, advocating changes in the English system. Perhaps, as Macaulay (who spent some days in Paris just a few weeks after the July Revolution) pointed out in one of his reform speeches, it did not so much generate liberal sentiments as show the extent to which those sentiments had already advanced. They were strikingly demonstrated in the great victory won by Brougham, the outstanding political figure on the Whig side, in the county of Yorkshire, where, as a tribute to him, his election expenses were paid for him by the freeholders.

The Wellington ministry, with little more than a technical majority, returned to office, but was not secure. Even the main body of the Tories was gradually becoming convinced that some reform of the representation had become inevitable.

Then, in the autumn of 1830, disturbances broke out in the country districts of southeastern England. The causes varied: exorbitant tithes and rents, low wages, and the harsh game laws were chief among them. The protest movement was set off by the introduction of threshing machines which threatened to deprive people of work. Their reaction was to smash the machines and to set fire to ricks. Rural incendiarism, or "Captain Swing" (so named after the swinging stick or flail used in threshing) was abroad; and the disturbances spread westwards and northwards from Kent.[5] At the same time strikes broke out in some of the northern industrial towns. The grievances involved in both movements were physical and economic; those who took part in them, not by any means the lowest of the low but respectable workingmen, felt, rightly, that Parliament was not doing anything to ameliorate their conditions. To them it seemed to

5. See George Rudé, *The Crowd in History: A Study of Popular Disturbances in France and England* (New York, 1964), 150–6; also E. J. Hobsbawn and George Rudé, *Captain Swing* (London, 1969).

be in the grip of the landed aristocracy and gentry, indifferent to their privations and sufferings. The existing constitutional structure appeared to be bound up with the appalling conditions they had to face during this miserable autumn. And it was now, on November 2, 1830, that the Duke of Wellington chose to declare that the English constitution needed no reform, for the very simple reason that it was perfect. "If," he said,

I had imposed on me the duty of forming a legislature for any country, and particularly for a country like this, in possession of great property of various descriptions, I do not mean to assert that I could form such a legislature as you possess now, for the nature of man is incapable of reaching such excellence at once; but my great endeavour would be to form some description of legislature which would produce the same results.[6]

This declaration on the part of the Duke, so patently untrue, so clearly expressive of that very upper-class arrogance which, as much as any specific measures, continually irritated those outside the pale, meant the end of any hopes Wellington might have entertained of staying in office. As Macaulay was to put it in his speech of July 5, 1831:

What followed? Everything was tumult and panic. The funds fell. The streets were insecure. Men's hearts failed them for fear. We began to move our property into German investments and American investments. Such was the state of the public mind, that it was not thought safe to let the Sovereign pass from his palace to the Guildhall of his capital.[7]

Francis Place, the Radical tailor, who played such a prominent part in organizing popular pressure for the passage of the Reform Bill, noted that the cancellation of the King's visit to the City marked the first time that apprehension of violence by the people against an administration induced it openly to change its plan of proceeding, and thus constituted the beginning of what he called the "British Revolution."[8] Rumors of violence and insurrection became widespread. Reform petitions poured in from all over the country. The inevitable end of Wellington's ministry came on November 16.

After a generation in the wilderness, the Whigs returned to power.

6. Quoted by J. R. M. Butler, *The Passing of the Great Reform Bill* (London, 1914), 97.

7. *Works*, XI, 437.

8. Place to Hobhouse, November 8, 1830, quoted by Joseph Hamburger, *James Mill and the Art of Revolution* (New Haven, Conn., 1963), 17.

Lord Grey accepted the royal request that he become Prime Minister after the King agreed to his condition that he should be able to bring in parliamentary reform. His cabinet was really a coalition, including as it did not only Lord Durham, Grey's son-in-law and a Radical Whig, representatives of the Foxite tradition such as Lords Lansdowne and Holland (the latter Fox's nephew), but also several Canningites, and even one ultra-Tory. It was a cabinet that could hardly have been more aristocratic in its composition. Only two men in it were not either themselves peers or heirs to peerages. It exemplified strikingly the workings of the Whig "cousinhood," not merely by its roll call of names—Spencer, Russell, Richmond, Stanley, Ponsonby—but also by its nepotism. Lord Grey, for instance, not only had a son-in-law in the cabinet, but a son at the Colonial Office, a cousin in charge of Woods and Forests, and a brother-in-law at the Treasury. On the other hand, Brougham, by all odds the most brilliant of the Whigs, but outside the charmed circle, was considered too edgy and unreliable a personality to become leader of the party in the House of Commons. After he had turned down as an insult the offer to become Attorney-General, he went to the Lords as Lord Chancellor.

All this should serve as a reminder that the Reform ministry seemed, on the face of it, to hold out no great threat to the established order. The Tories were not too unhappy about it. They had reconciled themselves to the fact that some reform would probably have to come. And the passage of Roman Catholic emancipation had removed what had up to that point been the principal issue between the two parties. From the other side of the fence, the vantage point of the working class, the Whigs seemed, to put it mildly, not much better than the Tories. Between November 1830 and March 1831, over 1,400 rioters were brought to trial, of whom 9 were sentenced to hang, 657 sent to prison, and 464 transported.[9] That, of course, was the work of the courts; but it was done with the full approval and, through the Home Secretary, Melbourne, with the assistance of the ministry.

At the same time, those articulate Radicals who had been working for a major reform of the "unstamped" press, in order to bring cheaper reading on current events to the working classes—men such as Hetherington, editor of the *Poor Man's Guardian*—were also severely punished, on charges of evading stamp duty, or—in the case of Richard Carlile—of inciting to riot. It would certainly be a grave

9. Figures from Rudé, *Crowd in History*, 154–5.

error to regard this Whig ministry as notably humanitarian and liberal. William Cobbett, prosecuted for incitement to incendiarism, said that the Whigs had started more political prosecutions in seven months than the Tories had in as many years.

Yet when its parliamentary reform proposals were actually presented to the House, they surprised friend and foe alike by their scope. Lord Grey's instructions to the committee drafting the bill had been that the measure should be "large enough to satisfy public opinion and to afford sure ground of resistance to further innovations," while maintaining the essential character of the constitution. The drafting committee of four—among whom were Grey's son-in-law, "Radical Jack" Durham, and Lord John Russell—interpreted this commission very broadly, and when Russell revealed the plan, kept secret until then, to an expectant House of Commons on March 1, it caused general amazement and much dismay, not only among the Tories, but among men of both parties.

No less than sixty boroughs—those with a population of less than two thousand inhabitants—were to lose both their representatives. Forty-eight more—those with a population of less than four thousand inhabitants—were to lose one respresentative in Parliament. Of the seats released in this way, forty-two were to go to boroughs hitherto unrepresented, such as the great industrial centers of Birmingham, Manchester, and Leeds, and to increase the representation of metropolitan London. Fifty-five were to go to the counties—a significant proposal revealing the extent to which the ministry was still thinking of the landed interest as the most important in the state. Nine seats were to go to Scotland, Ireland, and Wales. The rest would not be reassigned, and this would result in a decrease in the total size of the House. The vote from now on was to be given in the towns to all those occupying houses of which the annual rentable value was at least £10 a year. The vote in the counties remained with the forty-shilling freeholders. The effect of these proposals, Russell stated, would be to give the property of the country, whether landed, industrial, or commercial, proper representation.

To many in the House of Commons, Russell's proposals seemed to indicate nothing less than a major revision of the constitution. One-quarter of the English borough seats were to be wiped out at a single stroke. While Members of Parliament were shocked, many in the country at large were delighted. Radicals of all shades had not dared to hope for this much, and were pleased. And popular support of the measure was such that some of the moderate Whigs, initially unfavorable, quickly came around to the proposals.

In view of Lord Grey's previously hesitant attitude on the question of parliamentary reform, why had the government gone so far? Several reasons lay to hand. For one thing, the Whigs had seen two of "their" measures, repeal of the Test and Corporation Acts and Catholic emancipation, passed by the other side, and themselves, though they had helped from the Opposition benches to ensure their passage, deprived of any credit. They did not want this to happen again. For another, with much of public opinion now regarding the borough-mongers as exemplifying a corrupt and outworn system, a bold rather than a timid measure seemed indicated; especially since it was assumed that the Tories stood to lose more by the terms of the bill than the Whigs. Durham, one of the four who drafted the bill, was in touch with public opinion of all shades; and it was he who saw that a daring rather than a lukewarm measure would best satisfy it. Another advantage of presenting a bold proposal was the finality implicit in it. A large amount of concession at this time would bring to the side of the governing classes forces that otherwise, disgusted with mild and merely temporizing measures, might well join hands with forces the Whigs feared as much as the Tories—the "lower orders," bent on a real social upheaval, with no respect paid to property.

THIS IS NOT THE PLACE TO RECOUNT ONCE AGAIN THE COMPLEX STORY of the passing of the Reform Bill. But it is well to be aware of the critical points in the long struggle, and we are fortunate that, thanks to his letters, we can observe some of them through Macaulay's own eyes. The second reading of the bill, crucial for its successful passage through the House of Commons, took place three weeks after its introduction, during the night between March 22 and March 23, 1831. Macaulay, in a letter to his friend Thomas Flower Ellis, has left us a famous description of this event which, however often it is quoted, never seems to lose its power and immediacy:

Such a scene as the division of last Tuesday I never saw, and never expect to see again. If I should live fifty years—the impression of it will be as fresh and sharp in my mind as if it had just taken place. It was like seeing Cæsar stabbed in the Senate House, or seeing Oliver taking the mace from the table, a sight to be seen only once and never to be forgotten.

The crowd overflowed the House in every part. When the strangers were cleared out and the doors locked we had six hundred and eight members present, more by fifty five than ever were at a division before. The Ayes and Noes were like two volleys of cannon from opposite sides of a field of battle. When the opposition went out into the lobby,—an operation by the bye which took up twenty minutes or more,—we spread ourselves over the benches on both sides of the House—For there were many of us who had not been able to find a seat during the evening—When the doors were shut we began to speculate on our numbers—Everybody was desponding—"We have lost it—We are only two hundred and eighty at most—I do not think we are two hundred and fifty—They are three hundred. Alderman Thompson has counted them—He says they are two hundred and ninety nine." This was the talk on our benches. I wonder that men who have been long in Parliament do not acquire a better coup d'œil for numbers. The House when only the Ayes were in it looked to me a very fair House,—much fuller than it generally is even on debates of considerable interest. I had no hope however of three hundred. As the tellers passed along our lowest row on the left hand side the interest was insupportable,—two hundred and ninety one:—two hundred and ninety two:—we were all standing up and stretching forward, telling with the tellers—At three hundred there was a short cry of joy, at three hundred and two another—suppressed however in a moment—for we did not yet know what the hostile force might be. We knew however that we could not be severely beaten—The doors were thrown open and in they came. Each of them as he entered brought some different report of their numbers. It must have been impossible, as you may conceive, in the lobby, crowded as they [were] to form any exact estimate. First we heard that they were three hundred and three—then the number rose to three hundred and ten, then went down to three hundred and seven. Alexander Baring told me that he had counted and that they were three hundred and four. We were all breathless with anxiety, when Charles Wood who stood near the door jumped on a bench and cried out—"They are only three hundred and one." We set up a shout that you might have heard to Charing Cross—waving our hats—stamping against the floor & clapping our hands—The tellers scarcely got through the crowd:—for the House was thronged up to the table, and all the floor was fluctuating with heads like the pit of a theatre. But you might have heard a pin drop as Duncannon read the numbers. Then again the shouts broke out—and many of us shed tears—I could scarcely refrain—And the jaw of Peel fell; and the face of Twiss was as the face of a damned soul; and Herries looked like Judas taking his neck-cloth off for the last operation. We shook hands and clapped each other on the back, and went out laughing, crying, and huzzaing into the lobby. And no sooner were the outer doors opened than another shout answered that within the house.

All the passages and the stairs into the waiting rooms were thronged by people who had waited till four in the morning to know the issue. We passed through a narrow lane between two thick masses of them; and all the way down they were shouting and waving their hats; till we got into the open air. I called a cabriolet—and the first thing the driver asked was, "Is the Bill carried?"—"Yes, by one."—"Thank God for it, Sir."— And away I rode to Gray's Inn—and so ended a scene which will probably never be equalled till the reformed Parliament wants reforming; and that I hope will not be till the days of our grandchildren. . . .[10]

After the second reading, the bill came before a committee of the whole House for discussion in detail; and it was during this phase, in April, that a Tory motion against reducing the total number of Members of Parliament for England and Wales was carried by eight votes. The King then consented to a dissolution of Parliament so that elections could be held, and the electorate, such as it was, could express its feelings. This election, as Halévy has pointed out,[11] was not to decide on a legislature to govern the country for a number of years, but on a species of constituent assembly whose sole task it would be to pass a Reform Bill. The election constituted a triumph for the Whigs, increasing their parliamentary majority. They thereupon brought in a new Reform Bill in June 1831, and this had passed through all its stages in the Commons by September.

In mid-September, Macaulay had become convinced that the next three weeks would bring to an issue the question of reform or revolution. For the bill was about to go to the House of Lords, predominantly Tory, where it was sure to be turned down. And public opinion and agitation, getting stronger with every week's delay, were becoming increasingly vigorous in favor of the bill and in opposition to those who were putting obstacles in its path. Even at this point, there was some feeling that the only possible way in which the bill could ever be passed by the House of Lords was through the creation by the King—or at least the threat of such a creation—of sufficient Whig peers to outweigh those opposed to the bill. And this is exactly what Macaulay told his patron, Lord Lansdowne, never a very energetic reformer at best. The latter, Macaulay reported to his sister Hannah, "with the feeling natural to a nobleman of such ancient and such high rank, demurred." He expected the bill to be lost in the Lords, and foresaw, following upon this defeat, the return of the Tories. Macaulay, on the other hand, did not want to give up

10. T.B.M. to Ellis, March 30, 1831, Clive and Pinney, eds., *Macaulay*, 427–30.
11. *The Triumph of Reform, 1830–1841* (New York, 1961), 32.

easily. "If nobody else will move an address to the Crown against a Tory Ministry," he wrote, "I will."[12]

At the end of September, Macaulay, like most Whigs, found himself "extremely blue" about the forthcoming division in the House of Lords. The phrase is Margaret's. She informed a correspondent that Tom, "whose imagination you know often exaggerates," was talking in the strongest terms about the dangers to be apprehended, and prophesied that blood would flow in London before the end of the week. Some people, she reported, expected Peel, one of the bill's chief opponents, to be pelted to death.[13] Before the bill went to the Lords, it was given its third reading after an all-night session in the Commons, with the final vote taken at half-past four in the morning. We have a vivid description of this scene by Bulwer-Lytton, an eye-witness:

The candles, with the exception of the centre lustre, were burnt down to the sockets, and the continued fatigues and the series of late hours we had undergone for so many weeks made themselves strikingly visible at that hour and by that light in the persons of most of the dark mass that filled the chamber.

It was broad daylight when Members emerged. " 'Thank Heaven,' said we all, 'we have done with the Bill at last!' "[14] But they had not done with it after all.

In the event, the House of Lords rejected the second Reform Bill on October 8. Riots broke out in Nottingham and Derby; and at the end of the month, the Bishop's Palace and a number of other buildings were burned by an angry crowd in Bristol. Parliament was prorogued. The ministers proved less pusillanimous than Macaulay had feared and announced that they would go ahead with a third Reform Bill, which was duly introduced in December. It was substantially the same measure as its predecessors; with some reduction, however, of the number of boroughs condemned to lose one MP. Once again it was clear that the real crisis for the bill would come when it reached the Lords. And once again Macaulay, for his part, saw the only solution in the royal willingness to create more peers upon the recommendation of the ministry. In March 1832, his sister

12. T.B.M. to Hannah Macaulay, September 13, 1831, Trinity Correspondence.

13. Margaret Macaulay to Henry J. Thatcher, September 30, 1831, Huntington MSS.

14. Earl of Lytton, *The Life of Edward Bulwer, First Lord Lytton* (2 vols., London, 1913), I, 419, 421.

Margaret quoted Tom's parody of the nursery song "Twenty Pounds Shall Marry Me":

> *What though now opposed I be?*
> *Twenty peers shall carry me.*
> *If twenty won't, thirty will,*
> *For I'm his Majesty's bouncing Bill.*[15]

He was distressed, at the same time, at the thought that some of the ministers were still shrinking from advising the King to create peers. He went so far as to tell Margaret that if ministers failed to do this, he would take the Chiltern Hundreds, that is, resign from Parliament.[16]

The House of Lords passed the second reading of the bill in April, by a majority of nine; but in the subsequent debate carried a motion postponing its disfranchisement clauses until the rest of the bill had been settled—a direct challenge to the Commons. Lord Grey thereupon asked the King to create fifty new peers, but William IV refused to go beyond twenty. Upon which the ministry resigned. The King then asked Wellington to form a government, in order to introduce a more moderate measure of reform. Now public opinion, overwhelmingly in favor of the Whig bill, made itself felt in strength. Macaulay later commented that France could boast of its July days. "But I will boast of our ten days in May." For they had witnessed "the pacific and blameless triumph of a great people."[17] The threat of general disorder, in the background all along, became more intense as Francis Place and other Radical leaders organized a run on the banks. Wellington's own party was not with him, since now as before Peel refused to participate in bringing forward a parliamentary reform measure. Thus the Duke was unable to proceed, leaving the Whigs in a position to write their own terms for their return. These were that the King should now pledge himself to create as many peers as were required to carry the bill through the House of Lords. This pledge they received, and when the royal promise became known, the Tory leaders in the Lords dropped their intransigence, and the Reform Bill was finally passed on June 4, 1832.

Demonstrating a conspicuous (and calculated) lack of royal grace, the King did not himself give his assent to the bill, but left it to be

15. Trevelyan, *Life and Letters*, 138. 16. Margaret Macaulay, *Recollections*, 96.
17. Trevelyan, *Life and Letters*, 206.

given by commissioners—a proceeding in which Macaulay saw proof of William IV's enmity to his ministers and to his people. "What madness!" he wrote to two of his sisters. "To give more to his subjects than any King ever gave, and yet to give in such a manner as to get no thanks!"[18]

MACAULAY'S GREAT REPUTATION AS A PARLIAMENTARY ORATOR DE-rived from the part he played in the Reform Bill debates. But he had delivered his maiden speech almost a year before these debates began, on the affirmative side of the question as to whether Jews should be admitted to sit in Parliament. The speech, like the essay he wrote on the same subject, showed at their best his common sense and his remarkable ability to get to the root of the matter. To the argument that the Jews were "a people," who could therefore never become Englishmen, he replied: Let us first try the experiment by making Englishmen of them. Then we shall see whether or not they will become members of the national community. What was the point, Macaulay asked, of depriving the Jews of *political* power and its symbols—maces, gold chains, skins of parchment, with pieces of wax—while letting them possess what in fact was *real* power, that is, the power to own property and to obtain knowledge? A Jew could be the richest man in England, he could own all of London; which made depriving him of the ability to sit in the House of Commons ludicrous. The argument from legal prescription made no sense, either. Laws could and should be changed. Three hundred years ago, the Jews had had no legal right to be in England, six hundred years ago they had had no right to have teeth in their heads. It was up to the opponents of the measure to prove that some danger to the state existed in admitting Jews to Parliament. Failing such proof, their exclusion would be sheer persecution.[19]

Sir James Mackintosh, who had written a memorable reply to Burke's *Reflections,* and who was probably the leading intellect among the Whigs, rose to say that he could find no defect in Ma-caulay's speech, that it was in every way worthy of the name the speaker bore. The honor of receiving such praise from so distin-guished a figure was followed by more tangible rewards from the

18. T.B.M. to Hannah and Margaret, June 8, 1832, Morgan MSS.
19. April 5, 1830, *Hansard,* n.s., XXIII (1830), 1308–14.

Jewish community. One of their number, the banker Isaac Lyon Goldsmid, a leading figure among the English Jews pressing for emancipation, gave a great party in the precincts of the House of Commons for all supporters of Macaulay's speech. Tom reported the party to his sister Margaret the following day "in a sort of recitative manner":

> *I dined with a Jew,*
> *Such Christians are few,*
> *He gave me no ham,*
> *But plenty of lamb.*
> *And three sorts of fishes,*
> *And thirty made dishes.*
> *I drank his champagne*
> *Again and again.*
> *I drank up his hock*
> *Until ten o'clock.*
> *I drank up his claret*
> *Till up came my char'ot.*
> *And when 'twas eleven,*
> *I thought 'twas but seven.*
> *O Christians whose feasts*
> *Are scarce fit for beasts,*
> *Example take you*
> *By this worthy old Jew.*[20]

Things must have gone very well, for when Margaret asked him how he felt after his maiden speech, her brother replied: "Oh, desperate, you know! Quite desperate!"

Macaulay spoke again, in the course of the debate on the bill to abolish the death penalty for forgery, on June 7, 1830. His sister Selina noted in her journal that the speech was admired extremely as to matter, "but all who heard it agree in saying that he speaks far too rapidly and thus weakens very much the effect of what he says." Tom spoke so fast that the reporters were unable to follow him. He himself was determined in future to talk more slowly, but felt that he would find it exceedingly difficult to do so when animated in debate.[21] It was a fault he was never able to correct. One knowledgeable listener compared his "inconceivable velocity" with that of an

20. Margaret Macaulay, *Recollections*, 10.
21. Selina Macaulay, Journal, June 12, 1830, Huntington, MSS.

express train which did not stop, even at the chief stations.[22] Great speed was not an entirely negative factor. It meant, as one admiring witness of the Reform Bill speeches remarked, that Macaulay got over the ground he covered so rapidly that there was never a moment of tedium or satiety for his hearers.[23] Yet he was bound at times to leave them behind.

His voice was far from ideal for an orator. One listener called it "pitched in alto, monotonous, and rather shrill."[24] A famous description of one of Macaulay's Reform Bill speeches depicted "a little man of small voice, and affected utterance, clipping his words, and hissing like a serpent."[25] But what made up for these technical defects was the force of the argument, the depth of learning, the aptness of the historical illustrations—what Peel, no ally of Macaulay's, called "that wonderful flow of natural and beautiful language" with its "rich freight of thought and fancy."[26] With all that, he was, as his parliamentary colleagues soon came to realize, not a good debater, ready to reply on the spur of the moment to points of detail made by other speakers. As the diarist Greville put it: "Macaulay is very brilliant, but his speeches are harangues and never replies."[27] This criticism was just, and the object of it agreed with the critic. It may have been partly because of his own inability to excel in the art of debate that Macaulay later called it the most serious evil of popular government, since it demanded the separation of the faculty of argument from the capacity of belief. Talent for debate tended to impair talent for close reasoning and enlarged speculation.[28]

This is how Bulwer-Lytton, who heard him speak during the Reform Bill debates, recalled Macaulay's oratorical manner:

22. The listener was G. H. Francis. See G. H. Jennings, ed., *An Anecdotal History of the British Parliament from the Earliest Periods to the Present Time* (New York, 1881) , 281.

23. Hardcastle, ed., *Campbell,* II, 56.

24. *Anecdotal History of Parliament,* 281.

25. Arnold, *Public Life of Lord Macaulay,* 85.

26. Margaret's Journal, March 15, 1832, Trevelyan, *Life and Letters,* 138–9. It is worth noting the following reminiscence of the effect of T.B.M.'s oratorical skill: "One great speech of his on the Reform question I heard. . . . The House was entranced, almost breathless: and I recollect that, when I overtook him the same night walking home, I could hardly believe that the little, draggled, ordinary-looking man plodding by himself up the Strand was the same creature whom I had seen holding the House of Commons absorbed as the Opera house is by a first-rate singer." John L. Adolphus to H. H. Milman, December 14, 1861, Trinity MSS.

27. September 24, 1831, Wilson, ed., *Greville Diary,* II, 164.

28. T.B.M., "Gladstone on Church and State" (1839) , *Works,* IX, 113.

> *. . . first the speaker view,*
> *The bold broad front paled to the scholar's hue,*
> *And eye abstracted in its still, clear blue.*
> *Firm on the floor he sets his solid stand,*
> *Rare is his gesture, scarcely moves a hand,*
> *Full and deep-mouth'd, as from a cave profound,*
> *Comes his strong utterance with one burst of sound,*
> *Save when it splits into a strange wild key,*
> *Like hissing winds that struggle to be free.*
> *And at the close, the emotions, too represt*
> *By the curb'd action, o'erfatigue the breast,*
> *And the voice breaks upon the captive ear,*
> *And by its failure, proves the rage sincere.*
> *His style not essay, if you once admit*
> *Speech as sense spoken, essay as sense writ.*[29]

Macaulay's approach in his speeches was primarily philosophical; though, as we shall see, he was not above strategic considerations when he thought them warranted. He meticulously prepared his speeches, not by writing them down—for, as he once told Bulwer-Lytton, he never put into writing what was intended to be spoken on the principle that, writing them down, words would lose the vivacity essential for effective oratory—but by composing, revising, and rehearsing them all in his head, relying on his memory to serve him in the course of actual delivery. He tried out his speeches on his sisters who, he told them, served him as public tasters.[30] It was to one of them, Margaret, that he confided what he considered to be the secret of real eloquence—plan and order, the right thing said in the right place, but all with apparent carelessness and unconsciousness: "A mighty maze, but not without a plan."[31] His speeches were so thoroughly prepared with a particular date of delivery in mind that Margaret noted in her journal about one of them that it was "spoken a day sooner than was intended and the last touches were not put to it."[32]

This extensive preparation was perhaps responsible for the criticism made by some of his friends that his manner of speaking was too cold. "I feel this myself," he wrote. "Nothing but strong excitement,

29. Bulwer-Lytton, "St. Stephen's," *Blackwood's* (1860) , 288–9.
30. Ibid., 289; Margaret Macaulay, *Recollections*, 90; Arnold, *Public Life*, 352–3.
31. October 10, 1831, Margaret Macaulay, *Recollections*, 44.
32. December 30, 1831, ibid., 70.

and a great occasion overcomes a certain reserve and *mauvaise honte* which I have in public speaking," and which kept him from putting sufficient fervor into his tone or action. This defect, however, had another, more advantageous side. "For," he wrote, "when I *do* warm, I am the most vehement speaker in the House, and nothing strikes an audience so much as the animation of an actor who is generally cold."[33]

One occasion upon which he certainly did "warm," to immense effect, was that of his first speech on the Reform Bill, delivered the day after its introduction into the House of Commons. By the time the Reform Bill debates got under way, he had become used to the unique atmosphere of the House. "I feel the whole character of the place growing upon me," he had noted a few weeks before. "I begin to like what others about me like, and to disapprove what they disapprove."[34] Thus he now addressed the House no longer as a novice, feeling his way, but as someone familiar with its standards of judgment and with what it expected from those who rose to speak.

The date was March 2, 1831, and his sister Margaret was quite right in confiding to her journal a few days later that her brother, whom she called her "hero," now stood before the world a different man from what he had been on the morning of that fateful day. He had had a bad cold, which had affected his voice. This, added to his over-excitement, made him scream at times, at which some of the Opposition tittered. He became exhausted by the passionate tone in which he delivered parts of his speech, so that Sir James Mackintosh offered him refreshment in the form of some oranges.[35] And he rallied. Even now as one reads the peroration of that speech, one can easily imagine the excitement that must have overtaken the House as it listened to the short, squat figure, in a frenzy of passion, deliver this earnest appeal:

Now, therefore, while every thing at home and abroad forebodes ruin to those who persist in a hopeless struggle against the spirit of the age, now, while the crash of the proudest throne of the continent is still resounding in our ears, now, while the roof of a British palace affords an ignominious shelter to the exiled heir of forty kings, now, while we see on every side ancient institutions subverted, and great societies dissolved, now, while the heart of England is still sound, now, while old feelings and old associations retain a power and a charm which may too soon pass away,

33. T.B.M. to Hannah, August 5, 1831, Trinity Correspondence.
34. T.B.M. to Whewell, February, 1831, *Anecdotal History of Parliament*, 284.
35. Margaret Macaulay, *Recollections*, 26.

now, in this your accepted time, now, in this your day of salvation, take counsel, not of prejudice, not of party spirit, not of the ignominious pride of a fatal consistency, but of history, of reason, of the ages which are past, of the signs of this most portentous time. Pronounce in a manner worthy of the expectation with which this great debate has been anticipated, and of the long remembrance which it will leave behind. Renew the youth of the State. Save property, divided against itself. Save the multitude, endangered by its own ungovernable passions. Save the aristocracy, endangered by its own unpopular power. Save the greatest, and fairest, and most highly civilized community that ever existed, from calamities which may in a few days sweep away all the rich heritage of so many ages of wisdom and glory. The danger is terrible. The time is short. If this bill should be rejected, I pray to God that none of those who concur in rejecting it may ever remember their votes with unavailing remorse, amidst the wreck of laws, the confusion of ranks, the spoliation of property, and the dissolution of social order.[36]

The triumph was complete. It was no wonder that many years later he was to call this day an epoch in his own life as well as in that of the nation.[37] He had accomplished with a single speech what six years before he had accomplished with a single article. "Milton" had made him famous as an essayist of dazzling talents. His first speech on reform repeated and extended that earlier success. Friend and foe were quick with compliments and felicitations. The Speaker sent for him and told him that in all his long experience he had never seen the House in a comparable state of excitement. Mackintosh, no mean judge, thought the speech one of the finest ever spoken in Parliament.[38] Peel remarked that parts of it were as beautiful as anything he had ever heard or read. It reminded him, he said, of the old times.[39]

Comparison with the great parliamentary orators of the past—

36. *Works*, XI, 425-6. That T.B.M. must have studied Brougham's speeches with some care becomes evident when one compares this peroration with that of Brougham's speech in defense of Queen Caroline, October 4, 1820: "Save the country—save yourselves. Rescue the country; save the people, of whom you are the ornaments; but, severed from whom, you can no more live than the blossom that is severed from the root and tree on which it grows. Save the country, therefore, that you may continue to adorn it—save the crown, which is threatened with irreparable injury—save the aristocracy, which is surrounded with danger—save the altar, which is no longer safe when its kindred is shaken." Roger Fulford, *The Trial of Queen Caroline* (New York, 1968), 135.

37. Trinity Journal, February 23, 1854.

38. Mackintosh to Miss Allen, March 8, 1831, R. J. Mackintosh, ed., *Memoirs of the Life of the Rt. Honourable Sir James Mackintosh* (2 vols., London, 1835), II, 480.

39. Margaret Macaulay, *Recollections*, 27.

Burke, Fox, Canning—became a stock form of the compliments paid Macaulay as he continued to deliver his set speeches during the long and arduous debates that followed the introduction of the bill. And the debates were arduous. Many of them continued into the early morning—in Macaulay's words, "hallooing, crying *question* and dividing" until 5 A.M.[40]—in a chamber so hot and stuffy that he compared it one July afternoon to the hold of a slave ship, with 450 people stowed together.[41] The topic of reform caused so much concern in the outside world that a prominent physician solemnly told the singer-poet Tom Moore about "more than one or two instances" he had encountered in his practice of illness brought on by anxiety and alarm about the bill.[42] Inside Parliament, the toll, according to Macaulay, was far greater. He believed that by the autumn of 1831 there were about fifty MP's who had done irreparable injury to their health by attending the debates.[43]

Macaulay himself retained good health. He reported to his sister Hannah in August that he blushed to say that he was still "a dumpling of a fellow," as *Blackwood's* had just then called him.[44] In the August issue of that Tory periodical, he had been referred to as "an ugly, cross-made, splay-footed, shapeless little dumpling of a fellow, with a featureless face too—except indeed a good expansive forehead—sleek puritanical sandy hair—large glimmering eyes—and a mouth from ear to ear. He has a lisp and a burr, moreover, and speaks thickly and huskily for several minutes before he gets into the swing of his discourse." But even *Blackwood's* had had to concede that once Macaulay got into his swing, nothing could be more dazzling than his performance. Even though what he was saying was "of course" mere stuff and nonsense, "it is so well worded, and so volubly and forcibly delivered—there is such an endless string of epigram and antithesis—such a flashing of epithets—such an accumulation of images—and the voice is so trumpetlike and the action so grotesquely emphatic, that you might hear a pin drop in the House."[45]

As one of his parliamentary colleagues said, "He has the power of coming forward on great occasions with a speech that commands the

40. T.B.M. to Hannah, August 3, 1831, Trinity Correspondence.
41. T.B.M. to Hannah [July 30, 1831], Trevelyan, *Life and Letters*, 172.
42. April 27, 1831, Peter Quennell, ed., *The Journal of Thomas Moore, 1818–1841* (New York, 1964), 204.
43. T.B.M. to Ellis, October 17, 1831, Trevelyan, *Life and Letters*, 179.
44. T.B.M. to Hannah, May 8, 1831, Trinity Correspondence.
45. August 1831, [Wilson], *Noctes*, IV, 356.

House."[46] All the world certainly agreed with this judgment, from the anonymous fat man in the House of Commons Gallery who had been greatly upset about the dullness of the previous speaker, but who, when Macaulay had spoken just a little while, turned to his neighbor (who happened to be Tom's brother Charles) to remark with relief: "Well, now this is something like,"[47] to the principal Whig leaders who agreed that his speeches were the best that had been heard in the House since the death of Fox.[48]

How did he achieve this overwhelming effect, when his voice and his manner left so much to be desired; when it was clear that he was delivering previously memorized orations? The best answer to this question is to be found in an eyewitness description by a Whig Member of Parliament, E. J. Littleton, who commented as follows in his diary on Macaulay's speech of December 16, 1831:

Macaulay made one of those brilliant speeches, his third on the Reform question, which carried the House away in the same furious whirlwind of mixed passions which seemed to seize himself. Never was a more extraordinary compound of deep philosophy, exalted sentiments, and party bitterness, enunciated with a warmth, a vigour, and rapidity inconceivable. The public can collect but little of its character from the papers. It is like the course of the meteor, never to be forgotten by those who have the fortune to see it, but seen but by a few, and to be known to others only by description.[49]

It was the combination of the intellectual weight of the speeches with the whirlwind of passion which seized Macaulay when he delivered certain passages that made his auditors ignore the lisp, the excessive speed of his delivery, and the unpleasantly pitched voice.

From whence did Macaulay draw those reserves of passion which enabled him, in the word of another who was present, to wrap "himself in the Reform Bill as in a mantle," and throw "its brilliant and attractive forms around him"?[50] Emphasis in any answer to this question should probably fall equally on his sense of history and his sense of drama. He was not, let it be said, "putting on a show," saying things he really did not believe, merely for effect. On the contrary,

46. Le Marchant's Diary, December 12, 1831, Arthur Aspinall, ed., *Three Early Nineteenth Century Diaries* (London, 1952), 169.

47. Margaret Macaulay to Henry Thatcher, September 30, 1831, Huntington MSS.

48. So Lady Holland told him. T.B.M. to Hannah, July 8, 1831, Trevelyan, *Life and Letters*, 166.

49. Littleton's Diary, December 17, 1831, Aspinall, *Diaries*, 171.

50. Arnold, *Public Life*, 86.

he was sincerely convinced that he was privileged to be among the participants in a historic occasion, and that there could only be one verdict—in favor of those committed to the bill—that history would pass on the actors. In the course of his memorable depiction to Ellis of the division on the second reading of the bill, he had (as we know) compared the spectacle to seeing Caesar stabbed in the Senate House, or Cromwell taking the mace from the table—sights to be seen once only and never to be forgotten.[51] He was filled with a sense of the historic uniqueness as well as the historic drama of the occasion and this lent force to his utterances.

He could well feel that all his life up to this point had in some measure been a preparation for the role he was now playing. We remember him at an early age, vehemently debating Roman history; later, taking the part of one of Harley's accusers in a historical re-enactment put on by his school. We remember him scoring his oratorical triumphs at the Cambridge Union, later delighting his father with his first public speech against slavery. No one was more conscious of historical precedents in English history for the crisis of 1831; no one was temperamentally more susceptible to the special atmosphere of the place and of the occasion.

It is easy to say, with Bagehot, that Macaulay "delivered marvellous rhetorical exercises on the Reform Bill"; to wonder at his looking for rotten boroughs in the Civil Wars; to point out humorously that he was so obsessed with the future that he regarded existing men as painful prerequisites for great-grandchildren.[52] Yet it was precisely his deep conviction that future generations would judge these debates, that the decisions being made *were* of crucial importance in the history of England, which raised his own dramatic awareness to a fever pitch he was able to convey to his listeners. It goes without saying that ministers did not conduct their deliberations on this philosophical and passionate level. They were hardheaded men, who wanted to save their order, and who were, in the words of G. M. Trevelyan, trying to save the Tories' (and, it should be added, their own) estates in the country and their seats in the

51. T.B.M. to Ellis, March 30, 1831, Trevelyan, *Life and Letters*, 146.
52. Norman St John-Stevas, ed., *The Collected Works of Walter Bagehot* (8 vols., Cambridge, Mass., 1965), I, 400, 403-4.

upper Chamber, by wresting from borough owners their irregular privilege of nominating members of the House of Commons.[53] But it would be a mistake to sum up Macaulay's part in the Reform Bill debates as one merely of spreading an oratorical mantle of history and philosophy over the hard realities that lay underneath.

This is not to say that many of his listeners on both sides of the House may not have dismissed his speeches as largely irrelevant display pieces. We know that some did. Even someone like John Cam Hobhouse, sympathetic to Macaulay's cause, dismissed the great peroration of his first speech on reform as "too long and too laboured."[54] But as far as Macaulay himself was concerned, the heightening of style and of manner was not so much distortion as something akin to the exhortations of a preacher to his congregation. It is not merely the biblical imagery to be found in the speeches that makes this comparison apt. Into them, Macaulay poured all the moral fervor that was his by inheritance and that he had not been able to bring to the faith of his father. His reform speeches were secular sermons. He was imbued not only with the righteousness of his cause, but also with the need for all reasonable men to act accordingly. At the same time, the drama of the hour exalted both his historical and his histrionic imagination. Thus he could speak, in the words of his sister, "burning words," to achieve, as she put it, "that mightiest of triumphs, the triumph of mind over mind."[55]

In his speeches on the Reform Bill, Macaulay was, of course trying to do more than merely score an impression on those present in the House. As he wrote in his essay on Chatham, the real audience of parliamentary orators had now become the nation. The three or four hundred persons in the Chamber during the delivery of an actual speech—and that meant a crowded House—might be pleased or disgusted by the voice and the action of the orator. "But, in the reports which are read the next day by hundreds of thousands, the difference between the noblest and meanest figure, between the richest and the shrillest tones, between the most graceful and the most uncouth gesture, altogether vanishes."[56] It should be remembered that parliamentary reporting in the early 1830's still left much

53. G. M. Trevelyan, *Lord Grey of the Reform Bill: Being the Life of Charles, Second Earl Grey* (London, 1929), 284.

54. March 2, 1831. Lady Dorchester, ed., Lord Broughton, *Recollections of a Long Life, with Additional Extracts from His Private Diaries* (6 vols., London, 1909–11), IV, 89.

55. February 9, 1832, Margaret Macaulay, *Recollections*, 78.

56. T.B.M., "Chatham" (1834), *Works*, VIII, 377.

to be desired in terms of accuracy and completeness. Still, *The Times* printed fairly reliable versions of what was said; and many of the major speeches were published separately by their authors. Thus, while there was not a little exaggeration in Macaulay's talk of "the nation" following the debates (characteristically, he automatically excluded from this category the many who could not read, and the many who could read but could not afford to buy newspapers), it was certainly true that his speeches were meant to reach a public outside the walls of Westminster as well as Members of Parliament.

The arguments in these speeches may be divided into two principal categories, positive and defensive. In positive terms, Macaulay argued that the chief aim of the Reform Bill was to admit the middle classes to a larger and more direct share in the representation, without administering a violent shock to the institutions of the country. The elective system had to be adapted to changes in society that had taken place since it was first devised. Some of the opponents of the bill claimed that the middle classes were already "virtually" represented in Parliament, as one of the many interest groups of which it was a "mirror." Macaulay dealt with this argument simply but forcefully, countering that if the function of indirect representation was to accomplish in a different way what direct representation accomplished, then why be afraid of direct representation? Passage of the bill, he argued repeatedly, would result in security against revolution, because by satisfying the middle classes with the vote, and giving representation to such large and wealthy cities as Manchester, Leeds, and Birmingham, it would be possible to prevent them from being driven to the side of radicalism and revolution. Landed and commercial property would be united, which was desirable not only in itself, but because in the face of a threat to property from below, it would be fatal for different kinds of property to engage in internecine warfare.

All this was hardly original. In fact, Lord John Russell had introduced his reform motion in March by stating that it would place the country "between the abuses we wish to amend, and the convulsions we hope to avert."[57] And, just to take one example, during the previous autumn the *Manchester Guardian* had stated that popular opinion was now moving strongly "in favour of an adaptation of our institutions to the present condition of society."[58] Nor were Macaulay's defensive arguments strikingly novel. Here, however, his

57. March 1, 1831, *Hansard*, 3rd series, II (1831), 1062.
58. *Manchester Guardian*, October 9, 1830, quoted by Butler, *Reform Bill*, 96.

task was more difficult, since he had to deploy them against a variety of opponents, ranging from extreme left to extreme right.

For it must be remembered that if that wing of the Radicals most closely tied to middle-class aspirations, men such as Francis Place, for instance, welcomed the Reform Bill and helped the ministry at strategic junctures by bringing to bear outside pressures in order to instill sufficient fear into the governing class to ensure its passage, there were also those on the Radical and working-class side who would not be satisfied with anything less than universal (male) suffrage and the secret ballot. On the other side of the political spectrum were those who felt that even a moderate measure of reform was too much; who, in the name of order, regarded any change in existing constitutional arrangements as tantamount to sacrilege. Macaulay's defensive arguments were directed against these two extreme groups; and, as many politicians have done since, he often tried to link the two in the popular imagination.

In answer to the democrats, very sparsely represented in the House by men like "Orator" Hunt and Daniel O'Connell, the Irish patriot, Macaulay took up the question: Why not universal suffrage? Why was there a need for any kind of pecuniary qualification? His answer showed much of the smugness and self-satisfaction that were to characterize Victorian attitudes to the working class. It also showed the convenient extent to which classical economics lent itself to rationalizations for withholding political rights from that class. The argument ran as follows: English workingmen, at times, found themselves in miserable circumstances. Some of these were beyond the ken of government action, that is, nothing could be done about them, they were inevitable. But a state of distress had the effect of blinding people's judgment, inflaming their passions, and thus making them an easy prey for flatterers who appealed to their coarser instincts. If they were sufficiently educated, they might be able to withstand such appeals. But they were not. Therefore, a pecuniary qualification (the £10 rate) was necessary, since it would serve to exclude from the vote those whose lack of education precluded them from making rational choices, but not from falling prey to evil flatterers. Workingmen must not be blamed for their political extremism, which was a product of their situation, in which they were particularly susceptible to doctrines taught them by "illiterate, incapable, lowminded flatterers." If universal suffrage were granted, then these doctrines would prevail; and, as a result, working-class distress would increase. Thus, it was in the interest of workingmen themselves that only the most industrious and respectable among them should be admitted to a share in the government of the state.[59]

There is something repelling about the tone in which Macaulay couched these arguments. "If only," he seemed to be saying, "the working classes were well enough educated to deserve the vote. But, alas, they are not, and so they cannot have it." It is not so much that, given his views and general orientation, one should have expected him to defend universal suffrage. But did he really have to adopt this attitude of—hardly genuine—regret at being prevented from doing so only by certain ineluctable circumstances? Did he have to speak of workingmen as children who could not be left alone, lest they be led astray by those offering them sweet things to eat? And, though his faith in education was undoubtedly genuine, one is also amazed by his curious assumption that once men had attained a modicum of wealth and education, they would be immune to flattery of this sort. In view of the fact that it was still a common occurrence for votes to be bought and sold by and to persons with a great deal of both money and education, it might well strike us as extraordinary for Macaulay to have advanced this particular claim at that time. Furthermore, Macaulay's emphasis on the benefits of education for the working classes came at a time when the Whig government was outdoing its Tory predecessors in attempts to enforce payment of stamp duty on newspapers; attempts which, had they been totally successful, would have made it virtually impossible for workingmen to further their political education by obtaining reading materials they could afford to buy.

Needless to say, this is a paradox that would never have occurred to Macaulay. He would doubtless have said, if confronted with this argument, that what *he* meant by "education" was not to be defined in terms of wicked Radical doctrines put about by the likes of Cobbett and Hetherington. To be educated, in his terms, meant, rather, to be immunized against these very doctrines. Echoes of the eighteenth-century charity schools seem still to resound with this definition. The truth was, of course, that neither Macaulay nor the great majority of his fellow reformers in Parliament had the slightest intention of enfranchising the working classes at this time. Thus he comforted those who were constantly talking about the danger of "a leap in the dark," who felt that Members elected by £10 householders would promote the interests of the journeymen against those of the capitalists, by recalling what solid men of character such

59. December 16, 1831, *Works*, XI, 487–8.

democratic boroughs as Westminster and Southwark had sent to the House of Commons.[60]

There exists a revealing letter from Edward Baines, the editor and proprietor of the Leeds *Mercury* and a prominent figure in Whig affairs in Yorkshire, to Lord John Russell, who had inquired from him "concerning the numbers and respectability of the £10 householders in Leeds." The answer was that in all of Leeds, not more than one in fifty of the working class would be enfranchised by the bill.[61] As it turned out, Macaulay campaigned for election in Leeds during the autumn of 1832. When asked during one of the election meetings whether he believed in household suffrage his answer, "in a tone of great animation and decision," was negative. "If a householder has a right," he countered, "why not a servant? Why not a lodger? These privileges are not a matter of right, but of utility." The nation had a right to be well governed, but there was no such thing as the natural right of every householder to the vote.

It would be in the highest degree unjust to upbraid Macaulay for not having wanted to enfranchise the working classes. He was, after all, a Whig, not a democrat; and, as we recall, had been brought into Parliament by Lord Lansdowne on the strength of his *Edinburgh Review* articles against the democratic tendencies of the Utilitarians. What could more justly be singled out for retrospective censure is the combination in him of complacent regret for the unfortunate inevitability of the workingman's lot with acquiescence in the repressive measures taken by the government; measures the intent of which was, in effect, to make sure that this state of inevitability was not to be changed.

There is one passage in his speeches on the Reform Bill—it occurs in one not included in his *Collected Speeches*—where Macaulay painted a moving description of the condition of the working classes. During the debate on the third reading of the third Reform Bill, he referred to those parts of the country

in which the rate of wages was scarcely sufficient for the support of animal life, in which the labourer, starved and wretched as he is, considers the parochial rates as a fund, not for his occasional relief, but for his daily maintenance; in which men may be met harnessed to cars like beasts of

60. September 20, 1831, *Works*, XI, 448–51. The phrase "leap in the dark" was, with Disraeli's use of it, to become a key one in the debates on the second Reform Bill.

61. Edward Baines to Lord John Russell, November 7, 1831, quoted by J. F. C. Harrison, ed., *Society and Politics in England, 1780–1960: A Selection of Readings and Comments* (New York, 1965), 135–7.

burthen, and in which the far-spreading light of midnight fires, and the outrages of incendiaries have but too often indicated wretchedness and despair, starvation and daring recklessness.[62]

But the passage was set in the context of his argument against those who claimed that no constitutional reform was needed, since the English people were the happiest under the sun.[63] There is something unpleasantly theoretical about Macaulay's use of the sufferings of the poor to make a debating point. In fact, his mention of incendiaries and midnight fires shows how real was the fear that underlay the rhetoric.

The major theme running through Macaulay's speeches during these turbulent months was that of fear of an outbreak of violence and revolution, unless timely concessions were granted. His speeches have been called unduly abstract. Bagehot wrote of them being captioned, "Now, a man came up from college and spoke thus."[64] This estimate is true up to a point. When Macaulay extolled the wonders of modern industry, for instance, one might well have wondered how many factories he had actually visited; just as his talk about the sufferings of the laboring poor might have made one wonder about the extent to which his sentiments were based on personal observation. Yet when he came to speak of the threat of violence, he was far removed from the realm of theory. Scholars are still arguing over whether at any point during the Reform Bill debates a "revolutionary situation" could be said to have existed. Arguments may be advanced on both sides of that question. Certainly, some of the fear of violence on the part of the governing classes may be accounted for by the excellent propaganda methods used by the Millite Radicals precisely for the purpose of inspiring it.[65] Yet we have seen that Macaulay, for one, was genuinely convinced of the possibility of major violence, if the bill continued to be blocked. Quite apart from the sacking of Bristol and the burning of Nottingham Castle at this time, there had after all been enough violence both in England and Ireland during the decade and a half preceding the Reform Bill debates for the "haves" to have gained a pretty good idea of what the "have-nots" were capable of doing.

It is interesting to find Francis Jeffrey, formerly editor of the *Edinburgh Review* and now Lord Advocate in the Reform government, writing early in 1831:

62. March 19, 1832, *Hansard*, 3rd series, XI (1832), 454-5.   63. Ibid., 453.
64. Bagehot, *Works*, I, 403.
65. See Hamburger, *Mill and Revolution*, for this interpretation.

the real battle that is soon to be fought, and the only one now worth providing for, is not between Whigs and Tories, Liberals and Illiberals, and such gentlemanlike denominations, but between property and no property—swing and the law.[66]

At the very same time, that die-hard Tory, John Wilson Croker, Macaulay's chief parliamentary opponent, expressed his belief that the names of Whig and Tory ought to be dropped, since the struggle was no longer one between two political parties, but one between the mob and the government, the conservative and the subversive principles.[67] It is in a way amusing—though it would not have amused them—that both Jeffrey and Croker were thus confirming the analysis put forward for some years by the Benthamites in the *Westminster,* to the effect that both major parties, Whig and Tory, in spite of all their apparent differences, at bottom represented opposite sides of the same coin: the governing class. And that class, it could be argued, included not merely the aristocracy, but middle-class publicists on either side, like Croker, Macaulay, and Jeffrey. Given this analysis, the difference between Whig and Tory during the Reform Bill period concerned means more than ends, with the Tories not sufficiently alert to the real motives that actuated the Whig ministry's policy of generous concession; and, even when alert to it, resenting the fact that the Whigs were not merely concerned, as Lord Grey put it, to save their order, but also out for political power at the expense of the rival party.

Macaulay, for one, was certainly convinced of the need for concession as a means of avoiding civil conflict. We recall that in the peroration of his first speech on the Reform Bill he held out the prospect of confusion of ranks and spoliation of property, of the dissolution of the social order, if the bill did not pass.[68] It was this peroration that led Lord Mahon, the Tory historian, to accuse him immediately afterwards of using arguments *"ad terrorem."*[69] During the debate on the second reading of the bill, on March 22, Mahon again adverted to this aspect of Macaulay's argument. Many people, he said, had been "terrified" into advocating the necessity of reform. "Mr. Macaulay had told them, they said, that there would be a

66. Jeffrey to Empson, January 31, 1831, Henry Lord Cockburn, *Life of Lord Jeffrey, with a Selection from his Correspondence* (2 vols., Edinburgh, 1852), II, 233.

67. *Quarterly Review,* January 1831, quoted by E. L. Woodward, *The Age of Reform, 1815–1870* (Oxford, 1938), 75.

68. March 2, 1831, *Works,* XI, 426.

69. March 2, 1831, *Hansard,* 3rd series, II (1831), 1207. Mahon sat in the House of Commons.

massacre unless the Reform Bill passed, and Mr. Macaulay wrote in the *Edinburgh Review,* and must be right."[70]

Macaulay, needless to say, was not deterred; he continued to employ this particular line of argument in the course of the debates on the second bill, during the summer of 1831. It entered, for instance, into his insistence that the franchise not be regarded as property. The Tories were claiming that it was, and that it was therefore illegal to deprive anyone of his right to vote. Macaulay was quick to remind them that they had themselves disfranchised the Irish forty-shilling freeholders just a few months before, as part of Catholic emancipation. But, from scoring a debating point of this sort, he extended his argument into a more general realm. To link the franchise and property was inadvisable, he pointed out; since the two might well end by *falling* rather than *standing* together. Some "weak and ignorant minds" might well be persuaded, in other words, that there was no more injustice in confiscating someone's estate than in disenfranchising his borough.[71]

Macaulay did not want to admit that the Whigs were reformers mainly from fear. That, in fact, was what he dubbed the Tories; contrasting their attitude of having in the past given way to the demands of public opinion only under duress, with the grace and dignity shown by Lord Grey's government in its own concessionary policy.[72] Nonetheless, in the very same speech he defended what he called an "honourable" appeal to fear, based in this instance on historical analogy. It was, he said, because the French aristocracy had resisted reform in 1783 that it was unable to resist revolution in 1789. "They would not endure Turgot; and they had to endure Robespierre."[73]

When it had become clear, in September 1831, that the House of Commons would pass the Reform Bill for a second time, and that the Tories' only hope of defeating it now lay with the House of Lords, Macaulay warned in a similar vein about the fatal consequences of the "firmness" recommended by some Tories to the other House. Again, he turned to France for his example, and reminded his hearers of what had happened in "that neighbouring country, which still presents to the eye, even of a passing stranger, the signs of a great dissolution and renovation of society." He conjured up pictures of the stately mansions that lined the silent streets of the Faubourg St. Germain sinking into decay and portioned out into lodging rooms;

70. March 22, 1831, *Hansard,* 3rd series, III (1831) , 726.
71. July 5, 1831, *Works,* XI, 429–30.   72. Ibid., 439.   73. Ibid., 443.

of ruined castles in the valley of the Loire; of an aristocracy "as splendid, as brave, as proud, as accomplished as ever Europe saw . . . driven forth to exile and beggary . . . to cut wood in the back settlements of America, or to teach French in the schoolrooms of London." And why had this happened? Because the French aristocracy had not properly discerned the signs of the times; because it had refused all concessions until the moment for concession had passed.[74]

His main parliamentary opponent, John Wilson Croker, drew a very different inference from this particular historical analogy. "Good God! Sir," he exclaimed, "where has the learned gentleman lived,—what works must he have read,—with what authorities must he have communed, when he attributes the downfall of the French nobility to an injudicious and obstinate resistance to popular opinion?" It was the French aristocracy's "deplorable pusillanimity," not its "high and haughty resistance," that had led to its overthrow. Croker, a speaker not without eloquence and learning, recalled the night of August 4, 1789, in France, when the sacrifice of the nobility's privileges was proclaimed not by the Third Estate, but by a Montmorency and a Noailles, in other words, by the nobles themselves. What followed? The Montmorencies went into exile, and Noailles died on the scaffold.[75]

Whatever the validity of this position—and perhaps it had more truth than Macaulay cared to admit—the House of Lords chose for the moment not to follow in the footsteps of its French predecessor. On October 8, 1831, it rejected the Reform Bill. Two days later the Member of Parliament for Devonshire, Lord Ebrington, moved a resolution in the House of Commons to the effect that the Members of that body still adhered firmly to the principle and to the leading provisions of that bill.[76] Macaulay used his speech in support of that resolution to point out that the country was now in greater danger than had ever threatened it from domestic misgovernment or foreign hostility; and that while there was little chance of open, armed insurrection, there was, on the other hand, a very good chance that the people would engage in a silent, extensive, persevering war against the legal order. Firmness could do no good. Resistance on the Irish model was to be expected. Any society could only be governed in two

74. September 20, 1831, *Works*, XI, 460–1.

75. September 22, 1831, Jennings, ed., *Croker Papers*, I, 523–4.

76. T.B.M. claimed to have been wholly responsible for this course of action and, thus, to have saved the ministry. T.B.M. to Ellis, October 17, 1831, Trinity Correspondence.

ways, by public opinion or by the sword. Public opinion was clearly in favor of the bill. And to govern England—in contrast to Ireland—by the sword was "a wild thought." The danger now was that men of more zeal than wisdom might obtain fatal influence; in other words, that democracy and revolution would be unleashed.[77] We have already seen that Macaulay's fears of what might happen, whether justified or not, were genuine. Greville was wrong when he noted in his diary after hearing what he called Macaulay's eloquent but inflammatory speech that men like Macaulay did not care into what confusion the country was thrown, as long as they had a market to which they could bring their talents.[78] Certainly, violence was the last thing Macaulay wanted. Whether he went too far in this instance of employing the threat of violence was another matter. His fellow Whig MP, John Cam Hobhouse, well disposed toward him, felt impelled to comment that the speech had gone "somewhat near the wind on the intimidation side; and I told him so, and I saw he was not pleased."[79]

The Tory reaction was harsher. Wetherell, one of the chief opponents of the Reform Bill in the Commons, accused Macaulay of exciting in his speech to a breach of the laws. For what else, he asked, was the moral of his having cited the Irish example, if not that while pronouncing a hope for peace, Macaulay in fact gave an instance of successful violence? Croker, in similar fashion, accused Macaulay of endangering the country's legal system by instructing the people how they could best resist and evade the law without armed insurrection. The speech, he declared, could only be dubbed "spendid mischief."[80]

The threat of the violence that would ensue if the bill were not passed certainly formed a major theme of Macaulay's speeches on reform. In the spring of 1832, during the brief period of Wellington's return to power, he went out of his way to deny that his purpose was one of exciting discontent by emphasizing the consequences of a failure to pass the bill. He was as anxious as any man, he declared, for the preservation of order and the security of public property. But he could not cry "Peace, peace" when there was no peace. "Let the Legislature depend on those who boldly declared their opinions as to the danger of rejecting Reform," he urged,

77. October 10, 1831, *Works*, XI, 469–75.
78. October 12, 1831, Wilson, ed., *Greville Diary*, II, 164.
79. October 10, 1831, Broughton, *Recollections*, IV, 138.
80. October 10, 1831, *Hansard*, 3rd series, VIII, 400–2; 438–41.

rather than upon the smooth-tongued Conservatives. The former, he contended, were the only *true* Conservatives.[81]

He was no doubt sincere in stating his feeling that he supported reform because he wanted to preserve the institutions of the country; because he considered it to be the principal safeguard against revolution. It turned out that way, of course. And Macaulay was proved correct by subsequent events.

81. May 10, 1832, *Hansard,* 3rd series, XII, 856.

VII

ORATOR

THE ATTEMPT TO PERSUADE PARLIAMENT TO ADOPT A CONCESSIONARY policy or face the consequences formed one major theme of Macaulay's reform speeches. But he did not rest his case entirely on the argument *ad terrorem*. It is in his presentation of the arguments for reform not just as concession but as historical necessity, that he emerged at his most eloquent.

He kept reminding his listeners that parliamentary reform was not merely a political question of the moment, a temporary disturbance in the state, but one of the decisive events in English history, and, what was more, an event in tune with the harmonies of the progressive history of mankind. It was here that Macaulay's capacious memory and the ease with which he could draw examples and illustrations from the past had full play and could assert themselves to greatest effect. In adducing instances of famous men and events from all the ages of the world's history and literature, he was able to buttress and at the same time to ornament his thesis that the reform agitation in England was part of a long and continuous movement of the public mind, the convulsion of a great society; that it could therefore neither be stopped like a street riot nor treated according to the maxims of a quarter sessions.

In thus ranging the question of parliamentary reform alongside other great milestones in the world's history, Macaulay wished to heighten the occasion, to do what great orators had always done, that is, to lend "philosophical" dignity and a sense of awe to proceedings which, deprived of them, might have degenerated into political squabbles. He had studied the great orators from Demosthenes to Burke and Fox, and was consciously attempting to enter into their inheritance. Knowledgeable contemporaries noted at the time that the standard of House of Commons oratory during the reform debates was deplorably low, and that only a handful of speakers, among them Stanley and Macaulay, redeemed a long and noble tradition. But the wealth of allusion and illustration he brought forward had another and more practical purpose. It was designed to act as a devastating counter to Tory arguments that the reform agitation was a temporary disturbance in the state evoked by the example of the French and Belgian revolutions of 1830; intensified, to be sure, by hunger and distress, but in no sense sufficiently significant to warrant such large-scale measures as those the Whig government was now proposing. A little firmness, possibly a very moderate measure of reform—such as giving representatives to a few of the larger cities, something even Croker was willing to do—would take care of the matter. Why tamper with a constitution that was working, if not perhaps quite as admirably as the Duke of Wellington had declared in his notorious statement of November 1830, but still on the whole very well?

It was on this issue that Macaulay brought to bear his historical knowledge, his sense of occasion, and his capacity for creating myths with the fullest impact. He entirely denied that the sentiment for parliamentary reform in England was a sudden or recent phenomenon, some sort of caprice. It went back, he said, seventy years in English history, to the Wilkes affair, and was only interrupted by the reaction that followed the French Revolution.[1] As far as the Reform Bill itself was concerned, it was nothing less than yet another stage in an unbroken series of steps forward that began with Magna Charta. "The Great Charter, the assembling of the first House of Commons, the Petition of Right, the Declaration of Right, the Bill which is now on our table, what are they all but steps in one great progress?"[2] Here, indeed, was the "Whig interpretation" in full flower, and quoted to some purpose.

But it was not merely the whole of English history that Macaulay called to witness. In his first speech on reform, he rifled world history in search of precedents for the present situation which saw the English middle classes ranged against what he called an aristocracy of

1. September 20, 1831, *Works*, XI, 456-8.   2. July 5, 1831, *Works*, XI, 433.

mere locality. Note the qualification here. He was not expressing anti-aristocratic sentiments *tout court*—how could he, given the composition of the Whig Reform cabinet? Indeed, he assured the House that no one wished to turn the Lords out of their House, except perhaps "here and there a crazy radical, whom the boys in the street point at as he walks along."[3] What he did was to protest against a principle that invested "a hundred drunken potwallopers in one place, or the owner of a ruined hovel in another, with powers which are withheld from cities renowned to the furthest ends of the earth, for the marvels of their wealth and of their industry." For this struggle between "the young energy of one class and the ancient privileges of another," he found precedents in the struggle in Rome between the plebeians and the patricians, in the battle of Rome's allies for full citizenship, in the American revolutionaries, the Third Estate during the French Revolution, indeed, in the struggle of the Jamaican Negroes against an "aristocracy of skin."[4]

Macaulay further widened the scope of his historical background by looking beyond particular incidents and struggles to what he spoke of as a general historical movement. He admitted that history in short installments, for example, such episodes as the role of the nobility in the French Revolution (was this perhaps a concession to Croker's acuity?), could be made to prove anything. History in the large, however, did offer insights into the laws that regulated the growth of communities. One of these laws was the ineluctable progress of property and intelligence, which, ever more widely distributed, would aspire to greater political power. This process could not be arrested by people who wanted to turn the clock back. "The feeble efforts of individuals to bear back are lost and swept away in the mighty rush with which the species goes onward. Those who appear to lead the movement are, in fact, only whirled along before it; those who attempt to resist it, are beaten down and crushed beneath it."[5]

Society moved on, institutions must follow suit. Did this mean that the present instalment of reform could not be final? Indeed, it did. Wealth and civilization would progress further. "Who can say that a hundred years hence there may not be, on the shore of some desolate and silent bay in the Hebrides, another Liverpool, with its docks and warehouses and endless forests of masts?" The present House of Commons was not called upon to legislate for its children.[6] In this manner, Macaulay tried to incorporate reform into what might

3. March 2, 1831, *Works*, XI, 417.   4. Ibid., 415–16.
5. December 16, 1831, *Works*, XI, 489–91.   6. July 5, 1831, *Works*, XI, 440–1.

almost be deemed a cosmological system, an act of nature. Indeed, in one of his speeches he called the passage of the Reform Bill a duty to bring the legal order of society into harmony with the natural order.[7]

To some, this elaborate piling on of historical precedents and illustrations, this absorption of the Reform Bill into the laws of nature, probably smacked of hyperbole. But there was no doubt that Macaulay firmly believed what he was saying; and that, once again, by bringing the process of parliamentary reform into conjunction with far broader and—according to him—historically inevitable processes, he intended to plane down sharpened contours and to gain wider acceptance for the reforms being considered. As he said in his speech of December 16, 1831: "Whether the change be in itself good or bad, has become a question of secondary importance . . . good or bad, the thing must be done . . . a law as strong as the laws of attraction and motion has decreed it."[8] In other words, those who opposed the Reform Bill were setting out to do battle with the spirit of the age, with history, indeed, with the physical laws of the universe.

This was, let it be said, hardly an adventurous line to have taken, since public opinion outside the House was largely favorable to reform, and since even the Tories admitted the need for some reform. But if the approach lacked subtlety, it is still interesting to watch how the style of Macaulay's speeches reinforced their message that the participants in these debates were privileged to be present at an event of world-historical significance. What had with some justification been found excessive in his rhetorical exercises at the Cambridge Union seemed appropriate to most of his hearers now, when their awareness that they were involved in great events was heightened by the names of famous men of the past, of foreign lands and institutions, of history from classical antiquity to their own times, all of which flashed through Macaulay's speeches: Socrates, the Caesars, the Roman Tribunes, the Cortes of Castile, Peter the Great, Constantinople, Montesquieu, Commines, the Dey of Tripoli, the Anabaptists, the Lisbon earthquake, Xerxes, Henry VIII, Richard II at Blackheath, Luther against Indulgences, the American Revolution—all these passed in review. And, above all, the events and the

7. February 28, 1832, *Works*, XI, 506. In another speech—December 16, 1831—he compared opposition to the laws of society to attempts to change the course of the seasons and the tides. *Works*, XI, 491.

8. December 16, 1831, *Works*, XI, 489.

men of the seventeenth century to which Macaulay returned again and again: the Long Parliament, Ship Money, the Levelers, Charles I, Laud, Cromwell, Strafford, the Revolution of 1688.

All of Macaulay's capacities, both as a historian and as an actor, were given full play; as when he turned to the Speaker and reminded him of the day "when a faithless King filled our house with his guards, took his seat, Sir, on your chair, and saw your predecessor kneeling on the floor beside him."[9] The reform speeches were studded with rhetorical questions to his audience—almost fifty of these in the first speech alone, usually in extended bursts. They were shot through with biblical language—Macaulay had discarded Clapham religion, but the Bible remained imprinted in his memory, and he drew on it to great effect, comparing the inefficiency of the House of Commons as a check for the people against the King and the nobility to the salt that had lost its savor; telling the middle-class party, in Job's phrase, to be "daysman" between the two extremes; remarking, in the language of St. John, that all those must be for reform who had eyes to see and who understood with their hearts; drawing on the Old Testament to buttress his admission that the Reform Bill could not do much to improve directly the lot of the poor, since Members could not rain down bread on the multitude from Heaven, nor smite the rocks to give them to drink; summing up the generosity of the Whigs in letting the Tory governments of the 1820's adopt "their" principles of trade, jurisprudence, and foreign and religious policy in words that echoed St. Matthew's parable of the laborers in the vineyard: "They were content that he who came into fellowship with them at the eleventh hour should have a far larger share of the reward than those who had borne the burthen and heat of the day."[10] And we have already seen how he climaxed his great peroration on March 2 with a paraphrase of St. Paul: "Now in this your accepted time, now, in this your day of salvation. . . ."

Macaulay's own phrases stick in the mind; though perhaps there remains about them a certain artificiality, as of a speaker who had almost too carefully studied his classical models, ancient and British, and was consciously attempting to gain a niche in the oratorical Pantheon. Here are some examples: "Sir, we are legislators, not antiquaries"[11] (in response to the argument that the constitution

9. October 10, 1831, *Works*, XI, 475.
10. Biblical allusions in order: March 2, 1831, *Works*, XI, 417; December 16, 1831, *Works*, XI, 489; March 2, 1831, *Works*, XI, 425; September 20, 1831, *Works*, XI, 447; December 16, 1831, *Works*, XI, 480.
11. March 2, 1831, *Works*, XI, 413.

was better than ever before) . "Revolutions produced by violence are often followed by reactions; the victories of reason once gained, are gained for eternity."[12]—"For our children we do not pretend to legislate. All that we can do for them is to leave them a memorable example of the manner in which great reforms ought to be made."[13] —And, a particularly fine example because we possess a specific record of the effect achieved: "I am willing to let others *have infamy and place,* only leave us honour and the Bill." An eyewitness commented: "The effect was electrical. Poor Hardinge's face seemed swollen with rage. He jumped up as if he was about to enter into some personal conflict, and vehemently complained of such language. His complaints were coldly received and Macaulay's explanation was if possible worse [i.e., more effective] than his charge."[14]

In Macaulay's speeches, as in his essays, antitheses and anecdotes abounded. He described a Member of Parliament, who was "too proud to bend to the wishes of a nation, yet ready to lick the dust at the feet of a patron."[15] Radicals "without talents or acquirements sufficient for the management of a vestry," he said, "sometimes become dangerous to great empires."[16] To reduce to absurdity the argument that some able men would be elected under any system, Macaulay cited the example of that King in ancient times who was elected by the neighing of a horse. He told the story of Cyrus taking away the big coat from the little boy and putting it on the big boy, to illustrate that this was something Parliament would have no right to do—take Members away from small constituencies and give them to large ones—if the franchise were really private property.[17]

But perhaps the most novel aspect of the speeches was Macaulay's romantic approach to the achievements of the Industrial Revolution. It is not surprising to find him surrounding the heroic Whigs of old with a romantic aura, pointing with pride and delight to the Talbots, the Cavendishes, "the princely house of Howard," and to the descendants of Marlborough, Russell, and Derby.[18] These were figures whom in his imagination he had endowed with almost mythical greatness. Merely from calling the roll of their names he could derive the vicarious satisfaction of being part of their company. But just as he had welcomed the Reform Bill proposals as

12. September 20, 1831. *Works,* XI, 458–9.   13. July 5, 1831, *Works,* XI, 441.

14. May 14, 1832, *Hansard,* 3rd series, XII (1832) , 923; Le Marchant's Diary, May 14, 1832, Aspinall, *Diaries,* 255.

15. February 28, 1832, *Works,* XI, 502.

16. October 10, 1831, *Works,* XI, 475.

17. March 2, 1831, *Works,* XI, 421; July 5, 1831, *Works,* XI, 428.

18. September 20, 1831, *Works,* XI, 461.

giving "additional lustre to a noble name [Russell], inseparably associated during two centuries with the dearest liberties of the English people" at the same time that it distributed power through the great mass of the middle order,[19] so also did he combine his romantic approach to the aristocratic Whig tradition with an equally lyrical attitude toward the achievements of the industrial age.

At the very beginning of his first speech on reform, he used one of his favorite devices, familiar to us from the essay on History, the imaginary visit of a foreign traveler to London, here more specifically to "that immense city which lies to the north of Great Russell Street and Oxford Street, a city superior in size and in population to the capitals of many mighty kingdoms." He would conduct such a visitor "through that interminable succession of streets and squares, all consisting of well built and well furnished houses," would make him observe the brilliancy of the shops, the crowd of well-appointed equipages, show him "that magnificent circle of palaces which surrounds the Regent's Park"—and then tell him that this whole area was unrepresented in Parliament.[20]

In a subsequent speech, he extended the stranger's wonderment from the city of London itself to the wonders of industry in general. Nowhere had manufactures been carried to such perfection, nowhere did there exist a comparable mass of mechanical power.[21] Compare this with the existing political system, in this case not the state of the franchise so much as the state of the law. Following the biblical maxim, "By their fruits ye shall know them," Macaulay employed the achievements of industry as a yardstick by which he tested the accomplishments of the legislators. Manufacturers must be judged by the cotton goods and the cutlery they produced, engineers by their suspension bridges, tunnels, and steam carriages.

Is, then, the machinery by which justice is administered framed with the same exquisite skill which is found in other kinds of machinery? Can there be a stronger contrast than that which exists between the beauty, the completeness, the speed, the precision with which every process is performed in our factories, and the awkwardness, the rudeness, the slowness, the uncertainty of the apparatus by which offences are punished and rights vindicated?

The English legal system and government—cumbersome, inefficient, chaotic—represented the barbarism of the thirteenth century, in

19. March 2, 1831, *Works*, XI, 418.   20. March 2, 1831, *Works*, XI, 412.
21. July 5, 1831, *Works*, XI, 435.

contrast to the highest civilization of the nineteenth, which belonged to the people. The legal system and the government therefore had to be brought into harmony with the people.[22]

It is easy today, looking back, to be critical of such an attitude of possessive pride in material things, more especially since we are very much aware of how much suffering and distress on the part of those who performed them went into the "beautiful" manufacturing processes. At the same time, it ought to be remembered that Macaulay was introducing something new into the political dialogue of his day. With all his romantic admiration for the Whig aristocrats and his identification of himself with the bearers of the Whig tradition, he no less enthusiastically sang rhapsodies upon the industrial system. But, more than that, he had the vision not merely to welcome the material aspects of the Industrial Revolution, but to find in them the source of something akin to what the Romantic poets were finding in nature. This may be—indeed, it has been—severely censured as Philistinism and blindness to the terrible realities of the factories. Yet one should at least recognize that Macaulay glimpsed, behind the squalor, the grime, the merely mechanical and quantitative orientation of the manufacturing system, a potential of beauty and splendor.

He himself, of course, was neither a Whig aristocrat nor a maker of suspension bridges and cutlery. It was his romantic imagination that permitted him to identify himself with Russells and Sidneys. It was his sense of fact and concretion, an inseparable though to some an incongruous part of his imaginative faculty, that permitted him to celebrate the engineers and cotton manufacturers of his day as well as their products. An odd combination, perhaps, but one that was true to the actual spectrum represented in the reform debates. The comment of one who was present during the debates seems particularly apt, since it encapsulated the two aspects, traditional and modern, of Macaulay's approach: "In listening to him you seemed to be like a traveller passing through a rich and picturesque country by railroad."[23] It might be said that Macaulay in his speeches tried himself to build a suspension bridge of his own, between two periods, two classes, two worlds.

The principal arguments Macaulay brought forward in the course of his speeches on parliamentary reform were by no means original. One look at a speech delivered during the Reform Bill debates by one of his few acknowledged intellectual mentors, Sir James Mackintosh, is sufficient to show that Macaulay's leading themes were not

22. Ibid., 435–6.   23. Hardcastle, *Campbell*, II, 57.

uniquely his. Mackintosh expressed his own conviction that the social revolution of the past sixty years had altered the condition of mankind more than had the history of the three previous centuries; that only the state of representation had not kept pace. The rising elements of wealth and intelligence in Britain had a right to be called into the councils of the nation. Disfranchisement was *not* robbery. All this has a familiar ring for those who have read Macaulay's speeches. But in order to understand why Mackintosh's words created so much less effect than Macaulay's, one need only compare one or two passages in their respective speeches. Here is Mackintosh on the danger of the people confusing the rights of property with political abuses:

Let us not teach the spoilers of future times to represent our resumption of a right of suffrage as a precedent for their seizure of lands and possessions.[24]

Here is Macaulay on the same subject, in a speech delivered the very next day:

You bind up two very different things, in the hope that they may stand together. Take heed that they do not fall together.[25]

Here is Mackintosh on the wonders of the industrial age:

All the marvellous works of industry and science are unnoticed in our representation.[26]

And here Macaulay:

Our fields are cultivated with a skill unknown elsewhere, with a skill which has extorted rich harvests from moors and morasses. Our houses are filled with conveniences which the kings of former times might have envied. Our bridges, our canals, our roads, our modes of communication, fill every stranger with wonder.[27]

What in Mackintosh remained general and abstract became in Macaulay's handling of the same subjects specific and concrete. It was this ability to lend vivid substance to ideas which, to be sure, were

24. July 4, 1831, *The Miscellaneous Works of the Rt. Hon. Sir James Mackintosh* (Boston, 1858) , 587.

25. July 5, 1831, *Works*, XI, 430.   26. July 4, 1831, *Mackintosh*, 584.

27. July 5, 1831, *Works*, XI, 435.

often well known, but which others could only express in lifeless terms, that distinguished Macaulay's contributions to the Reform Bill debates.

Two circumstances added special drama to Macaulay's speeches during the debates on the Reform Bill. One arose from the fact that the man who was now one of the leaders of the attack against nomination boroughs himself sat for one (Calne). The second arose from Macaulay's finding himself involved during these debates in three personal duels—with his old Cambridge friend, Winthrop Mackworth Praed; with the *Quarterly Review*'s waspish John Wilson Croker; and with the leading statesman in the House of Commons on the Tory side, Sir Robert Peel.

IT HAD BEEN LAID DOWN IN THE DETAILED PROVISIONS OF THE MINistry's reform proposals that Calne was to retain both of its Members. The technical reason for this was that according to the Census of 1821, its population was over 4,000. This entitled it to have two representatives. But the Tories claimed (a) that this figure was arrived at by combining the borough's population with that of "the liberty of Bowood"; (b) that the Census of 1821 should not have been used in the first place, since a more recent census was available; and (c) that the real reason why this notorious nomination borough was saved from the slaughter was that it belonged to Lord Lansdowne, a member of the Whig ministry. As it turned out, the government eventually changed its policy on the use of the 1821 Census (employing that of 1831 instead), and by the time of the third Reform Bill, Calne had been put into "Schedule B," which meant that it was to lose one of its two MP's. But until this change of mind on the part of the ministry, the alleged special treatment for Calne provided a target for Tory attackers who were certainly not opposed to nomination boroughs in principle.

For they argued that one of the great advantages of the "rotten boroughs" lay in the undoubted fact that by means of these boroughs, many able MP's had in the past been brought into Parliament, either by a particular ministry's use of such a borough as Crown patronage; or, more frequently, by individual aristocratic patrons. Young men of talent who could not have afforded the considerable expense of a contested election were thus introduced into the House of Commons, and both the House and the country had been the better for their presence. In the course of his first speech on reform, Macaulay admitted—as he was bound to—that some able men had indeed entered the House by means of these boroughs, but he saw this as the result of a series of happy accidents rather than of a system that therefore deserved to be perpetuated. A form of government, he said, should not be judged by these accidents which could, after all, occur under the most haphazard of systems (choice by lot, for example), but must be judged by its general tendency. If the country were provided with popular institutions, if Members were henceforth "chosen freely by the middle classes," then great men would without a doubt find their way into the House of Commons.[28]

But the Tory Opposition was not disposed to yield easily to this argument, especially in view of the fact that Macaulay's own position appeared to them to be so vulnerable. In his essay on Horace Walpole, published in the autumn of 1833, Macaulay stated that "no man ought to be severely censured for not being beyond his age in virtue"; adding that no one was now thought wicked or dishonorable because, under the old system of election, he was returned for East Retford, for Liverpool, or for Stafford.[29] This was true, but irrelevant, because the references to Macaulay's sitting for Lord Lansdowne's borough of Calne did not take the form of censure upon him for doing so; rather, they praised the system that had happily resulted in sending so brilliant an orator to the House of Commons.

The tone was set by Lord Mahon who, immediately after Macaulay's first speech on reform, offered his "humble tribute of admiration to the eloquence and talent with which the honourable member for Calne had addressed the House," finding in him another proof of the utility and advantage of the reviled close boroughs.[30] "Orator" Hunt then expressed his amazement at Lord John Russell's having passed over Calne, that "rottenest, stinkingest" of boroughs.[31] Peel took the line of agreeing with Macaulay's statement that tendencies, not accidents, be considered in the matter of nomination boroughs returning able men. The record, he said, showed just such a tendency, that is, names such as those of Burke, Fox, Pitt, Brougham, and Horner—Peel cleverly picked some distinguished

28. March 2, 1831, *Works*, XI, 420–1.

29. T.B.M., "Horace Walpole," *Works*, VIII, 336.

30. March 2, 1831. *Hansard*, 3rd series, II (1831), 1206. Sir Charles Wetherell seconded this point, stating that the brilliance of T.B.M.'s speech ought to give the government pause in its proposed disfranchisement of boroughs. Ibid., 1223.

31. March 2, 1831, *Hansard*, 3rd series, II (1831), 1210–11.

Whigs to complete his list![32] Croker adopted a more sarcastic tone. He referred to "a certain borough in the south of England" which had certainly never stood higher in the House than it did at this moment as a consequence of Macaulay's eloquent speech.[33]

Another Tory MP, North, had good sport with Macaulay's reference to those "happy accidents" that had led to the election of able Members from rotten boroughs; adverting to "the happy accident to which the House had been indebted for the display of the honourable Member's eloquence, and without which happy accident the honourable Member might have toiled and laboured for many years yet to come, before he obtained the just distinction which already awaited him."[34] Daniel O'Connell, the leader of the Irish Nationalists in the House, told Macaulay, after congratulating him on his fine speech, that, Calne or no Calne, he had now established his claim to sit in the House by his opening speech on reform. "Need that honourable Member now care for the influence of the Marquis of Lansdowne?" he asked.[35]

In his speech of December 16, 1831, Macaulay resumed the theme of the relationship between the nature of the franchise and the return to Parliament of men of talent. It was true, he admitted, that some such men would never have become known to the large constituencies for which they finally sat, had they not initially been brought into the House for nomination boroughs. But the reason for this was that election expenses were so high that they could not have afforded to sit for large constituencies in the first place. In a graphic image, he showed his listeners that

at present you close against men of talents that broad, that noble entrance which belongs to them, and which ought to stand wide open to them; and in exchange you open to them a bye entrance, low and narrow, always obscure, often filthy, through which, too often, they can pass only by crawling on their hands and knees, and from which they too often emerge sullied with stains never to be washed away.[36]

Even those men sitting for nomination boroughs controlled by men of virtue and honor—here Macaulay clearly had Lord Lansdowne and himself in mind—wore the badge, though they might not feel the claim, of servitude. "Is it nothing," Macaulay asked, that such a Member of Parliament "cannot speak of his independence without

32. March 2, 1831, ibid., 1349.
33. March 4, 1831, *Hansard*, 3rd series, III (1831) , 98.
34. Ibid., 160.   35. Ibid., 187.   36. December 16, 1831, *Works*, XI, 484.

exciting a smile? Is it nothing that he is considered, not as a Representative but as an adventurer?" The present bill, in part by doing away with the so-called outvoters (whose votes were customarily bought and sold), would reduce election expenses, and thus enable men of talent and genius to contest popular constituencies.[37]

Croker would still not let the subject go. Macaulay had said in his speech of December 16 that he did not like the present (third) Reform Bill as well as the previous one. "No wonder!" was Croker's reaction. Calne, after all, had been put into Schedule B. Macaulay had meanwhile received an invitation to stand for the newly enfranchised borough of Leeds, should the bill pass. Did he not owe this invitation, Croker asked, to his having represented a nomination borough first? How else would he have become known there?[38] Praed, on the other hand, took up Macaulay's point that MP's sitting for nomination boroughs could never be truly independent, and remarked that nobody could charge Macaulay with being more debased or broken in spirit at the present moment, while sitting for Calne, than when sometime hence he would be sitting for Leeds.[39]

On balance, Macaulay was not really hurt by sitting for Calne during the Reform Bill debates. It was embarrassing that the population figures for the borough were successfully questioned by the Tories; it was perhaps embarrassing that the borough was switched to Schedule B in midstream. Macaulay's very success in the House gave the Tories some talking points in praise of nomination boroughs. On the other hand, in terms of serious argument about the advantages of such boroughs, Macaulay got the better of his opponents. And there was something particularly appropriate in his transfer in 1832 from Calne to Leeds, one of the newly enfranchised industrial boroughs.

WINTHROP MACKWORTH PRAED, MACAULAY'S OLD FRIEND FROM CAMbridge Union days, sat on the Tory side of the House during the debates on parliamentary reform. When he had first heard of Macaulay's entry into Parliament, he had expressed his delight to his sister: "I cannot but think that he must be the greatest man there by-and-by, and I have bespoken his first frank, in the expectation of

37. Ibid., 484–5.
38. December 16, 1831, *Hansard,* 3rd series, IX (1831), 394, 400–1.
39. December 17, 1831, ibid., 489.

selling it for ten pounds thirty years hence."[40] Only a few days later, he wrote to her in the strictest confidence that he himself might be offered a seat for a (then Tory) government borough. Lansdowne's having brought Macaulay into Parliament had apparently had a great deal to do with Praed's candidacy. For, he wrote, ministers were a little alarmed at Macaulay's intrusion. They wanted someone of equal sharpness and wit to counterbalance Macaulay in the Commons, where Peel (according to Praed's letter) now remained the only speaker of outstanding ability upon whom they could rely.

There were two obvious difficulties. Praed was known to be a close friend of Macaulay's. Furthermore, he was known to have held progressive views while at Cambridge. On both these points, Peel took soundings from a (Tory) friend of Praed's, Vesey Fitzgerald. He inquired of him whether Praed's intimacy with Macaulay was very close, and "whether [Praed] should, in consequence of it, be unwilling to be pitted against Macaulay in the House." Fitzgerald's answer was that Praed and Macaulay were indeed very close friends; and that the former would certainly refuse to place himself in personal collision with any man. As to Praed's views, Fitzgerald told Peel that he had not observed anything in them which should prevent him from generally giving his support to the present (Tory) administration. Both these answers, Praed told his sisters, were in exact accord with his sentiments. At this juncture, nothing came of the plans to bring him into Parliament. And it was not until December 1830 that Praed took the step of purchasing a seat for two years at a cost of £1,000. By this time, of course, the Tories were out, and Praed took his seat on the Opposition benches.

The question of his former sentiments was a delicate one. For, as he informed his sister, "all this [i.e., the seat in Parliament] would not be satisfactory if I were convinced that I was sacrificing my integrity to what would be at best a doubtful hope of advancement in the world." He had therefore consulted his feelings as scrupulously as he could. He could not have supported a party opposed to Catholic emancipation; but that question had now been settled. Reform was the major stumbling block. For, Praed wrote, his opinions at Cambridge had certainly been strongly in favor of it. But, he added (somewhat weakly), "they were never in favour of such a reform as it is likely the Whigs will introduce." Interestingly enough —and apparently in contradiction to the previous statement—he

40. Praed to his sister, February 10, 1830, Sir George Young, ed., *The Political and Occasional Poems of Winthrop Mackworth Praed* (London, 1888), xiv.

added that it was not unlikely that the Tories might let Reform be passed quietly; so that upon their return to power, "if ever they return," it would be out of the way.[41]

This, of course, did not happen; though it might well have, had Lord John Russell's proposals been less sweeping. And Praed in Parliament spoke several times against reform. In view of his having been linked at Cambridge with Austin and Macaulay, this caused some surprise. As we have already noted, "it was said at the time . . . that he and Macaulay . . . discussed in a friendly and calculating spirit the parts they should take in Parliament, and it was settled between them that Macaulay should be *progressive* and Praed *retardative* in his speeches."[42] This, surely, was not a true story. But it may well have been the case that once Macaulay had entered Parliament, Praed would not have wished to be on the same side, in danger of being overshadowed. His hesitation about accepting a seat certainly showed that he himself was not altogether convinced that his rightful place was on the Tory benches. On the other hand, to have entered Parliament as a Tory in 1830 could not well have been interpreted as evidence of calculating ambition, for never had that party's prospects looked darker.

If anyone thought that the presence of both Praed and Macaulay in Parliament would ensure a series of sparkling oratorical duels between equals, he was soon disappointed. It was Croker—who became a great friend of Praed's—who turned out to be Macaulay's principal parliamentary adversary. At the beginning of his parliamentary career, in fact, Praed wanted it made quite clear that he was not in Parliament for the purpose "of opposing any particular *man*, and that man my friend and idol—T. Macaulay. . . . A falser calumny was never breathed." The scandal vexed him, because it ought to have been known that he was himself under great obligation to Macaulay, "his warmest admirer and his most zealous friend."[43] But, as the reform debates proceeded, the two old friends inevitably clashed. Praed spoke in March against Macaulay's thesis that lucky accidents were responsible for producing able Members of Parliament under the old system. If that was so, he said, let us keep the system.[44]

---

41. Praed to his sister, *Political Poems*, xv–xvi.

42. October 16, 1831, Morley, ed., *Henry Crabb Robinson*, I, 393.

43. Praed to J. C. Tarver, January 14, 1831, Derek Hudson, *A Poet in Parliament: The Life of Winthrop Mackworth Praed, 1802–1839* (London, 1939), 171–2.

44. March 8, 1831, *Hansard*, 3rd series, III (1831), 242.

It was at about this time that Macaulay wrote to his sister Hannah that, compared to the struggles between Tories and Whigs at the close of Queen Anne's reign, the rage of party faction had become so intense that "Praed and I become colder every day."[45] In the course of the debates of December 1831, Praed, it was true, defended Macaulay against the charge of inconsistency on the question of the ballot, saying that it was well known that Macaulay had never been favorable to it.[46] But something must have happened to produce a breach between the two men, and to account for Macaulay's statement in his journal some years later that "I would much rather forget than recollect all about him. He was the only friend I ever had who served me basely and malignantly."[47]

One can only conjecture here about what happened. Praed wrote political *vers d'occasion* in which he sharply attacked his contemporary opponents. In one such poem, "The Young Whig," he might well have had Macaulay in mind. At the time, it was not printed, and was preserved in manuscript only, but Macaulay could certainly have heard it quoted:

> *He talks quite grand of Grant and Grey;*
> *He jests at Holland House;*
> *He dines extremely every day*
> *On ortolans and grouse:*
> *Our salads now he will not touch,*
> *He keeps a different set;*
> *They'll never love him half so much*
> *As those he must forget!*[48]

There was an explicit reference to Macaulay in a poem of Praed's published in the Tory press on May 24, 1833, on the question of the government's grant of compensation to slaveowners after the slaves had been emancipated by act of Parliament. Macaulay, as we shall see, offered to resign from the government over this issue. And Praed wrote about him:

> *There was a youthful Tully,*
> *Determined not to sully*
> *His laurels so green and so bright, O;*

---

45. T.B.M. to Hannah, July 15, 1831, Trevelyan, *Life and Letters,* 169.
46. December 16, 1831, *Hansard,* 3rd series, IX (1831) , 483.
47. Trinity Journal, November 14, 1849.   48. Praed, *Political Poems,* 168–9.

And he sighed, "With heartfelt sorrow
I must leave my place tomorrow,
If you won't wash the Blackamoor white, O."[49]

The lines seem innocuous enough. And there may have been other factors at work, making for a breach between the two old friends. But it is just possible that Macaulay, particularly sensitive to such slights, could not forgive this lampoon.

JOHN WILSON CROKER WAS THE SON OF AN ANGLO-IRISH EXCISEMAN. He had made a successful political career on the Tory side, and had been First Secretary to the Admiralty for over twenty years. He was a man of great ability and learning, endowed with a caustic wit. Perhaps the mutual antipathy between himself and Macaulay had its root in the fact that they shared certain common traits, though Croker was twenty years older than Macaulay. They were both literary critics and historians—Croker had been a steady contributor on various subjects to the *Quarterly Review* since 1809—and both had succeeded in politics in spite of lack of high birth and station. Neither of them minced words when it came to political warfare. Neither was averse to drawing blood. The two men could not abide each other from the very time they first met in the political arena. Croker later recalled that he had disliked Macaulay "at first sight before I ever heard him open his mouth; his very person and countenance displeased me."[50] And Macaulay similarly recalled his strong antipathy to Croker.[51]

They first clashed in Parliament in November 1830, when it was Croker who reminded the Whigs that Brougham, who had just accepted the position of Lord Chancellor, had previously pledged himself to take no part in the new administration and not to leave the House of Commons. Macaulay, as we know, did not have the kindliest feelings toward Brougham. But at this point he rose to his defense, compared Brougham's "mighty powers" of mind to the detriment of Croker's, and accused the latter of lacking the courage

49. Ibid., 233.
50. Croker to Lockhart, January 1849, Myron R. Brightfield, *John Wilson Croker* (Berkeley, Calif., 1940) , 369.
51. Trinity Journal, November 29, 1857.

to attack Brougham to his face.[52] Macaulay wrote to Napier that he had given Croker this "dressing" because his insufferable impertinence and poltroonery had exasperated him beyond all patience.[53] From then on, the battle was joined. Croker showed himself indefatigable in attacking the provisions of the Reform Bill in detail. It was when the whole House sat in committee, when the detailed provisions of the bill were debated, and amendments hammered out, when Macaulay, whose set speeches were delivered on "the question," rarely spoke, that Croker demonstrated his encyclopedic knowledge of the bill. From the very beginning of the debates, he was among those who singled out the anomaly of Calne's still having the right to send two Members to Westminster.[54]

The political conflict between the two became exacerbated by a conflict in the arena of literary criticism. As early as March 1831, Macaulay had written to Napier, now editor of the *Edinburgh Review,* that he wanted to review Croker's forthcoming edition of Boswell's *Johnson.*[55] He read it for the purpose of the review in June, and wrote to his sister Hannah at that time that "it is wretchedly ill done. The notes are poorly written, and shamefully inaccurate. There is, however, much curious information in it."[56] Thus, Macaulay had made up his mind about what he considered to be the low quality of Croker's edition before his major parliamentary clashes with him took place in the House of Commons during the later summer and autumn of 1831. But, as we have seen, the two men had clashed already. And there can be little doubt that personal animus reinforced whatever reservations Macaulay had about the edition. In a letter of July 30, 1831, he had reported his latest encounter with Croker "the other night [July 26?]," in the course of which "that impudent leering scoundrel Croker" had congratulated him on speaking, fearing that Macaulay had been silent so long because of the many allusions that had been made to Calne. "See whether I do not dust that varlet's jacket for him in the next number of the Blue and Yellow [the *Edinburgh Review*]," Macaulay wrote his sister. "I detest him more than cold boiled veal."[57]

By early September, he had sent off more than half of his *Edinburgh Review* article: "I have—though I say it who should not say

52. *Hansard,* 3rd series, I (1830) , 647–8.
53. T.B.M. to Napier, November 27, 1830, *Napier Correspondence,* 98.
54. March 4, 1831, *Hansard,* 3rd series, III (1831) , 98–9.
55. T.B.M. to Napier, March 8, 1831, *Napier Correspondence,* 110.
56. T.B.M. to Hannah, June 29, 1831, Trevelyan, *Life and Letters,* 165.
57. T.B.M. to Hannah, August 5, 1831, Trinity Correspondence.

it—beaten Croker black and blue. Impudent as he is, I think he must be ashamed of the pickle in which I leave him."[58] Macaulay's demolition of Croker in the *Edinburgh Review*, then, had been largely prepared before the two collided head on upon the occasion of Macaulay's speech during the debate on the third reading of the second Reform Bill, September 20, 1831. Here Croker was at his most sarcastic. Gravely, he congratulated Macaulay on his speech. He was sure, he remarked, that Macaulay was about to be called to the exercise of his abilities in some high station in the ministry; since, "with so grave a tone of authority and confidence, he imparted to the House the first, and indeed the only information as to the measures H. M. Government had decided upon adopting in the event of the Bill being rejected elsewhere."[59] The reference here was to Macaulay's statement that even if the Lords turned down the bill, "let not the enemies of Reform imagine that their reign is straightway to recommence, or that they have obtained anything more than a short and uneasy respite."[60] Croker commented acidly that it was somewhat extraordinary to "see these high and delicate duties confided to a Gentleman who has never yet appeared in political office, and who, notwithstanding his great talents, has hitherto had little other opportunity of displaying them, than in the humbler station of a practising barrister."[61]

That was the unkindest cut of all—and we know from Macaulay's sister Margaret's journal that it hurt her brother. For this came at a time when Macaulay was complaining that he had not as yet been given office. If ever there was a barrister who did not practise, it was Macaulay. To be contemptuously called a "practising barrister" by Croker was nothing less than an insult.

The issue of the *Edinburgh* containing Macaulay's review appeared on October 8. He began in his most destructive vein, by proclaiming that Croker's performance was on a par with the leg of mutton on which Dr. Johnson had dined while traveling between Oxford and London—"as bad as bad could be, ill fed, ill killed, ill kept, and ill dressed. This edition is ill compiled, ill arranged, ill written, and ill printed."[62] What followed was, in great part, a sarcastic commentary on Croker's errors, misstatements, and inaccuracies. Most of those errors were minor; some of them were, *pace*

58. T.B.M. to Hannah, September 7, 1831, Trinity Correspondence.
59. September 20, 1831, *Hansard*, 3rd series, VII (1831), 311.
60. September 20, 1831, *Works*, XI, 461.
61. September 20, 1831, *Hansard*, 3rd series, VII (1831), 311–12.
62. T.B.M., "Croker's Boswell" (1831), *Works*, VIII, 56.

Macaulay, not errors at all.[63] But Macaulay was convinced that he had "smashed" Croker's book.[64]

This did not end the contest between the two. Croker continued to play the role in Parliament of Macaulay's particular opponent. The latter's speech of December 16, 1831, he called a "palinode." He poured scorn on Macaulay for not composing his own election addresses and for being content to remain one of "the mere signers of some miserable radical letter, written . . . by a low attorney." Again, he made a sarcastic reference to Macaulay as an "eminent lawyer."[65] He blamed Macaulay for having hinted in one of his speeches at how people could resist and evade the law, a piece of "splendid mischief."[66] A final confrontation between the two, by now archenemies, took place during the debate on the third reading of the third Reform Bill on March 19, 1832, when Croker once again predicted that the course Macaulay was pursuing would end in revolution; though at the same time he paid genuine tribute to "the beauties of the honourable and learned Member's oratory which I am sure must be so much felt by every other person that it would appear a sort of vanity in me to say how much I appreciate them."[67]

In Croker, then, Macaulay had an able opponent, who was not afraid to pay back witticisms and sarcasms in kind, who was familiar with both history and literature, who could match Macaulay in cleverness and acuity. Gladstone once remarked that Croker replied to some of Macaulay's reform speeches with talent and effect, and that Macaulay did not quite acknowledge the strength of those replies.[68] This was true. Croker was a Tory of the old school who, for instance, had not approved of Peel's change of stance in 1829, and who foresaw the worst as a result of reform. The fact that history vindicated Macaulay, that the latter was on the winning side, should not prevent us from giving his cantankerous adversary his due. In Croker, Macaulay had found an enemy worthy of his mettle.[69]

63. See Brightfield, *Croker*, 301–5.
64. T.B.M. to Ellis, October 17, 1831, Trevelyan, *Life and Letters*, 180.
65. December 16, 1831, *Hansard*, 3rd series, IX (1831) , 392, 407–8.
66. October 10, 1831, ibid., VIII (1831) , 441.
67. March 19, 1832, *Hansard*, 3rd series, XI (1832) , 466–7. This praise was probably sincere. See Croker's statement in a letter to Lockhart, January 1849, to the effect that after he and T.B.M. had been pitted against one another in Parliament, he could honestly say that his original dislike of T.B.M. was "if not lost, at least overpowered, by my sense of the brilliancy of his talents." Brightfield, *Croker*, 369–70.
68. Gladstone, *Gleanings*, II, 298.
69. For a denial that T.B.M. revenged himself on Croker for having been crushed by him in debate, see E. S. de Beer, "Macaulay and Croker: The Review of Croker's Boswell," *Review of English Studies*, n.s., X (1959) , 388–97.

SIR ROBERT PEEL WAS CLEARLY THE LEADING TORY FIGURE IN THE House. Macaulay repeatedly angered him by reminding him of his reversal over Catholic emancipation in 1829. High-minded almost to a fault, Peel naturally resented the implications of opportunism on his part with which Macaulay taxed him. It is important to remember that in Peel, Macaulay had an opponent who was no crusty country squire, but, rather, someone who went out of his way to dissociate himself from the disparagement of the middle classes in which some of his party were engaging. Peel, on March 3, 1831, repudiated this sort of attack, "sprung as I am from those classes, and proud of my connection with them."[70] Peel's aligning himself with the middle class sheds some light on the elastic qualities of the term, then as now. For his father had amassed immense wealth through his cotton factories, had become a baronet, and had, in classic fashion, purchased a country estate. There was little real connection here with shopkeepers and attorneys. Peel was first greatly provoked by Macaulay's speech of July 5, 1831, in which the latter had told the House that if the Tories were now to come in, they would, as in 1829, be forced to bring in the bill they were so vehemently opposing. Then, amidst the generous cheers of the Whigs and "the indignant murmurs of those staunch Tories who are now again trusting to be again betrayed, the Rt. Hon. Baronet opposite [Peel] will rise from the Treasury Bench" to prepare the bill on which the hearts of the people were set.[71] An eyewitness—sympathetic, to be sure, to Macaulay—reported that "Sir Robert winced a good deal."[72]

Peel replied the next day, refusing to acquiesce in either Macaulay's praise or his satire. As far as violence was concerned, he stated that during the last six weeks of the reform period, more lives had been lost in clashes with the police and the militia than during his own six years in charge of the Home Department. As for memories of Ireland, which Macaulay had evoked, let him wait until the severity of the new proposals of the Whig government about that country were revealed.[73] In September, Peel took up Macaulay's accusation that the late government had fled from office. While it was in office, Peel rejoined, its members had been charged with clinging to it. It was truly wonderful, was it not, what a change took place once an identical object was viewed from different quarters.

70. *Hansard*, 3rd series, II (1831) , 1338.   71. July 5, 1831, *Works*, XI, 442.
72. July 5, 1831, Broughton, *Recollections*, IV, 119.
73. July 6, 1831, *Hansard*, 3rd series, IV (1831) , 872–3.

Given—a Commissioner of Bankrupts as the spectator—flight from office as the object to be viewed—what will be the variation in the appearance of that object, when seen by the Commissioner from the back benches of the Opposition, and from the front benches of the Ministerial side of the House? This is a curious problem in moral optics, and as the learned Gentleman is, no doubt, a mathematician [Macaulay might justly have taken that as a hit below the belt], he probably will attempt to solve it.[74]

The acidulous tone shows that Macaulay had clearly drawn blood. Peel was not the person to take this sort of attack lying down. He fastened on Macaulay's statement that the Tories had carried Catholic emancipation against the wishes of the middle classes: "What, Sir, are the £10 householders ever in the wrong? Are they . . . sometimes on the illiberal and intolerant side?" Was it not sometimes wise to oppose popular opinion?[75]

Greville's comment on this rejoinder of Peel's was that Peel had cut Macaulay to ribbons.[76] Greville himself did not particularly like Macaulay, but it was doubtless true that Peel sometimes came off best in reply. Not always, though. Macaulay's constant harping on his change of mind about Catholic emancipation had some effect. One such reference, according to a witness, "seemed to *combler* him with suffering. His speech was one of almost unconditional surrender."[77]

Peel again showed signs of great annoyance after Macaulay's speech of December 16, in the course of which the latter had defended the changes made by the ministry in drafting the third Reform Bill against Tory accusations that those changes showed ministers had recanted. Such a charge, he said, ought not to be brought forward "by men whom posterity will remember by nothing but recantations."[78] "We cheered and huzzaed," one of the Whig MP's noted in his diary. "Peel looked as if sweating blood. I never saw him so scalded, not even in the days of Brougham."[79] Peel, in turn, "showed how he had been touched to the quick by Macaulay's observation—for he occupied the House half an hour with his old story in vindication of his honesty in ratting on the Catholic question, which was quite unnecessary."[80]

Peel said in his reply that for the fourth time Macaulay had made a

74. September 21, 1831, *Hansard*, 3rd series, VII (1831) , 449–50.   75. Ibid., 450.
76. September 24, 1831, Wilson, ed., *Greville Diary*, II, 164.
77. E. J. Littleton's Diary, October 11, 1831, Aspinall, *Diaries*, 150.
78. December 16, 1831, *Works*, XI, 480.
79. December 16, 1831, Broughton, *Recollections*, IV, 155.
80. E. J. Littleton's Diary, December 18, 1831, Aspinall, *Diaries*, 172.

personal attack upon him, and characterized his latest strictures as "sweltering venom." The condemnation of people who changed their minds, he remarked, came with an ill grace from someone like Macaulay, who had admitted to the House that he was still undecided about his own attitude toward the (secret) ballot. "How did it happen that, like a certain animal (to which he meant by no means to compare him) between two bundles of hay, the honourable and learned Gentleman remained still balancing, and unable to decide, between two series of arguments?"[81] On this occasion, however, Peel's answer was not effective. Macaulay and his friend John Cam Hobhouse walked home from Westminster together in great glee, with the former unable to refrain from indulging in some pleasantries about a recent speech of Peel's at Oxford.[82]

The battle between the two men was not yet over. In his speech of February 28, 1832, on the third reading of the third Reform Bill, Macaulay once again singled out Peel for attack, this time for his silence on the question as to what sort of parliamentary reform the Tories would introduce should they come in. The country had a right to know this.[83] Peel counterattacked, but at the same time expressed the hope that on the subject of the Catholic question, all unkindly feelings between himself and Macaulay were now at an end. He did not wish to revive them; and was willing to acknowledge that "he always listened, not only with great attention, but with great admiration, to that flow of chaste and pure language, which, however rapid, seemed scarcely able to sustain the rich freight of thought and fancy which it bore along." But his last word was simply this. The reason he had not brought in a Reform Bill was that, people or no people, he happened to be against reform. Once the bill had passed, Peel was to change his mind on this point, and to accept what had been done. As for Macaulay, in taking on Peel, he had tangled with a giant and, in the general view, had come out on the whole the victor.

The following anecdote, noted in his diary by E. J. Littleton, the Whig MP, after the bill was carried in March 1832, confirms the high respect in which Peel came to hold Macaulay:

It was amusing to observe the extreme deference with which he [Peel] treated Macaulay—paid him compliments with evidently great pain, showed him much very distant civility but studiously called him through

81. December 17, 1831, *Hansard*, 3rd series, IX (1831–2) , 527, 534.
82. December 17, 1831, Broughton, *Recollections*, IV, 157.
83. March 19, 1832, *Hansard*, 3rd series, XI (1832) , 460–1.

the debate only "the learned gentleman" instead of the "Honourable and learned," the established form to a lawyer, he, however, well knowing that Macaulay was only a nominal lawyer, having never acquired more right to the title than that of living at an Inn of Court and keeping his term. But he thought that keeping him in view as a *lawyer* would detract from his reputation with the House.[84]

It didn't.

GIVEN THE EFFECT OF MACAULAY'S SPEECHES, GIVEN THE FAME AND notoriety that suddenly descended upon him, it is hardly surprising that in his own mind, as well as in the minds of some of the ministers, there should have arisen some thought of the reward of office for such a valuable Member. Some months after the Whigs had come in, they had completely reformed the existing bankruptcy laws; and, as part of that reform, Macaulay's commissionership was abolished. Thus his income was considerably reduced. According to his nephew's biography, he was forced to sell the gold medals he had won at Cambridge.[85] But it was not merely his financial needs that underlay his desire for office. He was, as we know, both proud and ambitious. His speeches had established his fame in Parliament and in society. By the late summer of 1831, Sydney Smith was explaining Brougham's deprecation of Macaulay's reform speeches by saying that "it is because Macaulay is not content with being a moon, but 'wants to do a little bit in the *solar line.'* "[86] He had been, without question, useful to the ministry. Why should he not receive office?

In September 1831, walking with two of his sisters, he imagined a minister asking him: "Why walk you here all the day idle?" And his reply (paraphrasing St. Matthew): "Because no man has hired me."[87] A few weeks later, in mid-November, Lord Grey sent for him. We know of what happened from his sister Margaret's *Recollections.* "That he will be offered a place," she wrote in her journal,

I have not the least doubt. He will refuse a Lordship of the Treasury, a Lordship of the Admiralty, or the Mastership of Ordnance. He will

84. E. J. Littleton's Diary, March 22, 1832, Aspinall, *Diaries,* 213.
85. Trevelyan, *Life and Letters,* 127.
86. July 29, 1831, Broughton, *Recollections,* IV, 124–5.
87. Trevelyan, *Life and Letters,* 134.

accept the Secretaryship of the Board of Control, but will not thank them for it; and would not accept that, but that he thinks it will be a place of importance during the approaching discussions on the East Indian monopoly.[88]

Macaulay stayed overnight at Grey's house, and then returned to London in the early afternoon. He said to Margaret, "I have nothing to tell you. Nothing." But it seemed that Grey had confided to Tom some confidential matter, which the inquisitive Margaret, looking at some papers her brother had thrown into the fire, found to concern the Duke of W. (Wellington?) and a certain major-general. Tom stayed up until 3 A.M. the next morning, writing. Margaret suggested to him that the task Grey had set him might be some sort of test from which he would be able to form a notion of Tom's ability in council. She had apparently hit the nail on the head. For Tom then declared "against the insolence of sending him to come and show off before he was hired."[89]

At the end of the following month, Lord Howick, Grey's son, told Macaulay that his father wished to make him a member of the government, but that an unexpected difficulty had arisen. According to the usage of the time, any MP obtaining major office had to stand for re-election, as a check on the influence of the Crown in dispensing patronage. By this time Calne had been transferred to Schedule B (i.e., was to lose one of its Members). And, according to Lord Lansdowne, the local population was so angry about this that Macaulay could not be sure of success in such an election. Even if he were to get in, which Lansdowne admitted was possible, any sort of struggle at Calne would be prejudicial to the chances of Lord Kerry, Lansdowne's son, at the next election. Margaret felt that this objection was "vexatious." The truth was, she felt, that Lord Lansdowne did not approve of Tom's views, which he thought too violent.[90]

Lord Holland indicated to Brougham that Grey had had some sort of "arrangement" ready for Macaulay, but that "alas! Calne cannot be vacated."[91] One solution to this problem was, of course, the assignment of another parliamentary seat to Macaulay. This was being canvassed. A Whig MP named Macdonald offered to go out and let Macaulay into his place. But at this point, the Lord Chancel-

88. November 14, 1831, Trevelyan, *Life and Letters*, 134.
89. Margaret Macaulay, *Recollections*, 47.
90. Ibid., 71.
91. *The Life and Times of Henry Lord Brougham Written by Himself* (3 vols., Edinburgh, 1871), III, 452.

lor exerted his sinister influence behind the scenes. Relations between Brougham and Macaulay had continued to be strained. In the
autumn of 1830, Brougham, whose political influence over the *Edinburgh Review* was then still supreme, had countermanded the commission of an article on French politics, to be written by Macaulay,
after the latter had already put in a month's work on it. The reason?
He wanted to write the article himself. Macaulay, furious, had
imagined Brougham's train of thought—probably accurately—as
follows:

I must write about this French Revolution, and I will write about it. If
you have told Macaulay to do it, you may tell him to let it alone. If he
has written an article, he may throw it behind the grate. . . . I am a
man who acts a prominent part in the world: he is nobody.[92]

Brougham was clearly jealous of Macaulay's dazzling successes. Predictably, he made disparaging remarks about his reform
speeches.[93] Now, he did his best to pour cold water on Macaulay's
chances for office. Coldly, he wrote to Lord Holland about Macdonald's offer to let Macaulay into his place, adding: "I know his
[Macaulay's] father intimately—the son very slightly." Hardly true,
and hardly a recommendation! From what Grey had said about the
matter, Brougham had concluded that it was the Mastership of the
Ordnance that he had in mind for Macaulay. Brougham, more than
ever jealous of the younger man's spectacular successes, recommended to Holland that any promotion of Macaulay over Sir James
Mackintosh was not to be thought of since—"in plain words" it
would be "preferring interest to gratitude"; adding that he did not
much like Macdonald's going out to make way for Macaulay.[94]

Grey, we know, lamented that the situation at Calne should be
preventing Macaulay from taking up another seat.[95] In mid-Febru-
ary, Macaulay had an interview with Lord Lansdowne about the
matter. It was a confrontation that revealed the attitude of pride
and independence Macaulay assumed toward his patron. Lansdowne
told him there was no particular vacancy in the government at this
time, but that he wanted to know Macaulay's wishes in the matter.

92. T.B.M. to Napier, September 16, 1830, Trevelyan, *Life and Letters*, 144. See also
Brougham to Napier, September 8, 1830, *Napier Correspondence*, 88.
93. July 29, 1831, Broughton, *Recollections*, IV, 124–5.
94. Henry Brougham to Lord Holland, December 2, 1831, Holland House MSS,
British Museum.
95. Journal of 3rd Lord Holland, January 28, 1832, ibid.

Margaret, who knew her brother well, commented in her journal that "Tom, in answer took rather a high tone. He said he was a poor man, but that he had as much as he wanted, and, as far as he was personally concerned, had no desire for office." But he believed that after the Reform Bill was passed, it would be absolutely necessary that the government should be strengthened, and that, approving of its general principles, he would then not be unwilling to join it.[96] He told Lord Lansdowne that the government would find itself so weak after the bill had passed that he (Tom) would even be prepared for a coalition with those who had opposed the bill—a realistic view in odd contrast with the black-and-white rhetoric about Tories and Whigs that Macaulay had been employing in his speeches.[97] In the event, office did not come to Macaulay until after the Reform Bill was passed. It was then, in the summer of 1832, that he was appointed a commissioner of the Board of Control for India.

MACAULAY'S ENERGY WAS SUCH THAT HE WAS ABLE TO CONTINUE writing contributions for the *Edinburgh Review* in addition to performing his duties in Parliament and, after his appointment to the Board of Control, in office. It is instructive to observe the way in which his articles reinforced and reflected the major points he was making in his parliamentary speeches. In them, one finds his belief in progress, his conviction that in the course of time the general movement of political thought and practice must inevitably lead in an ever more liberal direction. Thus, reviewing the *History of the War of the Succession* by his Tory opponent but personal friend Lord Mahon, Macaulay noted that if the author were to live fifty years longer, there could be no doubt that, as he now boasted of the resemblance the Tories of the present time bore to the Whigs of the Revolution, he would then boast of the resemblance borne by the Tories of 1882 to "those immortal patriots, the Whigs of the Reform Bill."[98]

This statement was a more explicit proclamation of progress than Macaulay's observation in his essay on Mirabeau six months before

96. February 12, 1832, Trevelyan, *Life and Letters*, 138.
97. Margaret Macaulay, *Recollections*, 81.
98. T.B.M., "War of the Succession in Spain" (1833), *Works*, VIII, 303.

that if M. Dumont (the translator and disciple of Bentham) had died in 1799, he would have died, "to use the new cant word," a decided conservative. If the younger Pitt, however, had lived in 1832, *he* would have been a decided reformer. Why? Macaulay's answer was, once again, that men were creatures of circumstances.[99] This doctrine, on the face of it, did not necessarily imply continual progress. After all, circumstances could change in a conservative as well as a progressive direction. But here, too, progress was—so to speak—"built in." For the examples chosen by Macaulay conveyed the message that in 1799, during the French revolutionary wars, both Dumont and Pitt would have been, with some justification, on the conservative side; whereas the Reform Bill would have united them in its support. In other words, the passage of time brought greater political liberalism. The linkage of Dumont and Pitt was of some significance; for its implication was that the hero of the Tories and the hero of the Benthamites shared views that would unite them, as all sensible men must be united, when it came to the crucial issues of world history.

Another theme that reverberated through the *Edinburgh* essays was comparison of the Reform Bill to other great events in history. In the article on Hampden (December 1831), for instance, Macaulay praised Queen Elizabeth as "an admirable study for politicians who live in unquiet times." She had made concessions, not grudgingly or tardily, as Charles I was to make them, but promptly and cordially. "If her successors had inherited her wisdom with her Crown, Charles the First might have died of old age; and James the Second would never have seen St. Germains. "[100] This reinforced the lesson taught negatively by the hope of the French aristocracy during the great Revolution. "They would not have reform; and they had revolution. They would not endure Turgot; and they were forced to endure Robespierre."[101]

Naturally enough, the substance of Macaulay's analogies to the French Revolution changed as the passage of the Reform Bill moved closer to reality and at last took place. The question now was no longer merely one of concession against stubbornness on the part of the governing classes. It concerned the long-range effects of the Revolution. In the course of his French tour of 1830, Macaulay had noted in his journal on the subject of the Revolution of 1789: "The

99. T.B.M., "Mirabeau" (1832), *Works*, VIII, 221.
100. T.B.M., "Memorials of Hampden" (1831), *Works*, VIII, 122.
101. T.B.M., "Mirabeau," *Works*, VIII, 242.

general effect of that great change has been most salutary. A vast and thriving middle class has risen on the ruins of an exclusive and oppressive aristocracy."[102] So Macaulay was perfectly sincere when he wrote in his essay on Burleigh that just as the volcano of the Reformation had spent its rage, and the landmarks it had swept away had been replaced, while "desert" had been turned into "garden" by its lava, so also would the great French Revolution continue to fertilize the soil it had devastated; which led him to remark that the more he observed the signs of his own times, the more he felt his heart filled with good hope for the future destinies of the human race.[103]

Did this mean that Macaulay regarded the Reform Bill as yet another volcanic eruption? The answer was: No; or, rather, Yes, but only so far as its beneficial effects were concerned. For he took pride in the fact that the "great change" just effected was milder than any revolution in history, and was brought about by the force of reason, under the forms of law. "The work of three civil wars has been accomplished by three sessions of Parliament." Not a sword had been drawn, not an estate had been confiscated. And during the fiercest excitement of the contest, "that first fortnight of that immortal May," there had not been one moment at which a sanguinary act would not have filled the country with horror and indignation.[104] This was, of course, a statement after the fact. We need only recall that in September 1831 Macaulay was convinced that blood would flow in London.[105] Once the crisis was surmounted, it was easy to look with hindsight at its inevitably peaceful course, and to forget that there may have been a narrow escape from major violence. But the final peaceful triumph was undisputed. And Macaulay had, after all, some reason to become its most lyrical celebrant.

102. Trinity Journal, September 1830.
103. T.B.M., "Burleigh" (1832), Works, VIII, 189–90.
104. T.B.M., "Mirabeau," Works, VIII, 229–30.
105. Margaret Macaulay to H. J. Thatcher, September 30, 1831, Huntington MSS.

VIII

HOLLAND HOUSE
AND LEEDS

MACAULAY'S PARLIAMENTARY TRIUMPHS HAD THEIR COUNTERPART IN
London society. "For a century and more," Gladstone was to write,
"perhaps no man in this country, with the exceptions of Mr. Pitt and
Lord Byron, had obtained at thirty-two the fame of Macaulay." As a
result of his parliamentary and literary success, he received "an
amount and quality of social attentions such as invariably partake of
adulation and idolatry, and as perhaps the high circles of London
never before or since have lavished on a man whose claims lay only in
himself, and not in his descent, his rank, or his possessions."[1] One
wealthy Member of Parliament (E. J. Littleton) was so enraptured
with Macaulay's having said something civil about his house "that he
insisted on showing me all its beauties and actually carried me into
the nursery still filled with the slops of his children."[2] Talleyrand, a
living chapter of history himself, now French Ambassador in London, expressed the hope that he might hear Macaulay speak in the
House of Commons. "Il avait entendu tous les grands orateurs, et il
désirait à présent entendre Monsieur Macaulay."[3] Whig society and
the literati on its periphery had found a new lion.

One must remember the aristocratic tone of political and social
life at the time, in order to gain some perspective on Macaulay's

1. Gladstone, *Gleanings*, II, 268.
2. T.B.M. to Hannah, July 26, 1831, Trinity Correspondence.
3. February 6, 1832, Wilson, ed., *Greville Diary*, II, 152.

position. When Poulett Thomson, a merchant who became vice-president of the Board of Trade in Grey's cabinet, took his seat on the government benches, he was exposed to mortifying sneers.[4] The Whig cousinhood, which played a predominant part in the politics of the time, looked back with pride to the heroic period in the late seventeenth century that had witnessed the first Whigs taking up arms against the double threat of Stuart despotism and Roman Catholicism. Their watchword, then as now, was liberty; then as now, they aligned themselves on the side of "the people." But this alignment had no democratic implications. For they regarded themselves, then as now, not as comrades but as leaders of the people, fighting not alongside them but on their behalf for the liberties of freeborn Englishmen. They had their great families—Spencers, Richmonds, Stanleys, Ponsonbys—and they had their martyrs—heroes like Russell and Sidney, who had laid down their lives for "the good old cause." Nothing better symbolized for them the historical continuity of which they were so aware than that Lord John Russell, who introduced the Reform Bill in the House of Commons, was a descendant of one of those martyrs.

That this continuity was more imaginary than real did not weaken the myth. After all, both Whigs and Tories had made the Revolution of 1688; though it was true that (as Macaulay pointed out in his essay on Lord Chatham), the Whigs were "that party which professed peculiar attachment to the principles of the Revolution."[5] After the Hanoverians had become firmly established on the throne, the Whigs emerged as upholders of monarchy and the Establishment; and from then on, eighteenth-century politics became so much a matter of struggles for power between groups and factions that for some decades it made little sense to speak of an extended battle between a Whig and a Tory Party. The designation of the Rockingham group, which "crystallized" under George III, as in the great Whig tradition owed more to the eloquence of its publicist of genius, Edmund Burke, than to fact. And the platform of the greatest of the Rockinghams, Charles James Fox, patron saint of the Whigs of Macaulay's time—"peace, retrenchment, and reform"—was carried out as much by the nineteenth-century liberal Tories and the Canningites as by the Whigs who, as we know, had for long been unable to agree on anything but the desirability of Catholic emancipation.[6] However, in the period of the French revolutionary wars, Fox had

4. Halévy, *Triumph of Reform*, 14.   5. T.B.M., "Chatham," *Works*, VIII, 366–7.
6. See Donald Southgate, *The Passing of the Whigs, 1832–1886* (London, 1962).

stood up against the repressive policies of the younger Pitt; and it was temptingly easy to imagine the mantle of the heroic figures of the seventeenth century descending upon him.

But to stand midwife at the birth of English political democracy was far from the intention of this Whig élite. In some ways the Tories, henceforth known as "Conservatives," were far more in tune with the tendencies of the future than the Whigs, who seemed increasingly out of place in an ever more plutocratic society. They themselves survived as a part of the Liberal Party because they were kept in touch with reality by others: Benthamites, Canningites, Free Traders, Dissenters. In 1832 they were no closer to trade, business, and finance than the Tories, and in economic terms could be said to be more liberal than the opposing party only by virtue of the negative factor of not having the bulk of the country squires on their side. What they did possess in greater measure than their Tory opponents and what contributed to their survival in a deferential society was what Burke had called "the unbought grace of life." Into the nineteenth century, they preserved enclaves of the eighteenth at their great London houses, where literature and society commingled, where exquisite wit was as much a tradition as exquisite food and wine, where aristocracy meant not merely ownership of vast acres, but brilliant conversation, learning lightly carried, and perhaps above all an innate sense of social superiority. This feeling of superiority, derived from an awareness of spiritual as well as physical kinship and from a strongly developed sense of historical self-consciousness, contributed to the atmosphere of grand Whiggery so memorably depicted in the opening pages of Lord David Cecil's *Young Melbourne*.

Did Macaulay actually penetrate this citadel? Gladstone remarked that while as a rule a man not born a Liberal might become one, a Whig was born, not made.[7] Yet one perceptive later writer—a Russell to boot—called Macaulay "probably the only man who, being born outside the privileged enclosure, ever penetrated to its heart and assimilated its spirit."[8] G. M. Young was more cautious in writing that "without birth or manners he made his way into the inner, though never the innermost, counsels of the Whigs."[9] Who was right?

In considering the question, one must recall that these aristocratic coteries were not self-sufficient. The old eighteenth-century relation-

7. Gladstone, *Gleanings*, II, 288–9.
8. G. W. E. Russell. Quoted by Southgate, *Whigs,* 196.
9. G. M. Young, ed., *Speeches of Lord Macaulay with his Minute on Indian Education* (London, 1935), viii.

ship of patron to artist or writer had given way to a new relationship, in which the publisher gradually took the place formerly held by the patron. But in the Whig circles of the Regency and the 1830's, there still flourished figures like the poet-singer Thomas Moore, who actually lived at Bowood, and the banker-poet Samuel Rogers, who regularly dined and wined in high society, and lent intellectual and artistic distinction to it. It was at Holland House, now the home of its third Lord and his Lady, that this tradition was still in its fullest flower at the time of the Reform Bill. In a commemorative essay written after the death of Lord Holland, Macaulay recalled Holland House as the favorite resort of wits and beauties, painters and poets, scholars, philosophers, and statesmen. "The last debate was discussed in one corner, and the last comedy of Scribe in another; while Wilkie gazed with modest admiration on Sir Joshua's Baretti; while Mackintosh turned over Thomas Aquinas to verify a quotation; while Talleyrand related his conversations with Barras at the Luxembourg, or his ride with Lannes over the field of Austerlitz."[10]

In his *English Bards and Scotch Reviewers,* Byron had exclaimed:

> *Blest be the banquets spread at Holland House,*
> *Where Scotchmen feed, and critics may carouse.*

His reference had been to the chief *Edinburgh* reviewers—Horner, Jeffrey, Brougham, Sydney Smith (a Scotsman only by virtue of his close association with the others) —who, from the start of the century, had found a hospitable roof at Holland House, along with the leading statesmen of the day. The house itself, located in what was then still a rustic Kensington, dated from the early seventeenth century, and had been in the possession of the related Fox and Holland families for almost two hundred years. It was a big mansion, with spacious and beautiful grounds, built, as Macaulay put it, "in the very perfection of the old Elizabethan style."[11] He described the place in a letter to his sister Hannah: the fine avenue of elms leading up to the great entrance; the considerable number of very large and very comfortable rooms rich with antique carving and gilding, but carpeted and furnished with all the skill of the best modern upholsterers; the famous library, with little cabinets for study branching off from it, looking out onto the green park.[12] Every room breathed history. After all, this was the place William III had called home for a few weeks in 1688. This was where Addison had been married and

10. T.B.M., "Lord Holland" (1841) , *Works,* IX, 406.
11. T.B.M. to Hannah, May 30, 1831, Trevelyan, *Life and Letters,* 150.
12. T.B.M. to Hannah, May 27, 1831, Trevelyan, *Life and Letters,* 150.

spent the last few years of his life. This was where Lord Holland's uncle, Charles James Fox, had passed his youth, and where the Hollands had extended hospitality to all the leading statesmen and literary figures of the age.

It was in late May of 1831, in the course of a musicale at Lansdowne House, that Macaulay was first introduced, at her request, to Lady Holland, whom he described as "a bold-looking woman, with the remains of a fine person, and the air of Queen Elizabeth." She asked him to dinner at Holland House three days later, and he chronicled his arrival there in verse that revealed at the same time his delight in the invitation and his determination not to seem overawed by it.

> *Scene. The Great Entrance of Holland House. Enter Macaulay and two footmen in livery.*
> First Footman: "Sir, may I venture to demand your name?"
> Macaulay: "Macaulay, and thereto I add MP.
>   And the addition, even in these proud halls,
>   May well ensure the bearer some respect."[13]

One can imagine Macaulay's feelings of pride and pleasure, as Lady Holland personally showed him a Reynolds portrait of Fox, and Luttrell took him to the seat in the garden where Rogers liked to compose his verses and where Lord Holland had had inscribed his own lines:

> *Here Rogers sate; and here for ever dwell*
> *With me those pleasures which he sang so well.*[14]

The history of Lady Holland exemplified the libertarian atmosphere, aeons removed from Clapham Evangelicalism, that prevailed in the mansion. She had left her first husband, Sir Godfrey Webster, to elope with Lord Holland, and a son was born to them before they were married. She was a formidable figure, notorious for an imperious manner that brooked no contradiction. Sydney Smith once felt impelled to write that London apothecaries gave a particular draft to persons who had been frightened at Holland House.[15] When she told Macaulay that she hated the word "womanly," since men never

13. T.B.M. to Hannah, June 1, 1831, Trevelyan, *Life and Letters*, 153.
14. Ibid., 154–5.
15. Sydney Smith to Lady Ashburton, November 10, 1836, Nowell C. Smith, ed., *The Letters of Sydney Smith* (2 vols., Oxford, 1953) , II, 647.

used it except as a term of reproach, he thought to himself that it was a reproach he would scarcely be inclined to bring against her.[16] She herself liked male company better than female. "I never will go up to the hen coop with the ladies, and prefer not hearing the debate," she wrote to her son, dismissing the possibility of a visit to the House of Lords during the Reform Bill discussions.[17]

On Macaulay's first visit to Holland House, she was most gracious to him. Yet, even after all he had heard about her, he was surprised by her haughtiness. "The centurion did not keep his soldiers in better order than she keeps her guests. It is to one 'Go,' and he goeth, and to another 'Do this,' and it is done. 'Ring the bell, Mr. Macaulay.'—'Lay down that screen, Lord Russell; you will spoil it.'—'Mr. Allen, take a candle and show Mr. Cradock the picture of Buonaparte.' "[18] John Allen, a Scottish physician who resided at Holland House, was made to fetch and carry for her like a servant, and had to put up with her manifold eccentricities, such as her tremendous fear of even the slightest thunderstorm: when one was in the offing, she retired to her bedroom, closed all the windows, and lit candles.[19]

She clearly admired Macaulay, and even went so far as to ask him to take up residence at Holland House. But he declined the favor; since, as he wrote his sister Hannah, he was neither qualified nor inclined to succeed Allen in his post.[20] She was as affable to him as her manner permitted, praised some of his articles to the skies, and did not hold what she nonetheless called his "want of *pedigree*" against him.[21] Still, she tried his patience, lecturing him on the indecorum of talking about young ladies without adding "Miss"; falling into a violent rage with him, for no apparent reason that he could see, over his essay on Horace Walpole; and occasionally trying to order him about, as she did everyone, including her husband.[22] But, as Macaulay put it many years later, he was never very complying.[23] And his frank description of her for Hannah's benefit is by no means entirely complimentary:

16. T.B.M. to Hannah, May 30, 1831, Trinity Correspondence.
17. April 9, 1832, Earl of Ilchester, ed., *Elizabeth Lady Holland to Her Son, 1821–1845* (London, 1946), 132.
18. T.B.M. to Hannah, May 30, 1831, Trevelyan, *Life and Letters*, 151.
19. May 7, 1822, John Gore, ed., *The Creevey Papers* (New York, 1963), 175.
20. T.B.M. to Hannah, September 20, 1832, Trevelyan, *Life and Letters*, 199.
21. Lady Holland to her son, May 19, 1840, Ilchester, ed., *Lady Holland to Her Son,* 184.
22. T.B.M. to Hannah, May 21, 1833, and July 25, 1831, Trinity Correspondence; T.B.M. to Napier, November 15, 1833, British Museum Add. MSS 34,616, f. 194.
23. Trinity Journal, July 13, 1856.

A great lady—fanciful, hysterical, and hypochondriacal, ill-natured and good-natured, sceptical and superstitious, afraid of ghosts, and not of God—would not for the world begin a journey on a Friday morning and thought nothing of running away from her husband.[24]

Yet her very eccentricities lent, if perhaps not a special charm, at least a special character to Holland House, and in that way intensified the pleasure of regular guests at finding themselves there. By July 1831, Macaulay had become one of their number. He had even been to "dine and sleep" there, on the occasion of a splendid dinner that included among the guests the Duke and Duchess of Richmond, the Marchioness of Clanricarde, and his admirer, the aged Talleyrand. Macaulay graphically depicted the last, head sunk down between high shoulders, one foot hideously distorted, face pale as a corpse, wrinkled to a frightful degree.[25] For the delectation of his sister, he described some other Holland House dinners, one where "we dined like Emperors, and jabbered in several languages";[26] another where those present were "all Lords except myself," and the menu proceeded from soup, sole, and salmon to roast beef "with brown pratees," lamb chops, veal cutlets, and sweetbreads—ending with port, Madeira, sherry, champagne, claret, and Majorca wine.[27]

His host on these occasions, the third Lord Holland, embodied qualities particularly appealing to the young Macaulay. After his death, some verses were found in Lord Holland's handwriting which aptly summed up both his lineage and his character:

> *Nephew of Fox, and friend of Grey,*
> *Enough my meed of fame.*
> *If those who deign'd to observe me say*
> *I tarnished neither name.*

The lines savor of a veritable Roman modesty and virtue, familial piety, and a sense of history and tradition. That he himself was their author demonstrated his literary inclinations. He was, moreover, learned in Spanish literature; and his *Memoirs of the Whig Party*—he himself had served in Fox's "Ministry of all the Talents"—has remained an important source for the political history of the early nineteenth century.

24. T.B.M. to Hannah, June 10, 1833, Trinity Correspondence.
25. T.B.M. to Hannah, July 11, 1831, Trevelyan, *Life and Letters*, 167–8.
26. T.B.M. to Hannah, July 25, 1831, Trevelyan, *Life and Letters*, 170.
27. T.B.M. to Hannah and Margaret Macaulay, July 2, 1832, Morgan MSS.

By the time Macaulay came to know him, he suffered a great deal from a painful siege of the gout, and spent much of his time in a wheelchair. Macaulay, who described him to Hannah as "a fine old gentleman very gouty and good natured,"[28] grew to like him extremely. He had, so Tom reported to his sister Margaret, a good-natured way of contradicting in conversation that put one instantly at ease. "He lowers his eyebrows as his uncle used to do: 'Well, Mr. Macaulay, I cannot see that.' "[29] He bore pain heroically, was never cross, and always managed to inspire good humor in others. "I admire him more, I think," Macaulay declared, "than any man whom I know."[30] In his obituary tribute to Lord Holland in the *Edinburgh Review*, he praised him for carrying on his uncle's traditions of toleration and civil freedom, and recalled his face as "the most gracious and interesting countenance that was ever lighted up by the mingled lustre of intelligence and benevolence."[31] His life, Sydney Smith had written, was one incessant effort "to resist oppression, to promote justice, and restrain the abuse of Power."[32]

Lord Holland's political views during the period of the Reform Bill debates reflect a good-humored cynicism about the world and its madcap ways, as well as what Bulwer-Lytton called elements of indolence and frigidity mixed in with his good nature.[33] At the end of 1831 he wrote that failure to pass the bill would mean civil war and revolution, and above all the loss of the House of Lords, "to which our aristocracy is so strongly attached."[34] It was characteristic that he should refer to "our aristocracy," as if he were not himself a part of it, as if a man of his perception and position would place himself as a matter of course above anything so vulgar by virtue of its collective nature as class, even if that class consisted of members of the nobility. In a cabinet discussion a few days later on the question as to whether Lord Grey was to recommend the creation of six or ten peers to the King, Lord Holland declared himself for ten, "though I should have preferred *fifteen*, for I was an old tennis player and loved that way of counting fifteen/thirty/forty/game and had no objection to the risk to boot."[35] Finally, there was his comment on

28. T.B.M. to Hannah, June 10, 1833, Trinity Correspondence.
29. November 22, 1831, Margaret Macaulay, *Recollections*, 49.
30. T.B.M. to Hannah, September 25, 1832, Trevelyan, *Life and Letters*, 199.
31. T.B.M., "Lord Holland" (1841), *Works*, IX, 397.
32. "A Portrait" (1830), *Smith Letters*, II, 526.
33. Robert Bulwer-Lytton, *The Life, Letters, and Remains of Edward Bulwer, Lord Lytton* (2 vols., London, 1883), I, 252.
34. December 27, 1831, Holland House MSS, British Museum.
35. January 2, 1832, ibid.

the "National Fast Day" of March 1832, known among the working classes as the "farce day." Lord Holland's feeling was that nine-tenths or ninety-nine-hundredths of "the reasonable class of society" condemned in their hearts, just as "the rabble" did, the utter uselessness of the observance of "such superstitions." But "each in looking grave, abstaining from his usual avocations, and going to Church tickles his own vanity by flattering himself that he is of the humbugging and not humbugged portion of mankind and so encourages the hypocrisy he despises."[36] Here is the voice of the eighteenth century, speaking in the idiom of Gibbon, dividing mankind into a class of reasonable beings and the rabble (with no nonsense about popular virtues), utterly cynical about religion, contemptuous of the "humbug" everywhere around it. Not, perhaps, an altogether endearing set of attitudes; rather, one that confirmed Brougham's acute comment that Lord Holland regarded men with the eye not of a brother, but of a naturalist.[37]

It was hardly surprising then, that Dr. John Allen, permanent resident in Holland House, was widely known as what Macaulay called him—"atheist in ordinary to the household of my Lady Holland"; and that Lady Holland had never heard of the parable of the talents.[38] On one occasion, as one of Tom's sisters reported to another, Tom was about to call for a Bible to verify a quotation, but refrained from doing so, as he was afraid that his host and hostess might be ashamed at not being able to produce one. His sister Fanny's comment on this was: "I do not think in a house where an atheist is kept, he need have been very scrupulous in this matter."[39] She was right. The atmosphere at Holland House—skeptical, sophisticated, fashionable—was a far cry from the solid piety and devotion of the Macaulay household.

MACAULAY THOROUGHLY ENJOYED HIS ROLE AS SOCIAL LION. WE catch glimpses of him dining with a literary party including Samuel Rogers and the German philosopher Schlegel; listening to Sydney Smith, "rector-like [in his] amplitude and rubicundity," discoursing

36. January 3, 1832, ibid.

37. Cited in Bulwer, *Life, Letters, and Remains*, I, 253.

38. T.B.M. to Hannah, June 10, 1833, Trinity Correspondence; same to same, May 30, 1831, Trevelyan, *Life and Letters*, 151.

39. Fanny Macaulay to Margaret, [February] 1833, Huntington MSS.

on the evil wrought by strait-laced Tories like Perceval, "the most mischievous man that ever lived," because he made oppression and humbug respectable by his decent character, his admirable demeanor, and his skill in debating; and effecting his escape just in time from the inevitable tedium of a lecture by Robert Owen, a fellow guest at a fancy-dress ball given by Isaac Lyon Goldsmid.[40] This was the season that saw the London triumph of the legendary Paganini—Tom Moore noted in his journal that he could play divinely, "but then come his tricks and surprises, his bow in convulsions, and his enharmonics like the mewlings of an expiring cat."[41] Macaulay, who had no ear at all for music, wrote to Hannah:

> *The dull crowd that flocks*
> *To an opera-box*
> *Had much better come to the Jewesses' ball.*
> *For it costs a good guinea*
> *To hear Paganini*
> *And here are twelve fiddlers for nothing at all.*[42]

His letters to his sisters during this period are full of *joie de vivre*. They convey in lively fashion his delight at finding himself caught up both as actor and spectator in great events and in London's high society. At one of Lady Grey's "routs," he got into "the thickest and hottest jam of Duchesses and Countesses which I ever saw in my life."[43] The very next day, he dined in the company of a Polish prince, a Spanish general, the American Ambassador, and an English baronet.[44] These were private occasions. But through his letters, we can also participate in some of the public and ceremonial occasions of this period. Here, for instance, is his graphic description of a royal procession during the summer of 1831: "The whole had something of that hazy gorgeousness which characterises Turner's pictures. The long succession of State carriages, white horses, red liveries, heralds in coats of cloth of gold, life-guards with helmets and cuirasses, passed through a roaring ocean of heads and waving hats with a kind of dim magnificence which was quite delightful."[45] Two days later, Lord Althorp called him and the other Members of Parliament to the House of Commons in drawing-room dress, for the presentation of

40. April 2, 1832, Moore, *Journal*, 210; T.B.M. to Hannah, June 14, 1831, Trinity Correspondence; same to same, June 7 and 8, 1831, Trevelyan, *Life and Letters*, 158–9.
41. June 23, 1831, Moore, *Journal*, 206.
42. T.B.M. to Hannah, June 13, 1831, Trinity Correspondence.
43. T.B.M. to Hannah and Margaret, July 16, 1832, Trinity Correspondence.
44. Idem.   45. T.B.M. to Hannah, June 22, 1831, Trinity Correspondence.

the Address. They proceeded from the House to St. James's Palace in carriages. Macaulay was somewhat disappointed in the state staircase—"those at the London clubhouses beat it all to nothing." To make up for this, there was the sight of Lord Wellesley holding the white staff at the King's elbow, "looking as if he had just been taken out of a bandbox." There followed the awkward ceremony of two hundred people trying to bow out backwards: "We came out with broken shins and broken toes in abundance—vowing—many of us—that we would never Ko-tou [kowtow] more."[46]

At the great Guildhall dinner given by the City of London for Reformers in both Houses to celebrate the final passage of the bill, he ate two large dishes of turtle soup, and reveled in the spectacle of the great hall, hung with scarlet cloth, brilliantly lit, and in the sounds of the musicians playing in the gallery, the immense clapping of hands, stamping of feet, and thumping of tables as the Whigs celebrated their victory.[47] At the coronation of William IV, Macaulay appeared in court dress and, as he put it, "looked a perfect Lovelace in it."[48] He wore his official costume, ordered

from a topping tailor in Bond Street who makes uniforms for H. M. Guards. . . . A blue coat, with collar and cuffs blazing with gold lace,— and blue trousers with a lovely delicate stripe of gold running down them,—a hat enough of itself to break all the hearts in sixteen boarding-schools, a sword—such a sword—

> *A better never did sustain itself*
> *Upon a soldier's thigh.*[49]

All this conjures up the picture of Macaulay, basking in the applause of the great, delighting in the fruits of his success, enjoying to the full a way of life that happily combined parliamentary activity with dining and wining in society. Is such a picture valid?

MACAULAY HAS BECOME SUCH A FAMILIAR FIGURE IN CONTEMPORARY accounts of London society in the early 1830's that it is easy to assume he naturally belonged there, if not by right of birth, then at

46. T.B.M. to Hannah, June 24, 1831, Trinity Correspondence.
47. T.B.M. to Hannah and Margaret, July 12, 1832, Morgan MSS.
48. T.B.M. to Hannah, September 9, 1831, Trevelyan, *Life and Letters,* 176.
49. T.B.M. to Margaret, January 11, 1833, Morgan MSS.

least by right of ability; and that he moved easily and comfortably in those circles. This is not altogether so. It was not merely a matter of getting accustomed to unfamiliar situations. That he soon managed to do. Thus in July 1831 he reported to Hannah that at a dinner held in Littleton's "palace" in Grosvenor Place, wines of which he had never heard the names had been served, particularly the "intermediate wines" (as he put it), connecting hock and burgundy. More important, it was at this same dinner that he made the discovery that the best use of his conversational powers was to employ them *tête-à-tête:* "A man is flattered by your talking your best to him alone. Ten to one he is piqued by your overpowering him before a company."[50] It was a lesson he did not always take to heart. That he remembered it on occasion emerges in Greville's account of his first encounter with Macaulay at Holland House. Greville admired the extent and variety of Macaulay's information, and found that at the same time there was "no kind of usurpation of the conversation, no tenacity as to opinion or facts, no assumption of superiority. . . ."[51] For Macaulay, such deportment must have meant considerable exercise of self-control. For someone with his great learning and capacious memory, who was making his way in aristocratic circles by virtue of talent rather than birth, the temptation to dominate in conversation must have been almost irresistible; his triumphs in politics and society had not been achieved without some cost to himself.

After his first speech on reform, he had written to his friend Ellis: "My speech has set me in the front rank, if I can keep there; and it has not been my luck hitherto to lose ground when I have once got it."[52] The image here is one of battle; and he came back to it as he reminisced later in life about this period. Twenty years after the Reform Bill struggles he met his maternal cousin Henry Mills on a visit to Bristol, and entered this comment in his journal: "I was very friendly and cordial. There was a time when I was half ashamed of being related to vulgar people. That was when I was fighting my way against all sorts of difficulties."[53] And again, just before his death, he wrote to one of his nieces about what a kind friend Sir James Mackintosh had been to him when he was a young fellow, fighting his way uphill.[54] For a man of ambition and, in Lady Holland's

50. T.B.M. to Hannah, July 26, 1831, Trinity Correspondence.
51. February 6, 1832, Wilson, ed., *Greville Diary,* II, 152.
52. T.B.M. to Ellis, March 30, 1831, Trevelyan, *Life and Letters,* 147.
53. Trinity Journal, August 14, 1852.
54. September 1859, Trevelyan, *Life and Letters,* 162.

words, no pedigree, with no money to help make up for the lack of birth, trying to make a political career with the Whigs must indeed often have seemed like a battle. Like any victorious soldier, Macaulay enjoyed savoring the fruits of victory. But even in his songs of triumph there are to be found occasional touches of irony—or is it embarrassment?—touches befitting a champion of the Roundheads and a sturdy defender of the claims of the middle classes. Thus, in describing to Hannah the company at Goldsmid's costume ball, Tom could not resist adding that it was "not such as we *exclusives* think quite the thing. There was a little too much of St. Mary Axe[55] about it—Jewesses by dozens, and Jews by scores."[56] A few weeks later, after a fashionable dinner attended by various members of the peerage, he urged her to "listen, and be proud of your connection with one who is admitted to eat and drink in the same room with beings so exalted."[57]

Even at this time, when high life was new to him, he had doubts about some of its aspects. For instance, he was amazed at the literary tastes prevailing in Whig society: "that such men as Lord Grenville, Lord Holland, Hobhouse, Lord Byron, and others of high rank in intellect, should place Rogers, as they do, above Southey, Moore, and even Scott himself, is what I cannot conceive. But this comes of being in the highest society of London."[58] After a year or so, his strictures became more fundamental. He was still invited out to dinner night after night. But now he had become "sick of Lords with no brains in their heads, and Ladies with paint on their cheeks, and politics and politicians, and that reeking furnace of a House."[59] He expressed a heartfelt conviction when he wrote to his sister Hannah in the late summer of 1833:

I am the only parvenu I ever heard of who, after being courted into splendid circles, and after having succeeded beyond expectation in political life, acquired in a few months a profound contempt for rank, fashion, power, popularity, and money—for all pleasures but those which derive from the exercise of the intellect and the affections.[60]

55. A London district heavily settled by Jews.

56. T.B.M. to Hannah, June 8, 1831, Trinity Correspondence.

57. T.B.M. to Hannah, July 26, 1831, Trinity Correspondence.

58. T.B.M. to Hannah, June 3, 1831, Trevelyan, *Life and Letters*, 156. See also his remark in the essay on Horace Walpole (1833), to the effect that Walpole's judgment of literature was altogether perverted by his aristocratic feelings. *Works*, VIII, 321.

59. T.B.M. to Hannah, June 14, 1833, Trevelyan, *Life and Letters*, 217.

60. T.B.M. to Hannah, July 22, 1833, Trinity Correspondence.

How HAD THIS COME ABOUT? How DID IT HAPPEN THAT THIS FAVORITE of the gods, who had made his mark in Parliament, who had captured Whig society, and who, as much as anyone else, was aware of what those achievements meant and could put them into historical perspective, tired so quickly of the life of society and affairs, and talked so philosophically about relinquishing it? Part of the answer must be sought in his dissatisfaction with his own role in politics. For a person as high-minded as he was, determined to be his own man, government office did not supply the financial security and political independence he craved. Office came belatedly, in any event. As far back as August 1831, *Blackwood's* had commented that it was the fashion to talk of Macaulay as "the Burke of our age"; and that "had he happened to be a *somebody,* we should, no doubt have seen Tom in high places ere now."[61] But he had to wait for almost a year, until June 1832. It was only then that he replaced Mackintosh (who had just died) as one of the commissioners of the Board of Control for India, and was duly re-elected for Calne, as custom required.

"Dual Control" had been introduced into the system of Indian government in 1784, with the Board representing Parliament, and the Court of Directors representing the proprietors of the East India Company. The two bodies jointly administered Indian affairs; and the president of the Board of Control—in 1832 the Evangelical Canningite Charles Grant—occupied a seat in the cabinet. Macaulay at once immersed himself in a study of Indian politics, and reported to Hannah and Margaret in early June that he was deep in Zemindars, Ryots, Polygars, Courts of Phoujdary, and Courts of Nizamut Adawlut.[62] He found himself busier than ever, "with India and the Edinburgh Review on my hands—the life of Mirabeau to be criticized—the Rajah of Travancore to be kept in order, and the bad money which the Emperor of the Burmese has had the impudence to send us by way of tribute to be exchanged for better."[63] One of his duties was to examine the claims of moneylenders on the native sovereigns of India. The energy he applied to this and the other tasks demanded by his new position amazed Charles Grant. Shortly after assuming office, Macaulay drew up two reports in twenty-four hours, dealing with cases that occupied about a cartload of paper. "You know how fast I read," he wrote to his sisters; "and the President

61. [Wilson], *Noctes,* IV, 356.
62. T.B.M. to Hannah and Margaret, June 10, 1832, Trevelyan, *Life and Letters,* 186.
63. T.B.M. to Hannah and Margaret, July 2, 1833, Morgan MSS.

seemed ready to think me a conjurer."[64] And again, "This I will say for myself," he told Hannah in 1833, "that when I do sit down to work, I work harder and faster than any person that I ever knew."[65]

Yet office did not by any means give Macaulay undiluted satisfaction. He had to see a great deal of "such pests as those curry-coloured watering place Nabobs."[66] Then there were annoying colleagues on the Board to be dealt with—such as Gordon, Member of Parliament for Cricklade, "a fat, ugly, spiteful, snarling, sneering old rascal of a slave-driver," who caused much trouble by wanting to remodel everything.[67] At the end of the year, upon the death of Hyde Villiers, Macaulay succeeded him as secretary of the Board, a position that paid £1,500 a year and carried with it the privilege of unlimited franking—one greatly appreciated by this indefatigable letter-writer.

Now, his India Board duties became more onerous; and he had to get up at five o'clock in the morning and work before breakfast in order to write his articles for the *Edinburgh*.[68] In his role of "the judicious poet," he turned to verse during the spring of 1833 to point the contrast between the demands on his time now and before:

> *Oh the charming month of May*
> *When I was in Opposition,*
> *I walked ten miles a day,*
> *And lounged at the Exhibition.*
> *Oh the hateful month of May*
> *Now that I am in power.*
> *No longer can I ramble*
> *In the streets to the East of the Tower.*
> *The Niggers in one hemisphere*
> *The Brahmins in the other*
> *Disturb my dinner and my sleep*
> *With "An't I a man and a brother?"*
> *And May for the first time goes by*
> *And brings me no delight.*
> *I am stewed at the Board all day:*
> *I am stewed in the House all night.*[69]

64. T.B.M. to Hannah and Margaret, June 29, 1832, Trinity Correspondence.
65. T.B.M. to Hannah, July 8, 1833, Trinity Correspondence.
66. T.B.M. to Hannah and Margaret, June 10, 1832, Trinity Correspondence.
67. T.B.M. to Hannah and Margaret, June 25, 1832, Morgan MSS.
68. T.B.M. to Napier, December 17, 1832, British Museum Add. MSS 34,615, ff. 458–60.
69. T.B.M. to Hannah, May 21, 1833, Trinity Correspondence.

There were, it is true, occasional lighter moments in the House. "We are a very joyous assembly," Tom wrote to Margaret. "The other day Colonel Torrens made a tipsy speech about rent and profits, and then staggered away, tumbled down a stairway and was sick as a dog in the Long Gallery." On another occasion, Macaulay's friend Spring-Rice tried to address the House, having arrived, "drunk as a fiddler," from a Lord Mayor's banquet. Some of those sitting on the Treasury bench had to pull him down by his coattails.[70] But these diversions did not make up for what he considered the hardest part of his duties, the need to see so many boring people. "It is all I can do to be civil to them," he confided to Margaret. "I improve however; and in time I shall lie like a true courtier."[71] When he wrote this, the "courtier" was no longer MP for Calne, but had just been elected to represent the newly enfranchised city of Leeds.

THAT LEEDS ELECTION, THE FIRST TO BE HELD IN THE NEWLY ENFRAN-chised borough, presents to the historian a microcosm of the social and economic forces in conflict during the 1830's. One major reason why Macaulay lends himself so admirably to retrospective treatment as a representative figure is that he—and fate—picked his opponents so well. He defined himself by his enemies as much as by his allies. As an *Edinburgh* reviewer during the late 1820's, he had tangled with Bentham and Southey, both leading proponents of distinctive sets of attitudes toward the new elements in nineteenth-century English society. Now, in contesting Leeds as one of the two Whig candidates during the first post-Reform Bill election, he was once again aligned in a way that, in retrospect, seems neatly symbolic of the larger trends and currents of the period. There was, to begin with, the self-evident contrast between the pocket borough and the industrial town, one vividly painted by Macaulay in one of his election speeches when he compared "the squalid misery, the dependence, and I may say the comparative stupidity, which I regret to know, characterizes the agricultural population of that part of the country in which I have generally resided" with the vigor, intelligence, and activity of the men and women of Leeds.[72] Furthermore, it so fell

70. T.B.M. to Margaret, March 11, 1833, Morgan MSS.
71. T.B.M. to Margaret, January 1, 1833, Morgan MSS.
72. T.B.M. at Bramley, September 6, 1832, *Preliminary Proceedings Relative to the First Election of Representatives for the Borough of Leeds, Including the Speeches of Thomas Babington Macaulay, Esq. M.P. etc.* (Leeds, 1832) , 40.

out that the Whig candidate for the other contested seat was John Marshall, a local flax-mill owner and one of the leading employers of labor in Leeds; whereas one of the Tories standing against them was Michael Thomas Sadler, a prominent advocate, in and out of Parliament, of a legally enforced limitation on children's working hours in factories. In this election Sadler had the support both of Richard Oastler, another "Tory Radical," and of William Cobbett, still the most eloquent spokesman for the rights of the English working classes.[73]

There could have been no sharper confrontation of differing interests. On one side the factory owner and the apostle of the middle classes, both pressing for a revision of the Corn Laws to put an end to agricultural protection; on the other, the Tory who had cast his vote in Parliament against the Reform Bill and Catholic emancipation, but who at the same time was one of the leaders of a cause close to the hearts of radical workingmen. Sadler was a devout Evangelical, a friend of Wilberforce, and the author some years before of a piece of Wesleyan apologetics. Here is one contemporary view of him: "In his countenance there was such a seriousness and solemnity that a stranger might have mistaken him for a clergyman. . . . His voice was full and distinct, but it had a species of twang about it very much resembling that which is so often heard in the pulpit." Halévy, who cites this view, comments that it presents what is almost a caricature of an Evangelical preacher.[74] In 1830, Sadler had struck a wild blow against the classical economists in publishing his anti-Malthusian *Law of Population,* in which he expounded the theory that the prolificness of human beings varied inversely with their number. Macaulay had manhandled this book in two *Edinburgh Review* articles,[75] and had described the author as one who "foams at the mouth with the love of truth, and vindicates the Divine benevolence with a most edifying heartiness of hatred."[76]

Economic interests lined up in what might now be called textbook fashion behind the candidates. The shopkeepers, as one of them put it in his diary, supported "Mr. Marshall Our Townsman and Mr. Mackholy the Scotchman."[77] Thus it was hardly surprising that

73. See E. P. Thompson, *The Making of the English Working Class* (London, 1963), 824, and Briggs, *Age of Improvement,* 247.

74. Halévy, *Triumph of Reform,* 110.

75. T.B.M., "Sadler's Law of Population" (1830), *Works,* VII, 570–604; "Sadler's Refutation Refuted" (1831), *Works,* VIII, 18–55.

76. "Sadler's Refutation Refuted," *Works,* VIII, 54.

77. Thompson, *Working Class,* 824.

Macaulay informed Hannah that his leading friends in the contest were the substantial manufacturers who fed him roast beef and Yorkshire pudding.[78] Working-class Radicals, on the other hand, attacked Marshall and Macaulay as traitors to reform, who favored abolition of all monopolies except their own, namely, those of millmen and of placemen.[79] The Reform Bill had enfranchised precious few working-class voters in Leeds. But the Whigs tried to offset the effects of ten-hour bill demonstrations in favor of Sadler by compelling factory hands to show their support for Marshall and Macaulay.[80] The latter himself attempted to inject popular appeal into his speeches; not, as it turned out, with complete success.

In defending himself against the charge that his position on the Board of Control made him a paid "placeman"—a bit of Tory doggerel ran, "In my snug little berth keep me warm, To enjoy my TWELVE HUNDRED a year"—Macaulay said that if there were a law enacting that public service be gratuitous, offices of state would be exclusively occupied by proprietors. No avenue would then be left by which "men who spring from the people—and I spring from the people—[could take office]; as a distinguished statesman of the present day said, I have always stood and always will stand by my order."[81] This confession of faith shows how intense middle-class consciousness had become as a factor in English politics at this time.[82] Peel, too, as we remember, had boasted of having sprung from the people. And Macaulay's transposition of Lord Grey's expressed determination to "stand by his order" from an aristocratic into a middle-class key was intended to meet one line of criticism employed by his electoral opponents. They had called him an "adventurer"; pointing out that while he relied on popular feeling and on the popular side of politics, he owed his fortune primarily to an aristocratic clique.[83] There was an element of truth in this. Not that Macaulay was in any sense the "tool" of a clique; not that his hymn of praise to the middle classes was insincere—but he was, in fact, defending a state of society in which the aristocracy, having duly

78. T.B.M. to Hannah, September 20, 1832, Trevelyan, *Life and Letters*, 198.
79. Thompson, *Working Class*, 825.
80. Idem.
81. For Tory doggerel, see A. S. Turberville and Frank Beckwith, "Leeds and Parliamentary Reform, 1820–1832," *Thoresby Society Publications*, XLI (1946), 67; Leeds Election Speech, September 4, 1832, *Preliminary Proceedings*, 12.
82. See Asa Briggs, "The Language of 'Class' in Early Nineteenth Century England," Asa Briggs and John Saville, eds., *Essays in Labour History* (London, 1960), 43–73.
83. Arnold, *Public Life*, 95.

made concessions required by the times, would continue to flourish. This granted, Macaulay's pride in his middle-class origins was perfectly genuine and he was able to express it with passion and sincerity. Who else but a convinced defender of the middle class would have been able to phrase an endorsement of freedom in the following manner?

As I am for freedom of discussion and worship, so I am also for freedom of trade. I am for a system under which we may sell where we can sell dearest, and buy where we can buy cheapest.[84]

In the rough-and-tumble of election meetings at this time, even the best-prepared orator could be caught off his guard. This happened to Macaulay at Leeds on at least one embarrassing—and revealing—occasion. As he was delivering the speech just cited, he glimpsed some in the crowd who were carrying flags inscribed with mottoes favoring regulation of factory hours, a subject of burning interest in Leeds, where Oastler in 1830 had begun his campaign on behalf of the factory children. Macaulay announced that he would speak openly and at once about this issue. The view he took was, to say the least, a cautious one; though it may not have struck his chief supporters, the Leeds manufacturers, as such. He started by saying that since the evidence had not been printed, he could not give his opinion in detail. He felt that the employment of children in factories required regulation. Yet, "I do say, that if there should be any great expectations of relief from this measure by the lower orders—lower!—I ought to apologize for using the word, for they are lower only because Providence has decreed that some of us should earn our bread by the sweat of our brow; if the labouring class [note the change here!] expect great relief from any practical measure of this nature, they are under a great delusion." For the overworking of children was the effect, not the cause of distress. What was required to get at the real cause was "judicious legislation with regard to trade" (presumably repeal of the Corn Laws) , as well as strict economy in public expenditure.[85]

The cat was out of the bag, and the Tories made something of Macaulay's slip. "The creature of the ruling oligarchy," they argued, "had, for once, unwarily given utterance to his real sentiments about the industrial classes."[86] They had a point. The reference to the

84. September 4, 1832, *Preliminary Proceedings*, 9.   85. Ibid., 10–12.
86. Arnold, *Public Life*, 92.

"lower orders," obliged to earn their bread by the sweat of their brows, smacked of the patronizing tone adopted toward the poor by Hannah More and the first generation of Evangelicals—a linkage not without its ironies, in view of the fact that Sadler who, unlike Macaulay, had retained his Evangelical faith, was now sponsoring factory legislation far more in tune with working-class aspirations than his opponent's prescription of laissez faire. Hannah More, it goes without saying, would have seen no necessity to apologize for the use of the term "lower orders." That was the measure of the power they had gained in the interim.

The views of Sadler and Macaulay illustrate the differing directions in which tributaries from the stream of Evangelical social teaching could flow in the course of the nineteenth century. The patronizing spirit that suffused these teachings carried with it at least an assumption, however "feudal," of social responsibility that could eventually lead to a dutiful acceptance of the need for state intervention. Oastler's and Sadler's sponsorship of factory legislation reflected this attitude. On the other hand, the doctrine of a providentially ordered class system could all too easily be adapted to the iron decrees of the classical economists. The laws of supply and demand were no less ineluctable than the divine edicts, and both seemed to be dependent for their working on a reserve army of labor. Macaulay's sentiments reflected this adaptability. As far as he was concerned, a factory bill came under the heading of quack medicine: "To tell a man that he may have ten hours' work and twelve hours' wages is the same thing as to tell him that by swallowing a certain pill, he would get rid of all diseases of thirty years' continuance." In this case, swallowing the pill would result in driving the cloth trade out of England.[87]

Actually, Macaulay, like some of the leading Benthamites and many Whigs, was not opposed to protecting children from overwork and cruelty, nor to the sort of factory bill intended to do this that was in fact passed in 1833.[88] What Oastler and Sadler wanted, however, was a ten-hour day for all persons under eighteen, which would mean in practice a ten-hour day for all adult workers. It was this that Macaulay, along with the majority of the Whigs, was opposing now. He would eventually vote in favor of a genuine Ten Hours' Bill in 1847. But at the time of the Leeds election, his belief in the saving power of free trade won out over any solicitude he may have felt for the plight of the working classes there, a plight that left little room

87. Ibid., 141.   88. Ibid., 107.

for the exercise of the vigor, intelligence, and activity so highly lauded by their prospective Member.

It would be wrong to say that he was totally unconcerned about that plight. He gave active support, for instance, to the Mechanics' Institute in Leeds. For, as he told its members in an address the following autumn, education was bound to produce political moderation. Once again, one seems to detect echoes of Hannah More in his cautionary tale of the Paris cab driver who had assured him a month after the Revolution of 1830 that, unlike his father, *he* could read and write and had thus been able to learn that French workers would not be able to improve their lot by robbing the Paris shops. This time, however, Macaulay spoke only of the "labouring classes," not at all of "the lower orders."[89] He had learned his lesson.

The Leeds Political Union, formed as a counter-organization to the workingmen's Radical Metropolitan Political Union there, supported Macaulay's candidacy. The essential idea behind it was that it should be jointly representative of the working as well as of the middle classes. But the fact that it came out for Macaulay shows the extent to which it was under middle-class control.[90] Some of the Political Unions were attempting to introduce the principle of delegacy rather than representation into the new electoral system, by obtaining advance pledges on how they would vote on key issues from parliamentary candidates. Macaulay announced at the very beginning of his election campaign that he would have none of this, and did so (according to his nephew) with "an attitude of high and almost peremptory independence which would have sat well on a Prime Minister in his grand climacteric."[91] Having stated his opinions to the Leeds electors, he advised them, if they concurred, to choose him for their sake, not for his. In the tradition of Burke he declared that, once in Parliament, he would feel free to follow his own best counsel, as the representative, not the delegate, of the borough of Leeds.[92] When these remarks were taken amiss, he followed them up with a second letter in which he grandly declared: "Under the old system I have never been the flatterer of the great. Under the new system I will not be the flatterer of the people."[93] This was true within limits. One need only remember his lyrical tribute to the men and women of Leeds. But that probably con-

89. Ibid., 166–8.

90. Turberville and Beckwith, "Leeds," 46–8; see also Asa Briggs, "The Background of the Parliamentary Reform Movement in Three English Cities (1830–1832)," *Cambridge Historical Journal*, X (1952), 310–15.

91. Trevelyan, *Life and Letters*, 201.

92. August 3, 1832, Trevelyan, *Life and Letters*, 202. 93. No date, ibid., 204.

tained more truth than flattery, at least in Macaulay's own view of things. We know that he did not have to flatter that portion of "the people" demanding pledges on the secret ballot, triennial Parliaments, and a factory act. They did not have the vote.

The Leeds election was an urban contest, very different from an election at Calne, where, as the Tories gleefully pointed out, the returning officer had been Lord Lansdowne's butler, the chairman of the committee his cook, and the electors had numbered only a score or so.[94] In Leeds, Macaulay found himself, as he wrote to the editor of the *Edinburgh Review*, in the midst of a storm; making four or five speeches a day, riding in processions, shaking the hands of thousands.[95] The Tory leaflet campaign spared neither him nor his father, now a charity commissioner. Thus "A New Song for the Leeds Election" went, in part, as follows:

> *Each a gentleman at large*
> *Fed and kept at public charge.*
> *Tom for India now petitions,*
> *Dad for charities commissions;*
> *Charity begins at home,*
> *So thinks Dad, and so thinks Tom.*
> *Bumpers off for honest Tom,*
> *Charge your glass for Daddy Zack.*
> *What's the chorus to your song?*
> *Quack! Quack! Quack! Quack!*[96]

Macaulay found time, nonetheless, to write his essay on Lord Mahon's *War of the Spanish Succession*. That he was able to do so at all is a tribute to his powers of concentration. At one meeting, Oastler, in attempting to ask Macaulay some questions about his opposition to the factory bill, climbed up on the coach from the roof of which Macaulay was speaking, getting his coat torn all the way up his back in the process. When he and another questioner had gained a foothold, this platform became so dangerous that Macaulay beat a hasty retreat to the steps of the Cloth Hall.[97] At another meeting, someone in the crowd (it turned out to be Marmaduke Flower, a local Methodist preacher and schoolmaster) inquired into the religious beliefs of Marshall and Macaulay—the Tories had been spread-

94. Arnold, *Public Life,* 91.
95. T.B.M. to Napier, September 5, 1832, *Napier Correspondence,* 130.
96. Turberville and Beckwith, "Leeds," 85.
97. Arnold, *Public Life,* 107.

ing the rumor that Macaulay was an "infidel." Outraged at the very question, Macaulay made him stand up and identify himself, castigated him for having dared make an inquiry into what was a personal matter, and, amidst cheers, told the assembled throng: "My answer is short, and in one word. Gentlemen, I am a Christian."[98] A Christian he may well have been, but that did not prevent him from comparing Sadler, the advocate of reducing the hours worked in factories, to "a certain wild beast called the Hyaena" who, when it wishes to decoy the unwary to its den, has "a singular knack of imitating the cries of little children." His opponents, in their turn, then referred to him as "Thomas Babington Hyaena."[99]

In the end, Macaulay's punning prophecy proved correct. "What have I done to the horses," he had written to Hannah and Margaret in June, "that my chief opponents should be an *Ostler* and a *Sadler*. But no matter: my good cause *Marshalls* the way and *Leeds* me to victory."[100] The two Whigs won out over their Tory opponents. Marshall had received 2,012 votes, Macaulay 1,984, and Sadler 1,596. In her novel *Wooers and Winners,* Mrs. G. Linnaeaus Banks many years later described the final polling: "It lasted three days—three days, during which the borough was in a ferment of ill-feeling, drink, and disorder. Ale and other liquors were to be had for the asking. The end of the poll on the fourteenth of December confirmed the show of hands; Messrs. Macaulay and Marshall were declared duly elected."[101]

The taste of triumph was sweet. "I must own to you," Macaulay wrote to Hannah, ". . . that I enjoy my victory over him [Sadler] and his impotent, envious fury, more than anything else in this contest."[102] (We shall see in due course that the marriage of his sister Margaret also had something to do with his state of mind.) With an air of glee, Macaulay reported to Napier that Sadler was mad with rage, and that his public life seemed to be finished.[103] Less gleefully, Tom informed Margaret a few weeks later that his Leeds committee had had the gall to make him pay his own election ex-

98. Trevelyan, *Life and Letters,* 204. Trevelyan does not supply the name of the questioner at this meeting of September 4, 1832. It is given by Turberville and Beckwith, "Leeds," 75. See the same source, 48, for Tory rumors.

99. Cecil Driver, *Tory Radical: The Life of Richard Oastler* (London, 1946), 201.

100. T.B.M. to Hannah and Margaret, June 19, 1832, Trinity Correspondence.

101. Mrs. G. L. Banks, *Wooers and Winners* (3 vols., London, 1880), II, 246.

102. T.B.M. to Hannah, December 12, 1832, Trinity Correspondence.

103. T.B.M. to Napier, December 17, 1832, British Museum Add. MSS. 34,615, ff. 458–60.

penses. Had he known this, he added, he would never have stood for that borough.[104]

YET IT WAS WITH ILL-CONCEALED PRIDE THAT ON FEBRUARY 6, 1833, Macaulay told the House of Commons: "I stand here . . . for the first time, as the representative of a new constituent body, one of the largest, most prosperous, and most enlightened towns in the kingdom."[105] In this instance, however, he spoke not for enlightenment, but for repression, in defense of the Whig government's stern Irish Coercion Bill. He had to defend himself against the charge of "inconsistency" between his call for a policy of concession during the Reform Bill debates, and his support now for a measure suspending Habeas Corpus and giving police the right of search for arms. "Few absolute governments," so Palmerston commented on this bill, "could by their own authority establish such a system of coercion as that which the freely chosen representatives of the people are placing at the command of the Government of this country."[106] Macaulay's speech was a clever one. He pointed out prophetically, for example, that the argument that there should exist two separate Parliaments for England and Ireland could be urged even more strongly when it came to Northern and Southern Ireland. But there was something unbecomingly self-righteous about the manner in which he was now at such pains to remind the House that in 1830 he had never said that rioters ought not to be imprisoned, that incendiaries ought not to be hanged; that in 1831 he had never meant to imply that the excesses in Nottingham and Bristol ought not to be put down, if necessary, by the sword.[107] It almost seemed that he was protesting too much, especially when one recalls how in the course of one of his reform speeches, he had cried woe to the government that could not distinguish between a nation and a mob, and thought that a great movement of the public mind could be stopped like a street riot.[108]

Just a year before he delivered this speech, Margaret had artlessly remarked to him that she thought the Irish people had as much right to dissolve the Union and have a Parliament of their own as the people of England had to reform *their* Parliament. Her brother re-

104. T.B.M. to Margaret, January 21, 1833. Morgan MSS.
105. *Works*, XI, 526.　　　　　　　　106. Halévy, *Triumph of Reform*, 131.
107. February 6, 1833, *Works*, XI, 521-3.　　108. July 5, 1831, *Works*, XI, 443.

torted as he might have in days of old to a simple-minded opponent at the Cambridge Union. What did she mean by "right," he asked her. Right and might, it seemed, amounted to very much the same thing. Before long, he got her to agree that "right" was a mere cant phrase, and, she reported in her journal, "completely routed the rights of man, at least my feeble defence of them."[109] That this was more than mere brotherly banter emerges in the pages of Greville, who quoted Macaulay's statement, a few weeks later, that if *he* had had to legislate on Ireland, he would have suspended the laws there for five years, given the Lord Lieutenant's proclamation the force of law, and put the Duke of Wellington in charge.[110] One cannot help but remark on the rapid transformation of the liberty-loving Commonwealthman into the stern supporter of military force; though, remembering Cromwell's activities in Ireland, one might add that Macaulay here took over the tradition whole. The point was, of course, that like one of his masters, Edmund Burke, he dreaded Jacobinism above all. And he compared the organization and conduct of the Irish Volunteers of 1833 with those of the Jacobin clubs of the French Revolution.[111] In very plain terms, he linked his support for severe measures in Ireland with the Whigs' motives for having pressed the Reform Bill. He belonged, he said, to a party that had carried Reform in order to avoid revolution. "But that party had not fought the battle against the proudest aristocracy in the world, in order that an oligarchy which had since sprung up should rule in its stead."[112]

For an illuminating gloss on this statement, one must look ahead some months, to a conversation between Macaulay and his friend John Cam Hobhouse about Edward Stanley, then a rising star of the Whigs, later (as Earl of Derby) a Tory Prime Minister. Macaulay allowed Stanley the highest capacity in almost every respect, except that of seeing what was beneficial for the country. Therefore, he continued, Stanley, even more than the younger Pitt, "seemed born for the destruction of the aristocracy, by his honest, uncompromising defence of them."[113] There was no reason for Macaulay not to be

109. Margaret Macaulay, *Recollections*, 103.

110. February 27, 1833, Wilson, ed, *Greville Diary*, I, 450.

111. The Volunteers of 1833 were not to be compared, he added, either to the Irish Volunteers of 1782 or to the English Political Unions, February 28, 1833, *Hansard*, 3rd series, XV (1833), 1331-2. Professor W. O. Aydelotte has pointed out to me that T.B.M.'s reasoning may be seen as an interesting anticipation of the modern statistical technique of factor analysis.

112. Ibid., 1332.   113. December 2, 1833, Broughton, *Recollections*, IV, 327.

perfectly frank with Hobhouse. He was about to leave for India. This was a private conversation. In view of what he said, it is hard not to characterize his rhetoric about battling the proudest aristocracy in the world as humbug; or at least to add the rider that if he battled it, it was not to destroy but to save it.

Certainly, the language he used about the Irish Volunteers was considerably more impassioned than any he had ever employed against the English nobility. It can only be compared to Burke's anti-Jacobin tirades. He declared that he preferred the cholera to the moral pestilence now raging in Ireland; that he would prefer life in despotic Algiers to life in Kilkenny. His position on the Coercion Bill, he concluded, was one that he would certainly be prepared to justify to his constituents. And this is precisely what he did in a letter to one of them, in which he expressed his conviction that it was the duty of public men "to make a firm stand at this conjuncture in defence of order, property, and public credit."[114]

Those who threatened property or violence must be put down; though Macaulay was willing to admit that some anomalies and evils were bound up with property. But he comforted himself with the reflection that these anomalies and evils "were not only willingly but cheerfully borne by the many, in consideration of the manifold blessings which the institution of property conferred upon society at large."[115] He offered this thought, fathered, no doubt, by the wish, in the course of a speech in support of the Whig government's bill proposing to reduce the number of Church of England bishoprics in Ireland. That, he said, would be conducive to the preservation of property there; since by diminishing the power of the Establishment in a Roman Catholic country, some of the odium against the English Church would be removed.[116] Thus he was by no means insensitive to Irish grievances.

IN COMPARING MACAULAY'S ATTITUDE TO IRELAND WITH HIS ATTITUDE to India, the Burkean parallel once more comes to mind. It was Macaulay's task to present the ministry's proposals changing the financial role of the East India Company in the government of India,

114. T.B.M. to [George Rawson?], May 6, 1833, Rylands Library MSS, University of Manchester.

115. April 1, 1833, *Hansard*, 3rd series, XVI (1833) , 1386.   116. Ibid., 1390.

as a result of the termination of the company's Chinese tea monopoly. He made one of his most brilliant speeches, though to a very thin House. (A week later he wrote to Margaret that he could hardly comprehend the strange indifference of all classes to Indian problems.) [117] The speech presented an irrefutable case for the new proposals, which passed by a huge majority. They included the revolutionary principle that henceforth appointments to writerships in the Indian Civil Service would be made by competitive examination. Macaulay ended his speech with an eloquent peroration, envisioning not only tenure of the highest public offices by Indians, but also eventual Indian independence:

The destinies of our Indian Empire are covered with thick darkness. It is difficult to form any conjecture as to the fate reserved for a state which resembles no other in history, and which forms by itself a separate class of political phenomena. The laws which regulate its growth and its decay are still unknown to us. It may be that the public mind of India may expand under our system till it has outgrown that system; that by good government we may educate our subjects into a capacity for better government; that, having been instructed in European knowledge, they may, in some future age, demand European institutions. Whether such a day will ever come I know not. But never will I attempt to avert or to retard it. Whenever it comes, it will be the proudest day in English history. To have found a great people sunk in the lowest depths of slavery and superstition, to have so ruled them as to have made them desirous and capable of all the privileges of citizens, would indeed be a title to glory all our own. The sceptre may pass away from us. Unforeseen accidents may derange our most profound schemes of policy. Victory may be inconstant to our arms. But there are triumphs which are followed by no reverse. There is an empire exempt from all natural causes of decay. Those triumphs are the pacific triumphs of reason over barbarism; that empire is the imperishable empire of our arts and our morals, our literature and our laws.[118]

There was no more contradiction between Macaulay's Irish and Indian speeches than there had been between Burke's attitude toward India and his attitude toward the French Revolution. In Ireland, Macaulay saw the spirit of Jacobinism at work, and an immediate threat to the social order, there and in England. In India, he saw a people waiting to be enlightened, and to be gradually guided toward freedom, to be sure; but freedom in a far-distant future.

117. T.B.M. to Margaret, July 17, 1833, Morgan MSS.
118. July 10, 1833, *Works,* XI, 571, 585–6.

He may have had an inkling, as he spoke, that he himself was about to spend several years in India, to play a prominent part in the very reorganization of the Indian government he was proposing. The new bill provided that one of the members of the Supreme Council, henceforth to govern India, was to be chosen from among persons not servants of the East India Company. By mid-August 1833, Macaulay was almost certain that this position was going to be offered to him. In a letter to Hannah, in which he sucessfully attempted to persuade her to accompany him to India, he outlined the advantages of the post. The salary was to be £10,000 a year; which, for someone whose total wealth at about this time amounted to £709 (*if* his debtors paid him),[119] for someone, moreover, who was responsible for the support of his father and his sisters, was a princely sum indeed. Macaulay anticipated that he would be able to live "in splendour" in Calcutta on £5,000 a year, and save the rest with accruing interest. He would thus be able to return to England before the age of forty with a fortune of £30,000.

Were he to remain in England, he could afford to continue in public life only if he retained office. For without its emoluments, he would be dependent on the earnings from his writings. And it was utterly impossible to combine being a Member of Parliament with writing enough to earn a decent livelihood. To live by his pen alone, on the other hand, would make him a very different person in the estimation of editors and booksellers from what he was at present, when he wrote only for amusement or for fame.[120] Meanwhile, there was no guarantee that he would be able to continue in office, since a schism in the ministry—presumably Macaulay had the split over the question of Irish tithes in mind—was developing. "I tell you in perfect seriousness," he wrote to Hannah, "that my chance of keeping my present situation for six months is so small, that I would willingly sell it for fifty pounds down." Under the circumstances, either holding on to office or going into opposition would be unpleasant. In England, in sum, he saw nothing before him for some time to come but poverty, unpopularity, and the breaking of old connections.[121]

"Before I went to India," he recalled to Napier some years later, "I had no prospect in the event of a change of government, except that

119. T.B.M. to Hannah, June 21, 1833, Trevelyan, *Life and Letters*, 221.

120. Last sentence, T.B.M. to Ellis, November 23, 1833, Trinity Correspondence. The rest, T.B.M. to Hannah, August 17, 1833, Trevelyan, *Life and Letters*, 234–7.

121. T.B.M. to Hannah, August 17, 1833, Trevelyan, *Life and Letters*, 235.

of living by my pen, and seeing my sisters governesses."[122] He told Brougham at the time that his sisters would have to go out into the world as milliners, "if he stayed to fight with us." If, on the other hand, he accepted the position on the Supreme Council, he would be able to withdraw for some years from the contests of action, would find new political combinations and parties formed upon his return, old issues settled, and would be able to take his own line.[123] Perhaps he had Canning in mind here. For in 1822, despairing of making a mark in English politics, Canning had taken the Governor-General-ship of India, in the expectation that while he was away, both parties would be broken up and the field would then be clear for his return. The death of Castlereagh put an end to this scheme.[124] In any event, Macaulay would be able to return to England as rich (so he remarked with some hyperbole) as if he were the Duke of Northumberland or the Marquess of Westminster, and would then be free to act on all public questions "without even a temptation to deviate from the strict line of duty."[125]

In a letter to his old patron, Lord Lansdowne, written at the end of 1833, Macaulay expanded on the difficulty of being in office as a man without means. "Without a competence," he wrote, "it is not very easy for a public man to be honest; it is almost impossible for him to be thought so." The constant effort to show that one was not holding onto office merely for the sake of financial gain, that one was not a mere "placeman," would clearly be a considerable strain for a person of Macaulay's independence of spirit. He told Lansdowne that the thought that others might suspect he was actuated by unworthy motives in defending unpopular measures in the House of Commons had once or twice disordered his ideas, and deprived him of his presence of mind.[126] Twice during the course of the parliamentary session just concluded, he had tendered his resignation,

122. T.B.M. to Napier, July 27, 1841, ibid., 407.

123. Brougham to Henry Reeve, January 1, 1860, John Knox Laughton, ed., *Memoirs of the Life and Correspondence of Henry Reeve* (2 vols., London, 1898), II, 37. T.B.M. to Hannah, August 17, 1833, Trevelyan, *Life and Letters*, 234–6.

124. Lloyd Sanders, *The Holland House Circle* (New York, 1908), 18.

125. T.B.M. to Hannah, August 17, 1833, Trevelyan, *Life and Letters*, 234–6.

126. T.B.M. to Lansdowne, December 5, 1833, Trevelyan, *Life and Letters*, 249. This may lend some credence to the story in the scurrilous periodical *John Bull*, to the effect that ministers were afraid of T.B.M.'s further assistance, since he broke down during one of his speeches in the course of the last session of Parliament. Arnold, *Public Life*, 184. See also [J. A. Roebuck], "Diary of an M.P.," June 21, 1833, *Tait's Edinburgh Magazine*, III (1833), 645: "The grand speech-maker was actually laughed down. He had not courage to stand up ten minutes against an unfavourable audience."

something he would never have done had he been a man of fortune.[127] To hold office while not in the cabinet was difficult for one as independent-minded as himself. "I have felt the bitterness of that slavery once," he was to note in his journal. "Though I hardly knew where to turn for a morsel of bread, my spirit rose against the intolerable thraldom." The situation of a subordinate he had found unsuited to his temper.[128]

One of the occasions on which he tendered his resignation was supplied by the Whig government's bill to abolish slavery. The bill, as originally brought in by Stanley, allowed for a twelve-year period of legally controlled apprenticeship during which certain portions of the money earned by the slaves would, if they so chose, be set aside to purchase their freedom from their masters at the end of that time.[129] Zachary was adamantly opposed to this provision. Margaret noted that Tom with great reluctance therefore found it necessary to speak against the government, to please Zachary, "for whose sake alone" he took part in the whole business. His father would probably not be satisfied unless the criticism of the bill was of a vehemence that Tom did not wish to employ, since he was unwilling to help defeat the ministry on any question at such a critical time.[130]

Macaulay's sense of filial piety impelled him to speak. On the question of compensation to planters—they eventually received £20 million—he supported the ministry, even though the chief abolitionists opposed any such compensation. But on the apprenticeship provisions, he parted company with it.[131] Having decided to do so, he tendered his resignation. In the event, the government reduced the apprenticeship period to seven years, and the abolitionists declared themselves satisfied with this concession. Macaulay's resignation was refused.

It was, in part, to avoid situations of this kind that he accepted the Indian appointment as legal member of the Council, after Hannah had agreed to go out with him. His old antagonist James Mill, an important figure at India House, was consulted by the directors and gave his support. In early December, the Court of Directors, by a large majority, endorsed the appointment. On the day he was sworn in, the directors tendered him a dinner. An eyewitness remembered that Macaulay "rather gave himself the airs of a Lycurgus, and spoke

127. T.B.M. to Lansdowne, December 5, 1833, Trevelyan, *Life and Letters*, 248–9.
128. November 10, 1838, Trevelyan, *Life and Letters*, 357.
129. Halévy, *Triumph of Reform*, 82–3.
130. Margaret Macaulay, *Recollections*, 35.
131. July 24, 1833, *Hansard*, 3rd series, XIX (1833), 1204–9.

as if he were about to bestow on the swarming millions of India the blessings of rudimentary legislation."[132] Yet, it was this imaginative power, which indeed sometimes verged on the ludicrous, that was essential to Macaulay's vision of his own role, both in politics and in the intercourse of daily life. There was something of this same sense of self-dramatization in his congratulating himself on the calmness with which he had made the decision to accept the Indian appointment; the same sort of calmness, he wrote his sister, that a general showed before battle. "I wonder," he added, "whether I should be as tranquil as [Russell and Sidney] on the scaffold. Very likely I should."[133] There was something of it, also, in the account he gave Hannah of the secret history of the India Board, and the incredible turns of fortune there. Ministers shedding tears at one moment were ready to dance for joy an hour and a half later. Tom's comment to his sister was: "I have myself been an actor in these affairs; though I have shown a composure about them which has astonished most of my associates."[134] And it was this same feeling that impelled him to address this elaborately high-flown farewell to the electors of Leeds:

May your manufactures flourish; may your trade be extended, may your riches increase! May the works of your skill, and the signs of your prosperity, meet me in the furthest regions of the East, and give me fresh cause to be proud of the intelligence, the industry, and the spirit of my constituency![135]

A few days later, on February 15, 1834, he and Hannah sailed for India. The news of his departure had evoked a hysterical scene from Lady Holland, who accused Macaulay's family of making a tool of him, and stormed at the ministry for letting him go, until even her mild-mannered husband reprimanded her for her antics.[136] It had led Sir James Graham, with tears in his eyes, to regret the irreparable loss to the House of Commons and to the India Board, and to predict that if Macaulay preserved his health, he would make a far greater figure in public life on his return than if he stayed in England.[137] And it had led the editor of the *Edinburgh Review*, who promptly commissioned articles from Macaulay for all forthcoming alternate

132. Arnold, *Public Life*, 184.
133. T.B.M. to Hannah, November 2, 1833, Trinity Correspondence.
134. T.B.M. to Hannah, August 15, 1833, Trinity Correspondence.
135. February 4, 1834, Trevelyan, *Life and Letters*, 258.
136. T.B.M. to Hannah, January 2, 1834, Trevelyan, *Life and Letters*, 255–6.
137. T.B.M. to Hannah, November 26, 1833, Trinity Correspondence.

issues of the periodical, to predict that in the course of his "banishment," he would fix his name lastingly in the history of the improvement of India.[138]

Old Zachary was less affected by the news of his son's impending departure than any of these. Tom's own explanation to Hannah was that his father had traveled so much himself that separations of this kind did not shake him. Moreover, he added, people generally liked a fat sorrow rather than a lean one.[139] When, in due course, Macaulay and his sister sailed from Gravesend aboard the *Asia,* Hannah had three hundred oranges to sustain her. Her brother had to make do with the complete works of Gibbon, Voltaire, Richardson, Horace, and Homer.

138. Macvey Napier to T.B.M., December 8, 1833, *Napier Correspondence,* 143.
139. T.B.M. to Hannah, November 2, 1833, Trinity Correspondence.

IX

T.B.M. AND TOM

WHAT DID MACAULAY LOOK LIKE DURING THIS PERIOD? BY 1833 HE HAD become famous enough to attract painters. "I am sick of pictures of my own face," he wrote to Hannah. "I have seen within the last few days one drawing of it, one engraving, and three paintings. They all make me a very handsome fellow."[1] And that, it may safely be stated, was the one thing he was not. Reports of his ugliness had preceded his coming into Parliament. "I . . . hear he is not pleasant nor good to look at," Lady Holland wrote to her son at the time.[2] Lady Lynd-hurst, encountering him first at Holland House the following year, remarked to him: "You are quite different to what I expected. I thought I should find you dark and thin, but you are fair and really Mr. Macaulay you are quite fat."[3]

Like many others, Greville, on first meeting Macaulay, was struck by the ungainliness and vulgarity of his appearance. "Not a ray of intellect beams from his countenance; a lump of more ordinary clay never enclosed a powerful mind and a lively imagination."[4] The

1. T.B.M. to Hannah, July 27, 1833, Trevelyan, *Life and Letters*, 229.

2. Lady Holland to her son, February 9, 1830, *Elizabeth Lady Holland to Her Son*, 108; see also the Earl of Dudley to Mrs. Dugald Stewart, February 19, 1830: "This Macaulay that Lord L[ansdowne] has brought into parliament, where I think he will make some considerable figure, is a *very* clever, *very* educated, and *very* disagreeable man." S. H. Romilly, ed., *Letters to 'Ivy' from the First Earl of Dudley* (London, 1905), 347.

3. Margaret Macaulay to Henry Thatcher, September 30, 1831, Huntington MSS.

4. February 6, 1832, Wilson, ed., *Greville Diary*, II, 152.

OVERLEAF: Macaulay in 1833. This is the portrait Macaulay gave to his sister Margaret before he left for India.

ABOVE: Zachary Macaulay.
BELOW: Rothley Temple, Leicestershire, Macaulay's birthplace.

RIGHT ABOVE: Tom to his father: his first wholly preserved letter, July 1807. The postscript is his mother's.
RIGHT BELOW: View from southeast corner of Clapham Common, 1825.

write to her if you have occasion as I am here. and direct for me, to Mrs Lime, Hertbury near Bristol

I begin to long much to see you, and hope you do not think of cheating me after all, as your Bristol visit,

My dear Papa   Ever your affectionate
T. Macaulay —

I am sorry that my writing did not please you I hope that I shall improve in it . Selina is in the country, and I am going this evening. all Mama commands are readily and cheer fully obeyed. The Miss Mores gave me a guinea, a bank note-

ABOVE: Great Court, Trinity College, Cambridge. Macaulay lived in the ground floor rooms to the left of the staircase entrance, between the great gate and the chapel.
BELOW: Tom to his father from Cambridge, October 23, 1818.

ABOVE: An apostrophe, "To Woman," hitherto unpublished, written by Macaulay at Cambridge, July 1822.

LEFT BELOW: John Wilson Croker.
RIGHT BELOW: Winthrop Mackworth Praed.

ABOVE: Lord and Lady Holland.
BELOW: South view of Holland House, 1813.

OPPOSITE ABOVE: Macaulay's sister Hannah, Lady Trevelyan.
FAR RIGHT BELOW: Lord Brougham.

ABOVE: Lord Lansdowne.
BELOW: A view of the Houses of Parliament in the 1820's.

OPPOSITE: Macaulay at the time of the Leeds election, 1832.

CENTER ABOVE: The House of Commons, February 1833.
FAR LEFT AND ABOVE: A detail of Macaulay.
CENTER BELOW: Guildhall banquet celebrating passage of the Reform Act of 1832.
FAR LEFT AND BELOW: A detail of Macaulay.

LEFT: Lord William Bentinck.
BELOW: Sir Charles Trevelyan.

RIGHT ABOVE: Sir John Cam
  Hobhouse, later
  Lord Broughton.
RIGHT BELOW: Lord Auckland.

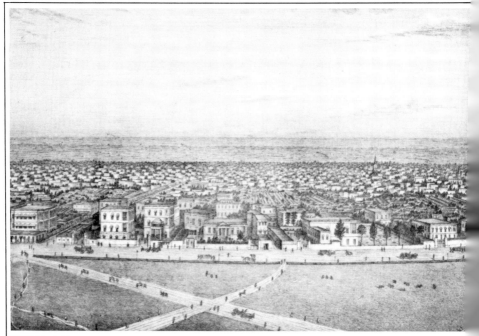

LEFT: Government House, Calcutta, 1824.

BELOW: Calcutta, 1845.

OVERLEAF: Macaulay in 1849.

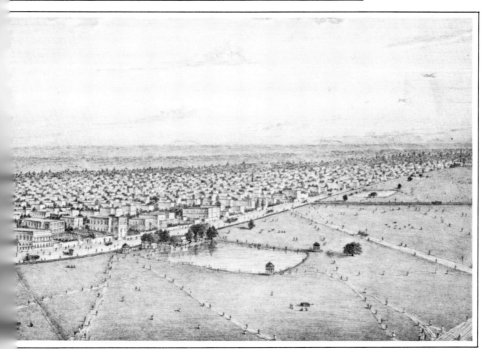

most detailed description of his appearance during the Reform
Bill period came from the pen of Thomas Carlyle, who, sometime in
1832, observed Macaulay in the lobby of the House of Commons,
where he was purchasing two oranges. This is what he wrote:

Macaulay is a short squat thickset man of vulgar but resolute energetic
appearance. Fair-complexioned, keen gray eyes, a large cylindrical head
close down between two round shoulders; the brow broad and fast reced-
ing, the crown flat. Inclines already to corpulence, tho' not five-and-thirty.
The globular will one day be his shape, if he continue. I likened
him to a managing ironmaster with vigorous talent for business [and]
little look of talent for anything else. He is the young man of most force
at present before the world. Successful he may be to great lengths, or not
at all, according as the times turn: meanwhile the limits of his worth are
discernible enough. Great things lie not in him, intrinsically common.[5]

Presumably it was a certain coarseness, a lack of delicacy in his features, what Greville called his "round, thick, unmeaning face," that
made the words "vulgar" and "common" come so readily to the minds
of those who observed him. When Sydney Smith advised Lady Grey
never to visit Holland, he gave the following reasons: "The roads all
paved—inns dirty, and dearer than the dearest in England—country
frightful beyond all belief; no trees but willows—no fuel but turf; all
the people uglier than Macauley [sic]."[6]

The effect he produced on people also depended to some extent on
their prejudices and preconceptions. The same features that led
Carlyle, who had no use for anything Macaulay stood for, to call him
"common" evoked a very different reaction from the more sympa-
thetically inclined Bulwer-Lytton. This was the impression the latter
received, as he watched Macaulay by flickering candlelight early one
morning in the House of Commons:

At a distance the full forehead, the firm lips, the large, cloven chin, the
massive, bold brow that overlays an eye small but full of deep, quiet light.
I scarcely ever saw a head so expressive of intellectual grandeur.[7]

His sister Margaret saw power as the most marked expression of his
face, with its "noble" expanse of forehead, the long and rugged mold
of his features, and the kindness and affection in his sparkling eyes.
The sisters' writing master had remarked to the two of them:

5. David Alec Wilson, *Carlyle to* The French Revolution (London, 1924), 279–80.
6. Sydney Smith to Lady Grey, May 12, 1837, *Smith Letters*, II, 655.
7. Bulwer, *Life of Bulwer Lytton*, I, 420.

"Ladies, your brother looks like a lump of good-humour!" Samuel Rogers, describing Macaulay, said that he had such a hearty way of giving his hand that "he would give it to the Devil if he met him, and would go up to him with a sort of polka step."[8]

All of which goes to confirm the saying that beauty lies in the eye of the beholder. Macaulay himself certainly had no illusions about his looks. When *Blackwood's* had called him an ugly dumpling of a fellow, with a mouth from ear to ear, he had written to Hannah: "Conceive how such a charge must affect a man so enamoured of his own beauty as I am."[9] It was in the same tone of wry amusement that he reported to her that the painter Benjamin Haydon, who had painted him into his immense canvas of the Reform Banquet, had pronounced his profile antique and a gem of art.[10] Haydon himself briefly chronicled that sitting in his diary. He did not comment on the sitter's appearance, but confined himself to the comment that Macaulay "was excited and turned round and looked and well he might, for I was roused beyond example. Macaulay is a clever fellow."[11]

That Macaulay was clever nobody who encountered him could deny. His talk was overpowering, so far-ranging in its learning, so abundant in its flow, that it left his interlocutors amazed and—if they did not try to compete—overawed. Sydney Smith, the leading wit of the age, expressed what many must have felt in a similar situation when he was said to have exclaimed after first hearing Macaulay talk: "I am now like Zacharias, my mouth is opened."[12] What was Macaulay's talk like? Good conversation is harder to preserve than almost any other historical source. It is evanescent by definition, and even when by some stroke of good fortune a few snippets survive, they generally reach us in a denatured state, wrenched out of context, and soundless. However, something is better than nothing. It is possible to convey some impressions of Macaulay's conversational powers by examples that have survived, some illustrating his learning, one his hectoring style and his predilection for scoring points, and yet another, his manner of talking *en famille*.

Early in 1832, Charles Greville found himself at a dinner in

8. Margaret Macaulay, *Recollections*, 33; Trevelyan, *Life and Letters*, 132; *Autobiographical Notes of George Denman, 1819–1847* (London, 1897), 83.

9. T.B.M. to Hannah, July–August 1831, Trevelyan, *Life and Letters*, 173.

10. T.B.M. to Hannah, July 27, 1833, ibid., 229.

11. July 21, 1833, Willard B. Pope, ed., *The Diary of Benjamin Robert Haydon* (5 vols., Cambridge, Mass., 1963), IV, 117.

12. Lord Houghton, *Academy*, IX (1876), 398.

Holland House, seated next to "a common-looking man in black."
Some obscure man of letters, he thought, or perhaps a cholera doctor.
The subject of early and late education came up, and "the man in
black" cited Alfieri as the most remarkable example of self-education.

Lord Holland quoted Julius Caesar and Scaliger as examples of late
education, said that the latter had been wounded and that he had been
married and commenced learning Greek the same day, when my neigh-
bour remarked "that he supposed his learning Greek was not an instantaneous act like his marriage." This remark, and the manner of it, gave
me the notion that he was a dull fellow, for it came out in a way which
bordered on the ridiculous, so as to excite something like a sneer. I was a
little surprised to hear him continue the thread of conversation (from
Scaliger's wound) and talk of Loyola having been wounded at Pampeluna.
I wondered how he happened to know anything about Loyola's wound.

Then someone addressed Greville's neighbor by name, and it turned
out to be, as the diarist noted in capital letters, "MACAULAY, the
man I had been so long most curious to see and to hear, whose
genius, eloquence, astonishing knowledge, and diversified talents had
excited my wonder and admiration for such a length of time, and
here I had been sitting next to him, hearing him talk, and setting
him down for a dull fellow." That evening Macaulay did not try to
usurp the conversation, but the variety and extent of his information
soon became apparent. He had quotations, illustrations, and anecdotes ready to hand for every topic.[13]

To observe Macaulay's omniscience in full operation, it is necessary to desert strict chronology for a moment, and to look ahead a
few years to another account by Greville of a gathering at Holland
House:

Before dinner some mention was made of the portraits of the Speakers in
the Speaker's House, and I asked how far they went back. Macaulay said
he was not sure, but certainly as far as Sir Thomas More. "Sir Thomas
More," said Lady Holland. "I did not know he had been Speaker." "Oh,
yes," said Macaulay, "don't you remember when Cardinal Wolsey came
down to the House of Commons and More was in the chair?" and then he
told the whole of that well-known transaction, and all More had said. At
dinner, amongst a variety of persons and subjects, principally ecclesiastical, which were discussed—for Melbourne loves all sorts of theological
talk—we got upon India and Indian men of eminence, proceeding from
Gleig's *Life of Warren Hastings,* which Macaulay said was the worst book

13. February 6, 1832, Wilson, ed., *Greville Diary,* II, 151–2.

that was ever written; and then the name of Sir Thomas Munro came uppermost. Lady Holland did not know why Sir Thomas Munro was so distinguished; when Macaulay explained all that he had ever said, done, written, or thought, and vindicated his claim to the title of a great man, till Lady Holland got bored with Sir Thomas, told Macaulay she had had enough of him, and would have no more. This would have dashed and silenced an ordinary talker, but to Macaulay it was no more than replacing a book on its shelf, and he was as ready as ever to open on any other topic. It would be impossible to follow and describe the various mazes of conversation, all of which he threaded with an ease that was always astonishing and instructive, and generally interesting and amusing. When we went upstairs we got upon the Fathers of the Church. Allen asked Macaulay if he had read much of the Fathers. He said, not a great deal. He had read Chrysostom when he was in India; that is, he had turned over the leaves and for a few months had read him for two or three hours every morning before breakfast; and he had read some of Athanasius. "I remember a sermon," he said, "of Chrysostom's in praise of the Bishop of Antioch"; and then he proceeded to give us the substance of this sermon till Lady Holland got tired of the Fathers, again put her extinguisher on Chrysostom as she had done on Munro, and with a sort of derision, and as if to have the pleasure of puzzling Macaulay, she turned to him and said, "Pray, Macaulay, what was the origin of a *doll?* when were dolls first mentioned in history?" Macaulay was, however, just as much up to the dolls as he was to the Fathers, and instantly replied that the Roman children had their dolls, which they offered up to Venus when they grew older; and quoted Persius for

Veneri donatae a virgine puppae,

and I have not the least doubt, if he had been allowed to proceed, he would have told us who was the Chenevix of ancient Rome, and the name of the first baby that ever handled a doll.

The conversation then ran upon Milman's *History of Christianity,* which Melbourne praised, the religious opinions of Locke, of Milman himself, the opinion of the world thereupon, and so on to Strauss's book and his mythical system, and what he meant by mythical. Macaulay began illustrating and explaining the meaning of a *myth* by examples from remote antiquity, when I observed that in order to explain the meaning of "mythical" it was not necessary to go so far back; that, for instance, we might take the case of Wm. Huntington, S.S.: that the account of his life was historical, but the story of his praying to God for a new pair of leather breeches and finding them under a hedge was mythical. Now, I had just a general superficial recollection of this story in Huntington's *Life,* but my farthing rush-light was instantly extinguished by the blaze of Macaulay's all-grasping and all-retaining memory, for he at once came in with the whole minute account of this transaction: how Huntington had prayed, what he had found, and where, and all he had said to the tailor by whom this miraculous nether garment was made.[14]

It was no wonder that Sydney Smith was impelled to call Macaulay "a book in breeches," as well as to observe that he not only over-flowed with learning, but stood in the slop. "I never heard such a man at conversation," Ruskin's Effie Gray reported to her parents some years later. "He goes from St. Chrysostom's sermon at Antioch to the people not to pick each other's pockets in church to M. Thiers speeches twenty years ago, gives them word for word, then back again to Greek Mausoleums four centuries B.C., gives you all the names of the people who built them contemporary with the battle of Salamis, then to Seringapatam streets and mud houses and going at such a pace, quite wonderful."[15] Macaulay's capacious memory helped to make his conversation a perpetual *tour de force*. James Stephen told Greville that Macaulay could repeat by heart all of Demosthenes, all of Milton, and a great part of the Bible in English, and the New Testament in Greek. As other men read by syllables, Macaulay had the faculty of reading by whole sentences, of swallowing entire paragraphs at once.[16]

However much Greville admired Macaulay's powers—"there is no more comparison between his brain and such a one as mine than between a hurdy-gurdy in the street and the great organ at Haar-lem," he once noted in his diary[17]—he nonetheless quickly became aware of one great defect in Macaulay's conversation: It astonished and instructed, but it failed to delight and captivate. "His proposi-tions and his allusions are rather too abrupt; he starts topics not altogether naturally; then he has none of the graces of conversation, none of that exquisite tact and refinement which are the result of a felicitous intuition or a long acquaintance with good society, or more probably a mixture of both."[18] Greville's comment exudes snobbery; but it was not without substance. It was not merely that Macaulay knew more than ordinary mortals, and delighted in showing it. In spite of all the good fortune showered upon him, he had had to fight his way up. Ungainly, practically penniless, aristocratic neither by birth nor appearance, naturally awkward and shy, he had long found that the best defense was attack. Thus in company—not in the family

14. January 21, 1841, ibid., II 157–8.

15. Effie Gray to her parents, February 12, 1848, Sir William James, ed., *The Order of Release: The Story of John Ruskin, Effie Gray, and John Everett Millais* (London, 1948) , 136.

16. February 9, 1836, and August 8, 1838, Wilson, ed., *Greville Diary*, II, 153, 156.

17. August 8, 1838, ibid., II, 156. 18. August 12, 1832, ibid., II, 155.

circle—he tended to overwhelm rather than to charm. "He is not *agreeable*," was Greville's comment.[19] Creevey, the other famous diarist of the period, found him noisy and vulgar.[20] There was something aggressive in his confrontation of the outside world, something that rarely evoked affection, though often awe and admiration, and at times hostility. Marianne Thornton, who loved and admired him, observed that "his first manner certainly has too much of the pedagogue about it. It will wear off—and no one who knows him can dislike him I think—but such a very authoritative way of speaking frightens so many people from entering into any discussion with him."[21]

In conversation, as in the *Edinburgh Review*, he loved to bait a victim. We possess a verbatim account of such a baiting, supplied by Macaulay himself in a letter to Hannah. The time was July 1833, the occasion one of those boisterously sadistic pranks that marked, then as later in English society, the continuation of a public school education by other means. It was a dinner, attended only by Members of Parliament, to which a prominent Quaker, Joseph Pease by name, who had just entered Parliament for the newly created constituency of South Durham, had been invited by one of the party to serve as a butt. They all laughed when, predictably, Pease began to preach against war. Macaulay then proceeded to argue with him. Pease maintained that God always miraculously protected the nonviolent. "What proof have you of that?" Macaulay inquired. The Indians did not burn Penn's settlement in America, was the reply. " 'Well,' said I [Tom wrote], 'but we know that the very Quakers who went to Pennsylvania had been driven by persecution from England, that Penn himself was twice imprisoned here, and that some of the sect were treated with the utmost cruelty. How was it that Providence which watched so carefully over them on one side of the Atlantic, left them quite exposed to tyranny on the other?' " Pease then denied that resistance ever prospered. " 'Why,' said I [Tom went on], 'what do you say to the resistance of John Knox and his Presbyterian followers to Mary Queen of Scots?' " By the time Macaulay began to lecture him on the Huguenots, poor Pease was utterly routed.[22] Admittedly, not a major challenge to Macaulay's dialectical abilities. But in the account to his sister of the actual exchange, we catch an authentic glimpse not merely of the extent of his knowledge, but also of something less admirable, a sort of conversational killer instinct, delight

19. Idem.   20. May 25, 1833, Maxwell. ed., *Creevey Papers,* 596.
21. Forster, *Thornton,* 136.
22. T.B.M. to Hannah, July 1, 1833, Trinity Correspondence.

in the demonstration of knowledge for the sake of victory rather than for its own sake.

Thanks to Margaret's faithful chronicle of her brother's sayings and doings for a period of some months (1831–2), we can hear Tom's voice once more, this time in the completely different setting of the family circle. Her diary makes it possible for us to eavesdrop on a conversation between him and his father during the winter of 1831. Zachary had just told his son that Brougham, now Lord Chancellor, had seemingly reneged on his promise to the older Macaulay of a Commissionership of the Public Charities. Tom had turned pale with rage. "Ah! I knew it would be so," he stormed, "profligate scoundrel, that he is! You will never get it—I knew he would never give it to you. I am not disappointed." "Papa," angry at his son's tone, then gave Brougham's reason for being unable to fulfill the promise: that he was being accused of favoritism to the Macaulay family. The following dialogue ensued:

TOM: Has he the effrontery to say that?
ZACHARY: There, again, Tom! I really must insist on hear-
           ing no more of such language.
TOM: Well, I am sorry, I am sorry; but I must tell you
           that I do not believe one single word Lord B.
           says. There never was a man who had done so
           much service to a Government used as I have
           been; and I know well that Lord Brougham's
           intense hatred of me will prevent any advance-
           ment as long as he is in power. What have we
           got as a family? Nothing but a place in Sierra
           Leone for Henry, which was done through other
           people mostly; and the loss of my Commission
           of Bankruptcy. And as anyone would rather
           have four hundred pounds a year in England
           than a much larger sum in Sierra Leone, I
           reckon we have lost and not gained by this Gov-
           ernment. We have got nothing, absolutely noth-
           ing, and I may certainly say that I had claims on
           the Government. Which of the Cabinet would
           tell him that we were favoured? Would Lord
           Grey? Would Lord Lansdowne? No; it is no
           more than one of his usual horrible lies.[23]

23. December 1, [1831], Margaret Macaulay, *Recollections*, 61–2.

Brougham, in one of his frequent quixotic reversals, awarded the commissionership, worth £800 per annum, to Zachary after all. And Margaret made her brother apologize to their father for his intemperate language. But what the dialogue reveals is far more significant than the topic that had produced it. As he exploded in righteous anger both against Brougham's treachery and against what he considered to be Zachary's pusillanimity in the face of it, he discarded the rhetoric of his essays and speeches in favor of the direct simplicity of familiar discourse. One can imagine the short, stout figure, pacing back and forth, hands clenched and muscles working with the exertion of his mind (as Margaret once described him), eyes blazing with fury, his high-pitched lisp turning into an angry scream. There was something boyish and intemperate about his outburst, both qualities that had struck some of those who knew him; perhaps even just a bit of that "rabid" quality by which the young Disraeli had characterized him in his first novel.[24] But, after all, the object of his wrath was Brougham. And he always made Macaulay bad-tempered, usually for good reason.

Anger was not his normal demeanor outside the columns of the *Edinburgh Review*. To observe Macaulay in the family circle during this period is to sympathize with his uncle Colin's reaction to Disraeli's characterization: "Rabid: dear me! dear me!—Tom is not rabid—I wonder what he means. He must be a very silly man. I am sure you are not rabid, my dear Tom."[25] Margaret once heard her brother express great disgust with those people who, lively and agreeable abroad, made themselves dead weights when they were *en famille*.[26] This was certainly not true of Macaulay, who liked nothing better than to be both the center of attention and the principal source of entertainment at home. Marianne Thornton, describing a joint family dinner of the Thornton-Macaulay clan some time during the 1820's, reported: "Tom as usual reigning King of the Mob, and amusing the young as much with his fun, as he might have delighted elders with his eloquence."[27]

By the time the Reform Bill had passed, the family circle was no longer what it had been. Macaulay himself had moved into barrister's chambers at Gray's Inn at the end of 1829. He still spent some

---

24. Ellis had found T.B.M. "boyish." Trevelyan, *Life and Letters,* 128. Lord Grey complained about the intemperate manner in which he expressed his views. G. M. Trevelyan, *Lord Grey,* 385. For "rabid," see Disraeli, *The Young Duke,* quoted by Trevelyan, *Life and Letters,* 162.

25. T.B.M. to Hannah, June 23, 1831, Trinity Correspondence.

26. Margaret Macaulay, *Recollections,* 17.

27. Forster, *Thornton,* 135.

time at home every single day; but, as his sister Selina noted in her journal, that was quite different from his living there.[28] Another sister, Jane, particularly close to their mother, died unexpectedly in the autumn of 1830. Tom wrote his father from Paris, where the news had reached him, that it had broken his heart. "We must love one another better," his letter concluded.[29] A few months later, his mother, for whom Jane's death had been a cruel blow, suddenly died herself. She had lived long enough to have witnessed her son's great triumph in Parliament. In Margaret's recollections, we catch a glimpse of her surrounded by newspaper accounts of Tom's first speech on reform, repeating the compliments that had been paid him.[30] Shortly thereafter, Macaulay, who had been away from London, came home to find the shutters darkened and all the family in tears.[31] Selina, who had rejoiced from the first in her brilliant son's successes; who, far more responsive to his sensitive nature than her husband, had brought him understanding and sympathy at critical moments, was dead. "His first burst of grief was indeed overwhelming," one of his sisters remembered, "and called our thoughts away from our own distress which had till then so much absorbed us."[32] Then calm returned, and he was a great comfort to the bereaved family.

Zachary, whose financial circumstances were steadily worsening, sold the house on Great Ormond Street; and the Macaulay family moved to a small and inexpensive house on Bernard Street, off Russell Square. It was there that Tom regaled his brother Charles and his sisters with streams of puns—he once won a bet he could make two hundred during the evening—there that he read to them from the *Spectator,* or organized parlor games in one of which he made the participants guess the following objects he had in mind: the slug that killed Perceval; the lemon Wilkes had squeezed for Dr. Johnson; the pork chop Thurtell had eaten after he had murdered Weare; and Sir Charles Macarthy's jaw, sent to George IV by the Ashantees.[33] When he and Hannah sailed for India in 1834, their sister Fanny compared the gap in the family circle created by Tom's departure to "something like what would ensue upon the sun's deserting the earth."[34]

28. Selina Macaulay, Journal, December 30, 1830, Huntington MSS.

29. T.B.M. to his father, September 26, 1830, Trinity Correspondence.

30. Margaret Macaulay, *Recollections*, 131.

31. T.B.M. to Napier, May 6, 1831, British Museum Add. MSS. 34,615, f. 83.

32. Selina Macaulay, Journal, December 27, 1831, Huntington MSS.

33. For puns and guessing game, see Trevelyan, *Life and Letters,* 131; for *Spectator,* see Selina Macaulay, Journal, December 3, 1830, Huntington MSS.

34. Fanny Macaulay to Margaret Macaulay, February 1834, Huntington MSS.

He must have been the life and soul of the family. At home, where young people were always present, he could unbend completely. His relations with his father were, on the face of it, completely harmonious; though to maintain that harmony must have required a good deal of forbearance on the part of the younger man. One need only recall his offer to resign from the ministry during the slavery abolition debates. Very rarely, one catches a glimpse of impatience and annoyance boiling up from below the solid rock of filial devotion. Once, while Tom was giving his brother Charles a lecture telling him not to ask him for patronage on behalf of his friends, Zachary broke in with: "No, Charles; you must not ask Tom for places for people. I want all that he has to give. I want a clerkship for Mr. Stokes, a place for Mr. Baines. . . ." At this point, reporting the scene to Margaret, Tom added, "and he was going to demand, I suppose, a partnership for the black man, when I stopped him by saying I had nothing to give."[35] The tone of exasperation that found vent in this letter gives some indication of the effort it must have cost Macaulay to control it under less uninhibited circumstances.

His evident distaste for the passionate intensity with which his father held his abolitionist convictions may be regarded as part of the continuous drift of his religious views away from Evangelical orthodoxy. The moral and ethical imperatives of the Evangelical creed had not lost their hold over him. He expressed shock and surprise, for example, at the coarseness of the conversation that passed between men and women in society; and taught his sisters and brothers to admire the healthfulness and animated nature of Walter Scott more than what he called the diseased mind and imagination of Lord Byron.[36] But as far as theology was concerned, the process of dilution may be seen at work in his correspondence and his conversations with Hannah and Margaret.

For one thing, they reflect his irritation with the modes of expression favored by Evangelicals. One of those modes was the confessional. When he found two of his sisters—Fanny and Selina—ecstatic over a personal letter they had received from one of their favorite preachers, Baptist Noel, he raged and stormed until he made both of them a little ashamed of their spiritual pastor and master. "I always hated confessors—Protestant as Catholic," was his summary comment about this scene.[37] There was a similar strain in his joking repri-

35. T.B.M. to Margaret, January 21, 1833, Morgan MSS.
36. Margaret Macaulay, *Recollections*, 19–22.
37. T.B.M. to Hannah, June 1, 1833, Trinity Correspondence.

mand to Hannah for having made up a list of novels she wanted to borrow from the circulating library:

> *You might have given to Noel's prate*
> *At least the space of one day . . .*
> *But now, for sermons you don't care,*
> *You bellow for romances.*[38]

The same note sounds in a little mock sermon he himself delivered to Hannah and Margaret, as part of one of his letters to them: "But I have thought it my duty to set before you the evil consequences of making vows rashly, and adhering to them superstitiously; for instance, my Christian brethren, or rather my Christian sisters, let us consider, etc. etc."[39] The Evangelicals' reaction in Parliament to the Jewish Emancipation Bill of 1833 he called "the merest praise-God-Barebones cant that had been obtruded on the House of Commons since the restoration." He used the same occasion to observe that all cabinet ministers had attended the running of the Derby, except Grant who (as a "Saint") thought it a sin, and himself, who thought it a bore.[40]

All this is hardly surprising on the part of one who, as we know, could not have been counted among the strict Evangelicals since his days at Cambridge. A prayer for his welfare in India, by one of the leading members of the Clapham Sect, James Stephen, simply assumed that a gulf now existed between the generations. He wrote to Tom's sister Fanny: "May the blessing of *his father's* God be with him in his going out and in his coming in."[41] What, then, were Macaulay's religious beliefs at this time? If religion was not a subject on which he frequently expressed himself, he shared that reluctance with many of his contemporaries. Tom Moore wrote in his journal in 1832 that the most worldly indifference prevailed in England when it came to people's true feelings on the matter, "while the slightest whisper of scepticism was sure to raise an outcry against him who dared to breathe it."[42] The Evangelicals had succeeded, if not in converting the country to their beliefs, in creating an atmosphere that made the display of theological doubts inexpedient. Not that

38. April 9, 1832, Margaret Macaulay, *Recollections*, 105.
39. T.B.M. to Hannah and Margaret, August 16, 1832, Trevelyan, *Life and Letters*, 196.
40. T.B.M. to Hannah, May 25, 1833, Trinity Correspondence.
41. Stephen to Fanny Macaulay, May 28, 1834, Huntington MSS (italics mine).
42. April 6, 1832. Quennell, ed., *Moore Journal*, 211.

there is any reason for assuming that when Macaulay told the electors of Leeds he was a Christian, he did not mean it. The great folly of the atheists, he told Margaret, was that they were unbelievers only in religion. He illustrated this point by an analogy whose first term was their father Zachary; its second, God. We cannot, he declared, prove the existence of our father any more than the existence of God. Yet, if we love and obey the former, why should we not love and obey God?[43] Considering the history of the relationship between father and son, and some of the stresses that had been put upon Tom's filial love and obedience, the analogy was probably more revealing than its author had intended.

The very playfulness of some of his other comments to Margaret at the time of the Reform Bill debates showed how much the milk of his father's vital religion had by now been watered down in the son. In order to be able to escape from the elderly bluestocking, Miss Berry, so that he could take a walk with his two favorite sisters, he told the old lady that his presence was required at the House of Commons. Margaret warned that his sin would find him out. "But I don't mind my sin finding me out," he replied, "if Miss Berry does not." Another day, he amazed Margaret by telling her that he did not believe that the pursuit of pleasure was any more harmful to character than any other pursuit that had self for its object. In response to her assertion that the effect of vice necessarily was to harden the heart, he averred that, on the contrary, men often preserved feeling hearts, even through a course of dissipation.[44]

One must remember the circumstances under which these talks took place—an adoring and adored older brother's raillery with a younger sister. Clearly, Macaulay could not resist the temptation of occasionally going counter to the conventional views of a twenty-year-old girl, brought up in the devout atmosphere of an Evangelical household. He was not above trying to shock her with his own daring. Still, when all due allowance has been made for the situation, these pleasantries show the distance he had put between himself and the stern piety of his father.

That distance became even more evident in the course of a serious discussion he had with Margaret about the meaning of Original Sin. He would have none of the black depravity that was part and parcel of Calvinist doctrine. "He would not allow more," she recalled in her journal, "than that we came into the world liable, from the consti-

43. Margaret Macaulay, *Recollections*, 42.   44. Ibid., 106–7, 93–4.

tution of mind and body, to certain temptations, and were led by their power to do wrong. He thought this quite sufficient for all practical purposes, and all that the Bible had laid down."[45] Both tone and substance of that last brisk sentence ring more of the comfortable latitudinarianism of Sydney Smith than of Clapham. They symbolize the change of outlook between the generations.

We owe the preservation of these revealing comments on religion, as well as the most intimate character sketch of her brother we possess, to Margaret's *Recollections,* privately printed after Macaulay's death. She had worshipped Tom from childhood, and felt sure in her heart that he would be counted among the great men of the century. And so, for some months in the winter and spring of 1831–2, as a tribute to his genius, she played the role of Boswell to his Dr. Johnson. The analogy is particularly apt, since she was herself very conscious of the similarities and differences between her brother and "the great Cham" of eighteenth-century English letters. Her candid and perceptive comparison between the two men gives us a picture of Tom as he appeared within the family circle—to a young girl who idolized him, it is true, but who, like most Evangelicals, had a passion for the truth that kept her critical sense ever sharp and alert.

In the autumn of 1831, Macaulay (as we know) delivered his own judgment of Dr. Johnson in an essay for the *Edinburgh Review.* He laid great stress there—many since have felt too great a stress—on the grotesque elements in Johnson's character and demeanor, painting the picture of a person of irregular habits, uncouth, diseased, irritable, full of odd prejudices and superstitions. He found an explanation for those qualities in Johnson's personal background of poverty and struggle. He had lived in what Macaulay called the period between the age of patronage and the age of curiosity, at a time when the position of a man of letters was at its most miserable and degraded.[46] Here, as elsewhere, he tempered moral judgment with reference to social context. Margaret, in her own, seemingly artless way, took a similar approach at just about the same time in trying to account for her brother's maladroitness and lack of good deportment. The reason for them, she thought (and confided to her journal), lay in his longstanding dislike of company, which meant that he had had little opportunity for improving manners "naturally

45. Ibid., 34.
46. T.B.M., "Croker's Boswell," *Works,* VIII, 85–107.

embarrassed and awkward."[47] Shyness is not a trait one usually tends to associate with Macaulay; and, when one thinks of him feasting at the great London houses, the cynosure of Whig society, one momentarily wonders at her characterization. Yet Margaret knew her brother well. And when one recalls the ways in which he compensated for that natural shyness she portrayed in him, one can better understand the unfavorable impression he left with many of those who encountered him. One can also understand why he tired so quickly of the heady round of social life open to him after his parliamentary triumph, and why he always longed with such fervor for the company of those who loved and understood him.

Johnson and her brother were alike, Margaret believed, not only in their lack of good manners, but in their hatred of humbug and cant, as well as in what she called their constitutional indolence; though both men, she added, were sometimes capable of great exertions. Both, she noted, had the habit of "tossing" people in conversation. Both disliked the laudatory mode. When Tom heard praise and general admiration for someone, it always spurred him on to find something to be blamed. Both loved London, and showed complete indifference to the beauties of nature. Her brother shared with Johnson, she thought, the habit of taking either side of the question in a discussion, depending on the opinions of their interlocutors. Tom was not as generous as Johnson. No consideration on earth, for instance, would have made him take disagreeable people into his house for charity. Johnson had not only done that, but had also given financial aid to those in distress, even while he himself was poor. This her brother would not have done. He was, she observed, generally too eager to forget unpleasant things, too fond of "reasoning himself out of feeling."[48]

Here Margaret had put her finger on a conflict that supplies a major clue to her brother's character. Naturally thin-skinned and tenderhearted, perpetually craving affection, attached with bonds of iron first to his mother, then to two of his sisters, he had gradually formed a hard shell of level-headedness and common sense around the vulnerable core of his delicate sensibilities. It had served first as a shield to guard him against his father's harsh discipline, had been toughened in the vigorous and disputatious atmosphere of Cambridge, and further reinforced in the course of his battle for fame in literature and politics. As reviewer and parliamentary orator, as the

47. Margaret Macaulay, *Recollections*, 32.   48. Ibid., 20–3.

conversational hero of Whig society, he had come to embody hard common sense, the merciless flash of wit, the confident assurance belonging to the solidly earthbound. He appeared to stand for the antithesis of all that tended toward the mystical, the sentimental, the self-revelatory, the heart rather than the head.

This hard shell could serve him as battering ram as well as shield. It also served to dam up the soft center of his innermost nature. For he knew from experience that without that dam, the floods of feeling within would pour out uncontrolled. He had parodied excessive sentimentality in his "Tears of Sensibility." He despised the emotional transports of Lake poets and Evangelical preachers. But in his heart of hearts he was often of their company, still the exiled schoolboy who yearned for home. "How dearly I love and how much I miss you," he wrote to Hannah and Margaret in the summer of 1832. "I am glad that I have business to transact, for I would find it in my heart to whimper as I used to do when I went to school at twelve years old."[49] It was because he was aware of these deep feelings in himself that he fought all the harder to hide them from the outside world. The mask was in place most of the time. But there were moments when "reasoning himself out of feeling" became an impossible task for him. And, above all, there was his pride.

The same shrewdness that led Margaret to gain insight into the conflict between reason and feeling in her brother's nature also gave her an understanding of the distinctive texture of his imaginaton. For she saw in Tom what she began by calling a "romantic" disposition, defined as "that love of living in the ideal world . . . that power of depicting . . . things that are not as though they were." Yet, at the same time, she observed in him (as well as in herself) a common sense way of looking at things which she was unable to reconcile with the belief that either of them could rightfully be characterized as "romantic." Her own experience was that after tearing herself away from some daydream, after turning from "some exquisite form I had worked up with the care of a Frankenstein, and which it had taken me long to place before myself in that perfection I desired"—after all that, she was yet left as cool-headed and as much disposed to view the world in its true colors as "the fattest alderman in London." In similar fashion, she saw that her brother's imaginative powers were increasing day by day, but not at the expense of his good sense. How could this be?

49. T.B.M. to Hannah and Margaret, June 7, 1832, Trinity Correspondence.

She found the answer in John Foster's essay entitled *On the Application of the Epithet Romantic.*[50] Foster there distinguished between people whose imagination might range far and wide, but could never make them do a foolish thing or indulge in extravagant expectations; and "romantic" people who believed that they had a special destiny, that their lovers would be perfect, and their friendships purer and more perfect than the world had ever seen. Tom, his sister noted, certainly did not belong to this latter category. For his powerful imagination did not inhibit his solid sense of reality.[51]

It is entirely true that Macaulay's imaginative faculty exemplified what, many years later, Walter Bagehot was to define as the rare union of a flowing fancy with a concern for the coarse business of life.[52] Writing from Paris in 1830, he was capable of describing individual items of furniture in the duc de Broglie's *salon* in such detail that he himself felt obligated to add: "You will think that I have some intention of turning upholsterer."[53] At the same time, he loved more than anything else to build castles in the air, to daydream; so that walking in the streets of London, he would fancy himself in Greece, in Rome, in the midst of the French Revolution. He felt that these two ways of looking at the world—which Margaret had noticed existing side by side in him—stood in a symbiotic relationship to each other. For, he told her, it was precisely when he built his castles in the air, when he daydreamed about the past, that factual accuracy became imperative. "Precision in dates, the day or hour in which a man was born or died, becomes absolutely necessary. A slight fact, a sentence, a word, are of importance in my romance."[54]

If anyone really understood Macaulay at this period of his life, it was Margaret. Chatting with him one spring day in 1832, she maintained that he was a happy man. There ensued a discussion between brother and sister on this subject. If, indeed, he was happy, Macaulay remarked in the bantering tone he liked to take with her, it was altogether due to the goodness of his disposition and the greatness of his mind. For his circumstances were not particularly good in any way. He was poor, for instance. True, unlike some men of great talents, *he* was not ashamed of his poverty. "This I never am," he remarked. "I tell everybody that I am a very poor man; I can't afford this or that: and never feel an instant who comes to see me at Gray's

50. The fifth edition of Foster's *Essays,* including this one, 167–245, appeared in London in 1813.
51. Margaret Macaulay, *Recollections,* 85–6.
52. Bagehot, *Collected Works,* I, 415.
53. Trevelyan, *Life and Letters,* 120.   54. Ibid., 133.

Inn." Thus he had to admit that it was not poverty that prevented his happiness. Well, then, he asked, what about his bad stomach? "You a bad stomach!" Margaret exclaimed. "You, who can eat a pound of tough beef and all sorts of things that no one else can take." She then proceeded to argue that what was most highly valued in the world could not be bought for money—it was the world's consideration. And that he had. But she was unable to budge him from his position that if he possesed any degree of superior happiness, it was due solely to his superior virtues.[55]

Once again, she had correctly seen into his character. For there could be no doubt that his success in Parliament and in London society, and the acclaim that had come with it, gave him immense satisfaction. Yet we have seen that political life, even for those who were successful, could bring with it its share of frustrations. Prophetically, Margaret put this question in her journal: "How will the unconquerable pride of Tom's spirit ever be able to support those necessary mortifications, checks, and vexations?"[56] She might have asked another question: To what extent was her brilliant brother's happiness dependent upon his possession of a secure and exclusive place in her own affections, and what would happen when he no longer occupied such a place? Perhaps she asked that question, too. But if she did, she did not record it in her journal.

55. March 15, 1832, Margaret Macaulay, *Recollections*, 88–9.   56. Ibid., 100.

X

HANNAH
AND MARGARET

WHY DID MACAULAY NEVER MARRY? THE QUESTION IS OF SOME IM-
portance. After all, did not Lytton Strachey ascribe the faults of the
historian's style to a lack of "the embracing fluidity of love"? Does
not J. H. Plumb conclude that the historian "lacked the roots of life,
sexual passion, and the sense of tragedy that it arouses—the biting,
painful sense of the transience of living and loving men"?[1] Thus an
answer to the question might not only shed light on Macaulay's personality, but also prove of some value in any consideration of his style
and subject matter.

At the age of seventeen or eighteen, Macaulay himself tells us, he
was half in love with his cousin Mary Babington. When he heard of
her death in 1858 (she was then Lady Parker) , he confided this to his
journal. But then he added: "Her conversation soon healed the
wound made by her eyes."[2] One thinks of Gibbon's "I must have a
wife I can talk to." In the early 1830's there was a widespread rumor
that Macaulay was showing romantic interest in someone he certainly could have talked to, Maria Kinnaird, a West Indian merchant's daughter, the ward and adopted child of "Conversation"
Sharp. The latter was a well-known London host who entertained
and moved in Whig literary society. Macaulay may well have en-

1. Lytton Strachey, *Portraits in Miniature, and Other Essays* (New York, 1931) , 177;
J. H. Plumb, *Men and Centuries* (Boston, 1963) , 255.
2. Trinity Journal, July 21, 1858.

countered Maria at Sharp's house. She sounds like a paragon—an admirable French and Italian scholar, as well as an excellent musician who sang Scarlatti, Handel, and Mozart to (among others) Wordsworth and Sydney Smith, both of whom liked her immensely. She was said to have been proficient in history and literature, and endowed with a good memory as well as with £70,000.[3] At the end of 1831, there was talk of their getting married. Macaulay was "very much annoyed," since that kind of gossip would make those very pleasant visits to "Conversation" Sharp's house rather awkward. He had once given Maria Kinnaird tea in the "ventilator" of the House of Commons; but his conscience was clear of all flirting imputation. "He says she is rather pretty, but she wears spectacles."[4]

The person to whom we owe this comment of Macaulay's was a girl who did not wear spectacles. In fact, he once remarked to her, after a reception at Lansdowne House where he had met a collection of fashionable women famous for their beauty, that one trouble with those women was that if they had good eyes, they spoiled them by squeezing them up and looking through glasses. They all appeared to him "parboiled, languid creatures." This conversation took place as he and she were taking one of their frequent walks of exploration through London. "Not one of them," Macaulay told his companion, "could take such a walk as you are taking now."[5]

His walking companion was, of course, his sister Margaret, and any search for the women in Macaulay's life must begin and end with her and her sister Hannah. For it was these two younger sisters, one (Margaret) twelve years younger, the other (Hannah) ten years younger than himself, upon whom alone was focused the strongly developed emotional side of his nature. Only they responded to his immense need for reciprocated affection. One should recall at this point the stern, unbending father, inculcating humility of spirit, modesty, and devotion to Christian duty upon his brilliantly precocious son; the gentle, protective mother, who tried to moderate her husband's relentless pressure on the boy, to supply the love and

3. [C. K. Paul], *Maria Drummond: A Sketch* (London, 1891), 27–8; Margaret Macaulay, *Recollections*, 51.

4. November 21, 1831, Margaret Macaulay, *Recollections*, 51. The House of Commons ventilator, where ladies could be taken to listen to the debates, was described by one of them as a room about 8 feet square, built like a ship's cabin, with a window, two chairs, and a table. The ventilator, "a thing like a chimney," was in the middle. Through it the sound from below ascended so perfectly that "with attention, not a word is lost." *The Diary of Frances Lady Shelley* (2 vols., London, 1912–13), II, 8.

5. Margaret Macaulay, *Recollections*, 19.

affection she felt he required more than constraint and reprimands. One should remember little Tom, already known as a wonderfully talented child, sent unwillingly away to school, aching to get home for the holidays, grievously afflicted with what he dubbed *la maladie du Clapham;* passionately fond of his mother; driven almost to breakdown by the paternal fury at his failure in the mathematical part of the Cambridge tripos examinations. As we know, the inevitable revolt against the father, largely repressed, came to the surface in the son's habits and appearance. Fat, slovenly, and ungainly, barely able to tie his shoe laces and completely unable to tie his neckcloth, more often to be found idling the time away reading novels than in steady application to work or, indeed, to prayer, he stood forth in all too visible contrast to his fanatically orderly and industrious Evangelical father. The galaxy of his triumphs, first at the Cambridge Union, then in print in *Knight's* and the *Edinburgh,* won for him many admirers and not a few jealous enemies; but few close friends to whom he could open his heart. Perhaps, then, it was not altogether surprising that he should have established a close relationship with his two youngest sisters, who totally adored him and who supplied for him on demand that element of secure domesticity so essential to his peace of mind.

The two sisters' special relationship to their brother dated back for both to late childhood. We have seen how when Tom was "gulfed" in the tripos examinations of 1822, his mother took Hannah, then twelve, into her room to inform her privately of what had happened; "for even then it was known how my whole heart was wrapped up in him, and it was thought necessary to break the news."[6] Margaret recalled that she, in turn, became very fond of her brother—at one point she had been rather afraid of him—about two years later. She was delighted when she found that Tom seemed to like talking to her and amusing her; and that he did not ever talk down to her. She was undoubtedly right in remarking that the clearness of Macaulay's style proceeded in some measure from his habit of conversing with very young people, to whom he had a great deal to explain and to impart. In some ways, he never ceased to regard the two sisters as children, long after they had passed that stage; and was only intermittently aware that their emotional needs might have changed with their ages. His role *vis-à-vis* these two young sisters was paternal as much as fraternal. Deterred from matrimony and fatherhood by his own severely repressed feelings of hostility toward Zachary, he could

6. Trevelyan, *Life and Letters,* 61.

now take satisfaction in being the sort of father to them that Zachary had never been to him.[7]

Of the two, Margaret was the more warm-hearted and affectionate, Hannah the more querulous and high-strung. Brought up in the strict Evangelical environment of the Macaulay family, both were properly devout, but their devotion did not inhibit their sharp-tongued comments about others or their natural high spirits. Both sisters, like everyone else in the family, tended to be introspective and highly emotional. In both, the imaginative faculty was strongly developed; though Margaret, as we know, shared with her brother a fundament of common sense. She was the more stable of the two.

One question that might well be asked is why Macaulay did not from the start enter into a similarly close relationship with those of his sisters—Selina, Jane, and Fanny—who preceded Hannah and Margaret. One can surmise, of course, that he subconsciously preferred the younger sisters because he wanted to act as their father, to outdo his own father in the realm in which the latter had so patently failed—the ability to maintain a bond of mutual trust and confidence with his children, to mold and influence the minds of much younger people without impairing their affective or imaginative capacities. That may be a part of the answer. But there is also the simple fact that there was less temperamental compatibility between the three older sisters and himself than there was between him, Hannah, and Margaret. Selina was the most serious-minded member of the Macaulay family, a chronic invalid in whom the Evangelical heritage had taken its strongest root. In November 1830, when Brougham was expected to bring in his motion for parliamentary reform, she noted in her diary that there was great interest in this motion in the family, since Tom might be involved; but that she herself could not help "strongly feeling the littleness and vanity of the objects of which the end is only to promote the temporal improvement of mankind."[8] A few weeks later she found herself suffering from a variety of physical and nervous symptoms, which became a great bodily and spiritual trial to her. Her only comfort was that she could legitimately pray for the improvement of her health, since the state she was in had

7. Joseph Romilly, who encountered T.B.M. with Hannah and Margaret at Cambridge in 1832, noted in his diary that they were "agreeable girls with sweet voices: not pretty but clever and conversible & very young." October 7, 1832, J. P. T. Bury, ed., *Romilly's Cambridge Diary 1832–42* (Cambridge, 1967), 20. On Margaret's early memories of T.B.M. and the relation of his style to his conversing with young people, see Trevelyan, *Life and Letters*, 130–1; Margaret Macaulay, *Recollections*, 6.

8. Selina Macaulay, Journal, November 16, 1830, Huntington MSS.

impeded her spiritual progress.[9] Hardly the sort of personality that would appeal to Tom. We know little about Jane, also an invalid since her youth, who died in 1830, much to Tom's sorrow. Fanny, who after the death of her mother devoted herself to the care of Zachary, now old and ailing, was more down-to-earth than her sister Selina; and thus proved more congenial to Margaret, who at one point expressed the hope of increasing friendship with her, something which she felt could never happen between Selina and herself. "Our minds are cast in a mould so totally different that we can never fit in," she wrote. And she could only regard her older sister with distant but kindly affection.[10] Fanny, then, was different; but Fanny lacked the quality to which Tom was particularly responsive, a sense of imaginative playfulness.

Perhaps because his father had attempted to push his gifted son too quickly into premature adulthood, had tried too hard and too early to shape and discipline his formidable talents into an instrument for the greater glory of God and the benefit of humanity, the son felt a correspondingly greater need to retreat as often as he could to an idyllic childhood of which he had never had enough. Perhaps, indeed, the elements of childishness in his character which he preserved to his dying day, were, as in many great men, an essential part of his genius. It may be that the tremendous internal tensions produced by having to "fight his way up" made it especially vital for him to be sure that during certain hours he could let his guard down and be himself.

Whatever the reason, the need existed, and Hannah and Margaret were there to fill it. In 1830, when the Reform Bill struggle loomed on the near horizon, Hannah was twenty, Margaret eighteen. It was in this and the following two years that the three of them lived what might be described as an urban idyll. Their close relationship must have begun after Macaulay came down from Cambridge to reside with the family in Great Ormond Street. Some years later, Margaret was to recall to Hannah the scene in Tom's room "when he used to lie in bed with his unshorn face, you opposite the window with your feet up on the bed, reading the *Spectator* resting on your knee, I opposite you, or at the foot of the bed, working." When Hannah left out an expression she thought "not *comme il faut*," Macaulay instantly corrected the omission.[11] Every afternoon, Tom took the two sisters

9. Ibid., December 30, 1830.
10. Hannah to Margaret, May 17, 1834, Huntington MSS.
11. May 21, 1831, Margaret Macaulay, *Recollections*, 39.

for a long walk. The three of them explored the City, Islington, Clerkenwell, and the parks—with Tom supplying anecdotes about every street, square, court, and alley. Margaret recorded their pacing up and down Brunswick Square and Lansdowne Place for two hours one day, deep in the mazes of what she called the most subtle metaphysics; and walking along Cork Street, discussing Dryden's poetry and the great men of that time; on another occasion, making jokes all the way along Bond Street and talking politics everywhere. Sometimes they would make puns on the names of the shopkeepers; for example: "I wish you had more No. 22 for me" (Love), or: "Is there any No. 27 you are afraid of seeing just now?" (Dunn).[12] After dinner, there would be more talk and punning, then singing, though none of the Macaulays had good voices.

Macaulay moved into chambers at Gray's Inn in 1829. His doing so reduced but by no means put an end to the companionable times the three of them had enjoyed together. When their mother died, he told Margaret how much more he would have suffered had it been she or Hannah.[13] His youngest sisters had by then become his sole confidantes, the two people on earth whom he trusted most. The only other person to whom he could speak freely, in fact, the only close friend he was destined to have in the course of his entire life, was Thomas Flower Ellis, a lawyer (and a former fellow of Trinity, though Macaulay had missed him there), whom he had met on the Northern Circuit in 1826. They were in effect neighbors throughout Macaulay's London years, since Ellis lived on Bedford Place, just a short distance away from Ormond Street and Bernard Street. Gray's Inn was not much farther away. What had brought the two together was a shared love and knowledge of the classics. Ellis, we are told by one who knew him, possessed a quick, keen intellect and a strongly developed sense of humor. His mind worked too rapidly to be easily followed by most people; and he had little sympathy for the ways and tastes of ordinary men.[14] He and Macaulay probably saw each other quite regularly during the late twenties and early thirties. But there can be no doubt that Macaulay's strongest personal bond at that time was the one to his two youngest sisters.

To this bond we owe some of the liveliest and most amusing letters in the language. Among them are many of Macaulay's sparkling descriptions of London politics and society, as well as his "hidden" verse

12. Trevelyan, *Life and Letters,* 134; Margaret Macaulay, *Recollections,* 99.
13. May 21, 1831, Margaret Macaulay, *Recollections,* 39.
14. Sir Frederick Pollock, *Personal Remembrances* (2 vols., London, 1887), I, 100–1.

letter to Hannah: "Why am I such a fool as to write to a gypsey at Liverpool, who fancies that none is so good as she, if she sends one letter for my three? A lazy chit whose fingers tire with penning a page in reply to a quire!"[15] Macaulay's fingers never tired. After all,

> *Be you Foxes, be you Pitts*
> *You must write to silly chits.*
> *Be you Tories, be you Whigs,*
> *You must write to sad young gigs.*[16]

But his sisters, sheltered and protected homebodies, for whom their brother's letters must have conjured up a strange and wonderful new world of high drama and solemn affairs of state, could not match his own steadfastness as a correspondent. At times his appeals to them to write sound a note almost of despair: "Write, my darlings, write. Give me whole conversations, if you have nothing else to tell. Above all tell me tales of each other."[17] Or, a few days earlier: "Write a little now and then to Poor Presto"—his own nickname for himself, derived from Swift's *Journal to Stella*.[18]

Two chief threads run through these letters. One is Macaulay's desire, or, rather, his need, to communicate his experiences in the great world to those he loved and knew best. Thanks to his "dear mother" and the interest she had always taken in his childish successes, he averred (and there is no reason to think that he was not candid in doing so) that affection had as much to do as vanity with his desire to distinguish himself. "From my earliest years," he remembered, "the gratification of those whom I love has been associated with the gratification of my own thirst for fame, until the two have become inseparably joined in my mind."[19] Certainly he obtained praise and appreciation, even to idolatry, from his sisters. This is how Margaret, for instance, faced the prospect of hearing him speak in the House of Commons:

It seems to me now as if it would be almost too much for me to witness that mightiest of all triumphs, the triumph of mind over mind, to hear those burning words, those streams of pure and lofty eloquence, to listen to music dearer to my ears than Pasta could ever make, in the enthusi-

15. T.B.M. to Hannah and Margaret, June 6, 1833, Trevelyan, *Life and Letters,* 215.
16. T.B.M. to Hannah, July 6, 1832, ibid., 188.
17. T.B.M. to Hannah and Margaret, June 21, 1832, Morgan MSS.
18. T.B.M. to Hannah and Margaret, June 18, 1832, Morgan MSS.
19. T.B.M. to Hannah, July 6, 1831, Trevelyan, *Life and Times,* 166.

astic applause of all about me, and to feel that he who was exercising this mighty influence prized the happy tears of my proud, devoted affection more than the compliments and applause of the first men of his country.[20]

But Macaulay obtained something more from his relationship with Hannah and Margaret—and this is the second chief thread that runs through their correspondence. With them he could give free rein to his fondness for self-dramatization and fantasy, a trait closely related to his achievements as a historian.[21] Whatever he did, whether he was making a speech in Parliament, delivering an address to the electors of Leeds, or merely taking a walk in London, in relating it to his sisters he gave the act, and his own role in it, another and more dramatic dimension by placing it in a context of fantasy, historical or otherwise. When Margaret expressed surprise at the great accuracy of his information, considering how desultory his reading had been, Macaulay told her that he owed his factual accuracy to his love of castle-building. He then went on to describe how the past in his mind was constructed into a romance:

With a person of my turn . . . the minute touches are of as great interest, and perhaps greater, than the most important events. Spending so much time as I do in solitude, my mind would have rusted by gazing vacantly at the shop windows. As it is, I am no sooner in the streets than I am in Greece, in Rome, in the midst of the French Revolution. Precision in dates, the day or hour in which a man was born or died, becomes absolutely necessary. A slight fact, a sentence, a word, are of importance in my romance. Pepys's Diary formed almost inexhaustible food for my fancy. I seem to know every inch of Whitehall. I go in at Hans Holbein's gate, and come out through the matted gallery. The conversations which I compose between great people of the time are long, and sufficiently animated: in the style, if not with the merits, of Sir Walter Scott's. The old parts of London, which you are sometimes surprised at my knowing so well, those old gates and houses down by the river, have all played their part in my stories.[22]

Hannah and Margaret were able to participate in those fantasies. He did not have to hide anything from them; for instance, the romantic satisfaction he derived from his involvement in great affairs of state, but which, in the role of the rising young politician, he

20. February 9, 1832, Margaret Macaulay, *Recollections,* 78.
21. On this aspect of T.B.M., see John Clive, "Macaulay's Historical Imagination," *Review of English Literature,* I (October, 1960) , 20–8.
22. Trevelyan, *Life and Letters,* 133.

could not really show to the outside world. It is likely that the knowledge on his part that he was not playing that role for himself alone, but for a secret audience which applauded his every move and dwelled with him in his imaginary as well as in his real universe, added zest and savor to his activities during the Reform Bill period. "But only think," he wrote to Hannah in July 1830, just before attending prorogation ceremonies,

I shall go to the House of Lords, and there the King will sit on his throne—so grand—with his crown of gold on his head, and his sceptre in his hand, and all his royal robes. And he will make a speech to us and he will call us his faithful commons. . . . Only think of a brother of yours being thanked for his munificence by a King in all his glory.[23]

He himself, it is clear, had thought of it.

To this same love of dramatizing himself, we owe some verbatim dialogue, reported from the House of Commons library, where on July 20, 1831, Macaulay was waiting for one of the Reform Bill debates to begin. In the same room was Thomas Duncombe—"a very honest good natured fellow Tom; but none of the soberest." At the other end, an MP named Gordon was preaching to Henry Maxwell—"a very dishonest, ill-natured fellow Gordon, though one of the most canting." Robinson (MP for Worcester)—"a bore"—was writing at one table, "and Mr. Macaulay Member for Calne—no bore—but a very promising young gentleman and a rising speaker—[is] writing at the other." The door opens, in comes another bore, "that stupid Irishman Ruthwen." Then follows the dialogue:

Sir J. G[raham]—Macaulay
M—What?
G—Whom are you writing to that you laugh so much over your letter?
M—To my constituents at Calne to be sure. They expect news of the Reform Bill every day.
G—Well writing to constituents is less of a plague to you than to most people, to judge by your face.
M—How do you know that I am not writing a *billet doux* to a lady?
G—You look more like it, by Jove.[24]

23. T.B.M. to Hannah, July 21, 1830, Trinity Correspondence.
24. T.B.M. to Hannah, July 20, 1831, Trinity Correspondence.

Macaulay liked the House of Commons library. Indeed, he had celebrated his affection for it in one of those doggerel verses with whose authorship he used to credit "the judicious poet":

> *If thou goest into the smoking-room*
> *Three plagues will thee befall;—*
> *The chlorate of lime, and the bacco-smoke*
> *And the captain who's worst of all—.*
> *The canting sea-captain,*
> *The lying sea-captain*
>   *The captain who's worst of all.*
>
> *If thou goest into the library*
> *Three good things will thee befall,—*
> *Very good books, and very good air,*
> *And M*c**l*y, who's best of all.*
> *The virtuous M—*
> *The prudent M—*
>   *M—who's best of all.*[25]

Best of all (among other things) at reporting overheard conversations to his sisters:

Here comes Vernon Smith.—"Well, Vernon, what are they doing?" "Gladstone has just made a very good speech and Howick is answering him."—"Aye, but in the House of Lords?"—"Brougham is firing into them."—"Is there a chance of our being beaten in the Lords?"—"They will beat us by twenty, they say."—"Well, I do not think it matters much."—"No, nobody out of the House of Lords cares either for Don Pedro or for Don Miguel."

"There," Macaulay writes, "is a conversation between two official men in the library of the House of Commons on the night of the third of June, 1833, reported word for word. To the historian three centuries hence this letter will be invaluable. To you, ungrateful as you are, it will seem worthless."[26]

As far as he was concerned, these letters were very far from having no value. "Nothing is worthless which affection sends affection," he added as a postscript to one of them, "and therefore nothing can be worthless which I send to you [Hannah], my darling."[27] Macaulay's

25. T.B.M. to Hannah and Margaret, July 30, 1832, Morgan MSS.
26. T.B.M. to Hannah, June 4, 1832, Trinity Correspondence.
27. T.B.M. to Hannah, July 20, 1831, Trinity Correspondence.

emotional investment in his relationship to his two favorite sisters was clearly far greater than merely that of a doting older brother. "The affection which I bear to you," he told Margaret in the summer of 1831,

is the source of the greatest enjoyment that I have in the world. It is my strongest feeling. It is that which will determine the whole course of my life. It has made me a better man and a far happier man than anything else would have made me. . . . The pleasures of dissipation end in disgust—those of vanity pall with repetition. Ambition itself passes away. But my love for my sweet sisters and friends becomes stronger and stronger from day to day and hour to hour.[28]

A year later, as we know, he addressed this unrestrained confession to both the sisters: "How dearly I love and how much I miss you. I am glad that I have business to transact, for I would find it in my heart to whimper as I used to do when I went to school at twelve years old."[29]

What strikes one particularly about the letter just cited is its date, June 1832, a time that found Macaulay at the zenith of his spectacular parliamentary, social, and literary career in the early 1830's: the hero of the Whigs for his speeches on the Reform Bill; the darling of Holland House for his fabulously erudite conversation and his seeming omniscience; the cynosure of London literary society for the scintillating essays from his pen that continued to appear in the *Edinburgh Review*. He had enemies, to be sure. But they castigated him for what they regarded as excessive arrogance, a tendency to be rude and overbearing, overweening ambition. What would they have said, had they been able to look over his shoulder and seen him write to Hannah after describing a breakfast at Holland House: "The great use of going to these fine places is to learn how happy it is possible to be without them"?[30] Or, again, a few weeks later: "Everybody flatters me from morning to night—and yet they cannot make me half so proud of anything as I am of your sweet affection, my dear sister."[31] To be beaten at the Leeds election, Macaulay wrote to Hannah and Margaret in the late summer of 1832, would not give him half as much uneasiness as he had felt about Hannah's toothache or Margaret's mumps.[32] To Hannah—he sometimes called

28. T.B.M. to Margaret, August 6, 1831, Morgan MSS.
29. T.B.M. to Hannah and Margaret, June 7, 1832, Trinity Correspondence.
30. T.B.M. to Hannah, June 1, 1831, Trevelyan, *Life and Letters*, 155.
31. T.B.M. to Hannah, June 27, 1831, Trinity Correspondence.
32. T.B.M. to Hannah and Margaret, August 11, 1832, Trinity Correspondence.

her "Nancy,"—he sent from Leeds his own version of a verse from Molière's *Misanthrope:*

> *If our good King would give me*
> *His London town this day,*
> *All for to leave my Nancy*
> *I know what I would say.*
> *Keep,—keep,—an't please your Majesty*
> *Your London east and west,*
> *And I'll keep my little Nancy,*
> *I love my Nancy best.*[33]

It may be argued that Macaulay's extravagant mode of expression should be discounted; that the epistolary style of the period was generally more openly fulsome than that of our time. People then had much less hesitation about giving vent to their feelings. Emotionalism and sentimentality were in the ascendant. Indeed, they derived their ascendancy in part from the pervasive influence of the Evangelicals, who couched their message in terms appropriate to the religion of the heart. But, as we know, Macaulay repudiated and despised just those aspects of his father's religion. Not for him the mawkishness, the maudlin outpourings of the heart, the confessional mode. One can almost see his own rhetorical style, full of hard common sense, self-conscious pomposity, elaborate irony, as a bulwark he set up against the intrusion of what he most disliked. Thus, the manner in which he addressed his sisters cannot be said to have been merely the conventional mode, and therefore discounted. The proof of this lies in his cautioning them on several occasions not to show what he had written them to the rest of the family. Surely, such a note of caution would not have been required, had the tone he employed fitted naturally into a conventional framework.

One should not assume, however, that Macaulay's emotions, even in his very personal correspondence, operated constantly at the same high level of intensity. He was moody and impulsive; quick to give way to the feelings of the moment. In one mood he could bring himself to write (to Hannah) :

Oxford, instead of being as it used to be, the magnificent old city of the 17th century—still preserving its antique character among the improvements of modern times, and exhibiting in the midst of upstart Birminghams and Manchesters the same aspect which it wore when Charles held

33. T.B.M. to Hannah, September 4, 1832, Trinity Correspondence.

his court at Christchurch, and Rupert led his cavalry over Magdalene Bridge,—is now to me only the place where I was so happy with my little sisters.[34]

An interesting passage, since the first part of the sentence shows Macaulay at his most pompous, artificial, and rhetorical, practicing, one might say, his "automatic" manner of historical composition, complete with built-in Whig interpretation; whereas the second has the artless simplicity that he permitted himself only in his intimate correspondence with those he loved most dearly. Another passage, dating from a few weeks before, illustrates the shift of mood that could take place even within the familiar epistolary context. In June 1832, as we have seen, Macaulay had to be re-elected for Calne. From there he wrote to the two sisters: "The bells are ringing. Flags are flying on the housetops. Music is playing in front of the inn. Macaulay for ever! Huzza!" From all the surrounding countryside, he reported, people had come to gaze upon and to listen to the great patriot—himself. Then the mood changes: "And I am wishing all the time that I were two hundred miles away, gazing upon and listening to my own little girls." Yet that mood does not last very long. For he goes on: "But here come the Guild-Stewarts and the Burgesses in their best. Here comes the music. Here come the beadles with fine coats and gold-headed staves; and here comes—is it? no—yes—it is Lord Kerry. I had no inkling that he was here. I must go and shake hands with him."[35] The ebullient side of his nature, then, could quickly be mobilized by the stimulus of action, and at times it won out. But the other, softer side always remained to assert itself once more when the stimulus had passed.

To the outside world, Macaulay wished to present above all an image of the independent man. What rankled most in the months during and after the Reform Bill debates was that because it was well known that he had no means, it might be thought he was interested in obtaining office for financial reasons. Yet in another realm, the personal, he was immensely dependent, at times to a truly pathetic degree, on two young girls. He himself was aware of the paradox. In talking once to Hannah and Margaret about his love of independence as a factor weighing with him against taking office, he told them: "I wish you two . . . would hang yourselves." Margaret chronicled their reaction: "We stared." Her brother went on: "Because then I should be the most independent man in the world."[36]

34. T.B.M. to Hannah, September 29, 1833, Trevelyan, *Life and Letters*, 200–1.
35. T.B.M. to Hannah and Margaret, June 13, 1832, Morgan MSS.
36. Margaret Macaulay, *Recollections*, February 12, 1832, 82.

Margaret did not hang herself. But within six months of the time her brother had made this remark, she did something that hurt him almost as much. She became engaged to be married. Her husband-to-be was Edward Cropper, a Quaker, a widower, and a member of a prominent Liverpool shipping family, active in the anti-slavery movement. Margaret had already spent long periods with the Croppers. In 1830 she had nursed the first Mrs. Cropper during her last illness. Hannah and Margaret spent the summer of 1832 with the Croppers; and it seemed as if Macaulay had some inkling of what was to come. For he wrote them in early July: "Tell me of every person who 'regards you with an eye of partiality'—be he a sleek Quaker or a Yankee ship captain with his heels in the air, and his mouth smoking like a chimney."[37] When news of the engagement reached him, in August, his initial reaction was one of stoicism. Unlike Mr. Woodhouse, he assured the sisters, he would not talk of "poor Margaret." "It has always been my wish," he wrote, "to see my dearest girls honourably and happily married."[38]

In the same mood of sensible resignation, he observed a little later that autumn that while attachments between brothers and sisters were blameless, amiable, and delightful, they were so liable to be superseded by other attachments that no man ought to suffer them to become indispensable to him. But for him, his attachment to his sisters had taken the place of a first love. During the years when the imagination was most vivid and the heart most susceptible, his affection for Margaret and Hannah had prevented him from forming any serious attachment of a different kind. That may have been a good thing. Half jokingly, he continued: "My reason tells me that, but for the strong attachment which is at this moment a cause of pain to me, I might, like my friend Charles Grant, have been crossed in love, or what is much more, might like his brother, have married a fool." Nature's laws decreed that men and women should contract ties closer than those of consanguinity. To repine against the nature of things would be "the basest and most absurd selfishness." He even reconciled himself at this juncture to the eventual (and inevitable) loss of Hannah, an event for which, when it arrived, he hoped to be prepared.

From that moment, with a heart formed, if ever any man's heart was formed, for domestic happiness, I shall have nothing left in the world but ambition. There is no wound, however, which time and necessity will not

37. T.B.M. to Hannah and Margaret, July 4, 1832, Trinity Correspondence.
38. T.B.M. to Hannah and Margaret, August 20, 1832, Trinity Correspondence.

render endurable: and, after all, what am I more than my fathers,—than the millions and tens of millions who have been weak enough to pay double price for some favourite number in the lottery of life, and who have suffered disappointment when their ticket came up a blank?[39]

Even here, the note of acquiescence appears somewhat forced, the tone of rational acceptance more that of a schoolboy repeating his lesson by rote than that of conviction. He was whistling in the dark. At the request of the artist, he had a portrait painted of himself (it is reproduced in this volume facing p. 238) which he intended to give to Margaret, not as a wedding present but as a "funeral relique," a memorial of one who, "though still living, is separated from you by a gulph like that which parts the living and the dead."[40]

When the wedding day (December 11, 1832) had come and gone, Macaulay was plunged into depths of depression. He was then just about to score his electoral victory over Sadler at Leeds. There he was, he wrote to Hannah, sitting in the midst of two hundred friends, all mad with exultation and party spirit, all glorying over the Tories, all thinking him the happiest man in the world. "And it is all I can do," he went on, "to hide my tears, and to command my voice, when it is necessary for me to reply to their congratulations. Dearest, dearest sister, whom have I on earth but thee? But for you, in the midst of all these successes I should wish that I were lying by poor Hyde Villiers."[41] The prospect of permanent separation from Margaret, he wrote Hannah from Leeds, had affected his temper. He found himself feeling bitterly toward Sadler, and resenting the very feeling. But suddenly there burned within him "a fierceness and restlessness, quite new and inexplicable." The explanation was not far to seek, of course. Sadler had become the object of Macaulay's anger and frustration over his loss of Margaret, a loss that had profoundly affected his psychological equilibrium.

At the very same time, less than a week after her wedding, Margaret was expressing her own feelings about Tom. "I think of him," she wrote, "with an earnestness and a love which are indescribable and feel as if absence and imagination only made him dearer to me."[42]

39. T.B.M. to Margaret, November 26, 1832, MS and typescript collection of T.B.M. letters in the possession of Mrs. Reine Errington (henceforth referred to as Errington MSS).

40. T.B.M. to Margaret, January 26, 1833, Errington MSS.

41. Secretary of the Board of Control, who had just died and whom T.B.M. succeeded. See above, p. 220.

42. Margaret to Fanny Macaulay, December 12, 1832, Huntington MSS.

After all, not so long before her engagement she had confessed to her journal that "if my dearest, dearest Tom still loves me, and I am not separated from him, I feel now as if I could bear anything. But the idea of being separated from him is what I cannot support." He had given her tastes no other person could satisfy, had for years been the object of her whole heart; every occupation almost had had him for its object, and without him would have been void of interest.[43] Her own marriage by no means put an end to this romantic adoration of her brother. Knowing all too well his probable reaction, it is quite possible that she suffered from real guilt feelings about the step she had taken; and, indeed, that a passage in a letter to Hannah some years later in which she made an autobiographical reference to "a struggle of mind in which every hope of future happiness appears to be destroyed by our determining on following what we believe to be the path of duty however hard to tread,"[44] concerned her marriage to Cropper. It is entirely conceivable that, in marrying, she did so with very mixed emotions; on the one hand, desolated at leaving her brother who meant so much to her; on the other, relieved to have effected an inevitable and necessary escape from an emotional bond which, however compelling, she knew could not and should not in the nature of things be permanent.

Perhaps anticipating that neither she nor Hannah would always remain single, she had tried to engage in a bit of matchmaking early in 1832. In a letter to her sister Fanny, she described a pleasant dinner party of the younger Macaulay set, where Tom had made himself extremely agreeable. He "looked his best and was as nice even as I could wish Selina Marriott to see him, on whom I very much wished him to make a favourable impression." Tom made jokes, and told all sorts of stories, evoking squeals of laughter. All the time, Selina kept her eyes fastened on him. A few days later, Margaret and Hannah went to call on her. "Oh," she said, "what a delightful evening I had at your house the other night! Such brilliant conversation! Such this. Such that! I was so [sad] when the coach came to take me away."[45] But we hear no more of Selina Marriott.

Macaulay had a different sort of domesticity in mind—to set up house with one, or, preferably, both of his favorite sisters. In July 1831, he had proposed this scheme to Hannah in a tone of ardent affection:

43. Margaret Macaulay, *Recollections*, 4–5.
44. Margaret to Hannah, January 11, 1834, Huntington MSS.
45. Margaret to Fanny Macaulay, January 4, 1832, Huntington MSS.

My dear girl, my sister, my darling—my own sweet friend—you cannot tell how, amidst these tempests of faction and amidst the most splendid circles of our nobles, I pine for your society, for your voice, for your caresses. I write this with all the weakness of a woman in my heart and in my eyes. We have difficulties to pass through. But they are not insurmountable; and, if my health and faculties are spared, I feel confident that, however the chances of political life may turn, we shall have a home, perhaps a humble one, but one in which I can be happy, if I see you happy.[46]

Though this appeal was addressed to Hannah alone, it seems that Macaulay was looking forward to settling down with both sisters. For in the autumn of the same year, Margaret noted in her diary that if Tom were to receive a sufficient salary, both Hannah and she herself would most likely live with him. "Can I possibly look forward to anything happier"—she added—"than living in such a manner as to draw us even closer than at present to one another. This would no doubt be the effect of that oneness of interest that would then exist between us."[47]

The affection that existed between brother and sisters, then, was by no means one-sided. The two girls worshipped Tom just as he worshipped them. This, for example, is how Hannah gave vent to her feelings during the spring of 1830:

. . . Mr. Noel preached one of the most beautiful sermons I have ever heard on the text "But this I say brethren the time is short" . . . it seemed as if he read my thoughts, when one inference he drew from the text was, that as the time is short we should idolize nothing on earth.—I felt that there was one I idolized, one I loved more than God, one on whom I depended alone for happiness, and in one moment we might be separated for ever. And yet I cannot endure the thought of ever loving him less than I do at this moment, though I feel how criminal it is—But I must leave off.[48]

There was a difference, of course, in what was at stake for the parties involved. It is doubtful whether either Hannah or Margaret ever thought of this *ménage à trois* as a permanent arrangement, a

46. T.B.M. to Hannah, July 13, 1831, Trinity Correspondence.

47. November 14, 1831, Margaret Macaulay, *Recollections*, 46; Trevelyan, *Life and Letters*, 134. See also Margaret to Mrs. Cropper, November 22, 1831, Huntington MSS: "I think it not improbable that before many months are over, Hannah and I may go and keep house with Tom."

48. Hannah to T. G. Babington, April 19, 1839, MS in the possession of Mrs. Humphry Trevelyan.

substitute for marriage and homes of their own. But while Macaulay, with one part of his mind, agreed with them, with another he clung to the hope that the innocent and delightful domesticity of which he promised himself so much would never end. He celebrated the advantages of such an arrangement in lyrical terms:

How sweet and perfect a love is that of brothers and sisters when happy circumstances have brought it to its full maturity . . .

> *My cousin is a bore,—*
> *My aunt she is a scold.—*
> *My daughter is too young,*
> *My grammam is too old.*
> *My mistress is a jilt—*
> *My wife—uh! Bad's the best,*
> *So give me my little sisters,*
> *And plague take all the rest.*[49]

"Let the world go as it likes," he mused to them some weeks later. "Let the Whigs stay in or be turned out. Let money be abundant or scarce. I do not know how love in a cottage may be with a wife. But I am sure it would suit me with a sister."[50] The date of this letter was July 6, 1832. In the very same month there appeared in the *Edinburgh Review* an article on Mirabeau. It contained the following sentence about the characters of the Regent Philip of Orléans and Charles II. "Both were more strongly attached to their female relatives than to any other human being; and in both cases it was suspected that this attachment was not perfectly innocent."[51] The author of that essay was, of course, Macaulay. Was he himself aware that this attachment to his female relatives might have been less than perfectly innocent?

To keep his relationship with his sisters in perspective, one must remember that such feeling between brothers and sisters was by no means unique among prominent English literary (and no doubt other) figures in the nineteenth century. Witness, among others, Wordsworth, de Quincey, Samuel Rogers, Disraeli, Harriet Martineau, and Charles Lamb. In a society in which up to a certain social level economic factors militated against early marriage, and moral factors against sexual experience before marriage, close attachments between brothers and sisters were to be expected. It may be relevant

49. T.B.M. to Hannah and Margaret, June 18, 1832, Morgan MSS.
50. T.B.M. to Hannah and Margaret, July 6, 1832, Trinity Correspondence.
51. T.B.M., "Mirabeau," *Works*, VIII, 240.

to note that none of the figures mentioned—Macaulay included—had attended public schools; especially if one recalls at the same time Fanny Macaulay's reflection some time after her brother's death that his character would have been improved, had he been trained at one of the great English public schools.[52] What she meant by that remark was almost certainly that Macaulay's self-centered and hyper-emotional tendencies would have been more severely curbed at a public school. Who knows whether, had his early education been different, the attachment to his sisters would have been equally close, or whether close male friendships would have taken its place? As it was, there were dangers of a different sort. One need only mention the name of Byron.

Rumor and scandal about Byron's relationship to his half sister Augusta were widespread when Macaulay was in his teens. In 1816, the year Byron had to leave England, Tom had written to his mother: "You have heard of course of the abominable, unmanly conduct of the peer-poet to whom we once paid much admiration."[53] There is no way of telling just what he had heard at the time, though this reference is almost certainly to the two poems Byron published on his separation from his wife. But it is certain that Byron and Augusta were in his mind fifteen years later. In a letter to Hannah during the autumn of 1831, he quoted from the poet's "Epistle to Augusta" (first published that same year) :

> . . . *two things in my destiny,*
> *A world to roam through and a home with thee.*

The next page of the letter is torn. But sufficient fragments of the following line are preserved for it to be reconstructed. It reads: "Lord [Byron to] his sister in the mids[t] of his tro[ubles]."[54]

Still, it is hard to be sure whether Macaulay himself was conscious of anything potentially dangerous in his own attachment to his sisters. What is certain is that his letters give evidence of a struggle within him: on one level between sense and sensibility; on a second level between selfishness and self-delusion on the one hand, renunciation and reality on the other. This emerges in the form in which

52. See above, p. 25.
53. T.B.M. to his mother, [April 21] 1816, Trinity Correspondence.
54. T.B.M. to Hannah, September 15, 1831, Trinity Correspondence. It has been suggested by Muriel Jaeger, *Before Victoria* (London, 1956) , 148, that the reason why T.B.M. took such a strong line against the general moral condemnation of Byron in his essay on the poet (1830) lay in his own personal circumstances.

he revived the idea of domesticity with Hannah alone after Margaret's marriage. It took him some weeks to recover from that blow. That he did so, at least temporarily, is evident from a letter of Margaret's to Hannah exactly one month after her wedding day. "Dear, dear Tom," she writes, "I knew it would be so. The violence of his emotions leads him necessarily to wish and to endeavour to escape from them, and such an endeavour when there are so many resources must succeed. Besides with his buoyant [?] spirits, the very reaction is enough." But it appears that Tom had regained his good spirits at the cost of his common sense. He was now trying to persuade Hannah that "husbands and wives are not so happy and cannot be so happy as brothers and sisters." "I cannot quite agree with him," Margaret wrote to her older sister, "and yet I think there is much in that relation which is the best part of married life."[55] It is clear that what Macaulay was exalting was an innocent bond between brother and sister. However, it is equally clear that while his common sense told him that Hannah, too, would eventually leave him and that this was inevitable, his fantasy conjured up for him the image of permanent domesticity with her. Whether at the conscious or the subconscious level, there was something in him that strove to prevent, or at least to delay her marriage. And he rationalized this element by identifying his happiness in her presence with hers in his, though he had no right to make such an equation.

Margaret's marriage did not put an end to the strange triangular relationship—so childlike in many ways and at the same time so heavily charged with passion and emotion—that antedated it. The two sisters continued to confide everything to one another, above all, everything that concerned their beloved brother. They were very different, though both shared the Evangelical capacity for introspection and self-analysis. Those who knew Margaret usually commented first of all on her affectionate nature, which had marked her personality from childhood. Those who encountered Hannah tended to be struck first of all by her cleverness.

Margaret, perhaps through her marriage, attained an inner harmony which Hannah—nervous, edgy, and rarely at peace with herself—lacked. It is the younger sister who plays the role of counselor at critical moments. Thus, a few days after her wedding she regrets (a bit sententiously) not seeing among Hannah's enjoyments the greatest of all—those springing from mutual affections and good offices. These she wants her sister to cultivate. "Live steadily in the world

55. Margaret to Hannah, Janaury 8, 1833, Huntington MSS.

around you," she advises her, "and I think you will find your position as favourable for happiness as any." Above all, she urges her to
devote herself to Tom, partly—she admits quite frankly—so that she
herself may continue to be closer to her brother: "The kind of
intercourse we shall maintain depends very much on the manner in
which you draw him towards me."[56] But mainly for Hannah's own
sake. "You will not know till you are parted from him as I am," she
writes her,

how much you love him. When if ever you are tempted to leave him, be
sure first that you know what you are going to, and for whom you
exchange him, but be sure above all that you know your own mind, that
you know how far your readiness to form new ties of affection is propor-
tional to the pain you experience in the breaking up of old. If you are
called some day to hold the balance and let fleeting passion weigh down
the scales, adjust them if you can with a steady hand, and I will throw in
a few grains of experience gratis to help you if I can to remain happy or
to become happier.[57]

In this extraordinary game of hearts, then, Margaret, too, driven on
by conflicting emotions, was playing in all innocence a double hand;
repudiating, for her sister's sake, Tom's derogation of the pleasures
of marriage; yet at the same time egging on Hannah, for his sake, to
devote herself to him.

The truth was, of course, that Margaret's marriage had not diminished by one whit her attachment to her brother. She knew her own
feelings better than anyone: "My love for him [Tom] is one which
cannot know diminution," she wrote a few weeks after her wedding,
"a feeling standing by itself within me and in which is concentrated
all the little romance of which I am capable."[58] Here she underrated
herself—as is evident from the Boswellian diary she had earlier kept
of Tom's sayings and doings, a diary redolent with romantic hero
worship. From the time of her engagement to Cropper, she had made
it a point never to look at that diary; though, as she confided to
Hannah, she sometimes could not bear even to glance at the side of
the room where she kept it. Then, a few days after her marriage, she
read some of it to her husband, "who was certainly interested in it,
but I began some passages I could not get through, and I felt almost
as I had broken faith, as if I was reading my love letters to my first
love."[59]

56. Margaret to Hannah, December 18, [1832], Huntington MSS.
57. Margaret to Hannah, January 28, 1833, Huntington MSS.
58. Margaret to Hannah, February 11, 1833, Huntington MSS.
59. Margaret to Hannah, January 28, 1833, Huntington MSS.

The Dingle, a sheltered valley located two miles upriver from Liverpool, was indeed a very different world from that in which Margaret, through her famous brother, had previously been able, if only vicariously, to live. And Edward Cropper, who owned a small estate there, was indeed very different from Tom. A Quaker, who had left the connection in order to marry Margaret, he was dedicated to good causes. He had been named for the author of *Night Thoughts;* but his disposition was stodgy rather than gloomy. Margaret's letters to Hannah occasionally indicate the difference in temperament between husband and wife; and, incidentally, supply a genre painting of the mode of life among the well-to-do, pious circle of the Croppers, a counterpoint to the great world of Holland and Lansdowne House in which Macaulay moved. Edward and Margaret became members of a book society, and her first choice was a book entitled *Memoirs of the Court of Charles the First.* "We are to have none but grave, solid, sensible books," was her slightly plaintive comment.[60] True, within a few weeks she had persuaded Edward to read *The Bride of Lammermoor* aloud to her. "We get through it pretty well," was her report, "but I see that Edward will never be a Scottian for many good and sufficient reasons."[61]

The days of computing the number of fainting fits in the novels of Mrs. Kitty Cuthbertson, the days of parlor games and puns, of careless laughter, and talk about all subjects under the sun—in other words, the days of life with Tom, were over. Edward was kind and affectionate, but hardly capable of any sort of frivolity. Their home life was a model of Christian seriousness. They rose at seven for prayer. In the evening, readings from the works of Henry Martyn, Evangelical missionary and martyr, followed the singing of a hymn. They retired at ten.[62] As befitted an anti-slavery family, religion reached outside the home. Margaret was active in the Negro's Friend Society, and in due course became secretary of the Ladies' Bible Society.[63]

A son, Charles James (was it due to Margaret that he was named for the Whig rather than the Quaker Fox?), was born to them; and Edward was so delighted with him that "he says he cannot think of a pleasanter sight than half a dozen of them in a bath together."[64] Still, when her sister Fanny inquired from Margaret about her future "expectations," she replied:

60. Margaret to Hannah, February 13, 1834, Huntington MSS.
61. Margaret to Hannah, May 13, 1834, Huntington MSS.
62. Margaret to Hannah, January 31, 1833, Huntington MSS.
63. Margaret to Hannah, June 10, 1834, and May 4, 1834, Huntington MSS.
64. Margaret to Hannah, February 4, 1834, Huntington MSS.

You are indeed in a much greater hurry than I am or than you would be, if you had once undergone such a business. I have no expectation of expectations and think that one in two years is quite enough for any body. . . . I should be sorry never to have another. But really one must have a little enjoyment now and then, some respite from all the troubles preceding and consequent on a confinement.[65]

Did a waltzing party that she and Edward attended count as "a little enjoyment"? From her description, one would hardly think so. "Making all allowance for habit and so forth," she wrote to Hannah, "I cannot but think that to a greater or less degree delicacy must be impaired by it." The day before, she had said to Edward that he would be rather surprised by the waltzing. He had denied it, having been used to seeing the waltz danced "as we have, brothers and sisters," in the family circle and with decorum. "When it began however, he coloured crimson, and I really felt quite ashamed. It is danced so fast that the ladies are given to panting which a[dds] coarseness to the thing and there was a something about it all that appeared to me very disagreeable."[66]

Much more agreeable were weddings—to be anticipated, to be attended, to be gossiped about. Marriage and talk of marriage dominated society and conversation, as in an Austen novel. There was Edward's cousin, Robert Thompson, who married a girl "the Miss Hancocks" had called remarkably interesting and very pretty, but who seemed to Margaret "like a nursery-maid dressed up in a white silk and a high comb." Then there was Edward's sister Eliza, who in April 1834 married the Birmingham Quaker, grain merchant, and philanthropist Joseph Sturge. She wore a gown of Margaret's own choosing, "and therefore of course pretty." But the bridegroom! He looked "so different, so painfully different, so clownish, so lumpish, so short, thick, fat, hot, heavy, everything that was bad, unutterably bad." Still, Margaret was charitable enough to add that this was merely the outward man, and that he would make Eliza a good husband.[67]

Margaret certainly believed in marriage as an institution. When a female acquaintance of hers ventured to maintain at a ladies' social gathering the doctrine of the general indifference of married people and the unsatisfactory nature of the married state, "I challenged her to show that old-maidism had less disastrous [effects?] or greater

65. Margaret to Fanny Macaulay, [April] 1834, Huntington MSS.
66. Margaret to Hannah, March 27, 1833, Huntington MSS.
67. Margaret to Hannah, April 30, 1834, Huntington MSS.

pleasure, and our conversation became so animated that it got to be general." Curiously enough, only one of the ladies, Agnes Hodgson, spoke in favor of marriage. She, Margaret remarked, was a sensible woman.[68]

This and much intimate news and gossip Margaret poured out in long letters to Hannah, for whom she continued to play the role of counselor and comforter. Hannah's character was much discussed. Someone had compared it to Emma's in the novel. "I do not think the resemblance just," was Margaret's rejoinder. "The difference between you in natural temper is I think great. Emma had a very easy, joyous contented turn, you have a much more restless and irritable frame."[69] Fanny, too, had noticed in Hannah a constitutional irritability and excitability that proved impervious to medicine.[70] Even as she commented on this, early in 1833, the possibility of Macaulay's going to India for a period of years had arisen. Fanny reported that Hannah and Tom had joked about it, but that Hannah had not taken the prospect seriously. A few months later, however, the joke became reality. On his appointment to serve in India, he asked Hannah to accompany him. In fact, as she was to recall many years later, it was clear that he would not have gone out himself, had she not agreed to go with him.[71]

"I know what a sacrifice I ask of you," he wrote her.

I know how many dear and precious ties you must, for a time, sunder. I know that the splendour of the Indian Court, and the gaieties of that brilliant society of which you would be one of the leading personages, have no temptation for you. I can bribe you only by telling you that, if you will go with me, I will love you better than I love you now, if I can.[72]

It was principally on her account, he told her, that he was willing to accept the Indian position. "It is that I may have a home for my Nancy, that I may surround her with comforts, and be assured of leaving her safe from poverty, that I am ready to leave a country which I love and a sister who is dearer to me than anything save one in this world."[73] No mention here of his own lack of political prospects in England, nor of his financial obligations to the rest of

68. Margaret to Hannah, March 13, 1834, Huntington MSS.
69. Margaret to Hannah, March 27, 1833, Huntington MSS.
70. Fanny Macaulay to Margaret, [February] 1833, Huntington MSS.
71. Hannah, Lady Trevelyan, "Reminiscences," 59, Trinity MSS.
72. T.B.M. to Hannah, August 17, 1833, Trevelyan, *Life and Letters*, 236.
73. T.B.M. to Hannah, August 21, 1833, Trinity Correspondence.

the Macaulay family, now finding itself in an ever more parlous condition. In couching his appeal to Hannah purely in terms of their mutual affection, he made it extremely difficult, if not impossible, for her to refuse it. No other act of his demonstrates so strikingly not merely his dependence on his sister, but his self-centeredness, born of the illusion that he was as much the sole center of her existence as she was of his.

Her brother's request plunged Hannah into a state of anxiety and turmoil. Greatly as she loved him, to be suddenly faced with leaving the rest of her family for such a long time, and for a strange destination a six months' voyage away, was a severe test. She had a special horror of India as a region of disease and death.[74] Going to India, Macaulay wrote later, nearly broke her heart.[75]

In any event, she was not satisfied with herself, or the sort of life she was leading; and she communicated her unhappiness to Margaret, who replied that it was her sister's single state that had a good deal to do with her difficulties. "There is no doubt," she told her, "that marriage is at your age the natural and accustomed change from the pursuits and pleasures of our first youth which with our first youth lose much of their charm." In this respect, Hannah's complaints were by no means unique. With all the wisdom of her twenty-one years Margaret informed her older sister that there was in almost all young people, "however pure and domestic their tastes, however sweet and contented their disposition, a desire for change at the bottom of their hearts, a disposition to look with something of dissatisfaction and anxiety on their present lot." Still, much of what Hannah complained of was peculiar to her alone. Margaret's advice was to leave everything to the blessings of God, to her own good sense, and to circumstances. Let her hope and trust, and look as cheerfully as she could on all that surrounded her.[76] Sound advice, no doubt, but not easy to put into practice for a young girl about to abandon family, friends, and homeland for a period of some years.

Margaret had, in fact, advised Hannah to accompany Tom to India. Later, she analyzed her own motives for doing so. The occasion was her reading Archdeacon Paley on selfishness. "Paley would say I suppose," she imagined, "you thought it would give you less pain to part with her [Hannah] than to think of Tom going alone

74. Hannah, Lady Trevelyan, "Reminiscences," Trinity MSS, 58.
75. T.B.M. to Margaret, December 7, 1834, MS in the possession of Mrs. Humphry Trevelyan.
76. Margaret to Hannah, September 7, 1833, Huntington MSS.

and being unhappy. Well but if selfishness had really been the ruling feeling of my heart, I should not have felt nearly as sorry for him as for myself."[77] Her brother was still the central concern of her life. And, even more so, she (as well as Hannah) of his. Shortly before leaving England, in a letter that he could not trust himself to finish without locking the door—lest he be found crying like a child—Tom wrote her that the separation that made him weep was not that which would result from his going to India, but that which had taken place a year earlier, when she married. That wound was still fresh. No successor had taken her place. She was as necessary to him as when he used to call for her every day in Golden Square (in the West End of London) , as when he had walked through the streets of the City with her on fine Sunday afternoons. "My loss is all pure loss. Nothing springs up to fill the void. All that I can do is to cling to that which is still left to me."[78]

And cling to Hannah he did, to the point of writing her that Margaret's marriage had created an impassable gulf between himself and his youngest sister. "She is dead to me. . . . The bitterness of that death is past. . . . Instead of wishing to be near her, I shrink from it."[79] Only ten days separate the two letters just quoted. Was Macaulay's mood so variable that he believed in each case what he was writing? Or did he feel that because of the enormous sacrifice she was making for him, he now had to assure Hannah of an exclusive place in his affections? His gratitude to her certainly knew no bounds. To express his feelings, he even had resort to the biblical language familiar to him since babyhood. There was a love which many waters could not quench, and for which if a man should give his whole substance, it would be utterly condemned. "Such love," he wrote, "is mine for Nancy, and, I think, hers for me."[80] Margaret, for her part, seemed to agree. "You may live long and go far," she told her sister, "and never meet with such love again."[81]

The letters addressed by the younger to the older sister before and after the latter's departure exude more than ever the atmosphere of an emotional hothouse. If one needed to be reminded of the extent to which the fervor, the inwardness, the passionate intensity of Evangelicalism colored the language as well as the substance of domestic relations, this correspondence would serve to supply such a

77. Margaret to Hannah, April 15, 1834, Huntington MSS.
78. T.B.M. to Margaret, January 2, 1834, Morgan MSS.
79. T.B.M. to Hannah, December 23, 1833, Trinity Correspondence.
80. T.B.M. to Hannah, November 2, 1833, Trinity Correspondence.
81. Margaret to Hannah, March 1, 1834, Huntington MSS.

reminder. "Though here present in body," so Margaret bursts out to Hannah, "this is not the world in which I live. All my love my heart is as it were within you and every fibre suffers in the wrench."[82] And, some weeks later, when Tom and Hannah were still on the high seas: "Oh my love my love it is as Anne's Fanny used to say of her leaving. It is just a heart-break, just a heart-break."[83]

She had a miniature of herself executed by Hargreaves, a Liverpool painter. Unfortunately, this has not been preserved. But Margaret described to her sister the sort of picture it was to be; and the description supplies reassurance, if any were needed, that her preoccupations had not become wholly spiritual. She wanted to be depicted in a perfectly plain white dress, with the folds on the bosom confined in the middle by a hand, rather than on the shoulders and in front. Over this Hargreaves said he could put in an open "pelisse" for her, "the fall of which around gives a very pretty turn to the shoulders and bosom which it first skirts." She liked this because it prevented the introduction of large sleeves which looked so ill in a picture. She sent the miniature to Hannah, expressing the hope that the latter would keep the original always in her heart.[84]

Yet, with all this love, the obverse of the Evangelical coin, unconstrained criticism of the weaknesses one observed in others (as well as in oneself), never remained hidden for very long. "There is one thing my dear Hannah I would gladly impress upon you," Margaret observed,

which is the old-fashioned lesson "beware of men." You must remember that to a man whose prospects are Indian you are as great a catch as you would [be] in England had you been an heiress. . . . Remember how very pleasant a flirtation you may have with a man who has no quality that will make you really happy, and how much a man of any quickness and knowledge of the world can affect as to his sentiments, feelings, and tastes according to what he sees of the mind of a woman he wishes to win. Above all do not become a flirt. I have no doubt that is your tendency and therefore I honestly warn you against.[85]

Poor Hannah! Lady Holland, who did not know her at all, had in her brusque way said much the same about her some weeks before;

82. Margaret to Hannah, February 14, 1834, Huntington MSS.

83. Margaret to Hannah, May 8, 1834, Huntington MSS.

84. Margaret to Hannah, January 25, 1834, and February 14, 1834, Huntington MSS.

85. Margaret to Hannah, May 28, 1834, Huntington MSS.

and Tom had duly passed on her comment. "Is she pretty?" the mistress of Holland House had asked Macaulay. He had replied that he thought so, but that he was too fond of her to be a judge. " 'Well,' said my lady,—'she will marry some rich Nabob within six months—no three—I won't allow her more than three. That's what you are taking her out for.' " Macaulay had assured Lady Holland that this was not the case, that his sister was making a great sacrifice in coming with him. "I was not allowed to finish—'Sacrifice—dear Macaulay—don't don't—sacrifice. Oh what dupes you men are. How women turn you round their fingers. Make me believe that any girl who has no future would not jump at visiting Calcutta as the sister of such a man in such a situation!' "[86]

"Such a man in such a situation." Macaulay's own mood, once Hannah had agreed to accompany him, corresponded far more than hers to Lady Holland's characterization. He was now looking forward to his role as the Lycurgus of India; and anxious to prepare his sister for her new position, that of presiding, as he put it, over "seventy or eighty Hindoos and Mahometans who will compose my household."[87] He wanted her, he told her, to "appear among the dancing, pianoforte-playing, opera-going damsels at Calcutta as one who has seen society better than any that they ever approached." To prepare her, he prevailed upon "Conversation" Sharp to give a few breakfast and dinner parties for the two of them—where Hannah would be able to meet celebrities like Rogers, Luttrell, Rice, Moore, and Sydney Smith—"the best set in town."[88]

Hannah, however, was forced to refuse at least some of these invitations. Her spirits were too low. "Poor girl!" Tom exclaimed to Margaret, to whom he promised to send the battered, ragged, and thumbed copy of the Spectator which she and Hannah used to read to him. "She feels the separation cruelly, though she does her best to bear up."[89] But this did not unduly dampen his own spirits. The news about Hannah's depressed state followed his telling Margaret that his own traveling library would be very good, "not large, but excellently chosen and all very readable."[90] From on board the Asia, he took delight in proclaiming that he was as well as he had ever been in his life, and infinitely better than he had been for months. "I

86. T.B.M. to Hannah, January 2, 1834, Trinity Correspondence.
87. T.B.M. to Napier, December 5, 1833, Napier Correspondence, 141.
88. T.B.M. to Hannah, December 21, 1833, Trevelyan, Life and Letters, 254–5.
89. T.B.M. to Margaret, January 13, 1834, Morgan MSS.
90. T.B.M. to Margaret, January 3, 1834, Morgan MSS.

enjoy the renovation of my health so much," he wrote to Margaret, "that I feel the sacrifice which I am making less than under other circumstances I should feel it." To which he added: "Dear Nancy has behaved like an angel."[91]

That was exactly the impression Hannah wanted to give him. "If I had any person to talk to I should be better," she wrote in a heart-breaking letter to Fanny from the *Asia*. "But I try to spare Tom as much as I can." She had not counted the cost when she had agreed to "this dreadful separation. . . . I have taken leave for years of almost anything I care for on earth and given up all chance for happiness." Her cabin—"I shall spare nothing to make a pretty little boudoir for you," Tom had promised her[92]—seemed cold and cheerless. "Why is it," she now asked herself, "that we are so very blind. I have sealed my destiny for the next six years and after that what will be left."[93]

This was her lowest point. In the course of the long voyage, she gradually recovered her equanimity, as opportunities for good deeds and gossip presented themselves on board. All the ladies gathered in her cabin in the mornings, to be assigned topics for reading. The captain proved well disposed to religion, and held prayers every Sunday. A "nice little Frenchman" gave dancing lessons, and she danced every night. It seemed (so Tom thought) that Miss Haldane was in love with the second mate. "I rather wonder at her choice," was Hannah's reaction, "for he is a round-shouldered vulgar-looking man." She had always been quick to spot vulgarity—Margaret had reprimanded her at one point for overstating the vulgarity of houses with little gardens facing the road, and Tom, in describing his factory-owning friends at Leeds to her as honest and substantial, had found it necessary to add, "whatever you may think of their refinement."[94] If she had been Miss Haldane, she now decided, she would have chosen the first mate, Mr. Wolfe, "for he is really a pleasant looking gallant frank young sailor. But then," she added rather coldly, "perhaps Miss Haldane had no choice."[95]

And so, in one sense, the story ends: with Macaulay and his sister on their way to Calcutta, there to set up house in a fashion they had surely never imagined in their dreams of domesticity; with Margaret settled at the Dingle near Liverpool with Edward and their

91. T.B.M. to Margaret, February 16, 1834, Morgan MSS.

92. T.B.M. to Hannah, December 21, 1833, Trevelyan, *Life and Letters*, 254.

93. Hannah to Fanny Macaulay, February, 1834, Huntington MSS.

94. Margaret to Hannah, December 18, 1832, Huntington MSS; T.B.M. to Hannah, September 4, 1832, Trinity Correspondence.

95. Hannah to Fanny Macaulay, February 28, 1834, Huntington MSS; see also Fanny Macaulay to Margaret, May 26, 1834, Huntington MSS.

young son; and with the rest of the family in London, helped financially by Tom, who undertook to contribute £800 a year to their support. But the story does not end here, after all. Within six months of Macaulay's arrival in India, Hannah had become engaged not to a Nabob, but to a young officer of the East India Company, Charles Trevelyan. In a long letter to Margaret, dated December 7, 1834, Macaulay gave vent to his grief and his disillusionment. The letter, like some others he had previously written to his sisters, was a strange mixture of reason and unrestrained emotion; and one can almost watch the transition from one to the other within him as one reads it. He began by telling Margaret that Hannah was to be married to Trevelyan, deputy secretary in the political department of the Supreme Indian Government. The marriage had his fullest and warmest approbation. "I can truly say," he wrote, "that if I had to search India for a husband for her, I could have found no man to whom I could with equal confidence have entrusted her happiness." Trevelyan, he went on to point out, was a person of the highest character and talents, author of a model state paper on the subject of Indian internal transit duties. He belonged to one of the oldest and best families in England; and (Macaulay added) what was more important, had capital worth £5,000 there as well as his Indian salary of £2,000.

He had fallen in love with Hannah from the start of his acquaintance with her; but she was cold to him at first because his conversation seemed to be confined to long disquisitions on political and economic problems. But, after a while, she began to reciprocate his feelings for her. At one point Macaulay had found her poring over some Minutes of the education committee, written by Trevelyan, which she had purloined from her brother's possession. Macaulay knew what was happening. And "could most easily have prevented it by treating Trevelyan with a little coldness, for he is a man whom the smallest rebuff would completely discourage." But, he asserted in a sentence that contains its own contradiction, no thought of such selfishness ever passed through his mind. In his most rational and resigned mood, Macaulay informed Margaret that he knew how painful a sacrifice he had to make, and that he had no right to enjoy Hannah's society at the expense of her happiness.

Whatever prudes may chuse to say, nature made the two sexes for each other. It is the fundamental law on which the whole universe rests that they should mutually attract each other. The celibacy of women has always been to me an object of more pity than I can express. I never see an amiable girl passing the prime of life unmarried without concern. And as to my dear Nancy I would as soon have locked her up in a nunnery as have put the smallest obstacle in the way of her having a good husband.

And so common sense and right reason had their day. But now, when he came to talk of himself, the storm broke, and all his grief and disillusionment revealed themselves:

My parting from you almost broke my heart. But when I parted from you, I had Nancy. I had all my other relations. I had my friends, I had my country. Now I have nothing except the resources of my own mind, the consciousness of having acted not ungenerously and the contemplation of the happiness of others. This is to make war on nature. This it is to form a scheme of happiness inconsistent with the general rules which govern the world. My Margaret and my Nancy were so dear to me and so fond of me that I found in their society all the quiet social happiness of domestic life. I never formed any serious attachment—any attachment which could possibly end in marriage. I was under a strange delusion. I could not see that all the qualities which made them so dear to me would probably make them dear to others. I could not see that others might wish to marry girls whose society was so powerfully attaching to keep me from marrying. I did not reflect—and yet I well know—that there are ties between man and woman dearer and closer than those of blood, that I was suffering an indulgence to become necessary to me which I might lose at any moment, that I was giving up my whole soul to objects the very excellence of which was likely to deprive me of them. I have reaped as I have sowed. At thirty-four I am alone in the world. I have lost everything and I have only myself to blame. The work of more than twenty years has vanished in a single month. She was always most dear to me. Since you left me she was everything to me. I loved her, I adored her. For her sake more than for my own, I valued wealth, station, political and literary fame. For her sake far more than for my own I became an exile from my own country. For her society and affection I found an ample compensation for all that brilliant society which I had left. She was everything to me: and I am to be henceforth nothing to her. . . .

Then Macaulay quoted some lines from the old nursery rhyme:

> *There were two birds that sat on a stone,*
> *One flew away and then there was but one.*
> *The other flew away and then there was none,*
> *And the poor stone was left all alone.*

He had tried to control himself; not to let Hannah know the extent of his suffering. Yet during the last few days he had been unable even at church or in the council room to command his voice or to restrain his tears. He had known poverty, he had known exile, but he had never known unhappiness before. He was putting his heart before her with all its inconsistencies and weakness; and was sending the letter to Margaret only because there was a pleasure in reposing confidence in someone, in exciting sympathy somewhere.[96]

In a second letter to Margaret, written the day after Hannah's wedding, he reported that he had accepted the Trevelyans' request that they live with him in his house; but only because they had made it a condition of their marriage. Hannah seemed to imagine that his sufferings (which he had done his best to hide from her) arose merely from the dread of parting. She was wrong: "It is the moral much more than the physical separation which I dread and the very course which she has taken for the purpose of preventing the physical separation will make the moral separation a slow torture instead of a quick decisive pang."[97]

Many years later, Hannah was to recall that after hearing the news of her engagement, her brother became mentally disturbed to such an extent that Lord William Bentinck, the Governor-General, was (to use her word) "frightened" about him.[98] The living death of her marriage, he later told her, had been a greater trial than the actual death of Margaret who, in the event, did not live to see the long confessional letter intended for her. She had died, in August 1834, of scarlet fever.

That he had not utterly sunk under this final blow, Macaulay wrote to Ellis in England, he had owed chiefly to literature. "What a blessing it is to love books as I love them; to be able to converse with the dead, and to live amidst the unreal!" He continued,

Many times during the last few weeks I have repeated to myself those fine lines of old Hesiod: "For if to one whose grief is fresh, as he sits silent with sorrow-stricken heart, a minstrel, the henchman of the Muses, celebrates the men of old and the gods who possess Olympus; straightway he forgets his melancholy, and remembers not at all his grief, beguiled by the blessed gift of the goddesses of song."[99]

He himself was to find fame and fortune both as minstrel and as henchman of the Muses, celebrating the men of old. Yet he remem-

96. T.B.M. to Margaret, December 7, 1834, Errington MSS.
97. T.B.M. to Margaret, December 24, 1834, Errington MSS.
98. Hannah, Lady Trevelyan, "Reminiscences," 63, Trinity MSS.
99. T.B.M. to Ellis, February 8, 1835, Trevelyan, *Life and Letters*, 311–12. The quotation appears in Greek in Trevelyan.

bered his grief all his life. More than twenty years after Margaret's death, he found himself "crying for her as if it were yesterday."[100] Hannah, at least, was still partially left to him. She and her husband, and later their children, did their utmost to provide for Macaulay the domesticity he continued to crave. And upon them, in Hannah's words, he poured out in return a world of love.

There exists an illuminating and oddly touching footnote to this story. When Trevelyan's *Life and Letters* of his uncle appeared in 1876, Macaulay's sister Fanny, then almost seventy, commented on how the book had revealed her brother's "singular devotion" to his two youngest sisters. There was another man in the household— namely, old Zachary—who, in her view, had needed all the devotion and care he deserved. "But the son was so brilliant and loveable that he overshadowed the father." Nonetheless, some of the children (in other words, she herself) did devote themselves to the father. As for Tom, he "never was happy but with entire attention and self-devotion, and this he found he could have from his youngest sisters. But it is curious to see how little their ideas corresponded with his, for the *first* men who asked them they accepted, whilst he imagined they would be his and his only forever."[101]

Fanny's sentiments carry with them some of the bitterness of an old lady who had never married herself, and who had not shared with Margaret and Hannah the adulation of her now world-famous brother. We are certainly aware that her remarks are less than just to her sisters' very real reciprocation of Tom's affection for them. Still, Fanny knew whereof she spoke as well as anyone, and her comment carries a large element of truth. Macaulay's imagination, that powerful instrument, often so beneficial to the orator and the historian, had tragically misled him in his personal life, where, just as in his view of the past, the concrete and the imagined were indissolubly linked. It was quite true that Margaret and Hannah both adored him. It was quite true that for a time he was the very center of their existence. But, youthful and inexperienced as they were, they knew that the idyll they lived with their brother was bound to be but a stage in their own lives, that it could not and should not last. This was an insight that Macaulay himself, in spite of all his learning, did not attain until it was brought home to him in India. Then his eyes, like those of the hero in one of his beloved Greek tragedies, were indeed opened. He had built his castle in the air; and now it lay in ruins about him. He was never able to rebuild it.

100. April 1856, Trevelyan, *Life and Letters*, 642–3.
101. Fanny Macaulay to "Annie" [Lady Cardwell], April 14, [1876], Morgan MSS.

XI

LEGAL MEMBER
OF COUNCIL

A SUMMARY COMMENT ON MACAULAY'S INDIAN YEARS PECULIARLY
lends itself to one of his own favorite devices in his historical writing
—pointing up unexpected paradox and contradiction. On the surface, those years represent a continuation of the pattern of general
success and good fortune which had thus far marked his life and
career. He went out to India in 1834 almost penniless, and in debt to
his brother-in-law. He returned to England, three and a half years
later, a man of substance who would never again have to give a
thought to his financial situation. And he returned not as some
latterday Nabob, loaded down with ill-gotten gain; but, rather, as the
proud boast on his Trinity College Chapel statue puts it, *India
litteris et legibus emendanda.* Indeed, he had played a major role in
shaping Indian education for at least a century to come and in giving
India a penal code which, in its essentials, is still in force today.

Yet Macaulay's Indian career was considered by many—and by no
means all of these were what might be called his natural enemies—to
have been a failure. His educational ideas in their pure form, and,
even more, the manner in which he enunciated them in his famous
Education Minute, pleased almost no one, Indian or English. His
code, on which, he later wrote, he had "bestowed the labour of two
of the best years of my life,"[1] was severely criticized, and set aside for
a generation. Indians were (and continue to be) offended by his
dismissive remarks about their culture and history. The British

1. October 1854, Trevelyan, *Life and Letters,* 337.

community in Calcutta was put off by his lack of solicitude for what it believed were its rightful privileges; and the Whig government at home was displeased with the headstrong and undiplomatic impetuosity of his reforming methods.

What is more, Macaulay's personal equilibrium, so dependent on his attachment to his two favorite sisters, was severely disturbed during his Indian sojourn by the marriage of the one and the death of the other. He immersed himself in work and in the great literature of the past, and regained his spirits to some extent. When he came back from India, his memory and his conversational powers were as strong as ever. There were, to be sure, those occasional flashes of silence welcomed by Sydney Smith. But it was Smith who noted that people in Macaulay's company burst for want of an opportunity of dropping in a word, since he seemed to confound soliloquy and colloquy; and who recommended that he take two tablespoonfuls of the waters of Lethe every morning in order to contract his retentive powers.[2] Yet much of his youthful exuberance, much of the fun and fantasy so readily summoned up for Hannah and Margaret, had left him forever.

If paradoxically minded, then, one can talk with some justification of the historian, said by S. R. Gardiner to have mastered the art of judging political situations, misjudging his own political situation in India. One can discourse about the Whig un-Whigged and the golden child of fortune come upon bad days at last. Yet all was not lost. He returned with the *Lays of Ancient Rome* in part composed and the project of the *History of England* firmly fixed in his mind; reconciled to bachelor life led in close personal if not geographical propinquity to the Trevelyans. And, whatever the immediate verdict on his achievements in India, they were of such a nature that the test of time and history was still to come. Above all, the least Indian of Indian civil servants (as Gladstone was to call him) had come home. And there could be no doubt at all that he was happy to see the end of his voluntary exile.

For, more than most of his compatriots who spent a limited number of years in India, Macaulay considered that period one of exile. To be sure, as he wrote to Lord Lansdowne shortly before his departure, he could scarcely conceive a nobler field than that of India for a statesman.[3] We have seen that at a dinner in London on

2. John Knox Laughton, ed., *Memoirs of the Life and Correspondence of Henry Reeve* (2 vols., London, 1898), I, 104.

3. T.B.M. to Lansdowne, December 5, 1833, Trevelyan, *Life and Letters*, 250.

the day he was sworn in as fourth member of the Council of India, he "rather gave himself the airs of a Lycurgus; and spoke as if he were about to bestow on the swarming millions of India the blessings of rudimentary legislation."[4] This was his way of making a virtue of necessity; of using his powerful imagination, not for the first or the last time, in order to invest his own role with glamour and romance. But, though he poured all his energies into his Indian tasks, he never thought of his sojourn in India as anything but an obligation, to be fulfilled as rapidly as possible. "I have no words," he wrote to his sisters from India,

to tell you how I pine for England, or how intensely bitter exile has been to me, though I hope that I have borne it well. I feel as if I had no other wish than to see my country again and die. Let me assure you that banishment is no light matter. No person can judge of it who has not experienced it. A complete revolution in all the habits of life, an estrangement from almost every old friend and acquaintance; fifteen thousand miles of ocean between the exile and everything that he cares for: all this is, to me at least, very trying. There is no temptation of wealth, or power, which would induce me to go through it again.[5]

He began to make plans for his return home almost as soon as he had got to India. During his stay in Calcutta he read Cicero's letters to Atticus, written during Cicero's banishment; and he entered in the margin: "Poor fellow! He makes a pitiful figure. But it is impossible not to feel for him. Since I left England I have not despised Cicero and Ovid for their lamentations in exile as much as I did."[6] Upon one thing he had determined: not to allow his mind to rust while in India. That was why, as he wrote to Margaret upon arriving at Madras ninety days after having left Falmouth, he was so pleased that, left to his own resources for that length of time, he had been able to devour with keen and increasing enjoyment the large library of classic and modern literature he had taken on board with him.[7]

The *Asia* had reached Madras, on the southeast coast of India, on June 10, 1834. The first Indian Macaulay glimpsed was a black fisherman, who came on board with nothing on but a yellow cap, "and walked among us with a self-possession and civility which,

4. Arnold, *Public Life*, 184.

5. T.B.M. [to Fanny and Selina Macaulay, September 11, 1837], Trevelyan, *Life and Letters*, 307.

6. Trevelyan, *Life and Letters*, 712.

7. T.B.M. to Margaret, June 15, 1834, Errington MSS.

coupled with his colour and his nakedness, nearly made me die of laughing." Macaulay himself, as befitted a new member of the Governor-General's Council, was welcomed by a salute of fifteen guns as he landed. He was less awed by this tribute than by his first impression of India:

To be on land after being three months at sea is of itself a great change:—but to be in such a land—nothing but dark faces and bodies with white turbans and flaming robes,—the trees not our trees,—the very smell of the atmosphere like that of a hothouse,—the architecture as strange as the vegetation, I was quite stunned.[8]

The original plan had been that he and Hannah would proceed by the *Asia* northward along the coast to Calcutta, capital of Bengal and, since the India Act of 1833, the principal seat of the British government in India. But it so happened that the Governor-General, Lord William Bentinck, had for reasons of health taken up temporary residence in the more salubrious climate of the Nilgiri Hills, and was holding a Council there. He had sent word to Macaulay to join him. So Hannah went on by herself to Calcutta, to stay with the Bishop of Calcutta—the bishop being none other than Daniel Wilson, the Evangelical clergyman at whose London church the Macaulay family had so frequently worshipped in the past. And Macaulay proceeded by himself to Ootacamund, 7,000 feet above sea level in the mountains west of Madras. "A new discovery," Macaulay wrote to his friend Ellis, "a place to which Europeans resort for their health, or, as it is called by the Company's servants,—blessings on their learning,—a *sanaterion.*"[9]

The journey from Madras to Ootacamund took over a week and was made (mainly at night, because of the intense heat during the day) by palanquin, a covered litter carried by two alternating teams of six bearers; who, while they carried their exalted passenger, chanted and grunted in rhythmic unison. Macaulay was subsequently told that the late Sir John Malcolm, once Governor of Bombay and an excellent linguist, had been able to make out the gist of one song his bearers had sung while carrying him. It went: "There is a fat hog—a great fat hog—how heavy he is—hum—shake him—hum—shake him well—hum—shake the fat hog—hum." Macaulay's characteristic comment about this story to his sister was:

8. Idem.   9. T.B.M. to Ellis, July 1, 1834, Trevelyan, *Life and Letters,* 267.

"Whether they paid a similar compliment to me I cannot say. They might have done so, I fear, without any breach of veracity."[10]

Thanks to Macaulay's long and lively account of his journey from Madras to the hills in his letters to Margaret—letters reminiscent in their gaiety and *élan* of those he used to send to her and Hannah about London politics and society—we get vivid glimpses of his first reactions to India. Some of these, seen within the wider context of the three and a half years that were to follow, take on in an almost uncanny fashion the quality of themes tentatively sounded early on in a musical composition, to be fully developed only later in the course of the work. At Bangalore, part way up into the hills, where a British colonel now ruled over a country probably as large and as populous as Scotland, Macaulay was told of a Rajah who "had the audacity, a few months ago, to go to war with us." He was defeated, but made a formidable enemy. "The truth is," Macaulay continued,

that every enemy is formidable in India. We are strangers there. We are as one in two or three thousand to the natives. The higher classes whom we have deprived of their power would do anything to throw off our yoke. A serious check in any part of India would raise half the country against us.[11]

From Bangalore Macaulay made an excursion to Seringapatam, once the capital of Tipu, Sultan of Mysore, who was killed during its capture by Wellesley in 1798. There he recalled how he used to hear the place talked of every day during his childhood. His uncle, General Colin Macaulay, had been imprisoned there for four years and had distinguished himself during the siege. In a shop window in Clapham there had hung a picture of the taking of Seringapatam that he remembered staring at as a boy of ten with the greatest interest.[12] And he had welcomed the general back from India with verses beginning

> *Now safe returned from Asia's parching strand*
> *Welcome, thrice welcome to thy native land.*[13]

The Rajah of Mysore, a puppet ruler placed on his throne by Wellesley and recently totally deprived of all power, struck Macaulay as a person of considerable natural abilities, who had reached his

10. T.B.M. to Margaret, October 3, 1834, Errington MSS.
11. T.B.M. to Margaret, June 27, 1834, Errington MSS.
12. Idem.   13. Trevelyan, *Life and Letters*, 26.

manhood without having acquired a taste for anything but toys, fine clothes, betelnut, and dancing girls. This was the fault of the British, who had neglected his education. "If he had been made an accomplished English gentleman," Macaulay commented, "what a different aspect his court would have exhibited. . . . If we had done our duty by him in the first instance, we never should have been forced to depose him."[14]

Macaulay was made to admire the Rajah's pictures—the glory of his collection turned out to be a head of the Duke of Wellington as large as life—his elaborately ornamented formal dress, and his state horse, a richly caparisoned white Arab. Then,

having seen his Highness's clothes, and his Highness's horse, I was favoured with a sight of his Highness's Gods, who were much of a piece with the rest of his establishment. The principal deity was a fat man with a paunch like Daniel Lambert's, an elephant's head and trunk, a dozen hands, and a serpent's tail.[15]

Macaulay arrived at Ootacamund (known to later generations of British officials as "Ooty") on the twenty-sixth of June and was immediately received by Lord William Bentinck. It was a cordial meeting. Lord William had welcomed news of Macaulay's appointment a few weeks before as providing the British government with a "giant" who would be able to conquer both European and native prejudices.[16] And Macaulay found the Governor-General just as he had expected him to be—"rectitude, openness, and good nature personified."[17] It was midsummer. But high in the Nilgiris it was colder than Scotland in April or September. In Madras the temperature had been 95 degrees in the shade. Here, inside Macaulay's "charming little cottage," Hannah More's Barley Wood in miniature, it was 65. The change was refreshing, and the vegetation delightful. But one still had to be careful, on a sunny day, not to venture out around noontime. And to beware of tigers, who preferred the mountains to the plain for the very same reason which had attracted so many

14. T.B.M. to Margaret, June 27, 1834, Errington MSS.

15. Idem. The *D.N.B.* describes Lambert (1770–1809) as "the most corpulent man of whom authentic record exists."

16. Bentinck to Bishop of Calcutta, May 1, 1834, A. F. Salahuddin Ahmed, *Social Ideas and Social Change in Bengal, 1818–1835* (Leiden, 1965), 156.

17. T.B.M. to Margaret, June 27, 1834, Errington MSS. On Bentinck, see John Rosselli, *Lord William Bentinck and the British Occupation of Sicily, 1811–1814* (Cambridge, 1956).

Europeans to India: "They encounter an uncongenial climate for the sake of what they can get."[18]

Then the rains came, such torrents that for an entire month Macaulay was unable to walk outside for more than two hours. He had some official business to transact; and he had his books. But the monotony of the daily round became almost intolerable to him. He hated watering places, in any event. But this was much duller than any spa. Even the *Asia* had been amusing, in comparison to Ootacamund. To be sure, the place was enlivened by a few pretty girls for whom the Governor-General's aides-de-camp were ready to pistol each other and themselves. "For my part," Macaulay wrote to Margaret, "I did not keep my liberty in Berkeley Square and Curzon Street to lose it in the Neilgherries."[19]

Macaulay did his best to be entertaining. A traveler—himself later to gain notoriety as the author of *Confessions of a Thug* (1839) — who encountered him briefly at Lord William's house never forgot his conversation, "his seemingly boundless knowledge of life, his acquaintance with history and philosophy, his fiery zeal in argument, and his calm eloquence in oratory," which opened up new subjects for future study.[20] Thanks to Macaulay's recommendation, *Clarissa* put the entire station into an uproar; with the Governor-General's physician, a Jacobin freethinker, crying so copiously over the last volume that he found himself too ill to appear for dinner.[21]

Macaulay entertained himself in a very different manner. On the way to the mountains, in the jungle at the foot of the Nilgiris, there had occurred to him the plan of telling the early history of Rome as its epic poets must have sung it. And it was during his stay at Ootacamund that he began to write what were to become the *Lays of Ancient Rome*.[22] At last, toward the end of August, Bentinck gave Macaulay permission to depart. He was about to start for Madras, when his servant—"such a Christian as the missionaries make in this part of the world, that is to say a man who superadds drunkenness to the other vices of the natives"—was accused of having gained the affections of the wife of one of Lord William's under-cooks. Macaulay, anxious to leave Ootacamund and in need of his servant, wanted to settle the matter by giving some money to the under-cook.

18. T.B.M. to Margaret, July 6, 1834, Errington MSS.

19. T.B.M. to Margaret, July 6, 1834, August 10, 1834, and October 3, 1834, Errington MSS.

20. Philip Meadows-Taylor, *The Story of My Life* (2 vols., London, 1877) , I, 118.

21. Trevelyan, *Life and Letters,* 273.

22. Peter Clark, "A Macaulay Letter," *Notes and Queries,* CCXII (1967) , 369.

But those who had brought the case against the man—contempt for a convert apparently played a role here—insisted on bringing him to trial, "in order that they might have the pleasure of smearing him with filth, beating kettles before him, carrying him round the town on an ass with his face to the tail, and giving him a good flogging."[23]

Macaulay asked the native judge to try the case instantly, which the latter was willing to do. But the plaintiffs insisted that it be postponed for three days, and that the servant be meanwhile put in prison. Macaulay tried to reason with them, but to no avail. Indeed, "the gentle and reasoning tone of my expostulations made them impudent. They are in truth a race so much accustomed to be trampled on by the strong, that they always consider humanity as a sign of weakness." But at this point, Macaulay reported, he was at the end of his sweet words, and handed the matter over to the British station commandant who was in charge of the administration of justice there. The latter ordered an immediate trial, and the judge pronounced Macaulay's servant not guilty. What Macaulay did not find out until some days later was that the judge had received 20 rupees as a bribe on this occasion.

The servant was due to leave three hours before Macaulay on the following morning, August 31. But his accusers, unhappy about the verdict, pulled him out of his palanquin, tore off his turban, stripped him almost naked, and—it seemed—were about to pull him to pieces, when Macaulay snatched up his sword stick and rushed to his servant's defense. It turned out that he himself was in no danger; since, "even in their rage, they retained a great respect for my race and station." The commandant was called in; and within a few minutes the rioters were marched off to jail, and the servant was on his way. Macaulay called the attack on him, after he had been legally acquitted, a gross and intolerable outrage; even though he himself had grave doubts about the servant's innocence, and did not know at the time that the judge had been bribed. "And even if I had known it, such is the state of Indian morality that there would have been nothing uncommon or disgraceful in the transaction."[24]

On September 10, Macaulay was back in Madras, and six days later he went on board the *Broxbournebury* to begin the voyage to Calcutta. In the course of it he amused himself with learning Portuguese and read the *Lusiads*—twice. At 2 A.M. on September 24 the ship entered the Hooghly River; and some hours later, from the special steamboat that had been sent to meet him, he saw the elegant villas

23. T.B.M. to Margaret, October 3, 1834, Errington MSS.   24. Idem.

of Garden Reach in Calcutta peeping indistinctly from amidst wooded groves. Had he and Hannah, with whom he was now re-united, decided to live in one of those fine houses, he wrote to Margaret, they would have been obliged to employ a man whose sole business it would have been to push away corpses from the garden into the stream.[25] When they could afford the fuel, the Hindus burned their dead. "The poor usually left partially burned bodies by the side of the river until they were borne away by the tide."[26]

This close juxtaposition of pleasure gardens and death was char-acteristic of Calcutta, then as now a place of contrasts. Here were to be seen the imposing neo-classic façades of Government House and other official buildings—not for nothing was Calcutta known as "the city of palaces." But nearby were to be found the mud huts of thousands of Indians who lived and died in abject poverty in "Black Town." The first impression made on a new arrival from England by the chief seat of British power in India, then a city with a popula-tion of about half a million people, has nowhere been better de-scribed than by Matthew Arnold's brother William, in his novel *Oakfield; or Fellowship in the East:*

There were the scorching sun and almost fearful verdure of Bengal; the ceaseless hum of unseen animal life; the white, flat-roofed, hundred-domed palaces of the European inhabitants, the mud hovels of the swarming natives; the natives themselves, and their strange language; the dull, broad Hooghly, bearing down the dead bodies of Hindus, glad to have their last home in its holy waters.[27]

It has been estimated that at this time there were about 40,000 Europeans in all of India, most of them British. Of these, 37,000 were soldiers—officers and men; about 1,000 "civilians," that is, officials of the East India Company; and the rest merchants, lawyers, missionaries, and adventureres. This amidst a total population of about 150 million native Indians.[28] Macaulay had observed in Madras, when he saw that the showy European villas there were not kept in the state of repair in which people usually kept houses they meant to leave to their children, that the rulers of India were pil-grims and sojourners in the land.[29] They came out to India for gain,

25. Idem.
26. Michael Edwardes, *Bound to Exile: The Victorians in India* (London, 1969) , 46.
27. William Arnold, *Oakfield; or Fellowship in the East* (2 vols., London, 1854) , I, 12–13.
28. Edwardes, *Exile*, 12.   29. T.B.M. to Margaret, June 15, 1834, Errington MSS.

for duty, for service. Some company officials, it is true, sent to India while still schoolboys, got used and often attached to the ways of the country. As Macaulay put it, they became "Orientalised," and by their mid-thirties came to prefer India, as a residence, to England.[30] But the great majority looked forward from the time they arrived to the day of their eventual departure. Meanwhile, they and their wives—for, in contrast to the previous century, when few British women had ventured out to India, the *memsahibs* played an increasingly important role in Calcutta society—tried to preserve, to the best of their ability, a Western way of life within a totally alien environment.

Here, too, there were exceptions—men who by dint of great and devoted effort learned, understood, and came to value the languages and customs of the country and who had nothing but contempt for the perpetual orbit of balls, dinners, visiting, matchmaking, and gossip in which the colony of officials moved in a place like Calcutta, the most important of the British settlements in India. The powers of the Governor-General were vast, and the greater because of the distance, in space and time, from his masters in London. "I can see," Emily Eden wrote about her brother Lord Auckland's tenure of the position in 1836, "how despotic power without the bother of Parliament, and immense patronage, may be rather pleasant."[31] His residence, Government House, was the social as well as the political center of British India. But within its spacious halls the constant battle against the heat was waged just as intensively as in every other British house in Calcutta.

For the climate was atrocious; and sickness and death all too frequent among the British residents. "We are annually baked for four months, boiled four more, and allowed the remaining four to become cool if we can," Macaulay wrote to a correspondent. And added: "Insects and undertakers are the only living creatures which seem to enjoy the climate."[32] Yet Macaulay's own health remained surprisingly good. J. L. Adolphus, son of the historian, who encountered him in London just before he left for India, thought that there was very little chance that he would ever return. His complexion then was "foul," his aspect "jaded," his skin "blotched." Adolphus felt that he was going to sacrifice his life.[33] Yet, in the

30. T.B.M. to Fanny and Selina Macaulay [September 11, 1837], Trevelyan, *Life and Letters*, 307.

31. July 2, 1836, Emily Eden, *Letters from India* (2 vols., London, 1872) , I, 182.

32. T.B.M. to Mrs. Drummond [September 20, 1837], Trevelyan, *Life and Letters*, 307–8.

33. John L. Adolphus to Dean Milman, December 14, 1861, Trinity MSS.

event, Macaulay did not suffer from the heat as much as others, "yellow, spectral figures which surround me." "J'ai le diable au corps," he wrote to Ellis, quoting Napoleon.[34] But though he found the climate "beyond all comparison, better than that of the House of Commons," he could not but observe its destructive effects. It is amusing to find the great apostle of progress and improvement chronicling the change and decay he saw all around him: "Steel rusts; razors lose their edge; thread decays; clothes fall to pieces; books moulder away, and drop out of their bindings; plaster cracks; timber rots; matting is in shreds." Sun, steam, and infinite armies of white ants wrought such havoc with buildings that houses needed to be completely repaired every three years.[35]

The inhabitants of those houses valiantly fought the heat by various means: punkahs—canvas-covered frames suspended from the high-ceilinged rooms and endlessly moved back and forth by native servants—ice (shipped from the United States along with apples and novels), and heroic quantities of soda water and lemonade.[36] And the official British colony showed the flag by carrying on with formal dinners and strenuous dancing as if the temperature were something to be ignored. Thus Macaulay made his first appearance in Calcutta society at a dinner where the ladies appeared in fancy dress. On that occasion, he declared himself somewhat indisposed.[37]

Indeed, he was the last person to enjoy the sort of official occasion he was often forced in his position of councilor to attend, where, in this strictly hierarchical society, it nearly always fell to his lot to be placed next to the lady of highest rank, "or in other words next to the oldest, ugliest, proudest and dullest woman in the company."[38] He much preferred a very different sort of evening, during which he and a few friends—men such as his old Trinity contemporary Benjamin Malkin, now a Supreme Court judge—would dine together and discuss a subject such as (on the particular occasion recorded in the diary of one of those present) Pope's theory of the ruling passions.[39] In a situation where English political news and the latest

34. T.B.M. to Ellis, July 25, 1836, and May 30, 1836, Trevelyan, *Life and Letters,* 326, 322.

35. T.B.M. to Ellis, February 8, 1835, and May 30, 1836, Trevelyan, *Life and Letters,* 314, 323.

36. Emily Eden to Mrs. Lister, August 24, 1836, Violet Dickinson, ed., *Miss Eden's Letter*s (London, 1919), 272.

37. Arnold, *Public Life,* 188.

38. T.B.M. to Fanny and Selina Macaulay, January 1, 1836, Trinity Correspondence.

39. Sir Auckland Colvin, *John Russell Colvin* (Oxford, 1895), 48.

novel were almost half a year out of date by the time they reached Calcutta, subjects such as this no doubt produced a maximum of intellectual excitement. When Macaulay landed in Calcutta, a local newspaper had assured him that he would find there a tolerable imitation of the luxuries and fashions of London. The diversions, he was informed, included drama, Italian opera, "French vaudevilles," and a *Literary Gazette* that reprinted *Nicholas Nickleby* in monthly instalments.[40] All this was part of the effort to create a cultural enclave within which a life of exile could be led as normally as possible.

But, if only in their role as personal servants, native Indians were always present to remind the British that the soil over which they ruled was alien. And all too many of the rulers felt it necessary to demonstrate in no uncertain terms that they were indeed the masters. One gets a very vivid sense of this in the letters home of the Eden sisters, who accompanied their brother to Calcutta early in 1836. One of them was immediately shocked by the subservience of natives to whites; and provided a glimpse in a letter home of "young officers driving fast through the streets under the burning sun, with their servants running after them just for show." The other, Emily, noted matter-of-factly that Government House was one of the few in Calcutta where native servants were not beaten. It was Emily who commented so memorably upon the omnipresence of the native servants, to the effect that "it sometimes strikes me that we Europeans are mad people, sent out here because we are dangerous at home, and that our black keepers are told never to lose sight of us, and the ingenious creatures never do."[41]

Macaulay had, to use his own phrase, an "army" of servants, but no such feelings of paranoia. He knew exactly why he had come to India. It was in order to save sufficient money to enable him to return to England, financially independent, as soon as possible. Even in describing his magnificent establishment in Calcutta, which included two carriages, his thoughts turned to the snug house near Russell Square where he longed to be with his family. "My tastes are not Oriental," he wrote to Fanny and Selina.[42] By the spring of 1836 he was already as rich as he cared to be if he had only himself to take

40. Arnold, *Public Life*, 187–8. *Pickwick* was one of the few current English novels of which there was a Calcutta reprint, woodcuts and all. See Emily Eden to Mrs. Lister, April 28, 1838, Dickinson, ed., *Eden Letters*, 298.

41. F. H. Eden, March 9, 1836; Emily Eden, March 22, 1837, and June 17, 1837, Eden, *Letters from India*, I, 92, 337; II, 52–3.

42. T.B.M. to Fanny and Selina Macaulay, October 19, 1834, Trinity Correspondence.

care of. And he wrote to his sisters that he would not stay in India until he was forty for all the Duke of Westminster's streets and all Lord Durham's mines.[43] By 1838, he informed a friend in England, he would have saved £20,000, which would enable him to do his duty to his family and to live comfortably.[44] A few weeks after he made these calculations, he found out that his uncle Colin had left him a legacy of £10,000. This, in addition to his accumulated savings, would make him "quite a rich man" by the end of 1837—"richer than I even wish to be as a single man; and every day renders it more unlikely that I should marry."[45]

Saving money all around was an argument in favor of the Trevelyans establishing a joint household with Macaulay in Calcutta after their marriage, in December 1834. At the time he scarcely knew, as he put it in his long *cri de coeur* to Margaret, whether their sharing a house was the right course to pursue; whether "it would not be wiser in me to bear the pain of separation once for all than to see the gradual growth of new feelings, the multiplication of new objects of attachment, the progress of that inevitable estrangement" which it would not be in Hannah's power to avert.[46] As it turned out, it was just as well that the Trevelyans, who rushed back to Calcutta from their honeymoon spent in the grounds of Bentinck's country residence at Barrackpore, could provide company and comfort after news of Margaret's death reached him early in 1835.

Not that even the most generously bestowed comfort and sympathy could assuage the pain this blow had inflicted. On his thirty-fifth birthday (October 25, 1835) Macaulay penciled into his copy of the Greek tragedians the bleak words of Sophocles: "The happiest destiny is never to have been born; and the next best, by far, is to return, as swiftly as may be, to the bourn whence we came."[47] At year's end he confided to Ellis that Margaret's death had left marks he would carry to the grave. "Literature," he went on, "has saved my life and my reason." But, even so, in the intervals of business he did not dare to remain alone for a single minute without a book in his hand.[48]

By the summer of 1836 he felt able to write to Ellis that his sorrow

43. T.B.M. to Fanny and Selina Macaulay, May 9, 1836, MS in the possession of Mrs. Humphry Trevelyan.

44. T.B.M. to Spring-Rice, February 8, 1836, "Macaulay Writes Home," *Bodleian Library Record,* I (1941), 252.

45. T.B.M. to Ellis, July 25, 1836, Trevelyan, *Life and Letters,* 326.

46. T.B.M. to Margaret, December 7, 1834, Errington MSS.

47. Trevelyan, *Life and Letters,* 728. The quotation appears in Greek in Trevelyan.

48. T.B.M. to Ellis, December 30, 1835, ibid., 319.

at Margaret's death had at last subsided.[49] He gradually recovered his spirits somewhat. And when a daughter, Margaret ("Baba"), was born to the Trevelyans, Macaulay became fonder of her "than a wise man who has seen and suffered so much as I have done should be of any thing but himself."[50] But the other Margaret remained in his thoughts. The first letter he could bring himself to address to her widowed husband, Edward Cropper, was written at the end of 1837, shortly before he left India. "My omission to write," Macaulay explained to his brother-in-law,

has been caused by no want of kindness for you, but by feelings of which it is enough to say that, after three years of mourning, they still retain their bitterness, and that however long my life may be, they will go with me to the grave. Even now I cannot bear to talk of her. The sight of anything that was hers is too much for me.[51]

That he had been able, after the initial shock of Margaret's death, to recover and sustain a certain equilibrium at all was due in large measure to his plunging into an immense program of work and reading. In his essay on Bacon, one of the two (along with that on Mackintosh) written during his Indian sojourn, Macaulay expressed the incalculable debt owed by a man of liberal education to the great figures of the past. "They have stood by him in all vicissitudes, comforters in sorrow, nurses in sickness, companions in solitude. These friendships are exposed to no danger from the occurrences by which other attachments are weakened or dissolved."[52]

There can be little doubt that these words were the fruit of his own experience. "I mean to go fairly through the whole literature of Greece and Rome before I return," he wrote to "Conversation" Sharp in February 1835.[53] And the marginalia published by Trevelyan in his *Life and Letters* provide proof of how well Macaulay carried out his intention. It was not merely the ancients whom he read and reread, and who elicited praise, criticism, and, at times, laughter. (Plato he found so amusing that "I often sink forward on my huge old Marsilius Ficinus in a fit of laughter."[54]) Among

49. T.B.M. to Ellis, July 25, 1836, ibid., 325.
50. T.B.M. to Fanny and Selina Macaulay, May 9, 1836, MS in the possession of Mrs. Humphry Trevelyan.
51. T.B.M. to Edward Cropper, November 5, 1837, Errington MSS.
52. T.B.M., "Bacon" (1837), *Works*, VIII, 498.
53. T.B.M. to Sharp, February 2, 1835, Paul, *Drummond*, 42.
54. T.B.M. to Ellis, May 29, 1835, Trevelyan, *Life and Letters*, 316.

his annotated authors, with marginalia dating from his Indian period, are to be found Gibbon, Swift, Pope, Coleridge, Samuel Parr, and one of his favorite victims, Anna Seward. He began to read the complete plays of Calderón in four volumes on January 29, 1835. "A very poor and absurd play indeed," was his comment about *La Vida es Sueño*, carefully dated the next day.[55] One by one he read eighty-five of Calderón's plays until, after thirteen months, he stopped, well into Volume 4, with *La Cisma de Inglaterra* (the eighty-fifth) which, on February 13, 1836, garnered one of his favorite forms of dismissal: "Stupid trash."

But one must not take away the impression from these two marginal notes that Macaulay read only to condemn. Here, as elsewhere in his reading, his marginalia give evidence of his constant effort to do justice to the achievements of the great writers of the past; never accepting with docility the judgment of former critics, but always willing, by rereading, to revise his own. It was his reading, rather than events in India, that helped him to keep track of the passage of time. "If I want to know when an event took place," he wrote to Ellis, "I call to mind which of Calderón's plays, or of Plutarch's Lives I was reading on that day." The reason for this was, that the days were so like one another.[56]

This is how he described his routine in 1836. He had to attend two Council meetings a week as well as two meetings of the Law Commission over which, as we shall see, he had come to preside in the summer of the previous year. Each of these meetings took six to seven hours. He had also become President of the Committee on Public Instruction, and a member of the Prison Discipline Reform Committee. "The hours before breakfast," he casually added, "I have all to myself; and I give them to literature."[57] This schedule makes one marvel once again at Macaulay's energy, which seemed to be in no way impaired by the climate. In justice, it should be added that not all Council meetings were strenuous. The very letter in which he described his routine was written during one such meeting, at which

Sir Charles [Metcalfe] is alternately yawning and punning. The Commander in Chief has gone into the antechamber to take a cup of coffee.

55. Calderón, *Comédias* (Houghton) , I, 25.
56. T.B.M. to Ellis, March 8, 1837, Trevelyan, *Life and Letters*, 333.
57. T.B.M. to Spring-Rice, February 8, 1836, "Macaulay Writes Home" *Bodleian Library Record*, 251–2.

One of my colleagues is writing a note, and another is drawing a man and horse on his blotting paper. I, who have no vote on the question, and who, if I had, should not know which way to vote, conceive that I cannot employ the next hour better than in writing to you.[58]

After lunch he sometimes read to Hannah, in French or translating Greek at sight. "And," so Sir George Trevelyan has described the scene, "Scribe's comedies and Saint Simon's Memoirs beguiled the long languid leisure of the Calcutta afternoon, while the punkah swung overhead, and the air came heavy and scented through the moistened grass-matting which shrouded the windows."[59] Then back to work again. Before dinner, Macaulay, like the rest of British officialdom, took the air in a drive along the Hooghly. More often than not, he spent the evening quietly with the Trevelyans. One of the Calcutta newspapers went out of its way to criticize him for his indifference to "all beauty and fashion" of Calcutta.[60] Little did the writer know the extent to which the double blow of Hannah's marriage and Margaret's death had affected his attitude toward any kind of social life. Furthermore, he was extremely busy. Hannah wrote to one of her correspondents that the three of them led "most un-Indian lives, for we have a great deal to do, and we mix in none of the parties. I do not care for them, and Tom and Charles have no time. By the evening they are both generally pretty well worn out, and are glad to get early to bed, to be up by four the next day to resume the unceasing round."[61] It was that unceasing round which took up most of Macaulay's time and energy. What did it involve?

In order to answer this question, one must keep in mind the successive stages of England's relationship to India.[62] There had been significant changes in this relationship since the East India Company first set up warehouses in Surat more than two hundred years before Macaulay's arrival. What had begun as trade in the seventeenth century became conquest in the eighteenth, a process hastened by the collapse of the Mughul Empire and by British rivalry with France. And what had begun as the venture of a commercial corporation increasingly came under the aegis of the British Crown. A group of merchants turned gradually into a political and military force, with

58. Ibid., 248.   59. Trevelyan, *Life and Letters,* 305.
60. Arnold, *Public Life,* 207.
61. Hannah to Mrs. Cropper, July 16, 1835, Huntington MSS.
62. The following account of the historical background is greatly indebted to Eric Stokes, *The English Utilitarians and India* (Oxford, 1959) and Michael Edwardes, *Raj: The Story of British India* (London, 1969) .

its private armies fighting and winning major battles such as Plassey and Buxar. Then this same group of merchants found itself in serious financial straits. When, in 1772, it was forced to request a major loan from the British government, a parliamentary investigation was set on foot. That revealed the extent to which the company's servants had enriched themselves by accepting personal tribute and gifts. The consequence was North's Regulating Act of 1773, which established parliamentary supremacy over the company and resulted in the appointment of a royal Governor-General. (Warren Hastings was the first.) Eleven years later, Pitt's India Act expanded the powers of the Governor-General, placing him in a position of superiority over the governors of Madras and Bombay, and set up a government-appointed Board of Control, whose president, from 1812, always sat in the cabinet, and whose function it was, under the new system of "dual control," to supervise the political and administrative operations of the Court of Directors of the East India Company. The twenty-four directors, elected by the shareholders and headed by the two "Chairs," the chairman and his deputy, remained the executive and decision-making body of the company, always subject to the Board of Control's veto. They retained their traditional power of patronage, which left them with a certain amount of political leverage since they still had in their gift the appointment of the company's servants in India.

Meanwhile, the economic basis of Anglo-Indian relations was changing, and with it the entire complex of social and cultural contacts between the two civilizations. In the course of the eighteenth century, the major economic objective of the company had gradually become not so much trade with India as the extraction of surplus revenue, mainly from land rents, for the benefit of its shareholders. But with the tremendous manufacturing potential released by the Industrial Revolution, and with British merchants on the lookout for new worlds to conquer, India could be regarded in a totally new light, as a major trading area as well as a great market for British goods. In the economic realm, with the winds of free trade blowing ever more powerfully, this meant that a trading monopoly such as that of the East India Company (for which Adam Smith had reserved his strongest terms of condemnation) began to appear increasingly anachronistic. In fact, the India Act of 1813, which renewed the company's charter for a period of twenty years, left it only with a monopoly of the China tea trade. With the next Charter Act (1833), which Macaulay in his capacity as secretary of the Board of Control helped to draft, and shepherd through Parliament, the company lost even that, and ceased altogether to be a trading company. Under the terms of the act, European merchants and speculators could now freely settle and do business in India; internal transit duties were gradually abolished—a measure in which Charles Trevelyan's reports played a major part; and steam navigation began to transform communications and transport. Between 1834 and 1856, the export trade of India increased by 188 per cent, her import trade by 227 per cent.[63]

But the shift in economic objective had other, even more momentous consequences. As long as India had served primarily as a source of profit and revenue, the necessity for interfering with native Indian administration and customs had appeared minimal. Indeed, most of the company's servants who governed British possessions in India during the eighteenth century—and it must be remembered that those possessions were small and scattered, and, in geographical terms, could not with any accuracy be referred to as "India"—regarded themselves as the inheritors of an old system rather than as shapers of a new. Indian culture, laws, and institutions, whether Hindu or Muslim, were respected, and often studied and admired into the bargain. There was a certain amount of mutually friendly contact between the British and the Indians. The very assumption on the part of many of the company's servants that they were in India, not in order to found a permanent Empire nor as a ruling caste, but for the purpose of enriching themselves and the company's proprietors, led on their part to tolerant, sympathetic, and easygoing attitudes toward the native Indians.

There has undoubtedly been a certain amount of sentimentalizing about the harmonious personal relationships between rulers and ruled in this period. But the contrast with what was to come in the nineteenth century is clear enough. Hundreds of millions of people came to be looked upon as potential customers for British goods rather than as mere contributory agents to landed revenue. A program of "Westernization" was bound to follow, to prepare them for their new role. At the same time, India was increasingly looked upon as a vital part of the British Empire. And once the idea, or, as it has been called, the "illusion," of permanence took hold, it was inevitable that "Westernization" should also be regarded as means to that end. "Westernization" implied superiority of West to East, lack of respect for Indian ways; in a word, the sort of racial and cultural tensions which had largely been avoided by the "Inheritors" who

63. Woodward, *Age of Reform*, 389.

could afford the luxury of collecting tribute without giving offense beyond that of merely being considered rapacious.

This is the larger economic framework within which changing British attitudes must be seen. But economic factors do not by any means tell the whole story. For as Parliament became more closely involved, as successive Governors-General tried to keep in check those abuses of personal power by servants of the company such as Clive and Hastings that had first called forth investigation by the government at home, the resulting reforms, while leading to greater probity and efficiency all around, also led to a greater spirit of alienation between the two races. A dialectical process was at work here: The financial excesses of men such as Clive and Hastings constituted nothing less than crimes, and had to be curbed. Henceforth, the British were to view their work in India as a "trust," and were thus obligated to see to it that this sort of thing did not happen again. But the idea of trusteeship carried with it the seeds of two alternative possible approaches to Indian affairs. One of these, eloquently stated by Edmund Burke, placed primary emphasis upon the need, indeed, the moral obligation to conserve time-honored Indian traditions and institutions, and to protect the native Indian population against violence and exploitation on the part of its masters. The other, more aggressive approach implied that it was only the trustees who could be trusted; and was based on the proposition that the Indian people, sunk in weakness and ignorance, must be helped out of their slough of despond, and infused with the invigorating values of the West.

The history of British rule in India from the eighteenth century on witnessed in the main the triumph of the second approach. What is significant above all is that British possessions in India were increasingly drawn into the cultural as well as the economic orbit of those sent out to govern them; and that, in consequence, it is possible to regard British India as a distant stage on which an English touring company came to act plays that had created some stir at home. The setting and costumes were different; there was a totally new supporting cast; and, at times, the principal actors unaccountably forgot their lines or spoke them with unaccustomed emphasis. But the texts were familiar.

Thus the Governor-Generalship of Lord Cornwallis (1786–95) could be summarized as Whiggism in action. In the realm of administration that meant separation of the judicial and revenue-collecting powers of local government, and a general minimization of government interference. In the realm of agriculture, it meant land settlement which replaced the old communal structure with a system of landlords and tenants à l'Anglais. That system was to have disastrous results for the Indian peasants. Meanwhile, natives were excluded from high administrative posts, and the Indian upper classes put into a position of isolation. The next of the great Governors-General, Richard Wellesley (1798–1807), pursued an expansionist military policy which enormously increased the company's territories. But as far as his domestic policy was concerned, he stuck to Cornwallis's Whiggish principles, combined, in the case of both men, with an attitude of contempt for their subjects.

It was a group of Wellesley's subordinates—Munro, Malcolm, Elphinstone, and Metcalfe—who took exception to these principles as embodying a wrongheaded application of British constitutional doctrines to an alien situation. Eric Stokes has called them "Romantics" because they wanted to conform to Indian history and experience, to avoid the artificialities of European forms of rule, and because they had the notion that simple peasants could best be governed by a frank paternalism tailored to local circumstances and traditions. As administrators, they had a chance to apply their principles outside Bengal. In their view, Cornwallis and Wellesley were misguided Anglicizers.

But even Cornwallis and Wellesley appear as conservatives when viewed from the vantage point of the upholders of those doctrines— Evangelical, free-trading, and Utilitarian—that exerted ever greater influence in India as the nineteenth century advanced; doctrines which carried with them in germ attitudes that would one day help to create what we have come to think of as the classical ideology of modern imperialism. In England the Evangelicals did their best to preserve the established order from the virus of Jacobinism released by the French Revolution. But their remedy of conversion and Christian renewal had anything but conservative social and political consequences, when applied to what seemed to them a society sunk in superstition, vice, and idolatry. How could the true Christian possibly respect—as the early company officials had respected, and as even Cornwallis and Wellesley had still to some extent respected— customs and institutions that had produced such evils? They were a result of ignorance and they had to be extirpated. The weapons lay to hand: missionaries and Western education.

By 1813 the Evangelicals had become powerful enough, in and out of Parliament, to provide in the Charter Act of that year for the appointment of a Bishop of Calcutta, the opening up of India to voluntary missionary efforts, and the appropriation of an annual parliamentary grant for the purpose of native education. Their principal manifesto, then and for some time to come, was the elder Charles Grant's *Observations on the State of Society among the Asiatic Subjects of Great Britain* (1797). In it, Grant, one of Cornwallis's aides and subsequently chairman of the East India Company, gave vent to his conviction that India had been providentially put into British hands, not merely in order to provide commercial profit, but in order to enable Britain to diffuse there the benign influence of truth, the blessings of a well-regulated society, and the improvements and comforts of active industry. But that was not all. In every progressive stage of this great work, "we shall also serve the original design with which we visited India, that design still so important to this country—the extension of our commerce."[64]

It was a moment of considerable symbolic as well as practical significance when in the 1820's the younger Charles Grant, later Macaulay's chief at the Board of Control, joined hands with the free trade forces in and out of Parliament who wished to put an end to what remained of the company's monopoly, and looked forward to a time when hundreds of millions of Indians would have been sufficiently "improved" to be able to become customers for British goods. It was this Grant who, with Macaulay's help, drafted the act which in 1833 put an end to the company as a trading body. Lest one think of England at this time as imperially minded, it is well to remember that Macaulay's great speech on that occasion[65] was delivered to a House of Commons audience whose small size (only 130 Members were present) was indicative of that indifference to Indian affairs which, as he put it, meant that a broken head in Cold Bath Fields produced a greater sensation in the House than three pitched battles in India. A week after his speech Macaulay wrote to Margaret that he found it hard to understand the strange indifference of all classes of people, Members of Parliament, reporters, and the public, to Indian politics. Yet he did not complain of this, since it had enabled the government to effect some most valuable improvements against little or no opposition.[66]

In Macaulay's speech advocating these improvements were to be

64. Quoted by Edwardes, *Raj*, 70.

65. "I made the best speech, by general agreement, and in my own opinion, that I ever made in my life," T.B.M. to Hannah, July 11, 1833, Trevelyan, *Life and Letters*, 225.

66. T.B.M. to Margaret, July 17, 1833, Morgan MSS.

found elements of the aims and attitudes of both Evangelicals and free traders. On the one hand, he spoke of toleration strictly maintained, yet of bloody and degrading superstitions gradually losing their power; of the morality, philosophy, and taste of Europe beginning to produce a salutary effect on the hearts and understanding of Indian natives; and of the public mind of India, "which we found debased and contracted by the worst forms of political and religious tyranny, expanding itself to just and noble views of the end of government and of the social duties of man." On the other hand, he looked forward to a time when the people of India would be ruled by their own kings, "but wearing our broad cloth, and working with our cutlery," and neither too ignorant to value nor too poor to buy English manufactures: "To trade with civilized men is infinitely more profitable than to govern savages."[67]

When, in the course of the same speech, Macaulay came to consider the question of whether India was as yet ripe for representative institutions, he cited in support of his negative reply "the author of a History of India, which, though certainly not free from faults, is, I think, on the whole, the greatest historical work which has appeared in our language since that of Gibbon." That author was James Mill, whose book had, ever since its appearance in 1817, exerted an immense influence on the attitudes to India of the company's civil servants. In the *History* James Mill had demonstrated to his satisfaction the cultural and political backwardness of the Hindus—their ignorance, the absurdity of their history, geography, and literature; their barbarous state of tutelage to despotism and priestcraft. The principal message of the book was that any government measures taken to ameliorate this situation must be tailormade for a people in a low state of civilization. Otherwise, grave mistakes would occur.[68]

The prominence given to Mill's views in 1833 by Macaulay, who had so savagely attacked him and his school just four years before in the *Edinburgh Review,* demonstrates the importance of the Utilitarian strain amid the new forces making for dynamic change in India. Where India was concerned, it was the authoritarian rather than the libertarian potential of Utilitarianism that was in the

67. July 10, 1833, T.B.M., *Works,* XI, 567, 584.

68. See James Mill, *The History of British India* (9 vols., 4th ed., London, 1848), edited by H. H. Wilson, II, 44-7, 152-3. For the extent to which Mill's *History* was a disguised attack on English institutions, see Duncan Forbes, "James Mill and India," *Cambridge Journal,* V (1951-2), 19-33. The *History* was revised by H. H. Wilson. On the inadequacy of his revisions, see Gerald and Natalie Sirkin, "Of Raising Myths for Fun and Profit," *Columbia Forum,* XI (1968), 33-5; and Natalie Sirkin, "Horace Hayman Wilson and Gamesmanship in Indology," *Asian Studies,* III (1965), 301-23.

ascendant. The happiness of the greatest number of Indians mattered more than their freedom; and that, in terms of governance, meant, if possible, an all-powerful legislative and executive authority. Furthermore, while Mill shared with the Evangelicals their alarm at the evil consequences of centuries of Indian despotism, his own remedy, unlike theirs, lay not so much in trying to change individual attitudes by means of education as in establishing good government through good laws, including above all provisions for light taxes.

James Mill was extremely influential in all that concerned British relations with India, not only as the author of the *History,* but as assistant (1819) and then chief (1830) examiner for the East India Company, a post second in importance only to those of the "Chairs" of the Court of Directors. (His son John Stuart joined him in the examiner's office in 1823.) Lord William Bentinck so admired James Mill that he told him that it was *he* who would really be Governor-General when he assumed his post in 1828. And, in a very real sense, Macaulay owed his position as legal member of the Governor-General's Council directly to Mill. For not only had Mill, in 1833, strongly recommended him to the directors for this appointment; he had himself defined the position Macaulay went out to assume, and which was actually established by the Charter Act of 1833.[69] He did so in the course of the testimony he gave before the parliamentary committee which in 1832 held hearings on the bill before it became law.

In the course of his evidence, Mill stressed the need for an Indian legislative council whose business it should be first to study what laws were required and then to frame them. Those laws would apply throughout British India, and would replace the previous system of separate "regulations" made by the Governors-in-Council of the three presidencies of Madras, Bombay, and Bengal. There could not, he said, be good government in India until there came to exist a uniform system of law that applied to all who lived there, including British citizens, who would no doubt complain about being deprived of the special tribunals to which they had the traditional right to appeal, but who ought nonetheless to be put under the ordinary jurisdiction of the country.[70] Mill suggested the establishment of a small legislative body, composed of an English lawyer, one or two

69. T.B.M. to Hannah, November 1, 1833; telling her that his "old enemy," James Mill, had advised the East India Company to appoint T.B.M.—"for, as public men went, I was much above the average." Trevelyan, *Life and Letters,* 244.

70. Evidence of James Mill, February 21, 1832, *Parliamentary Papers,* IX (1831-2), 44–5, 51.

company officials, and possibly a native Indian. Then he went on to say: "It is indispensable to add a man capable of bringing to the great work the aid of general principles; I mean, in short, a person thoroughly versed in the philosophy of man and of government."[71]

In the event, the Charter Act of 1833 endorsed the principles of centralized authority and uniformity set forth by Mill in his evidence, though it did not follow exactly his recommendations in regard to the composition of the new legislative authority. The entire civil and military government of India was placed under the Governor-General and his Council of three company officials at Calcutta, who were henceforth charged with promulgating what were to be no longer known as "regulations," but as "Acts of the Government of India." The Charter Act envisioned an eventually uniform legal code, and provided for a Law Commission to advise the Governor-General's Council on ways and means to go about producing this.

With the passage of the Charter Act of 1833, the Council itself began to fulfill a double function. It remained the supreme executive authority in British India. But, with the addition of the so-called law member, it could now also act as a lawmaking body. The law member (or fourth member of Council) was to devote himself entirely to the business of legislation. He was not entitled to sit or to vote at those meetings held by the Council as an executive body. He was to assist in the preparation of laws. But his concurrence was not required for the passage of any law. He was, in fact, to be that person, thoroughly versed in the philosophy of man and of government, whose presence Mill had considered so desirable.

Macaulay now assumed this position. But had he not, in his slashing articles against the Utilitarians, and more specifically against James Mill, denied the very premise that there existed any single philosophy of man and of government capable of universal application? Yet, in his Charter Act speech of 1833, almost as if putting himself forward for the position, he publicly took the risk of being called "that nickname which is regarded as the most opprobrious of all nicknames by men of selfish hearts and contracted minds," a philosopher.[72] It is worth recalling that Macaulay's articles against the Utilitarians were elicited as much by their democratic politics as by their propensity to excessive system-building in defiance of human nature. Macaulay's own reforming drive was strong; and the role of supreme legislator certainly appealed to his historical imagination, as did the knowledge that in his own person he was to carry

71. Ibid., 46.   72. July 10, 1833, T.B.M., *Works*, XI, 583.

on the Burkean tradition of protecting the native Indian population against the depredations of their rulers. One of the chief reasons for the new system of centralized legislation inaugurated by the Charter Act of 1833 was that another provision of the same act lowered the barriers against the unlimited admission of British subjects into India. As a consequence, there was a strong feeling that Indians had to be protected against possible abuses and injuries from a greatly enlarged privileged caste of settlers; and that this could only be effectively accomplished by giving the new legislative Council power to make uniform laws, equally applicable to all Indian residents, including the British.[73]

That being the case, the fourth or legal member of Council (as Macaulay wrote to Hannah shortly before they left England) was charged with a special responsibility for the Indian native population. He pointed out that she had to be particularly careful, in choosing an English maid to accompany her, to pick a girl of good character who would not ill-treat the native servants under her control. For "the fourth member of Council is to be, in a peculiar manner, the guardian of the people of India against the European settlers. I must not suffer abuses against which I am to provide in my public capacity to bring scandal on my own house."[74]

The question as to just how the legal member of Council was to operate in his new role was one that naturally occurred with great force to someone who knew his English constitutional history as thoroughly as this particular legal member did. Almost as soon as he had reached India, and had taken his seat on the Governor-General's provisional Council at Ootacamund, Macaulay recorded a Minute in which he outlined the difficulties and uncertainties inherent in his position. The line between the Council as an executive and as a legislative body seemed vague to him. Did the Council sitting as a legislature correspond to Parliament, and sitting as an executive, to the Crown? If so, the fourth member would not have the right to vote on going to war, but would be able to withhold supplies for war. Until an explanation came from the home authorities in London, he would leave it to Lord William Bentinck, the Governor-General, to determine just what share of public business he should be allowed to transact.[75]

Bentinck's own Minute on the subject, forwarded to London

73. See C. D. Dharker, ed., *Lord Macaulay's Legislative Minutes* (Madras, 1946), 18.
74. T.B.M. to Hannah, November 21, 1833, Trinity Correspondence.
75. Minute dated June 27, 1834, *Parliamentary Papers*, XXVII (1852–3), Appendix 10, 530–1.

along with Macaulay's, contained an interpretation of the fourth member's role which, he wrote, was less complicated and theoretical than Macaulay's and "more within the reach of my humble judgement." It was his view that the Governor-General's Council had remained the same as it had been before the Charter Act, that is, it could both make war *and* grant supplies—with the single additional proviso that in making laws it must henceforth have the advice of the fourth member.

In their specific response to these two Minutes, the directors of the East India Company did not enter into the general question, raised by Bentinck, of the exclusion or inclusion of the fourth member from Council meetings; but confined themselves to agreement with Macaulay's supposition that while entitled to vote on supplies, he was not entitled to vote on making war.[76] But meanwhile, in a despatch written by James Mill, the Court of Directors had entered more fully into what it understood to constitute the function of the fourth member. He was not entitled to sit or vote in Council except for the purpose of making laws and regulations. But it was up to the Governor-General to invite or not to invite him to participate in any or all meetings. The fourth member's presence must be regarded as a *substitute* for the sanction of the Supreme Court at Calcutta, hitherto necessary to give validity to presidency regulations. Laws would still be valid, even without his concurrence. But Parliament clearly intended that the whole of his time and attention, as well as all the resources of knowledge and ability he might possess, be employed in promoting the due discharge of the Council's legislative functions. It was he who should help to give shape and connection to the several laws as they were passed, and who should have a principal share

76. Ibid., 532. Also see despatch of February 27, 1835, India Legislative Department, India Office Library (henceforth referred to as I.O.L.). The question of the fourth member's legitimate functions became entangled with politics at home. Apparently, T.B.M. signed some Council papers both in a legislative and executive capacity. His former friend, and more recent enemy, Winthrop Mackworth Praed, who served as secretary of the Board of Control during the Tories' brief tenure of office under Peel between December 1834 and April 1835, took note of this and used it during a House of Commons debate to censure T.B.M., and to imply that the matter was serious enough to have warranted his recall by a Tory government, in view of the fact that the Whigs, upon returning to office, had annulled the appointment of a Tory Governor-General. John Cam Hobhouse, now president of the Board of Control, denied that T.B.M. had committed any gross error of a nature that would have justified his recall; and also denied any merit to the Tories for not recalling him. *Hansard,* 3rd series, XXIX (1835), 39, 49.

in the mighty labour of collecting all that local information, and calling into view all those general considerations which belong to each occasion, and of thus enabling the Council to embody the abstract and essential principles of good government in regulations adapted to the peculiar habits, character, and institutions of the vast and infinitely diversified people under their sway.[77]

That last sentence of James Mill's is noteworthy for its confident assumption that the great battle of the abstract versus the concrete, the general versus the individual, that battle which in the sphere of historiography helped to mark the dividing line between Enlightenment and Romanticism, could be settled by a compromise. Somehow, it would be possible to bring "the abstract and essential principles of good government" into harmony with the "peculiar traits, character, and institutions" of the different nations of the world.

It is one of those not infrequent ironies of intellectual history that Macaulay, of all people, was now charged with this task by James Mill. Not only had the conflict between the general and the particular been at the crux of his own historical writing. But in 1829, in an article specifically directed against Mill's *Essay on Government*, he had explicitly denied that the "abstract and essential principles of good government" could be deduced from the principles of human nature. A science of government, he had then maintained, could be constructed only by means of induction—

by observing the present state of the world,—by assiduously studying the history of past ages,—by sifting the evidence of facts,—by carefully combining and contrasting those which are authentic,—by generalising with judgment and diffidence,—by perpetually bringing the theory which we have constructed to the test of new facts,—by correcting, or altogether abandoning it, according as those new facts prove it to be partially or fundamentally unsound.[78]

Now, knowing (by his own admission) very little of Indian habits, character, and institutions, Macaulay found himself entrusted with the task of amalgamating them with certain general principles of government. Where was he to derive those principles? His own definition of his role was closer to Bentinck's than to Mill's. For in defining the function of the fourth member of Council, Bentinck

77. Despatch of Court of Directors, December 10, 1834, *Parliamentary Papers*, XXVII (1852-3), Appendix 10, 530. For Mill's authorship, see J. W. Kaye, *The Administration of the East India Company* (London, 1853), 137, and Stokes, *Utilitarians*, 193.

78. T.B.M., "Mill's Essay on Government," *Works*, VII, 365, 369-70.

had written that he should be able to provide most useful advice in drawing up laws, "so that they shall contain nothing either repugnant to the laws of England, or at variance with the enlightened spirit of the age."[79] It was the "enlightened spirit of the age" that had characterized Bentinck's own administration in India; and it was the same spirit that Macaulay, who was so sure of what it represented that he did not have to "deduce" it, brought to his Indian concerns.

In the event, Bentinck willingly admitted Macaulay to all Council meetings, let him see every official document, relied on his judgment, and referred to him more than once in letters to his wife as "un miraculo."[80] For his part (we have it on Hannah's authority), Macaulay thought Bentinck was the greatest man he had ever known, and paid him the ultimate compliment of comparing him to William III.[81] One of Bentinck's ancestors had, of course, been that monarch's closest friend and adviser. In the more recent past, Bentinck's father, the third Duke of Portland, a prominent Whig grandee, had presided over a cabinet including Fox and Shelburne. Those historical associations alone would have attracted Macaulay to him. But, in addition, Bentinck himself possessed the sort of personality which, whether in history or in real life, always elicited Macaulay's warmest sympathies. An aristocrat as well as a soldier, Bentinck has been described as never happier than when in the saddle or the camp, his favorite company that of men of action. An enemy of all theorists, he prided himself on his common sense.[82] In politics he represented the kind of fusion between Foxite Whiggism, Utilitarianism, and classical economics that was not so far removed from Macaulay's own position. In 1812 he had been instrumental in reforming the Sicilian constitution, while commander-in-chief of British forces there. In 1830 he had expressed his delight with the French Revolution of that year. And no wonder, since in 1827 Louis Philippe had congratulated him upon his appointment as Governor-General, and had urged him on to do good for India.[83] With his political liberalism he combined deep religious feelings and Evangelical inclinations. In this respect, he resembled his lieutenant, Charles Trevelyan. His sister-in-law, Lady Olivia Sparrow, was a well-known Evangelical, and she was on friendly terms with prominent

79. Minute of July 31, 1834, *Parliamentary Papers*, XXVII (1852–3), 531.
80. Trevelyan, *Life and Letters*, 276.
81. Hannah, Lady Trevelyan, "Reminiscences," 60, Trinity MSS.
82. T. G. Percival Spear, "Lord William Bentinck," *Journal of Indian History*, XIX (1940), 102.
83. Salahuddin Ahmed, *Bengal*, 3.

Evangelical families such as the Grants, as well as with some of the leading missionaries in India.[84] His most recent biographer is convinced that the roots of his reforming zeal were Evangelical rather than Benthamite.[85]

Bentinck had been sent out to Bengal as Governor-General in 1828, at a time when the company was anxious to stabilize its finances and to increase the efficiency of its civil service before its charter came up for parliamentary renewal five years later. The appointment was something of a personal vindication for him since, in 1807, he had been recalled from his position as Governor of Madras because the directors held him partly to blame for the events leading to the Vellore mutiny. (He had forced the sepoys to change their habits of dress and hygiene and had thus offended their religious susceptibilities.) Now he carried out what was expected of him, applying the financial ax to such good effect that he became known as "the clipping Dutchman." He was also called "the Pennsylvanian Quaker" because of the plainness of his appearance and style of life.

It was Bentinck's quite explicit aim to bring Western liberal and enlightened principles to bear upon India; to infuse, in the words of Macaulay's inscription on his monument in Calcutta, the spirit of British freedom into Oriental despotism. He was an active reformer, very much akin in spirit to the men of '32 in England. His favorite motto was "The happiness and improvement of the condition of the people." He abolished *suttee,* the custom of widows immolating themselves upon their dead husbands' funeral pyres, and initiated a vigorous campaign against *thuggee,* the ritual murder of travelers carried out by marauding gangs. He reorganized the company's civil service, and set up the system of district commissioners afterwards copied in all parts of the British Empire. He fostered freedom of assembly as well as of the press, and, as we shall see, Western education.[86] In short, to quote Macaulay's inscription again, it was his constant study "to elevate the intellectual and moral character of the nations committed to his charge." The words have a patronizing ring. Indeed, so does the whole concept of the white man's burden of which, it has been said, Bentinck was as conscious as any later imperialist.[87]

84. Cynthia Barret, "Lord William Bentinck in Bengal, 1828–1835," D. Phil. Thesis, Oxford, 1954, 13.

85. John Rosselli, in conversation with the author.

86. For details, see Barret, "Bentinck."

87. Nancy G. Cassels, "Bentinck: Humanitarian and Imperialist–the Abolition of Suttee," *Journal of British Studies,* V (1965) , 87.

But it should also be remembered that it was Bentinck who was responsible for the first real departure from the Cornwallis system of a European monopoly of higher government posts by creating two new grades of Indian judges; and that he was the first royal Governor-General who seriously tried to ascertain Indian opinion on matters relating to Indian affairs.[88] There is no mistaking the importance of his administration for modern India. "If the British dominion had come to an end in the year 1828," Percival Spear has written, "the British would have meant no more to India than the Huns or the Sakyas or the Scythians."[89]

Given the Governor-General's moral fervor and his determination to raise the standards of the company's civil service, it should come as no surprise that he had found in the much younger Charles Trevelyan a kindred spirit. Trevelyan had come out to India after compiling a brilliant record at the company's civil service training college at Haileybury, where he had been greatly influenced by the lectures of T. R. Malthus. He first made his mark in India when, at the age of twenty-one, he courageously exposed the corrupt practices of his chief in Delhi, the popular and powerful Sir Edward Colebrooke. Trevelyan publicly accused him of receiving bribes from Indian natives, and stubbornly stuck to his charges—which in the end he was able to prove. Colebrooke was sent home in disgrace, and Trevelyan had begun to build his formidable reputation for probity and energy. He was a man after Bentinck's own heart. The Governor-General appointed him to be undersecretary for foreign affairs, and in that position he wrote a report recommending the abolition of Indian internal transit duties, which Macaulay called "a perfect masterpiece of its kind."[90]

At the time of his engagement to Hannah he was twenty-eight years old and deputy secretary to the supreme government in the political department. In the words of his future brother-in-law, he stood "quite at the head of that active party among the younger servants of the company who take the side of improvement." He was of the Evangelical as well as of the improving party. "His religious feelings," Macaulay wrote to Margaret, "are ardent, like all his feelings, even to enthusiasm." His mind was so full of schemes of moral and political improvement that even when he was courting Hannah,

88. Percival Spear, A History of India (Harmondsworth, Middlesex, 1965), 125; Salahuddin Ahmed, Bengal, 3.

89. Spear, "Bentinck," Journal of Indian History, 100.

90. T.B.M. to Margaret, December 7, 1834, Errington MSS.

his topics of conversation were steam navigation, the education of the natives, the equalization of the sugar duties, and the substitution of the Roman for the Arabic alphabet in the Oriental languages.[91]

It was that kind of zeal for reform which characterized Bentinck's administration, and which found Macaulay's favor. But Macaulay possessed something that both Trevelyan and Bentinck lacked, something that may be said to have played the same role in his own reforming zeal as religion played in theirs: a firm conviction that European history was the history of progress, and a profound knowledge and love of the highest achievements of Western literature. This he combined with a belief that this history and those achievements gave convincing proof of a superior civilization, and, as such, warranted the introduction of the values they represented to a benighted continent so evidently in need of improvement and enlightenment. Freedom of expression and contract as well as equal justice before the law stood high among those values; and Macaulay did his best to champion them within the limits of the Indian situation.

He had no illusions about those limits, just as he had no doubts about the excellence of Western values. In his Charter Act speech of 1833 he had made it plain (and had cited James Mill's authority to that effect) that it was not possible to give India representative government, that here was a situation where the blessings which were the natural fruits of liberty had to be engrafted upon despotism.[92] He saw very clearly that the ultimate sanction for British rule in India was the sword; and that he and his countrymen were, in his own words, strangers in India.

In one of his Minutes, Macaulay commented that the political vocabulary used by the English in India, more especially by those Englishmen who wanted to be given a maximum of special privilege, was that of their compatriots at home. But his own sense of realism and his dislike of cant were too strong to be deceived by such phrase-mongering. He pointed out that the same words meant entirely different things in London and in Calcutta. Thus, "public opinion" in the Indian context meant "the opinion of five hundred persons who have no interest, feeling, or taste in common with the fifty millions among whom they live." "Love of liberty," in its turn, meant the strong objection the five hundred felt to every measure which could prevent them from acting as they chose toward the fifty

91. Idem.   92. July 10, 1833, T.B.M., *Works*, XI, 555–6.

millions. One might argue, of course, that the logical consequence of such insights was that the British should at once remove themselves from India. But Macaulay was no more an anti-imperialist than he was a democrat. Rather, he went on to repeat that India could not at present have a free government. "But she may have the next best thing," he continued; "a firm and impartial despotism."[93] That sentence was frequently cited against him. But, at least, there was no humbug about it. And within the framework he posited, Macaulay did his best to carry out his special charge, which was to protect Indian natives against abuses of power on the part of their rulers. It is a tribute both to his earnestness and his energy that the Indian editor of his legislative Minutes found himself able to conclude that while Macaulay was a member of Council, that body "indeed stood more often than not for the fifty million as against the five hundred."[94]

It would be wrong to sentimentalize Macaulay's attitude toward the Indians. He was appalled by their apathy and suspicious of their probity. "Everybody knows," he wrote, "that a Hindu witness is not generally deserving of so much credit as an English witness."[95] But, in the matter before him on that particular occasion—whether Indian judges should or should not be able to sit in suits involving any amount of money—he vigorously argued the positive side of the case. His argument was largely pragmatic. Hindu evidence might be less credible than that of the English. But it had nonetheless to be accepted, even in capital cases. For society could not be left altogether without protection. In the same way, it was essential to put one's trust in native judges, if only for reasons of economy, since the revenue of India could not bear the charge of additional hundreds of English judges. "We may regret," Macaulay wrote, "that they [the Indian judges] have not the honourable feelings of English gentlemen. But what can we do? We cannot change the heart and mind of a nation in a day."[96]

That last sentence is important for an understanding of Macaulay's view of reform in India. The hearts and minds of the people could not be changed in a day; but they *could* (and should) be changed, just as abuses *could* (and should) be corrected. History, as well as his own experience in the struggle for parliamentary reform in England, had taught him that major reforms could only be carried out when powerful interests in society combined in the endeavor. The best means of galvanizing those interests into action was joint

93. March 28, 1836, Dharker, ed., *Minutes*, 179–80.   94. Ibid., 37.
95. May 15, 1837, ibid., 230.   96. Idem.

suffering under similar inequities. We have seen that Macaulay's reaction to the proposition that native judges should try cases involving small amounts of money, while those involving large amounts were to be left in the hands of English judges, was unequivocally negative. Even on the assumption that native judges were bad and corrupt, what sense did it make to leave all the cases of the poor and almost all those in which the middle classes were concerned in their hands, and to make separate provision for the higher orders and the very rich? It was not merely a matter of special privilege, though it was certainly that. "I must own," Macaulay wrote, "that I am unable to comprehend this solicitude for the welfare of the few and this indifference to the welfare of the many."[97] But, more important, the result of this special treatment would be the indefinite postponement of reform. "While such abuses exist," he concluded, "I think it desirable that all classes should suffer from them alike. Then they will be exposed, and I trust speedily reformed."[98] That was how reform had come about in England, and Macaulay was sure that the same dynamic would be effective in India.

It was up to the government, then, to try to provide a uniform system for the administration of justice. But this did not mean that the government must regularly intervene in the everyday affairs of native Indians. Far from it. Just as the anti-aristocratic tendencies of Macaulay's thought, by no means totally obliterated by his Whiggism, were mobilized by the prospect of the perpetuation of caste and privilege in India—indeed, more readily mobilized there than in England, because less was at stake that could affect his own social and political stance—so also did the Indian situation elicit and confirm his faith in laissez faire. One could argue that if this faith was misguided in England, given the social problems there which cried out for state intervention, it was even more misguided in India, where only government intervention on the largest scale could even begin to cope with the immense amount of poverty and suffering that prevailed. But to argue thus would be to fail to understand that Macaulay carried his basic ideas and attitudes to India along with his Gibbon and his Voltaire. One can blame him for this, but one must also try to see the positive side of his inflexibility, his avoidance of the condescending paternalism which led some of his contemporaries and many of his successors to treat Indians as backward children who would and should never grow up.

Thus, when it came to the question as to whether ryots (peasants)

97. May 15, 1837, ibid., 231.   98. Ibid., 232.

should be enjoined from making contracts for terms longer than one year, he answered in the negative; and justified his position with a classic statement of the doctrine of negative freedom:

Grown up men, not idiots or insane, should be suffered to make such contracts as are not injurious to others and as appear to them to be beneficial to themselves. To say that the ryots of this country are mere children and ought to be specially protected is, I conceive, quite incorrect.

They were not intellectually inferior to peasants in other countries, and there was no reason why contracts entered upon by them should be set aside. If those contracts were not freely concluded, if force and deception were used in getting them to enter upon them, then that was a matter for the law; but not the actual conclusion of the contract. "A Government cannot be wrong in punishing fraud or force, but it is almost certain to be wrong if, abandoning its legitimate functions, it tells private individuals that it knows their business better than they know it themselves. . . ." If any one political truth had been proved by a vast mass of experience, it was "that the interference of legislators for the purpose of protecting men of sound mind against the inconveniences which might arise from their own miscalculations or from the natural state of markets is certain to produce infinitely more evil than it can avert."[99] The only sound principle of legislation, so Macaulay averred in yet another Minute opposing government restriction, this time of the activities of the Bank of Bengal, was that "freedom is the rule and restraint the exception; that the burden of the proof lies on him who proposes to prohibit any thing."[100] To readers in the final third of the twentieth century, and familiar with the problems even of an independent India, this doctrine has an almost antediluvian sound. But it would be a serious misunderstanding of Macaulay to depict him holding any other. He did not change his basic principles within the Indian context.

The Governor-General's Council took little official notice of Indian opinion; though Bentinck went further in this direction than his immediate predecessors. Macaulay himself argued in one of his legislative Minutes that the residents of Kaira were better judges than the government of Bombay as to whether it was worth their while to submit to a local tax for a purely local object, the repair of their walls.[101] But, apart from this, his main concern with the views of the Indians for whom he helped to legislate was to keep them

99. November 13, 1835, ibid., 275–6.   100. November 14, 1836, ibid., 282.
101. January 16, 1836, ibid., 163.

informed about the laws that were passed by the Council. While, following Bentham, he strongly objected to the use of the preamble in the framing and publication of legal enactments—on the ground that no brief and clear preamble could possibly contain a summary of the whole range of arguments for a particular law which different Council members were likely to have brought forward in its support—he also agreed with Bentham, "that eminent writer . . . from whose opinions on a question of jurisprudence it is rarely safe to dissent," that a government owed the public an accounting of the reasons for its legislative measures.[102] He considered the possibility of publishing the legislative Minutes of individual Council members to accomplish this end. But this was not, in fact, done.

Some segments of Indian opinion, though not systematically consulted, managed on occasion to make themselves heard to good effect. But it was English rather than Indian opinion that raised a storm over two of the Council's measures in which Macaulay had a major part: the Act of 1835, which by abolishing the licensing system formally instituted freedom of the press in India; and the so-called Black Act of the following year, which abrogated the special privileges British subjects possessed in matters of legal appeals and jurisdiction. Both these measures were based on liberal principles which must have seemed axiomatic to Macaulay—freedom of the press and uniformity in the dispensation of justice. Furthermore, neither of them really wrought a great deal of practical change in an existing situation. For the press was free in fact; and the use made by British subjects of special courts of appeal was minimal. Nevertheless, two different sections of English opinion were seriously provoked by the two measures. The authorities in London most strenuously objected to the Press Act; whereas the anger of the English community in Calcutta was aroused by the "Black Act." In both instances Macaulay was a principal target. And the nature of the criticism in each case throws a significant amount of light on some basic prevailing British attitudes to India, and thus on some widely accepted presuppositions of imperial rule at the time.

The act to free the press was passed by the Council in April 1835, at a time when Sir Charles Metcalfe—"the ablest civil servant I ever knew in India" (so Macaulay was to describe him in his India speech of June 24, 1853) [103]—was Acting Governor-General, Lord William Bentinck having returned to England a few weeks before. It may

102. May 11, 1835, ibid., 148. Lord Auckland was to call T.B.M.'s views regarding preambles one of his favorite crotchets. See below, p. 341.

103. Quoted by Trevelyan, *Life and Letters*, 590.

seem ironical that Metcalfe, who belonged to that group of "romantic" conservatives who had done their best to resist the Westernization of India according to British constitutional principles, should now be the chief sponsor of this particular measure. In the period of reform under Bentinck, Metcalfe had found himself in an alien world.[104] Still, the formal end of the licensing system in British India had quite properly become associated with his name. It was he who was behind the measure.[105] But it was Macaulay who strongly supported him and who wrote the Minute which justified the act and evoked such a sharp reaction from the home authorities.

The position in regard to the press in British India differed from place to place. In Madras no restrictions whatever existed on printing and publication. In Bengal, a different presidency, regulations passed in 1823 forbade the establishment of printing presses without a license; and there were restrictions on the circulation of printed books and papers there and in Bombay. But it was a fact that in Bengal those regulations had not, in recent years, been enforced; and that editors were therefore free in practice to print what they wished. It should be remembered that Indian as well as English language newspapers possessed this practical freedom. Between 1828 and 1835, sixteen Bengali and four Persian newspapers were started in Bengal. But most of the vernacular press was conservative in tone. It was the English newspapers that tended to be reformist.[106] During Bentinck's tenure of office, he invoked the Press Law on only one occasion, in order to prevent criticism not of himself but of the Court of Directors. It is worth noting that on this occasion, Metcalfe, then a member of Council, recorded his opinion against that act of censorship.[107]

In 1834, toward the end of Bentinck's term of office, a meeting was held in Calcutta with the avowed purpose of discussing the Press Law and the existing restraints on the right of public assembly. Out of that meeting emerged a petition to the Governor-General in Council, signed by eight Europeans and four Indians on behalf of the inhabitants of Calcutta, requesting the repeal of the existing laws and confirmation of the right of assembly. The reply of the Council,

104. Stokes, *Utilitarians*, 18, 239. But see also D. N. Panigrahi, *Charles Metcalfe in India: Ideas and Administration 1806–1835* (Delhi, 1968), 20–1, 212–20, who argues that there was nothing strange or anomalous about Metcalfe's freeing the press.

105. This is the view of H. T. Prinsep, "Three Generations in India," typescript, II, 219, I.O.L., who, as T.B.M.'s prime antagonist, had every reason to hold him chiefly responsible.

106. Salahuddin Ahmed, *Bengal*, 95, 99.   107. Dharker, ed., *Minutes*, 44.

drafted by Macaulay, supplied that confirmation, forecast a change in the Press Law in the near future, and indicated that Bentinck himself, who, during most of his term in office, had favored retention of the Press Law in order to deal with emergencies, had changed his mind about the subject.[108]

Shortly after Metcalfe became Acting Governor-General, the Council repealed the existing press restrictions in Bengal and Bombay. A uniform regulation was set up for all of British India, which merely stipulated that printers and publishers of all periodical works containing news or comment thereon must carry their names on what was published and inform the appropriate authorities about the time of printing and publication of their periodicals. Macaulay summed up the reasons for this decision in an eloquent Minute.[109] His main point was that since the press in India was, in fact, free in practice, the government need not and should not bear the odium of tyranny and suppression which derived from the continuing legal existence of restrictions. In some countries, there was perhaps something to be said for putting restraints upon political discussion. But that was not the issue here: "The question before us is not whether the press shall be free but whether, being free, it shall be called free."[110] The very words "license to print" had a hateful sound to the ears of Englishmen everywhere. Yet the licensing system, as currently administered, did not really prevent anyone from publishing the bitterest and most sarcastic reflections on any public measure or functionary. As for the argument that the government should keep emergency power in its hands, in order to take "the sharp, prompt and decisive measures, which may be necessary for the preservation of the Empire," it retained that power in any event.

No government in the world is better provided with the means of meeting extraordinary dangers by extraordinary precautions. Five persons who may be brought together in half an hour, whose deliberations are secret, who are not shocked by any of those forms which elsewhere delay legislative measures, can, in a single sitting, make a law for stopping every press in India.[111]

Thus, why keep the offensive form and ceremonial of despotism before the eyes of those who were permitted to enjoy the substance of freedom?

108. Barret, "Bentinck," 67–9.   109. April 16, 1835, Dharker, ed., *Minutes*, 165–7.
110. Ibid., 165.   111. Ibid., 166.

One could argue that Macaulay himself was guilty of exalting the shadow above the substance here. For, if the government indeed retained its emergency powers in the way he described, then how genuinely free would the Indian press actually be, even without licensing regulations? But that very safeguard might have been expected to placate the Court of Directors and the Board of Control in England, neither of which had been consulted before the new Press Act was passed by the Council. Far from it. The president of the Board of Control at this juncture (i.e., from April 1835 when the Whigs, who had been out of office since December 1834, came back in again) was John Cam Hobhouse, inventor of the phrase "His Majesty's Opposition," once Byron's bosom friend, and at one time known as "Radical Hob." By now he had made the transition from youthful radicalism to cabinet office in Melbourne's government. It will be recalled that during the Reform Bill days he had fought along with Macaulay, whose prose style he once characterized as "all flash, dash, and splash," but whom he greatly admired.[112] That did not, however, prevent him from sending an explosive despatch to the new Governor-General when he received news of the Press Act.

The Earl of Auckland's appointment shows the extent to which the position had become a political one. While the Tories under Peel were in power, they had nominated Lord Heytesbury to replace Metcalfe and to succeed Bentinck as Governor-General. But the Whigs, upon returning to office, rescinded that nomination, and instead sent out Auckland, who had been First Lord of the Admiralty in Melbourne's first cabinet. Hobhouse and Auckland were friends; and their personal correspondence constitutes one of the best sources for the study of Macaulay's Indian years. For in it they discussed issues and personalities involved in the governance of British India with the greatest frankness. Technically, the Governor-General was still selected by the Court of Directors; it was with the court that he conducted his official correspondence, and from the court that he received the despatches that laid down the policies he was to pursue, despatches so voluminous that with a single one there were sometimes sent along no less than 45,000 pages of elaboration.[113] But the real power over Indian policy had gradually passed to the president

112. Michael Joyce, *My Friend H: John Cam Hobhouse, Baron Broughton of Broughton de Gyfford* (London, 1948), 345.

113. Karl Marx, "The Government of India," New York *Daily Tribune*, July 20, 1853, quoting evidence of Lord Broughton before Official Salaries Committee, Shlomo Avineri, *Karl Marx on Colonialism and Modernization* (New York, 1969), 121.

of the Board of Control, that is, to the government of the day; though, given the distance between London and Calcutta, and the time it took for letters and despatches to be sent back and forth, a great deal of initiative inevitably remained with the Governor-General, who was on the spot.

The Press Act was a case in point; and Hobhouse, writing to the newly appointed Lord Auckland on this subject, castigated Metcalfe for his imprudence. It appeared that the Court of Directors wished to have the measure annulled by Parliament, a procedure provided for by the Charter Act of 1833. Thereupon Hobhouse took the matter before the cabinet, where a majority at first agreed with the court. And, Hobhouse went on, they would have been perfectly justified had they proceeded accordingly. "For such wretched unsubstantial pretexts for a great change in a system of government never, I am sure, were before invented by the most inconsiderate reformer." It was Hobhouse himself who finally managed to persuade the cabinet as well as the King—William IV—that the entire press business be placed in Auckland's hands forthwith, and that his decision be final.[114] The official despatch (far milder than that originally proposed) subsequently sent to the government in India on the subject of the Press Act was drafted by the president of the Board of Control himself, and formally approved by the cabinet.[115]

Hobhouse stressed the fact that Melbourne, as well as the King, had specifically given his approval to the reformulated despatch. This left the new Press Act intact, on the ground that an immediate repeal might produce mischievous results. But it was still a very stern document. The measure had been passed, it stated, in opposition to all previous orders from the home authorities, and had been adopted by what was after all only a provisional government, under an Acting Governor-General. Insufficient reasons had been adduced for the necessity of the act. No information had been supplied about the number of newspapers in operation, and about similar important facts. Instead, the home authorities had been furnished—presumably by way of Macaulay's Minute—with "only . . . the dogmatical assertion of certain principles, which may be admitted, and, indeed, are never denied with reference to one state of society and amount to mere idle declamation when applied to another." No real grievance

114. Hobhouse to Auckland, January 30, 1836, Home and Miscellaneous, Vol. 833, I.O.L.
115. Hobhouse to Auckland, November 30, 1836, Home and Miscellaneous, Vol. 837, I.O.L.

seemed to exist, since the press was said to possess ample practical liberty. Furthermore, "your legislative counsellor, with whom the proposal seems to have originated"—Macaulay—had declared that in an emergency the press could still be easily controlled. So the whole business was one of appearances. The press would not actually become any more free, nor the government (except momentarily) more beloved through its action.[116]

Thus, even in this toned-down reprimand, Macaulay was severely censured for his part in the Press Act. In his personal letter to Auckland, Hobhouse was far more outspoken. "Let me add my earnest entreaties, at Melbourne's desire," he wrote to the new Governor-General, "that you will keep B.M. [Babington Macaulay] a little more quiet. It is extremely unfair upon the Home Government to rush into these reforms, without previous consultation with them." What resulted were squabbles either with the Court of Directors or with Parliament, sometimes with both; "to say nothing of the King, who somehow or the other has been taught to take a very lively and troublesome interest in Indian affairs." Macaulay had, it seemed, written to Hobhouse that in his capacity as president of the Law Commission he hoped to squeeze all the laws of India into a small octavo volume within a year or two, though the other commissioners believed him to be sanguine in his expectation. "Of his vigour and genius," Hobhouse concluded, "I have no doubt, tho' I say to you, confidentially that I entertain some alarm. However you are the master, and will repress his ardour."[117]

It was unjust on the part of Hobhouse to have singled out Macaulay as the sole source of the Press Act. But it is an interesting commentary on Macaulay's reputation in the highest quarters in London that it was at once assumed that the measure must have been his idea. It was (as H. T. Prinsep recalled) the *belief* that the Press Act proceedings had been primarily due to Macaulay's influence that had provoked the severity of the terms in which they were condemned. That is why Metcalfe was later determined to make it quite clear that he, and not Macaulay, had instigated them.[118]

Still, there is no doubt that Macaulay had strongly favored the Press Act, and clearly thought that he was acting nobly as well as

116. Despatch to Governor-General, India Legislative Department, No. 1 (1836), February 2, 1836, I.O.L.

117. Hobhouse to Auckland, January 30, 1836, Home and Miscellaneous, Vol. 833, I.O.L.

118. Prinsep, "Three Generations," I, 219.

correctly in lending his support to it. The home authorities evidently did not take the same view. It must be kept in mind that the Education Minute, the subject of the next chapter, predated the Press Act; and, while Hobhouse supported Macaulay's views on education, there had been strong feelings among the directors concerning both its style and substance. As far as Melbourne's view of Macaulay was concerned, it should be remembered that not since Walpole had there been a Prime Minister more inclined to let sleeping dogs lie, and to avoid rocking the boat at any cost. "Dammit, why can't they be quiet?" had been his complaint about the Benthamites. He was hardly the man to warm to the sort of dangerous rhetorical gesture that he felt the Press Act represented. Hobhouse, as a member of Melbourne's cabinet, was duty-bound to pass on the Prime Minister's strictures. But his personal letter to Auckland shows that he, too, was concerned about what he felt was Macaulay's overly ardent approach toward his Indian responsibilities. One senses a feeling on the part of Hobhouse, himself an example of someone who had accommodated his ideals to political realities, that those high-minded principles and sentiments whose eloquent statement during the Reform Bill debates had established Macaulay's fame in politics were hardly suitable for translation into precipitate action in the Indian Empire.

It was because they feared for the security of that Empire that the home authorities were so nervous about the potential effects of the Press Act. "Now . . . this is a fine country; but it is nothing without its colonial possessions, especially India," William IV said to Hobhouse during the very year of the Press Act crisis.[119] A free press, and more especially a free vernacular press, could be viewed as a real threat to British rule. Sir Thomas Munro, like Metcalfe one of the "romantic" school of Indian administrators, had differed from the latter in regarding it as such. In answer to the question as to what the first duty of the Indian press consisted in, he had given an unequivocal answer: "It is to deliver the country from a foreign yoke; and to sacrifice to this one great object every meaner consideration; and if we make the press really free to the natives as well as to Europeans, it must inevitably yield to this result."[120]

Munro was afraid that a free press would inevitably carry disaffection into the army, and lead to a mutiny supported by the Indian masses. That is what Sir Robert Grant, brother of Macaulay's former chief at the India Board and now Governor of Bombay, had in mind

119. October 5, 1836, Broughton, *Recollections*, V, 64.
120. Quoted by Dharker, ed., *Minutes*, 44–5.

when he warned Hobhouse about the dangers of utilizing a free press in order to make a despotic government free. "We are a government of the sword," he declared, "and the sword, except for foreign warfare, is a peacock's feather. We are a government of opinion, and all opinion, throughout India, is fast poisoning at its very sources."[121] H. T. Prinsep, Macaulay's chief adversary in India, who as a councilor had reluctantly supported the end of licensing, made the same point when he quoted the dictum: "When you have a free press on board of a man-of-war, then you may think of giving one to India."[122]

As against this view, Macaulay's defense of the Press Act minimized the dangers that could result from it. In a Minute addressed to the directors, clearly intended to soothe their feelings, he made no mention at all of the eventual role of the vernacular press; nor did he on this occasion employ the argument of his Milton essay, that it was foolish to believe that no people ought to be free until they were fit to use their freedom. Rather, he confined himself to stressing the differences between newspaper readers in England and in India. In England, a great deal of evil as well as good could be caused by the press. In India, on the other hand, the number of English residents was very small. The circulation of English newspapers was mainly confined to civil servants, army officers, bankers, landed proprietors, barristers, and master manufacturers. A large proportion of these was engaged in government service, and therefore had an interest in maintaining established institutions. No threat to British rule emanated from them; and less possibility of sedition than in England. For in India there existed no class "analogous to that vast body of English labourers and artisans whose minds are rendered irritable by frequent distress and privation, and on whom, therefore, the sophistry and rhetoric of bad men often produce a tremendous effect."[123]

One must bear in mind that Macaulay wrote this Minute with the specific intent of alleviating the fears of the Court of Directors, and that it may therefore be regarded as not entirely candid. Still, it is

121. Sir Robert Grant to Hobhouse, September 26, 1837, Home and Miscellaneous, Vol. 841, I.O.L.

122. Dharker, ed., *Minutes*, 45–6.

123. "State Paper" to Court of Directors, September 1836, quoted by Trevelyan, *Life and Letters*, 285. T.B.M. made the same point many years later when, in 1853, as a member of a Select Committee on Indian Territories he asked: "Would it be possible to conceive that the utmost license of the press in England could do any harm if nobody read the newspapers except Masters in Chancery, Directors of the East India Company, the judges and justices of the peace?" *Parliamentary Papers*, XXVII (1852–3), 304.

worth comment that his defense of press freedom for India was so largely based on the lack of danger to be apprehended from granting it; that he saw the measure entirely in terms of the English rather than of the vernacular press; and that he regarded the Indian population as still so backward and passive that it could not in any sense be equated with the English working class. The implication was that once it had reached a stage where it could be thus equated, some form of censorship might be defensible. Much of nineteenth-century English history can be explained only in terms of constant awareness on the part of the governing classes of the ever-present threat posed by sedition and revolution from below. It was this threat, actual or potential, that served to define the limits of freedom, not just in the minds of the aristocracy, but also in the minds of the middle classes, fresh from their triumph in the Reform Act. Macaulay was no exception to this rule.

In spite of the acrimonious correspondence between London and Calcutta, one thing is clear. Neither the home authorities nor Metcalfe and Macaulay advocated press freedom without limitation. True, Macaulay wanted the existing practical freedom confirmed by legislation, in order to nip in the bud criticism on the part of those who were exercised over the disparity between practice and theory. But since the government retained its emergency powers, it could be argued that he was simply retreating to a second level of disparity. In the event, the press measure, adopted by Metcalfe and his Council without prior reference to London, was the most significant of several such that led to a stern legislative despatch—signed, in the usual manner, by "your affectionate friends"—from the Court of Directors to the Governor-General, giving him positive orders to stop adopting significant new measures inconsistent in principle with the instructions and recorded opinions laid down by the company.[124] If Macaulay saw or heard about this despatch, he was probably not greatly disturbed by it. The court was traditionally conservative, and opposed to the kind of innovations desired by Bentinck, Trevelyan, and himself. Karl Marx, writing for the New York *Daily Tribune* in 1853, reported that

Mr. Macaulay, in the course of the pending debates, defended the Court by the particular plea, that it was impotent to effect all the evils it might intend, so much so, that all improvements had been effected in opposi-

124. Despatch to Governor-General, India Legislative Department, No. 1 (1836), April 14, 1836, I.O.L.

tion to it, and against it by individual governors who acted on their own responsibility. Thus with regard to the suspension of Suttee, the abolition of the abominable transit duties, and the emancipation of the East India press.[125]

Lord Auckland decided not to repeal the new Press Act. By the time he reached India, he found it no longer a matter for comment. The powers of the government had not been dangerously weakened by it. On the contrary, he reported to Hobhouse, they appeared to be stronger than before, since the passage of the measure had removed what had previously been a topic of irritation.[126] However, if Auckland thought that was the end of the matter, he was wrong. For one thing, he had not yet received (at the time he wrote) the despatch of April 1836, from the Court of Directors, which ordered him to consult the home authorities before any important measures were passed. For another, he had, as a matter of routine, forwarded Metcalfe's own comments in defense of the Press Act to the chairman of the Court of Directors, Sir James Carnac. When these came to the attention of Hobhouse, the latter responded by sending Auckland what he called a "homily," couched in very strong language.

Hobhouse dismissed Metcalfe's comments out of hand as both impertinent and unsuitable, and went on to reiterate the necessity for the Governor-General's checking with the home authorities before important measures such as the Press Act were adopted, except in cases of clear emergency. Otherwise, there would have to come about a complete change in the system of administering the Indian Empire, with the home authorities formally abdicating a power they were unable to maintain in substance. He continued: "I shall, however, if I remain at this office, struggle hard to prevent this consummation; and, most assuredly, would recommend the recall of the best friend I ever had, were he to act in decided and repeated defiance of his masters at home." If the authorities in India did not stop acting on their own, how would it be possible to avoid terrible conflicts in England between the Court of Directors and the Board of Control? And how could their actions be defended in Parliament?[127]

In reply, Auckland expressed his vexation at apparently being put upon a footing different from that of his predecessors. "From day to

125. Marx, "Government of India," Avineri, ed., *Marx*, 119.
126. Auckland to Hobhouse, June 20, 1836, Home and Miscellaneous, Vol. 837, I.O.L.
127. Hobhouse to Auckland, January 26, 1837, Home and Miscellaneous, Vol. 837, I.O.L.

day I am called upon to decide questions which may involve war or peace, ruin or safety, honour or disgrace, and who knows, until it is tried, what is an 'important measure'?" Hobhouse had assured him that he would not hesitate to recall his best friend, if he defied his masters. Would not Hobhouse's opinion of that friend be lowered if the latter served his masters an hour longer than he could do so with credit and efficiency? As for Metcalfe's despatch about the Press Act—Metcalfe was a good man who insisted upon his right to be heard so that others, "Macaulay in particular," should not have to bear undue censure.[128]

That was a generous act on the part of Metcalfe, who must have heard, presumably from Auckland, that Macaulay was being blamed in London as the person principally responsible for inspiring a law whose passage had led to a crisis of confidence in the relations between Calcutta and London. And, moreover, a crisis in which the very highest authorities—the president of the Board of Control, the cabinet, the Prime Minister, and the monarch himself—had become enmeshed. Macaulay had certainly not intended to provoke such a crisis. What he had failed to take into account was the strength of feeling on the part of the British government that nothing must be done that might serve to endanger the security of its Indian possessions. There is a double irony here. For, in the first place, it was only because Macaulay was, in fact, convinced that the measure would *not* endanger that security in any way that he had supported it so strongly. In the second place, he could well have been wrong in this conviction; since a free press may have been among the contributory factors which made the Mutiny possible.

On the issue of the press, Macaulay had taken what he felt to be both the sensible and the high-principled side, only to find himself violently criticized, and almost repudiated, by the Court of Directors and by the Board of Control under Hobhouse. On the issue of how members of the British community in Calcutta were to be treated in the Indian law courts, he took up the same stance, was supported this time by Hobhouse in the teeth of opposition from the Court of Directors, and found himself violently criticized and totally repudiated by a powerful section of the British community in Calcutta. What was at stake here was the "Black Act" of March 1836.

That act had two major provisions. First, it annulled a clause in the Charter Act of 1813 allowing British suitors to appeal from the

128. Auckland to Hobhouse, April 16, 1837, Home and Miscellaneous, Vol. 838, I.O.L. This confirms Prinsep's version of the matter.

lower courts of the East India Company directly to the Supreme Court (i.e., the King's Court) in Calcutta in cases where native Indians were entitled only to appeal to the highest company court, the Sadar Dewani Adalat. The second provision laid it down that no person should by reason of place of birth or descent be exempted in civil cases from the jurisdiction of any but the very lowest courts of the company. Both these provisions stemmed directly from the Charter Act of 1833, which, at the same time it allowed unlimited admission of British subjects to India, recommended that steps be taken to protect Indian natives against the wrongs that might be apprehended from the new settlers.

In testimony given prior to the Act of 1833 James Mill had made it quite clear that he thought that, whatever their putative objections to such a procedure might be, Englishmen in India should be put under the ordinary jurisdiction of the country.[129] He repeated this conviction in the despatch he wrote to brief the new legal member of Council about his duties.[130] Macaulay was determined to proceed in this direction. So determined, in fact, that when he landed in Madras, he was at once reported to have let fall the remark that within two years' time no English law courts would any longer exist in India, an indiscretion which immediately set some of his country-men against him.[131]

The "Black Act" did not, in fact, apply to British-born residents of Calcutta, who continued to fall under the jurisdiction of the Supreme Court there. Nonetheless, an outcry went up against it, and more particularly against the provision disallowing appeals to the Supreme Court. The outcry came primarily from members of the Calcutta Bar, who evidently feared the loss of legal business provided by the former appeals procedure. The record showed that since 1813 there had only been two such appeals by British citizens from the company courts in the interior. But with many more settlers about to arrive, these lawyers no doubt hoped that they would benefit from an increased number of appeals to the Supreme Court. That was not, of course, the motive they adduced for their opposition to the projected act in the memorials they submitted to the Governor-in-Council. Those memorials laid stress on their outrage at the prospective loss of formally recognized superiority. The petitioners claimed that British

129. *Parliamentary Papers*, IX (1831–2), 51–3.

130. Despatch of October 10, 1834. Sir Courtenay Ilbert, *The Government of India: Being a Digest of the Statute Law Relating Thereto* (Oxford, 1898), 506–15.

131. Arnold, *Public Life*, 136.

citizens in India had a right to more privileged treatment in law than native Indians, merely by virtue of their citizenship; and that they must not under any circumstances be placed upon the same legal footing as the people over whom they ruled. It was this claim that Macaulay refuted, with eloquence and passion, in the three Minutes he devoted to the subject of the "Black Act."

The desirability for uniformity in judicial administration was one of Bentham's fundamental precepts, and, as such, certainly played a major part in Macaulay's reasoning on the subject. "All special exemptions," he wrote, "carry with them an appearance of unfairness and the burden of the proof lies on those who claim them."[132] But the sentiment which, to Macaulay's great credit, emerged most powerfully from his replies to the Calcutta protesters was his determination not to legalize the existence in India of a superior and specially privileged case of British rulers. The chief reason, he wrote, why the Sadar Dewani Adalat was to be preferred as a court of appeal to the Supreme Court was that

it is the court which we have provided to administer justice in the last resort to the great body of the people. If it is not fit for that purpose, it ought to be made so. If it is fit to administer justice to the body of the people, why should we exempt a mere handful of settlers from its jurisdiction?[133]

That provision of the Charter Act of 1813 which gave Englishmen special rights of appeal contained at least the semblance, if not the reality, of partiality and tyranny. For it seemed to indicate that the native of India might well put up with something less than justice, or that Englishmen in India had the right to something more than justice; that there were two kinds of justice, a coarse one good enough for Indians, and another of superior quality reserved for the British rulers.[134] This was pernicious doctrine. The very worst state into which those rulers could be placed would be the recognition by the government of a privileged order of free men in the midst of slaves.[135]

In one of their memorials, the Calcutta petitioners against the act had argued that they should be exempted from the jurisdiction of the local courts because native judicial officers were generally corrupt. Even if he granted its premise, that sort of argument called

132. Minute of March 21, 1836, Dharker, ed., *Minutes*, 173–4.
133. Minute of March 28, 1836, ibid., 177.   134. Ibid., 177–8.
135. Ibid., 180.

forth all of Macaulay's reforming zeal, as well as a personal confession of the extent to which this impulse was being frustrated by what he took to be the lethargy of the Indian people. "What is the great difficulty which meets us whenever we meditate any extensive reform in India?" he asked. His answer was that there was no way of helping men who would not help themselves.

The phenomenon which strikes an observer lately arrived from England with the greatest surprise, and which more than any other damps his hope of being able to serve the people of this country, is their own apathy, their own passiveness under wrong. He comes from a land in which the spirit of the meanest rises up against the insolence or injustice of the richest and the most powerful. He finds himself in a land where the patience of the oppressed invites the oppressor to repeat his injuries.[136]

Thus, to exempt English settlers from any of those evils under which their Hindu neighbors suffered would merely serve to perpetuate such evils. They should be felt, "not only by the mute, the effeminate, the helpless, but by the noisy, the bold and the powerful."[137] It was only by giving the settlers a common interest with the Indians in exposing abuses that those abuses could eventually be amended.[138] This was the voice of Macaulay the activist reformer, to whom India offered above all a vast area ripe for improvement, and who was continually exasperated because the population either did not seem to desire such improvement or, when it did, lacked the will and energy to go about achieving it in the right way.

The conclusive argument in favor of the wisdom of the "Black Act," according to Macaulay, was the nature of the opposition it aroused. While that opposition was at its height, its spokesmen "repeated every day that the English were the conquerors, the lords of the country, the dominant race, the electors of the House of Commons whose legislative power extend[ed] both over the company at home and over the Governor-General in Council here." The firmness with which the government withstood their protests was designated by them as insolent defiance of public opinion. "We were enemies of freedom because we would not suffer a small white aristocracy to domineer over millions."[139] Macaulay had already remarked on this view of things in his charter speech, when he had exclaimed: "God forbid that we should inflict on her [India] the

136. Minute of October 3, 1836, ibid., 190. 137. Idem.
138. Ibid., 190–1. 139. Ibid., 194.

curse of a new caste, that we should send her a new breed of Brahmins, authorised to treat all the native population as Parias!"[140] Now his comment was no less to the point: If the British government in India were to be conducted on such principles, at variance with reason, justice, honor, and the dearest interests of the Indian people, then he himself was "utterly disqualified by all my feelings and opinions from bearing any part in it, and cannot too soon resign my place to some person better fitted to hold it."[141]

Macaulay's resignation would certainly have rejoiced the hearts of that portion of the English community of Calcutta which, stirred to fury by the "Black Act," made use of the press, whose freedom he had helped to ensure, in order to conduct a campaign of vilification against him. At one of the public protest meetings against the hated measure, a proposal to lynch Macaulay was received with rapturous applause.[142] There were many mornings when the attacks against him in the Calcutta press were so virulent that he took steps to hide the newspapers from Hannah. Even on "decent" days, he was reviled as a cheat, a swindler, and a charlatan.[143] During the spring of 1836 Macaulay wrote to Ellis that the last "ode in my praise" he had perused began

> *Soon we hope they will recall ye,*
> *Tom Macaulay, Tom Macaulay.*

The last piece of prose on the same subject had compared him—of all people—to Strafford.[144]

Macaulay did not let this obloquy affect him very much. "To a person accustomed to the hurricanes of English faction," he informed Ellis, "this sort of tempest in a horsepond is merely ridiculous."[145] Furthermore, English opinion outside Calcutta was on his side. In one of his Minutes on the "Black Act," he had noted that in 1826 some of the settlers in the interior had actually petitioned to be deprived of the right of appeal to the Supreme Court in certain kinds of cases, presumably because the procedure was both too lengthy and

---

140. July 10, 1833, *Works*, XI, 575.
141. Minute of October 3, 1836, Dharker, ed., *Minutes*, 194.
142. S. C. Sanial, "Macaulay in Lower Bengal," *Calcutta Review*, CXXIV (1907), 77.
143. Trevelyan, *Life and Letters*, 283-4. See also Hannah, Lady Trevelyan, "Reminiscences." 65, Trinity MSS, in which she comments on T.B.M.'s unpopularity resulting from the "Black Act," and recalls that his private as well as his public character was vilified.
144. T.B.M. to Ellis, May 30, 1836, Trevelyan, *Life and Letters*, 323.   145. Idem.

too expensive for them.[146] Aware of this, Auckland reported to Hobhouse during the summer of 1836 that while Macaulay was unpopular with a large party in Calcutta, "from hence up to Meerut, with every paper published, native or English, there is but one tone, and that is in favour of the measure against which the lawyers of the Supreme Court, and the Party which follows them are about to petition Parliament."[147]

In this instance, Hobhouse was actively—and effectively—on the side of Macaulay. Once again, the Court of Directors was dubious about the measure, and wished to do no more than grant it qualified approval. The Calcutta Bar had sent an emissary named Turton to London in order to stir up opposition in Parliament. But Hobhouse decided to confirm the "Black Act" nonetheless. "This will inflame Mr. Turton's patriotism, but never mind," was his wry comment to Auckland in June 1837. He successfully insisted upon an unqualified approval of the act; approval which, he wrote to Macaulay, would not have been forthcoming without his insistence.[148] With William IV on his deathbed, he felt—rightly—that English public opinion would have little excitement to spare for Oriental politics.[149] When the matter was finally debated in Parliament, during the spring of 1838, a motion to abrogate the "Black Act" brought on behalf of Turton and the Calcutta petitioners was, in the end, withdrawn. Reporting this to Auckland, Hobhouse added a compliment intended primarily for Macaulay, who at the time was already on his way back to England. "I agreed to publish your minutes," he wrote, "which will do you all much credit."[150]

In making any judgment upon these efforts of Macaulay's on behalf of a free press and a uniform system of justice, one must note first of all that in spite of all opposition, the two acts were not countermanded, but remained in force. This in itself is perhaps more of a tribute to Hobhouse's adroit management in London than to the

146. Minute of March 28, 1836, Dharker, ed., *Minutes,* 176.
147. Auckland to Hobhouse, June 20, 1836, Home and Miscellaneous, Vol. 837, I.O.L.
148. Hobhouse to T.B.M., August 30, 1837, Home and Miscellaneous, Vol. 838, I.O.L.
149. Hobhouse to Auckland, June 13, 1837, Home and Miscellaneous, Vol. 838, I.O.L.; same to same, June 1, 1837, Home and Miscellaneous, Vol. 838, I.O.L. A few weeks later, Auckland reported to Hobhouse that the whole subject had by now been nearly forgotten in India. Auckland to Hobhouse, September 8, 1837, Home and Miscellaneous, Vol. 841, I.O.L.
150. Hobhouse to Auckland, April 14, 1838, Home and Miscellaneous, Vol. 841, I.O.L.

energy and eloquence which Macaulay put at the service of these liberal measures. Still, it should not prevent due recognition of his role. He brought to the Indian situation the impulses of his rather advanced form of English Whiggism, heavily shot through with common sense, a concern for justice, and a strong feeling against shirking the realities. The press was in fact free; so why keep it confined in a state of apparent censorship? The existing machinery of appeals by British subjects to the Supreme Court in Calcutta was in fact rarely used; so why retain it at the price of perpetuating the image of a privileged caste, legally superior to the native population? That was the sort of argument Macaulay, along with other reformers, had turned against aspects of the old régime in England. Now he applied it to India.

As a proving ground for liberal ideas, India was, of course, very different from England. If a similarity existed—where Macaulay was concerned—it was that in both countries there existed definite constraints upon his reforming zeal at certain danger points. In England, the danger point was democracy; in India, the abrogation of imperial rule. But just as, in the case of England, he was convinced that universal suffrage was something to be deferred rather than eternally denied, in the case of India, he was not one of those misled by the "illusion of permanence." He was certainly conscious of the need to maintain imperial dominance—witness his stress upon the emergency powers of the Governor-General in Council in the matter of the freedom of the press, and his acceptance of the fact that however impartially it was exercised, British rule was in its essence despotic, and was bound to remain so for the foreseeable future.

With that as a "given," there is at first sight something almost bordering on the fanciful in his insistence that the ruling caste (for that is what it was bound to be as long as the rulers ruled) should not *really* become a caste; just as there may be, to us, an element of the bizarre in his preaching the gospel of laissez faire in early nineteenth-century British India. At the same time, Macaulay's meliorism was so strongly ingrained that he was convinced that, given proper stimulation, India could, and would, in her turn pass through the same stages of development experienced historically by western Europe, eventually taking her place alongside of rather than in subjection to Britain. In his own mind, these two attitudes were concurrent rather than contradictory. But there *was* contradiction in this view of things. Those who did not share his premises or his historical imagination would accept neither his remedies nor his rhetoric. For officials in London, from the King and the Prime Minister down, dramatic phrases about the freedom of the press in India merely meant opening the door to indiscriminate criticism as well as to the possibility of revolution. For some of the British actually resident in India, equal treatment before the law meant the extinction of the very privileges which they believed to be inseparable from their position.

No wonder Hobhouse asked Auckland to keep "B.M." a bit more quiet. The Governor-General's reply to this request, dated June 1836, is worth quoting at some length, for its estimate of both the positive and the negative aspects of Macaulay's accomplishments in India up to that time. Auckland began by remarking that it was neither easy nor agreeable for him to qualify the admiration and regard he bore to Macaulay by any observations about the manner in which he had served. He then continued:

Certainly his conduct has not been prudent; he has weakened his own just influence, and he is not popular here [in Calcutta]. But this feeling against him is aggravated by the interests and the prejudices with which his high vocation of jurisprudence and education must interfere, and he has not dealt with it skillfully. He was encouraged to act too much alone, by the implicit reliance which my two predecessors [Metcalfe and Bentinck] placed in him, and he loved always rather to provoke than to conciliate the antagonists whom he has found in the Council, and to disregard the opposition which he might otherwise raise. In his general views, I for the most part feel warmly with him. In his doctrines and in his details I have often thought him wrong, but his great defect has been, and he does himself great injustice by it, in the exaggeration with which, when provoked to controversy, he states his own views and opinions.[151]

It is both instructive and amusing to compare Auckland's judgment of Macaulay with Macaulay's judgment of Bentinck: "The art of conciliating was one of the few parts of an excellent ruler which were wanting to my friend Lord William," he wrote to Spring-Rice. "Had he possessed that art, he would have been incomparably the best governor that England ever sent to India."[152] It was certainly an art that Macaulay himself lacked to a conspicuous degree; though Auckland, continuing his letter to Hobhouse, went on to remark that for himself he could truly say that he found Macaulay the

151. Auckland to Hobhouse, June 20, 1836, Home and Miscellaneous, Vol. 837, I.O.L.

152. T.B.M. to Spring-Rice, February 8, 1836, "Macaulay Writes Home," *Bodleian Library Record*, 251.

reverse of unreasonable and unyielding. They had differed, but had made some concessions to each other, on Macaulay's "favourite crotchet" of preambles. And Macaulay had willingly abandoned a projected act allowing appeals to a single judge, because the Governor-General thought it ill-timed. Macaulay had also agreed with Auckland about the propriety of the Council's obligation to obtain the support of the judges of the Supreme Court in every case of legal importance; even though, by the Charter Act of 1833, it was no longer required to do so. The Governor-General concluded as follows:

I know that in his great work of a code for India, he has none of the faults that have been charged upon him. His first ambition of doing good, and of gaining honour for his career in India rests on this; all the application and all the energies of his mind are given to it.[153]

A very fair and balanced estimate on the part of Auckland, lending perspective to that image of the meddlesome and injudicious reformer which had induced Melbourne to ask his president of the Board of Control to calm Macaulay down.

153. Auckland to Hobhouse, June 20, 1836, Home and Miscellaneous, Vol. 837, I.O.L.

XII

INDIAN EDUCATION: THE MINUTE

IT WAS HIS TENDENCY TO EXAGGERATE IN CONTROVERSY THAT LORD Auckland had singled out as the trait most damaging to Macaulay's work and reputation in India. Nowhere did that tendency show itself more strikingly than in the great battle over the future of Indian education. And it was his part in that battle which, along with his principal authorship of the Indian penal code, constitutes, in retrospect, Macaulay's major and most controversial activity during his Indian years.

In spite of thirty years of scholarship to the contrary, there is still widely current a simplistic version of Macaulay's role in the education controversy, which runs more or less as follows: In 1834 there raged a controversy over what form Indian education should assume in the future. Several questions were at issue. Was higher education in India mainly to be carried on in Arabic, Persian, and Sanskrit? Were the Indian vernacular languages to be used and fostered in elementary education? Above all, what about the place of English? Macaulay arrived; wrote his famous Minute on the subject in the spring of 1835; and the decision in favor of English was taken as a result, with all its fateful consequences.

The actual story of what happened is far more complex; and the issues it involved went beyond language and education. In order to understand them and to arrive at a proper estimate of Macaulay's part in them, it is essential to know something about the historical background of the Orientalist-Anglicist controversy; to look upon it not merely as a dramatic flare-up in 1834, but, rather, as a conflict that had been in the making for at least a generation. Its roots lay in those changing attitudes of the English toward India and its inhabitants which we have already had occasion to note. The Warren Hastings tradition, based primarily upon the desire on the part of Englishmen in India to acquaint themselves to the fullest extent with its languages and culture, in order to assimilate themselves to their surroundings, gradually gave way to the proposition that it would be more desirable for Indians to become acquainted with Western culture and the English language, so that they might be able to assimilate themselves to their rulers.

In 1781 Hastings himself had founded the Calcutta Madrassa (or Arabic College), where Muslims were trained in the principles and practice of Islamic law. Ten years later, Jonathan Duncan, an Orientalist scholar-administrator, founded Sanskrit College at Benares for the preservation and cultivation of the laws, literature, and religion of the Hindus. Both these institutions, supported by the government, were concerned with Indian learning and intended for Indians. But in 1800 Wellesley established the College of Fort William in Calcutta, intended for the higher education and training of servants of the East India Company who had come out to India in their teens and who were to be prepared at the new college to play their parts as judges, officials, and administrators.[1] Here Arabic, Persian, and Sanskrit as well as six Indian vernaculars were to be taught. Students were to have available to them courses in Hindu and Muslim as well as English law. And there were to be opportunities for studying Indian as well as European history and civilization.

Fort William College was financed by means of small deductions from the salaries of all company servants in India. It drew both inspiration and faculty from the Asiatic Society of Bengal, whose first president had been the great Sir William Jones, and whose activities continued to be built around the sympathetic scholarly study of Indian civilization. Two Orientalists, Horace Hayman Wilson and James Prinsep, who in succession held the position of secretary to the Society from 1811 to 1833 and from 1833 to 1838, were both closely associated with the college. It served not only as a training center for civil servants, but also, in part through literary patronage, as a link between Bengali intellectuals and the English.

1. For the story of Fort William College, see David Kopf, *British Orientalism and the Bengal Renaissance* (Berkeley, Calif., 1969), 43–126.

In 1807 the European curriculum of Fort William College was transferred to the new Indian Civil Service College at Haileybury, founded two years earlier; henceforth, new servants of the company such as Charles Trevelyan received a portion of their training in England, before completing it with Oriental studies in Calcutta. Lord Minto, Governor-General from 1807 to 1813, continued Wellesley's policy of reserving top government posts for those students who performed best at Fort William. It should be kept in mind that, as David Kopf has recently made clear in his book on the subject, the ethos of the college was not exclusively based upon a kind of antiquarian preservation of Sanskrit, Arabic, and Persian philology, literature, and history; though these subjects, of course, provided the principal fields of study. The vernaculars also received due attention; and there was general agreement among the faculty that social and cultural change in India was inevitable. But it was to come about by means of a rediscovery on the part of the Indians of the roots of their own civilization; to be organically "engrafted" rather than crudely imposed.

The basic attitudes inculcated at Fort William College were undoubtedly sympathetic to Oriental traditions and culture. Most of those who studied there, among them James Prinsep's brother Henry Thoby, who was to become Macaulay's chief antagonist in India, retained that outlook. A few, including Charles Trevelyan, turned against it. It was the latter who, in 1834, noted gleefully that

among other honours with which the administration of Lord William Bentinck will descend to posterity, it will not be the least, that in his time the Oriental mania, which broke out under Lord Wellesley's Government; advanced under Lord Minto's; was in the height of its career under Lord Hastings's; and began to flag under Lord Amherst's, has completely exhausted itself.[2]

Part of the evidence for this statement was that the period of Bentinck's administration had witnessed the virtual cessation of Fort William College as an educational institution, under an order of the Governor-General's, dated 1830, which brought professorships and lectures delivered to students to an end. But this event, as well as the victory of the "Anglicists" on the General Committee of Public Instruction five years later, represented not so much sudden reversals of policy as the final triumph of anti-Orientalist currents, mainly

2. Charles Trevelyan, J. Prinsep, et al., *The Application of the Roman Alphabet to all the Oriental Languages* (Serampore, 1834) , 21.

Evangelical and Utilitarian in origin, that had already exerted their influence for some time.

In 1792 Charles Grant, in his *Observations on the State of Society among the Asiatic Subjects of Great Britain* (which he submitted to the Court of Directors of the company in 1797, and which for many years remained the key document expounding Evangelical views on what was to be done in India), had proposed English rather than the Indian vernaculars as the most effective weapon with which to undermine the Hindu fabric of error. The use and understanding of the English language would enable the Hindus to reason, and to obtain new and better views of their duty as rational and Christian creatures. The absurdity and falsehood of their myths would be dispelled. With the spread of English arts, science, and philosophy going hand in hand with the spread of Christianity, the Indian people would be able to rise in the scale of human beings.[3] Grant noted the fact that some of the opponents of this view, with the loss of the American colonies in mind, had expressed fears about the unfortunate political effects that widespread dissemination of English and Christianity might have upon the Indian people. Grant had no such fears. It was, after all, a lack of religion that had left the French lower orders a prey to Jacobin ideas. As for the American example, that was irrelevant. For "the spirit of English liberty is not to be caught from a written description of it, by distant and feeble Asiatics."[4]

When the charter of the East India Company came before Parliament for renewal in 1813, the Evangelicals (including Zachary Macaulay as well as Grant) had become sufficiently influential to include in the Charter Act of that year not only a provision legally entitling missionaries to enter India, but also the first legislated assignment of public revenues for Indian education. In assessing the significance of this measure it should be kept in mind that the first such grant for education in England was not made until twenty years later. The Act of 1813 stipulated that

a sum of not less than one lac of rupees [£10,000] in each year shall be set apart and applied to the revival and improvement of literature and the encouragement of the learned natives of India, and for the introduction

3. Quoted in H. Sharp, ed., *Selections from Educational Records 1781–1839* (Calcutta, 1920) , 81–6.

4. Quoted by Ainslie T. Embree, *Charles Grant and British Rule in India* (London, 1962) , 154.

and promotion of a knowledge of the sciences among the inhabitants of the British territories in India.[5]

The intention of this provision seemed to be to accomplish two different aims at one and the same time: to foster both Oriental learning and Western science.

The precise meaning of the provision was to become the subject of intense dispute and, indeed, the main subject matter of Macaulay's Education Minute of 1835. But for the first ten years after enactment of the charter renewal, they meant nothing at all. For nothing was done. Somewhat surprisingly, in view of Grant's membership of and influence in that body, the Court of Directors in 1814 despatched a directive on education to the Governor-General, now Lord Hastings, which discouraged the setting up of any new colleges, on the ground that native Indians by caste and reputation would not submit to the subordination and discipline of such institutions; and recommended instead that pecuniary assistance might be given to learned Hindus teaching in private houses. For the rest, the directive emphasized the importance of consulting the feelings and even of yielding to the prejudices of the Indians. Sanskrit ethics and laws were recommended as subjects of study to those preparing for a judicial career. The company's servants were encouraged to learn Sanskrit. Sanskrit tracts dealing with plants and drugs were recommended to European medical men for useful study. Sanskrit tracts on astronomy and algebra, though they would not constitute a significant addition to the achievements of European science, "might be made to form links of communication between the natives and the gentlemen in our service, who are attached to the Observatory and to the department of engineers, and by such intercourse the natives might gradually be led to adopt modern improvements in those and other sciences."[6]

Here, then, was the idea of "engrafting" Western knowledge and innovations upon Indian cultural traditions by means of Sanskrit and Arabic, the same idea that was being advocated by some of the leading Orientalists at the College of Fort William. Lord Hastings himself, however, after following the advice of the Court of Directors to visit the holy city of Benares in order to see what could be done to improve existing Hindu institutions of higher education there, was so discouraged by the decadence he found that he came to feel that the money appropriated by the Act of 1813 might be utilized far

5. Sharp, *Educational Records*, 22.   6. Ibid., 23-4.

more advantageously to foster vernacular schools.[7] But the prospect of providing education for the Indian masses presented a daunting task, whether in terms of finance, staffing, or sheer geographical coverage. It was probably for this reason that nothing at all was undertaken with the parliamentary grant for about a decade, and that the proposal which led to the establishment of a General Committee of Public Instruction in 1823 was couched in more limited terms.[8]

That proposal stated that the government should concern itself mainly with the instruction of those who would themselves become teachers, and with the publication of useful works in the Indian vernaculars. The great mass of the Indian people was described as too poor, as well as too anxious to have their children find some gainful employment, to allow them to remain for any length of time under tuition. So the spread of education to the people at large had to come indirectly, by way of an educated élite. Here is the first appearance of the theory of "downward filtration" that was to constitute such an important part of Macaulay's thinking about Indian education. It was combined in this proposal of 1823 with the view that the difficulties of English as a common language were generally overrated, and that the new committee should concern itself with its practicability.

It is of some significance that the author of this proposal was Holt Mackenzie, like Charles Trevelyan one of the brilliant graduates of the College of Fort William who had come to repudiate the Orientalism inculcated there in favor of Utilitarian views.[9] For these views gradually came to play an ever larger role in the debate on the future of Indian education. In 1819 James Mill had been appointed assistant examiner for the Court of Directors of the East India Company, and during the 1820's the keynote of the despatches from the court on the subject of education increasingly reflected the sentiments of the author of the *History of India*. Thus, in a despatch which he had a principal part in writing in 1824 on the subject of the Calcutta Madrassa and the Hindu College at Benares, it was laid down that "the great end should not have been to teach Hindoo learning, but useful learning." It had been wrong to set up institutions for the purpose of merely teaching Indian and Muslim literature since these subjects contained much that was probably

7. Kopf, *Bengal Renaissance*, 152–3.
8. Sharp, *Educational Records*, 59–61.
9. See Kopf, *Bengal Renaissance*, 105.

mischievous, and in only a small portion of them was utility in any way involved.[10]

The current Governor-General, Lord Amherst, passed this despatch on to his newly appointed General Committee of Public Instruction. He had instructed that committee to submit from time to time "the suggestion of such measures as it may appear expedient to adopt with a view to the better instruction of the people, to the introduction of useful knowledge, including the sciences and arts of Europe, and to the improvement of their moral character."[11] The new committee's tough and defensive reaction to the despatch shows the extent to which in its early days it was dominated by the Orientalists. It pointed out in reply that the actual state of public feeling still constituted an impediment to any general introduction of Western literature or science; that the metaphysical sciences, as found in Sanskrit and Arabic writings, were fully as worthy of being studied in those languages as in any other; and that poetry was a legitimate object of study.[12]

Until the Bentinck era, the committee's actual policy consisted of a series of compromises. On the one hand, it did encourage—and, indeed, spent the greater part of its funds on—English education at various levels. On the other hand, having taken the Calcutta Madrassa and Sanskrit College at Benares under its charge, it also continued to do its best to foster Oriental learning. It sponsored the opening of a new Sanskrit College at Calcutta (1824) and, in the following year, of Delhi College, for instruction in Arabic, Persian, and Sanskrit. It should be noted that the courses at the new Sanskrit College were by no means entirely concerned with Oriental subjects. H. H. Wilson, largely responsible for the curriculum, saw to it that an extensive schedule of science courses was also available. And English was taught at the college.[13] Still, voices of protest against the inutility of any Oriental learning were making themselves increasingly heard. Not all came from Utilitarian or Evangelical sources.

From 1823 until the time of his death in 1826, the Bishop of Calcutta was Reginald Heber, author of the hymn "From Greenland's Icy Mountains" and of a *Narrative of a Journey Through the Upper*

10. Despatch of directors to Governor-General, February 18, 1824, *Parliamentary Papers*, IX (1831-2), Appendix 1, 488. On the extent of Mill's authorship of the despatches of that year, see Kenneth Ballhatchet, *Social Policy and Social Change in Western India, 1817–1830* (London, 1957), 257.

11. H. Woodrow, *Macaulay's Minutes on Education in India Written in the Years 1835, 1836, and 1837 and now first Collected from Records in the Department of Public Instruction* (Calcutta, 1862), 3.

12. Sharp, *Educational Records*, 95-8.   13. Kopf, *Bengal Renaissance*, 183.

Provinces of India.[14] That book contained some scathing comments about the Sanskrit colleges at Benares and Calcutta. Students there were said to be wasting their time with a science that knew nothing of Galileo, Copernicus, and Bacon; a literature that amounted to nothing but a series of endless refinements of its grammar, versification, and poetry; and a geography that enumerated six earths and seven seas supported on the back of a huge tortoise. The bishop wanted English grammar, Hume's *History,* Western geography, and the Gospel taught instead.[15]

Some of Heber's enthusiasm for English education derived from his delight at the extent to which certain Calcutta Hindus had become Anglicized by the early 1820's. He was pleased to find that some wealthy Indians "now affect to have their houses decorated with Corinthian pillars, and filled with English furniture." It was indeed true that much of the impulse for more useful learning and for the greater use of English in its teaching came from within the Hindu community of Bengal. The motive was largely practical. Those Hindus who wished to work for or with English merchants, administrators, and judges naturally had very pragmatic reasons for learning the language. But it was not merely a matter of job-seekers wanting to better their lot.

In his excellent book *Social Ideas and Social Change in Bengal, 1818–1835,*[16] Salahuddin Ahmed has shown that in the Bengal of the 1820's and 1830's there had come into existence an Indian middle class ranging from landowners, merchants, and bankers at the top to artisans and clerks at the bottom. It was a class in which wealth was the basis of leadership; and a great deal of social mobility existed within it. Calcutta was its cultural center. Many Hindus there favored British rule, participated actively in the free trade campaign waged by the British merchant community between 1813 and 1833, and willingly exposed themselves to the impact of the West. By 1816 the desire on the part of the urbanized and wealthy Bengali Hindus to study European literature and science had become so great that, at their own expense, they established Hindu College for that purpose. It came under the aegis of the General Committee of Public Instruction in 1824, at a time when it was in a rather parlous financial state. And it received a certain amount of assistance from the committee, including faculty, buildings, and English books.[17]

14. London, 1828.
15. Elmer Cutts, "The Background of Macaulay's Minute," *American Historical Review,* LVIII (1952–3) , 849–50.
16. Leiden, 1965.   17. Kopf, *Bengal Renaissance,* 182–3.

Professor Kopf has been at pains to show that the founders of Hindu College did not want to repudiate their religious heritage, and that its original aim was "useful knowledge from the West transmitted without ethnocentric bias," rather than "secular knowledge in Western dress."[18] But the founders did insist that the college not teach Hindu theology and metaphysics; and its curriculum emphasized Western history and literature as well as the natural sciences. Hindu College had the support not only of the conservative, upper-caste Hindus who wrote its charter, but also of the great liberal reformer and syncretist Ram Mohan Roy, a leading advocate of English culture and education until his death in Bristol in 1833, and the man Bentham once addressed as "intensely admired and dearly beloved collaborator in the service of mankind."

It was Ram Mohan Roy who protested to Lord Amherst at the end of 1823 about the projected Sanskrit College for Calcutta. He had hoped, he wrote, that the English would instruct Indians in mathematics, natural philosophy, and the useful sciences. Instead, they were setting up yet another institution to purvey knowledge already current in India. In any event, to learn Sanskrit properly took a lifetime, and was too difficult for most students. No improvement could be expected from it or from Vedantic speculations such as "In what manner is the soul absorbed into the deity?" or "Why is the killer of a goat sinless on pronouncing certain passages of the Veda?" He asked the Governor-General to compare the condition of science and literature in Europe before the time of Bacon with the progress of knowledge since Bacon wrote. If the intention had been to keep the British nation in ignorance of real knowledge, the Baconian philosophy would not have been allowed to displace the system of the Schoolmen. In the same way, the Sanskrit system of education was best calculated to keep India in ignorance. What the country required instead was a more useful and liberal system of instruction, based on the European model.[19]

Ram Mohan Roy, reformer rather than revolutionary, wanted to bring Eastern and Western learning and culture together. To the left of him were far more thoroughgoing Indian "Westernizers" such as Henry Derozio, who attacked Roy and his supporters as "half-liberals." The struggle of such Westernizers against what they considered to be the absurd and irrational aspects of Hinduism, along with the currents of thought represented by Hindu Colllege and Ram

18. Ibid., 181.

19. R. Roy to Amherst, December 11, November 12, 1823, Sharp, *Educational Records,* 99–101.

Mohan Roy, helped to create a climate of opinion that could be utilized by Bentinck, by Trevelyan, and eventually by Macaulay in the campaign on behalf of English as a linguistic and cultural force. For Bentinck, who arrived as Governor-General in 1828, that campaign was to some extent a very practical matter, divorced from ideology. He had been sent to India to economize. The East India Company's charter was coming up for renewal in 1833, and the directors wanted the finances of the company to be in good order. One of Bentinck's principal means of carrying out these economies was to make increasing use of Indians in judicial and administrative posts, and thus to reduce the cost of the English establishment. It was, in fact, at Bentinck's insistence that the Charter Act of 1833 contained the clause—so eloquently defended by Macaulay—which provided for the equal admission of Indians to every office in India, irrespective of religion, birth, descent, or color.[20] It was essential for those Indians to be able to speak and understand English; and the old educational policy was simply not producing a sufficient number of qualified candidates. What was policy on Bentinck's part coincided, as we have seen, with a widespread demand on the part of the growing urban middle class in Bengal for English books and instruction. That demand, based largely on worldly considerations, was increasing at a phenomenal rate in the early 1830's.[21] Here again, an economic factor entered in. Resources were limited. While it took a certain amount of money to supply the demand for English textbooks, the cost of doing so was as nothing compared to the really exorbitant expense of translating those books on a large enough scale into the Indian vernaculars.[22]

But more than merely practical considerations of this sort made Bentinck the partisan of an Anglicizing policy from the very moment of his arrival in India. A moderate Evangelical as well as an admirer of Bentham, he was convinced of the superiority of Western to Indian ideas and institutions. He was also certain that English must be the means by which those ideas and institutions were introduced into India. As Governor of Madras in 1806, he had endorsed a plan for the establishment of free English schools there. Twenty-three years later, he spoke of "the British [sic] language" as "the key of all improvements."[23] It was due to his efforts that English replaced

20. Bruce T. McCully, *English Education and the Origins of Indian Nationalism* (New York, 1940) , 63.
21. Salahuddin Ahmed, *Bengal*, 165.
22. Edwardes, *Raj*, 138.
23. Lord William Bentinck to Metcalfe, September 16, 1829, quoted by Spear, "Bentinck," *Journal of Indian History*, 109.

Persian (a heritage of the Mughuls) as the official government language and as the language used in the higher courts of justice.

Meanwhile, despatches from the Court of Directors continued to stress utilitarian considerations. We are told on good authority that by 1830 a decisive change of feeling had taken place among the directors; that there was by then far less respect than there had at one time existed among them for Indian culture and learning.[24] A despatch sent by them at the time pointed out that the sort of education that must commence with a thorough study of English could be placed within the reach of only a small proportion of Indians; but that

intelligent natives who have been thus educated, may, as teachers in colleges and schools, or as the writers and translators of useful books, contribute in an eminent degree to the more general extension among their countrymen of a portion of the acquirements which they have themselves gained, and may communicate in some degree to the native literature, and to the minds of the native community, that improved spirit which it is to be hoped they will themselves have imbibed from the influence of European ideas and sentiments.

The despatch ended with the recommendation that it be made known that those Indians who undertook an extensive program of English study were to be held in high honor by the government.[25]

Testifying before the Select Committee which looked into the affairs of the East India Company in 1832, prior to the Charter Act of the following year, James Mill (for whom law, not language, was the principal key to improvement) echoed that portion of the despatch just cited which had expressed pessimism about the prospect of more than a very small number of Indians being able to master English thoroughly. Mill favored the introduction of more Indians into the government, but denied that a knowledge of English would make them any fitter for most of the positions in which they would find themselves. True, knowing English literature would enlighten their understandings. But that could be accomplished better and more quickly by translating European texts into their own languages. When asked whether community of language between the English and the Indians would not help to identify the

24. Percival Spear, "Bentinck and Education," *Cambridge Historical Journal,* VI (1938) , 84.
25. Court of Directors to Governor-General, September 29, 1830, *Parliamentary Papers,* IX (1831–2) , Appendix 1, 495.

Indian people with their governors, Mill gloomily commented that such linguistic community had not, after all, identified the Irish people with their governors. He conceded that it was desirable that the people of India should speak English; but maintained that the prospect of this was chimerical.[26]

The Select Committee's report (1832) reflected more optimism about English than Mill's testimony. The committee, of which Macaulay was a member, concluded that the general cultivation of English was most desirable, "both with a view to the introduction of the natives into places of trust, and as a powerful means of operating favorably on their habits and character." The considerable partiality prevailing in favor of the English language and of English literature among the Indians, the report continued, had not hitherto met with the consideration and encouragement it deserved from the government.[27] Bentinck himself certainly did not merit such a reproof. All his own appointments to the General Committee of Public Instruction were of convinced Anglicists; among them (in 1833) Charles Trevelyan, who at once began to attack his colleagues on the committee with righteous fury.

In describing the character and personality of his prospective brother-in-law to Margaret early in December 1834, Macaulay spoke of him as "indeed quite at the head of that active party among the younger servants of the company who take the side of improvement. In particular he is the soul of every scheme for diffusing education among the natives of this country." Trevelyan had been on the warpath for some months. Records of the battle he waged exist in a volume entitled *The Application of the Roman Alphabet to All the Oriental Languages,* a collection of letters previously printed in various Calcutta periodicals and subsequently published in book form.[28] From this volume one derives a vivid sense of how vehement the Anglicist-Orientalist controversy had already become by 1833. In a letter dated January 1834, Trevelyan had lashed out at John Tytler, director of the Native Medical Institution in Calcutta, who had called the project of printing Oriental books in Roman characters a waste of money, and at James Prinsep, Oriental linguist and philologist, who had dubbed it "ultra radicalism." Trevelyan (whose pet project it was) replied that while scarcely any encouragement was offered to Muslims who were studying English in Calcutta, they were bribed to the tune of 30 rupees a month to cultivate Arabic. As

26. Evidence of James Mill, February 21, 1832, ibid., 55–7.
27. Quoted by McCully, *English Education*, 62.   28. Serampore, 1834.

a result, it was hard to find a single Muslim in Calcutta who had received a tolerable education. Delhi offered a striking contrast. There, both Muslims and Hindus were encouraged to study English literature and science, and did so with enthusiasm. If this was ultra radicalism, so be it. Printing Oriental books in Roman letters would end the curse of Babel and would help the gradual formation in India of "a national literature embodying in itself the selected knowledge of the whole civilized world."[29] Writing with all the considerable sense of moral superiority at his command, Trevelyan announced that it was particularly desirable to engraft upon the popular languages of the East such words as "virtue," "honour," "gratitude," "patriotism," and "public spirit," for which at present it was difficult to find synonyms. He threw Prinsep's accusation of ultra radicalism back in his face in asking whether, "in his ultra toryism," he would express English words in Sanskrit, Arabic, or Persian characters.

It was hardly an accident that political terminology was being employed in the linguistic battle. The controversy had political overtones, certainly from the point of view of the reforming party. But what emerged most forcefully from Trevelyan's polemics, apart from his contempt for the moral deficiencies of the Indian people, was his real hatred of Orientalism, and particularly of the sort of academic Orientalism which, he felt with some justice, dominated the General Committee of Public Instruction. That committee, he wrote, had been set up not in order to raise the reputation of Calcutta as a seat of Oriental literature, but in order to provide a cheap and easy means of instruction for the people of the Bengal presidency. Wellesley's aim had been to educate Europeans in the languages of the East. "Our object is to educate Asiatics in the sciences of the West."[30]

The general tenor of Trevelyan's attitude toward his Orientalist colleagues may best be gathered from his sarcastic and waspish remark that "we never meant to aspire to the honour of knighthood, nor did the prospect of filling the Oriental chairs in the universities of England ever enter into our imaginations."[31] This anti-academicism, directed at men like H. H. Wilson who had just been elected to the chair of Sanskrit at Oxford, was something that Bentinck, Trevelyan, and Macaulay had in common; and there is no doubt that it intensified their sense of solidarity as Anglicists. They saw themselves representing utility and public responsibility, as against the Ori-

29. *Roman Alphabet*, 4, 13.   30. Ibid., 16.   31. Ibid., 18.

entalists who, from their point of view, represented uselessness and the ivory tower. Trevelyan listed a number of books printed under the direction of the General Committee of Public Instruction—13,000 in Sanskrit, 5,600 in Arabic, 2,500 in Persian, 2,000 in Hindi. Not a single book had been printed by the committee in Bengali or Urdu, nor had translations into popular languages been undertaken. Instead of using the funds intended by the British Parliament to be spent on popular education for that purpose, the committee had been printing erotic Sanskrit dramas teaching lechery in its most seductive forms.

Meanwhile, according to Trevelyan, the Oriental mania that had begun under Wellesley had completely exhausted itself. Public opinion had come alive to the fact that the shortest and most effective way of communicating knowledge to the people of India was by teaching Indian youths English literature; and, when this was impracticable, by providing them with translations of scientific works in their own languages. But as the general public had gradually advanced toward this view of things, the General Committee on Public Instruction had retreated from it. Instead of instructing the Indian people, some of its members were mainly concerned with their own reputation for Oriental learning. "It seems to have been overlooked," Trevelyan remarked, "that the annual lakh of rupees was assigned by Parliament *for the education of the youth of India,* and that it was never intended from this source to provide matter for the lucubrations of Messrs. Bopp and Schlegel, or even to gratify the taste of the professors in English Universities."[32] What was required was not a Babel of dead languages, but rather living languages as English and the Indian vernaculars: "We do not want an ocean of words, but an influx of ideas."[33]

Here, then, was Trevelyan's conception of the British role in Indian education: not to foster Oriental studies in any way, but to bring Western knowledge to the people, either by means of English or through the vernaculars. James Prinsep's reply, dated January 2, 1834 is by no means a defense of academic Oriental studies; but, rather, a definition of what he and other Orientalists meant by "engrafting." The instruction, the business, and eventually the literature of India, Prinsep wrote, must be in the vernacular.

Our main aim ought to be to foster that, and transfuse into it the substance of our own advanced knowledge. Those whom we instruct in

32. Ibid., 24.   33. Ibid., 26.

English are to be the pioneers and interpreters of this peaceful and insensible innovation, not the uncompromising guerillas of a violent and *ultraradical* subversion of all that now exists.[34]

Trevelyan, in his turn, reverted to what was transpiring at the Calcutta Madrassa, "where the youth of India are bribed, by the offer of excessive emoluments, to imbibe systems of error, which we all know have been exploded, and their falsehood demonstrated years ago." These students were being bribed to study Ptolemy, whereas at Hindu College, they got nothing for studying Newton and had to pay besides.[35] Trevelyan agreed with Prinsep that those who received English instruction were to be the pioneers and interpreters of a peaceful and insensible invasion. They must be the translators, "the noble artificers of the literature which will hereafter constitute the medium through which the treasures of knowledge will be laid open to the mass of their countrymen."[36] But Prinsep seemed to want these creators of a new vernacular literature to learn Persian; whereas Trevelyan wanted them to learn English. It was only those who had mastered English who would be able to translate European science into the Indian vernaculars.[37]

In yet another letter published in this volume, John Tytler, active as a translator of books into Arabic, conceded in his turn not only that the poetry and romances of the East were greatly inferior to those of the West, but also that "Eastern sciences bear scarcely more proportion to those of Europe, than the first lispings of an infant to the ratiocinations of man."[38] Oriental studies helped to develop the students' speculative faculty; and because the Indian classical languages were so closely linked to the vernaculars, a knowledge of the former was absolutely essential for those who wished to make the latter into receptacles for Western science and knowledge.[39]

From these polemical letters emerge some significant points of agreement and disagreement between Trevelyan and his opponents, which can be supported by other evidence. It appears, for example, that there was no dispute between Orientalists and Anglicists about the superiority of Western to Eastern literature and learning. Thus Henry Thoby Prinsep, James's brother and himself a leading member of the Orientalist Party, stated that there was nothing he desired more than that the taste for the languages and science of Europe should be communicated to the rising generation of Mohammedans

34. Ibid., 35.   35. Letter dated January 4, 1834, ibid., 37–8.   36. Ibid., 38.
37. Ibid., 39.   38. Ibid., 55.   39. Ibid., 56.

and deeply implanted amongst them: "Encourage English and European science say I as earnestly as the hottest of the enthusiasts of fewer years and less experience." What he opposed was promotion rather than encouragement of English, and the deprecation of all but Western knowledge. But he referred without hesitation to "the direction to true science and good taste in literature which the superior lights of Europe ought to enable us to bestow."[40]

There was also general agreement about the ultimate desirability of vernacular education for the mass of the people of India, based on a vernacular literature infused to some extent with Western ideas and values. In the India of the 1830's, very little popular elementary education was available, and vernacular learning and literature were at a low ebb.[41] Something had to be done to revive them. Even H. H. Wilson, the most extreme of the Orientalists, spoke of rearing an indigenous literature on the basis of Western models, as part of the intellectual, moral, and religious improvement of the people of India.[42] Trevelyan granted in 1838 that both sides agreed that while the vernacular languages contained as yet neither sufficient literary nor scientific vocabulary for a liberal education, vernacular instruction at the lower levels was the ultimate object desired. There was, at the time, some prejudice against the vernaculars on the part of educated Hindus. But Bentinck had no such prejudices. In fact, he gave a great impetus to the vernaculars when, after abolishing Persian and introducing English as the language of the higher law courts, he stipulated that the vernaculars be the language of the lower courts.[43] It is probably true that the Orientalists cared more about the classical Indian languages than about the vernaculars; just as most Anglicists cared more about English than about vernacular education. But that does not invalidate the point that in their thinking about Indian education, both parties had the vernaculars very much in mind.

What, then, were the matters at issue? They revolved about the *means* to be employed for revitalizing the vernaculars, and about the

40. H. T. Prinsep, August 13, 1834, and March 9, 1834, Indian Public Consultations, LXVI (1835), I.O.L.; Minute of May 20, 1835, Sharp, *Educational Records*, 139.

41. Edward Thompson and G. T. Garratt, *Rise and Fulfilment of British Rule in India* (London, 1934), 313.

42. H. H. Wilson, "Education of the Natives of India," *Asiatic Journal*, n.s., XIX (1836), 15. But Gerald and Natalie Robinson Sirkin, "The Battle of Indian Education: Macaulay's Opening Salvo," *Victorian Studies*, XIV (1971), 412, have pointed out that there was calculated ambiguity here, and that Wilson's support for vernacular education was not genuine.

43. Thompson and Garratt, *Rise and Fulfilment*, 315.

scope of the educational system to be instituted. The Orientalists maintained that the only possible way of breathing new life into the vernaculars was through the Indian classical languages. There were in existence, of course, literally hundreds of different Indian vernacular dialects. But of the principal ones in the region of Bengal, apart from Bengali, Hindi was pure Hindustani derived from Sanskrit, and Urdu was an Arabicized and Persianized kind of Hindustani. For someone like H. H. Wilson, who believed that an Indian vernacular literature had to be constructed out of a mixture of European ideas and "home-spun," it was absolutely essential that Sanskrit and Arabic be cultivated, if the Indian people were eventually to have a literature of their own. No man ignorant of Sanskrit or Arabic could write Hindustani or Bengali with elegance, purity, or precision.[44] Testifying before the House of Lords Select Committee on the Government of Her Majesty's Indian Territories in 1853, Wilson (then Boden Professor of Sanskrit at Oxford) stated that in the country districts outside Calcutta, between half and three-quarters of the words an educated native who was sent there would have to use would be Sanskrit, so intimately was it related to both Hindi and Bengali.[45]

The Anglicists, on the other hand, believed, in the words of V. G. Kiernan, that the Indian vernaculars were *harmfully* tied to Sanskrit and Arabic, whose professors they regarded as religious obscurantists. "The Indian mind had walled itself up inside such a prison that only a new language could give it a ladder of escape."[46]

That new language, so far as Trevelyan was concerned, had to be English. A vernacular literature consisting not of dull translations, but of original works, could come only from minds saturated with English knowledge and tastes formed by the study of English masterpieces. He had, so he claimed in his tract *On the Education of the People of India,* nothing against Oriental learning. The Asiatic Society must continue its researches; India's past must continue to be studied. The Hindus "were a literary people when we were barbarians; and after centuries of revolution, and anarchy, and subjection to foreign rule, they are still a literary people, now that we have

44. Wilson, "Education," *Asiatic Journal,* 14–15. See G. and N. Sirkin, "Macaulay," *Victorian Studies,* 420, for evidence for the contrary view.

45. July 5, 1853, *Parliamentary Papers,* XXXII (1852–3), 263–4, 274. See also A. Troyer, "Report on the Sanskrit College," January 31, 1835, Sharp, *Educational Records,* 41.

46. V. G. Kiernan, *The Lords of Human Kind: European Attitudes Towards the Outside World in the Imperial Age* (London, 1969), 41.

arrived at the highest existing point of civilization." But Trevelyan refused to admit that what the Orientalists had been doing contributed anything at all to the instruction of the Indian people at large. "Education was conducted [by them] in a way more adapted for the lecture-room of a German university, than for the enlightenment of benighted Asiatics."[47]

The last sentence contains a clue concerning the second major difference between the Orientalists and the Anglicists, which had to do with the extent rather than the fact of English instruction. The Orientalists, so H. H. Wilson testified in 1853, had not been disinclined to encourage the study of English, but they had not wanted to make it the sole means of diffusing useful knowledge.[48] This is confirmed by a letter that Wilson, shortly after his return from India, wrote to a Bengali friend, Ram Camul Sen, in the summer of 1834. In it he described Bentinck as "an ignorant man who has a vigorous mind and quiet observation but who never reads and therefore, often judges wrongly." Neither he nor Trevelyan knew what he was doing. English "should be extensively studied, no doubt," but the improvement of the native dialects depended upon Sanskrit. Thus Sanskrit as well as English must be cultivated. "It is a visionary absurdity to think of making English the language of India."[49]

Twenty years earlier, there had been a split among the members of the Fort William College council between those Orientalists, the "classical" group, who favored an élitist, Sanskritic, high-culture program, and those, the "vernacularists," who preferred a scheme that would reach the mass of the people mainly through the indigenous languages.[50] That conflict had ended in a compromise, with the Orientalists on the General Committee of Public Instruction very much aware of the desirability of pursuing Oriental learning at a high level as well as reinvigorating the vernaculars by means of the classical languages. But there is no doubt that, in the nature of the case, a considerable amount of cultural élitism continued to mark the Orientalist position. This helps to explain why those who held it considered Trevelyan's educational schemes as "ultra radical"; and why the prospect of English, not as the language of a specially qualified élite, but as the national language of India, not only struck them as totally unrealistic, but literally appalled them.

47. Charles Trevelyan, *On the Education of the People of India* (London, 1838), 175, 183, 184.
48. July 15, 1853, *Parliamentary Papers*, XXXII (1852–3), 264.
49. Wilson to Sen, August 20, 1834, quoted by Kopf, *Bengal Renaissance*, 242.
50. Ibid., 149.

How seriously Trevelyan and Bentinck were really contemplating that English, in conjunction with the vernaculars, might one day play such a role is revealed by their correspondence during 1833 and 1834, from which it emerges that much of the battle over English education had, in fact, been fought and won before Macaulay ever set foot in India; though the Anglicist victory remained to be proclaimed and consolidated. Charles Trevelyan was the driving force behind the Anglicist effort. On March 18, 1833, having completed the report on Indian customs and internal duties that was to impress Macaulay so greatly, Trevelyan wrote to Bentinck that, henceforth, he wished to devote himself to what he had long considered to be the great enterprise of his life: "the moral and intellectual regeneration of the people of India." To achieve this, he wanted to see established a system of education so comprehensive as to embrace every class of public teachers and so elastic as to be capable of gradual extension to every village in the country. This was to be interwoven with the constitution of the state in such a way that the highest honors and emoluments of which the government was able to dispose would be awarded to the most distinguished students. Thus, what Trevelyan called the highest motives for intellectual exertion would be operative in the entire population.

What he had in mind, he went on, was the sort of comprehensive system of national education currently in existence in New York and in New England as well as in Prussia—and also contemplated by some for England and France. The introduction of such a system would change the face of India within twenty-five years; and countless millions would bless Bentinck's memory. The entire country craved education. Thus his scheme would meet no opposition, nothing but cooperation from everyone. Trevelyan concluded by remarking that he considered the project so important that he would be willing to spend the rest of his life on it. In fact, however, he was confident that it would not take more than a year to set it up; after which superintending it would be comparatively simple.[51]

Bentinck's reply to this letter is not available. But he probably suggested a waiting period before starting this grandiose project. For, little more than a year later, when Trevelyan addressed the Governor-General once again on the subject of education, he praised the latter's wisdom, which had dictated his resolution to put off the development of his views on the great question until public opinion was better prepared. There were, Trevelyan went on, two incom-

51. Trevelyan to Bentinck, March 18, 1833, Portland MSS, University of Nottingham.

patible systems of education: what he called the Mohammedan-Hindu, employing Arabic, Persian, and Sanskrit; and what he called the Anglo-Indian, based on English and the Indian vernaculars. If what Trevelyan, possibly with a certain amount of politic flattery, termed "your Lordship's scheme" had been publicly revealed a year before, the "old leaven" would have had to be included. But now, the Anglo-Indian system—and this is clearly the one that Bentinck and Trevelyan had in mind for their project of national education—was being increasingly favored by public opinion outside the General Committee of Public Instruction. Within the committee, the "anti-popular" cause of Sanskrit, Arabic, and Persian, zealously defended by Henry Thoby Prinsep, had won temporary ascendancy. But outside the committee, adherents to the "popular" cause were having it all their own way. All the influential members of the Indian community now thought alike in its favor. As soon as a "popular" character had been given to the General Committee of Public Instruction, no defenders of the old system would remain.

Like a prophet inspired, Trevelyan went on to depict India on the eve of a great moral change. The impending abolition of Persian in courts and government offices would shake Hinduism and Mohammedanism to their core, and would firmly establish "our language, our learning, and ultimately our religion in India." Thus, Bentinck's own situation was "the most solemn and responsible that ever fell to the lot of an individual in any age of the world." It was for him that the glorious privilege of becoming the regenerator of a hundred million of his fellow creatures in all their successive generations had been reserved. As if carried away by his own vision, Trevelyan went on to assert that India was merely a stepping stone to the rest of Asia; that Providence "was evidently concentrating her means of improvement here in order that, setting out from India as a base of operation, these may afterwards be applied with greater effect to the surrounding nations." In speaking "thus largely," he was, of course, addressing Bentinck alone. As far as the general public was concerned, he suggested that only "the practical part of the scheme" be unfolded. On that, all parties, whether Anglicans, Dissenters, Deists, Mahommedans or Hindus, would cordially agree.[52]

Three weeks later Trevelyan triumphantly reported to Bentinck (somewhat in the manner of a general in the field announcing a

52. Trevelyan to Bentinck, April 9, 1834, Portland MSS, University of Nottingham. Also cited in part by Kenenth Ballhatchet, "The Home Government and Bentinck's Educational Policy," *Cambridge Historical Journal*, X (1951), 228.

victory to his commander-in-chief) that the "liberal" part of the General Committee on Public Instruction had gained a decisive majority. The last stronghold of the old system had been taken. Some of its outworks were still unoccupied; but, as the citadel had been vanquished, they, too, must soon surrender at discretion. The great principle of English education had been established. The foundation stone of the old edifice of Sanskrit and Arabic learning had been removed. One committee member, and its president in 1834, Henry Shakespear, had proposed a reform of Sanskrit College. Another, John Colvin, had succeeded in getting adopted a rule that obliged all students in the Madrassa to learn English. Yet another member, William Bird, had proposed that a grant of 20,000 rupees procured by H. H. Wilson for the purpose of printing Hindu scriptures be rescinded. And Tytler's Arabic translation of Hooper's *Anatomist's Vade Mecum* would probably not be printed. Victory was complete. All that needed to be done now was to gather up the spoils.

Trevelyan went on to relate how that victory—one for which he had been laboring for seven years—had been achieved. It had not been easy. In Calcutta all the important posts in the field of education had been, and indeed still were, occupied by Orientalists. Yet "we have carried our point and laid the axe at the root of the old system in spite of them all." For nine months "we [i.e., Trevelyan and the other Anglicists] had laboured, as it were, underground," within the General Committee of Public Instruction. But they had remained in a minority. It was only when they began to have recourse to the (Indian) newspapers and thus to put outside pressure on the committee that anything effective was accomplished. Making the Calcutta press a party to the struggle had had "almost magical results." The thunderstorm that followed had cleared the air. Now, no further strong measures were required. The way was cleared for "your Lordship's plan of national education." On that subject, Trevelyan's heart was "full to overflowing." The most religious, that is, the missionaries, as well as the most profane, would be able to participate with equal zeal and cordiality in helping to institute one great system of national instruction.[53]

These letters of Trevelyan's accentuate the importance of the role he played in the education controversy: putting pressure on Bentinck, and not disdaining the use of inordinate flattery in so doing; going outside the General Committee of Public Instruction in order to mobilize Indian public opinion in favor of the Anglicists; and

53. Trevelyan to Bentinck, April 30, 1834, Portland MSS, University of Nottingham.

organizing the plans to achieve his aims with the ruthless strategy of a military campaign. From his own account, it would appear as if it was Trevelyan who had been the mainspring behind the new educational policy. There is no reason to doubt that this was substantially true. Some allowance must be made for hyperbole. Trevelyan was hardly the sort of person to underplay his own achievements. The fact that in spite of all his talk of total victory for the Anglicists, the committee actually remained so badly divided on the education question that it had to be submitted to the Governor-General for adjudication early in the following year should suffice to guard one against accepting without a grain of salt Trevelyan's talk of total victory. Still, he had certainly lent his energy and fanaticism to the Anglicist cause with some effect.

Another reason why Trevelyan's letters to Bentinck hold such interest has to do with the vocabulary he used to characterize the parties in the General Committee of Public Instruction. For it reveals dimensions of the educational controversy not usually found in historical accounts of it. The Anglicist cause was the "popular" as well as the "liberal" cause. The Orientalist side was, therefore, anti-popular as well as conservative. This does not merely indicate that the fight over the future of Indian education was waged—at least on the part of Trevelyan and his allies—in terms of English political party warfare. It also shows that far more was involved than a struggle over languages. The reason why Trevelyan regarded his side as the "popular" one was that he wished eventually to see the new educational policy, based on English and the vernaculars, as part of a comprehensive system of national education—with the most proficient students duly rewarded with government jobs. Regarded from Trevelyan's point of view, the Orientalists were élitist in their approach, and had little interest in popular education on the scale he envisaged. Finally, one cannot help but be struck by Trevelyan's ultimate vision of a Christianized Asia which he expounded to the Governor-General in such Machiavellian fashion. Since official British policy in regard to Indian religion was supposed to be one of the strictest neutrality, he had good reason to urge Bentinck to be discreet about this aspect of his strategy. So far as Trevelyan was concerned, the education controversy went far beyond linguistic and instructional policy. The stakes were very much higher.

In fact, financial and other practical considerations made the kind of comprehensive system of education Trevelyan and Bentinck had in mind a far from immediately realistic proposition. Still, it is significant that the prospect of English (in conjunction with the vernaculars) as the national language of India, which appeared chimerical as well as not particularly desirable to Orientalists such as H. H. Wilson, fired the imagination of Trevelyan and, to a lesser extent, that of Bentinck. Their correspondence shows that it was no coincidence that in March of 1834 the Anglicist position received support from a petition presented by former students of Sanskrit College to the secretary of the General Committee of Public Instruction, complaining that they found themselves jobless after having studied Hindu law at the college; and that at the same time Bengali radicals were vehemently criticizing current policies of the committee in the Calcutta press.[54] Trevelyan had been hard at work.

That is how matters stood when Macaulay arrived in India, and Bentinck, in view of the new law member's literary fame, offered him the presidency of the General Committee of Public Instruction. Macaulay declined to take any active part in the committee's proceedings until the government had officially pronounced on the question at issue in the committee. For, he later wrote,

as it seems to be the opinion of some of the gentlemen who compose the Committee of Public Instruction, that the course which they have hitherto pursued was strictly prescribed by the British Parliament in 1813, and as, if that opinion be correct, a legislative Act will be necessary to warrant a change, I have thought it right to refrain from taking any part in the preparation of the adverse statements which are now before us, and to reserve what I had to say on the subject till it should come before me as a member of the Council of India.[55]

In late January 1835, the two factions on the committee—Orientalist and Anglicist—laid their respective cases before the Supreme Council. The legal point at issue was that clause in the Charter Act of 1813 which had provided for "the revival and promotion of literature and the encouragement of the learned natives of India, and for the introduction and promotion of a knowledge of the sciences among the inhabitants of the British territories." The Orientalists claimed what the Anglicists denied, that any substantial reduction of Sanskrit and Arabic instruction would contravene that particular provision of the act. On February 2, Macaulay, as the legal member of Council, produced his famous Minute in which he adopted and

54. Salahuddin Ahmed, *Bengal*, 152–3.
55. T.B.M., "Minute on Indian Education" (February 2, 1835), Clive and Pinney, eds., *Macaulay*, 237–8.

defended the views of the Anglicist party on the committee. On the basis of his Minute, Lord William Bentinck decided "that the great object of the British Government ought to be the promotion of European literature and science among the natives of India."

What we now know is that the actual decision had in fact been taken by the beginning of December 1834, and had been in the making for some time before that. In a portion of Macaulay's long letter to Margaret dated December 7, 1834, in which he told her of Hannah's engagement to Trevelyan, he informed her that when he had arrived in Calcutta in September, he found his future brother-in-law engaged in a furious contest against half a dozen of the oldest and most powerful men in India on the subject of native education. "I thought him a little rash in his expressions," Macaulay continued,

but in essentials quite right. I joined him, threw all my influence into his scale, brought over Lord William,—or rather induced Lord William to declare himself,—and thus I have, I hope, been the means of effecting some real good. The question was whether the twenty thousand pounds a year[56] which Government appropriates to native education should be employed in teaching the natives Sanskrit and Arabic, as heretofore, or in teaching them English and thus opening to them the whole knowledge of the Western world. You will not doubt on which side Trevelyan and I were found. We now consider the victory as gained. Lord William has made me President of the Education Committee, and intends, very speedily, to pronounce a decision in our favour of the points at issue.[57]

In a letter to James Mill in which he appealed for Mill's support more than eight months later, Macaulay gave a more detailed version of these events, beginning with the fact that "last winter" (1834) he had found the General Committee of Public Instruction divided into two equal parties, and split so badly that all its proceedings had been at a standstill for several months. The question dividing the committee, Macaulay went on, had been whether its funds should be employed in teaching the learned languages and the scientific systems of the East, or in communicating English knowledge. On the side of Arabic and Sanskrit were "the most powerful of the old servants of the company, Macnaghten, Prinsep, and Shakspeare [sic], particularly"; on the other side, the rising young men, including Colvin and

56. In a later letter to James Mill, August 24, 1835, MS in the possession of Mr. Gordon Ray, T.B.M. explained that this total was made up of the statutory lakh of rupees from the public treasury and about as much more from other sources.

57. T.B.M. to Margaret, December 7, 1834, Errington MSS.

Trevelyan. "We had a most obstinate conflict, and at last referred the case to the Government." Bentinck then allowed Macaulay to draft his answer.[58]

In his letter to Mill, Macaulay sounded as if he himself had participated in the conflict within the General Committee of Public Instruction. Actually, he had not.[59] On the other hand, the impression given in Trevelyan's *Life and Letters*[60] that Macaulay withdrew totally from the whole question until the two parties in the committee had laid their briefs before the Governor-General is simply wrong. The briefs were dated January 21 and 22, 1835. But behind the scenes, as we know, Macaulay had already persuaded Bentinck to declare himself by the beginning of the previous month. In other words, thanks in large part to Macaulay's powers of persuasion, the decision had become a *fait accompli* by then.

When one looks at the actual briefs on behalf of the two parties in the committee, as transmitted to the Governor-General by the secretary of the General Committee of Public Instruction in late January, one is struck by the fact that, unlike Macaulay in his letters to Margaret and to James Mill, they do not present the conflict in the committee between English and the Indian classical languages as an either-or question; but, rather, as a debate over priorities. The Orientalists on the committee (Sutherland was one of them, along with Shakespear, the two Prinsep brothers, and Macnaghten) recognized the importance of creating a taste for English science and literature among the Indian natives, the extension of which could not but contribute to a wider diffusion of European knowledge in the vernacular dialects; but thought it their first duty "to revive and extend the cultivation of the literature of the country, and re-

58. T.B.M. to James Mill, August 24, 1835, MS in the possession of Mr. Gordon Ray. It should be pointed out that the "answer" was not the famous Minute, which preceded it by more than a month.

59. This is confirmed by the account given by H. T. Prinsep, who stated that T.B.M. took no part in discussing the three issues that actually led to the submission of the conflict to the Governor-General: (1) The propriety of maintaining an order passed by a subcommittee of two members of the General Committee of Public Instruction, making English compulsory for stipendiary students at the Calcutta Madrassa; (2) the amount of Oriental literature that was to be taught at Agra College; (3) the question as to whether preference should be given in public employment to natives who spoke English. Prinsep's son added to this account that T.B.M. justified his abstention on the ground that, as law member of Council, he would have had to deal with any legal objections that might arise against a new educational policy. That, the younger Prinsep remarked, was putting the cart before the horse. Prinsep, "Three Generations," II, 176–9, I.O.L.

60. Trevelyan, *Life and Letters*, 290, 292.

gard[ed] the introduction of the science and literature of Europe as an improvement to be engrafted thereupon, rather than an object to be pursued exclusively, or with any marked and decided preference."[61] The Anglicists, on the other hand (Bird, Saunders, Bushby, Colvin, and Trevelyan), pressed the paramount value and obligation of administering direct instruction in English literature and science in seminaries for higher education endowed and supported by the government, as well as the justice and expediency of making changes in existing institutions of this kind, so as to render such instruction a principal branch of the studies pursued in them.[62]

Thus the issue submitted to higher authority concerned preference and priority for English instruction over Arabic and Sanskrit instruction, rather than the complete elimination of English. But in the brief detailing the position of the Orientalists, self-styled "the conservative portion" of the committee, they were reported as feeling that the cause advocated by the Anglicists, who were said to represent "the spirit of innovation," was really not that of science and literature at all, but, rather, that of "rudimental English as a means of eventually pursuing the course into Literature and Science, should life be long enough and the inclination last."[63] Here again one receives the distinct impression that behind the conflict over priority for English or Sanskrit and Arabic in higher education—and it is worth noting that the briefs of both parties concerned themselves solely with higher education—lay another, more fundamental conflict. This was between those who were prepared to advocate the spread of English per se as widely as possible, regardless of whether the level of competence reached by those who studied it would in fact enable them to reach literary standards; and those who regarded English solely as a means for engrafting European knowledge upon the Indian vernaculars, and had no hope or desire of ever seeing it become the principal means of communication in India. It was in this rather than in the ostensible conflict that the battle lines were drawn between populists and élitists, as well as between those who were looking ahead to a culture and people as far as possible assimilated to the West (and, more specifically, to Britain) and those who were looking ahead to an Indian culture and people revitalized by means of Western knowledge, but in their essence still Indian—in

61. Sutherland to secretary of government in the general department, January 21, 1835, Sharp, *Educational Records*, 105.

62. Ibid., 104.

63. January 22, 1835. India Public Consultations, LXVI (1835), No. 14, I.O.L.

part because that knowledge would have reached them through the medium of their own languages.

One of those who took the latter position was John Tytler, who, toward the end of January 1835, addressed a letter to Macaulay in which he maintained that "English should be taught thoroughly to as many as have opportunities to learn it, but . . . Science is to be diffused generally by means of the languages of the Country and these it is the Natives [sic] duty to cultivate and ours to learn." But the vernaculars had to be rendered precise, regular, and elegant; and this could only be accomplished by means of a knowledge of Arabic, Persian, and Sanskrit. Therefore, those languages should be encouraged and diffused as much "as can be done with propriety" among all classes above the very lowest. Furthermore, error could not be confuted except by those who knew in detail of what such error consisted. Thus it was up to the English to master Indian systems of science as well as Indian languages.[64]

Macaulay's reply was brisk and vehement. What was the point, he asked, of trying to perfect the Indian vernaculars at this time? That would come in due course.

What we now want are necessaries. We must provide the people with something to say, before we trouble ourselves about the style which they say it in. Does it matter in what grammar a man talks nonsense? with what purity of diction he tells us that the world is surrounded by a Sea of butter? in what neat phrases he maintains that Mount Meru is the centre of the world?

He denied that as a part of teaching truth it was essential to confute all forms of error. "The same reasoning which establishes truth does ipso facto refute all possible errors which are opposed to that truth. If I prove that the earth is a sphere, I prove at the same time that it is not a cube, a cylinder, or a cone." Life was too short to study everything. It was impossible to teach one's pupils both truth and all the various forms of error in the short time allotted to education. "I think myself entitled to laugh at astrology though I do not know its very rudiments—to laugh at alchemy though I have no knowledge of it but what I have picked up from Ben Johnson [sic]." There was indeed some truth in Oriental science. "So there is in the Systems held by the rudest and most barbarous tribes of Caffraria and New

64. Tytler to T.B.M., January 26, 1835, 421, G. and N. Sirkin, "Macaulay," *Victorian Studies,* 421–6.

Holland. The question is why we are to teach any falsehood at all."[65]

This letter of Macaulay's, which only recently came to light, bears all the hallmarks of the famous Minute. And no wonder. For the Minute (February 2, 1835) dates from the same week. It was officially produced for the information of Bentinck on the basis of the briefs submitted by Sutherland in his two letters; ostensibly to assist the Governor-General in making up his mind about the question at issue. Actually, he had already made his decision, a fact to which Macaulay alluded with the phrase: "If the decision of his Lordship in Council should be such as I anticipate."[66] Thus the Minute was less an attempt to persuade Bentinck than an attempt to justify a policy already decided upon. It is one of Macaulay's most powerful productions—ingeniously argued, vigorously composed, sharply polemical; containing that special mixture of arrogance, common sense, illustrative brilliance, sarcastic humor, and prophetic vision so characteristic of his most memorable speeches and essays.[67]

Macaulay began by trying to show that the language of the Act of 1813 did *not*, in fact, compel the present British administration to continue to foster the teaching of Sanskrit and Arabic. It will be recalled that Parliament had then set aside an annual sum "for the revival and promotion of literature and the encouragement of the learned natives of India, and for the introduction and promotion of a knowledge of the sciences among the inhabitants of the British territories." Macaulay took on the difficult task of denying that by "literature" the act could have referred only to Arabic and Sanskrit

65. Ibid., T.B.M. to Tytler, January 28, 1835, 426–7.

66. T.B.M., "Indian Education," Clive and Pinney, *Macaulay*, 250. An additional piece of evidence, hardly required, for the view that the whole matter had already been decided is the fact that by January 1835, a medical college had been set up in Calcutta with instruction in English only. Thus the new policy was anticipated. Salahuddin Ahmed, *Bengal*, 157.

67. The Education Minute did not become widely known in England until many years later. In his *Education of the People of India* (1838), Trevelyan quoted from it at length, without mentioning the author. In the course of the same year, Sydney Smith asked a correspondent to read T.B.M.'s papers on the "Black Act" and Indian education: "They are admirable for their talent and their honesty, we see why he was hated in India and how honourable to him that hatred was." Sanial, "Macaulay in Lower Bengal," *Calcutta Review*, CXXIII (1906), 467. See also Sydney Smith to Lady Grey, September 1838, *Smith Letters*, II, 672. It is hard to know where Sydney Smith read the Minute; for it was not published until 1853 in C. H. Cameron, *Address to Parliament on the Duties of Great Britain in India* (London). H. T. Prinsep, who is the source for this information, claimed that T.B.M. did not wish to have the Minute published at all. "Three Generations," II, 190, I.O.L.

literature. It must be said that he did this more by assertion and a sneering tone than by argument. Thus, echoing Ram Mohan Roy, he summarized the Orientalist position as one that would have it that Parliament

. . . never would have given the honourable appellation of a "learned native" to a native who was familiar with the poetry of Milton, the metaphysics of Locke, and the physics of Newton; but that they meant to designate by that name only such persons as might have studied in the sacred books of the Hindoos all the uses of cusa-grass, and all the mysteries of absorption into the Deity.[68]

Macaulay was on more solid ground when he pointed out that the Act of 1813, after all, also assigned the money it appropriated for "the introduction and promotion of a knowledge of the sciences among the inhabitants of the British territories." Those words, he asserted, were sufficient to authorize all the changes he was about to advocate in his Minute. But, perhaps recalling that this aim had been only part of the act's purpose, he envisaged the contingency that the Council might not agree with his construction—in which case he would simply prepare a short act rescinding the other and, to him, more ambiguous clause. He then went on to take up the Orientalist argument based on legal prescription, which, if true, would be decisive against all change. Here he was really back in the Reform Bill debates, tearing into Tory claims in favor of the inalienable rights of property. The Orientalists, he wrote, felt that the public faith was pledged to the present system, and that to alter the appropriation of any of the funds hitherto spent in order to encourage Sanskrit and Arabic would amount to downright spoliation. This was, indeed, the position of Macaulay's chief antagonist, H. T. Prinsep, who noted in his diary at the time that he was less concerned with the language question than with the rights of pre-existing institutions such as the Madrassa, whose endowment and purpose, he felt, were perpetual, whether or not youths desired to study there.[69] But Macaulay argued that the rights of property, while "undoubtedly sacred," ceased to be so when patent abuses resulted from their existence: "Those who would impart to abuses the sanctity of property," he proclaimed, "are in truth imparting to the institution of property the unpopularity and fragility of abuses."[70]

68. T.B.M., "Indian Education," Clive and Pinney, eds., *Macaulay*, 238.
69. Prinsep, "Three Generations," II, 184–6.
70. T.B.M., "Indian Education," Clive and Pinney, eds., *Macaulay*, 239.

Here Macaulay's polemical eloquence hardly did justice to the Orientalist case. For he maintained that between 1813 and 1835 Oriental languages and sciences had, respectively, become useless and exploded, that is, had turned into "abuses." In fact, the Orientalists had been arguing that Sanskrit, for example, was extremely useful as a means of enriching the vernaculars and were promoting Indian science only insofar as it could serve as a stem upon which the new branches of Western science could be successfully engrafted. But for the purposes of his argument, Macaulay assumed that here was yet another instance of an abuse being defended purely on the ground of ancient prescription—"promises, of which nobody claims the performance, and from which nobody can grant a release"; "property without proprietors"; "robbery, which makes nobody poorer." As far as he was concerned, this plea for the sanctity of property was merely "a set form of words, regularly used both in England and India, in defence of every abuse for which no other plea can be set up."[71]

Having decided that the Governor-General was just as free to direct that the parliamentary grant be no longer employed for the encouragement of Arabic and Sanskrit as he was "to direct that the reward for killing tigers in Mysore shall be diminished, or that no more public money shall be expended on the chanting at the cathedral,"[72] Macaulay turned with evident relief to the question of what, from his own point of view, would be the most useful way of employing a fund for the intellectual improvement of the people of India. Percival Spear has argued that it was because of the weakness of his legal case that Macaulay concentrated in his Minute on a slashing attack upon Oriental learning: "He brought in the new learning to redress the balance of bad law; and he succeeded so perfectly that from that moment the legal issue was forgotten in discussion of the rights and wrongs of Arabic, Sanskrit, and English."[73]

There was general agreement, Macaulay wrote, that, given the state of the vernaculars, the intellectual improvement of those classes of people who had the means to pursue higher studies—and it is important to remember that he was here primarily concerned with that group—could at present be brought about only by means of some other language. What language should that be? In taking sides with

71. Ibid., 240.   72. Idem.

73. Spear, "Bentinck" *Cambridge Historical Journal*, 84. It is worth noting that Trevelyan had used similar words in a very different sense when he described T.B.M. as "one who, after having embellished the literature of Europe, came to its aid when it was trembling in the scale with the literature of Asia." Trevelyan, *Education*, 13.

the Anglicists, Macaulay now began his assault upon the languages and learning of the Orient. First, he cited the valuation of the Orientalists themselves, remarking that he had never found one among them "who could deny that a single shelf of a good European library was worth the whole literature of India and Arabia."[74] As one proceeded in one's estimate from poetry to prose, from works of the imagination to works in which facts were recorded and general principles investigated, European superiority became more obvious and more decisive.

As for the English language, it stood pre-eminent among the languages of the West. It abounded with works of the imagination "not inferior to the noblest which Greece has bequeathed to us"; with models of eloquence; with great histories; with "just and lively representations of human life and human nature"; with profound speculations on metaphysics, morals, government, jurisprudence, and trade; and with "full and correct information respecting every experimental science which tends to preserve the health, to increase the comfort or to expand the intellect of man." Whoever knew English had ready access "to all the vast intellectual wealth, which all the wisest nations of the earth have created and hoarded in the course of ninety generations. It may safely be said that the literature now extant in that language is of far greater value than all the literature which three hundred years ago was extant in all the languages of the world together."[75]

In India, English was the language of the rulers and of those natives employed in the higher seats of government. It was likely to become the language of commerce "throughout the seas of the East." It was the language of "two great European communities which are rising, the one in the south of Africa, the other in Australasia, communities which are every year becoming more important, and more closely connected with our Indian empire." Thus, whether one looked at the intrinsic value of English literature or at the particular situation of India, there was the strongest reason to think that English would be most useful "to our native subjects." That being the case—and here followed the sentence that was to offend generations of Indians and will no doubt continue to do so—why, when it was possible to patronize sound philosophy and true history, should there be countenanced, at the public expense, "medical doctrines, which would disgrace an English Farrier—Astronomy, which would move laughter in girls at an English boarding school—History, abounding

74. T.B.M., "Indian Education," Clive and Pinney, eds., *Macaulay*, 241.
75. Ibid., 241–2.

with kings thirty feet high, and reigns thirty thousand years long—and Geography, made up of seas of treacle and seas of butter"?[76]

Historical analogies pointed clearly in the direction of English. If, during the Renaissance, "our ancestors" had printed and taught nothing at the universities but chronicles in Anglo-Saxon, and romances in Norman French, would England have been what she is now? "What the Greek and Latin were to the contemporaries of More and Ascham, our tongue is to the people of India." The second analogy was supplied by the example of Russia. A hundred and twenty years before, that country was in as barbarous a state as "our ancestors before the Crusades." Now there had come to exist there a large educated class,

abounding with persons fit to serve the state in the highest functions, and in nowise inferior to the most accomplished men who adorn the best circles of Paris and London. There is reason to hope that this vast empire, which in the time of our grandfathers was probably behind the Punjab, may, in the time of our grandchildren, be pressing close on France and Britain in the career of improvement.

How had this been accomplished? Not by filling the head of "the young Muscovite" with lying legends about St. Nicholas: "not by encouraging him to study the great question, whether the world was or was not created on the thirteenth of September: not by calling him 'a learned native,' when he has mastered all these points of knowledge"; but, rather, by teaching him the languages of western Europe. "I cannot doubt that they will do for the Hindoo what they have done for the Tartar."[77]

Macaulay then turned to the argument that the British could secure the cooperation of the Indian public only by teaching Sanskrit and Arabic. The answer to that argument was to be found in the records of the Calcutta Madrassa for December 1833, which showed that the students of Arabic there received stipends; whereas those students who attended only the English course willingly paid for the privilege. In other words, it was necessary to bribe students to get them to learn Arabic, while other students were willing to pay in order to learn English. There were those who maintained that it was not the custom for students in India to pay for their own studies. In fact, as Percival Spear has pointed out, patronage and religious duty were keynotes of Indian higher education. Everyone who could do so studied at home by preference, receiving private instruction. Public

76. Ibid., 242–3.   77. Ibid., 243–4.

institutions were regarded as concessions to the poor. And the Madrassa existed on so definite a basis of charity that students were paid to attend it as a matter of course. But Macaulay simply declared that "nothing is more certain than that it never can in any part of the world be necessary to pay men for doing what they think pleasant and profitable."[78] As far as he was concerned, the state of the market was the decisive test. We do not have his reply to the question James Prinsep asked upon resigning from the General Committee on Public Instruction after its educational policy was newly determined from above: Which was the greater bribe, an allowance of 500 rupees a month during hard study for four or five years with no prospect beyond, or the promise of appointments of 50, 100, nay 500 and 1,000 rupees a month for a moderate acquaintance with English?[79]

In further support of his case, Macaulay cited the petition presented a few months earlier by the jobless ex-students of Sanskrit College. Surely those students had been right in protesting. Under British auspices, they had wasted the best years of their lives in learning what procured for them neither bread nor respect. Bounties and premiums, "such as ought not to be given even for the propagation of truth," had been lavished by the government upon the dissemination of false taste and false philosophy.[80] Moreover, the bounty money was being spent to raise up champions of error and to help in creating Indian opposition to Western languages and learning, opposition that did not at present exist. It is easy enough to smile at a phrase such as "champions of error" and to regard it as simply yet another example of Macaulayesque hyperbole and cultural intolerance. But Edward Thompson has pointed out that, with *suttee* only so recently abolished by Bentinck, awareness of the more cruel aspects of Indian religion on the part of Macaulay must be kept in mind as one reads his Minute on education.[81] In this connection it is by no means irrelevant that H. H. Wilson, the leading Orientalist on the General Committee of Public Instruction until he left for Oxford in 1833, had opposed the legal prohibition of *suttee*.[82] One is again reminded of the fact that the controversy over Indian education concerned more than languages and books.

78. Spear, "Bentinck," *Cambridge Historical Journal*, 87–8.

79. India Public Consultations, LXVIII (1835), April 30, 1835, I.O.L.

80. T.B.M., "Indian Education," Clive and Pinney, eds., *Macaulay*, 246.

81. Edward Thompson, *Suttee: A Historical and Philosophical Enquiry into the Hindu Rite of Widow-Burning* (London, 1928), 129.

82. Kopf, *Bengal Renaissance*, 175.

Which is not to imply that actual books were not involved. Macaulay made the point that there seemed to be no great demand for those Arabic and Sanskrit books of which the committee had printed such large quantities at so great a cost. Twenty-three thousand surplus volumes, most of them folios and quartos, "fill the libraries, or rather the lumber-rooms, of this body." At the same time, the School-book Society was selling 7,000 or 8,000 English books every year, and realizing a profit of 20 per cent on its outlay.[83] It was said by some that Hindu law was to be learned chiefly from Sanskrit books, and Muslim law from Arabic books. But the task of the Law Commission just appointed by act of Parliament was to promulgate a new law code for India. Thus it would be absurd to teach a kind of law which, within the space of a few years, would no longer be valid.

It had been said that Sanskrit and Arabic must be encouraged, since the sacred books of the Indian people were written in those languages. Macaulay's reply to this argument was that while it was the duty of the British government to be not merely tolerant but neutral on all religious questions, this did not imply that it was bound to encourage "the study of a literature admitted to be of small intrinsic value only because that literature inculcates the most serious errors on the most important subjects." While not publicly encouraging Christian missionaries (though it admitted them), could the government reasonably bribe students at state expense "to waste their youth in learning how they are to purify themselves after touching an ass, or what text of the Vedas they are to repeat to expiate the crime of killing a goat?"[84]

The advocates of Oriental learning seemed to take it for granted that no Indian native could possibly master more than a mere smattering of English, and looked down on the education recommended by their Anglicist opponents as a mere spelling book education. But this was simply not the case. Macaulay had himself heard "native gentlemen" in Calcutta discuss the question on which he was writing at that very moment "with a liberality and an intelligence which would do credit to any member of the Committee of Public Instruction." Nobody would contend that English was as difficult to learn for a Hindu as Greek for an Englishman. "Less than half the time which enables an English youth to read Herodotus and Sophocles ought to enable a Hindoo to read Hume and Milton."[85]

Macaulay did not make the Minute a platform for expounding Trevelyan's scheme for a national system of comprehensive educa-

83. T.B.M., "Indian Education," Clive and Pinney, eds., *Macaulay*, 247.
84. Ibid., 248.   85. Ibid., 248-9.

tion. Rather, he signalized his agreement with the Orientalists that, given the limited means available, it was impossible to try to educate the great mass of the Indian people. "We must at present do our best to form a class," he wrote, "who may be interpreters between us and the millions whom we govern; a class of persons, Indian in blood and colour, but English in taste, in opinions, in morals, and in intellect." It would be up to that class to refine the vernaculars and to enrich them with Western scientific terms, "and to render them by degrees fit vehicles for conveying knowledge to the great mass of the population."[86]

Having put forward this idea of "filtration," Macaulay then turned to the practical steps that he felt ought to be taken. Existing interests must be respected. "But I would strike at the root of the bad system which has hitherto been fostered by us." In order to do this, he proposed that an immediate halt be put to the printing of Arabic and Sanskrit books. He also recommended that both Sanskrit College in Calcutta and the Madrassa be closed down. To retain Sanskrit College at Benares and the Madrassa at Delhi would be doing more than enough for Eastern languages. If those colleges were retained, no stipends should be awarded to any students who chose to attend them. They would be left to make up their own minds about which of the rival systems of education they preferred. With the funds thus made available, more financial assistance could be given to Hindu College in Calcutta, and schools established in the larger cities where English could be well and thoroughly taught.[87] Macaulay ended his Minute dramatically, by tendering his resignation as president of the Education Committee in the event—most unlikely, as he well knew— that the government decision should turn out to be that of sticking to the present system. He wanted no part of a committee that was wasting public money; printing books of less value than the blank paper on which they were printed; and giving artificial encouragement to absurd history, absurd metaphysics, absurd physics, and absurd theology.

This, then, was the Minute which Macaulay submitted to Lord William Bentinck in order to confirm him in a decision he had already arrived at. Not unexpectedly, the Governor-General minuted after reading it: "I give my entire concurrence to the sentiments expressed in this Minute."[88] To some extent, of course, Macaulay's Minute was very much an occasional piece, written for a particular

---

86. Ibid., 249.   87. Ibid., 250.   88. Sharp, *Educational Records*, 117.

purpose. It is plain that he had carefully studied the records of the General Committee of Public Instruction and, in particular, Trevelyan's contributions to the debate, which even he had found too vehement and, in terms of the long-range plans they entailed, too ambitious, certainly too ambitious for public discussion. He was no doubt familiar with the feelings of liberal Hindus in Calcutta on the subject of education. Indeed, his example of time-wasting Hindu theology—which text of the Vedas one had to repeat in order to expiate the crime of killing a goat—was the very one employed by Ram Mohan Roy in his letter to Lord Amherst twelve years earlier.[89]

But the Education Minute was something more than a mere *pièce d'occasion,* cleverly argued to deal with a set of special circumstances. In some ways it was, as one scholar has called it, "a typical Whig document [which] reflected the Whig tendency to charge old laws with new meaning."[90] In other ways, for example in its condemnation of Hindu theology and culture and its faith in the educational value of the English language, it was in the direct line of Evangelical doctrine about India as set forth many years before in Charles Grant's *Observations.* Some of the sentiments expressed in the Minute were already to be found in Macaulay's Indian speech of 1833, in which he had spoken of "the morality, the philosophy, the taste of Europe, beginning to produce a salutary effect on the hearts and understandings of our subjects," and had noted the amount of attention already being paid "by the higher classes of the natives to those intellectual pursuits on the cultivation of which the superiority of the European race to the rest of mankind principally depends."[91] It will also be recalled that as he set down his first impressions of India in the course of his trip from Madras to Ootacamund, he had given vent to his regret that the Nabob of the Carnatic and the Rajah of Mysore had not been educated in such a way as to have been turned into accomplished English gentlemen.

Some of the ideas in the Minute simply reflected Macaulay's general views about education, formed years before and now unhesitatingly applied to the Indian situation. Thus, in his early essay on the new London University (1826) he had struck out at the enormous bounties that were lavished in the form of scholarships upon students of Greek, Latin, and mathematics, with the result that there had come to exist a lamentable scarcity of other subjects. In that instance,

89. R. Roy to Amherst, December 11, 1823, ibid., 100.
90. Salahuddin Ahmed, *Bengal,* 159.
91. July 10, 1833, T. B. M., *Works,* XI, 567, 571.

also, he had made utility and the state of the market decisive criteria. If the dead languages and the exact sciences were useful, they did not need peculiar encouragement. If useless, they should not receive it. London University deserved praise because it had no means of bribing one man to learn what it was of no use to him to know, or exacting mock attendance from another who learned nothing at all.[92] As far as Macaulay was concerned, then, scholarships and stipends at the Madrassa were not so much a particularly Indian abuse; but, rather, yet another example of a general abuse that required curbing in Calcutta as well as in Oxford and Cambridge.

But if he felt free to employ such contemporary analogies in spite of the thousands of miles and the many cultural differences separating England and India, it was his use of historical analogies to back his case that was really most characteristic of Macaulay's approach to the question of education. Just as in the Reform Bill debates his main rhetorical contribution had been to set the struggle over the extension of the franchise within the context of European economic and social history, so also in the debate over what language was to be the principal instrument of Indian education, he confronted the issue not as one that was in any sense new or unique, but as another version of a situation that had occurred in fifteenth-century England as well as in eighteenth-century Russia. He himself clearly felt that this sort of historical approach was essential. In January 1835, Bentinck had appointed William Adam to make a study of the actual state of indigenous education in Bengal. Writing to Bentinck on February 7, Macaulay expressed his approval of that appointment on the ground that Adam, like himself, had been struck by the parallel between the educational problems of India and those of the old Russian empire. As soon as the General Committee of Public Instruction had been remodeled, Macaulay assured the Governor-General, measures would be taken to find out what the present state of Russian education was like.[93]

In making his suggestions for the remodeling of the committee—anticipating Orientalist resignations which duly took place after the new policy was instituted—Macaulay recommended the names of three new members (Birch, Mangles, and Cameron), and proposed that henceforth its proceedings be regularly held in public. He also suggested that henceforth two Indians should have votes on the

92. T.B.M., "The London University," Clive and Pinney, eds., *Macaulay*, 18, 32.

93. T.B.M. to Lord William Bentinck, February 2, 1835, Portland MSS, University of Nottingham.

committee, and that those votes should go to the managers of Hindu College. Bentinck, he proposed, should hold out hope to the Muslims that if they exerted themselves in the cause of education—presumably, like Hindu College, in the Anglicist direction—they, too, would be represented on the committee. The remodeling should take place, he felt, as soon as the decision on the Anglicist-Orientalist controversy had been announced. "I see that our opponents are resolved to die game," he observed, "and that, even after the decision on the general principle, we shall have to fight every question of detail."[94]

Macaulay was right about the tenacity of the opposition, especially insofar as it was represented by Henry Thoby Prinsep. Prinsep, whose father had founded the local indigo industry, had come out to Calcutta at the age of sixteen, and had graduated from Fort William College in 1810. Like his brother James, one of the founders of Indian archeology, he was a learned and dedicated Orientalist. He had no use for either Bentinck or Macaulay. Bentinck he considered honest, but paranoid; someone who loved to meddle with every institution and practice found prevalent; who constantly tried to court popularity with the party of progress, and generally acted on the basis of insufficient information. Bentinck, for his part, did not like Prinsep. And the fact that, as Prinsep recalled in his "Memoir," it was he rather than his like-minded fellow committee member Macnaghten who had to "bell the cat" in the education question, accentuated Bentinck's antagonism toward him.[95]

Prinsep's relations with Macaulay were strained from the start. He became the Indian equivalent of a Croker for Macaulay, and there can be little doubt that the tensions between them had political undertones. It will be recalled that according to his own account, Prinsep's chief motive in preserving the Madrassa was his respect for perpetual endowments. One is not surprised to discover that upon his return to England, in 1843, he stood for Parliament as a Conservative. His differences with Macaulay were temperamental as well as political. A man who, in later life, became a close friend of Theodore Watts-Dunton and of Burne-Jones—both of whom resided for a time in his household—could hardly have been expected to develop much affinity for Macaulay's brand of common sense. In the educational records of the government of India there is to be found Prinsep's reply to Macaulay's Minute, dated February 15,

94. Idem. On Indian appointments, see same to same, February 27, 1835, Portland MSS, University of Nottingham.

95. Prinsep, "Three Generations," II, 202, 207–8.

1835, with marginal notes by Macaulay. It is a fascinating document, since it reveals the clash between two diametrically opposed but equally stubborn mentalities.

Prinsep began his reply by stating that it was clearly native literature the framers of the Act of 1813 had in mind when they referred to "the revival and promotion of literature and the encouragement of learned natives." Macaulay's marginal note here reads: "On the legal question I have had the opinion of Sir E. Ryan.[96] He pronounces that there is not the shadow of a reason for Mr. Prinsep's construction." Underneath this comment, Prinsep in his turn wrote: "I do not feel overwhelmed by this authority."[97] Prinsep was not easily overwhelmed.

The real question, as far as Prinsep was concerned, was not whether, when it was in the committee's power to sponsor the teaching of English, it should be sponsoring instruction in other languages. Prinsep, in fact, agreed with everything said in Macaulay's Minute on the subject of the superiority of English. The real question for him was whether the British in India had it in their power to teach English as well as European science *everywhere*. It was because he and his party held that this was impossible that they maintained the expediency of letting the natives pursue their present course of instruction, and endeavouring to "engraft" European science upon it. Macaulay's Renaissance analogy was false, since, in fact, Arabic and Persian were to the Muslims and Sanskrit to the Hindus what Latin and Greek had been to Europe in the fifteenth century: "To the great body of the people of India English is as strange as Arabic was to the knights of the dark ages." Macaulay's marginal note at this point reads: "It cannot be more strange than Greek was to the subjects of Henry the Eighth."[98] Prinsep went on to point out that the Russian analogy was false in its turn, since German was not exclusively taught in Russian schools. Macaulay's marginal comment here was that the Russian-educated class had acquired all it knew by means of English, French, and German. Now it was beginning to imitate and to translate. "This is exactly the course which I hope and trust that the educated class of our native subjects will follow."[99]

96. A judge of the Calcutta Supreme Court, and a close friend of T.B.M.'s. He was also the sole agent in India of the Society for the Diffusion of Useful Knowledge, and succeeded T.B.M. as president of the Education Committee.

97. Prinsep, Minute of February 15, 1835, Sharp, *Educational Records*, 118.

98. Ibid., 121. See John Gross, ed., J. R. Seeley, *The Expansion of England* (Chicago, 1971), 199, for the point that all three languages—Arabic, Sanskrit, and English—were alike in being utterly strange to the Indian population.

99. Prinsep, Minute of February 15, 1835, Sharp, *Educational Records*, 122.

Prinsep admitted that the Hindus desired to learn English. On the other hand, there was no reason to believe that Muslims in any part of India would ever become reconciled to it. His own position remained that of trying to engraft Western knowledge on an Oriental base. After all, the philosophy of Bacon, Locke, and Newton, which the British were attempting to inculcate, had grown out of that very philosophy of the Schools which had also been the highest point of knowledge reached in Sanskrit and Arabic. Why, then, despair of engrafting similar fruit upon a similar stock? It was not Macaulay, but one of his successors as legal member of Council, Drinkwater Bethune, who noted in the margin: "Monstrous assertion!" Finally, Prinsep argued that the new policy would mean that some natives would have to study the English ABC rather than being able to pursue those advanced courses for which they were qualified. Macaulay's comment reads: "Of course every body must begin a language at the beginning. The only question is whether we may reasonably expect in a few years to make an intelligent native youth a thoroughly good English scholar. And I do not now find that this is disputed."[100]

Underneath Prinsep's Minute, Macaulay wrote this:

I remain [not only] unshaken but confirmed [in all my] opinions on the general question. I may have committed a slight mistake or two as to [details], and I may even have occasionally used an epithet which might with advantage [have been] softened down. But I do not retract the substance of a single proposition I have advanced.[101]

Hardly a change of mind, let alone a retraction. But it shows that Macaulay was quite aware of the fact that the rhetoric of his Minute had not been calculated to soothe.

According to Prinsep, Macaulay's proposals for action in his Education Minute went further than the warmest advocates on the Anglicist side had yet ventured.[102] But in the course of the relatively short period of time that elapsed between the Minute and Bentinck's resolution, which put it into effect (February 2 until March 7), some of Macaulay's harsher recommendations were softened. That was not due to Prinsep, who was asked by the Governor-General's private secretary to stop circulating his protest against the Minute; since, he was told, it would be fully discussed in the Education Committee. He complied, but the opportunity for

100. Ibid., 126, 128.   101. Ibid., 130.
102. Prinsep, Minute of May 20, 1835, Sharp, *Educational Records*, 137.

such a discussion never arose. Bentinck was unalterably determined to proceed in the Anglicist direction. Thus, he ignored the protest of one of his councilors, Colonel Morison, who was sure that a sudden decision in favor of English would alarm the natives into thinking that even greater changes were coming and who wanted the whole matter to be referred back to London.[103] We shall see in due course that from his point of view, Bentinck felt that he had good reason for refusing to do this. In the end, the Governor-General would not even grant his permission for Prinsep's memorandum to be placed on record.[104]

But, as we have already had occasion to note, the power of public opinion, even in the Calcutta of 1835, could not be underrated. In part manipulated by Trevelyan, it had helped the Anglicist cause in the General Committee of Public Instruction. Now—whether it was similarly manipulated by Prinsep there is no way of knowing—it helped to ward off the full strength of the blows Macaulay wished to direct against the Orientalists. Through John Colvin, one of the Anglicist members of the Education Committee, word leaked out that the government was about to abolish Sanskrit College and the Madrassa.[105] Within three days, thousands of Hindus and Muslims had signed petitions to prevent this from happening. As a result, the "Resolution " of the Governor-General, which actually put the new educational policy into effect on March 7, 1835, contained the proviso that the government had no intention of abolishing any college or school of native learning, "while the native population shall appear to be inclined to avail themselves of the advantages which it affords."[106] This stipulation, which saved the Madrassa and Sanskrit College, was not in the original draft of the resolution, drawn up for Bentinck by Macaulay. Otherwise, except for some changes in the order of paragraphs, it was virtually identical with

103. India Public Consultations, LXVI (1835), No. 17, February 18, 1835, I.O.L.
104. Prinsep, "Three Generations," II, 180-1, and his Diary in Sharp, *Educational Records*, 134. Needless to say, the course of events just described did not serve to improve relations between Prinsep and T.B.M. Three months later, Prinsep, temporarily a Council member during the Metcalfe interregnum, proposed that the Executive Council alone—*without* the necessary presence of the legal member—carry out all legislative activities except the final passage of laws. Not unexpectedly, T.B.M. called this proposal "in the highest degree pernicious." *Parliamentary Papers*, XXVII (1852-3), 533.
105. Prinsep, Diary, Sharp, *Educational Records*, 133-4. T.B.M. suspected Prinsep himself of having been responsible for this leak. He denied it.
106. Sharp, *Educational Records*, 130.

Macaulay's original draft.[107] Macaulay himself was certainly convinced that in this way he had played a vital role in resolving the education controversy. "Lord William," he wrote to James Mill,

who placed a confidence in me for which I shall feel most grateful as long as I live, suffered me to draw the answer [to the briefs submitted by the General Committee of Public Instruction]. . . . There are very few things in my life on which I look back with so much satisfaction as the part which I took in deciding this question.[108]

The resolution stated that the Governor-General was of the opinion "that the great object of the British Government ought to be the promotion of European literature and science among the natives of India; and that all the funds appropriated for the purpose of education would best be employed on English education alone."[109] All currently active professors and students of Oriental learning at institutions under the control of the Education Committee would continue to receive their stipends, but no stipends were to be awarded to new students entering those institutions. Any Oriental professorships falling vacant could not be filled, unless the government specifically decided to do so in individual cases. No committee money was to be employed henceforth for the purpose of printing Oriental works. All funds made available in this way were to be used for imparting to the native population a knowledge of English literature and science through the medium of the English language.[110] In fact, the order to withdraw stipends, though not formally rescinded, was never actually carried into operation. The next Governor-General, Lord Auckland, modified it by granting pecuniary scholarships to industrious Indian students.[111] Thus, Bentinck's resolution turned out to be considerably less uncompromising than the practical policies advocated by Macaulay in his Minute.

Still, the die was cast. In the words of Prinsep, who had lost his battle: "English has ever since been the study preferentially encouraged by Government in connection with vernacular literature."[112] In anticipation of funds expected to be freed by the new measures,

107. In the Portland MSS, University of Nottingham.

108. T.B.M. to James Mill, August 24, 1835, MS in the possession of Mr. Gordon Ray.

109. Resolution of March 7, 1835, Sharp, *Educational Records*, 130.

110. T.B.M., Draft of Resolution, Portland MSS, University of Nottingham.

111. Evidence of H. H. Wilson, July 5, 1853, *Parliamentary Papers*, XXXII (1852–3), 259.

112. Prinsep, Diary, Sharp, *Educational Records*, 134.

five schools for teaching English language, literature, and science were at once opened in some of the principal towns of Bengal. The Orientalists were furious. After Bentinck left India, they appealed to his temporary successor, Sir Charles Metcalfe, who (so Macaulay reported to James Mill) "would never have taken so bold and decisive a measure as that of deciding for English education. But he is not at all a man to rescind such a measure when taken by another. He declared himself decidedly favourable to the new system." But this did not silence the opposition. The Asiatic Society sent a memorial to the Court of Directors in London, bitterly complaining about the new policy. Macaulay appealed to James Mill for his support, in case an attempt were made at home to reverse the decision taken in India. But the elder Mill who, as we know, disagreed profoundly with the Anglicizing policy advocated by Macaulay, was hardly the person to intervene in its favor. Moreover, the proposal made by the court to reverse the new policy came from the pen of none other than James's son, John Stuart.

When Lord Auckland took up his post in the spring of 1836, he wrote to Hobhouse at the Board of Control that he trusted that the "clatter" about the respective educational value of English and Oriental literature, which had prevailed in Calcutta just a few months before his arrival there, had made no impression in London.[113] His trust was misplaced. The Court of Directors had not taken kindly to the new policy; and, on its behalf, John Stuart Mill, in his capacity of assistant examiner, submitted a so-called Previous Communication ("P.C.") for the consideration of the president of the Board of Control. This was to be sent as an official despatch to the government in India, provided that Hobhouse's endorsement was forthcoming.[114]

It is a highly interesting document, not only on account of its author, but also because one of the copies preserved in the India Office Library contains Hobhouse's marginal comments on it. As was his right, Hobhouse rejected the "P.C." *in toto;* and it was therefore never sent as an official despatch. On its cover, the president of the Board of Control minuted: "I dissent from almost the whole of this P.C.—and see not how it is to be amended. *Nulla litera potesta sine*

113. Auckland to Hobhouse, April 12, 1836, Home and Miscellaneous, Vol. 833, I.O.L.

114. On the authorship of the despatch, see Sir James Carnac to Hobhouse, December 14, 1836, Home and Miscellaneous, Vol. 835, I.O.L.: "The draft was chiefly prepared by Mr. John Mill." See also Ballhatchet, "Home Government," *Cambridge Historical Journal,* 229.

littera."[115] It was this veto on the part of Hobhouse that finally confirmed the new educational policy adopted in Calcutta.

Mill who, as he wrote to Henry Taylor,[116] had the entire support of the directors for the sentiments he was expressing on their behalf, made it unmistakably clear that Bentinck's new policy had been undertaken "in opposition to our recorded opinions, and without any previous reference to us." But, quite apart from that, one could only deprecate the sudden change of course the policy represented. (Hobhouse's marginal comment: "This does not at all follow—some changes are more safe for being sudden.") Sudden changes of this sort were especially harmful because of the traditional attachment of the Indian natives, especially the Hindus, to ancient systems and establishments. (Hobhouse: "Those *ancient* systems date from 1813.") Indians regarded the prospect of an increased diffusion of English as a threat to their religion, and were immediately and intensely excited about it. (Hobhouse: He had heard from Auckland that the excitement had completely subsided. Indeed, a recent communication of Auckland's to Carnac, cited by Hobhouse in a covering letter which he enclosed with the rejected "P.C." on returning it to Sir James Carnac, chairman of the East India Company,[117] reported that the Muslims had calmed down upon learning that their institutions were still open to those who chose to attend them; and that the ill feeling that had resulted from the roughness and want of conciliation with which the new policy was put into effect had been nearly forgotten, except by a few.)

Mill went on to claim that the previous system, with its quiet and unobtrusive encouragement of English, had worked well. To accelerate its diffusion by unnecessary innovation was imprudent. There followed a direct attack on Macaulay whom—it is worth noting—both Mill and Hobhouse held chiefly responsible for the new policy. (Hobhouse's marginal note penciled alongside this attack on Macaulay breathes a spirit of disdain and *hauteur*: "It is unbecoming in a master to enter into a controversy with his servant.") Mill main-

115. The Latin is execrable, but he presumably meant to say: "No learning without letters." Previous Communication, 1836, India Public Department: "Recent Changes in Native Education." Revenue, Judicial, and Legislative Committee, Miscellaneous Papers, IX, I.O.L. (referred to henceforth as J. S. Mill, "P.C.").

116. John Stuart Mill to Henry Taylor, Monday [1837], F. E. Mineka and D. N. Lindley, eds., *The Later Letters of John Stuart Mill, 1849–1873*, 4 vols. (*Collected Works*, XIV to XVII, Toronto and London, 1972), XVII, 1969–70.

117. Hobhouse's letter is attached to J. S. Mill's "P.C." The letter he refers to is Auckland to Carnac, June 17, 1836, quoted by Abram L. Harris, "John Stuart Mill: Servant of the East India Company," *Canadian Journal of Economic and Political Science*, XXX (1964), 196.

tained that those members of the General Committee of Public Instruction who had had the most extensive experience in India wholly
disagreed with Macaulay's assessment that the Indians craved English
instruction and were indifferent to Oriental languages. Furthermore,
given the Indian tradition of public or private endowments for
learning, Macaulay was wrong about the question of stipends. True,
certain classes of natives wanted to learn English—but their motive
was not disinterested. (Hobhouse: "What does it signify?") They
believed it would help them to obtain public employment. (Hobhouse: "As if this was not a praiseworthy motive.") They would
learn a minimum of English—no literature and no "principles"—and
would thus, in fact, remain on a level with those who did not learn
English at all. (Hobhouse: "I do not believe that any men or set of
men who know one useful thing more than their countrymen can be
said to be only on a level with them.")

The Court of Directors, Mill wrote, did not want the new English
schools to be closed down. But if the government's object was "the
intellectual and moral improvement of the people of India," the
cultivation of Oriental languages was necessary in addition. It was
chimerical to think that the mental cultivation of a people could
mainly take place through the medium of a foreign language. All
that could be done was to teach the teachers, and raise up a class of persons who, having derived improved ideas and feelings from European
literature, would spread them among their countrymen. (Hobhouse:
"This is all that Macaulay and his friends propose to do.") But not
everyone who was motivated to learn English would also be motivated
to diffuse English ideas. (Hobhouse: "Certainly not—but he will diffuse them insensibly and without labour.") Those who were actually
helping to diffuse these ideas must needs do so either by way of the
Oriental languages, as schoolteachers or writers, or else in colloquial,
that is, vernacular, discourse with families, friends, and neighbors.

That brought Mill to the state of the Indian vernaculars, which,
he wrote, were presently fit only for the purposes of everyday life.
Words treating scientific and philosophical subjects had to be drawn
from Sanskrit and Arabic. Macaulay seemed to think that a knowledge of Sanskrit for this purpose would be provided without government help. (Hobhouse: "I think so.") But that, Mill countered,
presupposed a consciousness of their intellectual wants on the part of
a people "such as has never yet existed in the most civilised nations."
(Hobhouse: "The P.C. writer seems to know many curious facts.")
Mill agreed with Macaulay that a class of "diffusionists" must be
created. But it had to consist, he maintained, not of those who

studied English in order to assure themselves of employment and profit, but, rather, of those very men of learning who had been most alienated by the recent measures. It was these Indian scholars, Mill asserted, who invariably turned out to be the best English scholars.

For all these reasons, so the proposed despatch went on to state, the Court of Directors would have vetoed the proposed changes, had they not already begun to be put into effect. The problem now was how the "error" could be repaired with the least possible inconvenience. The government's main aim must be to encourage the study of English as a *classical* language. (Hobhouse: "Quite a mistake. Let the natives learn English as a vernacular and make what use of it they like.") English studies must not be supported at the cost of Oriental instruction, lest the Indian learned class become jealous and hostile. Thus, grants to existing Hindu and Muslim colleges should not be retracted. (Hobhouse: "Has any such resumption been threatened? Only that where there are no scholars there shall be no school.") Indian classical languages, as well as both Hindu and Mohammedan law, should continue to be taught and studied at these institutions so that the vernaculars could be improved, and justice duly administered. Stipends must be maintained. (Hobhouse: "No— this has been done and why undo.") A sum of money should be granted to the Asiatic Society so that it could take over the unused stocks of books. Finally, no governmental funds should be devoted to elementary schools. Only those parties directly benefiting from it should ultimately pay for knowledge of English when it was required as a means of livelihood or professional advancement. (Hobhouse: "I entirely differ from the P.C.") Public money must be spent only for the purpose of engaging qualified teachers for the higher branches of English education.

Thus, Mill and Hobhouse agreed that the end of education was to be the moral and intellectual improvement of the people of India; and that to carry this out, a specially trained class of people must act as diffusionists downward for Western ideas. But Mill thought that: first, the changes initiated by Bentinck and Macaulay—he was seemingly not aware of Trevelyan's preparatory maneuvers—were imprudent and impolitic in their suddenness; second, the class of cultural mediators should consist of men learned in Indian classical languages as well as in English since the vernaculars, crucial for the instruction of the people at large, had to be reinforced by Sanskrit and Arabic in order to communicate Western ideas efficiently; and third, public money should be devoted solely to English studies at such a high level that they would attract only "disinterested" students eager to acquire and to disseminate knowledge of science and literature, and that it should not be spent to finance the teaching of elementary English to those who merely wished to learn it in order to pursue careers in business or government.

Judging by the similarity of their arguments, it is likely that Mill was familiar with H. H. Wilson's article on "Native Education" in the *Asiatic Journal* (1836), a slashing attack upon the new policy and, in part, on Macaulay in person, for example: "The laws of Manu and the *Koran* will scarcely be set aside altogether, it is to be presumed, by the luminaries of the new legislative council."[118] Wilson tried to hoist Bentinck and Macaulay by their own petard in arguing that to teach natives only a little English was quite compatible with gross ignorance and inveterate superstition. Only by teaching English knowledge, not speech, at the highest levels to an élite which could pass on European ideas, first in translation and eventually in original works, could the natives really be "improved." But stopping the funds used to translate authors such as Euclid and Hutton into Sanskrit and Arabic had delivered a fatal blow to this process. "Such, however, is the mischievous consequence of acting upon a theory, and diverting the funds appropriated to education from purposes of practical utility, in order to apply them to the unnecessary and unprofitable scheme of teaching English to all the natives of India."[119]

There is more than a little irony in this broadside delivered by the Boden Professor of Sanskrit at Oxford against "theoreticians" like Bentinck and Macaulay, in the name of practical utility and improvement. Moreover, it must be emphasized that neither Mill and Wilson (who opposed it) nor Hobhouse (who supported it) paid strict attention to the actual words of Macaulay's Minute which did *not*, in fact, propose that all natives be taught English, but rather that, for the moment, the best that could be done was for a limited class of educated natives to filter down their knowledge to the masses. On the other hand, while Wilson's interpretation may have been unjust to Macaulay's text, it was not unjust to the spirit that animated the Anglicist position. We need only recall Trevelyan's letters to Bentinck for reassurance on that point. What strikes one time and again in rereading the documents is that the Orientalists were far more élitist and the Anglicists far less élitist than they claimed to be. The real issue, as Mill's despatch and Hobhouse's marginal notes on it show, was English for all as against English for a few.

118. H. H. Wilson, "Education," *Asiatic Journal* (1836), 14.   119. Ibid., 13.

In one sense, the difference between the two approaches was purely tactical. Mill's caution and prudence were just as much at the service of "improvement" as the more grandiose plans of the Anglicists. That this was the case emerges from an angry letter addressed by Mill to Henry Taylor, after Hobhouse had rejected his "P.C." "You will sympathise," he wrote,

in the annoyance of one [who] having for years (contrary to the instincts of his own nature, which are all for *rapid* change) assisted in nurturing and raising up a system of cautious and deliberate measures for a great public end, and having been rewarded with a success quite beyond expectation, finds them upset in a week by a coxcombical dilettante littérateur who never did a thing for a practical object in his life.[120]

Hardly a kind or even a fair description of Thomas Babington Macaulay, to whom Mill owed a considerable intellectual debt, gracefully acknowledged in his *Autobiography;* and who, at the very moment Mill wrote his letter, was completing a new criminal code for India which, whatever its ultimate merit, could hardly fail to qualify as something undertaken for a practical end. Later, in *On Liberty,* Mill was to enunciate the doctrine that no community had the right to force another to be civilized. Presumably, he had no objection to the procedure when it was carried out with the requisite caution. In some ways, a comparison between Macaulay's "coxcombical" and Mill's prudential approach to Indian education might well lead one to prefer the former to the latter; since, for all its crude arrogance, it possessed at least one negative quality which the other lacked. It did not beat about the bush quite so much.

But to put the matter thus, to see the conflict in purely tactical terms, is hardly just to Mill, whose attitude toward English as a means of education as set forth in his proposed despatch was in some ways very much like his father's, in others like that of the Orientalists on the General Committee of Public Instruction. Like the elder Mill, John Stuart regarded the prospect of an English-speaking India as totally unrealistic as well as undesirable. Though they agreed that English for all was at present impracticable, and that, for the immediate future, the vernaculars had to remain the *vox populi,* Macaulay and Hobhouse did not share this pessimistic view. Certainly, Hobhouse had nothing against encouraging spoken English at any level. And while Macaulay, in his Minute, had made the creation

120. Mill to Henry Taylor, Monday [1837], Mineka and Lindley, eds. *Later Mill Letters,* XVII, 1969–70.

of a small educated class the first order of business, he had by no means excluded the possibility that once sufficient teachers had become available as a part of that class, these in turn would be able to pass on not only Western ideas, but also the language in which those ideas were best expressed, that is, English, to all their pupils. At the very least, both Macaulay and Hobhouse wanted the vernaculars to become totally dependent upon English rather than on Sanskrit and Arabic. "I believe my friend Macaulay, to whom remember me kindly," Hobhouse had written to Auckland in the spring of 1836,

wishes to discourage Eastern literature, in order to leave the ground clear for the cultivation of our own language. But there is a strong party here who think that the rights of conquest do not extend to the destruction of language; and who believe it would be extremely impolitic to withhold all support from the propagation of Oriental learning.[121]

Unlike the Orientalists, Mill was more preoccupied with policy than with the preservation of Oriental literature. But there is no doubt that he sympathized with their desire to preserve the classical Indian languages, as well as with their academic élitism, which made them regard themselves as guides and coadjutors of the Indian intellectual aristocracy. It was the chosen few who were to absorb and pass on the best of what the West had to offer within a framework that remained, and was to continue to remain, essentially Indian. The idea of using public money to teach Indians English on practical grounds, Mill, as well as the Orientalists, considered foolish and vulgar. In the context of Indian educational policy, those two Radicals-turned-Whigs, Hobhouse and Macaulay, were more genuinely democratic, more "popular," than that sworn enemy of Whiggery, the leader of the Philosophical Radicals.

The real reason why neither Hobhouse and Macaulay nor those who shared their views objected in the slightest to the prospect of financing English instruction even for nonscholarly natives was that they were aiming not merely for an engrafting of Western ideas upon Indian civilization, but for the eventual assimilation of the inhabitants of British India to their rulers. This emerges from a letter of Lord Auckland's to Hobhouse sent in the spring of 1836, which the latter no doubt had very much in mind as he read through Mill's "P.C." at the end of that year. "All must wish the Hindoos and Mahometans to assimilate, and to attach themselves to us," the

121. Hobhouse to Auckland, April 1, 1836, Home and Miscellaneous, Vol. 833, I.O.L.

Governor-General had reported to the president of the Board of Control. "And," he went on,

there is a disposition with many of them to become Englishmen as nearly as possible, and all must wish to encourage them; but on their side, there are prejudices and superstitions; and interests; and party violences have been raised upon them, and they had had their eruption, and have subsided, and the system appears to be working well every where.

The Calcutta Muslims, to be sure, were still exercised about the recent measures. But those in the country felt far less strongly about them than those in town. "And I think there is a very reasonable prospect of our seeing a good system of English education eagerly and cheerfully adopted by all sorts and all classes."[122]

We may smile at Auckland's undue optimism. One ground he had for it was probably the fact that, much to the annoyance of the Orientalists, even conservative Hindus were cooperating with the government's new educational policy.[123] But the importance of Auckland's letter is that it reveals clearly what Macaulay and his friends had in mind, and why it stuck in the craw both of the Orientalists, who feared that it would mean the complete supersession of Indian civilization, and of hard-headed Utilitarians such as John Stuart Mill, who were afraid that it would give such offense to Indian traditions and religion that it must inevitably turn out to be self-defeating. In some ways it was a very strange alliance. Sir James Carnac, replying as chairman of the Court of Directors to Hobhouse's rejection of Mill's "P.C.," adverted to its strangeness in pointing out that "Mr. John Mill . . . was not likely to have any extravagant prepossessions in favour of ancient oriental literature." He himself agreed with Mill. But he knew that the Board of Control had the legal right to do exactly what Hobhouse had done: reject despatches proposed by the court. And so he assured Hobhouse that the draft would be duly withdrawn.[124]

Hobhouse who, above all, did not want to start a new debate over education in Calcutta, had recommended to the Court of Directors

122. Auckland to Hobhouse, April 12, 1836, Home and Miscellaneous, Vol. 833, I.O.L. On Mill's élitism in general, see Maurice Cowling, *Mill and Liberalism* (Cambridge, 1963).

123. Salahuddin Ahmed, *Bengal*, 166–7.

124. Carnac to Hobhouse, December 14, 1836, Home and Miscellaneous, Vol. 835, I.O.L. For a similar, very reluctant acquiescence to Hobhouse's veto of J. S. Mill's "P.C.," see W. B. Bailey to Hobhouse, October 17, 1840, Home and Miscellaneous, Vol. 836, I.O.L.

that nothing but a short acknowledgment of the new educational policy was to be sent to Calcutta, expressing no opinion one way or the other on the substantive issues.[125] To Auckland he wrote far more frankly, informing him that the "Chairs" had put into his hands "a very long P.C. essay on the confounded education question; and, having worn my eyes out in reading some hundreds of folios of controversy, I came to a distinctly contrary opinion to that contained in the proposed despatch to you." He then summarized what he considered to have been the faults of the "P.C.," and continued as follows:

In short I take part with Macaulay, and he may rest assured I shall stand by him on this occasion, but I do wish he had delayed the change or brought it about more gradually. His paper on the subject bears the stamp of his genius, but he must excuse me for saying that it is not a state paper. It is a declamation, eloquent, vehement, and argumentative but I repeat, too controversial, too much inviting and defying opposition. Give my kind regards to him—thank him for two letters to me, and if he will bear criticism, tell him what I venture to think of this business.[126]

Two things strike one about this part of Hobhouse's letter. The first, that he was convinced—wrongly, as we know—that Macaulay was the principal if not the sole architect of the new educational policy; the second, the tone, both gingerly and respectful, in which the president of the Board of Control chose to communicate his criticism of the Minute to Auckland. The respect was genuine. Macaulay was an old and valued friend. But Hobhouse no doubt remembered the cabinet's reaction to the Press Act, and his own subsequent injunction to Auckland to keep "B. M." a little more quiet. Now he wished to make amends and did not want to hurt Macaulay, for whose sensitivity to criticism he showed great regard.

He had, of course, paid him the even greater and historically more significant compliment of taking sides with him in the dispute over education. This is how he concluded his letter to Auckland:

I think you are right in wishing to drop the matter altogether, and leave the encouragement of learned natives and their language, by occasional translation of instructive works, to your discretion. I feel quite sure you will not allow of any harsh step being taken to wound even the preju-

125. Hobhouse to Carnac, December 12, 1836, attached to J. S. Mill, "P.C.," I.O.L.
126. Hobhouse to Auckland, December 15, 1836, Home and Miscellaneous, Vol. 837, I.O.L.

dices of the native, but as to the paramount importance of encouraging the diffusion of the English language, I should have thought there could not have been two opinions on the subject. I see however that party has found its way to India, for in one of Mr. Prinsep's furious protests, I find the words, "the conservative portion of the Committee." Pleasantry apart, this is intolerable, as is indeed the general tone and tenor of the same gentleman's correspondence; and yet he is Secy. to Govt. and, they say, a valuable functionary.[127]

We know that Auckland showed this letter from Hobhouse to Macaulay.[128] The latter was so gratified to hear that the president of the Board of Control had sided with him that (as he put it in a letter to him) "I should have easily pardoned your criticisms on my minute, had they been less gentle than they were."[129] The remarks about Prinsep must have given Macaulay particular pleasure. Hobhouse was quite right in fastening on the political aspects of the education battle. He might have gone on to point out the Whiggish aspects of Macaulay's own part in the controversy. But that, no doubt, would be asking too much from a Whig cabinet minister.

Auckland, too, was pleased that Hobhouse had made no attempt to stop or impede the new policy. "Macaulay was right in everything but manner, and perhaps in degree," he wrote to Hobhouse, "and in these, happily, those who were opposed to him were at least as wrong as he." If the president of the Board of Control could see his way clear to relaxing so far as to enable the Education Committee to conciliate the Muslims by creating a few scholarships to the Madrassa, he, Auckland, would have no objection.

But any complete change of system would be fatal to the progress of improvement in India. The appetite for English education is eager and general amongst the Hindus, and it will grow, as, from year to year, success in commerce and advancement in private and in public shall become more difficult without it. Let it be borne in mind too that it will do more "emollire mores" and to reform the abominations which are grafted upon the manners and religion of the nation than all the law giving and all the interference of government can accomplish.

He agreed with Hobhouse's strictures on the violence with which the education controversy had been carried on, but, in justice, had to

127. Idem.
128. Auckland to Hobhouse, April 9, 1837, where he explicitly says so. Home and Miscellaneous, Vol. 838, I.O.L.
129. T.B.M. to Hobhouse, April 17, 1837, Home and Miscellaneous, Vol. 838, I.O.L.

testify to Prinsep's abilities as a public functionary. Prinsep knew more about India than all the rest of the service put together—and was always ready with his knowledge, and almost too ready with his tongue and pen. In addition, he was honest, hardworking, able, and good-humored. But when he was wrong, he was not wrong by halves; "and, in this case, he and Macaulay butted at each other like wild bulls, blind to everything but their own joust of brains, and the contest was not advantageous to either." As for Macaulay, to whom he had shown Hobhouse's letter, he "most entirely forgives your criticism, though he begs you to be reminded that the controversial minute of a member of Council is not of the grave nature of a State paper—and you have gladdened his heart by the just view you have taken of the measure in which he has worked so hardly."[130]

The tone of Auckland's next letter to Hobhouse three months later was somewhat less cordial. For he had by then received what Hobhouse had called his "homily," in which the president of the Board of Control had made it clear beyond all doubt that he resented the independent line taken by Bentinck and Metcalfe in adopting important measures for India, without even the pretext of an emergency situation that required them. Auckland had expressed his unhappiness with a despatch of the previous spring[131] instructing him to consult London before settling on any major new policies. That despatch, Hobhouse now informed him, had referred to the new measures concerning currency, military discipline, and the press. He was not aware that it had had reference to the Indian government's proceedings in respect to steamboat navigation and education.[132]

In his reply to the "homily," Auckland admitted (as we have seen) he was vexed with Hobhouse, who seemed to be putting him on a footing different from that of his predecessors: "From day to day I am called upon to decide questions which may involve war or peace,

130. Auckland to Hobhouse, April 9, 1837, Home and Miscellaneous, Vol. 838, I.O.L.

131. April 1836. See above, p. 331.

132. Hobhouse to Auckland, January 26, 1837, Home and Miscellaneous, Vol. 837, I.O.L. This must be kept in mind when reading the late Abram Harris's article in the *Canadian Journal of Economic and Political Science* (1964). Harris assumed that the April 1836 despatch *had* referred to the new educational policy. That he had some grounds for this is demonstrated by the fact that in the margin of the India Office copy of the despatch of April 14, 1836, "Native Education" is listed among the five issues to which Hobhouse's reprimand is said to refer. But that is clearly not the version that reached Auckland. See Legislative Despatches to India, Despatches to India and Bengal, Vol. 747, I.O.L. I owe this reference to Professor Ballhatchet.

ruin or safety, honour, or disgrace, and who knows until it is tried, what is an 'important measure'?" The steam business had not been important. The Press Act might have been referred to London, but it, too, had not been important. The new currency measures had been approved by the court two years previously. Auckland, whose own endeavor it was to minimize any offense that might be given to Indians by the new educational policy, of which he approved, went on as follows: "The English education was a matter of infinite importance; and Sir Alexander Johnston would have defeated it single-handed, if it had been referred to England."[133]

Auckland himself had not arrived in India until March 1836. Thus, it would have been up to Bentinck and Metcalfe, his temporary successor, to consult the court about the new policy. Furthermore, there was no need for Auckland to refer to the education policy at all since Hobhouse (who, in any event, favored it) had gone out of his way to make it clear that, as far as he was concerned, that policy had not been the subject of the reprimand from him. The fact that Auckland, nevertheless, felt impelled to state so categorically that the new policy would surely have been vetoed, had the court been consulted, confirms that Bentinck, certainly with the support of, and quite possibly upon the advice of Trevelyan and Macaulay, deliberately went ahead with his resolution of March 7, 1835, without first checking with the authorities in London.

Who, then, was Sir Alexander Johnston? The answer to that question illuminates the fact that the Orientalist party was neither confined geographically to Calcutta nor politically to Tories. A descendant on his mother's side of the great mathematician John Napier of Merchistoun, Johnston had spent his youth in India (where he was born in 1775) and had mastered Tamil, Telugu, and Hindustani in the course of it, thus laying the foundation for his lifelong interest in Indian history and culture. A lawyer by profession, he had become chief justice (1806) and president of the Council (1811) of Ceylon, and had initiated wide-ranging reforms there, including popular education, trial by jury, and a law code which had paid special attention to Hindu, Muslim, and Buddhist custom and tradition. Lord Grey later said of this code that it had immortalized Johnston's name. In 1806, in a paper submitted to

133. Auckland to Hobhouse, April 16, 1837, Home and Miscellaneous, Vol. 838, I.O.L. For Auckland's policy, see D. P. Sinha, *Some Aspects of British Social and Administrative Policy in India During the Administration of Lord Auckland* (Calcutta, 1969), 11–66.

Charles James Fox, with whom he had become acquainted, he proposed that Indian natives be given a major share in their own government.[134] Upon returning to England from Ceylon, he continued to work in that direction.

Thus, in testifying before the parliamentary committee hearings preceding the Charter Act of 1833, he proposed that legislative councils with representation from all classes of Indians be set up. After all, he remarked, India had been governed by natives for two thousand years before Europeans got there. "It is therefore to be inferred that the natives are just as competent as Europeans can be to legislate for their own wants and their own country."[135] He did not even exclude the possibility that Indians might be in the majority on his proposed legislative councils. In this respect he was willing to go very much further not only than Macaulay, but than almost any other contemporary English statesman concerned with Indian affairs. The same was true of the unreservedly positive attitude he took toward natives holding the very highest positions in government and in the company's civil service.

As we know, Macaulay spoke with great eloquence of the desirability of this in his Charter Act speech. And, in his official capacity in India, he favored the appointment of natives as long as they remained under direct European supervision. But when, in 1836, the Lieutenant Governor of the Northwest Provinces wanted permission to appoint certain classes of native officials to act as assistants to European magistrates, Macaulay agreed with his fellow councilor Henry Shakespear that natives at a distance from European control could not be trusted with the power of fining or imprisoning; though he expressed the hope that in not too distant a future it would be possible to employ some of the principal native officers in the administration of criminal justice.[136] However, twenty years after the Charter Act of 1833, which had made it legal for natives to hold higher offices, none as yet did. "There is a practical exclusion, and so there must be, until the natives are very much improved in character," John Stuart Mill then testified before the House of Lords Select

134. For this as well as other papers of Johnston's, see *Parliamentary Papers,* XII (1831–2) , July 9, 1832, 147–84.

135. Ibid., July 6, 1839. T.B.M., as a member of the committee, was present during part of Johnston's testimony. In a letter written to Hannah and Margaret, July 4, 1832, Trinity Correspondence, while the committee was in session, he referred to "Sir Alexander Johnstone [sic] . . . on whom be all the curses of bores, palavering at the table." And added for good measure: "That Sir Alexander's eternal prosing puts all my imaginations to flight."

136. Indian Legislative Proceedings, LXXXIV (1836) , December 19, 1836, I.O.L.

Committee.[137] During the subsequent debate in the House of Commons, Macaulay, while reiterating his hope that eventually the effect of Western education in India would permit talented natives to gain positions in the "covenanted" civil service (i.e., its higher ranks) in competition with English candidates, expressed his belief that "there is not in India a young Native whom it would be a kindness to the Native population to place, at the present moment, in your civil service."[138]

Johnston's view more than two decades earlier had been in striking contrast to this. Since, he said, there were in India natives of high caste, high rank, great wealth, great talents, and local influence, why not make them immediately eligible for higher state offices? Like Mill and Macaulay, Johnston wanted the British to remain in India for the foreseeable future. But where he differed from them was in his conviction that the sooner the government made use of the natives in this way, the more attached to Britain they would become; since the more they would have to lose by overthrowing their rulers.[139] He, too, saw the need for circulating historical, political, and moral knowledge among the Indian people; but he felt that the only way to do this was in their own languages, and through the traditional media of drama, sculpture, and pictorial representation.[140]

He was, in fact, that rare phenomenon, someone with advanced liberal political ideas who combined with them great love and respect for (as well as great scholarly interest in) Indian culture, history, and institutions. In 1823 he helped to found the Royal Asiatic Society, of which he became a vice-president and chairman of its Committee of Correspondence. By the 1830's the Society had come under the patronage of William IV, and counted the Duke of Sussex and Lord Wellesley among its other patrons. Its list of members included the most distinguished Orientalists the world over. It had close ties with the Court of Directors of the East India Company, whose chairman was the Society's vice-patron *ex officio*, and with similar local societies in India. Thus, its Oriental Translation Committee, of which Sir Alexander was deputy chairman in 1836, had branches in Calcutta, Madras, and Bombay.[141]

137. June 22, 1852, *Parliamentary Papers*, XXX (1852–3), 324.

138. June 24, 1853, *Hansard*, 3rd series, CXXVIII (1853), 757.

139. July 6, 1832, *Parliamentary Papers*, XII (1831–2), 139.

140. For his very interesting proposals in this regard, see ibid., IX (1831–2), July 19, 1832, 254–6.

141. As one looks at the list of contributors to the activities of that committee in the Society's Annual Report (1836), one's eye is struck by "Macauley" (*sic*). But the 10 guineas had been sent by Uncle Colin, the major-general. *Journal of the Royal Asiatic Society*, III (1836), cxiii. Needless to say, neither Trevelyan nor T.B.M. was a member.

Johnston played a prominent part in the Society's proceedings. If one seeks a contemporary counterfoil to Macaulay's Minute of 1835, one could not find a more striking one than his report, as chairman of the Committee of Correspondence, to the Society's anniversary meeting of the same year. In the course of that report he asserted that the Hindus had (1) made the same progress in logic and metaphysics by 1500 B.C. as the Greeks during the most enlightened period of their history; (2) possessed centuries before the Greeks laws equal to, and in some cases, superior to theirs; (3) possessed early knowledge of the numeral system which had proved to be essential for the achievements of Kepler, Newton, LaPlace, and Johnston's own ancestor Napier; and (4) devised astronomical tables of great scientific worth around 3000 B.C.

At the time Johnston delivered this report, he was a member of the Judicial Committee of the Privy Council—now the court of ultimate appeal in colonial litigation; and had clearly become, as Auckland's despatch indicates, a figure whose influence was to be reckoned with. That he would indeed have advised strongly against the new educational policy, had he been consulted, becomes crystal clear from the report of the Royal Asiatic Society's anniversary meeting of 1836. By that time news of the Anglicist victory had reached London; and some of the leading members of the Society condemned the new policy in no uncertain terms. Charles W. Williams Wynn (Canning's "Mr. Squeaker")—president of the Board of Control from 1822 to 1828 and now president of the Royal Asiatic Society—led off. "He was not sanguine," so the account of his speech went,

as to the introduction of the English language into the East; but this attempt at forcing the natives to adopt it, would, in his opinion, produce a complete reaction, and defeat the plan. When he considered how attached the people of India were to their own language, it was not probable, that out of compliment to their rulers, they would all at once adopt another. A striking example of the truth of his observations might be found in the case of his own country, Wales. . . . Poland was another instance of what he alleged.

Other speakers, Sir George Staunton and Sir Ralph Rice, echoed their president, with Rice endorsing Wynn's Welsh example with particular fervor—"for, if there was one thing which the Welsh loved far above all others, it was the sweet sound of their own language."

He also adduced the bitter hatred that Napoleon had elicited from the Dutch as a result of his attempt to put down their language.[142]

Wynn informed the meeting that a delegation consisting of himself and other prominent members of the Society (undoubtedly including Sir Alexander Johnston, in his capacity of vice-president) had paid calls on the "Chairs," as well as on Hobhouse at the Board of Control, to protest the decision; "and the answer given by these gentlemen led him to hope that the application would be attended with good effect."[143] Had he known of Hobhouse's real feelings regarding the Society, of which he was (*ex officio*) a member, he would have been less sanguine. In reporting to Auckland in the autumn of 1837 that the education question had reposed during the whole of the parliamentary session just concluded, and that he thought it would be heard of no more, "at least not in a loud or complaining tone of voice," the president of the Board of Control felt bound to add that there was "a certain Asiatic society inclined to be troublesome, and talk nonsense on that as well as other subjects."[144] Hobhouse himself did not seem greatly perturbed by that "nonsense." "If you like a few Mahometan scholarships," he informed Auckland with studied nonchalance, "you shall have them, i.e., I will recommend them to the Court: But I see no cause for haste in this matter."[145]

It happened no more than once in a hundred times, John Stuart Mill was to testify to the Lords committee of 1853, that a despatch prepared by the Court of Directors underwent alteration in principle and substance by the Board of Control.[146] His own "P.C.," seventeen years before, had met such a fate. Barring a few sops to Indian public opinion—such as the scholarships for the Madrassa—the Bentinck-Macaulay policy was secure. And so it remained.

142. Ibid., lv, lvii–lviii. For Johnston's report, see ibid., II (1835), x–xvii.
143. Ibid., lv.
144. Hobhouse to Auckland, August 30, 1837, Home and Miscellaneous, Vol. 838, I.O.L.
145. Idem.   146. June 22, 1852, *Parliamentary Papers*, XXX (1852–3), 317.

XIII

INDIAN EDUCATION: THE CONSEQUENCES

In August 1835, Macaulay wrote to James Mill: "We have now fallen to work in good earnest. Instead of paying away our funds in jaghires to students of Mahometan and Hindu theology, we opened schools at the principal towns in the two presidencies. The stir in the native world is certainly very great."[1] As president of the newly constituted General Committee of Public Instruction, Macaulay became actively involved in the day-to-day running of these schools; and the Minutes he wrote about some of the problems that arose provide instructive glimpses of his thought, style, and methods. John Stuart Mill, who so cavalierly dismissed Macaulay as someone who had never in his life devoted himself to any practical object, might have had second thoughts, had he been able to observe the way in which the man he called a "coxcombical dilettante littérateur," but whom many others would have, even then, called one of the leading English men of letters, found time to devote time and energy to what were often bound to be matters of trivial detail.

One of Macaulay's most characteristic qualities, and one that keeps coming to the surface in these Educational Minutes, is his irrepressible sense of the ludicrous. Thus, his comment on the application for a mastership of a former clergyman:

1. T.B.M. to James Mill, August 24, 1835, MS in the possession of Mr. Gordon Ray.

Mr. —— seems indeed to be so little concerned about proselytising, that he does not even know how to spell the word, a circumstance which, if I did not suppose it to be a slip of the pen, I should think a more serious objection than the Reverend which formerly stood before his name.

On the subject of overindulgence on the part of the committee in allowing masters to transfer from one school to another: "We have a collection of rolling-stones which, as the proverb says, gather no moss. Our masters run from station to station at our cost, as vapourish ladies at home run about from spa to spa." On the subject of the proposal to deprive a successful candidate named Balmokund at Agra College of an essay prize he had been awarded on the ground that he was not a Christian: "That would be too much in the style of Diocletian, who is reprehended very justly, though not very much *apropos,* in Balmokund's Essay."[2]

The humor was an integral part of Macaulay's particular brand of common sense, at no time demonstrated to better advantage than in these Minutes. One can argue that they were not, in the long run, significant; and that they should therefore be left in the comparative oblivion of Woodrow's collection. Yet for anyone who wishes to understand Macaulay's cast of mind they supply an invaluable record, an essential supplement to the more formally significant products of his Indian years. The problems, to be sure, were not always major ones. There was the question, for instance, as to whether the committee could afford to supply paper for the use of the students at Gowhatta School. Macaulay's decision? The great majority of the boys could do very well for some time using slates. In any event, the paper sent for scrawling ought to be the largest and cheapest obtainable.[3] What about financing punkahs and punkah pullers for college students? "I approve. I would make them physically as comfortable as possible while they are studying." Should the *Edinburgh* and *Quarterly* reviews be put into the Hooghly College library? No. The library was for the students, not for the professors.[4]

Then there was the matter of prizes. Too many were being awarded at the Patna school. "The practice of giving almost as many prizes as they [*sic*] are students is in the highest degree pernicious," Macaulay minuted. It destroyed all emulation. It was also very expensive. "The most trifling honourary distinction, a copper medal or book worth two rupees, if given only to one highly distinguished

2. Woodrow, *Educational Minutes,* 49–50, 54.   3. August 29, 1836, ibid., 63.
4. April 6 and May 4, 1837, ibid., 101, 102.

student, will do more to excite industry than a thousand rupees laid out in making presents to the majority of the boys of the school.''[5] The number of prizes should also be reduced at Hindu College. And, above all, a stop must be put to the grotesque dramatic exhibition that followed the prize distribution. Even in England, acting by boys deserved no more than indulgence at best. In India, such recitations were particularly out of place. "I can conceive nothing more grotesque than the scene from the Merchant of Venice, with Portia represented by a little black boy.'' There were other subjects, equally ill chosen and out of place, as well as offensive to good taste.

The society of Calcutta assemble to see what progress we are making; and we produce as a sample a boy who repeats some blackguard doggerel of George Colman's about a fat gentleman who was put to bed over an oven, and about a man-midwife who was called out of his bed by a drunken man at night. Our disciple tries to hiccup, and tumbles and staggers about in imitation of the tipsy English sailors whom he has seen at the punch houses. Really, if we can find nothing better worth reciting than this trash, we had better give up English instruction altogether.

Macaulay's advice was to put a stop to the oaths and the buffoonery. He felt it was sufficient if the author of the best essay read it aloud after the prizes had been awarded.[6]

What should the prizes consist of? It was "absolutely unintelligible" to Macaulay why Pope's *Works* and "my old friend Moore's Lalla Rookh" should have been selected from the mass of English poetry as prize books. He undertook to frame a better list:

Bacon's Essays, Hume's England, Gibbon's Rome, Robertson's Charles V, Scotland, and America, Gulliver, R. Crusoe, Shakespeare, *Paradise Lost,* Milton's smaller poems, *Arabian Nights,* Parke's Travels, Anson's Voyage, Vicar of Wakefield, Johnson's Lives, Gil Blas, Voltaire's Charles XII, Southey's Nelson, Middleton's Cicero.

Those were books that would amuse and interest the prizewinners. To give a boy "Abercrombie on the Intellectual Powers, Dick's Moral Improvement, Guy's Intellectual Philosophy, Chalmers' Poetical [*sic*] Economy (in passing I may be allowed to ask what that means) " was quite absurd. There was a difference between prize books and schoolbooks. Prize books were those a boy received with pleasure, and turned over and over again, not as a task but spontane-

5. December 2, 1835, ibid., 35.   6. May 10, 1837, ibid., 35.

ously. Macaulay recalled that he himself had never been better pleased than when at the age of fourteen he had received Boswell's *Johnson* as a prize: "If my master had given me, instead of Boswell, a Critical Pronouncing Dictionary, or a geographical class book, I should have been much less gratified by my success."[7]

Even when it came to schoolbooks rather than prize books, Macaulay did not think much of grammars and treatises on rhetoric.

Give a boy Robinson Crusoe. That's worth all the grammars of rhetoric and logic in the world. . . . Who ever reasoned better for having been taught the difference between a syllogism and an enthymeme? Who ever composed with greater spirit and elegance because he could define an oxymoron or an aposiopesis? I am not joking, but writing quite seriously when I say that I would much rather order a hundred copies of Jack the Giant Killer for our schools than a hundred copies of any grammar of rhetoric or logic that ever was written.[8]

At a more advanced level, there was such a thing as knowing too much about English literature. After examining students at Hindu College, Macaulay found a disproportionate amount of attention given to it: "They all had by heart the names of all the dramatists of the time of Elizabeth and James the First, dramatists of whose works they in all probability will never see a copy: Marlow [*sic*], Ford, Massinger, Decker [*sic*], and so on. But few of them knew that James the Second was deposed."[9] English history, then, was an essential subject. And so was geography. "I am not sure that it is not of all studies that which is most likely to open the mind of a native of India." But astronomy was less essential. Macaulay knew many enlightened English gentlemen who could not tell Aldebaran from Castor and Pollux. So he gave instructions that ten times as many terrestrial as celestial globes had better be ordered.[10]

It is illuminating to look at these practical, day-to-day "housekeeping" memoranda and decisions in the light of Macaulay's Minute of February 7; since, in doing so, one gets some idea of how the author, when given the chance, went about putting its recommendations into effect. The English language, he wrote in one of these "minor" Minutes, was the great avenue by which the people of India could arrive at all valuable knowledge. Without it, a native could never have more than a smattering of science. With it, he had ready access

7. December 21, 1836, ibid., 82–3.   8. May 6, 1835, ibid., 74–5.
9. Sanial, "Macaulay," *Calcutta Review*, 480.
10. March 25, 1835, Woodrow, *Educational Minutes*, 72.

to full and accurate information on every subject; and, if his natural talents were great, he could make very considerable advances in knowledge, even without the aid of a teacher. Thus, Macaulay favored native students teaching each other English as far as possible so that a greater number of them could learn it.[11] There was no point, he remarked in another Minute, in imposing a maximum age limit on students of English. After all, in the sixteenth century—historical analogies came so naturally to Macaulay that one finds them even in the briefest and most casual of his writings—"it was not at all unusual to see old Doctors of Divinity attending lectures side by side with young students." He would be sorry to deny Indians of any age facilities for studying English.[12] The more, the better.

On the other hand, he did not want the committee to have any part of infant schools. In England it was, after all, only the children of the poor who were sent to such schools; to be "safe, cheerful, and harmlessly, if not profitably, employed while their parents are at work." But in India, it was not the function of the British to educate the lower classes directly. "We aim at raising up an educated class who will hereafter, as we hope, be the means of diffusing among their countrymen some portion of the knowledge which we have imparted to them." "Our schools," he asserted in another of these Minutes, "are nurseries of School-masters for the next generation. If we can raise up a class of educated Bengalees, they will naturally, and without any violent change, displace by degrees the present incompetent teachers."[13]

It is quite clear from these Minutes that Macaulay continued to remain attached to the position he had enunciated in his Minute of February 1835: that direct education of the Indian masses was, for the moment, a pipedream; and that the best that could be done at present with the funds available was to train a group of intermediaries who would themselves become teachers and pass on what they had learned. It is also quite clear that Macaulay was strongly in favor of combining vernacular with English instruction whenever possible. "Indeed," he wrote,

I conceive that an order to give instruction in the English language is, by necessary implication, an order to give instruction, where that instruction is required, in the vernacular language. For what is meant by teaching a

11. October 2, 1835, ibid., 26. This was in the tradition of the Bell-Lancaster monitorial system, which Zachary had helped to promote.
12. November 3, 1835, ibid., 23.
13. July 31, 1837, and September 28, 1836, ibid., 145, 149.

boy a foreign language? Surely this, the teaching him what words in the foreign language correspond to certain words in his own vernacular language, the enabling him to translate from the foreign language into his own vernacular language and *vice versa*.

Teaching the boys at Ajmere School to read and write Hindi, therefore, seemed to Macaulay to be *"bona fide* a part of an English education."[14]

The idea of creating an indigenous Hindi literature, however, was a different matter, and one far beyond the powers of the General Committee of Public Instruction. "Languages grow. They cannot be built."[15] All the committee could try to do was to raise up a class of enlightened natives. "I hope," Macaulay wrote,

that twenty years hence there will be hundreds, nay thousands, of natives familiar with the best modes of composition, and well acquainted with Western science. Among them some persons will be found who have the inclination and the ability to exhibit European knowledge in the vernacular dialects.

That was the only way in which a good Indian vernacular literature could be encouraged to grow. But no funds at all were to be expended on Persian or Arabic, whether for purposes of teaching or translation. "That the Saracens a thousand years ago cultivated mathematical science is hardly, I think, a reason for now spending any money in translating English treatises on Mathematics into Arabic."[16] Thus, Macaulay emphasized once again that the educated class he had in mind was to consist not of the traditional Indian learned men, who would use Oriental languages to reinforce the vernaculars and to engraft the knowledge of the West upon them, but of a new élite of natives fully conversant with English.

On one important question, whether an educated English-speaking class would not find itself totally and fatally separated from the rest of their countrymen if public employment were to be exclusively reserved for it, Macaulay found himself in difficulties. When the issue first came up, shortly before he left India for home, he had come to no conclusion about the matter, since, he wrote, his opinion was altogether founded on general reasoning and on what he had observed in England.[17] But when the matter was put to the

14. July 3, 1836, ibid., 41.   15. November 25, 1836, ibid., 43.
16. August 30, 1837, and April 9, 1835, ibid., 44, 72.
17. November 4, 1837, ibid., 51. He did not always show such restraint in similar circumstances.

vote, he showed remarkable foresight. Reserving a monopoly of public positions for students educated under the aegis of the committee was bound to separate them from the great body of their countrymen. That would be the disadvantage of the education they had received, and it had to be set off against its advantages: "We mean these youths to be conductors of knowledge to the people, and it is of no use to fill the conductors with knowledge at one end, if you separate them from the people at the other." To some degree it was inevitable that these specially educated students would become estranged from the rest of the Indian people by the mode in which they had been brought up. But the proposal to reserve special places of employment, situations not open to their countrymen, for them would only increase the evil. Still, having voiced his reservations, Macaulay in the end voted for the proposal.[18] A few days later he was on the high seas, bound for England. But the problem he had foreseen duly arose; and there are those who have called it his chief legacy to India.

That was a long-term consequence of the new policy. In the short run, there was considerable enthusiasm among the Hindus in Bengal for the new English schools. Thousands wanted to be enrolled. By 1838, forty "seminaries," where English was taught, were under the control of the General Committee of Public Instruction. Boys from every caste were admitted to them.[19] The Calcutta Book Society sold more than 30,000 English books over a period of two years. On the other hand, Muslims everywhere were hostile to the new educational policy. And, in contrast to Bengal, there was considerably less activity or interest in English education in Bombay and Madras.[20]

In Bengal, however, the funds of the Education Committee were now spent almost exclusively for English education. Trevelyan exulted in the columns of the *Edinburgh Review* (1836) that at the newly established Hooghly College, 1,100 students flocked to the English, as against 300 to the Oriental department.[21] At the lower levels of education the committee, in spite of its expressed interest in the vernaculars (which, as we have seen, Macaulay endorsed), did little more than set up English schools in the chief towns. Meanwhile, from 1835 to 1838, William Adam conducted his statistical

18. December 3, 1837, ibid., 51.
19. Trevelyan, *Education*, 16, 19. Trevelyan, optimistic as usual, expressed the view that caste would not long survive, when all were trained to disregard it.
20. Edwardes, *Raj*, 142.
21. Charles Trevelyan, *Hinduism and Christianity Contrasted* (1837), 83. This is a reprint of his article.

inquiry into existing conditions of native education in Bengal. His reports recommended the establishment of vernacular schools in every "thana"; and his views found support in pamphlets such as B. H. Hodgson's *Pre-Eminence of the Vernaculars; or, the Anglicists Answered: Being four Letters on the Education of the People of India.* It was Hodgson who, in a preface to the republication of his letters (1843), coined the term "Macaulayism" to denote the actual policy of the new General Committee of Public Instruction.[22]

That policy had turned out to be one of using available funds primarily for English rather than vernacular education.[23] As far as Bengal was concerned, it was endorsed by Lord Auckland in a Minute dated 1839. He was convinced that the primary task of the government was to diffuse wider information and better sentiments among the upper and middle classes; and that it was not possible as yet to try to educate the masses. However, he used the occasion to report on an experiment involving elementary vernacular schools that was being conducted in Bombay. On the whole, he felt that even at that level English instruction would attract more students.[24] In 1841, the Court of Directors, silent on the subject of education since 1835, endorsed a policy (proposed by Auckland) lending limited countenance to the study of Oriental literature, but stressing above all "the importance of supplanting Persian by English in the public services and in everyday business and of satisfying the increasing demand among the natives for a knowledge of the English language as a means towards public and private employment."[25] This was clearly a victory for the Bentinck-Macaulay point of view. But, in fact, approaches to the immense problem of educating the Indian masses differed from area to area.

In Bengal, Auckland was proved correct in his supposition that English would attract the greater number of students by the failure of a vernacular education experiment in 1844. The inhabitants there expected the government to give them English schools. In Bombay, on the other hand, efforts to establish vernacular schools in every village of more than 2,000 inhabitants, on condition that the people contributed to their cost, resulted by 1842 in 120 such schools, with about 7,000 pupils. In the Northwest Provinces the Lieutenant

22. Brian H. Hodgson, *Miscellaneous Essays Relating to Indian Subjects* (2 vols., London, 1880), II, 255.

23. Barret, "Bentinck," 101–4.

24. Auckland, Minute of November 24, 1839, Sharp, *Educational Records*, 152–65.

25. Harris, "Mill," *Canadian Journal of Economic and Political Science*, 200.

Governor, James Thomason (1843–53), conducted his own experiment in vernacular education, whose aim it was to bring local peasants up to a minimal standard of literacy, sufficiently high to defend themselves against exploitation. But here, as elsewhere, what the government was able to do in the face of the vast numbers involved was no more than a drop in the bucket. This becomes apparent from the official statistics reporting the total number of pupils educated at government expense in all parts of the British dominions in India on April 30, 1845: 17,360, for the most part Hindus.[26]

In 1853 there took place yet another of those parliamentary inquiries into the administration of Her Majesty's Indian territories, the last one to deal with the affairs of the company, which ceased to exist five years later. A Select Committee of the House of Lords heard evidence; and the result of the new educational policy was one of the subjects upon which witnesses were interrogated. Trevelyan testified, of course; and, not surprisingly, displayed great enthusiasm for what English education had already accomplished. After Persian was dropped as the official language, he said, it had "melted away like snow." English was much easier to learn than Sanskrit or Arabic, and more useful. Some of the Hindus spoke purer English "than we speak ourselves." For—and here it is hard to tell whether the irony was conscious or unconscious—"they take it from the purest models; they speak the language of the Spectator, such English as is never spoken in England."[27]

But by far the most interesting part of Trevelyan's testimony consisted of his elaboration of a theme he had already enunciated some years before in his *On the Education of the People of India* (1838), a section of which he had devoted to a discussion of the political tendencies of different systems of education. Here he had developed some of the strategic concepts that underlay and reinforced his advocacy of English as the principal means of instruction. Both Hinduism and Mohammedanism, he had written, were in their nature exclusive. If they were to become popular through a system of national education, they would be "perpetually reminding the Mahommedans that we are infidel usurpers of some of the fairest realms of the Faithful, and the Hindus, that we are unclean beasts, with whom it is a sin and a shame to have any friendly intercourse."[28]

26. This and preceding paragraphs based on Edwardes, *Raj*, 143–4.

27. June 16, 1853, *Parliamentary Papers*, XXXII (1852–3), 148–9.

28. Trevelyan, *Education*, 188–9. For a different view, see Azizur R. Mallick, *British Policy and the Muslims in Bengal, 1757–1856* (Dacca, 1961).

On the other hand, the spirit of English literature was favorable to the Indian connection with England. Indian youths, "educated in the same way, interested in the same objects, engaged in the same pursuits with ourselves . . . become more English than Hindus, just as the Roman provincials became more Romans than Gauls or Italians." Instead of brooding over former independence and making their sole aim the expulsion of the English, they would themselves have a stake in English protection and instruction. In the nature of things, the Anglo-Indian connection could not be permanent. Ultimately, the Indians were bound to regain their independence. But whereas a Muslim or Hindu despotism might be re-established in a month, a century would scarcely suffice to prepare India for self-government on the European model. And during that time, "we shall be as safe as it will be possible for us to be. The natives will not rise against us, because we shall stoop to raise them."[29] The educated classes would have to cling to their rulers, since they themselves would have everything to fear from premature independence. Eventually, in other words, when they had learned to make good use of it, independence would come. And then—here Trevelyan took a leaf out of Macaulay's speech of 1833—"we shall exchange profitable subjects for still more profitable allies."[30] Strictly speaking, there would be no separation at all. For a commercial union between the first manufacturing and the first producing countries in the world would replace the present connection with one of even greater attachment.

Even today, Trevelyan's testimony before the Select Committee makes dramatic reading. If the British government took the proper course in regard to education, Trevelyan asserted, India, like Canada and Australia, might then go through an intermediate period, a sort of gradual transition toward independence. At this point, Lord Ellenborough, a Tory and a former Governor-General of India, interjected: "Why should we ever leave it [India] at all?" To which Trevelyan replied: "I hold that this is the way to keep it as long as possible."[31] If and when the political connection ceased, Trevelyan continued, India would be left a highly improved country so that trading with her would probably be more advantageous than before. This, after all, had been true of the United States, where England now had trade advantages it could never have possessed before

29. Trevelyan, *Education*, 190–3.   30. Ibid., 194.

31. June 23, 1853, *Parliamentary Papers*, XXXII (1852–3), 170–1. A little later, he reiterated that the ultimate result of "improving" and educating Indians would be to postpone India's separation from Britain for "a long indefinite period." Ibid., 173.

American independence. Here is the "Imperialism of Free Trade" spoken plain.

It will be recalled that twenty years previously, in one of his letters to Bentinck, Trevelyan had expressed his private conviction that English education was destined to sound the death knell of the idolatrous religions not only of India, but of all Asia. In his *On the Education of the People of India,* he had more publicly reiterated his belief that Hinduism—"not a religion which will bear examination"—would give way at once before the light of European science; and that, though Mohammedanism was "made of tougher materials," Muslim youths, too, would become different persons after receiving an English education.[32] Now, in his testimony before the House of Lords Select Committee, he stressed once again his certainty that English education could not but lead to the triumph of Christianity in India. Sounding very much like his brother-in-law, he declared: "It is sufficient to prove that the world does not rest on the back of a tortoise, or is not composed of concentric circles of wine and cake and milk, and so forth, and their religion is gone." The natives were now in a "middle state" of enlightened heathenism. But they could not remain in that state. They needed a religion, and were bound to go on to Christianity.[33]

Thus, for someone like Trevelyan, the introduction of the English language and of English literature into India had a significance that far transcended educational innovation. In part, that significance was political: the extension for at least a century of British rule; in part, economic: the continuance of that rule by other, commercial means, even after the formal connection ceased; in part, religious: the end of idolatry and the triumph of Christianity, brought about with the official policy of "religious neutrality" still intact. Trevelyan was at pains to underline the fact that all these benefits would result not from any Machiavellian maneuvers, but from nothing more than the simple performance of their duty by the rulers of India. When Lord Wharncliffe asked him during the Select Committee hearings whether it was not "our plain duty" to promote the improvement of the people of India, whatever the result, Trevelyan replied in the affirmative. "It is a plain moral duty," he averred, "to govern India as well as we possibly can for the benefit of the Natives; and Providence has so arranged, that the performance of duty shall always be found to be conducive to the best interests of mankind. Honesty in

32. Trevelyan, *Education,* 203.
33. June 23, 1853, *Parliamentary Papers,* XXXII (1852-3) , 183-4.

this, as in everything else, is the best policy."[34] What is more, he believed it.

To what extent did Macaulay share this faith in the incidental benefits of the new educational policy? He certainly agreed with Trevelyan that it would help to cushion the shock of ultimately inevitable separation by bringing into existence a nation able and willing to buy as well as to think British. After all, he himself had first sounded this theme in his Charter Act speech of 1833; and Trevelyan, for whom his brother-in-law had quickly become, in his own word, an "oracle," probably owned some of his ideas on the subject to Macaulay. Whether Macaulay shared to the full Trevelyan's confident belief that English education would hasten the providential triumph of Christianity in India is more problematical. A letter to his father, often quoted, seems to indicate that he did. On October 12, 1836, he wrote to Zachary:

Our English schools are flourishing wonderfully. We find it difficult,—indeed, in some places impossible,—to provide instruction for all who want it. At the single town of Hoogly fourteen hundred boys are learning English. The effect of this education on the Hindoos is prodigious. No Hindoo, who has received an English education, ever remains sincerely attached to his religion. Some continue to profess it as a matter of policy; but many profess themselves pure Deists, and some embrace Christianity. It is my firm belief that, if our plans of education are followed up, there will not be a single idolater among the respectable classes in Bengal thirty years hence. And this will be effected without any efforts to proselytise; without the smallest interference with religious liberty; merely by the natural operation of knowledge and reflection. I heartily rejoice in the prospect.[35]

What must be borne in mind in reading this letter is the person to whom it was addressed. In commenting upon the periodical insertion on Macaulay's part in his letters to Zachary some years before of anecdotes and observations regarding slavery, Sir George Trevelyan aptly noted that they reminded the reader "of those presents of tall recruits with which, at judiciously chosen intervals, Frederick the Great used to conciliate his terrible father."[36] True, Macaulay firmly (and wrongly) believed that a knowledge of Western science, geography, and history would be inimical to Eastern religions.

34. Ibid., 178.
35. T.B.M. to his father, October 12, 1836, Trevelyan, *Life and Letters*, 329–30.
36. Ibid., 98.

"Every young Brahmin, therefore, who learns geography in our colleges, learns to smile at the Hindoo mythology," he wrote in his essay on Ranke.[37] But where he differed from Trevelyan—and, *a fortiori,* from his father—was in the way in which he regarded the forthcoming collapse of Indian religion not so much as the triumph of Christianity over idolatry, but rather as the triumph of civilization over barbarism. During the summer of 1838, shortly after his return from India, Hobhouse met him at a social gathering and subsequently noted:

He seemed to me not to have the slightest taint of fanaticism, which somewhat affected, in those days, our Indian servants.[38] Indeed, he told me that the religious controversies which disturbed society at Madras had no existence in Bengal. Of the latter Presidency he said laughingly, "that every man was either a sinner or a saint"; either a hypocrite or an atheist—at least, so called by the opposite party.[39]

This attitude of Macaulay's, more genuinely characteristic of his views than his letter to his father, may explain why in his essay on Gladstone's *Church and State* (which appeared a few months later) he asserted that it was not necessary to be a Christian in order to wish for the propagation of Christianity in India. It was sufficient to be a European not much below the ordinary European level of good sense and humanity. For in no part of the world was heathenism "more cruel, more licentious, more fruitful of absurd right, and pernicious laws."[40] In similar fashion, in his speech on "The Gates of Somnauth" four years later, he called the great majority of the population of India "idolators, blindly attached to doctrines and rites which, *considered merely with reference to the temporal interests of mankind* [my italics], are in the highest degree pernicious." It was not only that the Brahminical mythology was absurd in itself, and bound up with an absurd system of physics, an absurd geography, and an absurd astronomy. It was an immoral, as well as an inelegant and an irrational superstition. "But for our interference human victims would still be offered to the Ganges, and the widow would still be laid on the pile with the corpse of her husband, and burned

37. T.B.M., "Ranke's History of the Popes" (1840) , *Works,* IX, 293.
38. Hobhouse to Auckland, August 30, 1837, Home and Miscellaneous, Vol. 838, I.O.L.: "I am afraid of the violence of your Saints and our Saints, and I prefer attempting some compromise with that fierce and foolish party."
39. June 17, 1838, Broughton, *Recollections,* V, 138.
40. T.B.M., "Gladstone on Church and State" (1839) , *Works,* IX, 148-9.

alive by her children." In view of this, how could there be any question about the superiority of Christianity to that kind of heathenism? To countenance Brahminical idolatry and to discountenance Christianity was "to commit high treason against humanity and civilisation."[41]

In an address delivered at the opening of the Edinburgh Philosophical Institution on November 4, 1846, Macaulay spoke of British literature, "before the light of which impious and cruel superstitions are fast taking flight on the banks of the Ganges."[42] That English literature might also serve to aid the spread of Christianity was certainly not a prospect that caused him any dismay. But his own religious feelings were not, in the words he had used about his brother-in-law, "ardent . . . even to enthusiasm." In this respect, therefore, his attitude toward the future of India was very different from Trevelyan's.

In the course of his testimony before the Lords Select Committee in 1853, Trevelyan came out strongly for setting up vernacular schools in India to the largest extent possible in order to educate the whole body of the people and to engraft upon them, whenever feasible, the means of learning the elements of English.[43] The next official statement of educational policy from London, Sir Charles Wood's despatch of the following year, fell into line with this emphasis, one for which, as we know, Trevelyan had stood for twenty years. Wood's despatch tried to provide for a shift in Indian education, away from inculcating Western literature and philosophy at the higher levels to teaching more practical subjects at the lower.[44] It called for expanded government support in setting up a comprehensive system of elementary and secondary education, as well as a grant-in-aid scheme; so that, as Michael Edwardes has put it, "private institutions could take over the burden of higher education and release government funds for the education of the predominantly rural masses. Essentially, this was no more than a pious hope. The government's main aim was still to be the extension of English education. . . ."[45]

Both Macaulay and Trevelyan were shown a draft of Wood's despatch before it was sent. The latter wrote to the former that it was so comprehensive and complete, and that the views taken in it were so

41. March 9, 1843, T.B.M., *Works*, XII, 22–5.   42. Ibid., 231.
43. June 21, 1853, *Parliamentary Papers*, XXXII (1852–3), 166.
44. R. J. Moore, *Sir Charles Wood's Indian Policy, 1853–66* (Manchester, 1966), 114–15. Wood was president of the Board of Control at the time.
45. Edwardes, *Raj*, 144.

just and liberal, that he had nothing to suggest in addition.[46] But, in fact, these views differed in some degree from those expressed in Macaulay's Minute of 1835. For the stress in Sir Charles Wood's despatch fell not so much on "filtration" as on direct mass education. The reason for this shift in emphasis was clear. "Filtration" had not been successful. And Wood's despatch did not really change the occurrence of what Macaulay had foreseen, but, given his basic policy, could not have prevented: the separation of an English-speaking élite from the rural masses of India. Sir George Trevelyan, writing in 1876, triumphantly recounted the success of the new educational policy. He told of hundreds of thousands of natives who could appreciate European knowledge in English and reproduce it in the vernaculars; more than a thousand works of literature and science published annually in Bengal alone, at least four times that number in all of India; 6,000 students enrolled in colleges, 200,000 receiving a liberal education in schools of the higher order; nearly 7,000 young men in training as certificated masters; the budget allotted to public instruction increased more than seventy-fold since 1835, supplemented by fees willingly paid by parents of all classes, generous contributions to Indian higher education by wealthy natives. And behind all of this, Macaulay, "the master engineer, whose skill and foresight determined the direction of the channels, along which this stream of public and private munificence was to flow for the regeneration of our Eastern Empire."[47]

Those figures are impressive, and one must not fail to recognize what was accomplished as a result of the course charted in 1835. Macaulay's forecasts, as Thompson and Garratt point out, did prove to be partly true. An English-speaking class of persons did, after all, come into existence. The vernaculars did become considerably more important, though more by means of the press than textbooks.[48] English did help to enrich the Indian dialects. But there seems to be general agreement that the master principle of filtration failed to work in the end. Perhaps it was too much to hope for. In using the analogy of Russia, V. G. Kiernan has recently written, Macaulay should have remembered that there, in spite of the influence of Western ideas on the upper classes, the peasants remained as ig-

46. Charles Trevelyan to T.B.M., April 17, 1854, Trevelyan MSS, University of Newcastle Library.
47. Trevelyan, *Life and Letters*, 298.
48. Thompson and Garratt, *Rise and Fulfilment*, 316.
49. Kiernan, *Lords*, 40.

norant as they had been before Peter the Great.[49] The gap between the few with Western knowledge and the many without it remained in India as well. One explanation for this is that the "sieve" through which Western ideas were to flow turned out, after all, to have no vernacular openings in it. The result was estrangement rather than communication, a divisive wall of literary pride and knowledge.[50] Another explanation speaks of the Hindu social system as "most unsuitable for filtration," since it divided the population both socially and culturally into watertight compartments. The educated *Zemindar* (landowner) simply did not return to his village in order to educate his tenants.[51]

Quite apart from the difficulties connected with "filtration," there was the barrier of pride—to some extent foreseen by John Stuart Mill in his "P.C."—which prevented upper-caste Hindus from absorbing the new learning. And there was the barrier of caste. A recent book on western India shows that Mountstuart Elphinstone, Governor of Bombay from 1819 to 1827, tried to rear there a class of new, Western-educated brahmans. But, except for a brief period, these "new" brahmans did not assume the leadership of rural Maharashtra.[52] The "old" brahmans, there and elsewhere, did not take to Western political and social ideas. The new educational policy tended to produce in the end not a learned class imbued with the best that the English language, English literature, and European ideas had to offer but, rather, a large English-speaking secretarial and professional class, without a tradition of responsibility and power.[53] "Education for clerks"—that is how Nehru summed up British educational policy in India during the nineteenth century; adding that supply soon outstripped demand, leaving many of the educated unemployed.[54]

This situation had been foreseen by Radha Kanta Dev, a progressive Calcutta merchant as well as an upholder of Brahminism, whose comments on the new educational policy show that Indian opposition to the widespread introduction of English was by no means entirely "Tory."[55] In 1851, Dev warned against a system,

50. Spear, "Bentinck," *Cambridge Historical Journal*, 98.
51. Thompson and Garratt, *Rise and Fulfilment*, 315–16.
52. Ravinder Kumar, *Western India in the Nineteenth Century: A Study in the Social History of Maharashtra* (London, 1968).
53. Spear, "Bentinck," *Cambridge Historical Journal*, 98–9.
54. Jawaharlal Nehru, *Glimpses of World History* (London, 1942), 434.
55. Barun Dé, "The Influence of Macaulay on India," Curzon Memorial Prize Essay, Oxford, 1957.

whereby, with a smattering knowledge of English, youths are weaned from the plough, the axe, and the loom, to render them ambitious only for the clerkships for which hosts would besiege the government and mercantile offices, and the majority being disappointed (as they must be), would (with their little knowledge inspiring pride) be unable to return to their trade, and would necessarily turn vagabonds.[56]

Dev favored agricultural and industrial schools, where useful skills could be taught. For him the prerequisite for these was a solid vernacular education. Lord Curzon made the same point half a century later when, as Governor-General, he called a conference on the state of Indian education. Making English education the key to government employment, Curzon maintained, had resulted in an overemphasis on pure memory demanded by examinations. He deplored the excessive Anglicization, the contempt for the vernacular literatures of India, and the decline of elementary education in the vernacular, for all of which he blamed "the cold breath of Macaulay's rhetoric." He himself called for an expansion of vernacular education and for emphasis on science and technology rather than literature. But it is worth noting that his opposition to excessive Anglicization was in part motivated by his feeling that an English liberal education tended to foster political speculation and thus threatened order and authority.[57] Whereas Trevelyan and Macaulay had believed that the inculcation of British institutional principles would help to extend the period of British rule, Curzon (who had the same aim) thought that it could best be achieved by greater emphasis on the study of Indian culture which sanctioned order and authority. The strategy and the ultimate aim were the same; only the tactics were different.

Quite apart from these strategic considerations, it could be argued that it was not so much the linguistic medium but the content of English education that had come to be at fault in the Indian educational system as a result of the policy confirmed and proclaimed by Macaulay's Minute; that what was taught was far too literary and academic, and not practical enough. Sir George Trevelyan might celebrate the young Hindu who had made the most of his time at college and who was able to "write by the hour a somewhat florid and stilted English with perfect ease and accuracy; and . . . [to]

56. Jogesh Chandra Bagal, *Radha Kanta Dev, 1784–1867* (5th ed., Calcutta, 1957), 47.
57. Edwardes, *Raj*, 279–83.

enjoy, and criticise any of our authors, from Chaucer down to Robert Browning and Carlyle."[58] But as far as the British in India were concerned, that same young Hindu tended to turn far too easily into "Babu Jabberjee," a figure of fun.[59] "Education," Malcolm Muggeridge has written, "was about the worst thing we did to India and, appropriately enough, contributed to our departure. Was it not predominantly enraged and unemployed graduates who chased us out, hurling after us curses and copies of the *Oxford Book of English Verse*?"[60]

Nationalism was certainly one of the by-products of the new educational policy. As one writer has put it: "Macaulay had . . . stated that at some time in the very distant future a new anglicized class would demand and deserve self-government. This was rhetoric, not policy, but educated Indians—many of them afire with Western liberal ideas—chose to believe him."[61] The English-educated class, Nehru wrote, was destined to take the lead in Indian nationalist movements.[62] It was only natural, after all, that ideas of independence should grow in the minds of professional people, lawyers in the lead, who, after acquiring the same education as their rulers, were more than ever aware of the fact that they themselves were still in positions of dependence.[63]

But nationalism meant more than trying to get rid of the British. The constant reiteration of Western superiority, exemplified by the contemptuous remarks about Indian culture in Macaulay's Minute, still known and quoted by all educated Indians today, led to self-assessment and to a heightened awareness of India's cultural and spiritual heritage. "If Anglicists such as Trevelyan and Macaulay believed that they were writing the obituary for Hindu cultural customs and civilisation as they had succeeded in doing for the Orientalist movement," it has been pointed out, "they proved to be poor prophets."[64] Indian religions have not collapsed in the face of Western knowledge. What did result from the new educational policy was increased social divergence between Muslims and Hindus, as well as a weakening of the cultural links between them since most Muslims, unlike most Hindus, were opposed to the stress on English.

58. G. O. Trevelyan, *The Competition Wallah* (London, 1864) , 425.
59. Kiernan, *Lords*, 48–9.
60. Malcolm Muggeridge, "Twilight of Empire," *The Listener*, LXXII (1964) , 966.
61. Edwardes, *Raj*, 169.
62. Nehru, *Glimpses*, 435–6. See also McCully, *English Education*, 388–95.
63. Spear, "Bentinck," *Cambridge Historical Journal*, 98.
64. Kopf, *Bengal Renaissance*, 272.

As a result, Muslims were slowly ousted from government posts, and their places taken by Hindus.[65]

In view of what has happened in this century, this increased divergence might fairly be called one of the evil consequences of the educational policy Macaulay helped to initiate. Another, similarly deleterious, lies in the realm of identity. Truth, Erik Erikson has pointed out, becomes something hazy when official business and everyday life are conducted in stilted and broken English. It becomes impossible to say what one "really" means.[66] This situation has been nowhere better described than by V. S. Naipaul in his *Area of Darkness*. "The clerk using English in a government office," he writes, "is immediately stultified. For him the language is made up of certain imperfectly understood incantations, which limit his responses and make him inflexible. So he passes his working life in a sub-world of dim perceptions; yet in his own language he might be quick and inventive."[67] But, of course, the previous official language, certainly in Bengal, had not been the vernacular either.

Gandhi's solution was the substitution of Hindi for English. It was nothing less than scandalous, he said, that people should devote the best years of their lives to mastering a foreign tongue.[68] But Hindi is spoken and understood by less than half of India. And the violence that followed the recent introduction of Hindi as the Indian official language shows that the problem cannot be solved that simply. The Indian constitution of 1950 decreed that during the first fifteen years of independence English and Hindi were to be joint official languages. Then, in 1965, Hindi became *the* official language of India, with civil servants being granted higher seniority as a reward for mastering it. But while Hindi was the language of 190 million Indians in the north (representing 40 percent of the country's population), in southern India 111 million people spoke four different languages—Tamil, Telugu, Kaunala, and Malayalam. After the new law went into effect there were suicides, riots, and demonstrations in the south. As a result, the government retained English as the "associate" language of India and permitted the use of regional

65. Frank Moraes, *India Today* (New York, 1960), 55. In his book *The Emergence of Indian Nationalism: Competition and Collaboration in the Later Nineteenth Century* (Cambridge, 1968), 308–9, Anil Seal differs from this assessment. He points out that by mid-century, Calcutta's upper-class and more respectable Muslims were already showing a growing desire for English education; and that what held Muslims back from the new learning was poverty rather than religious prejudice.

66. Erik H. Erikson, *Gandhi's Truth: On the Origins of Militant Nonviolence* (New York, 1969), 259.

67. V. S. Naipaul, *An Area of Darkness* (London, 1968), 213–14.

68. Erikson, *Gandhi*, 282.

languages in civil service examinations. It has been estimated that Indians today speak fourteen major tongues and over eight hundred dialects. In 1965 English, though regarded by many in this century as the tool of British imperialism, proved to be indispensable as the only truly common language spoken by educated Indians.

In view of this recent experience, it might well be questioned whether there was a viable vernacular alternative that might have been pursued in the course of the nineteenth century. Perhaps equivalents for scientific and technological terms could have been found in or added to the vernaculars. Perhaps English was not an essential prerequisite for industrialization. On the other side it has been pointed out that particularism based on the use of vernaculars alone "would have grown so greatly as to break up even the idea of Indian unity."[69] Furthermore, as two other recent scholars have argued, "once the modern Western world had broken in upon India, it was impossible for Indian education to be confined to the traditional paths." Modernization was essential, and it could not come from the traditionalist program of the Orientalists. The linguistic controversy was on the surface. Useful knowledge was the real key. The situation "called for Macaulayan language and Macaulay delivered it."[70]

Impressive testimony as to the correctness of the policy defended in Macaulay's Minute appears in a letter addressed in 1908 by Charles Freer Andrews, a vigorous supporter of Indian independence, to Sir James Dunlop-Smith, Lord Minto's private secretary:

English as the language of education has justified itself, in spite of great drawbacks. It has had a supreme political justification. It has made India no longer only a geographical expression but a political unity. It has created the hope and the possibility of an Indian Nation. English history and literature have fashioned the political thought of modern India and fashioned it inevitably on national lines.[71]

Furthermore, as V. G. Kiernan has written, even had a decision totally in favor of vernacular education been taken, it would not have made the British immune from criticism by Indian nationalists. He instances Indonesia, where there existed widespread suspicion that Dutch talk of indigenous education really meant a plan to keep

69. K. M. Panikkar, *A Survey of Indian History* (4th ed., London, 1964), 211.
70. G. and N. Sirkin, "Macaulay," *Victorian Studies* (1971), 408–9, 428.
71. Andrews to Dunlop-Smith, March 1, 1908, Martin Gilbert, *Servant of India: A Study of Imperial Rule from 1905 to 1910 as Told Through the Correspondence and Diaries of Sir James Dunlop-Smith* (London, 1966), 132.

Western knowledge hidden from the Indonesians.[72] Similar accusations have been brought in South Africa.

They cannot be brought against Macaulay. He had the vision to see that English was on the way to becoming a world language, and he wanted India to become and to remain part of the world community.

English either is or is rapidly becoming the second language in those great regions [India, Africa, Asia], useful because it allows people of even the same race or nation to surmount their own internal linguistic frontiers, to address themselves to the world at large, and to acquire the knowledge essential to their national development.

The author of these lines credits Macaulay with the prophetic gift of having foreseen this. But he praises him even more for going beyond utilitarian considerations to envisage the creation of a class of people educated not because they would be able merely to read and speak English (though we have seen that Macaulay was not dismayed by the prospect of as many people as possible doing just that), but because the knowledge of English would enable them to study Milton, Locke, Newton; in other words, to become truly educated.[73]

Since the deleterious consequences of English for the Indian psyche have been mentioned, it is only just to cite the beneficial consequences in that realm, as described by Nirad Chaudhuri. For him the impact of the English language and English literature resulted in his awareness of a new kind of life,

with psychological dimensions whose existence we had not suspected before. . . . To put it in brief, the greatest human passions which have arisen in the course of evolution of western civilisation, the passions which the western civilised man would consider as basic to his being, did not exist at all amongst us, and we came not only to know about their existence, but even to feel them with intense power, after reading English literature, and only after that.

Without a knowledge of English literature, Hindus would not have had any idea of Western values: of God, of country and nature, of religion and spirituality, of love and of physical beauty. The result, at least as far as Chaudhuri is concerned, was indeed schizophrenia induced by a simultaneous hatred of foreign rule and a love of Western values. But it was, he writes, "a happy and exultant schizo-

72. Kiernan, *Lords*, 40.   73. *Times Literary Supplement*, August 10, 1962, 567–8.

phrenia." And he asks those who were taking so much pride in developing an underdeveloped country to recall "that in a former age they developed an underdeveloped mind."[74]

It remains to ask how much of the praise and blame for the new educational policy of the 1830's should be assigned to Macaulay. For a long time it was assumed that Macaulay was alone responsible for that policy, that it was he who singlehandedly charted the new course that emphasized English instruction. And there are still people today who credit, or debit, him, and him alone, with the policy and its consequences. It was Edward Thompson who, in 1937, pointed out that "more secondhand nonsense is talked about what he is supposed to have done by his own single deed, than about almost any other event in British-Indian history."[75] Thompson maintained that what really settled the question was a combination of Indian insistence, insofar as it could make itself felt, and financial necessity on the part of the British. The course of action Macaulay proposed in his Minute, Thompson said, was one already determined upon by most influential people in the government. Three years later, Percival Spear amplified the same point. After dwelling on the practical considerations that reinforced Bentinck's own inclinations in support of the Anglicists, he summed up as follows: "Macaulay has been too much praised and too much blamed; his contribution was like the lightning flash which vividly illumines the storm and reveals the landscape, albeit in fantastic proportions and bewildering lights; but which neither directs its course nor ordains its conclusion."[76] It was Spear's contention that one must look to England for the decisive factors that produced the change in Indian educational policy, in other words, to Utilitarian and Evangelical currents of thought, and to the fact that by 1830 the Court of Directors of the East India Company had lost its respect for Indian learning and culture. Macaulay and Bentinck, according to Spear, were accessories after the fact rather than instigators of the new policy.

In 1951 Professor Kenneth Ballhatchet took issue with this view. True, the despatch of 1830 had stressed useful knowledge; but it had also warned that it did not necessarily have to be communicated in English. Furthermore, J. S. Mill's "P.C." of 1836 was blocked only by the intervention of Hobhouse. Even in 1841, the home authorities were still not prepared to do more than endorse Auckland's com-

74. Nirad Chaudhuri, "The Impact of England," *The Listener*, LXXVIII (1967), 664–5.

75. Edward Thompson, *The Life of Charles, Lord Metcalfe* (London, 1937), 302.

76. Spear, "Bentinck," *Cambridge Historical Journal*, 83.

promise solution. All this went to show that Bentinck's policy was made in India, and supported from India by Auckland, who successfully persuaded London not to reverse it.[77]

An examination of some of the evidence tends to bear out Professor Ballhatchet on this point; though it would appear that Hobhouse, whose role in rejecting Mill's proposed despatch was, after all, crucial, did not need much persuasion by Auckland to help him reach his decision. One is struck time and again by the very great practical advantages that slow communications between England and India gave to the men on the spot in Calcutta. By the time word of new policies concerning education or anything else reached London, months had passed; and even those who fundamentally disagreed with those policies (e.g., Mill in his "P.C.") were wary of vetoing what, by the date the veto in its turn had reached India, would already have been in force for a considerable period of time. Thus, a Governor-General bent upon instituting certain reforms was hard to stop, except by recall. Speaking in the course of the debate on the Charter Act of 1853 Macaulay recalled that while he was in India, "every measure of which history will hereafter make mention was taken without any authority from home." Almost every such measure had been disapproved at home, yet none had been rescinded or annulled. The language of the home authorities had generally been that the men on the spot had done wrong, but that what they had done was done. "That," Macaulay continued, "was most eminently the case with respect to that great reform made in 1835 by Lord William Bentinck, before his departure from India, on the subject of the education of the Natives in European literature." Other examples were the abolition of transit duties, the Press Act, and the measure establishing a uniform coinage.[78] The initiative lay not in London, but in Calcutta, and the Governor-General was the key figure.

By the time of Macaulay's arrival in India, Bentinck was well on his way to being flattered and cajoled into publicly endorsing an Anglicizing policy, toward which he inclined in any event, by its fanatical champion Charles Trevelyan. There is no reason to doubt Auckland's supposition that authorization from London for the new policy was deliberately not sought on the assumption that it would not be received. The putative influence of Sir Alexander Johnston and the Royal Asiatic Society was one factor here. It should also be remembered that the King had dismissed Melbourne and the Whigs

77. Ballhatchet, "Home Government," *Cambridge Historical Journal* (1951), 224–9.
78. June 23, 1853, *Hansard,* 3rd series, CXXVIII (1853) , 744–5.

in November 1834, and that news of this step had reached Calcutta by the time of Bentinck's resolution. The assumption must therefore have been—correctly—that Charles Grant, who might have been expected to be favorable to the new educational policy, was no longer at the Board of Control. Hobhouse, who was distinctly favorable to the policy, did not assume his post until the Whigs came back in April. He and the Court of Directors were confronted by a *fait accompli* when they received word of the new course in Indian education.

Macaulay's role in helping to engineer that *fait accompli* had been considerable. The full text of his letter to Margaret shows that it was he who induced Bentinck to declare himself in favor of the Anglicists, some weeks before the rival parties in the General Committee of Public Instruction submitted their respective briefs. Thus, victory for Trevelyan's side was "in the bag" some time before Macaulay wrote his famous Minute in February 1835. But it was Macaulay himself who had finally helped to ensure it. It was Macaulay, also, who, at the Governor-General's request, drafted the actual resolution that implemented the new policy. True, in the face of Indian public opinion, Bentinck somewhat softened that resolution before he issued it. But when Auckland reported to Hobhouse that Macaulay had worked "hardly" in the cause of English education, he was not exaggerating. In London, both supporters, such as Hobhouse, and opponents, such as John Stuart Mill, simply assumed that Macaulay's role had been decisive. In one sense, of course, it had been. His case may have been dubious; but in his capacity as legal member of Council he had attested to the legality of the Bentinck resolution. Thus, Hobhouse wrote to Macaulay upon receipt of his resignation as law member, that "although, I fear, I have had the misfortune to differ from you on one or two points, yet in your two main *decisions* [my italics] on the Education Question and the Black Act I have entirely concurred with you."[79] Certainly, Macaulay's persuasiveness, enhanced in Bentinck's eyes by the dazzling reputation that had preceded him, had played its part in bringing the new policy into being.

Macaulay himself took great satisfaction in the role he had played. As we have seen there were then, as there are now, many who did not share his satisfaction. On the very day these lines are being written, a reviewer in the *Times Literary Supplement,* trying to explain the lack of interest in Urdu literature, turns for an explanation in the

79. Hobhouse to T.B.M., August 30, 1837, Home and Miscellaneous, Vol. 838, I.O.L.

first place to "the blighting influence of Macaulay."[80] This anonymous reviewer is only the most recent representative of a point of view which had its beginning in the 1830's. It was certainly Macaulay who was the target of H. H. Wilson's remark in 1836 that

individuals of undoubted talent, but of undeniable inexperience; of unquestionably good intents, but of manifestly strong prejudices, have set themselves impatiently to undo all that was effected by men, at least, their equals in ability, their betters in experience, and who can never be surpassed in an ardent desire to accelerate the intellectual, moral, and religious amelioration of the natives of India.[81]

Wilson did not change his mind. There was a dramatic confrontation between him and Hobhouse, now Lord Broughton, during the House of Lords Select Committee hearings of 1853. Broughton asked Wilson whether he was aware that Macaulay—by this time, of course, famous as the author of the *History of England*—had been one of those who had advocated an English system of education. Wilson replied in the affirmative. "Of course, like everybody else," he added,

I have a great respect for Mr. Macaulay's talents, but he was new in India, and he knew nothing of the people; he spoke only from what he saw immediately around him, which has been the great source of the mistakes committed by the advocates for English exclusively. They have known nothing of the country; they have not known what the people want; they only know the people of the large towns, where English is of use and is effectively cultivated.

A few minutes later, Broughton inquired of Wilson as to whether he had ever seen Macaulay's Minute. He had, of course—"and a very clever minute it is; very ingenious, like all his writings; but there is throughout an evident want of experience and knowledge of the country."[82]

Fair comment, certainly; though it ignores the fact that the likes of Trevelyan, who possessed both experience and knowledge of India, had taken the same line Macaulay took in his Minute. The struggle between Orientalists and Anglicists had political and philosophical dimensions that transcended any conclusions to be drawn from the observation and study of India. All the parties involved

80. *Times Literary Supplement,* January 29, 1970, 104.
81. H. H. Wilson, "Education," *Asiatic Journal* (1836) , 8.
82. July 5, 1853, *Parliamentary Papers,* XXXII (1852–3) , 263–4.

acted strategically, attempting in various ways to bring Western learning and science to bear upon Indian education. Prompted by very different motives, the Orientalists in Calcutta as well as the Mills, father and son, in London, wished to pursue a policy of Burkean caution. Macaulay threw caution to the winds and charged. In many ways there is something refreshingly straightforward about his frontal attack, an attraction lacking in Trevelyan, who shared to the full and even exceeded his brother-in-law's combativeness, but tended to regard the Indian people as potential Christians in a way that Macaulay, who regarded them more reasonably as potential customers, never did. This is not to palliate the crudity of Macaulay's strictures upon Oriental learning and civilization, fated to survive in the purple patches of his Minute. On very little evidence he made up his mind that Indian history and religion were "absurd"; and that was that. In the course of his visit to Rome in the autumn of 1838, shortly after his return from India, he encountered an old Indian gentleman at a dinner party. In his journal he noted that he seemed "exceedingly absurd," adding: "I have since heard what is quite compatible with his absurdity that he is a great Orientalist."[83]

It is perhaps because of this attitude toward Oriental studies that Macaulay, unhesitatingly applying historical analogies from ancient and modern European history to the Indian situation, never suspected those analogies might be inappropriate; that, as one critic has pointed out, Indian social institutions and mental attitudes possessed a resilience which enabled them to absorb the impact of other civilizations without ever finally yielding to them.[84] There is a significant sentence in one of his minor Educational Minutes, in which Macaulay opposed the division of the students of Benares College into rich and poor. It was a difficult matter, he wrote, "and *if society in India be not altogether in a different state from that which exists in Europe* [italics mine], must produce evils."[85] The question of the extent to which allowances had to be made by English administrators for special cultural and historical factors that made India and its people different from Europe and Europeans was one Macaulay had to face constantly and directly in his capacity of law reformer; and it will be considered in that connection. But the Minute just cited would seem to indicate that he did not seriously confront the possibility that India was, in fact, a unique historical and cultural entity.

83. Trinity Journal, November 25, 1838.
84. B. K. Boman-Behram, *Educational Controversies in India* (Bombay, 1943), 231.
85. Woodrow, *Educational Minutes*, 65.

His failure to do so may have led him on occasion into making false analogies. Yet the very same failure may have saved him from passing the sort of condescending judgments upon India and its inhabitants often passed in the course of the nineteenth century by those of his countrymen who assumed that here was a more primitive people, destined to remain for all time in a state of tutelage. Macaulay can certainly be justly accused of underestimating the Indian heritage and Indian cultural achievements. But, as far as he was concerned, the same forces of progress that had operated in Europe to bring general improvement to society as a whole, as well as wealth and power to the middle classes in particular, would also operate in India, once Western seed had taken root. The fact that progressive Hindus such as Ram Mohan Roy regularly used Bacon as the touchstone of intellectual and material progress for India was not lost on Macaulay, and is reflected in his own essay on Bacon, written during his Indian sojourn.

One can argue, as Percival Spear has, that the implication of the Bentinck-Macaulay policy was that Indian civilization had no value; that it was ripe not for enrichment by Western knowledge, but for replacement by Western civilization.[86] The most ardent partisan of Macaulay today cannot turn him into an Orientalist sympathizer, any more than the great Max Müller could more than a century ago. The translator of the Rig-Veda was granted an interview by Macaulay at the end of 1855, when,

primed with every possible argument in favour of Oriental studies, [he] had to sit silent for an hour while the historian poured out his diametrically opposite views, and then dismissed his visitor who tried in vain to utter a single word. "I went back to Oxford," he said, "a sadder and wiser man."[87]

But, however much one may deplore this attitude on the part of Macaulay, one can hardly disagree with the judgment, brief and to the point, that he himself set down in his journal when, almost twenty years after he had written it, he came once more across his Minute on education: "It made a great revolution."[88]

86. Spear, "Bentinck," *Cambridge Historical Journal,* 96.
87. Quoted by Sir H. Verney Lovett, "Education and Missions to 1858," *Cambridge History of India* (6 vols., Delhi, 1964) , VI, 114.
88. Trinity Journal, January 23, 1853.

XIV

THE INDIAN
PENAL CODE

IN HIS CHARTER ACT SPEECH OF 1833 MACAULAY PROPOSED THAT THE reconstituted government of India be given, for a time, the assistance of a Commission for the purpose of digesting and reforming the laws of India so that those laws might, as soon as possible, be formed into a code. India needed such a code, since all her previous conquerors had brought their respective laws with them; and since, at the time, those different systems of law clashed with one another. Macaulay did not call for one identical code for all inhabitants of India. That was unattainable, because feelings generated by differences of religion, of nation, and of caste had to be respected. The principle that was to underlie the new code, best prepared by a small knot of jurists, was to be: "Uniformity where you can have it; diversity where you must have it; but in all cases certainty."[1]

The Act of 1833 duly empowered the setting up of such a Commission, with the task of inquiring fully "into the nature and operation of all laws whether civil or criminal, written or customary, prevailing and in force in any part of the said territories, and whereto any inhabitants of the said territories whether Europeans or others are now subject."[2] Eventually, the act envisioned a general system of justice and police as well as a code of law for all of India. Meanwhile, the Governor-General-in-Council, a Council which, with Macaulay's

1. July 10, 1833. *Works*, XI, 578–82.
2. Cited in Indian Legislative Despatches, No. 4 (1837) , March 1, 1837, I.O.L.

arrival, now included a fourth "legal" member, was invested with new legislative powers. These he was authorized to exercise without awaiting the results of the Law Commission's labors.

Guidelines for the new Council were laid down in a despatch from the home authorities almost certainly written by James Mill.[3] Macaulay's work as legal member of Council evidently owed a great deal to those guidelines. Mill stressed the need for mature deliberation and discussion of the new laws as well as the importance of having them properly authenticated. With the unlimited admission of British citizens to India under the new act, it was essential that their legal status be clearly determined, and the rights of natives protected. Macaulay's "Black Act" had really followed from the sentence: "It would only be necessary to render British subjects truly amenable to the jurisdiction of the native tribunals, and all would be well." Mill allowed for a modicum of variation, since it was inevitable that what would operate as a severe penalty to a Hindu would not be felt as such by an Englishman. But the principle remained. Thus, Englishmen had no inalienable right to a trial by jury. "The only inalienable right of an accused Englishman is justice; and if he resides in the interior of India, he must be content with such justice as is dispensed to the natives."[4]

Mill who, as a leading Benthamite, had no use whatever for the current state of English criminal law, strongly deprecated the transfer to India "of all the peculiarities of our criminal judicature," not being satisfied that those peculiarities were virtues. There was no inherent perfection in the number twelve, no mysterious charm in the enforced unanimity of opinion of a jury. Legislating for the Indian people, the British should not shrink from seeking precedents in the ancient usages of India rather than in the modern practice of England.[5] The principal task of the new legislative body must be to repress rapine, to secure property, and to create confidence. And the fourth or legal member would have to take a principal share in giving shape and connection to the several laws.

Macaulay, as we know, was by no means averse to playing the role of latterday Lycurgus that Mill envisaged for him. After all, his great hero Bacon had devoted his energies to the reduction and recompilation of English law, a task that Macaulay called "the most arduous, the most glorious, and the most useful that even his mighty powers could have achieved."[6] Bacon had exerted a major influence on

3. December 10, 1834. Ilbert, *Government of India*, 492–532.
4. Ibid., 506, 515.   5. Ibid., 516.   6. T.B.M., "Bacon," *Works*, VIII, 546.

Bentham, for whom, as far as matters of jurisprudence were concerned, Macaulay had unreserved admiration.[7] Even in the course of violently attacking the Utilitarians in his essays of 1829, Macaulay had declared that he revered in Bentham the father of the philosophy of jurisprudence.[8] In his article on Mackintosh (written in India) he praised the subject of his essay along with Bentham and Dumont as men who had had nothing but observation and reason to guide them, and who had obeyed the direction of those two guides.[9] For Macaulay, the challenge of reforming laws in the direction of clarity, simplicity, and uniformity was one he was more than ready to accept.

On May 25, 1835, the Acting Governor-General, Sir Charles Metcalfe, asked Macaulay to become head of the Law Commission. In his reply—he was clearly anxious to occupy the position, and, according to Sir George Trevelyan, had in fact instigated the appointment himself[10]—Macaulay wrote that even though he had been permitted to attend all Council meetings and to read all the documents connected with them, he still felt that his official duties did not occupy as much of his time as the public had a right to require. "I cannot better employ my leisure," he went on, "than by taking part in the labours of the law commission; and I shall forthwith enter with the greatest alacrity on the important duties of my new office."[11] That Macaulay, given the time-consuming tasks he was already carrying out, not to mention his own literary projects, should have found it possible to speak of "leisure" is certainly yet another demonstration of his formidable energies. One should remember, however, that after the double blow of Hannah's marriage and Margaret's death, the plunge into ceaseless activity was bound to be therapeutic. Furthermore, law reform was something to which Macaulay could bring real enthusiasm.

When he informed Ellis that "the Government have determined on putting me at the head of the Law Commission," he added, *con brio*: "I have immense reforms in hand,—such as you big Templars would abhor, but such as would make old Bentham jump in his grave—oral pleadings—examination of parties—single-seated justice—

7. On Bacon and Bentham, see Mary Mack, *Jeremy Bentham: An Odyssey of Ideas, 1748–1792* (London, 1962), 130–8.

8. T.B.M., "Defence of Mill," *Works*, VII, 373.

9. T.B.M., "Mackintosh" (1835), *Works*, VIII, 430.

10. Trevelyan, *Life and Letters*, 299.

11. Letter offering post, and T.B.M.'s reply in Indian Judicial Proceedings, LXIV (1834–5), May 2, June 1, and June 15, 1835, I.O.L.

no institution fees—and so forth."[12] At the time of writing Macaulay had reason to believe (wrongly) that Peel and the Tories were still in office, and that a Tory Governor-General would be sent to take Metcalfe's place. "A Tory Governor-General is not very likely to agree with me about the very important law reforms I am about to bring before the Council," he wrote to Ellis.[13] Far from being Tory, the reforms he had mentioned were, in fact, very similar to those suggested by James Mill in his evidence (1832) before the parliamentary committee set up in connection with the Charter Act renewal of the following year. And Mill, in turn, as Eric Stokes has pointed out, had been following Benthamite principles.[14] No wonder that Macaulay had visions of Bentham jumping—presumably for joy—in his grave; though, since the great man's skeleton was (and still is) preserved in University College, London, it would have been amid the classical splendors of Gower Street rather than in subterranean privacy that such a leap would have had to occur.

Macaulay embodied his official proposals for a reform of the procedure, constitution, and jurisdiction of the East India Company's civil courts in the *mofussil* (interior) of British India in a Minute dated June 25, 1835, a Minute marked by a mixture of Benthamite ideas of jurisprudence and his own robust common sense. He inveighed against the existing system of four orders of courts, where the magnitude of the sums involved in a particular case determined the court in which it was adjudicated. "Every person who has ever attended a court of law as a spectator for a single day," Macaulay wrote, "is aware that the intricacy of the case bears no proportion whatever to the magnitude of the sum in dispute."[15] The real measure of the importance of any particular case was not the sum of money involved in it, but rather the quantity of pain and pleasure the decision produced; and this did not depend on the magnitude of the sum, but on the magnitude of the sum in relation to the means of the parties at law. That being so, why should there be one class of judges for small money cases, and another for large? This was manifestly unjust to the poor.

Macaulay wanted only two categories of judicial functionaries in the *mofussil*. The higher class, he wrote, "must inevitably, for a long time, consist chiefly of Europeans," the lower class chiefly of natives.

12. T.B.M. to Ellis, June 3, 1835, Trinity Correspondence.
13. T.B.M. to Ellis, May 29, 1835, Trevelyan, *Life and Letters*, 315.
14. Stokes, *Utilitarians*, 185–6.
15. Minute of June 25, 1835, Dharker, ed., *Minutes*, 206.

English judges excelled in energy, powers of general reasoning, extent of general information, integrity, and humanity. But native judges knew the language, manners, and modes of thinking and feeling of their countrymen in a way that foreigners would never be able to come to know them. Thus they were far more competent to judge the value of evidence than Europeans. It was also cheaper to make maximum use of them. Macaulay wished to proceed on the principle of employing natives under European supervision. As we have seen, he was wary of presently employing natives in the administration of criminal justice.[16] But he was willing to leave original jurisdiction in all civil suits to native magistrates in the subordinate courts, with English *zillah* (district) judges acting as inspectors of these proceedings. Additional funds would be needed to set up more subordinate courts. But "no Government has a moral right to raise twenty crore from a people, and then to tell them that they must put up with injustice because justice costs too much."[17]

In all cases, pleading was to be oral; and, as far as possible, the parties to a case were to confront one another in making their pleas. As for the law of evidence, this was a subject "on which, as indeed on most parts of the philosophy of jurisprudence, it is not easy to add to what has been said by Mr. Bentham."[18] The great principle on which that law ought to be framed was that all evidence be taken at what it might be worth, and that no consideration which had a tendency to produce conviction in a rational mind be excluded from consideration by the tribunals. Evidence of both plaintiff and defendant was to be universally admitted. This was a considerable innovation. Macaulay granted that it was certainly true that parties to a case had a tendency to falsify. But of all partial witnesses, the parties were the least likely to mislead a judge since their bias was, after all, known. English legal procedure in Macaulay's time voluminously concerned itself with the kinds of evidence *not* admissible in court. Macaulay, willing (like Bentham) to admit the maximum of evidence, had no need to take up space in this way. In fact, he had written to Ellis that "the very wigs of the Judges in the Court of King's Bench would stand on end if they knew how short a chapter my Law of Evidence will form."[19] Simplicity and rationality were his principal aims. "I cannot but hope," he remarked, "that when we have brought justice near to every man's door, when we have made pleading oral, when we have made the law of evidence simple and

16. See above, p. 396.   17. Dharker, ed., *Minutes*, 207–9.   18. Ibid., 214.
19. T.B.M. to Ellis, July 1, 1834, Trevelyan, *Life and Letters*, 270.

rational, the number of unjust prosecutions will shrink to a small amount, and that the decisions will generally be just and speedy."[20]

No part of the jurisprudence of Bengal seemed to Macaulay to be so defective as the law of appeal. Thus, Europeans were allowed to appeal from company courts in the interior to the King's Courts in Bombay, Calcutta, and Madras, that is, from courts administering one system of law to courts administering another entirely. In some cases, courts of appeal took new evidence, and thus improperly transformed themselves into courts of original jurisdiction. In other cases, courts that had not heard the evidence took it upon themselves to revise decisions pronounced by courts that had heard it.

Macaulay's reform proposals were based on what he called the natural division of appeals into those on matters of law and those on matters of fact. Those on matters of law, he proposed, should always be made directly to the highest company court, the Sadar Dewani Adalat; and the decision should be made by no more than one of the judges of that court. This exemplified Bentham's principle of "single-seated justice." As for appeals on matters of fact, Macaulay would not, in the strict sense of the word, allow them. The fundamental principle of the law of appeal was that appeals be made from less competent to more competent tribunals. But an appeal from a judge who had heard the evidence to one who had not was just the opposite, an appeal from the more competent to the less competent. The native judge of first instance was probably at least as competent as an English judicial functionary to weigh the value of native testimony. And when such a judge had actually heard and seen the witnesses—unless he was what he ought not to be, "an absolute idiot"—he must be the better able of the two to decide the case. In vivid fashion Macaulay drew the contrast between that judge who had merely read written depositions and that judge

who has looked the witnesses full in the face, who has noted not merely their words, but the tones in which those words were uttered, who has read the lines of their countenances, who has observed in one the stammering of a man conscious of fraud, in another the suspicious fluency of a man who is repeating a tale learned by rote.[21]

Thus, Macaulay did not want the judgment of the court of first instance reversed on a matter of fact by a court that had not heard the evidence. But he did want to make it possible for either of the parties to demand a new trial.

20. Dharker, ed., *Minutes*, 215.   21. Ibid., 218.

The language of record in oral pleading must be the language spoken by the parties to the suit, in other words, the vernacular, Macaulay maintained. And no taxes were to be levied on the institution of suits. In a letter to James Mill written not very long after he drew up his Minute, Macaulay referred to "that vile system of institution fees and stamps in judicial proceedings which is my utter aversion."[22] In the Minute itself, his language was almost equally strong. "It has been said by gentlemen for whom I have the highest respect," Macaulay wrote,

that in this country nothing but an institution fee prevents the poor from harassing the rich with vexatious prosecutions. I own that I found some difficulty in believing, on the authority of any person however eminent, that a state of things so utterly unlike anything that exists elsewhere could really exist here. Make your legal proceedings as simple, as cheap, as expeditious as you can, the rich man must still have an advantage over the poor man. To diminish that advantage is one of the chief ends which a legislator should propose to himself.[23]

But while Macaulay thus condemned a mistaken regard for the interests of the rich, he also went out of his way to condemn what he called a mistaken tenderness for the poor by proposing to abolish the suits *in forma pauperis* in which the government undertook to find good lawyers free of charge for those who could not afford them. Macaulay's reasoning here showed the extent of his belief in laissez faire. "Good legal advice may be important to a suitor," he wrote. "But surely it is not more important to him than good medical advice to an invalid. And why the State which suffers its poor subjects to die by thousands for want of good physicians should be bound to find them good advocates, I am unable to comprehend."[24] Some today may feel that Macaulay should have advocated free medical care for the poor as well as free legal advice. But to argue in this fashion is to apply the values of the welfare state to the early nineteenth century, and to underestimate the degree of Macaulay's commitment to self-help and against state intervention, except in strictly defined areas such as education. One historian's comment on this part of Macaulay's Minute is very much to the point. He finds a significant break between the outlook of Bentham, who favored a state organization to provide free legal aid to the poor, and that of

22. T.B.M. to James Mill, August 24, 1835, MS letter in the possession of Mr. Gordon Ray.

23. Dharker, ed., *Minutes*, 222-3. 24. Ibid., 224.

Macaulay, who stood in this matter "for an individualism that was tinged with an element of puritanical sternness."[25]

Few of the reforms contemplated by Macaulay in this Minute were actually put into effect. An act was passed at the end of 1837 empowering the Governor-General in Council to dispense with the Persian language and script in judicial and revenue proceedings. And the same year saw some reform of appeal and judges of first instance which Macaulay had proposed. Macaulay himself abandoned, at Auckland's request and against his own opinion, his projected act for the appeal to a single judge, because the Governor-General thought it "at least ill timed."[26]

Prinsep did his bit to stop or delay proposals that seemed to him to constitute a wholly new system of civil law and procedure, as well as being too expensive. And he had powerful support in his opposition: "The opposition which Macaulay encountered was doubtless in some measure partisan, and also partly the natural hostility of long-experienced Indian civil servants to the scheme of a transient and brilliant speculative reformer."[27] For that is how he was regarded by some. He was reprimanded by one member of Council (T. C. Robertson) for basing himself too much on *a priori* reasoning and reliance on Bentham, and too little on experience; and the secretary to the government in the political and secret departments (W. H. Macnaghten) opposed his projected reforms because he was firmly convinced that "the country will be ruined if the philosophers get the upper hand."[28] He might have added that it was Macaulay himself who, just six years before, had savaged Mill and his friends in the *Edinburgh Review* for not sufficiently rooting their thought in concrete human experience.

It is, however, a mistake to take too seriously the picture of Macaulay as an *a priori* reasoner. It would be hard to find any piece of writing by him in which practical common sense is not predominant—and that includes his legal Minutes. Yet, if some discrepancy between the Macaulay of 1829 and the Macaulay of 1835 remains, it is one for which it is not too hard to account. Macaulay's attack on Mill and his friends was directed against the Benthamites' political theory; whereas in India, Macaulay acted on the basis of Bentham's

25. Stokes, *Utilitarians*, 208–9.

26. Auckland to Hobhouse, June 20, 1836, Home and Miscellaneous, Vol. 837, I.O.L.

27. Stokes, *Utilitarians*, 211.

28. Robertson's opposition cited in ibid., 212; Macnaghten's in T.B.M. to J. Mill, August 24, 1835, letter in the possession of Mr. Gordon Ray.

jurisprudential rather than his political teachings. In the realm of legal reform, he could justly consider himself among the "philosophers." For he was not merely trying to patch up an existing legal structure, but to construct an entirely new system of law and procedure for British India. The penal code he devised, still largely in force today, has remained the most enduring monument to his efforts in India.

The idea of drawing up a complete criminal code for India was Macaulay's. The Charter Act of 1833 had conceived of the inquiries undertaken by the law commissioners as *preliminary* to whatever alterations of the law might be judged necessary. Thus, as Prinsep was quick to point out, drafting a penal code went beyond the terms of the act.[29] But Macaulay was not the man to be held back by such restraint. As we have seen, he contemplated an entirely new code of civil procedure for India, and he wanted to supplement it not merely with a new penal code, but with a new code of criminal procedure and of civil rights as well. Bentham regarded the construction of such a complex of codes, or "pannonium," as the masterwork for philosophic reformers.[30] It was nothing less than this that Macaulay wished to produce. To have given himself the airs of a Lycurgus before his departure from England may have been a way of dramatizing his own role. But here was the chance to give substance to his rhetoric.

There were several reasons for his eagerness to begin with a new criminal code.[31] One, as he explained in the Minute of June 4, 1835, in which he proposed that project to the Indian Council, was that Parliament had directed the government of India to frame laws as early as possible that would prevent European settlers in India from oppressing the natives of the country. To achieve this aim, Europeans ought really to be subject to the criminal jurisdiction of the company's courts in the interior. But before this could be done, the laws had to be changed.[32] There was another, more personal motive for Macaulay's readiness to devise a new penal code. "One reason for beginning with the criminal law," he wrote in the same Minute,

---

29. Prinsep, Minute of June 11, 1835, quoted by Stokes, *Utilitarians*, 223.

30. Ibid., 219.

31. For the view of the home authorities that this was, in fact, the wrong place to begin, see testimony of David Hill before House of Lords Select Committee of 1853, *Parliamentary Papers*, XXX (1852–3), 338. Hill, representing the Judicial Department of India House, made the case that what had been most urgently required was administrative rather than statutory reform.

32. Board's Collections, Vol. 1555 (1835–7), No. 63507, ff. 7–9. Not reprinted in Dharker.

is that there is no department of law which so early attracted the attention of philosophers or which still excites so general an interest among reflecting and reading men. It is now more than seventy years since the famous treatise "Dei delitti e delle pene" [by Beccaria] acquired an European reputation, and from that time down to the present day a succession of men eminent as speculative and as practical statesmen has been engaged in earnest discussion on the principles of penal jurisprudence. There is perhaps no province of legislation which has been so thoroughly explored in all directions.[33]

Reform of the English criminal law had indeed engaged the attention of leading statesmen—Mackintosh, Romilly, Peel, and Brougham among others. After Romilly's suicide in 1818, Macaulay had written to his father: "How long may a penal code at once too sanguinary and too lenient, half written in blood like Draco's, and half undefined and loose as the common law of a tribe of savages, be the curse and disgrace of the country?"[34] About twenty years later, English criminal law was still in a state of chaos, with serious reforms just being put in train. And it was no doubt because it was still both "undefined" and "loose" that Macaulay suggested to the Council that its instructions to the law commissioners should emphasize that the Indian code was to cover all contingencies. "Not only ought everything in the Code to be law; but nothing that is not in the Code ought to be law." The code was to be more than a mere digest of existing usages and regulations, and to comprise all the reforms that the Law Commission might think desirable. Two principles were to underlie it: That of suppressing crime with the smallest possible infliction of suffering, and that of ascertaining truth at the smallest possible cost of time and money.[35]

The terminology to be employed in the proposed code was to be clear and unequivocal, the language concise and perspicuous. The Council was to warn the commissioners against using vague terms such as "treason" and "manslaughter," taken from English law—"words which include a great variety of offences widely differing from each other." Every criminal act was to be separately defined, no indictment to be good which did not follow the words of the definition, no culprit convicted whose act did not come distinctly within that definition. Uniformity as far as possible was to be the chief aim of the code; and special definitions of crime, modes of procedure, and

33. Idem.
34. T.B.M. to his father, November 9, 1818, Trevelyan, *Life and Letters,* 65.
35. Board's Collections, Vol. 1555 (1835–7), No. 63507, ff. 7–9.

measures of punishment designed to cater to different races or sects were not to be included without clear and strong reasons.[36]

Predictably, Prinsep objected to what Macaulay had proposed, mainly on the ground that the Charter Act of 1833 had merely provided that the law commissioners were to inquire into the state of the existing Indian laws, and to report on this; not to devise a new code before they had made their inquiries. "I look upon it as contrary to the spirit and letter of the law," he wrote in his dissenting Minute, "that the whole of what is now in existence should first be laid prostrate in the idea that a new system can readily and with ease be established." Macaulay's proposals implied such a "demolition." But Prinsep pointed out that it was unwise to build before the bricks had been made and the materials collected.[37] He was in a minority of one. The Council adopted Macaulay's suggested instructions to the law commissioners, and duly issued them on June 15, 1835.[38] When a copy reached London, the directors of the company commented that the instructions appeared to have been transcribed from Macaulay's proposals, while Prinsep's remarks, so much more in conformity with the provisions of the Act of 1833, did not seem to have been taken into consideration. Their despatch to the Indian government expressed confidence that "the course of proceeding recommended by Mr. Prinsep must substantially have been pursued by the Law Commissioners."[39] By the time that despatch reached India, the new penal code was almost completed. Once again, Prinsep's conservative gradualism had lost out to Macaulay's drive for wholesale reform.

At the time the commissioners began their labors, the actual state of criminal justice in India was a patchwork of Muslim and Hindu law overlaid with the East India Company's regulations. Muslim law permitted a "blood price" as the punishment for murder, did not consider the infliction of personal injury a crime against the state, and did not permit Muslims to be prosecuted on the evidence of non-Muslims. The different presidencies—Madras, Bombay, and Bengal—had made different provisions for modifying the effect of Muslim law on non-Muslims. The result was a variable standard of criminal justice throughout British India.

A counterfeiter, for example, was well advised to pursue his trade in Bombay rather than in Madras or Bengal, where the punishment was

36. Idem.   37. Ibid., ff. 11–16.   38. Ibid., ff. 16–19.
39. India Legislative Despatch No. 4 (1837), March 1, 1837, I.O.L.

almost twice as severe. In Bengal, a man selling stamps without a licence was subject only to a fine; in Madras, to a short term in jail. The purchaser went unpunished. In Bombay, however, both seller and purchaser could be sentenced to corporal punishment and five years' imprisonment.[40]

The new penal code was intended to get rid of discrepancies of this sort and to ensure, as far as possible, a single standard of justice. Such a standard was also a necessity if—as Macaulay desired—the "Black Act" should ever be made applicable to criminal as well as civil jurisdiction. By August 1835, Macaulay had warmed to his work on the code, and wrote to Ellis: "It is indeed one of the finest employments of the intellect that it is easy to conceive."[41] Besides doing good for India and gaining honor for his career—the two motives Auckland adduced for his devoting all his application and energies to the code—Macaulay had another, which he expounded in a letter to James Mill, aware, no doubt, that Mill would be particularly receptive to it. That was the utility of the code, not only for India, but also for England. "When once the English people see the whole criminal law of a vast empire, both substantive and adjective, contained in a volume smaller than one of the hundred volumes of statutes and reports which a Templar must turn over to know whether a particular act be larceny or forgery," he wrote to Mill, "they will, I think, turn their minds to the subject of law-reform with a full determination to be at least as well off as their Hindoo vassals."[42]

In the same letter, written in August 1835, Macaulay expressed strong hopes that the work on the code would be finished by himself and his fellow law commissioners "in a few months." His colleagues included Charles Hay Cameron, who, according to John Stuart Mill, was made a member of the Commission because he had successfully carried out a complete reform of judicial procedure and the courts of justice in Ceylon. As a consequence of his reforms, the younger Mill wrote, Ceylon had now (1838) become the only country which actually enjoyed a judicial system

constructed on the best conceptions of philosophic jurists—a system in which, without any servile deference to the authority of Bentham, the principal improvements made in the theory of the subject by that great

40. Edwardes, *Raj*, 93.
41. T.B.M. to Ellis, August 25, 1835, Trevelyan, *Life and Letters*, 318.
42. T.B.M. to James Mill, August 24, 1835, MS in the possession of Mr. Gordon Ray.

man have been, with due consideration of local circumstances, adopted and carried into practice.[43]

Macaulay thought very highly of Cameron, and found himself in agreement with him on all the general principles upon which the code was to be based.[44]

He also had a high opinion of one of the other commissioners, John Macleod, whom he described to James Mill as a very acute man, with a mind fertile in objections. On the other hand, this meant that Macleod himself contributed little that was positive: "He refines so much that he does nothing. He has not been able to produce a single definition which satisfies himself. But he is invaluable as a critic, or rather a hypercritic on all that others do."[45] Macleod had had some experience with the Madras judicial system. The fourth member of the Commission, G. W. Anderson, was to contribute the experience he had gained in Bombay. But Anderson, though very willing to work, turned out to be totally incompetent. "He has absolutely no notion of any other jurisprudence than that which he has passed his life in administering," Macaulay wrote; "nor have we yet received from him even a single hint of the smallest value."[46]

For a year the Commission labored at full strength. Macaulay found himself pleasantly surprised, as he wrote to Hobhouse early in 1836, that two of the three judges of the Calcutta Supreme Court were not opposed to the new code. Both of them were zealous law reformers. One was Macaulay's old Trinity College contemporary, Sir Benjamin Malkin. The other was Sir Edward Ryan, who had supported him on the legal issue involved in the education controversy. At a dinner in 1832 he had been toasted as "the sergeant-major of the march of intellect," an encomium he had earned by his work in reprinting publications of the Society for the Diffusion of Useful Knowledge in Calcutta. The law commissioners submitted all their proposals to these two judges, who were always helpful. The third judge, Sir John Grant, was less helpful. In fact, Macaulay described him as "a wild elephant" (the phrase is Lord Ellenborough's) who, in spite of being restrained by Malkin and Ryan, would not long

43. [J. S. Mill], *Westminster Review*, XXIX (1838) , 395.
44. T.B.M. to James Mill, August 24, 1835, MS in the possession of Mr. Gordon Ray.
45. Idem.
46. Idem. See also T.B.M. to Napier, June 15, 1817, British Museum Add. MSS. 34, 618, ff. 163–6, where he refers to Anderson's "utter incapacity."

keep his trunk and his tusks from the Law Commission.[47] Still, good progress was being made.

Then the climate began to take its toll. In the course of the autumn of 1836, Macaulay wrote in a Minute explaining the delay in the completion of the code to the Governor-General, every member except himself had become wholly incapacitated for work. Anderson had been forced to leave Calcutta. Macleod was feeble. Cameron had been ill for four months. That left only the secretary, Frederick Millett, and Macaulay himself. And Millett had other duties to perform as well. Thus, the entire burden of completing the code had fallen on Macaulay, who reported to Auckland early in 1837 that in spite of all these difficulties the code had now actually been drawn up. All that remained was to revise it and to add notes and explanations. Full of righteous—and completely justified—anger, Macaulay heaped scorn on those who were complaining that progress had not been speedier. "People who have never considered the importance and difficulty of the task in which we are employed," he informed Auckland, "are surprised to find that a Code cannot be spoken off extempore or written like an article in a magazine."[48]

He was not ashamed to admit that the code contained several chapters which he himself had worked on for months, whose outline he had changed completely ten or twelve times, and with which he was still very far from satisfied. He certainly did not mince words when it came to dealing with those critics who had accused him of procrastination, and assured Auckland that he would not hurry his share of the work in order to gratify the childish impatience of the ignorant. After all, he remarked, when one compared the progress of the Indian code with the progress of codes undertaken under far more favorable circumstances, one had little ground for accusing the commissioners of tardiness. Napoleon's criminal code was started in 1801, and did not reach completion until 1810. Livingston's Louisiana Code had taken four and a half years to complete. "Indeed," Macaulay remarked,

when I remember the slow progress of law reforms at home and when I consider that our Code decides hundreds of questions, every one of which will bear considerable discussion, every one of which if stirred in England would give occasion to voluminous controversy and to many animated debates, I must acknowledge that I am inclined to fear that we have been guilty rather of precipitation than of delay.[49]

47. T.B.M. to Hobhouse, June 11, 1836, British Museum Add. MSS. 47, 227.
48. Minute of January 2, 1837, Dharker, ed., *Minutes*, 253.
49. Ibid., 254. See also 252-3.

For once, Macaulay was guilty of understatement. It is almost inconceivable that, in addition to all his other Indian duties, he was able to play the major part in drafting a penal code for India within two years. And it should not be forgotten that he wrote his immensely long essay on Bacon at the same time. After reading that essay in the *Edinburgh Review,* Hobhouse noted in his journal that it had Macaulay's usual faults; giving the reader not a moment's repose, but knocking him right and left like the boxer in Virgil, *nec mora nec requies.* "However," he added, "there is not a man in the world except Macaulay who could write it, to say nothing of his Indian occupations: *a criminal code* for all India."[50] It is difficult not to share his awe at the magnitude of Macaulay's achievement.

To make a penal code, the commissioners wrote in their covering letter to Auckland when they submitted the results of their labors to him in the autumn of 1837,[51] was "among the most difficult tasks in which the human mind can be employed." Any extant code was open to criticism. Inevitably, there would be omissions and inconsistencies. And the commissioners had only done what could reasonably be expected from them, namely, furnished the government with that which, by suggestions from experienced and judicious persons, might be improved into a good code. For one thing, it was hard to render a penal code clear and explicit when, as in India, the substantive civil law and the law of procedure were still dark and confused. "While the rights of individuals and the powers of public functionaries are uncertain, it cannot always be certain whether those rights have been attacked, or those powers exceeded."[52]

The system of penal law proposed in the new code, the commissioners went on to report, was not a digest of any existing system, "and . . . no existing system has furnished us even with a groundwork."[53] But they were at pains to make it clear—presumably in view of Prinsep's strictures to the effect that they had exceeded their brief as laid down by Parliament—that they had not gone out of their way to innovate. Had they found in India a system of criminal law favorably regarded by the people, they would have been inclined to ascertain it, to digest it, and to correct it moderately, rather than to propose a fundamentally different system. But all existing systems were foreign; and had been introduced by conquerors—Hindu, Muslim, and British. They differed widely from one another, and not one

50. September 5, 1837, Broughton, *Recollections,* V, 96.
51. This was the first printed version, dated October 14, 1837. The first version of the code was actually laid before Auckland on May 2, 1837.
52. T.B.M., "Introductory Report upon the Indian Penal Code," *Works,* XI, 4–5.
53. Ibid., 5.

of them possessed even the rudiments of a good code. Where British regulations were applicable in the interior, they were those made by three legislatures (in the three presidencies) and therefore contained very different provisions. True, people living under the jurisdiction of the King's Courts in the cities of Calcutta, Bombay, and Madras were subject to English criminal law. But that had been formulated without the slightest reference to India, and was itself so much in need of reform that it had just been pronounced by a commission composed of able and learned English lawyers to be so defective that reform was possible only by its being entirely taken to pieces and reconstructed.[54]

For these reasons the Indian law commissioners had not based their code on any of the systems of law presently in force in India. They had, indeed, compared their code with all those systems, just as they had compared it with the most celebrated systems of Western jurisprudence, specifically the *Code Napoléon* and Livingston's Louisiana Code. They particularly wished to acknowledge their indebtedness to Livingston because they had found themselves under the necessity of combating his opinions on some important questions.

The commissioners then proceeded to explain the technical features of their code. The "Notes" contained explanations for or a defense of those provisions which required them. The most original feature of the code, the "Illustrations," owed their existence to the fact that the definitions of crimes actually laid down in the code, if they were to convey the commissioners' entire meaning and nothing but that meaning, often had to be couched in language that was precise, yet, lacking neatness and perspicuity, harsh at the same time. But when each of those definitions was followed by a collection of cases falling under it, and of cases which, though at first sight they appeared to fall under it, did not really do so, then the definition itself as well as the reasons for its adoption, would be readily understood.

The illustrations will lead the mind of the student through the same steps by which the minds of those who framed the law proceeded, and may sometimes show him that a phrase which may have struck him as uncouth, or a distinction which he may have thought idle, was deliberately adopted for the purpose of including or excluding a large class of important cases.[55]

54. The commissioners appointed to inquire into the state of the *English* criminal law had just reported in this vein to Lord John Russell.

55. T.B.M., "Introductory Report," *Works*, XI, 13.

The principal aim of the commissioners had been to make their definitions precise, even at the cost of rugged or intricate phraseology. The definitions and the enacting clauses contained the whole law. The illustrations made nothing law that would not be law without them. "They only exhibit the law in full action, and show what its effects will be on the events of common life."[56] Thus, the code would serve at one and the same time as a statute book as well as a collection of decided cases; cases decided not by the judges but by those who made the law and who therefore knew better than any judge what the law was that they meant to make. As in the Roman imperial rescripts (and here Justinian was quoted at length), decisions on particular cases proceeded from the same authority whence the provisions themselves had emanated. But, unlike the imperial rescripts, these cases were not based *ex post facto* on actual cases; but, rather, condemned or absolved purely imaginary persons. "Therefore, whatever may be thought of the wisdom of any judgement which we have passed, there can be no doubt of its impartiality."[57]

Thus far the introductory report. What of the code itself? It was divided into three parts: the actual clauses: the illustrations; and the explanatory notes. The clauses of the proposed code, along with the illustrations and notes, were printed as part of the *Parliamentary Papers* of 1838.[58] The "Notes" alone are to be found in the "Albany" edition of Macaulay's *Works*.[59] For present purposes, all three parts will be discussed together and Macaulay's authorship assumed. This procedure is open to criticism on the ground that it was the commissioners as a body rather than Macaulay alone who took responsibility for compiling the draft of the code. Still, we have seen how large a portion of the burden Macaulay himself carried. One of his fellow commissioners, John Macleod, testified to this effect: "I may state a fact already generally known when I say that Mr. Macaulay is justly entitled to be called the author of the Indian Penal Code."[60] There can be little doubt that in the end it was he who wrote most of it singlehanded.

The first thing that strikes a layman as he looks at the actual code is the simplicity of its arrangement and its lack of technical language.

56. Ibid., 14.   57. Ibid., 15–16.
58. "Copy of the Penal Code Prepared by the Indian Law Commissioners, and published by Command of the Governor-General of India in Council," *Parliamentary Papers*, XLI (1837–8).
59. *Works*, XI, 22–198.
60. Sir John M. Macleod, *Notes on the Report of the Indian Law Commissioners on the Indian Penal Code* (London, 1848), iv.

"The more progress I make as a legislator," Macaulay had written to Ellis, "the more intense my contempt for the mere technical study of law becomes."[61] Conciseness and clarity rather than technicality and elaboration are hallmarks of the code. All of it, including the "Notes," occupies less than two hundred pages in octavo.[62] The chapter headings read as follows: Offenses against the state; against the army and navy; against public tranquility; of the abuse of the powers of public servants; contempts of the lawful authority of public servants; offenses against public justice; offenses relating to revenue; to coin; to weights and measures; to public health, safety, and convenience; religion and caste; illegal entrance into and residence in territories of the East India Company; offenses relating to the press; affecting the human body; against property; relating to documents; to property marks; illegal pursuit of legal rights; breach of contracts; of service; offenses relating to marriage; defamation; criminal intimidation, insult, annoyance. It has been remarked that this simple nomenclature—with such terms as "malice," "misdemeanour," and "libel" noticeable by their absence—represented a "natural" rather than a "technical" system of classification, and was modeled on Jeremy Bentham's principles of jurisprudence.[63]

Under each chapter heading the particular clauses are set forth, followed immediately by illustrations. For example, Clause 138 in Chapter VIII ("Abuse of the Powers of Public Servants") stipulates that "whoever . . . accepts or tries to obtain for himself or any other party any gratification other than legal remuneration for any official act, or for showing or forbearing to show in the exercise of his official functions favour or disfavour to any party" is to receive a maximum punishment—all penalties in the code are maximum penalties—of three years in prison or a fine or both. The first illustration that follows immediately, reads: "A., a public servant, obtains Z.'s consent that Z.'s sister shall live with A. as A.'s mistress, as a motive to A. for giving Z. a place in A.'s gift. A. has committed the offence defined in this clause."[64]

Macaulay pioneered in employing such "illustrations" in practical legislation. They were subsequently much criticized by judges for tending to impair judicial discretion. Indeed, they were partly in-

61. T.B.M. to Ellis, August 25, 1835, Trevelyan, *Life and Letters*, 318.

62. *The Indian Penal Code as Originally Framed in 1837, with Notes by T. B. Macaulay, J. M. Macleod, G. W. Anderson, and F. Millett and the First and Second Reports thereon dated July 23, 1846 and June 24, 1847 by C. H. Cameron and D. Elliott* (Madras, 1888), 1–185.

63. Stokes, *Utilitarians*, 231.   64. *Code* (Madras), 25–6.

tended to limit (though *not* to eliminate) such discretion.[65] But that was not their principal aim. John Stuart Mill came closer to the mark when he called their use

an idea by which the advantages of general language, and those which English statutes vainly seek to attain of an enumeration of particulars, are happily blended; and which, besides the great certainty and distinctness given to the legislator's meaning, solves the difficult problem of making the body of the laws a popular book, at once intelligible and interesting to the general reader.[66]

Mill here correctly recognized the essence of the role the illustrations were supposed to play in the code, which was to make it as plain and as easily comprehensible as possible.

Macaulay did his best to eliminate vagueness wherever he could. This was not always easy. For example, the distinction between theft, criminal misappropriation of property not in possession, and breach of trust "becomes fainter and fainter as we approach the line of demarcation, and at length the offences fade imperceptibly into each other."[67] This lack of distinctness would be greatly increased by unskillful legislation. But thinking as he did that it had its origin in the nature of things and the imperfection of language, he felt that it must remain, in spite of all that legislation could effect.[68] What Macaulay did was to insert a clause[69] that would serve to prevent judges from wasting their time and ingenuity in trying to devise nice distinctions. In cases on the frontier between theft and breach of trust, "they will not trouble themselves with subtle distinctions, but, leaving it undetermined by which name the offence should be called, will proceed to determine what is infinitely of greater importance, what shall be the punishment." For, as he noted elsewhere, "the more nearly the amount of punishment can be reduced to a certainty the better."[70]

On the intricate question of exactly what constituted "possession," Macaulay laid down a few rules[71] which he believed were in accord "with the general sense of mankind"; but, in general, left it to the

65. Cameron and Elliott, "First Report" (1846), ibid., 202–3. For critical comments by some judges on the device, see ibid., 190–200.

66. Mill, *Westminster Review* (1838), 402.

67. T.B.M., "Notes," *Works*, XI, 149.

68. In fact, the distinction was embedded in English law, and was not removed until 1968.

69. *Code* (Madras), 9.

70. T.B.M., "Notes," *Works*, XI, 152, 131.

71. Clauses 17, 18, 19, *Code* (Madras), 3–4.

tribunals, without any direction, to determine whether particular property was at a particular time in the possession of a particular person or not. Doing this, he wrote, avoided an error of Livingston's in the Louisiana Code, where an attempt to make elaborate technical distinctions had served to confuse the entire issue of what was theft, and had shown "how dangerous it is for a legislator to attempt to escape from a difficulty by giving a technical sense to an expression [in this instance, "possession"] which he nevertheless continues to use in a popular sense."[72]

These are just a few examples of how Macaulay applied his mind to an attempt to reduce the tangled technicalities and definitions that tended to obscure much of the law as it stood in England; and how, when faced with a confusion inherent in the nature of things, he stuck to common sense as far as possible, allowing judges latitude in individual cases. But it was a common sense based on wide knowledge that Macaulay applied to the code. Here is one example that may serve to illustrate that learning. At issue was the law of property in regard to pigeons in a dovecote:

By the English law, pigeons, while they frequent a dove-cote, are the property of the owner of the dove-cote. By the Roman law they were not so. By the French law they are his property at one time of the year, and not his property at another. Here it is evident that the taking of such a pigeon, which would in England be a violation of the right of property, would be none in a country governed by the Roman law, and that in France, it would depend on the time of the year whether it were so, or not.[73]

All of this complete with references to Blackstone, Justinian, and Paillet's *Manuel de Droit Français*.

Was it all merely learning for the sake of learning? Hardly. The instance just cited demonstrates the difficulty inherent in compiling a penal code providing for punishment in case of violations of the right of property at a time when a new code of civil law had not yet been framed. Given the unsettled state of Indian jurisprudence, not all disputable questions of civil right could be determined in the penal code. But one had to begin somewhere; knowing full well that

that portion [of the law] be it what it may, which is selected to be first put into the form of a code, with whatever clearness and precision it may be expressed and arranged, must necessarily partake to a considerable

72. T.B.M., "Notes," *Works,* XI, 151.   73. Ibid., 146.

extent of the uncertainty and obscurity in which other portions are still left.[74]

Uncertainty about the civil law, then, was one of the limitations imposed upon the scope and completeness of the penal code. Another was imposed by Macaulay himself. A penal code, he wrote, was not a body of ethics. It must content itself with keeping men from doing positive harm, and must leave to public opinion and to teachers of morality and religion the office of furnishing men with motives for doing positive good.[75]

In pursuit of this aim of keeping men from doing positive harm, Macaulay's code was based upon what were for the time rather advanced humanitarian principles. Thus, the death penalty was reserved for murder and for treason, the highest offenses against the state; and neither flogging nor the pillory—or its Indian equivalent, public exhibition of the offender on an ass—was permitted as a mode of punishment. More positive humanitarian provisions were not lacking. Thus, by stipulating that no act falling under the definition of an offense was to be exempted from punishment because committed by a master against his slave, the code "will at once deprive slavery of those evils which are its essence, and will insure the speedy and natural extinction of the whole system."[76] Here was one instance in which penal legislation was intended to aid in bringing about social change; though Macaulay showed himself quite aware of the fact that laws of themselves could not accomplish that purpose. In terse, epigrammatic language, he got at the root of the problem: "It is of little use to direct the judge to punish unless we can teach the sufferer to complain."[77] Writing to his father, and knowing as always what the latter had closest at heart, he took a more optimistic line: "We have got rid of the punishment of death, except in the case of aggravated treason and wilful murder," he reported to him. Then he added: "We shall also get rid indirectly of everything that can properly be called slavery in India."[78]

The London authorities looked favorably upon the proposed provisions in regard to slavery—a despatch recommending their enactment, put forward by Hobhouse, was endorsed by the Court of Directors in September 1838.[79] But another humanitarian recom-

74. Ibid., 144–5.   75. Ibid., 176, 115.
76. Ibid., 65.   77. Ibid., 67–8.
78. T.B.M. to his father, October 12, 1836, Trevelyan, *Life and Letters*, 329.
79. Hobhouse to "Chairs," September 17, 1838; Lushington to Hobhouse, September 20, 1838; Hobhouse to Lushington, September 21, 1838; Lushington to Hobhouse, September 25, 1838. Home and Miscellaneous, Vol. 836, I.O.L.

mendation, closely associated with the code, fared less well. That was
the reform of the Indian prison system. In a Minute dated December
1835, Macaulay had remarked that the best criminal code was of very
little use to a community, unless there existed proper means for the
infliction of punishment. A new penal code had to go hand in hand
with prison reform. Imprisonment must be a terror to wrong-doers
without in any circumstances shocking humanity. Indian prisons
required great improvement. They could not all be as good as those
in the United States. But Calcutta and a few other places might well
establish a prison system not greatly inferior to those of New York
and Philadelphia.[80]

A few days later, Macaulay wrote to Hobhouse that "our criminal
code, whatever credit it may do us in the opinion of Benthamites at
home, will do very little good to the people of this country, unless it
be accompanied by a thorough reform of prison-discipline." Macaulay had proposed that a special committee be appointed on this
subject, of which the law commissioners and the judges of the
Calcutta Supreme Court should constitute the membership. Such a
committee was now being appointed.[81] The committee's report
appeared in 1838. Its recommendations included the establishment
in the center of every six or eight districts of a penitentiary for all
prisoners sentenced to more than one year's detention. Each penitentiary was to be put under the charge of an able and trustworthy
superintendent, either European or native; and there was to be
provision for each prisoner to have a separate sleeping place. The
report also recommended extensive resort to solitary confinement;
enforcement of monotonous, uninteresting work indoors upon all
prisoners sentenced to labor; and the deprivation of prisoners of
every indulgence not absolutely necessary to health.[82]

Hardly humanitarian? Professor Stokes has a point when he
detects in the provisions the authentic (and stern) voice of the new
Poor Law, of Chadwick and Southwood Smith, and points to the
debt they owed to Bentham's ideas on penal law and to his "Panopti-
con." But it should be kept in mind that Macaulay's main aim here
was to *shorten* terms of imprisonment by making the prisoners' stay
as unpleasant as possible. "Where a good system of prison discipline
exists," he wrote in his "Notes" to the code,

80. Minute of December 14, 1835, Dharker, ed., *Minutes*, 278-9.
81. T.B.M. to Hobhouse, January 1, 1836, British Museum Add. MSS. 47, 227.
82. Legislative despatch to India, October 30, 1839, quoted by Stokes, *Utilitarians*, 218.

where the criminal, without being subject to any cruel severities, is strictly restrained, regularly employed in labour not of an attractive kind, and deprived of every indulgence not necessary to his health, a year's confinement will generally prove as efficacious as confinement for two years in a gaol where the superintendence is lax, where the work exacted is light, and where the convicts find means of enjoying as many luxuries as if they were at liberty. [83]

These sentiments may not be in accord with twentieth-century ideas of prison reform; but, for their time, they must be regarded as an innovation and as humanitarian in ultimate aim, if not in method. They were, however, rejected by the home authorities on financial grounds.

The code contained other innovations. Two of them have been emphasized by M. C. Setalvad, recently Attorney-General of India, in his book on *The Common Law in India:* the right of a woman to own property in her own person, which Macaulay adopted from Indian law, and which was not introduced in England until 1882, the year of the Married Woman's Property Act; and the liberal manner in which the code treated acts committed in self-defense.[84] Another innovation concerned civil claims for reparation in cases where injury was caused by a felony. English law did not allow such reparation; and Macaulay described the result in vivid terms, and in the antiphonal style familiar to readers of his *Essays:*

He [the injured party] is entitled to reparation if his coat has been torn, but to none if his house has been maliciously burned down. He is entitled to reparation for a slap on the face, but to none for having his nose maliciously slit, or his ears cut off. A woman is entitled to reparation for a breach of promise of marriage, but to none for a rape.[85]

The code stipulated that every person injured by an offense was legally entitled to compensation for the injury.

Yet another innovation in the legal realm was the distinction drawn in the code between murder and "voluntary culpable homicide by consent," which had never, as far as Macaulay knew, been as clearly recognized by any other code. He explained why this species of homicide should be less severely punished than murder in one of those marvelous illustrative sentences, full of incidents from history

83. T.B.M., "Notes," *Works,* XI, 26.
84. M. C. Setalvad, *The Common Law in India* (London, 1960) , 150, 153–4.
85. T.B.M., "Notes," *Works,* XI, 38.

and everyday life, the mastery of which had contributed to his fame as an author, and which he alone could have written:

The soldier who, at the entreaty of a wounded comrade, puts that comrade out of pain, the friend who supplies laudanum to a person suffering the torment of a lingering disease, the freedman who in ancient times held out the sword that his master might fall on it, the high-born native of India who stabs the females of his family at their own entreaty in order to save them from the licentiousness of a band of marauders, would, except in Christian societies, scarcely be thought culpable, and even in Christian societies would not be regarded by the public, and ought not to be treated by the law as assassins.[86]

One further innovation, at variance with English criminal law as well as with the French and the Louisiana codes, and going "beyond what even the boldest reformers of English law have proposed," was to be found in the clause laying it down that the truth of an imputation prejudicial to character should, in all cases, exempt the author of that imputation from punishment as a defamer. In defending the clause, Macaulay pointed not only to its "perfect simplicity and certainty" as a reason for adopting it, but gave various examples illustrating the manner in which public-spirited and courageous persons could act as auxiliaries to the law in exposing illegal practices.[87] One wonders whether, in adducing in this connection as an example the man who warned the mercantile community against a notorious client or advised families not to admit into their intimacy a practiced seducer of innocence, Macaulay did not have in mind in the first category his brother-in-law Charles Trevelyan, who had risked his career in exposing the corrupt practices of Sir Edward Colebrooke at Delhi. It seems likely.

If so, this was by no means the only instance of Macaulay's personal experience and attitudes intruding into the code's notes and illustrations. One seems to see him, for example—this time playing the fraternal role—in the following passage, part of a note dealing with injuries inflicted under gross provocation:

That a worthless, unfaithful and tyrannical husband should be guilty only of manslaughter for killing the paramour of his wife, and that an affectionate and high-spirited brother should be guilty of murder for killing, in a paroxysm of rage, the seducer of his sister, appears to us inconsistent and unreasonable.[88]

86. Ibid., 124.   87. Ibid., 183–90.   88. Ibid., 122.

The notes and illustrations reflected not merely the personality of their chief author, but also some of his general notions about society. The harsh tone sounded in his Minute on the reform of the *mofussil* courts regarding suits *in forma pauperis*[89] sounds again in a casual reference to artisans employed "in callings which are useful and indeed necessary to society, but which tend to impair the constitutions of those who follow them"; and in an allusion to "that idleness and that profusion which end in bringing a man into a condition in which no law will keep him from committing theft."[90] There is also no mistaking the heartfelt tone of the passage in which Macaulay expressed both amazement and dismay at that spirit of submissiveness on the part of the Indian people which allowed them to be patient in the face of depredations committed by gang robbers and ruffians. In giving considerable legal scope to acts of self-defense, Macaulay commented that "we are desirous rather to raise and encourage a manly spirit among the people than to multiply restrictions on the exercise of the right of self-defence."[91] In this way, Macaulay believed he could use the projected penal code as a device for helping to bring about those changes in the character of the Indian people which he felt were prerequisites for their entering upon a historical *cursus honorum* like that followed by Western nations. His exasperation with Indian passivity in the face of suffering, expressed elsewhere on many occasions, served in this instance to give shape to the laws he proposed.

One way of reading the code, then, is as a reflection of Macaulay's style, personality, and ideas. Another is as a series of glimpses of Indian life; or, perhaps more accurately, of Indian life as seen and experienced by the British rulers. Thus, one finds A. (doomed to be the perpetual villain) collecting "toddy" (palm wine) from the brabtree; making himself liable by omitting to take proper order with a furious buffalo in his possession and thus preventing Z. from passing along a road which Z. had a right to traverse; intending to rob Z., who is riding in a palanquin; introducing water into an icehouse belonging to Z., thus causing the ice to melt; and counterfeiting the mark of a Sheffield cutler on cutlery made by himself in India.[92] These are examples of crimes committed in an Indian setting. Yet in all these cases the setting is, in a sense, immaterial; for the acts described would be crimes in whatever setting they were committed. It

89. See above, p. 433.   90. T.B.M., "Notes," *Works*, XI, 50, 61.   91. Ibid., 56.
92. "Penal Code," *Parliamentary Papers*, XLI (1837–8), Nos. 212, 330, 340, 399, and 458.

remains to ask whether Macaulay went beyond using the Indian scene as an illustrative setting and how far he went in actually tailoring the code to the special situation and circumstances of British India.

The question is an important one, since it involves the whole problem of the universal versus the local, and the general versus the particular, which lawgivers have always faced; and which Macaulay himself had to confront as a historian. In historiographical terms, a similar problem could be subsumed under the general heading of Enlightenment versus Romanticism, Cosmopolitanism versus *Historismus*. But in the realm of legal codification, a single name can serve as a touchstone—that of Jeremy Bentham. As it happened, Bentham himself in his "On the Influence of Time and Place in Matters of Legislation,"[93] with which Macaulay was probably familiar, had singled out Bengal as his example of a country as different as it could possibly be from England. Bentham was sure that universal principles such as the maximization of pleasure and the minimization of pain were applicable just as much in Bengal as anywhere else in the world. But he proceeded to point out that allowance must be made for local prejudices and customs, though these should not of themselves be regarded as ultimate arbiters. Thus, since the Hindus held caste much dearer than life, that attitude must be taken into account when a code dealt with such matters as special sensitivity to certain injuries. The wise legislator should be conciliatory, and should refrain from enkindling passions that might lead to opposition to his code by the very people for whom he was legislating. He should conclude an alliance with time, "the true auxiliary of all useful changes, the chemist which amalgamates contraries, dissolves obstacles, and unites discordant parties." What the legislator should *not* do was to transplant English law, with all its defects, to Bengal.[94]

Macaulay made it clear in the introductory report to the code that it was not his intention to undertake such a bodily transplant; though expert legal critics, from Sir James Fitzjames Stephen on, have agreed that, in fact, English law formed a good deal of the code's substance. Thus Stephen wrote:

The point which always has surprised me most in connection with the Penal Code, is, that it proves that Lord Macaulay must have had a knowledge of English criminal law which, considering how little he had

93. John Bowring, ed., Jeremy Bentham, *Works* (11 vols., Edinburgh, 1843), I, 169–
94. First published in Dumont, *Traités de Législation Civile et Pénale* (Paris, 1802).
94. Bentham, "Time and Place," *Works*, I, 184.

practised it, may fairly be called extraordinary. He must have possessed the gift of going at once to the very root of the matter, and of sifting the corn from the chaff to a most unusual degree; for his Draft gives the substance of the criminal law of England, down to its minute working details, in a compass which, by comparison with the original, may be regarded as almost absurdly small.[95]

But, as one subsequent commentator, who agreed with Stephen's general conclusion, has pointed out, it was right reason that accounted for most of the code's departures from English law.[96] And that is a crucial point.

The philosophical, Benthamite, approach to codification was to think of law as it ought to be as well as law as it was; to dissect every idea; to ask of every rule what useful purpose it served. That was Macaulay's approach, and he was "never so happy (indeed one might almost say gleeful) as when pointing out the absurdity of this or that rule of the English law."[97] The scholar who has most thoroughly studied the influence of Bentham on Macaulay's code concluded in similar fashion that it must not be looked upon as a mere attempt to apply reformed English law to Indian conditions. Macaulay's aim, he believes, was a code that sprang from the universal science of jurisprudence; "and to neglect this universality of outlook, this cast of mind that was of the eighteenth-century *philosophe,* is to lose the historical atmosphere in which the Code took shape."[98]

Indeed, Macaulay was himself well aware of this universality of outlook on his own part. Writing to Hobhouse early in 1836, he singled out two of the Calcutta Supreme Court judges (Ryan and Malkin) for praise as being unlike those judges who were unable to see merit in any other system, "or to recur to those general principles

95. Quoted by Trevelyan, *Life and Letters,* 303. See also Setalvad, *Common Law,* 127–8: "It appears that Macaulay and his colleagues, striving all the time to keep away from the established systems of criminal law, and particularly the English system, so that they might arrive at a result truly suited to India's needs, travelled unconsciously but inevitably along the track of principles in which they had been trained and to which they were accustomed." See also Sir George Rankin, *Background to Indian Law* (Cambridge, 1946), 207; K. Lipstein, "The Reception of Western Law in India," *The Indian Year Book of International Affairs* (Madras, 1957), 287–8; and Cameron and Elliott, "First Report" (1846), *Code,* 194.

96. Rankin, *Background,* 208.

97. S. G. Vesey-Fitzgerald, "Bentham and the Indian Codes," in G. W. Keeton and C. Schwarzenberger, eds., *Jeremy Bentham and the Law: A Symposium* (London, 1948), 227.

98. Stokes, *Utilitarians,* 227. See also Dharker, ed., *Minutes,* 140–1, who agrees with Leslie Stephen that the Indian penal code was the first actual attempt to carry out Bentham's favorite schemes under British rule.

on which all such systems ought to be founded."[99] In the same letter he anticipated the credit the code would do its framers in the opinion of the Benthamites at home. Auckland's comment on the completed code is also relevant here. He was sure that it would be criticized on the ground that "an Indian Commission was little requisite for a law which throughout will be of almost general application."[100] But, then, so were Bentham's principles—always remembering that he, too, wished to have certain allowances made for time and place.

Macaulay's code certainly made such allowances. Some, to be sure, seemed to be primarily for the benefit of European residents. Thus, special problems arose from the rudimentary state of Indian transport. In England it was unnecessary to provide punishment for the stagecoachman who, however maliciously or dishonestly, drove on, leaving his passenger behind. At worst, the result was inconvenience or delay. But in India, the dangers connected with such a desertion—especially where ladies were concerned—were potentially so great, and the chances of recovering civil damages so small, that breaches of contract of this kind had to be treated as crimes.[101] That sort of special allowance for Indian conditions should probably be classed with the code's insistence that Europeans who had committed serious offenses should be sentenced to banishment rather than to long prison terms; since, for one thing, it would be cruel to subject them to severe prison discipline "in a country in which existence is almost constant misery to an European who has not many indulgences at his command," and, for another, the English national character would suffer in the esteem of the people of India if Englishmen were too frequently exhibited in degrading situations.[102]

Other allowances were intended to apply more widely. Discussing the giving and taking of bribes, for instance, Macaulay made a distinction between a country such as England, where it was generally the giver of the bribe who was far more deserving of punishment than the receiver, and a country such as India, where men gave bribes because without one no one could obtain justice. Macaulay doubtless had in mind his own experience with Indian justice on the occasion of his return trip from Ootacamund to Madras. In any event, the code stipulated that persons who complied with a demand

99. T.B.M. to Hobhouse, January 1, 1836, British Museum Add. MSS. 47,227.

100. Auckland to Hobhouse, August 26, 1837, Home and Miscellaneous, Vol. 841, I.O.L. See also same to same, July 14, 1837, rejecting James Young to fill a vacancy on the Law Commission: *"Between you and me,* I thought that enough of pure Benthamism was already secured to our Code." Quoted by Stokes, *Utilitarians,* 240.

101. T.B.M., "Notes," *Works,* XI, 169–70.   102. Ibid., 27–8.

for a bribe on the part of public servants were not considered guilty of inciting such public servants to receive bribes, and thus not liable to punishment.[103] When it came to the question as to whether practicing intentional deceit for purposes of gain ought always to be punished, Macaulay's answer was negative. After all, "a very large part of the ordinary business of life is conducted all over the world, and nowhere more than in India, by means of a conflict of skill, in the course of which deception to a certain extent perpetually takes place." The moralist might regret this. But the legislator must understand that as a result of such a conflict, articles were generally sold at the prices they ought to fetch.[104]

A more serious problem was whether to make adultery a criminal offense. In dealing with this, Macaulay's proposals went against existing Indian law in the name of Indian social conditions. Criminal laws against adultery were on the books in certain presidencies. Indeed, there was some feeling that the higher class of natives did not consider them harsh enough, and were unable to understand on what principle adultery was more tenderly treated than forgery or perjury. But a penal code, so Macaulay pointed out, should not be considered a body of ethics. The fact that an act went unpunished did not mean that a legislature approved of it. Some Indians considered nothing less than death fit punishment for adultery. In such a state of society it was far better that the law should not punish adultery at all than that it should punish it leniently. Furthermore, in a state of society where some husbands customarily had several wives (and "we are not so visionary as to think of attacking, by law, an evil so deeply rooted in the manners of the people of this country as polygamy"), a humane man must pause before determining upon punishing a wife's infidelity. "It will be time enough to guard the matrimonial contract by penal sanctions when that contract becomes just, reasonable and mutually beneficial." That was the work of time, not of law. Thus, since any enactment on the subject would be either nugatory or oppressive, the proposed code did not regard adultery as a criminal offense.[105]

It is possible to dismiss these particular allowances for "time and place" as minor. Not so those that touched on the subject of Indian

103. Ibid., 86.   104. Ibid., 157.

105. Ibid., 174–9. This particular proposal of T.B.M.'s was not accepted when the revised code went into effect in 1862. Adultery was punishable by prison terms up to five years. Only husbands could prosecute. Sir James Fitzjames Stephen, *A History of the Criminal Law of England* (3 vols., London, 1883), III, 318.

religion. Certainly, self-interest could be said to be involved here, since unrest and possible uprisings might be anticipated as a result of the law's sanctioning the wounding of religious susceptibilities. Indeed, religious toleration was the official policy of the home government. Thus, allowances in this sphere should not, perhaps, be considered surprising. Still, they went too far for the tastes of some of the British authorities, which shows that in this matter Macaulay erred, if he erred at all, on the side of "time and place." There was no other country, the "Notes" to the code pointed out, in which more cruel suffering could be inflicted, and more deadly resentment evoked, by injuries affecting mental feelings; for example, if someone deprived a high-born Rajput of his caste, or thrust his head into the covered palanquin of a woman of rank. Macaulay's comment was:

That on these subjects our notions and usages differ from theirs is nothing to the purpose. We are legislating for them, and though we may wish that their opinions and feelings may undergo a considerable change, it is our duty, while their opinions and feelings remain unchanged, to pay as much respect to those opinions and feelings as if we partook of them.[106]

So the code provided that whoever committed assault with the intent of causing a person to lose caste or induced that person to do ignorantly something by which he would lose caste was liable to a prison sentence up to six months or a fine.[107]

Because it was the policy of the home authorities to protect Indian natives in holding their religious opinions, the company was anathematized in Evangelical circles as "the Churchwarden of the Idol."[108] But Macaulay emphasized in the "Notes" that the truth or falsity of a person's religion must have nothing to do with the punishment of insults offered to it. The religion might be false; "but the pain which such insults gives to the professors of that religion is real."[109] As far as religious rites were concerned, the code specifically distinguished between acts which at one time and in one place were perfectly innocent, but which at another time and place were properly subject to punishment. Thus, "there are many Hindoo rites which in Hindoo temples and religious assemblies the law tolerates, but which could not with propriety be exhibited in a place which English gentlemen and ladies were in the habit of frequenting for purposes

106. T.B.M., "Notes," *Works*, XI, 123.
107. "Penal Code," *Parliamentary Papers*, XLI (1837–8) , No. 284.
108. A. P. Thornton, *Doctrines of Imperialism* (New York, 1965) , 165.
109. T.B.M., "Notes," *Works*, XI, 105–6.

of exercise." To forbid such rites was therefore left up to local authorities, and they could do it only in cases where they felt the rites endangered public tranquility, health, safety, or convenience.[110] The law of defamation in India had to be particularly flexible, in view of the diversities of opinion that existed about manners, tastes, and religion. Thus, when A. said of Z. that Z. drank wine, the question whether A. had defamed Z. might turn on whether Z. was a Muslim or a Christian. And when A. said of Z., a Hindu, that it was highly probable that he would be converted to Mohammedanism, the question whether or not defamation had taken place depended on whether that communication was made to Z.'s relatives or to a Muslim.[111]

Macaulay was therefore at pains to take cognizance of the special susceptibilities of India's various races and creeds. And it will have been noted that in doing so he showed particular awareness of people's psychological and emotional states. "The most striking feature in the content of the Code," it has been said, "is . . . the manner in which the mental circumstances involved in a criminal act are carefully distinguished and made use of."[112] Recognition of the mental element (*mens rea*) in criminal liability was inherent in the English common law. But since it was not until 1898 that the accused was permitted to give evidence in his own behalf, his mental state had up to that time to be inferred from what he had done and the circumstances in which he had acted. English statutes sometimes expressly specified a particular mental state, but more often than not were silent on the point. It was the originality of Macaulay's penal code "to incorporate into the common law crime the *mens rea* needed for that particular crime so that the guilty intention . . . [was] generally to be gathered not from the common law but from the statute itself."[113] Thus it avoided difficulties that later bedeviled English law, where the courts sometimes favored *mens rea* as a necessary ingredient in the commission of statutory offenses, and sometimes not. Since the full recognition of the problems of the mental state could not ensue until it became possible for the accused to testify, Macaulay's view of the matter in 1838, when the difficulties were only slowly becoming apparent, was remarkable.

It has been pointed out that in dwelling on the relevance of mental states Macaulay owed a general debt to Bentham, though he

110. Ibid., 90–2.
111. "Penal Code," *Parliamentary Papers*, XLI (1837–8) , No. 469.
112. Stokes, *Utilitarians*, 232.   113. Setalvad, *Common Law*, 137–40.

did not follow him exactly.[114] But the heritage of Bentham was supplemented by Macaulay's expert probing of motive or intention, whether in history, fiction, or, in this instance, a penal code. It is obvious that this aspect of the code fully engaged his ingenuity and imagination. Note "B," for example, which deals with "General Exceptions," takes up the question of the extent to which the fact that a person did not mean to cause death, but knew that he was likely to cause it, should be regarded as a justification for his having caused it. This would be true, for example, of the surgeon who, with the consent of his patient, carried out an operation which in a large proportion of cases had proved fatal, but which was the only method by which the patient's disease could possibly be cured.

Again; if a person attacked by a wild beast should call out to his friends to fire, though with imminent hazard to himself, and they were to obey the call, we do not conceive that it would be expedient to punish them, though they might by firing cause his death, and though when they fired they knew themselves to be likely to cause his death.[115]

The code stipulated that in neither case had an offense taken place.

In another place (a "Note" on "Offences against the Body"), Macaulay took up the more complex question of whether omissions intended to produce or known to be likely to produce certain evil effects should be made punishable. The Louisiana Code had laid it down that a person was considered guilty of homicide who omitted to save life which he could save "without personal danger or pecuniary loss." But, Macaulay objected, what of the surgeon summoned from Calcutta to Meerut to perform an operation? He might be offered a large fee; he might feel that he ran a greater personal risk in traveling to Meerut than in continuing to reside in Bengal. But if he refused to go, because he either expected some member of his family by the next ship or wished to go to Europe himself, should he be punished? Surely not.[116] The rule proposed by Macaulay was that such acts of omission should be punished only if and when illegal on other grounds as well. Thus, if A. omitted to give Z. food and by that omission caused Z.'s death, it was murder only if A. was Z.'s jailer or father or doctor; it was not murder if Z. was a beggar who had no other claim on A. than that of humanity. Another, similar example reads as follows:

114. Stokes, *Utilitarians*, 232. 115. T.B.M., "Notes," *Works*, XI, 52–3.
116. Ibid., 111.

A. omits to tell Z. that a river is swollen so high that Z. cannot safely attempt to ford it, and by this omission voluntarily causes Z.'s death. This is murder if A. is a peon stationed by authority to warn travellers from attempting to ford the river. It is murder if A. is a guide who contracted to conduct Z. It is not murder if A. is a person on whom Z. has no other claim than that of humanity.[117]

Macaulay went on to grant that only a very depraved man would suffer another to be drowned when he might prevent it by a word.

But if we punish such a man, where are we to stop? How much exertion are we to require? Is a person to be a murderer if he does not go fifty yards through the sun of Bengal at noon in May in order to caution a traveller against a swollen river? Is he to be a murderer if he does not go a hundred yards?—if he does not go a mile?—if he does not go ten?[118]

Macaulay's conclusion was that since a code did not exist to provide men with motives for doing good, such acts were not punishable. But just as important as the conclusion was the process by which he reached it, which involved not merely his imaginative powers, but also the necessity of making subtle distinctions and judgments in the realms of psychology and morality.[119] Throughout, Macaulay showed particular sensitivity to mental states; disagreeing, for instance, with Livingston's dictum that passion excited by insult was entitled to less indulgence than passion excited by pain.[120] It is partly because of this emphasis that Macaulay's code, with its apparatus, turns out to be at one level what Bagehot called *The Wealth of Nations*—an amusing book, imbued with the knowledge, learning, and stylistic vigor of its author.

Some of his legislative Minutes had the same quality. There is one, for instance, hitherto unpublished, in which he stated his objections to the proposed regulations for the establishment of a "Conservancy Department" in Bombay.[121] The Bombay authorities had proposed

117. Ibid., 113.   118. Ibid., 114–15.

119. Because he knew that she was particularly interested in the moral problems raised by crimes committed by omission, Sir James Fitzjames Stephen lent T.B.M.'s penal code notes to George Eliot when she was writing *Middlemarch*. That novel, he noted, "approaches the subject, but in *Daniel Deronda* a much more striking illustration of the principle is given." The reference here is probably to the Bulstrode-Raffles episode in *Middlemarch,* and to the death of Grandcourt in *Daniel Deronda*. See Stephen, *A General View of the Criminal Law of England* (2nd ed., London, 1890), 127.

120. T.B.M., "Notes," *Works,* XI, 121.

121. Board's Collections, Vol. 1,555 (1835–7), April 28, 1835, No. 63,501, I.O.L.

that the commissioners, whose duty it would be to supervise cleaning, the sale of liquors, and public works, should at the same time act as a tribunal to try offenders in these spheres. Macaulay's view was that the commissioners must not combine the role of public accuser with that of judge. They should be zealous in their inquisitorial function, in making Bombay "an example of cleanliness and order to all other towns in India . . . this should become, to use a vulgar phrase, their hobby." But that was not the same as acting in a judicial capacity. And then Macaulay dealt with the different psychological states of mind of executive and judicial officers. "It is natural and even desirable," he wrote, "that an executive officer should over-rate the importance of his own department, and should exert himself in it as if the whole safety of the state depended on his exertions." But that was hardly the judicial temperament. What would happen if the commissioners were to act as judges would be that they would take all offenses far too personally. They would see every transgression brought before them as a transgression against themselves, and every deliquent as someone who had defaced *their* buildings or *their* streets.

In other words, Macaulay tried to put himself in the place of a commissioner-judge; just as, in one of the "Notes" to the code, he tried to put himself in the place of an Indian condemned to a sentence of transportation: "The criminal is taken for ever from the society of all who are acquainted with him, and conveyed by means of which the natives have but an indistinct notion over an element which they regard with extreme awe, to a distant country of which they know nothing, and from which he is never to return."[122] Not only does the code yield such vintage examples of his own style, it also yields some examples of his putting his literary knowledge to good use. One appears in an illustration concerned with the fabrication of evidence, in which A. and Z. clearly had an earlier incarnation in *Macbeth:*

A. after wounding a person with a knife, goes into the room where Z. is sleeping, smears Z.'s clothes with blood, and lays the knife under Z.'s pillow; intending not only that suspicion may thereby be turned away from himself, but also that Z. may be convicted of voluntary grievous hurt. A. is liable to punishment as a fabricator of false evidence.[123]

Playful? Perhaps. But to good purpose.

What is more, the code is a storehouse of miscellaneous historical

---

122. T.B.M., "Notes," *Works,* XI, 25.
123. "Penal Code," *Parliamentary Papers,* XLI (1837–8) , No. 190.

information. The reader learns that Sir Joshua Reynolds took old pictures to pieces in order to discover the secret of their coloring; that many of history's most famous assassins—Jean Chatel, Damiens, Guiscard—aimed their blows at the heart of their victims, but wounded them only slightly because the knife glanced aside; and that the Sicilian Vespers as well as Wat Tyler's rebellion began because "a person [took] indecent liberties with a modest female, in the presence of her father, her brother, her husband or her lover."[124] Macaulay's knowledge of history, stored up ready for instant use in his capacious memory, helped not only to enliven but also to make more telling the concrete illustrations that formed so vital a part of the penal code. For, after all, here were incidents that had actually occurred, and that might therefore, in a different guise, occur again.

But if history helped the historian with the code, did writing the code help the historian? There are various ways in which it may well have done so. Writing history and compiling a penal code have this in common, that they both demand the formulation of certain general statements which must be supported by evidence and which are impaired by exceptions. In the case of the code, those general statements were the definitions of what constituted crime; and in the introductory report to the code, Macaulay had stressed the need for coming as close as possible to absolute precision in these definitions. That precision could only be attained by going through a mental process which assailed the tentative definition with hypothetical exceptions. If these made dents in the definition, and uncertainty about liability ensued, then the definition had to be changed in order to accommodate the exceptions. Ideally, any hypothetical situation advanced to test a definition must receive a clearly affirmative or negative answer from it. Either it depicted a criminal act or it did not. The by-products of this procedure ended up as "illustrations" in Macaulay's code. When he wrote to Ellis at the end of 1837 that he felt and knew that his work on the code had been of great use to his own mind,[125] he did not go on to specify what benefits his mind had derived from it. But the labor of constructing the definitions must surely have been useful to the historian.

Another obvious benefit—though he could not fully foresee it in 1837—was that he had had to refresh (or acquire) his knowledge of the major criminal law codes already in existence, and in particular of the English criminal law. Since, in the event, his major historical work dealt with a period of English history in which legal issues (and

124. T.B.M., "Notes," *Works*, XI, 50, 119, 122.
125. T.B.M. to Ellis, December 18, 1837, Trevelyan, *Life and Letters*, 337.

not infrequently issues involving criminal law) played a major role, such knowledge was to stand him in excellent stead. Perhaps one may not be amiss in speculating that his work on the code, beyond sharpening and refining his capacity to make verbal and logical distinctions and to accept no general statement without ruthlessly questioning it, also provided a searching test of his ability to make difficult matters clear and· comprehensible. The instructions to the law commissioners from the Governor-in-Council,[126] which Macaulay had himself suggested, stressed that conciseness ought to be carefully studied as far as it was consistent with perspicuity; and predicted that it would be found that the two qualities were not incompatible, but identical. Macaulay followed his own advice, and the finished code proved the accuracy of his prediction.

With his exceptional memory and wide learning, he had known how to ransack the past for illustrations and analogies ever since his Cambridge Union days. To these faculties he had always been able to add another: the ability to fantasize, to daydream, to become through his powerful imagination a part of a fictitious universe that rivaled the printed works of fiction he knew and loved so well. The composition of the code made use of these abilities and, at the same time, disciplined and enhanced them. Should one add that it may also have enhanced his tendency to award marks for good and bad behavior, to see the past, as it were, from the judge's bench, condemning and acquitting according to the bidding of clauses and precepts he had himself invented? Can one call the *History of England,* in a certain sense, a continuation of the penal code? It would be frivolous to press this particular argument too far. But the composition of the code left definite marks on his intellectual development. At the very least, it contributed further to the lucidity and precision of his style, and to his capacity to use concrete illustrations in order to bring home to his readers the meaning of historical issues and problems, often of great complexity.

Reviewing the code in the *Westminster Review,* John Stuart Mill singled out its style for special praise and—making amends for his negative reaction to Macaulay's Education Minute—referred in glowing terms to "the accomplished President of the Commission."[127] He called the code eminently successful, in that it had actually done what was deemed impossible, namely, framed adequate definitions of offenses expressed in general language. In his enthusiasm he went

126. Board's Collections, Vol. 1,555 (1835–7), June 15, 1835, No. 63,507, I.O.L.
127. Mill, *Westminster Review,* XXXI (1838), 395.

further than Macaulay himself, whose own judgment about his handiwork, as communicated to Ellis, was that it seemed ill done when looked at by itself, and well done when compared with Livingston's code, the French code, or with the English statutes that had been passed for the purpose of consolidating and amending the criminal law.[128]

Mill concluded his review by stating that the attacks against the code made thus far both in London and Calcutta derived from the worst motives, from people who were still venting their fury against Macaulay's "Black Act." This was only partly true. One of the code's leading opponents turned out to be Macaulay's successor as fourth member of Council, Andrew Amos, the first professor of English Law at University College, London, and himself an English criminal law commissioner from 1834. Auckland quoted Amos to Hobhouse in the summer of 1838, to the effect that the Madras judges and some of the lawyers there wanted to have the code superseded. Amos had also reported to the Governor-General that a great deal of excitement had been caused among the missionaries about the provisions against persons who interfered with Hindu religion. The missionaries had drafted a memorial against the code of which, Amos wrote to Auckland, "my colleagues" (presumably in Madras) seemed to approve. Amos himself shared the missionaries' misgivings to some extent. He thought that it should have been left to the discretion of individual magistrates to deal with interferences with Hindu religion, according as these affected the public peace. While he did not want to go so far as to drop the entire code, and believed that the promulgation of a few provisions would be beneficial, he hoped that it would be possible to steer clear of several "exciting" matters in the draft.[129]

Amos's adverse judgment, opposition in India, the need to consult experts, British involvement in the Afghan wars—and thus much less attention paid to Indian domestic affairs—all these were factors making for a delay of many years between the drafting and the promulgation of Macaulay's code. Meanwhile, the draft was submitted to all the Supreme Court judges in Bombay, Madras, and Calcutta, as well as to other experts, for criticism. Their comments were in turn forwarded to Charles Hay Cameron and Daniel Elliott, Indian law commissioners in the 1840's, who issued two exhaustive reports on

128. T.B.M. to Ellis, March 8, 1837, Trevelyan, *Life and Letters,* 333.
129. Auckland to Hobhouse, June 3, 1838, Home and Miscellaneous, Vol. 841; Lushington to Hobhouse, October 1, 1839, Home and Miscellaneous, Vol. 836, I.O.L.

the code in 1846 and 1847. The reports summarized the critical comments they had received—which ranged from doubts about the utility of the illustrations to skepticism about whether the code lent itself to translation into the Indian vernaculars—and then proceeded to a clause-by-clause examination and suggested revision of the entire code. Their verdict was that it should be enacted with very slight modifications.[130]

In 1848, John Macleod issued his *Notes on the Report of the Indian Law Commissioners on the Indian Penal Code,* a down-the-line defense of the original code in almost all respects.[131] It was Macleod who, testifying before the House of Lords Select Committee on India in 1852, stated that: "I think I may say safely, that I know of no work whatever which . . . was subjected to such severe scrutiny and criticism as the Indian Penal Code, and I do not see that the result has been to detect any great errors in it." But, much to Macleod's dismay, Macaulay's code was being sent back and forth between the Indian Council in Calcutta and the home authorities in London; and nothing had as yet been decided one way or the other. Meanwhile, even though it had not yet been enacted, the code was already being used by some judges in Bombay and in some other parts of India.[132]

What had underlined the urgency of enacting a new criminal code, either Macaulay's or someone else's, was the proposal, made in 1851, that the "Black Act" be extended from civil to criminal cases, in other words, that British-born subjects be put under the criminal as well as the civil jurisdiction of the company's courts in the interior. The then Governor-General, Lord Dalhousie, objected that such people would then be subject to Mohammedan law. He would not give his assent until a new and uniform code had been framed and enacted.[133]

The person who was put in charge of this was the then legal member of Council, Drinkwater Bethune, an old friend of Macaulay's from Trinity and the Northern Circuit. One of his objections to Macaulay's code was that its language was "totally unknown to an English lawyer." He saw no use in setting aside traditional terms of English law "which, if not etymologically correct, had acquired a settled and definite meaning." To do so was mere whim, mere love of singularity, which ought not to be indulged. Further-

130. Cameron and Elliott, "Second Report," *Code,* 328, 495.
131. London, 1848. Macleod had shown his "Notes" to T.B.M., who had read them carefully and fully agreed with them.
132. *Parliamentary Papers,* XXX (1852–3) , 287, 296.   133. Ibid., 334–5.

more, he did not like the illustrations, which he believed were contrary to scientific principle. Thus, Bethune drafted his own criminal code. Dalhousie sent Macaulay's and Bethune's versions to the home authorities, and asked them to choose between them.[134] Under the Charter Act of 1853 a Commission was set up by Parliament to make a definite recommendation. The president of the Board of Control at the time was Sir Charles Wood, who had no preference as between Bethune's and Macaulay's drafts. In the end, the adoption of Macaulay's code was recommended. It was then that Macaulay wrote to Hannah that at last his handiwork had had justice done to it. If that had happened sixteen years earlier, he added, he would probably have devoted much more attention to legislation, and much less to literature.[135] Actually, it took six more years before the code was finally enacted, with revisions primarily drafted by Sir Barnes Peacock, legal member of Council during the 1850's. The code went into effect on January 1, 1862.

Subsequent judgments about its merits have differed, just as they have differed about the new educational policy in the framing of which Macaulay played so large a part. Barun Dé in a recent essay on Macaulay (unfortunately not published) has criticized the code for making little or no attempt to change the Indian social system. Others have questioned the very attempt to apply Western ideas of justice to the Indian situation.[136] But, on the whole, the verdict has been favorable, ever since Sir James Stephen, who knew what he was saying, called Macaulay's code a "work of true genius."[137] In a sentence that has become famous, Sir George Trevelyan wrote (in 1876) that if it were asked whether or not the penal code fulfilled the end for which it was framed, the answer might safely be left to the gratitude of Indian civilians, "the younger of whom carry it about in their saddle-bags, and the older in their heads."[138]

A later and less prejudiced observer commented that

translated into almost all the written languages of India, it [the code] has familiarised the native mind with ideas of justice and humanity, the maintenance of public order and public morality, the rights of the indi-

134. Ibid., 335.

135. T.B.M. to Hannah, October 1854, Trevelyan, *Life and Letters*, 337.

136. Barun Dé, "Macaulay," 28. And, for a summary of such views, see Erikson, *Gandhi*, 272–5. See also Lloyd I. Rudolph and Susanne Hoeber Rudolph, *The Modernity of Tradition: Political Development in India* (Chicago, 1967), 254–68.

137. Quoted by Leon Radzinowicz, *Sir James Fitzjames Stephen, 1829–1894, and His Contribution to the Development of Criminal Law* (London, 1957), 13.

138. Trevelyan, *Life and Letters*, 301.

vidual to life, health, freedom, honour, and property, the possibility of expressing a law with clearness and authority, and of dealing systematically with a vast and complicated subject.[139]

A more recent Indian commentator, after noting that nowadays Macaulay was not popular in India, goes on to say: "It is the genius of this man, narrow in his Europeanism, self-satisfied in his sense of English greatness, that gives life to modern India as we know it. He was India's new Manu, the spirit of modern law incarnate."[140]

Whether, in 1837, Macaulay anticipated that such a tribute would one day be paid to his work must remain matter for speculation. What is certain is that once the code was finished, he was determined to return to England. During almost the whole of the past year, he wrote to Hobhouse in his letter of resignation dated April 17, 1837, he alone had really been the law commission, since all its other members had been too ill to contribute anything to its labors. Now that he had singlehandedly brought the code to completion, his mind was fully made up to leave India for home by one of the ships sailing during the next cold season.[141] Hobhouse, accepting his resignation, replied that he was in despair about finding a successor who would be favorably regarded by their friends in Calcutta.[142] Auckland had, in fact, advised him (and this he did not confide to Macaulay) that, beyond ability and the general requirements of the craft, the new law member should possess one further qualification: "We want good sense and temper, and address in conciliation in large proportions."[143] There can be no doubt that this particular request represented a critical judgment of certain aspects of Macaulay's personality. Whatever his achievements in India—and they had been considerable—a capacity for conciliation had not been among the chief qualities he had brought to his tasks.

TO OBSERVE MACAULAY IN INDIA IS TO SEE HIM IN A SETTING JUST about as different as can be from that to which he had been accustomed. He had exchanged the fetid heat of the House of Commons

139. Whitley Stokes, *The Anglo-Indian Codes* (2 vols., Oxford, 1887) , I, 71.

140. Panikkar, *Survey*, 210.

141. T.B.M. to Hobhouse, April 17, 1837, Home and Miscellaneous, Vol. 838, I.O.L.

142. Hobhouse to T.B.M., August 30, 1837, Home and Miscellaneous, Vol. 838, I.O.L.

143. Auckland to Hobhouse, April 9, 1837, Home and Miscellaneous, Vol. 838, I.O.L.

for the burning sun of Bengal, 10,000 miles and half a year away from London; the wit, elegance, and cosmopolitan sophistication of Holland House for occasional evenings of literary talk with a few kindred spirits among the judges and civilians of Calcutta; the tangential involvement in great affairs of state at the center of power for the squabbles of faction at the periphery, where, as he complained to Ellis, the Tories would be unable to take notice of his inveighing against them, since they could not understand Greek.[144] Above all, he had exchanged the problems created by pressure for reform on the part of those hitherto excluded from political power in England for the problems involved in the preservation of dominion over millions of Indians by the last of a long series of conquerors. Thus the fervent opponent of Stuart tyranny and the great advocate of Whiggish libertarianism found himself compelled to recognize the need for an impartial despotism as the most efficacious and desirable means of government.

There can be no question but that he took his duties seriously, and that by devoting his incredible energies to them, he accomplished the work of several men. For most, the completion of the penal code alone (which took him two years) would have meant the labor of a decade, if not of a lifetime. But although his intellect and his literary ability were engaged by his tasks, his heart and his inmost mind were not. All the time he was counting the days that had to pass before his return.

In 1833 he thought that six years in India would satisfy his financial needs.[145] At the end of that time, he hoped to return with a fortune of £30,000.[146] Once arrived in Calcutta, he discovered that his expenses would be smaller than he had anticipated. If he survived, he could grow rich fast. After Christmas 1834, he expected to lay by about £7,000 a year, he wrote to Fanny and Selina; and five years from the time of writing (August 1834), he hoped that the Macaulay family would be reunited in a comfortable house, "certain of a good fire, a good joint of meat, and a good glass of wine," not obliged to anyone, and perfectly indifferent, as far as money was concerned, to political changes.[147] But that was before Margaret's death and Hannah's marriage.

A few weeks after those blows had fallen, when he had to contemplate the possibility of a Tory Governor-General's blocking his law

144. T.B.M. to Ellis, May 29, 1835, Trevelyan, *Life and Letters*, 315.

145. December 2, 1833, Broughton, *Recollections*, IV, 326–7.

146. T.B.M. to Ellis, November 28, 1833, Trinity Correspondence.

147. T.B.M. to Fanny and Selina Macaulay, August 10, 1834, Trevelyan, *Life and Letters*, 270–1.

reforms, he wrote to Ellis that in a few months he would have enough to enable him to live, "after my very moderate fashion," in perfect independence at home.[148] By the beginning of 1836 he was able to inform Spring-Rice that two years thence he would have saved £20,000; that he could live in perfect comfort and independence on half that sum as a bachelor, and that it would not be worth his while to spend several additional years in India in order to enable him to marry—"which after all I might not choose to do." With £20,000 he would be able to do his duty to his family and to support himself in a manner quite as much to his satisfaction as if he owned all the Duke of Bedford's acres and all Lord Westminster's mines. By the summer of 1838 he hoped to be in England again, free to choose between politics and literature.[149] True to his word, he had indeed returned by that date.

His greatest fear while in India was that his sojourn there would dull his faculties, that his knowledge and his intellect would atrophy. That is why he spent his time in the early morning hours reading and annotating the classics; and why he kept on writing essays for the *Edinburgh Review,* in spite of the many other demands on his time. It has often been said that he might have used that time to learn Indian languages and to immerse himself in the classics of Indian civilization. He would have regarded such a suggestion as bizarre; not merely because he had made up his mind about the "absurdity" and inferiority of Indian literature and science, but also because he simply did not wish to make that sort of commitment to India. He was absolutely determined to regard his "exile" as an interlude. His real intellectual life while in India lay in his long letters to Ellis about disputed points of Greek philology. The only social life he cherished continued to be that supplied by the family circle, now consisting of the Trevelyans and their daughter "Baba." Thus, he strove to create as much continuity as he could with the mode of his existence in England.

Continuity with his activities before he had come to India was not confined to the realm of the private and personal. It occurred in the realm of public affairs as well. Once again, Macaulay found himself on the side of reform; battling for freedom of the press, equality before the law, and English education against the forces of reaction as represented by Prinsep and the Orientalists on the one hand, the

148. T.B.M. to Ellis, May 29, 1835, ibid., 315.
149. T.B.M. to Spring-Rice, "Macaulay Writes Home," *Bodleian Library Record,* 252.

Calcutta lawyers on the other. Once again, as in the battle over the Reform Bill, Macaulay's contribution to the struggle turned out to be largely that of supplying rhetorical and historical underpinnings for policies he himself had not originated. James Mill had outlined the policy of putting British subjects in India under the same legal procedures as native Indians. The freedom of the press was Metcalfe's hobbyhorse. Trevelyan and Bentinck had prepared the way for the new educational policy. In each instance, Macaulay's powerful prose and dialectical skill supplied arguments and illustrations to support those measures.

The Education Minute contained very little that had not been put forward previously by other "Anglicists." But it is still cited today, by both friend and foe, because Macaulay invested its arguments with the drama belonging to events of world-historical significance. His angle of vision, it is true, was derived from his knowledge of European history. He always saw the world, and that included the Oriental world, through Western eyes. This led him to look upon India as he might have looked upon Britain before the Roman invasions, or on Russia before Peter the Great. The negative side of such an approach resulted in that condescension to Indian culture and institutions that has offended so many generations of the country's intellectuals. On the other hand, it was that same angle of vision which prevented him from ever looking upon India and her inhabitants as doomed to remain indefinitely in a state of tutelage to England. On the contrary, he wished to see India begin the same advance toward prosperity and liberal institutions that had taken place in England.

He himself was quite aware of the paradox of a situation in which free institutions were to be engrafted upon a despotic form of government. He had only to take cognizance of the fiercely negative reaction in London to his Minute on the freedom of the press if he wanted to get some idea of the difficulties of what he was trying to do. The liberal approach to Empire suffered from such contradictions throughout the nineteenth century. For there existed a fundamental conflict between the liberal ideal and the imperial reality. It could not be resolved, though the date on which it would become fully manifest could be postponed by continually putting the ultimate fulfillment of the ideal backward in the time scale. There were those who were willing to put off that date to the Greek kalends; who, for instance, throughout the nineteenth and into the twentieth century found excuse after excuse for postponing the entry of Indian natives into the higher ranks of the civil service.[150] Thus, speaking in 1868 against allowing the regular competitive system (which he and his brother-in-law had helped to establish) to operate for natives, Sir Charles Trevelyan declared: "You submit them [the natives] to an intellectual test, by which the great number are pretty sure to pass. You dispense with the moral test, which the great number are pretty sure to fail."[151] There were others like Sir Alexander Johnston, and later Lord Ripon, who, though no less desirous of preserving the Anglo-Indian connection, were willing to be more generous. Macaulay fell in between. He regarded the English *mission civilisatrice* as a means to an end—Indian autonomy. But his preoccupation with the means was the stronger impulse.

Because of this, it can be argued that his vision of the future, which included eventual Indian independence at some distant date, was a convenient device that enabled him to have his cake and eat it too. Certainly, he occasionally laid himself open to that accusation of "humbug" which has so often been brought against the English rulers of India.[152] When he had replied to Hobhouse's strictures on the Press Act, he argued, in effect, that freedom of the press would not mean any danger for British dominion, since the newspapers were read for the most part by those who were there to sustain that dominion in the first place. But one must remember that the purpose of that particular communication was to calm ruffled tempers at home; and that Macaulay was not unwilling to accept the risks that freedom of the press might carry with it. We may now savor the irony of his maintaining (in 1848) at a dinner in honor of Lord Hardinge, who had just returned from a series of military victories in India, that (on the basis of his experience at the Board of Control and in the India Council) "no Government exists of which the intentions are purer, or which, on the whole, has done more to extend civilization and promote the happiness of the human species."[153] But there is no doubt that he believed what he was saying. He may

150. See Appendix One of Anthony Lester and Geoffrey Bindman, *Race and Law* (London, 1972), 383–418, for a good account.

151. May 5, 1868, *Hansard*, CLXXXXI (1868), 1845.

152. See William Arnold, *Oakfield*, I, 159, for an example. Ensign Oakfield remarks to Mr. Middleton of the Indian civil service: "Then you mean to say, that all the talk as to the magnificent work of civilizing Asia through British influence in India is . . ." and Middleton interjects: "Humbug in practice, and it has grieved many generous hearts before now to find it so."

153. *The Times*, April 6, 1848: "On the table, in front of the chairman, was placed a superbly gilt plateau, on which stood a beautiful equestrian group in frosted silver representing a charge by cavalry, and other military emblematic devices."

have deluded himself on occasion, but he was neither cynical nor hypocritical.

Macaulay did not leave his Whiggism behind when he took ship for India. This emerges not only from the fact that he had no intention of upsetting the Cornwallis system, with its separation of the revenue-collecting and judicial powers held by local administrative officials. It also emerges from the fact that he saw the best guarantee for India's future development in the growth of an articulate and active middle class, engaged in modernizing India with the help of Western science and technology. What disturbed him, time and again, was the passivity of the Indians in the face of suffering and injustice. And so, time and again, in his legislative Minutes, he emphasized the need for creating conditions that would make it possible for Indians to translate their dissatisfaction into active pressure for reform. It may be that when he talked of Indian independence he saw it as far away as he saw universal suffrage in England. But there is no reason to doubt his sincerity in trying to move British India onto the same historical tracks that had led other nations to material prosperity and free institutions. Situated as he was in Calcutta, he may be pardoned for believing that this development was already under way. For in the Calcutta of the 1830's there existed a class of liberal Indian merchants who, through the media of newspapers, meetings, and petitions, were beginning to press for measures in which they had a common interest. Needless to say, Calcutta was not all India. And Macaulay has often been accused, then and more recently, of forgetting that fact. Furthermore, it might be objected to Macaulay's vision with some force that to treat India in terms of Western historical experience was mistaken in the first place; that India could only be properly understood *sui generis,* and her putative progress charted in the same manner.

Macaulay may legitimately be taxed with several errors of judgment. But, whatever his views about Western cultural superiority, he cannot be taxed with treating Indians as inferior beings, perpetual servants to the white *sahibs.* He believed that given time, a good system of justice, and receptivity to Western ideas, India would (and should) advance toward prosperity and freedom. This is what he had said in his great Indian speech of 1833, when he talked about the necessity for bringing natives into Indian government. And this is what he continued to believe. There has been occasion earlier to note the limitations of his commitment to his own policy: the need, for the time being, for European supervision; the unsuitability of the *munsiffs* (native judges in the lower courts) for dispensing criminal justice; and the acquiescence on his part, in 1853, in the continued exclusion of Indians from the highest civil service positions.[154] But when he expressed the hope that it would be possible in time to employ some of the principal native officers in the administration of criminal justice, and that native civil service candidates would one day be able to compete successfully against English candidates, it was more than mere idle talk. His Education Minute and his penal code were intended to aid in bringing about conditions in which these things would one day happen as matter of course.

A hitherto unpublished legislative Minute of his shows that he was very much aware of the responsibility, with which he had been charged, to ensure that qualified natives were not deprived of their rights as proclaimed in the Charter Act of 1833. In this Minute he recommended the rejection of regulations proposed by the Bombay government for extending the jurisdiction of its Court of Requests.[155] His main reason was that he objected to the proposal that of three commissioners, two were to be Europeans and only one a native. He doubted whether that was legal; and was sure that it was both unjust and impolitic. It went against the wise and wholesome principle of Parliament that "fitness alone is henceforth to be regarded in the choice of public functionary and not colour, extraction or place of birth." He also objected to the proposal that while the European commissioners were to be paid, the native commissioner was to remain unpaid. Furthermore, he would have nothing to do with the plan that twelve natives should hold the office of commissioner of requests in monthly rotation. "The principle of the division of labour holds good in this as in most other cases," he asserted. "A militia is no match for a regular army. An amateur artist is hardly ever equal to a professional artist." Similarly, a man who tried causes for a year would be better at it than one who tried them for a month at a time. In other words, within the limitations already noted, he did what he could to give Indians a greater role in their own affairs.

So, beyond making allowances for India's current historical stage, Macaulay did not regard her as a special case, but as part of a general movement of world history, a movement whose momentum now emanated from the West. The tension between the situational and the universal which had marked his historical writing from the start

154. See above, pp. 396–7.
155. Board's Collections, Vol. 1,555 (1835–7), April 17, 1835, No. 63,502, I.O.L. I owe this reference to Vasudha Dhagamwar.

became actualized for him in his Indian tasks. In the penal code, as elsewhere, he came down on the side of the universal. That meant he came down on the side of Benthamism which, taking time and place into account to some extent, nevertheless operated on the basis of certain universally applicable principles of human behavior and psychology. Still, while the spirit and the substance of Bentham may be found in the code, it would be false to label Macaulay, even in his character as a penologist, as merely a disciple of Bentham. His imagination and his sense of concretion—conjoined as always—infused marrow into the dry bones of Bentham; just as his historical vision made the Education Minute something other than yet one more Anglicist manifesto. If one were to categorize Macaulay in terms of his work in India, it would have to be as one of the last representatives of the Scottish school: ready to approach a penal code, a Minute on education, a project to reform the courts of justice, not as disparate and specialized projects, but rather as varied manifestations of human endeavor in which his view of the world could find expression.

His contemporaries classified him in very different ways; and one of the benefits of studying his Indian career in some detail is that it affords us a sight of the variety of points of view from which he was regarded. To Bentinck he was "un miraculo"; to Trevelyan, an oracle. Hobhouse, echoing Melbourne, though within a context of affection and friendship, looked upon him with some trepidation as something of a hothead who had to be kept under control. Auckland regarded him as personally agreeable, but lacking tact and diplomacy; whereas Prinsep saw him as stubborn, unyielding, and wrong. John Stuart Mill's view was that he was, in some matters, a coxcombical dilettante; in others, able. To the English community in Calcutta, he appeared unsociable and conceited. He himself had made no secret of his dislike of Calcutta society, and his departure met with complete indifference—apart from a few insulting paragraphs in one of the newspapers.[156]

In London, *The Times* expressed its regret after his return that the vital power of effecting all sorts of changes in the relations between ranks and races throughout the vast Indian Empire had been left "to the dictates of a genius alternately rioting in abstraction, and enslaved by crotchety prepossessions upon difficult subjects of civil policy, of which, in the nature of things, he must be practically and profoundly ignorant." He had thrown the whole European

156. Arnold, *Public Life*, 207, 228.

community in British India into "a blaze of exasperation and confusion." As a member of society, he had been more disliked, and as a public functionary, more execrated, than "any Englishman that ever left the shores of the Thames to visit those of Ganges."[157]

That was one judgment. But surely, not one which an impartial observer is able to endorse. As always, in history and in life itself, the view of the man depended on the angle of vision from which he was regarded. There is no doubt that in his public dealings with others, especially when they did not share his views, he lacked what he himself had criticized the want of in Lord William Bentinck—the art of conciliating.[158] He tended to be carried away by his own eloquence, and to exaggerate the points he made in his polemical arguments. But those failures should not diminish the magnitude of his Indian achievement. Even a critic like John Stuart Mill, who had condemned both the timing and the strategy of Macaulay's Education Minute, came to hold a favorable view of the penal code. And one cannot but agree that he was right in his judgment. Macaulay was not just a latterday Nabob who took a high salary out of India and did nothing but harm in return. In the form of the code he gave India a rational and humane system of criminal law, which incorporated the humanitarian reforms carried out by Bentinck and which seems to have stood the test of time well. In its essentials, it is still in force today.[159]

On education, Macaulay's thesis will continue to be disputed. His cultural condescension cannot be excused. But his vision is not to be denied. Western science and Western ideas have indeed left their mark on India, and by no means entirely to her detriment. Even those who condemn the Minute for its Europe-centered point of view would find it hard to argue that, given the many vernaculars and linguistic fissures that existed (and still exist) in India, any viable nationalist movement could ever have come about without an English-speaking intelligentsia. And while "filtration" did not turn out to operate as Macaulay had anticipated, some enrichment of the vernaculars did, in fact, take place as a result of the Anglicist policy. It can indeed be claimed that he gave India laws and letters.

Macaulay, then, certainly made a difference to India. Did India make a difference to him? In a well-known passage, part of his essay

---

157. Ibid., 247.
158. See T.B.M. to Spring-Rice, "Macaulay Writes Home," *Bodleian Library Record*, 251.
159. See Setalvad, *Common Law*, 225.

on Macaulay, Bagehot commented on what he called the historian's *"in*experiencing nature," and illustrated this with his Indian so-journ. The Charter Act speech of 1833 had been one of the most remarkable ever made on India by an Englishman who had not been there. But after his return, one could not tell from his speeches that he had spent several years in India.

Before he went to India he recommended that writers shall be examined in the classics; after being in India he recommended that they should be examined in the same way. He did not say he had seen the place in the mean time, he did not think that had anything to do with it. You could never tell from any difference in his style what he had seen, or what he had not seen.[160]

There is something in this charge. Macaulay tended to try to dominate experience rather than letting it work on him. Still, one need look no further than his essays on Clive and Hastings to find echoes of his Indian sojourn—the company's servants at Madras enjoying the breeze from the Bay of Bengal at sunset; the languid and sedentary habits of the Bengalis; the season "when the fierce heat of Bengal can scarcely be rendered tolerable to natives of England by lofty halls and by the constant waving of fans"; the cloud of crows pecking a sick vulture to death; the English barrister working 15,000 miles from all his friends with the thermometer at 96 in the shade.[161] Those glimpses of India were certainly based on his own experi-ence. But it is also true that the range of his experience was limited; and it would be difficult to agree entirely with the admiring writer in the *Calcutta Review* (1847) who, after admitting that Macaulay's observation in India had not been very extensive, went on to add that because he was Macaulay, he "saw as much, one morning, from the verandah of his house in Chowringhi, as an ordinary person would have seen in a year."[162]

In one very concrete sense, if in no other, his Indian stay certainly affected him greatly. He had come out to India a poor man in search of financial independence. With what he had saved from his salary plus the legacy from his uncle Colin, he returned to England com-fortably off, without money worries. He could now devote himself to literature or politics as he chose; and it was toward literature that he

160. Bagehot, *Works*, I, 399–401.
161. T.B.M., "Lord Clive" (1840), *Works*, IX, 190, 220, 223; "Hastings" (1841), ibid., 446, 468.
162. [Anon.], "Sir Elijah Impey," *Calcutta Review*, VII (1847), 453.

tended more and more. The Indian years had not been useless to him. To have drafted the code had in itself been a major intellectual achievement. It had not only supplied him with legal knowledge that would stand him in good stead in the *History,* but had further developed and refined those qualities in his style that he valued so highly: conciseness and clarity; the ability to bring home to the general reader through concrete examples and illustrations the most complicated issues and arguments. India had strengthened some of his long-held convictions. When he wrote in his essay on Bacon that the progress of mankind was furthered not by metaphysicians, but by scientists and utilitarian philosophers such as the subject of his essay, it is not improbable that he had his Indian experience in mind. The obverse of this was his increased contempt for mystical and irrational attitudes and streams of thought—regressive forces, he believed, in Indian society.

India saw the germination not only of the *Lays of Ancient Rome* but also of the *History of England.* As early as the end of 1835 he had written to Ellis, in a letter that contained the first adumbration of the *History,* that he was more than half determined to abandon politics, to give himself entirely to letters, and "undertake some great historical work which may be at once the business and the amusement of my life; and to leave the pleasures of pestiferous rooms, sleepless nights, aching heads, and diseased stomachs to Roebuck and to Praed." He admitted that he might feel differently about things when back in England. But in India—"in the quiet of my own little grass-plot,—when the moon, at its rising, finds me with the Philoctetes or the De Finibus in my hand"—he wondered what it was that led men to squander their intellect, health, and energy on such subjects as most statesmen pursued. Fame? But compare Townshend to Hume, North to Gibbon, Chatham to Johnson. Even Burke and Cicero would have been happier as literary figures. But, Macaulay had the candor to add, these were meditations in an Indian garden. "What I might feel if I again saw Downing Street and Palace Yard is another question." A year later he wrote to Mahon that he had no intention of again taking part in politics—once more, however, adding a cautionary clause in which he admitted that he could not tell what effect the sight of "the old Hall and Abbey" might produce on him.[163]

Part of the reason why he found himself increasingly veering

163. T.B.M. to Ellis, December 30, 1835; T.B.M. to Mahon, December 31, 1836, Trevelyan, *Life and Letters,* 319–21, 308.

toward literature rather than politics may have lain in a sense of failure, at least in the short run, concerning his Indian endeavors. Many of his proposed reforms had not been adopted; and even the penal code had encountered immediate opposition which had made its ultimate enactment uncertain. All of this may have intensified his feelings about the frustrations of public life. But what really helped, to use his own phrase, to turn him into a bookworm in India was the death of Margaret and the marriage of Hannah. The shock almost cost him his reason. In order to recover from it, he had fled to his books. The family idyll he had imagined, in which he would have come home, as in the past, from triumphs in the House of Commons to delight his admiring sisters with his exploits, had now been shattered. He was to seek instead for a different sort of fame, that granted by posterity. When Macaulay landed in England on June 1, 1838, he found that his father had died while he was on his homeward voyage. The dreams as well as the burdens of his youth and early middle age had ceased to exist. James Stephen, who encountered him shortly after his return, found him in great force:

I am sorry to say that he has become almost reproachfully fat, but the evil is compensated for by an obvious improvement in another direction. A long course of study and reflection in India has manifestly added to the composure of his mind, and rendered him a wiser man without detracting anything from the brilliancy of his talents.[164]

With the coronation of Queen Victoria impending, London was in a great state of excitement that June. There had been a prodigious influx of foreigners and people from the country, which meant that there were crowds everywhere. "For my part," Macaulay wrote to Napier, "I am sick to death of the turmoil, and almost wish myself at Calcutta again, or becalmed on the Equator." What of his future? Should it lie in politics, in literature, or in both? His own wishes now led him to prefer literature to politics, but when he told some of his friends this, they thought he was out of his wits.[165] In the event, he was lured back into politics in the course of the following year by an offer of the Secretaryship-at-War, which carried with it a seat in the cabinet. But, for the moment, his plan was to visit Italy in the autumn, then come back to London the following spring. Upon his return he would commence his *History* which, as he saw it that summer, would cover the period from 1688 to 1832, from "the

164. James Stephen to Napier, June 25, 1838, *Napier Correspondence*, 255.
165. T.B.M. to Napier, June 14 and June 26, 1838, ibid., 255, 258.

Revolution which brought the Crown into harmony with the Parliament," to "the Revolution which brought the Parliament into harmony with the nation."[166] He was true to his word. Two entries in his journal tell the story:

March 9, 1839. Began my history—sketch of early revolutions of England—pretty well, but a little too stately and oratorical.

March 10, 1839. History—tolerable. Must verify many statements and turn over many books.[167]

The historian was at work.

166. T.B.M. to Napier, July 20, 1838, ibid., 264–5.
167. At Trinity College.

EPILOGUE

Before attempting to make any summary judgment of Ma-caulay's character and achievement at the time of his return from India, it is worth looking closely at the two essays he wrote in Calcutta, one on Sir James Mackintosh, the other on Francis Bacon. For not only do these essays, considered together, convey a good sense of his intellectual bearings at the point when he began to settle down to the *History of England,* but as much as anything he ever wrote, they are intimately related to his general outlook and personality.

The "Mackintosh," in the form of a review of his posthumous *History of the Revolution in England, in 1688,* was, in part, an impassioned defense of his old mentor against the editor's suggestion that Sir James had not been entirely disinterested when he abandoned those sentiments which had led him, in his *Vindiciae Gallicae* (1791), to attack Burke's *Reflections* as a counter-revolutionary tract. Mackintosh was by no means alone, Macaulay pointed out, in adopting a more conservative stance under the impact of the Reign of Terror and military despotism. Viewing the events of the French Revolution from the vantage point of the mid-1830's, Macaulay gave it as his deliberate opinion that in spite of all the crimes and follies associated with it, it had been a great blessing to mankind. But it had surely been inevitable that those who observed the events as they were taking place should have undergone some changes of mind about them.

A man who had held exactly the same opinion about the Revolution in 1789, in 1794, in 1804, in 1814, and in 1834 would have been either a divinely inspired prophet, or an obstinate fool. Mackintosh was neither. He was simply a wise and good man; and all the change which passed in his mind was a change which passed in the mind of almost every wise and good man in Europe.[1]

Mackintosh had never been captured for any length of time either by Jacobinism or by anti-Jacobinism. He sometimes leaned in one direction, sometimes in the other, but he kept his balance; never abandoning either his concern for the safety of property and the just authority of governments or his belief in peace, liberty, and toleration. As such he could serve as a prime example of that "middlingness," that golden mean between two absurd extremes, which appealed to Macaulay's own deepest inclinations, both in the realms of politics and literary style.[2]

What exasperated Macaulay in particular was the way in which Mackintosh's editor had diminished his stature by calling him a Whig of the Revolution who had progressed no further than the men of 1688. In the first place, that judgment was less than fair to Mackintosh; but it also savored of a certain contempt for the achievements of the Glorious Revolution. And this Macaulay could not stomach. He believed that the science of government, like all other sciences, was in a state of progression. Truth advanced, slowly but steadily. "The great progress goes on, till schoolboys laugh at the jargon which imposed on Bacon, till country rectors condemn the illiberality and intolerance of Sir Thomas More."[3] There were no grounds for believing that improvement would not continue. But for that reason one's ancestors had to be judged in the same manner that one expected to be judged by posterity. "In order to form a correct estimate of their merits, we ought to place ourselves in their situation, to put out of our minds, for a time, all that knowledge which they, however eager in their pursuit of truth, could not have, and which we, however negligent we may have been, could not help having."[4]

1. T.B.M., "Mackintosh," *Works*, VIII, 431.
2. The expression "middlingness" derives from Vincent E. Starzinger, *Middlingness: Juste Milieu Political Theory in France and England, 1815–1848* (Charlottesville, Va., 1965). On "middlingness" in T.B.M.'s style, see William Madden, "Macaulay's Style," in G. Levine and W. Madden, eds., *The Art of Victorian Prose* (New York, 1968), 127–53.
3. T.B.M., "Mackintosh," *Works*, VIII, 434–5. The mention of the jargon that imposed on Bacon may well have derived from a reference in Tytler's letter (see above p. 368) to Bacon's not having accepted the Copernican system.
4. T.B.M., "Mackintosh," *Works*, VIII, 436.

The benefactors of mankind were customarily reviled by the dunces of their own generation for going too far. But it was too much to bear that they should be reviled by the dunces of a future generation for not going far enough. On one side was the bigot, out to obstruct useful reforms, who pleaded "the wisdom of our ancestors" as a reason for not doing what he in our place would have been the first to do; who, for example, opposed the Reform Bill because Lord Somers had not seen the need for reforming Parliament. On the other side was the sciolist, the superficial pretender to knowledge, who spoke with scorn of the Revolution of 1688 because it had not purified the House of Commons. Both of these extreme positions Macaulay dubs "absurd"; the truth, he finds, not for the first or last time, lies in between. But his chief concern in the essay on Mackintosh was to attack those who sneered at the men to whom England owed its House of Commons because they had not allowed the parliamentary debates to be published, those who treated the authors of the Toleration Act as bigots because they had not gone the whole length of Catholic emancipation. "Just so we have heard a baby, mounted on the shoulders of its father, cry out, 'How much taller I am than Papa!' "[5]

The question to be asked about the great men of the past, whether statesmen or scientists, ought to be not where they were, but where they were going. "Were their faces set in the right or in the wrong direction? Were they in the front or in the rear of their generation? Did they exert themselves to help onward the great movement of the human race, or to stop it?"[6] Like James Mill in his *History of British India,* the historian should devote himself to tracing the progress of sound opinions from their embryo state to their full maturity. Thus, Mill "eagerly culls from old despatches and minutes every expression in which he can discern the imperfect germ of any great truth which has since been fully developed," never failing to bestow praise on those who, though far from coming up to his standard of perfection, yet rose in some degree above the level of their contemporaries. "It is thus that the annals of past times ought to be written. It is thus, especially, that the annals of our own country ought to be written."[7] And then Macaulay spelled out his own program for writing the history of England which, to him, was emphatically the history of progress. In the course of seven centuries, a:

5. Ibid., 439. For the genealogy of that image, see Robert K. Merton, *On the Shoulders of Giants: A Shandean Postscript* (New York, 1965).

6. T.B.M., "Mackintosh," *Works,* VIII, 440.   7. Ibid., 442.

wretched and degraded race have become the greatest and most highly civilised people that ever the world saw, have spread their dominion over every quarter of the globe, have scattered the seeds of mighty empires and republics over vast continents of which no dim intimation had ever reached Ptolemy or Strabo, have created a maritime power which would annihilate in a quarter of an hour the navies of Tyre, Athens, Carthage, Venice, and Genoa together, have carried the science of healing, the means of locomotion and correspondence, every mechanical art, every manufacture, every thing that promotes the convenience of life, to a perfection which our ancestors would have thought magical, have produced a literature which may boast of works not inferior to the noblest which Greece has bequeathed to us, have discovered the laws which regulate the motions of the heavenly bodies, have speculated with exquisite subtilty on the operations of the human mind, have been the acknowledged leaders of the human race in the career of political improvement.[8]

That was the main action of English history. In the political realm, it had progressed from Magna Carta to 1832 as a series of great struggles—Saxon against Norman, Villein against Lord, Protestant against Papist, Roundhead against Cavalier, Dissenter against Churchman, Manchester against Old Sarum. Those who, in the contest that raged in their particular period, distinguished themselves on "the right side," were entitled to the historian's gratitude and respect. Those on the "wrong" side had presumably earned, and richly deserved, his obloquy. Progress was not invariably continuous. Indeed, in the short run, recoil often followed a great advance. Thus, comparing 1640 and 1660, 1680 and 1685, 1708 and 1712, 1782 and 1794, one finds regression. "But, if we take centuries, if, for example, we compare 1794 with 1660 or with 1685, we cannot doubt in which direction society is proceeding."[9]

The best comment on this general approach to history is still that of Sir Herbert Butterfield, in his *Whig Interpretation of History:*

Instead of seeing the modern world emerge as the victory of the children of light over the children of darkness in any generation, it is at least better to see it emerge as the result of a clash of wills, a result which often neither party wanted or even dreamed of, a result which indeed in some cases both parties would equally have hated, but a result for the achievement of which the existence of both and the clash of both were necessary.[10]

8. Ibid., 443.   9. Ibid., 444–5.
10. Herbert Butterfield, *The Whig Interpretation of History* (New York, 1951) , 28.

Macaulay did not approach history in this way. And to the extent that he did not, far more than in any narrowly political sense, he must certainly be ranked among the Whig historians. As such, he was very much aware of the solemn duty of the historian to deliver moral judgments. On the one hand, as he tried to make clear in the essay on Mackintosh, he must attempt to place himself in the situation of past generations in order to estimate their contribution to human progress from the proper perspective. Like Sir James Mackintosh himself, he must make ample allowance for the state of political science and political morality in former ages. On the other hand, "there are no errors which are so likely to be drawn into precedent, and therefore none which it is so necessary to expose, as the errors of persons who have a just title to the gratitude and admiration of posterity."[11]

One of those persons was Francis Bacon. It was to him that Macaulay devoted the longest of his essays, an enormous disquisition on Bacon's character and philosophy in the form of a review of Basil Montagu's edition of his *Works*. The thesis of this essay, which appeared in the *Edinburgh Review* in July 1837, was twofold: Bacon was a great benefactor of humanity, primarily because, unlike Plato and the Schoolmen, he had aimed his philosophy not at beautiful, useless abstractions, but at "fruit," practical benefits to be enjoyed by all mankind. At the same time, far from having been, as Montagu maintained, an eminently virtuous man, Bacon was a man cold of heart and mean of spirit, not above bribery and corruption. Montagu's case in extenuation of Bacon's conduct was that these were common practices at the time. Macaulay's rejoinder was that indeed they were—but not because people did not know what was right, but because people liked to do what they knew to be wrong.

Never, so Macaulay wrote to Macvey Napier, the editor of the *Edinburgh,* had he bestowed so much care on anything he had written; though he had previously admitted to the same correspondent that the part dealing with Bacon's philosophy was superficial. But he was certain that the essay would be popular with the many, "whatever the few who know something about the matter may think of it."[12] The second part of this prediction certainly proved to be correct. Though Francis Jeffrey read it "with throbbings of the heart, and tears in the eye," convinced that there had been nothing quite so fine since Bacon himself, other critics fastened on the essay

11. T.B.M., "Mackintosh," *Works,* VIII, 440.

12. T.B.M. to Napier, November 26, 1836, January 1, 1836, August 30, 1836, *Napier Correspondence,* 181, 174, 180.

from the start as mistaken and misleading. Bulwer-Lytton called Macaulay's view of Bacon's philosophy "merely brilliant declamation"; Brougham attacked Macaulay's reasoning—"his contemporaries at Cambridge always said he had not the conception of what an argument was."[13]

A leading Baconian of the time, James Spedding, himself a future editor of Bacon's *Works,* set to work in defense of Bacon's public and personal conduct, and produced two volumes, running to 800 pages, entitled *Evenings with a Reviewer: or, Macaulay and Bacon.* There were nineteen such evenings in all, each devoted to a dialogue between Macaulay and his critic. In the course of these dialogues, Spedding questioned the worth and accuracy of almost every single phrase in the biographical part of the essay.[14] Other critics, then and since, concentrated their fire on the philosophical part of the essay, generally regarding it as evidence of a quintessentially Philistine and materialistic turn of mind. And one cannot wholly blame them for taking this line.

Macaulay was at pains to show that after declaiming for eight hundred years, the ancient philosophers had not succeeded in making the world any better than when they began; that they had filled it with long words and long beards, and left it as wicked and as ignorant as they had found it. On the other hand, Bacon's philosophy of "fruit" had been triumphantly vindicated. Guns, cutlery, spy glasses, and clocks were better now than in the time of our fathers, and better then than they had been at the time of our grandfathers. In contrast, what had Plato and the other ancient philosophers done for humanity? No great moral or mental amelioration had resulted from their lucubrations. They had disdained to occupy themselves with the provision of bodily comforts. Not so Bacon. This is what his philosophy had accomplished:

It has lengthened life; it has mitigated pain; it has extinguished diseases; it has increased the fertility of the soil; it has given new securities to the mariner; it has furnished new arms to the warrior; it has spanned great rivers and estuaries with bridges of form unknown to our fathers; it has guided the thunderbolt innocuously from heaven to earth; it has lighted up the night with the splendour of the day; it has extended the range of the human vision; it has multiplied the power of the human muscles; it has accelerated motion; it has annihilated distance; it has facilitated

13. Jeffrey to Napier, May 2, 1837; Bulwer to Napier, August 23, 1837; Brougham to Napier, July 28, 1837; ibid., 191, 195, 197.

14. James Spedding, *Evenings with a Reviewer* (2 vols., Boston, 1882). T.B.M. never saw this work, which was published after his death. But he may have seen a manuscript version of it.

intercourse, correspondence, all friendly offices, all despatch of business; it has enabled man to descend to the depths of the sea, to soar into the air, to penetrate securely into the noxious recesses of the earth, to traverse the land in cars which whirl along without horses, and the ocean in ships which run ten knots an hour against the wind. These are but a part of its fruits, and of its first fruits. For it is a philosophy which never rests, which has never attained, which is never perfect. Its law is progress.[15]

It is important to remember that Macaulay wrote the Bacon essay in Calcutta, with the struggle between Orientalists and Anglicists fresh in his mind. In the course of that conflict, the champions of English, whose primary aim it was to make Indian education "useful," repeatedly referred to Bacon and his philosophy as their touchstone of modernity. As far as the Anglicists were concerned, the Orientalists were analogous to the medieval Schoolmen, preoccupied with dead languages and barren speculation. When Macaulay explained why Bacon sometimes appeared to ascribe too exclusive an importance to the practical arts, the explanation doubtless applied to himself as much as it did to Bacon. "Those arts had been most unduly depreciated. They had been represented as unworthy of the attention of a man of liberal education."[16] Macaulay's intellectual energies as well as his eloquence were often most effectively mobilized by anger or hatred; when he had been challenged or stung by an opponent, when he was fighting back. It is quite likely that this was the case here.

Quite apart from the Indian context, there was Basil Montagu himself, the man responsible for the edition of Bacon which Macaulay was ostensibly "reviewing." Not only did Montagu in his general essay on Bacon, a part of the edition, acknowledge his greatest debt to his "friend and instructor" Samuel Taylor Coleridge. But he then went on, very much in the manner of that friend and instructor, to wax ironical about how, "in these enlightened times," Bacon's views would be warmly welcomed by the political economists. The irony lay in the fact that these views had been, in actuality, strongly directed both against the worship of wealth and against the evil of sedentary mechanical labor performed indoors, especially by children. The factory bell of the nineteenth century, so Montagu went on to argue, would have sounded on Bacon's ear with a harsher impact than the Norman curfew.[17] At least part of Macaulay's overemphasis on the "practical" Bacon may well have

15. T.B.M., "Bacon," *Works*, VIII, 616.   16. Ibid., 619.
17. Basil Montagu, ed., *The Works of Francis Bacon, Lord Chancellor of England* (16 vols., London, 1834), XVI, 12; and cxviii.

sprung from his desire to save his hero from Coleridge, for whom Bacon was "the British Plato"; and to save him also from Coleridgean critics of classical economics and conditions of work in factories; just as, ten years before, in his "Milton," he wished to save 1688 from being exploited by the Tories.[18]

Walter Houghton has called Macaulay's essay on Bacon a *locus classicus* of Victorian anti-intellectualism; but, if it became that, it was against the intention of its author. Indeed, rarely can human genius, intelligence, and imagination have been so eloquently celebrated as in the passage Macaulay devoted to the workings of the poetical faculty and the capacity for imagination of Bacon's mind. Adopting Cowley's image, in which the poet had compared Bacon to Moses standing on Mount Pisgah, Macaulay conjured up the picture of

the great Lawgiver looking round from his lonely elevation on an infinite expanse; behind him a wilderness of dreary sands and bitter waters in which successive generations have sojourned, always moving, yet never advancing, reaping no harvest, and building no abiding city; before him a goodly land, a land of promise, a land flowing with milk and honey.[19]

It is precisely because Bacon could invest the prospect of that land of promise with the kind of vision, imagination, and intelligence hitherto reserved for ends less concrete that Macaulay (who doubtless wished to see his own, admittedly less exalted endeavors in the same light) admired him so greatly. Long before Huxley (and even longer before C. P. Snow), it was Macaulay's aim to expand the range of a liberal education to include science and the arts of human improvement. Those who disagreed with this aim regarded it as anti-intellectual. That was not how Macaulay saw it. He went out of his way to point out that the world for which Bacon (and, it may be assumed, Macaulay himself) wished was not "a world of water-wheels, power-looms, steam-carriages, sensualists and knaves." Bacon would have been as ready as Zeno himself to maintain that the skilled labor of a hundred generations would not give happiness to a man whose mind was dominated by licentious appetite, envy, hatred, or fear.[20]

This passage from Macaulay's "Bacon" is not often cited by those who follow Arnold in regarding it as the work of "the great Apostle of the Philistines." Nor is it often remembered that Macaulay was

18. Coleridge's "British Plato" in Barbara E. Rooke, ed., *The Friend* (2 vols., London, 1969), I, 488. On Coleridge's view of Plato and Bacon in general, see ibid., 482–95.

19. T.B.M., "Bacon," *Works*, VIII, 645.   20. Ibid., 619.

not among those who wrongly credited Bacon with the invention of the inductive method. According to Macaulay, Bacon's originality lay, rather, in turning the minds of speculative men from verbal disputes to practical improvements. "It was not by furnishing philosophers with rules for performing the inductive process well, but by furnishing them with a *motive* [my italics] for performing it well that he conferred so vast a benefit on society."[21] We should guard, then, against scoring off Macaulay by making a caricature out of the Bacon essay. Still, some questions remain to be asked. Why did he, who had shown in his essay on Machiavelli that he was very much aware of the pressures of a particular time and situation on moral standards, take such pains to dwell on Bacon's moral shortcomings? Was it, as Spedding suggested in his *Evenings with a Reviewer,* yet another instance of his love of rhetorical antithesis, a demonstration *in extenso* of Pope's line about "the greatest, wisest, meanest of mankind"?

Certainly, Macaulay liked to make paradox or antithesis the organizing principle for his biographical sketches. Brougham called this "Tom's snip-snap." One need only recall Boswell—"if he had not been a great fool, he would never have been a great writer"; and Horace Walpole—"as the *pâté de foie gras* owes its excellence to the diseases of the wretched animal which furnishes it, and would be good for nothing if it were not made of livers preternaturally swollen, so none but an unhealthy and disorganised mind could have produced such literary luxuries." But in those two instances, Boswell and Walpole, their negative qualities were said actually to have helped to enhance, or even to have made possible, their positive achievements. In the case of Bacon, Macaulay simply presents the two aspects—mean spirit and great philosopher—without linking them. Indeed, that was precisely the ground of attack upon the essay taken by an anonymous *Quarterly* reviewer, who "respectfully" inquired of Macaulay whether the conduct of Socrates before his judges compared with that of Bacon on the very seat of justice did not lead him to suspect his own comparative estimate of the two philosophies which those men had founded.[22]

John Henry Newman was to take a similar line in his sixth "Discourse on the Scope and Nature of University Education." If Bacon in the conduct of his life played false to his own professions, Newman there remarked, he was, after all, not bound by his own philosophy to be true to his friend or faithful in his trust. He had a right to be

21. Ibid., 633.
22. [Anon.], "Plato, Bacon, and Bentham," *Quarterly Review,* LXI (1838) , 505.

the meanest of mankind without any prejudice to his theory of induction. "His mission was the increase of physical enjoyment and social comfort; and most wonderfully, most awfully has he fulfilled his conception and his design." To the word "comfort" Newman added this footnote in his best ironical manner: "It will be seen that on the whole I agree with Mr. Macaulay in his Essay on Bacon's Philosophy. I do not know whether he would agree with me."[23] Three generations later, another conservative, Irving Babbitt, made the point more explicitly. Macaulay, he wrote, failed to see that the significance of Bacon's moral breakdown lay in the very fact that it had the same origins as his idea of progress. "In seeking to gain dominion over things he lost dominion over himself."[24]

Both Newman and Babbitt may be said to have faulted the Macaulay of the Bacon essay for his lack of true religion; for his making too sharp a separation of the personal and spiritual from the intellectual and practical. That was the kind of separation which Macaulay's father would have been incapable of making. For Zachary, it would have been axiomatic to judge the works by the man, the man by his works. For his son, it was still one of the first duties of the historian to judge the personal moral qualities of the men and women of the past; to judge them, indeed, within the context of the standards of their age, but, nonetheless, to judge them without mercy if they fell below those standards. No man, he had written with regard to Sir Robert Walpole, ought to be severely censured for not being beyond his age in virtue. Walpole had governed by corruption because, in his time, it was impossible to govern otherwise.[25] On the other hand, Bacon, by letting himself be influenced out of court and by allowing prisoners to be tortured, was not conforming to a usage then generally admitted to be proper.[26] He was distinctly behind his age. But the conclusion Macaulay drew from this was that here was yet another example of a bad action by an extraordinary man, of high intelligence united to low desires. He saw no necessary connection between personal character on the one hand, *Weltanschauung* on the other.

Ralph Waldo Emerson's acid comment on the Bacon essay was: "The critic hides his skepticism under the English cant of practical. To convince the reason, to touch the conscience, is romantic preten-

23. John Henry Newman, "Discourses on University Education," in Tillotson, ed., *Newman*, 470–1.

24. Irving Babbitt, *Literature and the American College: Essays in Defense of the Humanities* (Boston, 1908) , 39.

25. T.B.M., "Horace Walpole," *Works*, VIII, 336–7.

26. T.B.M., "Bacon," ibid., 548–51.

sion."[27] "Skepticism" is the wrong term by which to characterize Macaulay's own religious views. G. M. Trevelyan was probably closer to the truth when he expressed the view that the term "agnostic" in its stricter sense might have fitted his great-uncle. He cites a note of Macaulay's in the margin next to this passage in one of Conyers Middleton's controversial pieces:

But if *to live strictly and think freely; to practise what is moral and to believe what is rational,* be consistent with the sincere profession of Christianity, then I shall acquit myself like one of its truest professors.

Macaulay had underlined the words that are in italics, and had written: "Haec est absoluta et perfecta philosophi vita."[28] We shall probably never know the truth about Macaulay's most intimate beliefs. It is quite possible that Emerson's intuition was correct, to the extent that his paean of praise to "fruit" owed something to his reaction against Clapham. Some of the faith and fervor he could no longer bring to his father's religion he undoubtedly brought to the philosophy that he himself summed up as "Utility and Progress." But it would never have occurred to him to blame the Baconian philosophy for the moral failings of its progenitor. For he never came to regard Baconianism as a substitute religion from which ethical precepts and sanctions could or should be drawn. Rather, like so many of his contemporaries from Evangelical families, he continued to conduct his personal life by Christian standards, even after he had quietly discarded belief in the theological tenets from which those standards were derived.

To argue from the Bacon essay, as some have done, that Macaulay was personally someone who put material improvements above all else, who had no sense of the importance of the role played by man's higher faculties—intellectual, spiritual, emotional—in his existence, would be quite mistaken. After all, that essay begins with what must be one of the most moving tributes ever paid to the great minds of the past by one who was familiar with them:

The debt which he [the man of liberal education] owes to them is incalculable. They have guided him to truth. They have filled his mind with noble and graceful images. . . . Time glides on; fortune is inconstant; tempers are soured; bonds which seemed indissoluble are daily sundered by interest, by emulation, or by caprice. But no such cause can affect the silent converse which we hold with the highest of human intel-

27. H. M. Jones, ed., R. W. Emerson, *English Traits* (Cambridge, Mass., 1966) , 160.
28. G. M. Trevelyan, *Sir George Otto Trevelyan: A Memoir* (London, 1932) , 15.

lects. That placid intercourse is disturbed by no jealousies or resentments. These are the old friends who are never seen with new faces, who are the same in wealth and in poverty, in glory and in obscurity. With the dead there is no rivalry. In the dead there is no change. Plato is never sullen. Cervantes is never petulant. Demosthenes never comes unseasonably. Dante never stays too long. No difference of political opinion can alienate Cicero. No heresy can excite the horror of Bossuet.[29]

When, in the course of the essay on Bacon, Macaulay went on to exalt the Baconian over the Platonic philosophy, he did so in defense of an intellectual position firmly, even fervidly, held, but dissociated from his personal needs and desires. One is free to see this dissociation, with Newman, as paradigmatic of modern, liberal, secular man. But one should understand Macaulay's own situation: When he wrote the essay, he had tasted to the full the cup of personal grief and sorrow. Lacking the faith of his fathers, for whom death or personal tragedy offered the opportunity for familial and communal seeking of comfort and surety or for individual consolation, he had had to come to terms with his sorrow in his own way. Literature had saved his life. But his life had a public as well as a private dimension. And here Macaulay devoted that energy and that sense of mission which his father and his generation had committed to the preaching of salvation through Christ to the preaching of salvation through progress. In so doing he retained the ethical postulates of Evangelicalism—indeed, he made use of them in delivering his own moral judgments on history and its personages. But they had become static categories for him; for, unlike his brother-in-law Trevelyan, he no longer believed in Christianity as an animating force for the regeneration of mankind. That force, as far as he was concerned, was wholly secular, the force of progress and improvement.

Was he whistling in the dark? Is there any reason to believe that his optimism about the future was a "cover" for his own profound unhappiness? It seems unlikely. What seems probable is that the Baconian philosophy of "fruit" appealed to him not merely on substantive but also on psychological grounds. For, on the one hand, its message of material comfort and improvement could be raised to a higher level of poetry and imagination, when preached at large both to believers and unbelievers. On the other hand, it left his private, inner self untouched. It appealed to him, not because he lacked emotion and sensibility, but because he possessed them in excess. In taking up the cudgels for the "lower" needs of mankind, and investing these with intellectual content and poetic glamour, he was not

29. T.B.M., "Bacon," *Works*, VIII, 498.

only settling scores with those "mystics" and "theoreticians" who looked down on those needs; he was also staking out for himself a large public arena in which he could, in all sincerity, preach fervent secular sermons without really infringing upon his private self. His anti-Coleridgean, anti-Platonic fervor may have come, at least in part, from some secret or unconscious intuition that under the Augustan shell of common sense and no nonsense there existed an area of his personality which, in psychological terms, resembled that of his "enemies" more than it did that of his hard-headed Baconian allies. Yet he was not a hypocrite. Perhaps he was more of an élitist, humanist scholar than he always wanted to let on. His close friendship with Ellis seems to confirm that. But if he wanted to hide anything, it was his personality rather than his ideas. His intellectual convictions about the past and the future were the same, in public and in private.

Apart from Macaulay's family and Ellis, his contemporaries were not aware of the sensitive inner core of the man, and, while recognizing his extraordinary talents, tended to be repelled by him. Walter Savage Landor, meeting him at Monckton Milnes's house just after his return from India in the spring of 1838, concluded that he was "a clever clown." Queen Victoria encountered him in the course of the following year, and observed to Melbourne that she thought he was odd-looking. "Uncouth, and not a man of the world," Melbourne replied.[30] The ungainliness of his appearance no doubt contributed to these judgments. Having seen him speak during the Reform Bill debates, Maria Edgeworth had described him to a friend as "a mean whitey looking man. . . . Yellow hair all any-how except the right way." Harriet Martineau was put off by his appearance in society, "with his strange eyes, which appeared to look nowhere, and his full cheeks and stooping shoulders, which told of dreamy indolence." Sir Henry Taylor, the author of *The Statesman*, remarked that "his looks always seemed to me the most impudent contradiction of himself that Nature had ever dared to throw in man's face. I could not conceive how he came by them; and although I think I was rather disposed to like him personally, I never could quite get over them."[31] One of the striking features of the critical reaction to

30. Malcolm Elwin, *Landor: A Replevin* (London, 1958), 318; Viscount Esher, ed., *The Girlhood of Queen Victoria* (2 vols., London, 1912), II, 259.

31. Maria Edgeworth to Harriet Butler, March 16, 1831, Christina Colvin, ed., Maria Edgeworth, *Letters from England, 1813-1844* (Oxford, 1971), 488; Harriet Martineau, *Autobiography* (3 vols., London, 1877), I, 350; Sir Henry Taylor to Lord Blatchford, June 5, 1878, Edward Dowden, ed., *Correspondence of Henry Taylor* (London, 1888), 383.

Trevelyan's *Life* of his uncle (1876) was the frequency with which readers and reviewers expressed their surprise at the affectionate, avuncular, emotionally vulnerable figure revealed by his letters. Thus James Spedding, fiercely opposed to him in the matter of his view of Bacon, wrote that he had had no idea of "the tenderness which we now find was the predominant element in his mental constitution. And I cannot yet understand how it contrived to show so little of itself in his writings."[32]

Those of his contemporaries who judged Macaulay the man tended to be put off, then, by his manner, his appearance, and (if they judged him through his writings) his harshness. But harshness was only one of the negative qualities singled out for censure by the leading Victorians. For Arnold he was the great Philistine; for Morley, a writer disastrously preoccupied with the pursuit of vulgar effect. John Stuart Mill thought that he was not a genuine lover of the true and the beautiful, which was the reason why among his thousands of clever and brilliant things there were so few true things, and hardly one which was the whole truth and nothing but the truth. "He is what all cockneys are," he wrote in 1855, after reading his essays, "an intellectual dwarf—rounded off and stunted, full grown broad and short, without a germ of principle of further growth in his whole being." Gladstone admired his rare and marvelous power on the surface, but found wanting in him the capacity to fetch from the depths or soar to the heights. Carlyle described him as a man of truly wonderful historical memory, but otherwise definable as the sublime of commonplace; none of his ideas had the slightest tincture of greatness or originality or any kind of superior merit except neatness of expression. Acton, though convinced he was one of the greatest of historians, felt him lacking in "that vigilant suspiciousness of his own weakness, that look out for temptation, that betoken honesty. . . . He never starts except for the end in view. His hook and bait will only catch a particular fish,—there is no vague cast of the net."[33]

A study of his early life and writings tends to lend weight to some of these judgments. But one must not forget two things: Macaulay,

32. James Spedding to Henry Taylor, May 14, 1876, Dowden, ed., *Taylor Correspondence*, 356.

33. Acton to Gladstone, June 21, 1876, J. N. Figgis and R. V. Laurence, eds., *Selections from the Correspondence of the First Lord Acton* (2 vols., London, 1917), I, 260; David Alec Wilson, *Carlyle at His Zenith, 1848–1853* (London, 1927), 395; Gladstone, *Gleanings*, II, 338–9; J. S. Mill to Bulwer, November 23, 1836, Mineka, ed., *Mill's Earlier Letters*, I, 311; Peter Stansky, ed., John Morley, *Nineteenth Century Essays* (Chicago, 1970), 94; Matthew Arnold, *Essays in Criticism*, 1st series (London, 1889), 304; J. S. Mill, February 17, 1855, F. A. Hayek, *John Stuart Mill and Harriet Taylor: Their Correspondence and Subsequent Marriage* (Chicago, 1951), 223.

it is worth recalling, referred to himself at one point as a parvenu, as someone forced to fight his way uphill. Shortly after his return from India, he told Greville that if he had the power of recalling everything he had ever written and published and of destroying it all, he would do so, "for he thinks that his time has been thrown away upon *opuscula* unworthy of his talents."[34] There was a connection between those two judgments passed by himself on his early career and works. His writings were the means of his advancement; and, thus, from early on, he had to score with them. From the days of the Cambridge Union he remained something of a debater who almost required an opponent or enemy—Croker, James Mill, Sadler, Prinsep —to elicit his utmost energy and brilliance. As a reviewer and essayist he did not see himself as writing for posterity, and thus he did not always weigh his words as carefully as he might have. He was, after all, not a professor, but a journalist of a very high order, writing for an educated but not a learned audience. His reviews must be judged with that in mind.

The power of Macaulay's early essays, speeches, and state papers derives, in part, from their style, in part from the force with which he was able to direct the rugged empiricism of his common sense against all those who dogmatically thought themselves to be in possession of the truth—whether Tories, Millites, or Orientalists. Anyone writing after Dr. Johnson and employing this approach ran the risk of comparison, and, what is more, must have been fully aware of that risk. Macaulay's common sense, perhaps for that reason, seems to be a more artificial product than Johnson's—and, ultimately, less impressive because less idiosyncratic, less organically related to his own character and personality. Thus, even as one applauds the forthright sentiment in his essay on Byron to the effect that "we know no spectacle so ridiculous as the British public in one of its periodical fits of morality," one cannot help but remember his own censorious view of the Restoration dramatists whose works, to be sure, he wished to keep in print and accessible to English gentlemen but then went on to call "a disgrace to our language and our national character."[35] Yet, at its best, Macaulay's common sense could serve as a marvelously effective weapon, one that dented even the tough Utilitarian armor of the two Mills. When directed against a very different target, such as Indian art or Indian mythology, it could, of

34. August 8, 1838, Roger Fulford and Lytton Strachey, eds., *The Greville Memoirs* (8 vols., London, 1938), IV, 85.

35. T.B.M., "Byron" (1830), *Works*, VII, 533; "Dramatists of the Restoration" (1841), *Works*, IX, 339.

course, also create an effect both narrow and crude. Certainly, Macaulay often got things wrong. He underestimated Johnson and Walpole; he was neither a philosopher nor (as he was the first to admit) a literary critic.

But if these were some of his failings, what were his achievements? First, one comes away from studying his early life and writings once again impressed both by his energy and his many-sidedness. He was, to be sure, gifted with a phenomenal memory. Still, one cannot but share Hobhouse's amazement at his more or less singlehandedly producing a penal code for India, while writing the essay on Bacon, so to speak, with his left hand. Secondly, one should not underestimate the power of his style. There is a tendency nowadays to do so, to use words such as "rhetorical" and "glittering" purely as terms of dismissal, forgetting that parliamentary speeches are, after all, delivered in order to persuade and periodical essays written in order to be read. The most, and possibly the sole, convincing testimonial to an author's style is the survival of his works. Macaulay is still read. And he can still persuade. At a recent meeting of university teachers, young and old, convened to consider whether or not the language requirement for undergraduates in a certain field of study should be retained or abolished, the following passage from Macaulay's essay on "The London University" was read aloud:

It was justly said by the Emperor Charles the Fifth, that to learn a new language was to acquire a new soul. He who is acquainted only with the writers of his native tongue, is in perpetual danger of confounding what is accidental with what is essential, and of supposing that tastes and habits of thought, which belong only to his own age and country, are inseparable from the nature of man. Initiated into foreign literature, he finds that principles of politics and morals, directly contrary to those which he has hitherto supposed to be unquestionable, because he never heard them questioned, have been held by large and enlightened communities; that feelings, which are so universal among his contemporaries, that he had supposed them instinctive, have been unknown to whole generations; that images, which have never failed to excite the ridicule of those among whom he has lived, have been thought sublime by millions. He thus loses that Chinese cast of mind, that stupid contempt for every thing beyond the wall of his celestial empire, which was the effect of his former ignorance. New associations take place among his ideas. He doubts where he formerly dogmatised. He tolerates where he formerly execrated. He ceases to confound that which is universal and eternal in human passions and opinions with that which is local and temporary. This is one of the most useful effects which results from studying the literature of other countries; and it is one which the remains of Greece, composed at a remote period, and in a state of society widely different from our own, are peculiarly calculated to produce.[36]

The effect of this reading was almost magical. A century and a half after it was written, this essay written for the *Edinburgh Review* helped to persuade listeners in another country and in totally different circumstances with its message, not because it was original, but because it was put in terms that struck (and strike) the mind as well as the imagination with immediate impact.

What of the substance of the early essays? It goes without saying that they reveal a great deal about Macaulay's development as a historian. Not only do we get, in his essay on History, a programmatic statement of what he thought the function of the "new" historian was to consist of—poet as well as chronicler, concerned with English society as a whole rather than merely with politics, treaties, and wars. But we can also observe Macaulay using to good effect the method of situational analysis which, in the large, he probably derived from Hume and the Scottish school of historians, but which he made particularly his own in applying it to contemporary society as well as to social groups in the past. By its means he could bring into sharp focus the injustices done to Jews, Negroes, and Indians, as well as the mindless prejudices against an urban university; the relations of writers and patrons at the time of Dr. Johnson; the moral atmosphere of Italy in the age of Machiavelli; and the characteristics shared by the first generation of professional statesmen (of whom Bacon's father was one) in the reign of Queen Elizabeth. It was a sociological method severely limited by a stern moralism. Nonetheless, limited as it was, it yielded results still impressive today.

In their explicit search for the origins of those forces and tendencies that went into the making of what for Macaulay were the great and beneficent events of modern times—the Reformation, the Revolution of 1688, the Reform Act of 1832—his historical essays were certainly Whiggish, in the sense that Butterfield has familiarized us with the term. But it was Sir Herbert himself who in his *George the Third and the Historians*[37] demonstrated that in the essays on Walpole (1833) and Chatham (1834), Macaulay made the "Tory" case against the Whigs under George II, and did not for a moment pretend that in 1760 there had existed a happy constitu-

36. T.B.M., "The London University," Clive and Pinney, eds., *Macaulay*, 23.
37. London, 1957.

tional order which George III wickedly set out to overthrow. To characterize the Macaulay of the essays, any more than the Macaulay of the *History,* as naïvely and perpetually swayed by political prejudice would be wrong; though, from "Milton" to "Mackintosh" there is never any doubt about the party to which their author owed allegiance.

He was a loyal Whig. And as a member of that party his principal endeavor was to accommodate the new forces released by the French and Industrial revolutions; to contain democracy, on the one hand, and blind Toryism on the other; that is to say, to steer a middle course. Regarded from this perspective, Macaulay may, of course, be seen as a propagandist for the possessing classes, who helped to supply the ideological and historical dimensions for a holding operation on their behalf. According to his own lights, he still called himself a Radical after his return from India. Greville ran into him in the course of the summer of 1838, and Macaulay told him that he had not been prepared for the general tranquility and contentment he had found in England. For his part, he was "as great a Radical as anybody." He then went on to explain what he meant by that term. If ever the voice of the nation should be as clearly and universally pronounced for a reform of the House of Lords or for any other great change such as the Reform Bill, he would be for it, too. But at that moment he did not think it worth while to give such projects a thought, "and it no more occurred to him to entertain them in this country than it would to advocate the establishment of a representative Government in Turkey, or a Monarchy and hereditary Peerage in America."[38] In other words, societies went through various stages, in politics as well as in economy and literature. It was up to the "Radical" to keep pace with, but not to anticipate or to hasten these stages. A curious definition of radicalism, certainly, and one by no means acceptable to those in the vanguard, whether as politicians or (later) as historians, chronicling the sufferings and aspirations of the working classes. It cannot be said that Macaulay really sympathized with or understood those sufferings and aspirations, though he was certainly aware of the new forces that were transforming English society. There may be differing views about the gradualist, evolutionary pattern of modern English history, the soft-pedaling of the class struggle through the general acceptance of the mimetic process by which the working class, or at any rate a considerable proportion of it, shaped itself according to middle-class models. But if the case be

38. July 14, 1838, Fulford and Strachey, eds., *Greville Memoirs,* IV, 77.

granted that, on the whole, English society has been able to adapt itself flexibly to forces that led to violent struggle and revolution in other societies, then Macaulay must be given his due as one of those who, opposed to the democratic movements of his own time, yet held out the vision of an educated democracy in the future. Those who still insist on regarding this vision as a myth must, at least, agree that Macaulay proved to be a functionally effective myth-maker. But that is the lowest level at which to estimate his achievement in the political sphere.

Like all historical personages, Macaulay was time-bound. There are a few great figures in history who are able to transcend limits of time and situation and to become benefactors of the human race as a whole. It need hardly be said that Macaulay was not one of these. But there is no need to apologize for someone who spoke out as eloquently as he did not only for freedom as an abstraction, but concretely for the rights of Jews, Roman Catholics, and Negroes, and who not only prophesied but hastened along the independence of India. His Whiggism was not the genuine article, but the sort of amalgam one could be led to expect from a man with one foot in Holland House and the other in Great Ormond Street. His ideological underpinnings were also mixed—a mixture of ideas deriving from the seventeenth-century libertarians, Fox, Burke, the Scottish school, Bentham—all shot through and leavened with the moral *élan* of a secularized Evangelicalism.[39]

It has often been maintained that Macaulay "reflected" Victorian attitudes. It would be truer to say that he helped to mold them, not because he was an original thinker, but because the amalgam he popularized in his essays met the needs of a middle class, either educated or in need of education, which liked to see its own position glamorized. Macaulay helped to fulfill that wish. What he preached was not the pure milk of liberalism. That, as Sheldon Wolin and others have shown, was not a joyous but in many respects an austere and gloomy creed, leading to worry and neurosis along with freedom.[40] What Macaulay did was to infuse the Liberal creed with the spacious and sanguine spirit of humanism and history. The very fact that he was not to the manner born, but had himself "climbed," was significant for the effect he created. He was able to communicate the

39. For a similar mixture in the making of T.B.M.'s style, see Madden, "Macaulay's Style," *Art of Victorian Prose*, 127–53.

40. See Sheldon Wolin, *Politics and Vision: Continuity and Innovation in Western Political Thought* (Boston, 1960), 286–351.

sense that the middle class was not only respectable, but, like the aristocracy, had its own glorious historical traditions and achievements to sustain it.

In spite of his triumphs at Holland House and in Parliament, Macaulay himself never came close to conforming to the *beau idéal* of the Whig aristocracy. Shortly after his return from India, the Duke of Wellington reported to a friend the fact that Brougham knew "Lord Melbourne would prefer to sit in a Room with a Chime of Bells, ten Parrots, and one Lady Westmorland to sitting in Cabinet with Mr. Macaulay!"[41] Macaulay entered the Whig cabinet nonetheless, in the autumn of 1839, as Secretary-at-War. But he remained an object of amusement. Because of his learning and his "waterspouts of talk," Sydney Smith had remarked to Melbourne, Macaulay resembled a book in breeches. Melbourne repeated the remark to the Queen; "so whenever she sees her new Secretary at War, she goes into fits of laughter."[42] His undistinguished appearance, accompanied by his informality of manner, soon startled his colleagues. When the cabinet was discussing the murder of Lord William Russell by his valet, so Hobhouse related, "Macaulay repeated some lines of a ballad, which he had heard in the street about the murder; and some of us could not help laughing; others looked astonished at this strange want of decorum, and Baring, taking me to the window, whispered, 'What an odd fellow!' "[43]

That he disgraced himself among the Whigs by quoting a street ballad is not without significance. For, whatever his views of the metaphysics of the Lake school, he himself was deeply caught up in the Romantic movement, whether as a youthful imitator of Byron, a passionate collector of popular songs and broadsheets, or as a "new" social historian in the manner of Sir Walter Scott. The public persona he cultivated was, of course, very far from the popular image of the romantic wearing his heart on his sleeve. But we know that this was not the whole story.

S. C. Roberts relates that when he suggested to G. M. Trevelyan that the full text of Macaulay's diary ought to be published he was surprised by the vehemence of Trevelyan's outburst: " 'Over my dead body,' he said. 'I'm not going to have those Bloomsbury people laughing at my great-uncle.' "[44] What Trevelyan presumably had in

41. Wellington to Lady Wilton, September 5, 1839, 7th Duke of Wellington, ed., *Wellington and His Friends: Letters of the 1st Duke of Wellington* (London, 1965), 123.

42. November 30, 1839, *Reeve Memoirs*, I, 104.

43. Joyce, *My Friend H.*, 293.

44. S. C. Roberts, *Adventures with Authors* (Cambridge, 1966), 121.

mind was that Macaulay's close relationship with Hannah and Margaret would evoke the laughter of Bloomsbury. But, surely, what is required is understanding rather than laughter. The sisters provided a retreat, a "park," in which Macaulay, at odds with his own father, could himself play the role of father to his younger sisters. Many have remarked on the "boyishness" Macaulay retained for so long. It manifested itself in part by a continuing search for emotional security within the family rather than outside it in courtship and marriage. He found that security first with Hannah and Margaret, and then, after that world collapsed, with the Trevelyans.

The relationship with his father is, of course, crucial in any assessment of Macaulay. The bottled-up energy that exploded in his conversation was due, in part, to the repressed hostility which, like so many sons of Evangelical fathers, he could not possibly have dared to express openly.[45] In 1843, Sydney Smith told Maria Edgeworth, to her utter astonishment, that Macaulay's torrents of talk did not betoken vanity. "He only pours out talk and listens to no other mortal man or woman only because he cannot help pouring out. 'Did you ever see a beer barrel burst, Miss E? Well Macaulay bursts like a beer barrel and it all comes over you but he can't help it. He really has no wish to shew off.' " Miss Edgeworth recorded this, adding that she had a great mind to ask Smith whether Macaulay ever burst in private, alone in his own room. Why always burst in public? But she refrained.[46] It would have been a clever question. Yet Sydney Smith was right in not seeing Macaulay's proverbial dominance in conversation as mere vanity, but, rather, as a more fundamentally emotional, almost a physiological process. It was his aggression, let loose against the world. When Gladstone wrote[47] that "this favourite of fortune, this idol of society" seemed to have known nothing of the inward battle of life, that his mind was self-contained, coherent, and harmonious, he was unaware of the struggle that had gone into the making of that outward harmony. In more ways than one, Zachary had cast a long shadow.

45. For other examples, see E. Tangye Lean, *The Napoleonists: A Study in Political Disaffection, 1760–1960* (London, 1970) .
46. Maria Edgeworth to Harriet Butler, December 3, 1843, *Edgeworth Letters*, 600–1.
47. Gladstone, *Gleanings*, II, 278, 269.

A NOTE ON THE
MACAULAY MANUSCRIPTS

THE MOST IMPORTANT COLLECTION OF MACAULAY MANUSCRIPTS IS AT Trinity College, Cambridge, where the late Dr. G. M. Trevelyan deposited it. That collection includes not only a great many of T.B.M.'s letters—some hitherto unpublished, others only partially published in Sir George Otto Trevelyan's *Life and Letters* of his uncle—but also T.B.M.'s Journal, which begins in 1838, but which contains some interesting observations by T.B.M. about his early life and career.

The Henry E. Huntington Library and Art Gallery, San Marino, California, possesses a large collection of Macaulay family letters, indispensable for anyone who is interested in tracing T.B.M.'s relationship with his sisters. That collection is nicely supplemented by the Macaulay letters in the possession of the Pierpont Morgan Library, New York. A considerable number of T.B.M.'s letters, including many of those he wrote from India, are in the possession of Mrs. Reine Errington.

Professor Thomas Pinney is at work on the definitive edition of T.B.M.'s letters, which will contain many never published before. Dr. R. Robson of Trinity College, Cambridge, is editing T.B.M.'s Journal for publication.

A bibliographical essay on T.B.M. by John Clive and Thomas Pinney, part of a bibliographical volume, *Victorian Prose: A Guide to Research,* edited by David De Laura, is to be published by the Modern Language Association of America in the fall of 1973.

INDEX

Throughout the index, the name of Thomas Babington Macaulay has been abbreviated to TBM.

A NOTE ABOUT THE AUTHOR

JOHN CLIVE was born in Berlin in 1924, and received his early education in Germany and England. In 1943 he graduated from the University of North Carolina at Chapel Hill. After World War II, in the course of which he served in the United States Army as a member of the Office of Strategic Services, he did graduate work in history at Harvard University, where he obtained his doctorate in 1952. He taught at Harvard until 1960 when he joined the history department of the University of Chicago as its modern British historian. In 1965 he returned to Harvard as Professor of History and Literature, and has since divided his time between the history department and the Committee on Degrees in History and Literature of which he is at present chairman. In 1957 his *Scotch Reviewers,* a history of the early years of the *Edinburgh Review,* was published. He has also written numerous periodical articles, and has edited Carlyle's *History of Frederick the Great,* Mittelberger's *Journey to Pennsylvania* (with Oscar Handlin), and Macaulay's *Selected Writings* (with Thomas Pinney). Mr. Clive is general editor of the University of Chicago Press series Classics of British Historical Literature.

A NOTE ON THE TYPE

This book was set on the Linotype in a type face called Baskerville. The face is a facsimile reproduction of types cast from molds made for John Baskerville (1706–75) from his designs. The punches for the revived Linotype Baskerville were cut under the supervision of the English printer George W. Jones.

John Baskerville's original face was one of the forerunners of the type style known as "modern face" to printers—a "modern" of the period A.D. 1800.

Composed, printed, and bound by H. Wolff Book Manufacturing Co., Inc., New York, New York.

Typography and binding design by Clint Anglin.